THE
COLLEGE
PRESS
NIV
COMMENTARY

1 & 2 SAMUEL

THE COLLEGE PRESS NIV COMMENTARY

1 & 2 SAMUEL

JAMES E. SMITH

Old Testament Series Co-Editors:

Terry Briley, Ph.D.   Paul Kissling, Ph.D.
Lipscomb University   Great Lakes Christian College

 COLLEGE PRESS
PUBLISHING COMPANY
Joplin, Missouri

Library of Congress Cataloging-in-Publication Data

Smith, James E. (James Edward), 1939–
   1 & 2 Samuel /James E. Smith
     p.   cm. – (The College Press NIV commentary. Old
  Testament series)
   Includes bibliographical references.
   ISBN 0-89900-881-X
   1. Bible. O.T. Samuel—Commentaries. I. Title: 1 and
2 Samuel. II. Title: First & Second Samuel. III. Title:
First and Second Samuel. IV. Title. V. Series.
BS1325.3.S65 2000
222'.407—dc21

                                      00-022696

A WORD
FROM THE PUBLISHER

Years ago a movement was begun with the dream of uniting all Christians on the basis of a common purpose (world evangelism) under a common authority (the Word of God). The College Press NIV Commentary Series is a serious effort to join the scholarship of two branches of this unity movement so as to speak with one voice concerning the Word of God. Our desire is to provide a resource for your study of the Old Testament that will benefit you whether you are preparing a Bible School lesson, a sermon, a college course, or your own personal devotions. Today as we survey the wreckage of a broken world, we must turn again to the Lord and his Word, unite under his banner and communicate the life-giving message to those who are in desperate need. This is our purpose.

ABBREVIATIONS

ABD	*The Anchor Bible Dictionary*
ABW	*Archaeology and the Biblical World*
ALQ	*The Ancient Library of Qumran and Modern Biblical Studies*
ANET	*Ancient Near Eastern Texts Relating to the Old Testament*
ANEP	*Ancient Near Eastern Pictures Relating to the Old Testament*
AOTS	*Archaeology and Old Testament Study*
ARI	*Archaeology and the Religion of Israel*
ASV	*American Standard Version,* 1901
BA	*Biblical Archeologist*
BAR	*Biblical Archaeology Review*
BASOR	*Bulletin of the American Schools of Oriental Research*
BT	*Bible Translator*
BETS	*Bulletin of the Evangelical Theological Society*
BDB	Brown, Driver and Briggs, *A Hebrew and English Lexicon of the Old Testament*
BibRev	*Bible Review*
BibSac	*Bibliotheca Sacra*
BV	*The Berkeley Version in Modern English,* 1959
CBQ	*Catholic Biblical Quarterly*
CMHE	*Canaanite Myth and Hebrew Epic*
DSS	Dead Sea Scrolls
EAE	*Encyclopedia of Archaeological Excavations in the Holy Land*
EOR	*Ex Orbe Religionum; Studia Geo Widengren*
ET	*Expository Times*
FSAC	*From Stone Age to Christianity*
GK	*Gesenius' Hebrew Grammar*
GTJ	*Grace Theological Journal*
HS	*Hebrew Studies*
HUCA	*Hebrew Union College Annual*
IDB	*Interpreter's Dictionary of the Bible*
IDBSupp	*Interpreter's Dictionary of the Bible, Supplement*

IEJ	*Israel Exploration Journal*
Int	*Interpretation*
IPH	*Israel's Prophetic Heritage*
ITH	*In Time of Harvest. Essays in Honor of A.H. Silver*
JANESCU	*Journal of Ancient Near Eastern Society of Columbia University.*
JB	*The Jerusalem Bible,* 1966
JBL	*Journal of Biblical Literature*
JETS	*Journal of the Evangelical Theological Society*
JNES	*Journal of Near Eastern Studies*
JPOS	*Journal of the Palestine Oriental Society*
JSOT	*Journal for the Study of the Old Testament*
JSS	*Journal of Semitic Studies*
JTS	*Journal of Theological Studies*
KD	*Keil and Delitzsch Old Testament Commentaries: Judges 6:33 to Ezra*
KJV	*King James Version*
LB	*The Living Bible Paraphrased,* 1971
LXX	The Septuagint (pre-Christian Greek version of the Old Testament)
MBA	*The Macmillan Bible Atlas,* 3rd. ed.
MOT	*The Messiah in the Old Testament*
MS(S)	Manuscript(s)
MT	Masoretic Text
NAB	*New American Bible,* 1991
NASB	*New American Standard Bible,* 1960
NBD	*New Bible Dictionary*
NEASB	*Near East Archaeological Society Bulletin*
NICOT	New International Commentary on the Old Testament
NIV	*New International Version,* 1984
NKJV	*The New King James Version,* 1979
NRSV	*New Revised Standard Version,* 1993
NJPS	*Tanakh: The Holy Scriptures.* Jewish Publication Society, 1985.
OBA	*Oxford Bible Atlas*
PEPI	*Patterns in the Early Poetry of Israel*
PHOE	*The Problem of the Hexateuch and Other Essays*
POTT	*Peoples of Old Testament Times*
RR	*Reformed Review*
SBN	*The Sense of Biblical Narrative*
SJT	*Southwestern Journal of Theology*
SPDS	*Studies in the Period of David and Solomon*

ST	*Studia Theologica*
TB	*Tyndale Bulletin*
TDOT	*Theological Dictionary of the Old Testament*
TJ	*Trinity Journal*
TZ	*Theologische Zeitscrift*
TEV	*Today's English Version*, 1976
VT	*Vetus Testamentum*
WHJP	*The World History of the Jewish People*
WTJ	*Westminster Theological Journal*
YGC	*Yahweh and the Gods of Canaan*
ZA	*Zondervan NIV Atlas of the Bible*
ZAW	*Zeitschrift für die Alttestamentliche Wissenschaft*
ZPEB	*The Zondervan Pictorial Encyclopedia of the Bible*

Simplified Guide to Hebrew Writing

Heb. letter	Translit.	Pronunciation guide
א	ʾ	Has no sound of its own; like smooth breathing mark in Greek
ב	b	Pronounced like English B *or* V
ג	g	Pronounced like English G
ד	d	Pronounced like English D
ה	h	Pronounced like English H
ו	w	As a consonant, pronounced like English V or German W
וּ	û	Represents a vowel sound, pronounced like English long OO
וֹ	ô	Represents a vowel sound, pronounced like English long O
ז	z	Pronounced like English Z
ח	ḥ	Pronounced like German and Scottish CH and Greek χ (chi)
ט	ṭ	Pronounced like English T
י	y	Pronounced like English Y
כ/ך	k	Pronounced like English K
ל	l	Pronounced like English L
מ/ם	m	Pronounced like English M
נ/ן	n	Pronounced like English N
ס	s	Pronounced like English S
ע	ʿ	Stop in breath deep in throat before pronouncing the vowel
פ/ף	p/ph	Pronounced like English P *or* F
צ/ץ	ṣ	Pronounced like English TS/TZ
ק	q	Pronounced very much like כ (k)
ר	r	Pronounced like English R
שׂ	ś	Pronounced like English S, much the same as ס
שׁ	š	Pronounced like English SH
ת	t/th	Pronounced like English T *or* TH

Note that different forms of some letters appear at the end of the word (written right to left), as in כָּפַף (*kāphaph*, "bend") and מֶלֶךְ (*melek*, "king").

Vowels in Hebrew (except where the ו is used to represent a vowel sound), are represented by "vowel points" added to the consonant. For example: הַ (*ha*, "the"). The letter *yod* (י, y) also becomes a *part of* certain vowel sounds, as in the conjunction כִּי (*kî*, "that"). Originally, Hebrew was written as "unpointed" text, with just the consonants. For convenience, the different vowel points are shown below on the letter Aleph (א).

אָ	ā	Pronounced not like long A in English, but like the broad A or AH sound
אַ	a	The Hebrew short A sound, but more closely resembles the broad A (pronounced for a shorter period of time) than the English short A
אֶ	e	Pronounced like English short E
אֵ	ē	Pronounced like English long A, or Greek η (eta)

א	i	Pronounced like English short I
א	î	The same vowel point is sometimes pronounced like אִי (see below)
א	o	This vowel point sometimes represents the short O sound
א	ō	Pronounced like English long O
א	u	The vowel point ֻ sometimes represents a shorter U sound and
א	ū	is sometimes pronounced like the וּ (û, see above)
אֵ	ê	Pronounced much the same as א
אֵ	ê	Pronounced much the same as א
אֵ	î	Pronounced like long I in many languages, or English long E
א	ə	An unstressed vowel sound, like the first E in the word "severe"
א, א, א	ŏ, ă, ĕ	Shortened, unstressed forms of the vowels א, א, and א, pronounced very similarly to א

PREFACE

A commentator is a bridge builder. His task is to build a communication bridge from the present day to biblical days. The word of the Lord is communicated in words of ancient languages with which most modern students are unfamiliar. It lies intertwined with customs and figures of speech which are not clear to casual readers. If the meaning intended by a biblical writer is to be clear, his statements must be placed in a chronological and geographical context. They must be integrated into the message of a given author, and into the overall theological message of the Bible.

In part the communication gap is bridged by a good translation. Bible students who are restricted to English translations generally assume that the translation committees have rendered the best possible Hebrew or Greek text into the best possible English idiom. Needless to say, a perfect English translation has never been made.

The task at hand is to comment on the books of Samuel as rendered into English by the New International Version which is an acceptable, but not a superior, translation of the Hebrew text. At times the NIV abandons the Hebrew text altogether; at times it is more of a commentary on the text than a translation thereof. Regularly I have placed literal translations of the text side by side with the NIV rendering. I have noted where other standard English versions differ significantly from the NIV. The reader may judge for himself to what degree the NIV has given a clear and accurate rendering of the Hebrew text.

This commentary is not meant for scholars, yet hopefully it will be a resource for serious students of the word. I have assumed that most who make use of the volume will have little or no acquaintance with the Hebrew language. For this reason, Hebrew terms are transliterated. Technical discussion of the fine points of Hebrew grammar has been kept at a minimum. Literal translations (in quotation marks) are the author's.

In preparing this material I have perused both the classical commentaries on 1 & 2 Samuel as well as many of the more recent works. On controversial issues I have aimed to identify conclusions which differ from those I advocate. I have cited a fair representation of the voluminous scholarly literature on the Samuel books in order to facilitate research of various issues which arise in the study of this material.

I appreciate the opportunity extended to me by College Press to expand and refine my earlier comments on Samuel which were part of the volume *The Books of History* (1995). I am especially indebted to the Library staff of Florida Christian College for assistance in preparing the manuscript: to Debbie Jones, Assistant Librarian, for assistance in securing research materials; to Linda Stark, Librarian, who read the original draft and made many helpful suggestions.

Dedication

To
Dr. A. Wayne Lowen
Third President of Florida Christian College

Former Student of the Author
Colleague
Friend

INTRODUCTION

With regard to the names of the ninth and tenth books of the Old Testament, two ancient traditions can be documented. The Talmud (A.D. 500), representing the older tradition, regarded this historical material as one book called "Samuel."[1] Hebrew manuscripts continued to treat Samuel as one book until printed editions of the Hebrew Bible began to appear. The division into two books was first introduced into the Hebrew Bible edited by Daniel Bomberg in A.D. 1517.

In the Greek and Latin traditions the original book of Samuel appears as two separate books. Christian Greek manuscripts of the Old Testament (ca. A.D. 350) designate these two books as 1 & 2 Kingdoms. This tradition was followed in Jerome's Latin Vulgate. In later Vulgate tradition "Kingdoms" was shortened to "Kings." Older English versions combined both traditions in the headings of these books, e.g. in the King James Version, "The First Book of Samuel otherwise called the First Book of Kings." Most English versions of the twentieth century have opted to follow exclusively the Samuel tradition for naming these books.

A. BACKGROUND OF SAMUEL

The Philistines or "sea peoples," as they are called in nonbiblical sources, settled en masse in the coastal region of Palestine about 1200 B.C. About 1126 B.C. they began to extend their influence into the lowlands and mountains where they clashed with the Israelites. The chariots and weaponry of this powerful people intimidated the Israelites for forty years (Judg 13:1). Samson vented his personal

---

[1]There is no break in the MT between 1 and 2 Samuel. The Masoretic notes at the end of 2 Samuel give a total of 1,506 verses for the entire corpus and point to 1 Sam 28:24 as the middle verse of the *book* (sing.).

vengeance against the Philistines for the twenty years of his judgeship (1105-1085 B.C.).

Eli's ineffective judgeship of forty years (1 Sam 4:18) paralleled
the forty years of Philistine oppression. During the years of
Samson's exploits and Eli's decline, Samuel was growing to manhood at the tabernacle in Shiloh. The opening chapters of 1 Samuel
give the details of his birth and boyhood, his call to prophetic office,
and his moral and spiritual influence on Israel.

The name of Samuel came to be attached to the ninth and tenth
books of the Old Testament primarily because of the prominent
role this prophet played in this period. He was the last of the judges
and the first of a new line of prophets (cf. Acts 3:24). Samuel was the
instrument through whom God founded the monarchy in Israel. He
anointed Saul and David, the first two kings. In the career of David
the influence of Samuel lived on long after his death.

B. CIRCUMSTANCES OF WRITING SAMUEL

The Book of Samuel is anonymous. The Jewish tradition (*Baba
Bathra* 14b) that Samuel was the author seems untenable in view of
the fact that the history continues far beyond his death in 1 Samuel
25:1. Jewish tradition is most likely correct, however, in regarding
the author of the book as a prophet.

The fact that the death of David is not recorded in Samuel suggests that the book was written before he died. Because of the length
of time covered in Samuel no one person could have been a con-
temporary of all the events. Hence the author, guided by the Holy
Spirit, must have used some sources. According to 1 Chronicles
29:29 the acts of King David, from first to last, were written "in the
records of Samuel the seer, the records of Nathan the prophet and
the records of Gad the seer." The chronicles written by these three
prophets probably constituted the sources from which the Narrator
drew his materials.[2] It is not likely, however, that the Book of Samuel
appeared in its present form prior to the division of the kingdom
after the death of Solomon.[3]

---

[2]Probably Samuel was the source for most of what appears in 1 Samuel
1-24; Gad for 1 Sam 24-2 Sam 5:3; and Nathan for 2 Sam 5:4-1 Kgs 3:28.

[3]The statement "Ziklag . . . has belonged to the kings [pl.] of Judah ever
since" (1 Sam 27:6) points in this direction. Youngblood (554) comments:

C. LITERARY CONTEXT OF SAMUEL

In the Hebrew Bible the books of Joshua, Judges, Samuel and Kings are classified as Former Prophets (as distinguished from the Latter Prophets: Isaiah, Jeremiah, Ezekiel and The Twelve). These four books summarize the history of Israel over a span of eight centuries, from the conquest under Joshua (ca. 1407 B.C.) to the fall of Jerusalem to the Babylonians (586 B.C.) and even beyond.[4] While these four books are distinct literary compositions, there are similarities, which appear to be intentional, that link them together in narrative sequence. Certainly all four books reflect the spirit of Moses who set forth in Deuteronomy the legal foundation of monarchy (Deut 17:14-20) and who emphasized the blessing/curse alternatives related to covenant obedience/disobedience (Deut 27:9–28:68). This evidence falls short of proving, however, that a "Deuteronomic" historian who lived during the exile gathered together the books of the Former Prophets, christened them with his own Mosaic theology, and palmed them off on a gullible public as the ancient histories of his people.[5] The "Deuteronomic" spirit is the prophetic spirit. A succession of pre-exilic prophets, some of whom may have been contemporaries of the events they relate, would have produced works stamped with the theology of Moses.

D. THE PURPOSE OF SAMUEL

The Book of Judges sets the stage for Samuel thematically as well as chronologically. The author of Judges (perhaps Samuel himself) stressed the deplorable conditions which existed in Israel before the nation had a king (Judg 18:1; 19:1; 21:25). The immediate purpose of

---

"the possibility of a modest number of later editorial updatings and/or modernizations of the original work cannot be ruled out."

[4]The last chronological note is the thirty-seventh year of the exile of King Jehoiachin, ca. 561 B.C. (2 Kgs 25:27).

[5]Cf. M. Noth, *The Deuteronomistic History*, JSOT Supp. 15 (Sheffield: JSOT, 1981). Noth's thesis is that Deuteronomy to 2 Kings is a continuous narrative, compiled by one writer. He considered this historian to be antimonarchical and pessimistic. Noth can only arrive at his position by branding all passages which refute his thesis as later additions. Cf. D.J. McCarthy, "II Samuel 7 and the Structure of the Deuteronomic History," *JBL* 84 (1965): 131-138.

the Book of Samuel was to narrate the circumstances surrounding the founding of the monarchy in Israel. 1 Samuel relates the *birth* of the monarchy. 2 Samuel narrates the *expansion* of the kingdom of Israel into an important power. The ultimate purpose of the books was to reveal the divine origin of the messianic house of David, i.e., the family through whom the Messiah would one day come (2 Sam 7:12f.).

E. CHRONOLOGY OF SAMUEL

The books of 1 & 2 Samuel combined cover about 140 years. The opening event, the birth of Samuel, can be assigned to ca.1118 B.C. The closing event, the death of David, probably occurred in 970 B.C.[6] Breaking this down according to the two books, 1 Samuel covers about a century and 2 Samuel about forty years. At this period no great world power was seeking to dominate the near East. Israel's battles were waged against near neighbors. In particular the Philistines were a constant threat until they were finally subdued by David. By the end of David's reign, devastating raids by neighboring peoples were at an end. Cordial relations had been established with Phoenicia. Kingdoms to the east and north paid tribute to Jerusalem. The land promised to Abraham extended from the border of Egypt to the Euphrates river (Gen 15:18-21).

The anchor date for the life of David is 970 B.C., the date of his death and the accession of Solomon. For constructing the chronology of his life prior to 970 B.C. the key passage is 2 Sam 5:4-5. These verses establish that David (1) was thirty when he began to reign, (2) reigned seven and a half years in Hebron, and (3) thirty-three years in Jerusalem. From these data a fairly reliable skeletal chronology of David's life can be established. Other events of his life can then be inserted into the skeletal chronology, with hints from the text and occasional external data being utilized to inform the speculation on these matters. Authorities do not always agree on the details. The following table reflects the chronological conclusions which have been utilized in this commentary.

---

[6]E. Thiele (15, 31) has succeeded in establishing 931/30 B.C. as the date for the division of the monarchy after Solomon's death. Others argue for 932 (Barnes, 153-154), 945 (Falstich, 202-203), or 927-26 (Hayes & Hooker, 18-19).

Table 1
The Life of David

B.C.	Event	Reference	David's Age
1040	Birth of David		
1029	Privately anointed by Samuel	1 Sam 16:1-13	11
1028	Serves in Saul's court	1 Sam 16:14-23	12
1021	David defeats Goliath	1 Sam 17	19
1020	David serves in Saul's army	1 Sam 18	20
1016	Flight from Saul begins	1 Sam 19–26	24
1014	Samuel dies	1 Sam 25:1	26
1012	David serves King Achish	1 Sam 27–30	28
1010	Saul dies; David anointed	1 Sam 31; 2 Sam 5:4	30
1005	Ish-Bosheth begins two-year reign over Israel	2 Sam 2:10	32
1003	David anointed king of all Israel; Capture of Jerusalem; Philistine wars.	2 Sam 5, 21	37
1000	Begin three-year famine	2 Sam 21:1	40
997	Restoration of Mephibosheth	2 Sam 9:1-13	43
996	Begin Ammonite wars	2 Sam 10–12	44
995	The sin with Bathsheba	2 Sam 11	45
988	Birth of Solomon; Amnon rapes Tamar	2 Sam 12:24; chap. 13	52
986	Absalom kills Amnon	2 Sam 13:23	54
983	Absalom returns from Geshur	2 Sam 13:38	57
980	David battles Absalom	2 Sam 15–19	60
979	Sheba rebellion; Hiram builds David a palace	2 Sam 20; 5:11-12	61
975	David's census	2 Sam 24	65
971	Grandson Rehoboam born	1 Kgs 14:21	69
970	Adonijah revolt; David's death; Solomon anointed	1 Kgs 1–2	70

The chronological details for the life of Samuel and Saul are much more speculative. Key pieces of information are not related, e.g., Samuel's age at his death; the length of Saul's reign. The New Testament states that God gave Saul to Israel for the space of "forty years," after which he raised up David to be their king. If Acts 13:21-22 refers to the rule of Saul's dynasty, as seems likely, and if his dynasty ceased to have any royal power in 1003 B.C. when David was anointed, then it would appear that Saul was anointed about 1043

B.C. The following table reflects an attempt to reconstruct the chronology of Samuel's life.

Table 2

The Life of Samuel

B.C.	Event	Reference	Samuel's Age
1118	Birth of Samuel	1 Sam 1	
1105	Ark captured by Philistines	1 Sam 4–6	13
1085	Mizpah revival; Philistines defeated	1 Sam 7	33
1083	Birth of Saul		35
1048	Birth of Saul's son Ish-Bosheth	2 Sam 2:10	70
1043	Saul anointed	1 Sam 9	75
1041	Battle of Michmash	1 Sam 13:2	77
1040	Birth of David		78
1029	Amalekite war; David privately anointed	1 Sam 15–16	89
1014	Samuel's death	1 Sam 25:1	105

F. CONTENTS OF SAMUEL

For the most part the books of Samuel consist of historical narrative. Other literary forms which appear in the books are prayers, songs (e.g., 1 Sam 2; 2 Sam 22; 23), and lists (e.g., 2 Sam 21:15-22; 23:8-39).

Childs (271-277) has done commendable work in analyzing the structure of the books of Samuel. He regards 1 Sam 13:1 and 2 Sam 1:1 as formulas marking major divisions in this material. The division of the original book into two separate books recognized the structural significance of 2 Sam 1:1. The language of 2 Sam 21:1 is similar to that which was used in Ruth 1:1 to set off an historical appendix which is dischronological. Based on these indicators, the text of the Samuel books falls into four main divisions.

The first main division (1 Sam 1–12) focuses on the transition to monarchy.[7] The unit begins with the birth of Samuel and ends with his valedictory address. The text clearly indicates two major

---

[7]For a defense of the thematic unity of 1 Samuel 1–12, see Eslinger, *Kingship*, 48-53.

subdivisions. The first seven chapters cover the last days of judge-ship government. The high priestly judge Eli is depicted as a failure both in respect to his governance of the worship center, and in respect to his inability to cope with the Philistine menace. These failures led to the rise of a new type of judge. In Samuel the roles of prophet and judge were combined. The climax of this subsection is the victory over the Philistines which Yahweh granted in response to the prayer of Samuel (1 Sam 7).

The phrase "When Samuel grew old" in 1 Sam 8:1 clearly marks the beginning of the second subsection of the first main division. Here the focus is on the interaction between Samuel and Saul. Saul was selected by God, anointed privately and publicly by Samuel, and finally, after vindication through military leadership, embraced by the people. Once the people accepted their king, Samuel resigned from his role as judge. He indicated such by a marvelous farewell address (1 Sam 12).

The second main division of the material begins in 1 Sam 13:1. The kingship was now in place. This division, which terminates with the death of Saul in 1 Sam 31, also has two subdivisions. The account of Saul's disastrous reign comes to a climax in 1 Sam 16:13-14 where the Spirit of Yahweh departs from Saul and comes might-ily on David. The remaining chapters of 1 Samuel describe the rise of David to prominence and Saul's desperate efforts (1) to consoli-date his power and (2) to thwart the elevation of David to the throne. These observations are reflected in Chart 1.

Chart 1			
STRUCTURE OF 1 SAMUEL *Birth of the Kingdom* 1 Samuel 1–31			
Anticipation of Monarchy 1:1–2:10	**Transition to Monarchy** 2:11–12:25	**Failure in Monarchy** 13:1–16:13	**Promise to David in Jeopardy** 16:14–31:13

The third main division of material (2 Sam 1–20) focuses on the forty-year reign of David. The material has three subdivisions. The first (2 Sam 1–7) highlights the establishment of David's throne. This unit concludes with a prophetic word underscoring God's commitment to the dynasty of David (2 Sam 7). The second subdivision is concerned about the development of David's kingdom both in terms of territorial expansion and internal organization. Clearly the great sin with Bathsheba (2 Sam 11) marks a turning point in the narrative. This unit concludes with a prophetic word condemning David's adultery and announcing the commencement of a period of turmoil for the king (2 Sam 12). In the third subdivision David experiences one set of problems after another, for he was under a divine curse (cf. 2 Sam 12:11ff.).

The last four chapters of 2 Samuel serve as an appendix to the David narratives. These chapters are carefully crafted to present "a highly reflective, theological interpretation of David's whole career" (Childs, 275). The above data are displayed in Chart 2.

Chart 2
STRUCTURE OF 2 SAMUEL
Expansion of the Kingdom
2 Samuel 1–24

The Covenant with David Established	The Covenant with David Blessed	The Covenant with David in Jeopardy	The Covenant with David in Retrospect
2 Sam 1:1–7:29	2 Sam 8:1–12:15a	2 Sam 12:15b–20:26	2 Sam 21:1–24:25

G. TEACHING OF SAMUEL

According to Childs (272-275), three texts in the Samuel material indicate the main point which the author was attempting to get across. These texts are (1) the song of Hannah (1 Sam 2), (2) the oracle of Nathan (2 Sam 7), and (3) the last words of David (2 Sam 22–23).

In Hannah's song God is central. Hannah praised the character and the strength of God and the ultimate day when God would judge the ends of the earth through his anointed king. The history which unfolds in the Samuel material illustrates the truth of which Hannah sang. Virtually every line of her song finds its counterpart in the pages which follow. The Narrator placed this poem near the beginning of the work in order to indicate the perspective from which he presents the history of Israel.

The Nathan oracle is the pinnacle of the blessings which God showered on David in 2 Samuel 1–10. Here the general expectations of Hannah are made more specific. The blessings bestowed on David are projected into the distant future. God would bless the "house of [David] . . . forever." Thus David is regarded (1) as the fulfillment of

Yahweh's ancient promise to give his people a king, and (2) as a type
of the ultimate Ruler who would sit on God's throne forever.

The final passage with crucial significance for the message of
these books is 2 Sam 22:1-23:7. This passage contains two separate
poetic compositions, the first (2 Sam 22:1-51) coming from the time
when Yahweh had delivered David from all his enemies (2 Sam
22:1). The second composition comes from the last days of David
(2 Sam 23:1). This material has been placed at the conclusion of the
Samuel books for strategic purposes. The thanksgiving hymn in
ch. 22 echoes many of the themes articulated in Hannah's praise
hymn (1 Sam 2). The poem looks back over the career of David and
underscores the grand proposition which is the overriding message
of this material, viz., that God rewards the righteous, and brings
judgment upon the unrighteous.

The thanksgiving poem concludes with an allusion (2 Sam 22:51)
to the Nathan oracle which announced Yahweh's eternal involvement with the house of David. This theme is stated even more forcefully in the following poem (2 Sam 23:5). Thus in spite of the terrible sin with Bathsheba and the other shortcomings of David's
career, the promise of an enduring house was still valid.

Appearing as they do at the beginning of the material, (roughly)
the middle, and at the conclusion, the four poetic compositions cast
a messianic shadow over the books of Samuel. One cannot read
these passages without concluding that God had great things in
store for the house of David: an everlasting covenant, an eternal
throne, and a righteous king who ultimately would judge the very
ends of the earth. The testimony of the New Testament is that such
promises find their fulfillment in Jesus of Nazareth.

H. THE CANONICITY AND TEXT OF SAMUEL

Table 3 NEW TESTAMENT CITATION	
Samuel Reference	New Testament Citation
2 Samuel 7:8,14	2 Corinthians 6:18
2 Samuel 7:14	Hebrews 1:5
2 Samuel 22:50	Romans 15:9

The canonicity of the Samuel material has never been disputed
by Jews or Christians. While Samuel and David in particular are

mentioned frequently, only three direct citations of this material are found in the New Testament.

The text of the Samuel books is notoriously difficult.[8] In a number of places the NIV has chosen to follow the lead of the LXX rather then translate the standard Hebrew text (MT). The discovery of the Dead Sea Scrolls in 1948 produced three priceless fragments of these books which in some places have significantly different readings. These MSS antedate by centuries the oldest copies of the MT. In places these fragments support the LXX reading, and in other places they do not. At least one modern version has made wholesale use of readings from the LXX and the Dead Sea fragments.[9] This reliance on LXX and Qumran readings over against the MT has been challenged by some scholars (e.g., S. Pisano). Generally speaking, a large textual plus or minus (i.e., words added or missing) is most likely a further literary activity by the LXX or the Qumran fragments (Pisano, 283). Where obvious corruptions have occurred in the MT through faulty transmission, the LXX and Qumran fragments are helpful in making restorations. More important than the variety of small differences in the text is the astonishing similarity between the MT and the MSS which are a thousand years older (Cross, ALQ, 40-42).[10] Youngblood (559) proposes this rule of thumb: when two or more non-MT readings agree as over against the MT, careful attention should be paid to the evidence they present.

---

[8] Cf. Gordon, 57: "For some reason the books of Samuel have suffered more in the process of transmission than perhaps any other part of the Old Testament."

[9] The translators of the NAB record over four hundred emendations, the vast majority of them from the DSS. Of these some seventy-three are supported from a Qumran text, and twenty-two follow a Qumran text without further support. *Textual Notes on the New American Bible* (Paterson, NJ: St Anthony's Guild, n.d.), 342-351. In contrast, the NIV footnotes indicate preference for a reading other than that of the MT in about fifty instances.

[10] Recent studies of the Qumran texts of Samuel: E.C. Ulrich, Jr., *The Qumran Text of Samuel and Josephus* (Missoula, MT: Scholars Press, 1978); idem, "4QSam^c; A Fragmentary Manuscript of 2 Samuel 14-15," *BASOR* 235 (1979): 1-25; E. Tov, "The Textual Affiliations of 4QSam^a," *JSOT* 14 (1979): 37-53; E. Tov (ed.), *The Hebrew and Greek Texts of Samuel* (Jerusalem: Academon, 1980); Geza Vermes, "Biblical Studies and the Dead Sea Scrolls 1947-1987: Retrospects and Prospects," *JSOT* 39 (1987): 113-128.

OUTLINE

1 SAMUEL
THE BIRTH OF THE KINGDOM

I. ANTICIPATION OF THE MONARCHY — 1:1–2:10
 A. The Birth of the King-Maker — 1:1-20
 B. Report of Samuel's Birth — 1:21-28
 C. Prophetic Song of Anticipation — 2:1-10

II. TRANSITION TO MONARCHY — 2:11–11:15
 A. The Rise of Samuel — 2:11–7:17
 B. The Rise of Saul — 8:1–11:15

III. SAMUEL'S VALEDICTORY: RETROSPECT AND PROSPECT — 12:1-25

IV. THE FAILURE IN MONARCHY — 13:1–16:13
 A. Saul's Initial Rebuke — 13:1-15a
 B. Saul's Heroic Son — 13:15b–14:23
 C. Saul's Foolish Curse — 14:24-46
 D. Saul's Firm Control in the Kingdom — 14:47-52
 E. Saul's Final Rejection — 15:1-35
 F. The "Call" of David — 16:1-13

V. DAVID'S RISE TO PROMINENCE IN SAUL'S COURT — 16:14–21:9
 A. Initial Recognition and Danger — 16:14–17:58
 B. Post-Goliath Recognition and Danger — 18:1-12
 C. Military Recognition and Danger — 18:13-27
 D. Growing Recognition and Danger — 18:28–19:6
 E. Continuing Recognition and Danger — 19:7-24
 F. Jonathan's Recognition and Danger — 20:1–21:9

VI. DAVID'S RISE TO PROMINENCE AS AN OUTLAW — 21:10–27:4
 A. David in Gath — 21:10-15
 B. David at Adullam — 22:1-28

C. David at Keilah — 23:1-14
D. David at Horesh — 23:15-29
E. David near En Gedi — 24:1-25:1a
F. David in the Wilderness of Paran — 25:1b-35
G. Last Scenes of Fugitive Life — 25:36-26:25
H. David Seeks Sanctuary in Gath — 27:1-4

VII. DAVID'S RISE TO PROMINENCE OUTSIDE ISRAEL —
27:5-31:13
A. David in Ziklag — 27:5-28:2
B. A Word of Judgment for Saul — 28:3-25
C. David on the March — 29:1-30:6
D. A Word of Encouragement for David — 30:7-8
E. David in Battle — 30:9-31
F. Final Obstacle to Kingship Removed — 31:1-13

2 SAMUEL
THE EXPANSION OF THE KINGDOM

VIII. THE COVENANT WITH DAVID ESTABLISHED —
1:1-7:29
A. Enthronement of David over Judah — 1:1-3:5
B. Enthronement of David Prospects — 3:6-39
C. Enthronement of David over Israel — 4:1-5:16
D. Enthronement of David in Jerusalem — 5:17-6:23
E. Enthronement of David's Dynasty — 7:1-29

IX. THE COVENANT WITH DAVID BLESSED — 8:1-12:31
A. National Expansion — 8:1-18
B. Royal Benevolence — 9:1-13
C. Glorious Victories — 10:1-19
D. Personal Failing — 11:1-27
E. Prophetic Rebuke — 12:1-14
F. Divine Discipline — 12:15-23
G. Tokens of Grace — 12:24-31

X. THE COVENANT WITH DAVID IN JEOPARDY —
13:1-20:26
A. Tested by Family Turmoil — 13:1-14:33
B. Tested by Dynastic Upheaval — 15:1-19:43
C. Tested by Tribal Revolt — 20:1-22
D. David's Court — 20:23-26

XI. **THE COVENANT WITH DAVID IN RETROSPECT —**
21:1–24:25
A. **David's Discipline: A Famine** — 21:1-14
B. **David's Heroes: A List** — 21:15-22
C. **David's Testimony: A Song** — 22:1-51
D. **David's Hope: A Song** — 23:1-7
E. **David's Heroes: A List** — 23:8-39
F. **David's Discipline: A Census** — 24:1-25

BIBLIOGRAPHY

Ackroyd, P.R. *The First Book of Samuel*. In The Cambridge Bible Commentary on the New English Bible. Cambridge: University Press, 1971.

Aharoni, Y. *The Land of the Bible*. Philadelphia: Westminster, 1979.

_____. *The Archaeology of the Land of Israel*. Philadelphia: Westminster, 1982.

Ahlström, G.W. *The History of Ancient Palestine*. Minneapolis: Fortress, 1993.

Albright, W.F. *The Biblical Period from Abraham to Ezra*. New York: Harper & Row, 1963.

Anderson, A.A. *2 Samuel*. Vol 11 of Word Biblical Commentary. Dallas: Word Books, 1989.

Archer, G.L. *Encyclopedia of Bible Difficulties*. Grand Rapids: Zondervan, 1982.

Baldwin, Joyce G. *1 & 2 Samuel*. In Tyndale Old Testament Commentaries. Downers Grove, IL: InterVarsity, 1988.

Barnes, W.H. *Studies in the Chronology of the Divided Monarchy of Israel*. Atlanta: Scholars, 1991.

Berlin, A. *Poetics and Interpretation of Biblical Narrative*. Sheffield, 1983.

Bierling, Neal. *Giving Goliath His Due; New Archaeological Light on the Philistines*. Grand Rapids: Baker, 1992.

Bright, John. *A History of Israel*. 2nd ed. Philadelphia: Westminster, 1972.

Bruce, F.F. *Israel and the Nations*. Grand Rapids: Eerdmans, 1963.

Brueggemann, Walter. *First and Second Samuel*. Interpretation: A Bible Commentary for Teaching and Preaching. Louisville, KY: John Knox, 1990.

Caird, G. "The First and Second Books of Samuel." In Vol. 2 of *The Interpreter's Bible*. New York: Abingdon, 1953.

Campbell, A.F. *The Ark Narrative: A Form-Critical and Traditio-Historical Study*. Missoula, MT: Scholars, 1975.

Carlson, R.A. *David the Chosen King: A Traditio-Historical Approach to the Second Book of Samuel*. Stockholm: Almqvist and Wiksell, 1964.

Childs, B.S. *Introduction to the Old Testament as Scripture*. Philadelphia: Fortress, 1979.

Clarke, Adam. *The Holy Bible with a Commentary and Critical Notes*. Vol. 2. New York: B. Waugh and T. Mason, 1835.

Clines, D.J.A., and T.C. Eskenazi, eds.*Telling Michal's Story: An Experiment in Comparative Interpretation*. Sheffield: JSOT, 1991.

Conroy, C. *Absalom, Absalom! Narrative and Language in 2 Sam 13-20*. Rome: Biblical Institute Press, 1978.

Crockett, W. *A Harmony of the Books of Samuel, Kings, and Chronicles*. Grand Rapids: Baker, 1951.

Cundall, A.E., and L. Morris, *Judges and Ruth*. Tyndale Old Testament Commentaries. Leicester: Inter-Varsity, 1971.

Davis, John J. *Biblical Numerology*. Grand Rapids: Baker, 1968.

Dothan, T. *The Philistines and Their Material Culture*. New Haven: Yale University, 1982.

Driver, S.R. *Notes on the Hebrew Text and the Topography of the Books of Samuel*. 2nd ed. Oxford: Clarendon, 1913.

Erdmann, D. "Samuel." In J. Lange (ed.). *Commentary on the Holy Scriptures*. Grand Rapids: Zondervan, n.d. (reprint of the 1877 ed.).

Eslinger, L.M. *Kingship of God in Crisis; A Close Reading of 1 Samuel 1-12*. Sheffield: JSOT Press, 1985.

_____. *House of God or House of David: The Rhetoric of 2 Samuel 7*. Sheffield: JSOT Press, 1994.

Falstich, E.W. *History, Harmony, and the Hebrew Kings*. Spencer: Chronology Books, 1986.

Fokkelman, J.P. *Narrative Art and Poetry in the Books of Samuel*. 4 vols. Assen: Van Gorcus, 1981-1990.

Foresti, F. *The Rejection of Saul in Perspective of the Deuteronomistic*

School: A Study of 1 Sm. 15 and Related Texts. Rome: Edizioni del Teresianum, 1984.

Gardiner, F., and H.D.M. Spence. "I and II Samuel." Vol. 2 in *An Old Testament Commentary for English Readers.* Ed. Charles John Ellicott. New York: Cassell, 1901.

Glueck, Nelson. *Hesed in the Bible.* Cincinnati: Hebrew Union College, 1967.

Goldman, S. *Samuel.* Soncino Books of the Bible. London: Soncino Press, 1951.

Gooding, D. *The Story of David and Goliath: Textual and Literary Criticism.* Göttingen: Vandenhoeck and Ruprecht, 1986.

Gordon, R.P. *I & II Samuel: A Commentary.* Grand Rapids: Zondervan, 1986.

Gottwald, N.K. *The Tribes of Yahweh, A Sociology of the Religion of Liberated Israel, 1250-1050 B.C.E.* London: SCM Press, 1980.

Guillaume, A. *Prophecy and Divination.* London: Hodder and Stoughton, 1938.

Gunn, David M. *The Fate of King Saul: An Interpretation of a Biblical Story.* Sheffield: JSOT, 1980.

_____. *The Story of King David: Genre and Interpretation.* Sheffield: JSOT, 1982.

Haley, John. *An Examination of the Alleged Discrepancies of the Bible.* Grand Rapids: Baker, 1977 (reprint).

Hayes, John, and Paul Hooker. *A New Chronology for the Kings of Israel and Judah and Its Implications for Biblical History and Literature.* Atlanta: John Knox, 1988.

Herrmann, S. *A History of Israel in Old Testament Times.* 2nd ed. London: SCM Press, 1981.

Hertzberg, Hans W. *I & II Samuel, a Commentary.* The Old Testament Library. Trans. J.S. Bowden. Philadelphia: Westminster, 1964.

Herzog, C., and M. Gichon. *Battles of the Bible.* New York: Random House, 1978.

Hindson, Edward. *The Philistines and the Old Testament.* Grand Rapids: Baker, 1971.

Horner, T. *Jonathan Loved David: Homosexuality in Biblical Times.* Philadelphia: Westminster Press, 1978.

Jamieson, Robert. "Joshua–Esther." In vol. 2 of *A Commentary, Critical, Experimental, and Practical, on the Old and the New Testaments*. Philadelphia: Lippincott, n.d.

Jobling, D. *The Sense of Biblical Narrative*. JSOTSup 7. Sheffield: JSOT, 1978. 4-25.

Kaiser, W. *Toward Old Testament Ethics*. Grand Rapids: Academie, 1983.

Kalluveettil, P. *Declaration and Covenant*. Rome: Biblical Institute Press, 1982.

Katzenstein, H.J. *The History of Tyre*. 2nd rev. ed. Beer Sheva: Ben-Gurion University of the Negev Press, 1997.

Kirkpatrick, A.F. *The First and Second Book of Samuel*. 2 vols. The Cambridge Bible for Schools and Colleges. Ed. J.J.S. Perowne. Cambridge: University Press, 1880-81.

Klein, Ralph W. *1 Samuel*. Vol. 10. Word Biblical Commentary. Waco, TX: Word, 1983.

Knight, H. *The Hebrew Prophetic Consciousness*. London: Lutterworth Press, 1947.

Lindblom, J. *Prophecy in Ancient Israel*. Philadelphia: Fortress, 1962.

Mauchline, J. *1 and 2 Samuel*. New Century Bible. Greenwood, SC: Attic Press, 1971.

May, H.G. *Oxford Bible Atlas*. London: Oxford, 1962.

Mazar, Benjamin, "The Philistines and their Wars with Israel." *World History of the Jewish People*. 3:164-179. Tel-Aviv: Massada, 1971.

McCarter, P. Kyle, Jr. *I and II Samuel, A New Translation with Introduction, Notes and Commentary*. 2 vols.The Anchor Bible. New York: Doubleday, 1980, 1984.

McCarthy, D.J. *Treaty and Covenant*. 2nd ed. Rome: Biblical Institute Press, 1978.

McKane, W. *I and II Samuel: Introduction and Commentary*. Torch Bible Commentary. London: SCM, 1963.

Merrill, E.H. *Kingdom of Priests: A History of Old Testament Israel*. Grand Rapids: Baker, 1987.

Mettinger, T.N.D. *King and Messiah; The Civil and Sacral Legitimation of the Israelite Kings*. Lund: Gleerup, 1976.

Miller, P.D., and J.J.M. Roberts, *The Hand of the Lord: A Reassessment of the Ark Narrative of 1 Samuel*. Baltimore: Johns Hopkins, 1977.

Miscall, P.D. *1 Samuel: A Literary Reading*. Bloomington: Indiana University, 1986.

Myers, J.M. *I Chronicles*. In Anchor Bible. Garden City, NY: Doubleday, 1965.

Noth, M. *The History of Israel*. 2nd ed. Eng. trans. London: A. and C. Black, 1958.

Oesterley, W., and T. H. Robinson. *A History of Israel*. 2 vols. Oxford: Clarendon, 1932.

Pisano, Stephen. *Additions or Omissions in the Books of Samuel*. Göttingen: Vanderhoeck & Ruprecht, 1984.

Polzin, Robert. *Samuel and the Deuteronomist*. Bloomington: Indiana University, 1989.

Pope, M. *Song of Songs*. In Anchor Bible. New York: Doubleday, 1977.

Pritchard, J.B. *Gibeon, Where the Sun Stood Still: The Discovery of the Biblical City*. Princeton: Princeton University, 1962.

Robertson, E. *The Old Testament Problem*. Manchester: University Press, 1950.

Rogerson, John. *Atlas of the Bible*. New York: Facts on File, 1985.

Schniedewind, W.M. *Society and the Promise to David: the Reception History of 2 Samuel 7:1-17*. New York: Oxford, 1999.

Simons, J. *Jerusalem in the Old Testament*. Leiden: Brill, 1982.

Smith, H.P. *A Critical and Exegetical Commentary on the Books of Samuel*. International Critical Commentary. New York: Scribner's Sons, 1909.

Smith, J.E. *What the Bible Teaches about the Promised Messiah*. Nashville: Thomas Nelson, 1993.

Smith, R.P. "I Samuel: Exposition." *The Pulpit Commentary*. H.D.M. Spence and J.S. Exell, eds. New York: Funk & Wagnalls, 1907.

Stanley, A.P. *Lectures on the History of the Jewish Church*. 3 vols. New Edition. New York: Scribner's Sons, 1892.

Sternberg, M. *The Poetics of Biblical Narrative: Ideological Literature and the Drama of Reading*. Bloomington: Indiana University, 1987.

Tadmor, H., and M. Weinfeld, eds. *History, Historiography and Interpretation*. Jerusalem: Magnes, 1984.

Thiele, E. *A Chronology of the Hebrew Kings*. Grand Rapids: Zondervan, 1977.

Unger, M.F. *Israel and the Arameans of Damascus*. Grand Rapids: Baker, 1980, reprint.

Vannoy, J.R. *Covenant Renewal at Gilgal*. Cherry Hill, NJ: Mock, 1978.

Vaux, Roland de. *Ancient Israel: Its Life and Institutions*. Pb. ed. 2 vols. New York: McGraw Hill, 1961.

Vermes, G. *The Complete Dead Sea Scrolls in English*. New York: Penguin Books, 1998.

Wenham, G.J. *The Book of Leviticus*, NICOT. London: Hodder & Stoughton, 1979.

Whybray, R.N. *The Succession Narrative*. London: SCM, 1968.

Wiseman, D. ed. *Peoples of the Old Testament*. Oxford: Clarendon, 1973.

Woudstra, M. *The Ark of the Covenant from Conquest to Kingship*. Philadelphia: Presbyterian & Reformed, 1965.

Yadin, Y. *The Art of Warfare in Biblical Lands*. Jerusalem: International Publishing, 1963.

Youngblood, R. "1, 2 Samuel." In vol. 3 of *The Expositor's Bible Commentary*. Grand Rapids: Zondervan, 1992.

1 SAMUEL 1

I. ANTICIPATION OF THE MONARCHY (1:1–2:10)

A. THE BIRTH OF THE KING MAKER (1:1-20)

Appropriately the story of Israel's monarchy begins with an account of the early life of Samuel the king maker. God chose Samuel to anoint both Saul and David, Israel's first two kings. Each was to be the "leader" (נָגִיד, *nāgîd*) over his people (1 Sam 10:1; 13:14; 16:13).

1. Hannah's Plight (1:1-8)

1:1 The NIV does not render the conjunction *waw* (ו, "now," NASB) with which v. 1 begins in the Hebrew. The independent histories of Ruth, Esther, and Jonah also begin with this conjunction. Therefore, the *waw* appears to be the formal opening to a historical narrative, without any connecting force.[1] The opening verse here is unlike v. 1 of Joshua and Judges in that those books are linked to preceding events by the first line of text. First Sam 1:1 signals that Israel is about to march down a different path, one which does not have its genesis in recent events. The verse sketches the background for the events of the birth story utilizing a pattern of gradually increasing specificity.

A certain man: lit., "one man," is an idiom sometimes used to indicate a person without rank or position (2 Sam 18:10; Judg 9:53). Here the description of Samuel's father is very similar to that of Samson's father (Judg 13:2) in that the idiom is accompanied by

---

[1]*Contra* Kirkpatrick (1:43) who argues that the *waw* is intended as a linking device to the Book of Judges which immediately precedes the Book of Samuel in the Hebrew Bible.

(1) his town, (2) his tribal area, (3) his name, and (4) his marital status.[2] The "certain man" is more precisely identified in three ways.

1. As to location, the "certain man" was from "Ramathaim" ("the two Ramahs or heights").[3] This name, which appears only here in the Bible, is the more technical name for Ramah ("the height") in v. 19. The name suggests (1) that a new village had sprung up alongside an old Ramah or (2) that this village was built near or on two hills. The writer uses "Ramathaim" to distinguish Samuel's birthplace from the more prominent Ramah of Benjamin (Josh 18:25; Judg 19:13; et al.) and at least three other towns of the same name. Ramathaim has not yet been located.[4]

The Hebrew term rendered **Zuphite** by the NIV actually is part of the name of the town. A more accurate rendering would be "Ramathaim-zophim" (NASB).[5] Some understand *zophim* (צוֹפִים, *ṣôphîm*) to be a common noun meaning "Watchers," perhaps expressing the idea that at one time the hills of Ramah had been used as lookout posts. The name of the town in English would then be "Ramahs of the Watchers." The NIV connects *zophim* with Zuphites or descendants of Zuph, an ancestor of Elkanah. Ramathaim was located in an area called "the district of Zuph" (1 Sam 9:5f.). This region apparently had been settled by Zuph or Zophai (1 Chr 6:26,35).

Ramathaim was located in **the hill country of Ephraim**, lit., "the hill of Ephraim." The NIV rightly interprets this phrase as a reference to a range of hills. The mountainous backbone of Palestine is referred to as *har*, i.e., hill country. The southern part of this range of hills is called "the hill country of Judah," and the northern part took its name from the dominant tribe of the area, viz., Ephraim.

---

[2]The similarity between the introductions of the two fathers is probably intentional. It highlights the dedication of both Samson and Samuel as Nazirites to the Lord from birth (Youngblood, 570).

[3]"Ramathaim" appears to be a dual form. Youngblood (570), however, thinks it is not intended to be a grammatical dual, but rather possesses locative force.

[4]In Bible atlases Ramathaim is (1) equated with Ramah in Benjamin (ZA); (2) not listed (MBA); (3) identified with Rentis, New Testament Arimathea (OBA; Rogerson) located sixteen miles east of Joppa on the west slope of the hill country of Ephraim (Matt 27:57).

[5]The NIV translation is based on an emendation of the text, proposed by a number of scholars, who read *zuphi* for *zophim*.

The hills and valleys of this region are well watered and remarkable for their fertility.

2. As to ancestry, the "certain man" came from a family which elsewhere is traced back to Kohath, the son of Levi (1 Chr 6:1ff.). Here his genealogy to the fourth generation is recorded.[6] This may mean that Elkanah belonged to a noble and well-known family. More likely, however, the genealogy has been recorded because of the importance of Samuel, Elkanah's son, whose birth is the focus of the chapter. Why is Samuel not called a Levite in the book of Samuel? No doubt the reason was that the work of Samuel as the last of the judges and the first of a new line of prophets did not rest upon his Levitical descent, but upon his prophetic call. The fact that Samuel belonged to God by virtue of the vow made by his mother is not at variance with his Levitical descent. Levites were not required to serve at the central sanctuary until their twenty-fifth year, and even then only as they were needed. Samuel's mother offered him in lifelong service under the terms of a Nazirite vow.

The pedigree of Samuel appears also in 1 Chr 6:13-11 and 1 Chr 6:18-20. The variations are such as often appear in parallel lists of names in the Old Testament. While some attribute such variations to deliberate alteration for religious purposes, conservative scholars suggest these different readings are the result of (1) errors in scribal transmission, (2) name change over time, (3) genealogical selectivity of the narrator, or (4) double names for the same individual.

Table 4		
The Genealogy of Samuel		
1 Sam 1:1	1 Chr 6:26-28	1 Chr 6:33-35
(Samuel)	Samuel	Samuel
Elkanah	Elkanah	Elkanah
Jeroham	Jeroham	Jeroham
Elihu	Eliab	Eliel
Tohu	Nahath	Toah
Zuph	Zophai	Zuph

---

[6]Eslinger (*Kingship*, 66f.) thinks the names in Elkanah's genealogy are important only because of their unimportance. As stated here, the genealogy accomplishes nothing in the way of legitimation. "Samuel's natural lineage grants him no claim to any important rank. If he has or attains any status at all it is not because of his family tree."

3. As to civil standing, Elkanah was an **Ephraimite,** lit., *Ephrathite*. Two other times in the Hebrew Bible this term is applied to Ephraimites (Judg 12:5; 1 Kgs 11:26), and the NIV correctly has understood it here. Levites had no tribal territory of their own. They originally were assigned forty-eight cities scattered throughout the tribes of Israel. Apparently it was the practice to reckon Levites as belonging civically to the tribes to which they were attached (cf. Judg 17:7).[7] Elkanah is called an Ephraimite either (1) because he belonged to a Levitical family which originally had been assigned to the territory of Ephraim (Josh 21:20); or (2) because Ramathaim was located in the tribal territory of Ephraim, or at least in the hill country of Ephraim.[8]

1:2 Elkanah was the only commoner in the books of Samuel and Kings specifically mentioned as having more than one wife. One was named **Hannah** ("Grace"; cf. Anna in Luke 2:36) and the other **Peninnah** ("Coral" or "Pearl"). Perhaps he took the second wife because Hannah was barren. By her barrenness Hannah was being tested like several famous women before her (Gen 11:30; 25:21; 29:31; Judg 13:2).

1:3 Elkanah is represented as a pious man. The term translated **went up . . . to the LORD** is the technical language for a religious pilgrimage. The verb form has frequentative force. This verse sets forth four facts about Elkanah's worship.

---

[7]In certain passages an Ephrathite refers to a citizen of Bethlehem (1 Sam 17:12; Ruth 1:2) because Bethlehem was known as Ephrathah (Gen 35:19; 48:7; Ruth 4:11; Micah 5:2). In Ps 132:6 the term is perhaps applied to a district where Kirjath Jearim was located on the border of Judah and Benjamin. Both Ephrathah and Ephraim mean "fruitful." Baldwin (51) thinks that the text is claiming Elkanah had connections with Bethlehem. She points out that there were connections between Levites of Bethlehem and the hill country of Ephraim (Judg 17:7-12; 19:1-21). If Elkanah traced some family connections to Bethlehem, it would be natural that his son Samuel should return there to offer his sacrifice (1 Sam 16:2), even though the family more recently had been worshiping at Shiloh.

[8]Two unacceptable explanations of divergence between the Levitical and Ephraimite ancestry of Elkanah have been advanced: (1) because the Ephraimite Samuel was attached to the sanctuary by his Nazirite vow, the Levitical authorities could claim him as their own; and (2) Chronicles represents a later and inaccurate attempt of the priestly authorities to claim for this priest-like character a Levitical ancestry.

1. The time of his pilgrimage. **Year after year** is lit., "from days to days," a phrase which elsewhere refers to a statutory annual religious observance. Elkanah made annual religious pilgrimages with his family. Did he ignore the Mosaic requirement to attend three annual festivals (Passover and Pentecost in the Spring, Tabernacles in the Fall) at the central sanctuary? (cf. Exod 34:23; Deut 16:16). Not necessarily. Families were not required to attend any festival. Elkanah, however, took his family to the central sanctuary annually (cf. Deut 12:10-12). Perhaps as a Levite (see above) he had responsibilities at the other two annual festivals. On the other hand, Elkanah may not have been as circumspect in observing the law of Moses as he should have been. The annual festival here may have been Passover.[9]

2. The purpose of the pilgrimage. Elkanah went from his town (Ramathaim) **to worship and sacrifice** to the Lord Almighty. The term "worship" means lit., "to bow down or prostrate oneself before a superior, whether monarch or deity." The word speaks primarily to the attitude of the heart. "Sacrifice" refers to the presentation of an animal which was slain at the altar in a ritual jointly administered by worshiper and priest. Four basic sacrifices are described in the law of Moses: (1) the burnt offering which symbolized complete consecration, (2) the peace or fellowship offering, (3) the sin offering, and (4) the trespass offering. What follows in the chapter suggests that the peace or fellowship offering was the highlight of the festival (Lev 7:11-18).

The name of God here is literally "Yahweh of hosts." The NIV has followed the lead of most English versions by substituting the word LORD (small caps) for the tetragrammaton, the four-letter name for God (יהוה, YHWH). This name was regarded by Jews in post-Old Testament times as so sacred that it ceased to be uttered. In time the accurate pronunciation of the name was lost. Jews would substitute the Hebrew equivalent of the word "Lord" when they came across the tetragrammaton in the Bible. The best scholarly guess as to how the name was pronounced in ancient times is *Yahweh*. The name means something like "he who exists," or "he who causes things to exist."

---

[9]The Hebrew expression rendered "year after year" is found in Exodus 13:10 in reference to the Passover and Feast of Unleavened Bread which immediately followed. Youngblood (571) thinks the festival was Tabernacles in the fall of the year. On the other hand, the annual sacrifice may have been a traditional family gathering unrelated to any of the prescribed feasts.

Here the name Yahweh is combined with "hosts" to form a special title for the God of Israel. This is the first of some 260 usages of this title. The complete title would be "Yahweh God of Hosts" (e.g., 2 Sam 5:10). The term "hosts" is used in the Old Testament of (1) the stars (Gen 2:1; Deut 4:19; et al.), (2) the angels (1 Kgs 22:19; Ps 103:21), and (3) the armies of Israel (Num 1:52; 1 Sam 17:45; et al.). Attributing to God the authority over all hosts in heaven and on earth is a way of underscoring divine power. This majestic name for God, appearing at the inception of the Israelite monarchy, describes him in a way that is much more royal than military.[10] Polemically, the title "Yahweh of hosts" proclaims the Lord as superior to sun, moon and stars which were the objects of worship among the ancient peoples (Deut 4:19; Job 31:26-28).

3. The place of the pilgrimage. Elkanah went up to **Shiloh** (MBA, p. 82), a town in Ephraim, "east of the road that goes from Bethel to Shechem" (Judg 21:19). Archaeology has indicated that Shiloh (modern ruin called "Seilun") was a new city, first built by Israelites.[11] The tabernacle had been located here since the days of Joshua (Josh 18:1). A platform (400' × 70') roughly hewn out of the rocky hillside is still visible there. This may have been the site of the tabernacle (Goldman, 2).

4. The impediments to the pilgrimage. The piety of Elkanah in going up to Shiloh regularly is here contrasted with the inactivity with the Elides who were merely there. At Shiloh the leading priests were **Hophni and Phinehas**, the **sons of Eli**. Either due to age, or to the other duties of judgeship, Eli seems to have delegated priestly responsibilities to his sons. These two are mentioned because (1) they were ranking priests, likely in line to become the high priest; (2) they figure prominently in one of the greatest tragedies which befell the people of God prior to the monarchy; and (3) these two prominent

---

[10]J.P. Ross, "Jahweh S'bha'oth in Samuel and Psalms," *VT* 17 (1967): 76-92; T.N.D. Mettinger, "YHWH SABAOTH — The Heavenly King on the Cherubim Throne," SPDS, 109-138. Eslinger (*Kingship*, 70), however, thinks the name introduces Yahweh as "the warrior god [*sic*] who will play such an important role in connection with the ark in chs. 4–6." F.M. Cross (CMHE, 69-71) claims to have found parallels to this title in the Ugaritic texts. He concludes that this was a creation formula which originally meant "he who creates the (heavenly) armies."

[11]I. Finkelstein, "Shiloh Yields Some, but Not All, of Its Secrets," *BAR* 12 (Jan-Feb 1986): 22-41.

priests illustrate the terrible state of corruption into which the priesthood had fallen (Spence, 295). Hophni and Phinehas were reprobates and hypocrites. Yet Elkanah did not let their presence at Shiloh and their public leadership in ritual activities deter him from fulfilling the duty to express his worship at that shrine.

1:4-5 In the peace or fellowship offering, (1) the blood was poured out at the foot of the altar, (2) the fat was burned on the fire, (3) the breast and right shoulder were given to the priest, and (4) the rest of the animal was cooked and eaten in a joyous celebration by the worshiper and his family before the Lord in the courtyard of the tabernacle (Lev 7:11-34). Elkanah carved the meat for his family and dispensed portions to each family member. Hannah received **a double portion** (lit., "one portion for two faces"). Perhaps he gave to her his portion, as well as that which would normally be hers. In this way Elkanah (1) publicly proclaimed his love for her above his wife Peninnah and (2) expressed his sympathy for her barrenness. The words **the LORD had closed her womb** serve as (1) an implicit claim to inspiration (for who but the Lord could reveal such a fact) and (2) a signal that God was at work behind the scenes.

1:6-8 The Hannah story is one of several in the Bible where a barren wife is given a child by the Lord. Sarah, Rebekah, Rachel, and Samson's mother are examples of women who, for long periods of time, had to deal with the Eastern stigma of childlessness. These accounts serve to underscore the importance of the child who is born as well as the piety and faith of the parents involved. Four points are emphasized in these verses.

1. The plan of God (v. 6a). The statement that God had **closed her womb** is made twice. This suggests that God directly and actively restrained the womb of Hannah for his own sovereign purposes. This should not be viewed as a judgment for some sin in her life necessarily, but as a trial which would refine her priorities and faith. The painful experiences of life often drive a believer to make commitments and promises he otherwise would not be inclined to make.

2. The provocation of Peninnah (v. 6b). On **went up**, see v. 3. **The house of the LORD** refers to the tabernacle. Peninnah is called Hannah's **rival** (צָרָה, *ṣārāh*). Some think that a better rendering of the word here is "fellow-wife" (Goldman, 3). Peninnah's spitefulness was triggered by Elkanah's public display of affection for Hannah. She used her fertility to lord it over Hannah (cf. Gen 16:4; 30:1-24). She **kept provoking** Hannah, perhaps by making an ostentatious exhibition of

her children (Clarke, 107). One of the most detestable manifestations of malice is exultation over the misfortunes of others. Jealousy, grief, anger, and malice are some of the bitter fruits of polygamy. Peninnah had as her aim to **irritate** (lit., "to thunder against," i.e., browbeat or bully) Hannah.

3. The pain of Hannah (v. 7). Peninnah's provocation was an irritation to Hannah. Year after year the little family drama was played out. Elkanah gave Hannah the extra portion. Peninnah provoked Hannah to tears. Hannah would become so upset she could not participate in the religious meal. What was supposed to be a joyous feast became a miserable experience for all concerned.

4. The pity of Elkanah (v. 8). The Narrator emphasizes the special relationship between Hannah and Elkanah by attaching the seemingly redundant description **her husband** to the proper name. He is never described as Peninnah's "husband," though he of course was married to her. Elkanah addressed his grieving wife with exceptionally loving words of consolation. His four questions (v. 8), though of small comfort to his distraught wife, stress that in terms of their marriage she had nothing to worry about. **Why are you downhearted?** is literally "Why is your heart bad?" i.e., not so much sad, but resentful, angry and full of spite.[12] In response to Peninnah's provocation, Hannah had developed a bad attitude. The fourth question — **Don't I mean more to you than ten sons?** — may have been an effort to use humor to wipe away Hannah's tears. If taken more seriously, this question means something like "Am I not more devoted to you than ten sons would be?" He (wrongly) thought that his love for her would remove the pain of not having a child.

2. Hannah's Prayer (1:9-18)

1:9-11 1. The time of her prayer (v. 9a). Apparently Hannah humored her husband by eating, for the text next declares, literally, "And Hannah arose after eating[13] in Shiloh and after drinking."

---

[12]The only precise parallel for this phrase is Deut 15:10 which forbids giving with a "grudging" (lit., "bad") heart.

[13]The NIV has followed the LXX in supplying the third person masculine plural suffix to the infinitive construct, i.e., "after they had finished eating . . . ."

Perhaps Hannah **stood up** merely to leave the table where the religious meal was eaten. The words could also be taken to be a reference to the posture of her prayer. Presumably she was in the courtyard of the Lord's house. **In Shiloh,** as in v. 3, serves to reinforce the contrast between this pious woman and the Elide priest who just happened to be sitting there (Eslinger, *Kingship*, 76).

2. The witness to her prayer (v. 9b). Eli was a **priest**, indeed he seems to have held the office of high priest. He belonged to the house of Ithamar, Aaron's fourth son (1 Chr 24:1,3).[14] Eli was sitting on **a chair** (lit., "the chair," i.e., his special chair). He was a judge as well as a priest. The chair may have been his official seat of judgment. Eli was **sitting by the doorpost** or gateway. The seats of high officials were commonly placed close to posts or pillars (cf. 2 Kgs 11:14; Ezek 46:2). He was sitting in a prominent place where all the people could have access to him. From this position Eli could survey the courtyard where, presumably, Hannah was standing and facing the sanctuary itself. The **LORD's temple** could also be rendered "Lord's palace." That sanctuary was designated a "palace," not because of external magnificence, but because it was there that the King of Israel manifested himself from time to time in the glorious cloud called *Shekinah*. Some think the word "temple" suggests that the old tabernacle had been surrounded by a more permanent structure.[15]

3. The earnestness of her prayer (v. 10). She prayed **in bitterness of soul.** Her inward agony was expressed outwardly in that she **wept much.** Her faith and faithfulness are indicated in the fact that she **prayed to the LORD,** i.e., Yahweh. Under the circumstances she might have been tempted to follow the lead of many of her countrymen and address her prayer to some fertility goddess. Three times in the Hebrew in v. 11 she refers to herself as the Lord's **servant** (lit.,

---

[14]The last high priest mentioned prior to Eli was Phinehas, the son of Eleazar (Judg 20:28). Scripture says nothing about the circumstances which caused the high priestly succession to pass from the house of Eleazar to that of Ithamar.

[15]Other terms supposed to point to a permanent structure are "doorpost" (v. 9) and "doors of the house" (1 Sam 3:15). The Hebrew הֵיכַל (*hêkal*) is used of (1) a royal palace, (2) the temple, and (3) heaven as the true temple of Yahweh. It is applied to the tabernacle here and in 1 Samuel 3:3. In some psalms attributed to David, this term may be used of the tabernacle as well (cf. Ps 5:7). Psalm 27 describes God's sanctuary as a "temple" (v. 4) and a "tabernacle" (v. 6).

"handmaid"). By referring to herself in this manner, Hannah reveals her piety and humility.

4. The content of her prayer (v. 11). As part of her prayer, Hannah made a vow, a solemn and irrevocable commitment. Under the law of Moses, Hannah was duty bound to report this vow to her husband. As head of the family, he had until sundown to cancel the vow if he did not agree with it. The fact that the terms of this vow were in fact fulfilled, indicates that Elkanah, in effect, joined his wife in this vow.[16]

The vow was addressed to the LORD Almighty (lit., "Yahweh of hosts"; cf. v. 3). This vow was conditional. It was couched in an *If . . . then* format. Hannah asked that the Lord (1) take note of her misery, (2) remember her, and (3) give her **a son** (lit., "male-seed"). Childless women felt that they had been forgotten by God. The Lord would show that he had not in fact abandoned her, by giving her a son. In accordance with the custom of the time, Hannah asks, not for a child, or children, but for a son.

If God would give her a son, Hannah promised to give that son back to the Lord. In the light of what follows, Hannah meant to give the child to the service of the Lord in his sanctuary. She proposed to deny herself the pleasure of that child in the household. No greater self-denial was possible. As a Levite the son normally would serve at the tabernacle from age twenty-five or thirty to fifty. Hannah, however, proposed a dedication which would be **for all the days of his life.** The outward sign of the son's dedication to the Lord would be that **no razor will ever be used on his head.** The uncut hair was the outward badge of one who took a Nazirite[17] vow. The growth of the hair may have symbolized the complete dedication of all the man's powers to the Lord (Kirkpatrick, 1:47) or his separation from the usual customs of life (R.P. Smith, 12). In addition, Nazirites were not permitted to drink wine or touch any dead thing (Num 6).[18]

---

[16]The law of vows, with special limitations in the case of married women, is given in Num 30.

[17]Although the term *Nazirite* is absent in 1 Samuel, it is surely presupposed. The Dead Sea Scroll fragment 4QSam[a] states at the end of v. 22: "I gave him to be a Nazirite forever all the days of his life." Early Jewish tradition is unanimous in recognizing Samuel as a Nazirite.

[18]A Nazirite's abstinence from wine symbolized avoidance of any indulgence which might cloud the mind and render the man unfit for prayer or

1:12-14 As Hannah kept on praying (lit., "multiplied to pray," i.e., prayed long and hard), **Eli observed** (lit., "was observing") **her mouth**. Since she was praying inwardly (lit., "speaking upon her heart"), he noticed her lips quivering, but did not hear her voice. Eli jumped to the conclusion that a woman speaking to herself in the court of the Lord must be drunk. This priest could not recognize true piety when he saw it. Eli rebuked her with a question (**"How long will you keep on getting drunk?"**) and issued an order: **Get rid of your wine,** i.e., go away and sleep off your intoxication. This may be said in defense of Eli's actions: (1) The high priest had the responsibility to guard the courtyard of the Lord's temple from anything that would defile it. (2) Apparently drinking abuses were not uncommon in the precincts of the Lord's house during festival celebrations (cf. Judg 9:27). (3) Silent prayer was unusual at the time.

1:15-16 Eli's false accusation provided Hannah with the opportunity to proclaim her abstinence from alcoholic beverages, a basic requirement for a woman who would bear a Nazirite (cf. Judg 13:4). Though she had been injured by the harsh accusation, Hannah's response was polite but firm. She refers to the high priest by the respectful **my lord**. Again she referred to herself in a deferential way as **your servant**. Hannah had been drinking (v. 9), but not intoxicants. Her response proves that the term "drinking" in the Bible does not necessarily refer to drinking intoxicants. She explained her demeanor as due to the fact that she was **deeply troubled** (lit., "a woman of hard, difficult, or severe spirit"). She explained her actions by saying **I was pouring out my soul to the LORD,** a vivid idiom for praying earnestly. She was praying out of **great anguish** (caused by her childlessness) **and grief** or provocation (caused by Peninnah's taunting). Only a **wicked woman** (lit., "a daughter of worthlessness") — a good for nothing woman[19] — would appear drunk at the house of the Lord. She begged Eli not to regard her in this way. Here is a striking irony. The man who in the following

---

work for the Lord. Avoiding contact with the dead symbolized abhorrence for all moral defilement. The LXX inserts here "and he will not drink wine or any intoxicating beverage."

[19]The KJV rendered the word as a proper name, *Belial*. The word traditionally has been explained as a compound of *bᵉlî* ("without") and *ya'al* ("worth"). The term is used to describe one who rebelled against all authority and social order (Judg 19:22; 1 Sam 10:27).

chapter could not recognize that his own sons were "sons of worthlessness" here falsely accused a godly woman of conduct which might be expected from a "daughter of worthlessness."

1:17-18 Eli accepted Hannah's explanation, though without apology for his error in judgment. Once he saw the genuineness of her need and the sincerity of her faith, he did his best to reassure her. He dismissed her with the traditional salutation of peace (**go in peace**), and added the wish or promise that her petition will be fulfilled.[20] Jewish commentators generally opt for interpreting Eli's words as a promise. In any case, this is the only passage which actually shows a priest blessing an individual worshiper (Gordon, 75). Ironically, Eli is approving a request for his successor.

Hannah expressed the wish that she might continue to be viewed with favor by the old priest. This is an oblique request for his continued prayer. Hannah then **went her way,** i.e., returned to her regular activities. Though the formal religious meal had concluded (v. 9), Hannah was now ready to eat that of which she was unable to partake earlier (v. 7). **Her face was no longer downcast,** literally, "no longer to her [as it had been previously]." She was confident that now at last God had heard her prayer.

3. Hannah's Presentation (1:19-20)

1:19-20 The day following the religious festival, Elkanah's family again worshiped before the Lord at his sanctuary. Then the family returned home to Ramah, the Ramathaim of v. 1.

The Narrator notes that Elkanah **lay with Hannah,** literally, "knew Hannah his wife," a common euphemism for sexual intimacy. **The LORD remembered her,** as she had asked him to do (v. 11), and as he had remembered Rachel in a similar situation (Gen 30:22). This means that God heard her prayer and removed whatever impediment there may have been to conception. The words **in the course of time** (lit., "at the coming around of days") suggest that the

---

[20]Grammatically the words of Eli could either be a wish or a promise. The JB, NASB, and NIV render them as a wish; the BV takes this as a promise; the ASV, NKJV, and NRSV render Eli's words with the same ambiguity which they have in the Hebrew.

conception did not take place immediately,[21] but later as a result of the normal connubial intercourse between husband and wife.

Hannah named the child. The names of children were given sometimes by the fathers (e.g., Gen 4:26; 5:29), and sometimes by the mothers (e.g., Gen 4:1; 19:37). The child was named **Samuel**. Among the early Israelites names were frequently compound, with one part, as here, including an appellation of God. In this name the final *el* is one of the generic names for the Deity in the ancient world. The meaning of the first part of the name "Samuel" is disputed. Some interpret "Samuel" to mean "name of God" or "his name is God." The derivation of this name, however, is by way of assonance rather than of etymology. The name appears to be a contraction of the Hebrew expression which means "asked from God" or "heard of God." Hannah explained the reason for giving the boy this name when she said, **"Because I asked the LORD for him,"** (lit., "from Yahweh I asked him"). "From Yahweh" by position in the sentence is emphatic. The lackluster genealogy of v. 1 is now superseded by that which gives Samuel his true credentials: he is from Yahweh.

B. REPORT OF SAMUEL'S BIRTH (1:21-28)

1:21-23 When the time for the annual festival arrived the following year, Elkanah **went up with all his family.** He had a double reason for going to the central sanctuary at Shiloh: (1) to offer the **annual sacrifice** (lit., "the sacrifice of days"), and (2) **to fulfill his vow**. Elkanah himself must have taken a vow either in anticipation of the birth of the son, or in gratitude for the birth of that son.[22] His vow concerned offering special sacrifices. This is indicated in the Hebrew by the fact that the term **vow** is the second object of the verb "offer" or "sacrifice," the verb "fulfill" not being represented in the Hebrew text.

---

[21]W. McKane (34) points to a similar phrase in Exod 34:22 used in connection with the Feast of Tabernacles. If this is the case, then Samuel was born just as Elkanah was about to make the annual pilgrimage to Shiloh.

[22]Others contend that Elkanah had accepted Hannah's vow as his own in conformity with Numbers 30:1ff., and had ratified the same by adding to it a thank offering of his own. Eslinger (*Kingship*, 86) proposes a modest emendation of the text by taking the last words of v. 21 as the first of v. 22, which then would read: "but with a vow Hannah did not go up." In this case the text makes no reference to a vow by Elkanah.

Hannah did not accompany her husband on this trip to Shiloh. She wisely suggested that she wait until the child was weaned from the milk of his mother's breasts before presenting him **before the LORD** in an act of dedication. After that Samuel would **live there always** (lit., "forever"), equivalent to "for his whole life" in v. 28.[23]

Elkanah agreed, but prayed that the Lord might make good **his word**.[24] The reference probably is to the blessing of Eli the priest, which contained not merely the assurance of the birth of a son, but a general confirmation and approval of all for which Hannah had prayed. The birth of the child after the vow indicated that the vow was in accord with Yahweh's purpose. Both Hannah and Elkanah expected this child to be intended for some extraordinary work for the Lord.[25] Elkanah appears here as the one responsible before God to see that the vow was discharged correctly (Hertzberg, 28).

1:24 When Samuel was **weaned**, Hannah was prepared to fulfill her vow. Three years is mentioned as the usual period of lactation among Hebrew women in 2 Macc 7:27, but the rabbis make the time a year less.[26] **She took the boy with her** to Shiloh. Elkanah is not mentioned, but it is clear from 2:11 that he accompanied Hannah.

A great feast normally was held in conjunction with the weaning of a child (Gen 21:8), but in the house of Elkanah the participants must have had mixed emotions. Some object that a child possibly as young as two would have been a great burden to Eli. There were, however, women engaged in tabernacle service (1 Sam 2:22). One of them might have acted as surrogate mother to the lad in his most tender years. It was important that he be dedicated to the Lord as soon as possible. The earliest impressions of his youth were to be those of the sanctuary (Kirkpatrick, 1:50).

Along with the child, Hannah took to Shiloh materials for sacrifice. First, she took **a three-year-old bull**, lit., "three bulls." The NIV

---

[23]4QSam[a] has an additional line which is without versional parallel, though it may be reflected in Josephus (*Ant.* 5.10.3): "and I will dedicate him as a Nazirite for ever, all the days of his life" (cf. NAB).

[24]So reads the MT. 4QSam[a], the LXX, and Peshitta have "your word," a reading preferred here by Baldwin (54) and Klein (10).

[25]The rabbis generally suppose that God had given some special word directly to Elkanah and Hannah regarding the birth and vocation of Samuel.

[26]Weaning takes place late where there are no specially prepared foods for a baby's digestion (Baldwin, 53). Some commentators have interpreted the term *wean* figuratively as the age when Samuel was independent of his mother, i.e., about ten.

has chosen to follow the LXX in postulating one bull.[27] Probably the one bull in v. 25 was the special burnt offering used to accompany the dedication of Samuel to the Lord, while the other two bulls were for Elkanah's usual yearly sacrifice consisting of a burnt offering and a thank offering.[28] The choice of bulls when smaller animals would have sufficed (Lev 12:6) is indicative of the gratitude of both Hannah and Elkanah (Baldwin, 54). Second, she took an ephah (½ bushel) of flour. Three tenths of an ephah of flour were to be offered with each bullock (Num 15:9). Third, she took a **skin** of wine for a special sacrifice. Liquids were transported in animal skins which had been specially prepared for that purpose. A wineskin would hold a considerable quantity of wine, more than enough to satisfy the prescribed drink-offering with each bull of half an hin of wine (Num 15:10) which would be equivalent to about three pints. The **house of the LORD** here is equivalent to the "LORD's temple" in v. 9. See comments there.

The NIV has rearranged the word order of v. 24 and thereby obscured an important point. The words **young as he was** (lit., "and the child was a child")[29] actually stand last in the verse. The phrase contains a play on the word נַעַר (na'ar) which can mean "child" or "servant." Hannah brought the child to Shiloh and the child (hanna'ar) was/became a na'ar, i.e., he took up his role as a servant to the priests once he got to Shiloh. This play on words underscores (1) the exact compliance of Hannah with the terms of her vow; and (2) the commencement of Samuel's tabernacle duties at the tenderest of ages.

---

[27]The LXX reading is supported by 4QSam[a]. If this reading is the original, the animal's age would specify maturity for purposes of sacrifice (cf. Gen 15:9). E.A. Speiser pointed out parallels in the Nuzi texts. "The Nuzi Tablets Solve a Puzzle in the Books of Samuel," *BASOR* 72 (1938): 15-17.

[28]It is also possible that one or more of the bulls might have been intended as a gift for Eli. Wenham (79, n. 12) identified the three bulls as (1) the burnt offering; (2) the purification offering that was expected after childbirth (Lev 12); and (3) the peace offering in fulfillment of a vow. Wenham also points out that an ephah of flour is approximately three times the normal quantity of flour to be offered with a bull (Num 15:9), which would be in keeping with three bulls.

[29]The LXX and 4QSam[a] have a longer reading here: "and the boy was with them. And they came before the Lord, and his father killed the sacrifice as he did year by year before the Lord, and she brought the boy . . . ." Baldwin (54) thinks some words were lost from the original Hebrew text between the two occurrences of the word "boy" ("child").

1:25-28 The focus here is on the slaughter of that particular sacrifice which is connected with the dedication of the boy. The writer did not think it necessary to comment on the routine annual sacrifice of the two other bulls to which the Hebrew text alludes. **When they had slaughtered the bull** could be regarded as an impersonal passive, viz., "when the bull had been slaughtered," i.e., by the appropriate authorities. After the sacrifice, both parents presented the child to Eli.

Hannah first identified herself (v. 26). The words **as surely as you live** (lit., "as your soul lives") are an oath formula which occurs six times in the Samuel books and once in the books of Kings. The meaning is: As surely as you are a living soul, so surely am I the person who stood beside you (Eli) praying to Yahweh. These words confirm that the posture of prayer in v. 9 was standing.

Hannah next explained herself (vv. 27-28). She emphasized her point by a word play on the root שָׁאַל (ša'al, "to petition or ask").[30] Baldwin (54) brings out the thrust of the Hebrew in this translation: "the LORD has granted me my *petition* which I *petitioned* him. Therefore I have *petitioned* him to the Lord . . . he is *petitioned* to the LORD." She was formally giving Samuel to Yahweh as a living sacrifice.[31] She understood — and she wanted the priest to understand — that this gift was a lifelong proposition. The ceremony here is the equivalent to a modern parent terminating parental rights.

The chapter ends with creative ambiguity designed to engage the reader in a struggle to understand the text (Eslinger, *Kingship*, 97). Who is the subject in the sentence: **And he worshiped the LORD there**? Eli, Samuel and Elkanah have been nominated. Of these Eli is least likely, for he is not portrayed in a positive light in these chapters. Samuel is most likely, for he has been the subject of Hannah's speech in the two preceding verses (Spence, Jamieson). The sentence would then demonstrate Samuel's willingness to assume the role prescribed for him in the sanctuary. Nevertheless some argue that it was Elkanah who bowed in reverent worship in v. 28 while his wife poured out her heart in the hymn which immediately follows in the next chapter (Kirkpatrick, KD, R.P. Smith).

---

[30]On the basis of the connection between the verb *ša'al* and the name Saul (שָׁאוּל, *šā'ûl*), and points of contact with Judg 13, P. Kyle McCarter (1:65 f.) and others argue that an account of *Saul's* Nazirite birth has been here adapted for *Samuel*. For refutation, see Eslinger (*Kingship*, 92 ff.).

[31]The KJV "lent him to the Lord" gives the wrong connotation.

1 SAMUEL 2

Chapter 2 highlights the blessing which came to Elkanah and Hannah because they had given their son to the Lord. It places in juxtaposition the growing ministry of Samuel with the failing ministry of Eli's family.

C. PROPHETIC SONG OF ANTICIPATION (2:1-10)

Hannah's prayer in ch. 1 was a vow; her second prayer is both a poem and a prophecy. It is appropriate that she is said to have **prayed** this song because (1) parts of the song are addressed to God in the second person, and (2) the song includes thanksgiving and praise. While Hannah's song grows out of her own personal experience, the language here escalates into a dynamic statement of faith regarding God's universal and moral government of the world. She expressed not merely vague hopes for the future, but specific predictions of what God had revealed to her.

Critics argue that a song of such lofty expression of faith in God's rule and providence could not possibly have been composed by Hannah, a humble farmer's wife.[1] This composition is usually reckoned to be either (1) an already existing hymn which Hannah made her own or (2) a later composition put into her mouth by a compiler long after her time. Since such criticism is based on no objective criteria, it may be dismissed.[2]

---

[1]E.g., J.T. Willis thinks this song may have originated as a song of triumph at the Shiloh sanctuary in connection with Israel's victory over an enemy. It may have been one of Hannah's favorite songs. "The Song of Hannah and Psalm 113," *CBQ* 25 (1973): 139-154. W.F. Albright (*YGC*, 18) found archaisms in the hymn which made it highly probable that it dates back to the time of Samuel.

[2]For a discussion of the relationship of Hannah's song to the immediate context, see Eslinger (*Kingship*, 99-102).

1. Hannah's Praise (2:1-8)

Hannah certainly had something to sing about: she (1) had given birth to a son, (2) saw her prayers answered, (3) knew the joy of giving a costly gift to the Lord, and (4) grasped the truth that God is in sovereign control of the whole world (Baldwin, 56). The first half of Hannah's prayer is dominated by praise to the Lord. She praises God for his deliverance (v. 1), for his attributes (vv. 2-3), and for his actions (vv. 4-8).

2:1 Hannah's prayer hymn opens with four assertions about herself and the holy joy which she experienced since the birth of her son. *Inwardly* she rejoiced. With the Hebrews the **heart** was the center, not merely of the physical, but also of the moral and intellectual life. The word **rejoices** is a strong word with connotations of exulting or triumphing. Hannah's joy is not that of the world, for she rejoices **in the LORD.**

Outwardly her lot has changed. The phrase **in the LORD** stands first in the second poetic line for emphasis. Whatever joy, strength and self-confidence she experienced was derived from Yahweh. Lifting high one's **horn** is a symbol of strength (Deut 33:17) and self-esteem (Job 16:15). Hannah had been elevated to a position of power and importance. The figure is probably derived from the habit of horned animals tossing their heads in the air in proud display of their power and potency.[3]

Vocally, her mouth **boasts** (lit., "is opened wide"). This expression has received three interpretations. First, some think it merely affirms that Hannah was no longer silent (as she appears to have been in 1:7-8) in the face of the taunting of her rival. Her mouth opens wide to proclaim God's salvation, thus effectively silencing those who had set themselves as her enemies. Second, based on the use elsewhere of "to open wide the mouth against enemies," this phrase is taken to connote scorn, sneering, and perhaps sticking out the tongue[4] (cf. Ps 35:21; Isa 57:4). Third, the phrase may be taken as a proverbial or figurative expression of triumph. In this context the first or third views are appropriate. Certainly personal vindictiveness is out of character

---

[3]The figure of the horn being raised is a frequent metaphor in the psalms for victory (e.g., Ps 89:17; 92:10).

[4]Cf. Baldwin (57) who takes רָחַב (*rāhab*, "is opened wide") as figurative for defeat of one's enemy by swallowing him.

with the spiritual beauty of the rest of this song. Hannah boasts of the Lord and in the Lord over her **enemies**. She may be referring to Peninnah and perhaps other women who had made life miserable for her. Two factors in this song, however, suggest that **my enemies** are in reality *God's enemies*. First, in this song the works of God, and not personal experiences, are the object of praise. Second, Hannah speaks here from the position of one who is **in the LORD**. The enemies of one who is in the LORD are in fact the enemies of God.

Spiritually, Hannah experienced **deliverance** (i.e., salvation). The term "salvation" in the Old Testament means (1) *deliverance* from dangers or adversities of all kinds (Ps 9:14; 13:5) and (2) *help*, the power by which the deliverance is effected, whether divine or human (Ps 35:3). Here Hannah expressed **delight** in deliverance from the humiliation of childlessness, the taunts of her rival, and the subjective feelings of worthlessness.

2:2 Here Hannah gives the reasons for the holy joy expressed in v. 1. First, she regarded Yahweh as incomparable in holiness. To be **holy** is to be apart from this world, apart from sin and corruption. Second, she regarded God as incomparable in his existence: **there is no one besides you**. God alone absolutely exists. All other existence is secondary and derived (R.P. Smith, 26). Third, she regarded the God of Israel as incomparable in his durability. The title **Rock**[5] emphasizes his eternality and reliability. Because they were easily defended, huge rocks formed the nucleus of most ancient towns, and continued to serve as their citadels. God as "rock" pictures him as the ground of confidence and refuge (Mauchline, 50).

2:3 While Hannah had been delivered from her enemies (v. 1), those enemies were still active. They kept talking in proud and arrogant ways (lit., "proudly, proudly")[6] against God, against God's people, and against God's law. The prophetess gave a twofold warning that such people should not continue to lift themselves up against the holy and high God of Israel. First, Yahweh **is a God who knows**, lit., "a God of knowledges," the plural indicating varied and extensive

---

[5]Klein (16) prefers "mountain" as the rendering for צוּר *(ṣûr)* rather than the conventional "rock."

[6]The doubling of the word גְּבֹהָה *(gᵉbōhāh,* "proudly") is a characteristic feature of ancient Hebrew poetry and helps in dating the Song of Hannah early rather than late (Youngblood, 580).

knowledge. Second, **by him**[7] **deeds are weighed,** i.e., he evaluates deeds. The implication is that he evaluates deeds with a view to punishing those which are not up to his standards.

Seven contrasts follow v. 3 and illustrate the balancing or weighing of deeds by Yahweh. Hannah was inspired to discern in her own individual experience the general principles which undergird divine providence. While at any given time life is full of inequalities, circumstances in life have a way of evening out. God sees to that. This was Hannah's conviction. Changes of fortune are not the result of chance, but of that omniscience combined with holiness which Hannah attributed to Yahweh in vv. 3-4. She sets forth those principles (1) anecdotally (vv. 4-5), and then (2) theologically (vv. 6-8).

2:4-5 Hannah cited three illustrations of how things even out for people in the course of life. She had seen enough examples to convince her that extreme situations are frequently reversed. The perfect form of the verb suggests that Hannah had actually observed such divine interventions.

1. In military terms, **the bows of the warriors are broken.** Mighty warriors often find their bows broken, i.e., they find themselves defeated, their weapons destroyed.[8] The bow was one of the chief weapons of war (2 Sam 1:22). The broken bow is a symbol of defeat and the insignificance of human strength. On the other hand, those who stumbled to awkwardness and fearfulness toward the battle line are **armed with strength,** lit., "girded with strength." An example of cowardly stumblers girding on strength is found in the accounts of Saul's battles against the Philistines (1 Sam 14:22-23; 17:52).

---

[7]The NIV has followed the *Qere* or traditional reading of the MT which was לו (*lô*, "to him" or "by him"). The common interpretation is that God weighs the deeds of men. Scripture, however, never speaks of God weighing human conduct, but rather human character (Prov 16:2; 21:2; 24:12). This fact invites the translation "to him deeds are weighed," meaning the actions of God are weighed, i.e., equal or just. These weighed or righteous acts of God are then enumerated in vv. 4-8. Still better would be to follow *Kethibh* or written text which has לא (*lō'*, "not"). The *Kethibh* may be rendered either (1) "though actions be not weighed," i.e., God is aware of wicked actions even if they are not immediately punished; or (2) interrogatively, "and are not actions weighed?"

[8]KD argue that bows "of the warriors" stands for the heroes carrying bows. With the exception of Isa 51:6, the verb חתת (*ḥātath*) is not used to denote the breaking of outward things, but the breaking of men. Hence KD translate here: "Bow-heroes are confounded."

2. In economic terms, those who are **full**, i.e., they have plenty to eat — the wealthy — often lose all they have. They must hire themselves out in order to earn money to buy food. On the other hand, those who were once economically disadvantaged and hungry, **hunger no more**, (lit., "cease, come to an end"), i.e., they cease to hunger.[9]

3. In domestic terms, the humiliated and despised barren woman suddenly finds her womb opened. She bears **seven** children, the full number of the divine blessing in children (Ruth 4:15; Jer 15:9). On the other hand, the woman who has many sons to care for her **pines away**, i.e., languishes. She becomes psychologically devastated and perhaps physically destitute because she has lost those sons either to disease or to battle. In the previous two examples it was the strong who become weak followed by the weak becoming strong. Here the sequence is reversed. Hannah probably wanted to emphasize God's positive actions on behalf of the weak.

2:6-8 In these verses participles are used in order to transfer the emphasis from the specific acts of God to his customary actions. What appears here has been called "the theology of God the reverser" (Klein, 17).[10] Yahweh is the one who brings about role reversal and who levels the playing field. Hannah employed two figures, with an explanation attached to each.

1. The first figure and explanation (v. 6). **The LORD brings death and makes alive; he brings down to the grave** [lit., *Sheol*] **and raises up**. While it is true that Yahweh literally brings death and makes alive, it is unlikely that Hannah was thinking in this verse of either physical death or physical resurrection. The verse uses participles to express continuous action. Since returns from the grave are rare in the Bible,

---

[9]Others understand the sentence to say that the hungry (1) cease to labor and are able to enjoy the holidays, or (2) they cease to exist as a group in a society. D. Winton Thomas has adduced evidence to show that the verb חָדַל (*ḥādal*) may have had the meaning "to be plump, well-nourished" as well as "to cease." See *Supplement to VT* 4 (1957): 14f.; Theodore Lews, "The Sons of Hannah and Deborah: HDL-II ('Growing Plump')," *JBL* 104 (1895): 105-108; and additional references in Baldwin (*1 & 2 Samuel*, 57).

[10]The theology of God the reverser is also found in Ps 113. The basic idea is that winners become losers, and losers, winners. Scripture abounds with illustrations of God the reverser in action. The supreme example is found in the life of Jesus who was exalted to the right hand of the Father from the utter humiliation of the Cross.

and nonexistent prior to Hannah's time, it is most likely that she is referring in v. 6 metaphorically to death and resurrection. Death and Sheol in this verse are figurative for the depths of misfortune and peril. Life and revival would then point to recovery from such dire extremity. This is made clear by the statements of v. 7.

2. The second figure and explanation (vv. 7-8). Yahweh is responsible for poverty and wealth, for humiliation and exaltation. **He raises the poor from the dust and lifts the needy from the ash heap**. To "sit in the dust" (Isa 47:1) or "on the ash heap"[11] or city dump (Lam 4:5) are figures for extreme degradation and misery (cf. 1 Kgs 16:2-3; Job 2:8). To keep company with princes and occupy a **throne** or seat of honor are metaphors for social advancement and prosperity.

The last clause of v. 8, which offers an explanation of how Yahweh can make such radical changes in the structure of society, has received two very different interpretations. The issue is whether the verse affirms that God places the physical earth upon its foundations or whether he places the inhabited earth upon its rulers. (1) Some think that Hannah uses a traditional creation metaphor when she refers to **the foundations of the earth**.[12] These foundations or pillars **are the LORD's**, i.e., they belong to him. Upon these foundations or pillars **he has set the world** (Heb. תֵּבֵל, *tēbēl*, the inhabited earth). This poetical metaphor is derived from the construction of a building (Judg 16:26); it does not imply any theory as to the actual shape of the earth (Kirkpatrick, 1:54). The thought is that if Yahweh can lift up the inhabited world and place it upon its pillars, how much more easily can he raise up a man. Since he created the world and maintains it, God has the power and the right to intervene in its affairs and rearrange the fortunes of men according to his sovereign will. (2) Others think the emphasis here is on the sovereignty of God. He has established **the pillars** of the social and moral ordering of society (Baldwin, 58), perhaps earth's rulers. God's providence raised

---

[11]The term אַשְׁפֹּת (*'ašpōth*) is rendered "ash heap" (NIV, NKJV, NRSV); "dump" (BV); "garbage dump" (CEV); "dunghill" (ASV, JB), i.e., the place where a pile of horse, cow, or camel offal was heaped up to dry in the sun so as to serve as fuel (Jamieson, 138).

[12]The translation of מָצוּק (*māṣûq*) is difficult. The word only occurs here and in 1 Samuel 14:5 where it can only mean a crag or mass of rock. The word is translated "pillars" in the NASB, ASV, NKJV, NRSV, and NJPS; "props" in JB; and "foundations" in CEV. The poetic concept of "pillars of the earth" is found in Ps 75:3 and Job 9:6, but a different Hebrew word is used.

these men to their places of dignity and influence. He laid the government of the world upon their shoulders. The emphasis on the sovereignty of God in the placement of the world rulers seems more in keeping with the immediate context than the reference to physical creation. In either case the expression is metaphorical.

2. Hannah's Prediction (2:9-10)

2:9-10 The moral order requires judgment at some point. Hannah made four predictions. First, she predicted the fate of God's **saints**,[13] i.e., the faithful ones, they who are here contrasted with the **wicked** or, more properly, the "guilty." The Hebrew term חֶסֶד (*ḥesed*) refers to one who is pious, i.e., one who is lovingly drawn toward the Lord, and one who is the object of God's mercy. Based on her own experience, Hannah drew the conclusion that God **will guard the[ir] feet** or protect them. Slipping, falling, and stumbling feet are symbols of defeat, but the faithful have no need to fear defeat by circumstances or by adversaries.

Second, the **wicked** who oppose the Lord's people will be silenced by the darkness of adversity and death when God withdraws the light of his grace. In their misery they will recognize that they are the object of divine punishment for their misdeeds. In silent submission they will acknowledge the justice of the divine outpouring against them. The wicked shall be defeated because **it is not by strength that one prevails**. Victory over circumstances and adversaries, whether on a personal level or a national level, only comes through the strength which God supplies. In the preceding verses Hannah has named several who might be perceived to be strong, yet who ultimately are brought down. So the concluding verse of Hannah's hymn reverts to the thought presented in v. 1, viz., that it is in the Lord that the humble find their strength. God is omnipotent, and no power successfully can be asserted against him or his people. The classic statement of this truth in the Old Testament is found in Zech 4:6, and in the New Testament, in 2 Cor 12:9.

Third, Hannah predicted the universal judgment of God (v. 10a). Yahweh, the Creator of the world, is also the Judge of the world.

---

[13]The Hebrew written text (the *Kethibh*) has "his saint" (sing.). While this fact does not affect the meaning of the text, the singular does add force to Hannah's statement.

Ultimately those who **oppose**[14] him will be **shattered.**[15] The word translated "oppose" has reference to contentions in a court of law. This is in keeping with the thrust of this entire verse regarding the administration of justice. This shattering results from Yahweh's **thunder against them from heaven.**[16] Yahweh is depicted seated in the heavenly places. He is the supreme Judge. His voice throughout the Old Testament is compared to thunder. Thunder is a symbol for the approach of the Lord in judgment. That judgment would be unleashed to the ends of the earth, i.e., throughout the whole earth.

Fourth, Hannah spoke of the exaltation of God's ruler (v. 10b). In the Hebrew v. 10 actually begins with the name "Yahweh" set off from the rest of the verse for emphasis.[17] Hannah's intent was to give all glory to Yahweh, the God of covenant faithfulness. Not only is Yahweh the Judge of the world, he is the one who brings salvation in the person of a powerful king. God will **give strength to his king, and exalt the horn of his anointed.** The poem began with a reference to the exaltation of Hannah's "horn," and it concludes with the joyous prediction that God would exalt the "horn" of his anointed.[18] See on v. 1. The **anointed** (מָשִׁיחַ, *māšiaḥ*) is the first use in the Bible of the Hebrew term transliterated elsewhere as "Messiah." Here the terms **king** and **anointed** refer to the same person. A strong king brings deliverance to his people from all their adversaries. The king's welfare meant fertility, prosperity and abundance for the whole nation. Clearly the faithful in Israel had expectations of someday being part of a monarchy. Faced with anarchy and growing disintegration of the nation, and surrounded by internal corruption and external attack, the desire for a king must have been growing.

---

[14]"Those who oppose," i.e., adversaries, has a legal connotation which agrees well with the depiction of God as the judge of the earth.

[15]The Hebrew is more appropriately rendered: "As for Yahweh, all who oppose him will be shattered." In Hebrew the nouns in this verse are singular, though the verb is plural, showing that they are to be taken collectively.

[16]The NIV has departed from the MT which actually reads "against *him*," i.e., against every individual who contends against God. The term "shattered" is the same Hebrew term used of the bows of the warriors in verse 4.

[17]A better rendering of this verse might be: "Yahweh — his adversaries shall be shattered," etc.

[18]Hannah's horn raising was accomplished through her prayerful but submissive request for divine aid. Perhaps the thought is that the anointed one's horn will be raised up for similar reasons.

This expectation was based on promises, predictions and principles set forth centuries prior to Hannah's time.[19] It was always God's intention that his people some day have a king. According to many authorities, the **king** in Hannah's prayer is not any particular king, but an "ideal" king. According to this view, the passage is messianic only in the sense that the royal line culminated in Christ.[20] Hannah's prophecy must be interpreted in the context of royal messianic prophecy which preceded her utterance.[21] God promised the Patriarchs that kings would come from their descendants. Jacob predicted that the scepter would not depart from Judah until Shiloh came, and unto him would be the obedience of the peoples (Gen 49:10). A star and scepter would arise in Israel who would crush the enemies of God's people (Num 24:17). In the context of this emerging messianic hope, Hannah predicted the exaltation of an anointed one (Messiah) and king. The question is not, What would Hannah have understood when she uttered these words? but What did the Holy Spirit mean when he inspired her to speak them?

II. TRANSITION TO MONARCHY (2:11–11:15)

The material in this unit reflects a beautiful parallelism of thought in the rise of Samuel and of Saul after the rejection of the leadership of their predecessors. Along the way, each meets a challenge before general recognition.

---

[19]God had promised Abraham that kings would come from his loins (Gen 17:6,16). Moses set forth regulations to govern the rule of future kings (Deut 17:14ff.).

[20]In this scenario, the fulfillment of Hannah's prediction has four phases: (1) it *commenced* with David's victories over the enemies of Israel, (2) *continued* in every victory over the enemies of God and his kingdom gained by David's successors, (3) *culminated* in the advance of the kingdom of Christ, and (4) *concludes* with the judgment of the last day through which all the enemies of Christ are made his footstool.

[21]The Targum renders: "he shall multiply the kingdom of the Messiah." For an analysis of the role of Hannah's prediction within the context of royal messianism, see J.E. Smith, 76-78.

A. THE RISE OF SAMUEL (2:11–7:17)

1. Eli's Leadership Rejected (2:11-36)

The Sins of Eli's Sons (2:11-26)

2:11 Elkanah returned home to **Ramah**. See on 1:1. The failure to mention Hannah's homeward journey suggests that she may have stayed with her son for a time of adjustment. At least her heart was still at Shiloh.

The boy Samuel commenced his ministerial duties at Shiloh. On the term **boy**, see note on 1:24. The text uses a participle from the root שָׁרַת (*šārat*) to describe the activities of Samuel at the sanctuary. The same term is used elsewhere to denote the priestly ministry of Aaron and his sons (e.g., Exod 28:35,43; 29:30). As young as he was, Samuel was assisting the priests in their regular obligations in the Lord's house. The purpose of this verse is to paint the contrast between the innocent and faithful young lad Samuel, and the corrupt sons of Eli who served in the same place.

2:12 Eli's sons were בְּלִיַּעַל (*bᵉliyā'al*), i.e., worthless or good-for-nothing. The priest had judged Hannah to be a "worthless woman" (1:16), but apparently failed to see that his own sons were the real scoundrels. They were careless and irreligious, loose in their actions, scandalous in their conduct, and ruthless in their dealings with their fellowman. **They had no regard for the LORD,** lit., "they did not know [יָדַע, *yāda'*] Yahweh," i.e., they knew *about* the Lord, but they did not know *him* experientially. They knew the Mosaic rituals, but they had never experienced intimate communion with the Lord.

2:13-14 God had prescribed how both worshiper and priest should behave in the sacrificial ritual. When a person wished to present a peace offering, the offering was brought to the priest. After the Lord's part — the fat — was burnt on the altar, the parts designated respectively for the priests and worshipers were to be boiled in preparation for sacred meals. At Shiloh, however, the priests had substituted their own **practice** (lit., "right") for the prescribed ritual of Mosaic law. The priests — not just the sons of Eli, but all the priests — had usurped to themselves a right in respect to their relationship with the worshipers. Apparently they were not content with the modest share of the offerings assigned to them by Mosaic law (Lev 7:28-36; Deut 18:3). Their sin was fourfold.

First, the priests robbed the people of the portion of the sacrificial animal which was assigned to them. Using a three-pronged fork, the priests' servant would dredge up from the cook pot whatever stuck to his fork. That portion of meat that was boiled was intended for the worshiper after the sacrificial portion had been offered on the altar.[22]

2:15-17 Second, the priests took the sacrificial meat prematurely. The law (Lev 7:23-25,31; 17:6) prescribed that the fat portions — considered by people of that region the best pieces of meat — were to be burned on the altar to the Lord (v. 15). Nothing should have intervened between the presentation of the offering and the burning of the parts consecrated to God. To take the meat of the sacrificial animal and roast it before the burning of the fat portions to the Lord was certainly a contemptuous insult to the Lord; it may even be equivalent to a robbery of God.[23]

Third, the priests would accept no compromise from the people. A worshiper might offer to give the priests whatever piece of meat they might desire after the portion for the Lord had been placed on the altar. Ordinary worshipers at Shiloh were more scrupulous and conscientious than were their priests. They knew that the fat should be burned **first** (lit., "like the day"). Such compromises, however, were rejected.

Fourth, the priests caused the people to despise the sacrificial ritual. The sin of the **young men** — Hophni and Phinehas — was very great **in the Lord's sight**, lit., "with the face of Yahweh." The NIV follows the Septuagint in omitting a word from v. 17 which robs the verse of a significant thought. Literally the last clause reads: "Because the *men* despised the offering[24] of Yahweh." The misdeeds of **the young men** (Eli's sons) caused the men of Israel to treat **with contempt**[25] the sacrificial ritual.[26]The people observed that the priests had no piety; this caused them to treat with contempt the sacred services.

---

[22]Eslinger (*Kingship,* 117) argues that vv. 13-14 do not condemn the priests nor their servants, but rather are designed to establish the regular practice in order to highlight the irregularities of verse 15.

[23]The Hebrew in v. 15 indicates the seriousness of the priests' crime by use of the emphatic particle גַּם (*gam*).

[24]The term "offering" (מִנְחָה, *minḥāh*) is frequently used of the nonbloody or meal offering, but here seems to stand for the entire sacrificial system.

[25]The verb is Piel, and hence intensive.

[26]Goldman (11) suggests that the term "young men" refers to the servants, and "men" to the sons of Eli.

2:18 In contrast to the sacrilege of Shiloh's priests stands the piety of Samuel. The lad grew up in the sanctuary, performing such ministries as were appropriate to his age. Though he was a **boy** (Hebrew *na'ar* can also mean servant), he wore (lit., "was gird with") **an ephod**, a symbol of ministry worn by priests (1 Sam 22:18), Levites and even laymen who were engaged in religious service (2 Sam 6:14).[27] This was a small shoulder garment or apron secured round the waist by a sash or girdle. Samuel's ephod was of white **linen**[28] (v. 18). The point of the verse is that while the Elides were misbehaving as priests, Samuel was behaving as one both in appearance and conduct (Eslinger, *Kingship,* 120).

2:19-21 Samuel's mother and father continued to make their annual pilgrimage to the sanctuary. No mention is made of Peninnah on these pilgrimages. Each year Hannah would weave a new robe for her son to accommodate his growth. The **robe** was an outer garment of wool, woven throughout without seam, with holes for the head and arms, and reaching nearly to the ground. This garment was the ordinary dress of all classes of people. It has no special meaning except that in this handiwork, Hannah exhibited her motherly pride and care. The ephod was worn over this robe.

The annual visit to the sanctuary was more than merely a reunion with the boy Samuel. Eli pronounced an annual blessing on Elkanah and Hannah reminiscent of the blessing he pronounced in 1:17-18. He prayed that the Lord might **give**[29] to this couple several children to take the place of **the one she prayed for and gave to the** LORD, lit., "instead of the petition which he[30] asked for Yahweh" (v. 20). Hannah, and apparently her husband as well, had not simply asked the Lord for a son, but for a son that might be given to God. Eli's blessing was given in gratitude for the gift of the young child to

---

[27]N.L. Tidwell, "The Linen Ephod; 1 Sam. II 18 and 2 Sam. VI 14," *VT* 24 (1974): 505-507.

[28]The ephod of the high priest was of different color and material than that which is indicated here (cf. Exod 28:6-8).

[29]The LXX, supported by 4QSam[a], has "repay" (cf. NRSV). This reading differs from the MT by only one letter, and a case can be made for either reading as far as idiom is concerned (Gordon, 83).

[30]The third person masculine singular is an indefinite form which Eli may have used to express his belief that, whereas Hannah had prayed for the son, Elkanah had shared the petition of his pious wife. The form can legitimately be rendered as passive in English.

the sanctuary. After receiving the blessing of the high priest, the couple **would go home**, lit., "to his [Elkanah's] place."

Standard English versions ignore the opening word of v. 21 and miss an important thought. The verse begins with כִּי (*kî*) which appears here to have the meaning "for" or "because." The thought is that Eli's prayers were not empty and fruitless. Elkanah and Hannah went home blessed *because* Yahweh **was gracious to** (lit., "visited") **Hannah**. For the one child the couple gave to the Lord at the sanctuary, they received five others. While Hannah became increasingly occupied with her other children, Samuel grew to maturity **in the presence of the LORD**, i.e., at the Shiloh sanctuary. Yahweh was his family, and the things of Yahweh were the focus of his life. The verb **grew up** denotes mental and moral advancement as well as physical growth (Exod 2:10f.).

2:22 While Samuel was growing up, Eli was growing **very old**. According to one manuscript, he was ninety at this time (cf. 4:15). Old age accounts for his weak indulgence of his wicked sons, his failure to nip in the bud their sinful conduct, and his lack of energy to deal with the corrupt and ever-worsening situation. He **heard** at long last about the irreverent behavior of his sons in the ritual of the sanctuary.

Perhaps the immoral conduct[31] with **the women who served at the entrance to the Tent of Meeting**,[32] i.e., female sanctuary servants, was the activity that finally forced Eli to make some effort to correct his sons. What little is known about these women is conveyed here by the verb **served** (הַצֹּבְאוֹת, *haṣṣōbᵉ'ôth*).[33] The term is related to the divine title by which the God of Shiloh was known, viz., *YHWH ṣᵉbā'ôth* (1:11). These women were "hostesses" of Yahweh of Hosts (Eslinger, *Kingship,* 123). Most frequently this verb "served" is used of military activity, and so it may convey some idea such as standing in ranks. It is used several times of the service of Levites in sacred places (e.g., Num 4:3,23,30). These women appear to be a

---

[31]"They slept with the women" is literally, "they laid the women."

[32]See F. Cross, "The Tabernacle," *BA* 10 (1947): 45-68.

[33]J. Willis thinks these women were temple prostitutes. "Cultic Elements in the Story of Samuel's Birth and Dedication," *ST* 26 (1972): 56. Had they been hierodules, sleeping with them would not have evoked the condemnation which is here implied in the text. It seems more likely that these godly women were victims of the insatiable lust of Eli's sons (Eslinger, *Kingship,* 123).

regularly organized band of attendants. Such an institution can be traced back to the days of Moses (Exod 38:8). Classical Jewish commentators understood the verb to mean "assembled," i.e., for prayer, instruction and sacrifice. Surely, however, more than that is meant by the language here. It has been suggested by some that these women were responsible for keeping the entrance to the sanctuary clean; others think they provided music for services (cf. Ps 68:11). The sin was all the greater because the women the priests defiled were those dedicated to holy service.

2:23-25 Eli was a good man, but he erred on the side of parental indulgence. Though he had the authority to remove his sons from office, or to discipline them in some other way,[34] he chose only to scold them verbally. First, Eli rebuked his sons with a rhetorical question (v. 23a): **"Why do you do such things?"** They had been raised in a godly home. They had known from their youth the sacred law. They had seen the example of their godly father. They had accepted the holy ministry of priesthood and had been set apart for that service through the solemn services of ordination. Why would they now choose to walk away from God? His rebuke, however, was so gentle that he deserved the condemnation of 3:13 that "he failed to restrain them."

Second, Eli confronted his sons with the evidence of their guilt. Twice in vv. 23-24 Eli mentions the report that was spreading among the people about the evil deeds of his sons. He had heard reports from **all** the people concerning their wicked conduct. Eli had waited for a long time — obviously too long — to confront his sons with these charges. It is a telling condemnation of Eli's administration that he personally had not witnessed the deeds of the sons. Either they were too clever for him, or he too trusting of them. In any case, the evidence at this point could no longer be ignored (v. 23b).

Third, Eli indicated the public consequences of their sin. They had led others into sin. As rendered by the NIV, v. 24 lamely comments on the report of the people that (1) it was not good and (2) it was spreading. The verse appears, however, to add another dimension to the charges which Eli brought against the sons. Literally the verse reads: "not, my sons," i.e., do not do such things; "not good is

---

[34]Willis understands v. 23 to be accusing Eli of willful wrongdoing or at least culpable negligence. "An Anti-Elide Narrative Tradition from a Prophetic Circle at the Ramah Sanctuary," *JBL* 90 (1971): 292.

the report which I am hearing, causing the people of Yahweh to transgress."[35] The scornful disregard for the divinely established ordinances of the sanctuary on the one hand, and the unblushing immorality on the other, caused a disregard for morality and things sacred among the general population.

Fourth, Eli pointed out the serious nature of their sin. If a man sins against his fellowman, **God may mediate for him**[36] The verb וּפִלְלוֹ (ûphillô) comes from a root which has connotations of acting in the capacity of a lawyer. In transgressions between men, God or his representative (judge, priest, or prophet) can argue the case or smooth out the difficulty between the two. If, however, a man sins deliberately and directly against God, who will be the mediator? (cf. Job 9:32f.). God can no longer serve as an impartial moderator. By the very nature of the case, there is no superior third party to intercede as mediator or impose a just settlement. The transgression which appears to be beyond the limits of divine forgiveness is impenitence. When the priests despised the offering of Yahweh, they destroyed their sole link to forgiveness (Miller & Roberts, 29).

Eli's efforts led to no change in the sons: **his sons, however, did not listen to their father's rebuke**. These men had hardened their hearts in sin long before their father attempted to correct them. The Lord did nothing further to soften the hearts of these men **for it was the LORD's will to put them to death** (lit., "Yahweh was pleased to slay them"). He already had determined they should die for their many years of sinning against their God and their fellowman.[37]

---

[35]The root עבר ('ābar) means "to pass over, through, by, pass on" and by extension "to overstep or transgress." In the Hebrew the form is a Hiphil m. pl. participle. The NIV rendering would seem to require a Qal f. sing. participle. The objection that מַעֲבִרִים (ma'ăbirîm) without further definition cannot mean "to cause to sin" is met by the context which supplies the further definition (KD, 153). Two Hebrew MSS supply the second person pl. pronoun to serve as the subject for the Hiphil participle. Without the pronoun the sense is indefinite. The word order in this verse is difficult, but on the whole the rendering of the KJV and ASV is superior to the NIV.

[36]The NIV translates 'ĕlōhîm as "God," which is the usual meaning of the word. In the KJV and the NIV margin the word is rendered here "judge," a meaning which the word seems to have in certain contexts. See Exod 21:6; 22:8f.; Ps 82:1,6. Judges were viewed as God's representatives in executing justice on earth (Deut 1:17).

[37]The situation here has been likened to God's hardening of Pharaoh's heart in refusing to release the Hebrew slaves (e.g., Exod 9:12; 10:20,27), or

2:26 While the priests were declining, Samuel was increasing. Theirs was an evil reputation, while Samuel's was favorable. They were under God's judgment, while Samuel receives commendation. The boy Samuel was growing up (lit., "going and becoming big and good") to be the kind of spiritual leader that God desired and the people needed.

The Prophecy against Eli's House (2:27-36)

2:27 Before the Lord intervened at Shiloh, he sent a man of God or prophet to announce, as a warning for all ages, the judgment which was about to come. This man of God is one of many anonymous prophets who appeared during the history of Israel. Like all prophets, he spoke with authority, with a "thus says the Lord." Even though Israel's religious life was in a state of serious decline at this time, God still had his faithful messengers. This is the first prophet to appear in Israel's history since the time of Gideon (Judg 6:8).

The prophetic word began with a rhetorical question which anticipated a positive answer.[38] By this question the prophet affirmed to Eli that God had revealed himself **to your father's house** when they were still in Egyptian bondage (lit., "when they were in Egypt to the house of Pharaoh" (v. 27b).[39] This refers to the house of Aaron, the first high priest, from whom, through Ithamar, the fourth son of Aaron, Eli was descended.

2:28 The privileges and provisions of the Aaronic priesthood are enumerated in order to arouse the conscience of Eli regarding the current desecration of the sacred office. Upon Eli's **father** or ancestor

---

to the hardening of the Canaanites (Josh 11:20). Scripture does not affirm that God hardened Pharaoh's heart until after it states several times that Pharaoh had hardened his own heart. Thus when men harden their hearts, God withdraws any further influences to soften them. In this sense, God hardens hearts in that he permits people already hardened by their own free will to become ever more hardened in sin.

[38]1 Sam 2:27 is representative of a group of verses in which the interrogative particle *he* serves merely to express the conviction that the contents of the statement are well known to the hearer. See GK. ¶150:2e for other examples. Thus the sentence in English is more properly translated as an assertion rather than a question which necessitates the addition of the word "not" to make sense.

[39]The LXX and 4QSam[a] suggest that the word "slaves" has dropped out of v. 27, i.e., they were *slaves* in Egypt (cf. NRSV).

God had bestowed wonderful privileges. These are enumerated in ascending scale: First, Yahweh **chose**[40] this father out of all the tribes of Israel to hold the priestly office. Second, as priest of God, Eli's father had the privilege of ministering in the outer court at the bronze altar of sacrifice. He could **go up to**[41] the altar and present offerings on behalf of his people. Third, Eli's father had the privilege of ministry in the inner sanctuary, the holy place where he could offer up incense before the Lord (Exod 30:7f.). Fourth, Eli's father was placed in charge of the priestly oracle. He was privileged **to wear an ephod in my presence**, lit., "to carry an ephod before me." The reference is probably to the high priest's special ephod (Exod 28:6ff.), not the ordinary linen ephod worn at this time by all priests (cf. v. 18), since that is the only one mentioned in the Pentateuch. From his breastpiece, which was considered an extension of his special ephod, he was able, by means of Urim and Thummim, to offer divine guidance for the future. Along with these privileges of service, God gave to Eli's father's house, **all the offerings made with fire by the Israelites**, i.e., the priests received a portion of those sacrifices as the compensation for their faithful ministry (Lev 10:12-15). Clearly in these verses Eli's father or ancestor is Aaron, the first high priest of Israel.

2:29 By means of two rhetorical questions the prophet condemned Eli. First, he was the high priest. He was responsible for the abuse of the sacrificial system by his sons. The priests were showing **scorn** for God's sacrifice and offering. The word rendered **scorn** (lit., "kick") is a Hebrew term which occurs elsewhere only in Deut 32:15 where it refers to the efforts of a pampered ox violently to shake off the yoke.[42] To kick against God's sacrifices was to treat the ordinances which were the source of their prestige and wealth as if they were a grievous burden. The term **sacrifice** (lit., "slaying") includes all sacrifices of slain animals; the word **offerings** (lit.,

---

[40]The verb בָּחַר (*bāḥar*) when used of individuals denotes choice out of a group so that the one chosen discharges a function in relationship to the group.

[41]Klein (26) argues that the language which he renders "go up on (עַל, *'al*) my altar" presupposes that the altar was approached by steps which would seem to contradict the directive of Exod 20:26. The language, however, cannot be pressed that far. It simply means to approach the altar in order to perform the sacrificial duties. See 2 Kgs 16:12; 2 Chr 1:6.

[42]The LXX supported by 4QSam^a reads "Why then do you [plural] look with greedy eye?"

"gifts") when used in a narrow sense is applied to meal or grain offerings. **My dwelling** is the tabernacle (cf. v. 32).[43]

Second, by his inaction regarding the abuses, Eli had shown that he honored his sons above the Lord. The priests (including Eli) were guilty of **fattening** themselves **on the choice parts** of the sacrificial offerings (cf. v. 13). Eli was included in the reproach either (1) because his failure to correct his sons sanctioned their actions or (2) because it was inevitable that he would eat with his sons from time to time.

2:30-31 Based upon the twofold indictment of the previous verse, the Lord through his prophet announced that his commitment to the priesthood would be rescinded. In the NIV **declares** is really a noun (נְאֻם, *nə'um*) which introduces the most solemn divine utterance.[44] First, the man of God acknowledged that a commitment had been made to the family of Aaron in all of its branches that they would **minister**[45] **before me forever** (Exod 28:43; 29:9).[46] That promise, however, had been based upon a principle or condition which should have been understood by all involved: **Those who honor me I will honor, but those who despise me will be disdained.** Since Eli's house — current representative of the Aaronic priesthood — had failed to give Yahweh appropriate honor, the Lord was released from the commitment which he once had made (cf. Jer 18:7-10).[47]

---

[43]The word "dwelling" is an accusative of specification justifying the use in English of the preposition "for." The possessive suffix has been supplied by the NIV, NKJV and NASB for clarity.

[44]The technical word נְאֻם is used eight times in the Pentateuch, six times in the Historical Books, three times in the Poetic Books, and over three hundred times in the prophetic books of the Old Testament.

[45]Lit., "to walk to and fro." Walking before the Lord does not here denote a pious walk with God, as in Gen 5:22 and 17:1, but refers to the service of the priests at the sanctuary as walking before the face of God.

[46]According to Josephus (*Ant.* 8.1.3), Eli was the first in his branch of the family who was made high priest.

[47]In Num 25:13 the house of Eleazar, elder brother of Ithamar, was promised the high priesthood forever. Yet for some reason, unexplained in Scripture, that privilege had been revoked and given to the house of Ithamar of which Eli was the current representative. Thus there was historical precedent for the shifting of the high priestly office from one branch of the Aaronic family to another. The present passage, however, seems to anticipate the removal of the entire Aaronic priesthood.

The NIV ignores הִנֵּה (*hinnēh,* "behold") with which v. 31 begins. In prophetic speech this term serves to introduce a shocking, or at least unexpected, announcement. **The time is coming** (lit., "the days are coming") is another traditional prophetic formula. God would punish the house of Eli by cutting short his **strength**, lit. "arm," the usual metaphor for strength.[48] The young men who were part of that house would die prematurely. The same threat is stated against **your father's house**. Based on the use of this phrase in vv. 27,30 the entire Aaronic family is in view, not just the Ithamar branch. The judgment here announced unfolded gradually. The house of Ithamar (of which the Elides were representatives) suffered devastating blows, first at Shiloh (1 Sam 4:13-17), and later at Nob (1 Sam 22:18-19). Still later, Abiathar, the lone escapee of that slaughter, was deposed from office. Thus was the family of Ithamar removed from the priesthood and reduced to insignificance. Eventually, after the coming of Christ, God cut off all the family of Aaron from the honor of the priesthood.

2:32-33 Four additional judgments were announced to Eli. First, he would see **distress in my dwelling**, lit., "narrowness of dwelling." This might be taken (1) as metaphorical of distress in the personal life of Eli, especially in his domestic relations; or (2) taken more literally of the distress of a physical dwelling.[49] By inserting the word "my" the NIV has interpreted the **dwelling** as the tabernacle. This is probably correct and the fulfillment is found in ch. 4.

Second, although Israel would see glorious days under David and Solomon, the family of Eli would not fare well. The threat was repeated from the previous verse that none of Eli's family would live to see old age, but here the threat was intensified. There would

---

[48]To break or cut off one's arm in Scripture is equivalent to destroying his power (Job 22:9; 38:15; Ps 10:15; 37:17). The "arm" of Eli was either his priestly preeminence or his children. The rest of this passage points in the latter direction. For the idea of children as one's strength, see Gen 49:3; Deut 21:17; Ps 127:4f.

[49]The term צָר (*ṣar*) can be rendered "distress/affliction" as in the ASV, NIV and NASB or "rival/enemy" as in the KJV and NKJV. The first rendering seems to fit the context better. Those who take *ṣar* to mean "enemy" see a reference either (1) to the enemy who would destroy Shiloh and seize the ark; or (2) a high priest from a rival family, i.e., either Samuel or Zadok. Samuel, however, was not an enemy of Eli, nor was Zadok, years later, an enemy of Eli's descendant Abiathar.

never (lit., "all the days," i.e., so long as his house existed) be an old man in the house of Eli.

Third, the Elide priests who were not immediately cut off from the altar, i.e., removed from office or slain, would be overwhelmed with grief because of the degradation of their family and the distress into which the sanctuary would fall. The pronouns in v. 33 are singular, meaning that Eli is identified with his posterity. He would see through their eyes long after he was dead.

Fourth, all of Eli's **descendants** (lit., "all the increase of your house") would **die in the prime of life**, lit., "as men," at about the age of thirty, the legal age (Num 4:3) for the discharge of priestly duties.

2:34 The death of Hophni and Phinehas both in one day would be **a sign**.[50] It was not unusual for prophets to foretell the occurrence of some near event the fulfillment of which would be a pledge of the certainty of their long-range predictions (cf. 1 Sam 10:7).

2:35 The words **I will raise up for myself** suggest that this new priest would be from another line or family. The old priesthood would be replaced by a new priesthood led by one called **a faithful priest**, in contrast to the unfaithfulness exhibited by Eli's sons. Three predictions are made respecting the faithful priest. First, the faithful priest would do, not just what God commands, but **what is in my heart and mind**. Second, God would establish the **house** of the faithful priest. The same participle (נֶאֱמָן, *ne'ĕmān*) is used to describe the house as is used to describe the priest. The NIV's **I will firmly establish his house** is literally "I will build for him a faithful house."[51] Third, the house of the faithful priest would perform priestly ministry **before my anointed one always**, lit., "all his days."[52]

---

[50]Heb. אוֹת (*'ôth*) is an object, occurrence, or event through which a person is to recognize, learn, remember, or perceive the credibility of something. The significant thing is not the sign itself, but its function to confirm or corroborate something beyond itself. Helfmeyer, TDOT, 1:170,183.

[51]While it is true that the Niphal participle נֶאֱמָן often refers to that which is made firm, sure, or lasting, it is also used of reliable, faithful, or trustworthy persons. When used with the verb "build" the participle seems to have a durative sense (1 Sam 25:28; 1 Kgs 11:38). The other sense, however, might be appropriate here because (1) it would not be likely that the writer would use the same word in two different senses in one verse, and (2) the contrast with the unfaithful house of Eli would thereby be all the more obvious. Hence the faithful priest's house would also be faithful.

[52]The NIV renders "he will minister," taking the antecedent of the pronoun to be the faithful priest. The nearest antecedent of the pronoun, however, is

Verse 35 raises two crucial questions, viz., Who is the faithful priest? and Who is "my anointed"? To the first question, four answers have been given. First, some think that the "faithful priest" was Samuel (e.g., R.P. Smith, 1:56). A legitimate question, however, can be raised as to whether or not Samuel was a priest. Second, others think Zadok was the "faithful priest" (e.g., Goldman, 15). The author of Kings linked the banishment of priest Abiathar, a descendant of Eli, and the subsequent elevation of Zadok, with the prophecy of the man of God in the present passage (1 Kgs 2:27). The Zadokites held the high priesthood until the end of the monarchy. While it is clear, however, that the deposing of Abiathar fulfilled the threat against the house of Eli, the author of Kings does not in fact identify Zadok as the "faithful priest." Third, some see the "faithful priest" as a collective embracing all the priests whom the Lord would raise up as faithful servants, culminating in Christ (e.g., KD, 46f.). According to this view, the prophecy of the "faithful priest" found first fulfillment in Samuel, a new fulfillment in Zadok, and its highest fulfillment in Christ. Fourth, a better view is that the "faithful priest" is Christ who would replace the Aaronic priesthood.[53] He would carry out all that was in God's heart (cf. John 8:29).

Who, then, is the anointed one? Because of the mode of their consecration the kings of Israel were called "the Lord's anointed" (e.g., 1 Sam 24:6,10).[54] Like Hannah (2:10), this prophet anticipated a great king of the future. Most take the reference here to be to David. No high priest, however, is ever said to walk before the kings of Judah or Israel, and certainly the Faithful Priest (Christ) does not **minister** (lit., "walk to and fro") before any earthly king. The anointed one is here the Anointed One *par excellence*, Messiah. His **house**

"his house." Hence the last clause in v. 35 is better translated "it [the house of the faithful priest] will minister before *my anointed*." On this interpretation see J.E. Smith (78-82); and the concurring opinion of W. Kaiser (75f).

[53]Some of the church fathers sensed that this passage contained a prediction of the abrogation of the Aaronic priesthood by Jesus Christ, but their method of reaching this conclusion is untenable. They referred vv. 31-34 to Eli and his house, and then regarded the sentence pronounced upon Eli as simply a type of the messianic fulfillment. For references and discussion, see KD, 159.

[54]The title would also be appropriate to priests, since they too were anointed with consecration oil (Lev 4:3,5,16).

or priestly family,[55] walks before him in the sense that it is under his scrutiny and supervision.[56] Messiah's house is the New Testament royal priesthood (1 Pet 2:9).

2:36 Members of the old priesthood (the family of Aaron) would submit to the authority of the Faithful Priest. The Aaronic priests would **come and bow down before him**. They would be dependent on him for sustenance (**piece of silver and a crust of bread**). In their greed, Eli's sons had an abundance of food because they defrauded both the worshipers and God in the sacrificial ritual. The punishment here announced for their priestly descendants fits the crime. They would be reduced to the level of beggars. The former priests would have to turn to the Faithful Priest (Messiah) for appointment to the priestly office, an office which he cheerfully confers on all who embrace his gospel. An example of the fulfillment of the prophecy may be found in Acts 6:7.

---

[55]The term "house" usually refers to numerous offspring (e.g., Exod 1:21; 2 Sam 7:11). In some passages the term "house" is used metaphorically of assured posterity. To those who dwell in tents, a fixed and permanent dwelling was a mark of greatness. For "house" in this sense, see 1 Kgs 2:24; 11:38.

[56]The idea of a *walking house* is already found in v. 30, where the NIV again translates "minister." There a plural verb is used because the subject is compound ("your house and the house of your father"). Here a singular verb is used with בַּיִת (*bayith*), perhaps stressing the unity of the house or family of the Faithful Priest. While plural verbs are often used with *bayith* as subject, this is not inevitably the case. See e.g., Gen 45:2; Josh 7:14; Ruth 4:12.

1 SAMUEL 3

2. The Call of Samuel (3:1-18)

The narrative of the call of Samuel to prophetic service marks the beginning of the transition of spiritual leadership from the Elide priesthood to Samuel. Samuel was called by the providence of God to be the founder of the prophetic institution, which, as time marched on, would stand on equal footing with the priestly and royal offices in the preparation for the coming of the one who would be Prophet, Priest and King.

The Lad's Mistake (3:1-9)

3:1 As he was growing up,[1] Samuel **ministered before the LORD**, i.e., he had duties around the tabernacle which were appropriate to his age (cf. 2:11,18). He served **under Eli**, lit. "to the face of Eli," i.e., in his presence.[2] Perhaps he was the personal attendant to the old priest.

In those days after the formal rejection of the Elide priesthood, two conditions existed in respect to divine revelation. First, **the word of the LORD**, i.e., the divine revelation announced by prophets, **was rare** (lit., "precious"). This note is intended as (1) a commentary on the terrible times and (2) an explanation as to why Samuel did not

---

[1]Samuel is called here a *na'ar* which is not very specific as to age. Estimates of his age at the time of his call vary widely. Josephus preserves a Jewish tradition to the effect that Samuel had just completed his twelfth year when the word of God came to him (*Ant.* 5:10.4).

[2]English versions generally obscure a subtle distinction between 2:11 and 3:1. Eslinger (*Kingship*, 145) calls attention to the fact that in 2:11 Samuel served both *Yahweh* and *Eli*, lit., "the face of Eli the priest." In 3:1 he serves only Yahweh, doing so in the presence of Eli who is no longer designated as "the priest." In the eyes of the Narrator, Eli already seems to have lost his position.

recognize the meaning of his experience when God called to him.[3] Second, **there were not many visions** (lit., "vision[4] did not spread abroad"[5]). This means that prophetic visions were not granted (Klein, 29), or at least were not widespread in the land, i.e., God did not reveal himself often in visions. The implication is that God was punishing his people because of the spiritual malaise which was amply illustrated in the previous chapter. For these reasons an entire chapter is devoted to Samuel's first communication from God.

3:2-4 These verses set forth (1) the assertion that revelation came to Samuel (vv. 2a,4) and (2) the circumstances under which it came (vv. 2b-3). One **night** (lit., "it came to pass on that day") suggests that the day was special, a milestone in Samuel's rise to leadership, and consequently in redemptive history.[6] Though sleeping, the lad was awakened by the voice. He thought the sound proceeded from the chamber of Eli. **"Here I am,"** (lit., "behold me") is the regular formula for expressing attention to a call and readiness to obey (cf. Gen 22:1; Isa 6:8).

Five circumstances throw light on the initial revelation to Samuel. First, as respects Eli's physical condition, he was nearly blind. His condition is mentioned (1) to anticipate the statement in 4:15 where he is totally blind and (2) to explain Samuel's behavior as later described. Under these circumstances, when Samuel heard his name called out in the darkness, he might easily suppose that Eli was summoning him for assistance.

Second, as respects Eli's location, he was **lying down in his usual place**. Eli's sleeping place is left indefinite. He seems to have been somewhat removed from where Samuel was sleeping. He may have been sleeping in the vestibule of the sanctuary (Klein, 32).

---

[3]Eslinger (*Kingship*, 146) reads more into this notice. The scarcity of divine revelation could indicate (1) that Yahweh had nothing to say to Israel; or (2) the official receptors of the vision, the Elides, were unfit to mediate any revelations.

[4]The term "vision" (חָזוֹן, *ḥāzôn*) is a technical term for divine revelation mediated through a seer (חוֹזֶה, *ḥôzeh*).

[5]The text uses a Niphal participle of the root פרץ (*prṣ*). In the Qal stem this root is used of the publication of a royal decree (2 Chr 31:5). The idea seems to be that there was no publicly acknowledged prophet whose prophetic revelation was shared with all Israel.

[6]Others think the "day" was the day when the man of God appeared to Eli. The text, however, gives the impression that some time elapsed between the appearance of the man of God and the revelation to Samuel.

Third, as to the timing of the revelation, **the lamp of God had not yet gone out.** This lamp (נֵר, *nēr*) is probably the same as the lampstand (מְנוֹרָה, *mᵉnôrāh*) which stood on the south side of the holy place opposite the table of showbread (Exod 25:31-37; cf. Lev 24:2,4). It is here mentioned for the last time in Scripture. This lamp was lighted every evening and allowed to burn through the night until all the oil was consumed (Exod 27:21). Thus the language here is equivalent to "before morning light."

Fourth, as to the recipient of the revelation, he was **lying down in the temple of the LORD.** Some take **temple** (הֵיכָל, *hêkal*) here to refer to that area within the actual tent which is called the holy place (cf. 1 Kgs 6:5; 7:50); others think the entire tabernacle complex is encompassed by this term as in 1:9.[7]

Fifth, as to the source of the revelation, the historian notes that Samuel was sleeping **where the ark of God was.** The ark of God, as his most sacred throne, was housed in that tent-palace.[8] The presence of the ark in the temple/palace of Yahweh is mentioned (1) to suggest that the manifestation of God is to be linked in some way with the ark, (2) to enhance Samuel's credentials by associating him with the ark, and (3) to indicate that the revelation to Samuel came before the ark was captured and removed from Shiloh.

3:5-7 Upon hearing his name called, Samuel **ran** to Eli's side to present himself for whatever duties the old man might assign. His response shows (1) that his sleeping chamber was within earshot of that of the high priest and (2) that he was accustomed to being summoned to Eli's side during the night. Eli assured the boy that he had not called for him. So Eli sent him back to his bed. When the voice spoke the second time, Samuel did not immediately answer, "Here I am," and he did not *run* to the side of Eli. He only *went* to Eli. Samuel was beginning to wonder about who was calling him. Eli addressed Samuel this time as **my son,** obviously a term of endearment, and perhaps puzzlement over what must have appeared to be strange behavior by the youth.

---

[7]Several of the old commentaries, e.g. KD, Jamieson, Spence, Kirkpatrick, insist that both Samuel and Eli were sleeping in the cells which were built for priests and Levites around the courtyard of the tabernacle.

[8]For a fine study of the theological significance of the ark, see M. Woudstra. G.W. Ahlström evaluates the ark narrative from a far more skeptical perspective. "The Travels of the Ark: A Religio-Political Composition," *JNES* 43 (1984): 142-149.

How could Samuel make the same mistake twice? The sacred historian offers two explanations. First, Samuel did not yet **know** the Lord in a personal way. This language is not used in the same way as in 2:12 where Eli's sons did not *know* the Lord. Samuel certainly *knew* and *worshiped* the God of Israel prior to this night. In Samuel's case the text is asserting either (1) that he did not yet know it was Yahweh who was speaking, or (2) that he did not yet have the special relationship with the Lord which he would subsequently experience, or (3) that he did not have that immediate knowledge of God which is received in direct revelation. Second, the lad had never before heard a word from God. Perhaps this clause explains the sense in which Samuel did not *know* the Lord. Revelation was a new experience for him.

3:8-9 When Samuel came to Eli the third time, the old priest realized that it must be the Lord calling the boy. If Samuel had been simply dreaming, the dream would not have continued through two interruptions. Eli, therefore, concluded that the Lord must have called the boy. The old priest gave the lad a proper response to use if he should hear that voice again. The response expresses eagerness (**speak**), acknowledgment (**LORD**), humility (**your servant**), and attentiveness (**is listening**) which are appropriate for one to whom God is speaking.

The Lord's Manifestation (3:10-14)

3:10 At this point the Lord **came and stood** and called to Samuel as he had done before. In the previous calls the voice appeared to proceed from a distance; now the sound was as if the speaker stood beside him. In Old Testament times God often assumed bodily form in order to come and speak to his servants. As in the first call, the repetition of his name was intended to arrest the boy's attention and convey a sense of urgency and finality. Samuel responded to the Lord generally in the manner which Eli had directed him. He did not, however, use the personal name of God. Whether this was due to caution, ignorance, accident or awe cannot be determined.

3:11 The Lord revealed to Samuel that he was about to do something so shocking that the news of it would make everyone's ears **tingle**.[9] The catastrophe was the impending defeat of Israel by the

---

[9]This language is used in the Old Testament twice: here at the beginning of the monarchy and at the end of the monarchy in reference to the destruction of the temple by Nebuchadnezzar in 586 B.C. See 2 Kgs 21:12; Jer 19:3.

Philistines, the death of Eli's sons and Eli himself, the capture of the ark of God, and the desolation of the national sanctuary at Shiloh.

3:12 God would carry out against Eli and his family everything which the anonymous prophet had predicted in the previous chapter. **Carry out** is literally "raise up," i.e., initiate or stir up. Everything which God had spoken through that man of God **from beginning to end** (lit., "beginning and ending"), i.e., beginning with the death of Eli's two sons, and continuing until the whole prophecy of doom regarding the house of Eli and the Aaronic priesthood was fulfilled.

3:13-14 The reasons for the downfall of the house of Eli were enumerated to Samuel. First, through a prophet Yahweh had announced his intention to **judge,** i.e., "punish," that priestly family **forever,** i.e., with an eternal verdict. Eli's house would pass away.

Second, Eli himself was culpable because he had failed **to restrain**[10] his sons in their contemptible behavior. Apparently the Lord regarded Eli's efforts in 2:23 as being too little and too late. The clause **his sons made themselves contemptible,** is literally "were cursing for themselves," i.e., they had brought cursing upon themselves or made themselves accursed.[11]

Third, at this point the sin of Eli's house could not be **atoned for** (lit., "covered over") by any sacrifice or offering, i.e., either by bloody or nonbloody offerings. Deliberate and continuous sin, i.e., sinning "with a high hand" (Num 15:27-31), could not be forgiven. The appointed sacrifices would not avail in the case of Eli's sons because

---

[10]The Hebrew verb is more forceful than "restrain." In the Piel, the root כהה (*khh*) has the sense of "weaken, humble, reduce to powerlessness." Thus the condemnation here is that Eli should have stripped his sons of their office.

[11]Similarly "were bringing [brought] a curse upon themselves" (BV, NASB); "made themselves vile" (NKJV); "committed sacrilege at will" (NJPS). Jewish tradition lists v. 13 as one of the *tiqqune sopherim*, i.e., an emendation of the scribes. Supposedly the text originally read, "cursing me" (לִי, *lî*), which the scribes, out of reverence, changed to "cursing themselves" (לָהֶם, *lāhem*). If the original reading was "curse me," i.e., God, then the priests are being charged with blasphemy, a sin which the Mosaic law categorically condemns. See Exod 22:28; Lev 24:15. Gordon (90) mentions the possibility that a single *aleph* was dropped from the consonants of *lāhem*. The original text would then have read: were "cursing God" (אלהם, *'lhm* [*elohim*]). The LXX supports this reading which is also accepted by the NRSV, NEB, and JB, Klein (33) and Gordon (90).

they had hardened themselves in sin even after the solemn warning of 2:27-36.

Fourth, the doom of Eli's house was sealed with an oath of God (**I swore to the house of Eli**). The oath made the sentence irrevocable. A prophet already had pronounced the decline of Eli's house (2:31); now the Lord himself pronounced that inescapable doom.

The Priest's Question (3:15-18)

3:15 In the morning Samuel performed his usual duty of opening **the doors to the house of the Lord.** The nature of Samuel's ministry about the sanctuary is here indicated. He performed the duties of a subordinate Levite (cf. 1 Chr 15:18,23). The term **doors** seems to denote *double* or *folding* doors of wood. On the structural implications of "doors," see on 1:9.

Samuel was afraid to tell Eli the message which had been given to him. He was under no divine directive to do so. His fear was not of retaliation by the old priest, but of hurting him deeply. The text characterizes what happened that night to Samuel as **the vision** (מַרְאָה, *mar'eh*), i.e., something seen when wide awake, and in the full, calm possession of every faculty. Clearly the Lord made an objective appearance at Shiloh to Samuel; this was not a vision within the mind.

3:16-17 No doubt Samuel tried to avoid Eli for much of the day. Finally the old priest summoned him. With the prophecy of the previous chapter on his mind, he anticipated that the revelation to Samuel concerned the termination of his priesthood. His efforts to elicit information from the reluctant Samuel became more intense with each sentence. First, he merely **asked** what message the lad had received during the night. The old priest addressed the lad as **my son.** Everything in the narrative suggests that the priest and Samuel enjoyed a warm and loving relationship. Second, Eli **demanded** a complete accounting of what was said. Finally, Eli put Samuel under oath to tell the truth when he said: **May God deal with you, be it ever so severely, if you hide from me anything he told you.**[12] He did

---

[12]Lit., "so shall God do to you and so shall he add if . . . ." The words imply this: "If you do not tell me fully what God has revealed, may the same, and greater curses, fall on you." This form of adjuration appears eleven times in the books of Samuel and Kings. Elsewhere it is found only in Ruth 1:17.

not want Samuel to go easy on him. Any concealment on Samuel's part would have involved the sin of perjury.

3:18 In the light of the message he had already received (2:27-36), **Samuel told him everything, hiding nothing from him.** Eli was not shocked nor angry by what Samuel told him. In fact he expressed a twofold confidence. First, he recognized the message as coming from the LORD, i.e., Yahweh. He recognized that Yahweh was sovereign, and would do what he willed; he was righteous, and would do nothing unjust. Second, he expressed confidence that the Lord would do what was best. Eli left himself in God's hands.

3. The Initial Leadership of Samuel (3:19–4:1a)

3:19-21 These three verses form the transition from the call of Samuel to the account of his prophetic labors in Israel. **The Lord was with Samuel** in every respect as he grew up (cf. 2:21,26). The phrase **the LORD was with Samuel** can be used to describe any successful person, but here it refers to one who was especially blessed by God, the man of God. A specific example of this divine presence in his life was that God did not let any of his words **fall to the ground**, i.e., go unfulfilled.[13] Fulfillment of prediction is the main way in which the word of a prophet is shown to be true (Deut 18:22). The passage in effect is saying that Samuel quickly displayed prophetic gifts.

Samuel's reputation as a true **prophet** of God spread throughout the land. From **Dan** in the north **to Beersheba** in the south[14] Samuel was **recognized** to be **attested**, i.e., accredited, as a prophet of God.[15] These two towns marked the traditional limits of the Promised

---

[13]On the use of the root נָפַל (*npl*) in the sense of "go unfulfilled," see Josh 21:45; 23:14; 1 Kgs 8:56. Klein (34) thinks that it was Yahweh's promises to Samuel which were not allowed to fall to the ground. Spence (306) understands that it was Samuel who did not let the words of the Lord fall to the ground, i.e., he carried out all of God's commands. The metaphor appears to be derived from water being spilled on the ground.

[14]Samuel's status as a prophet was acknowledged throughout the land, though a more circumscribed jurisdiction is attributed to Samuel the judge in 7:15-17 (Gordon, 91).

[15]The word translated "attested" (נֶאֱמָן, *ne'ĕmān*) also means "faithful." It is used of Moses in Num 12:7, and of the faithful priest and his house in 2:35.

Land.[16] Whatever the etymological significance of the term "prophet" — and that is much discussed — the appropriate definition is indicated here in the context. A prophet was one to whom Yahweh appeared and to whom he revealed his word.

Shiloh regained its prestige as the central sanctuary of God's people, not because the ark was there, but because an accredited man of God was there. The text suggests that people would come to Shiloh to consult with the boy prophet. The reason Samuel could make such accurate predictions is that the Lord **continued to appear** (lit., "added to appear") to him **at Shiloh**. Yahweh would reveal himself to Samuel **through his word**, (lit., "in the word of Yahweh"), i.e., through a prophetic announcement of his word. Samuel then would take that word to all the people of Israel (v. 21).

4:1a The opening sentence of ch. 4 has been variously interpreted. Some see it as the summary statement regarding the growing influence of Samuel in the land, in which case it would more properly be considered the last line of ch. 3. The thought would then be, "because Samuel spoke by the word of Yahweh, therefore his word came to all Israel." Others see a connection between these words and the outbreak of hostilities with the Philistines, and this seems to be the intention of those who arranged the present text. Did the prophetic word of Samuel send the armies to the battlefield? (KD, 164). Did the growing influence of Samuel provoke Philistine incursions? (Jamieson, 144). The connection may be only chronological.

---

[16]The expression "from Dan to Beersheba" is found first in Judg 20:1 and thereafter five times in the books of Samuel. It disappears after the time of the division of the kingdom, and is used only one further time, and that after the fall of the northern kingdom (2 Chr 30:5).

1 SAMUEL 4

Because the focus in chs. 4–6 is on the ark of God, this material is frequently called "the ark narrative."[1] The unit is generally viewed as thematically separate from chs. 1–3. In a series of articles, John Willis has challenged this scholarly consensus as being too fragmentary. He sees in chs. 1–7 a well-attested biblical literary pattern: (1) Yahweh prepares a man to lead Israel through some crisis (1:1–4:1a), (2) the crisis is described (4:1b–7:1), and (3) the successful guidance of Israel out of the crisis is accomplished by the chosen man (7:1-17).[2] Samuel is absent from chs. 4–6. Willis suggests that this may be intended to emphasize that without him Israel's situation was rapidly deteriorating under the Elides. Though nothing is said in ch. 4 about Samuel or the sins of Eli's sons, a link is forged with the preceding unit by the mention of Shiloh, the ark and the priesthood.

4. The Challenge by the Philistines (4:1b–7:2)

The two battles of Ebenezer were fought ca. 1105 B.C. The Israelites were attempting to put an end to Philistine incursions into their land. Chronologically this preceded the exploits of Samson

---

[1]The extent of the material which should be assigned to "the ark narrative" is debated. A. Campbell defends the older view that 1 Sam 4:1b–7:1 + 2 Sam 6 are excerpts from a longer and continuous ark narrative. "Yahweh and the Ark: A Case Study in Narrative," *JBL* 98 (1979): 31-43. Miller & Roberts omit 2 Sam 6 but incorporate twenty verses from 1 Sam 2.

[2]J.T. Willis, "An Anti-Elide Narrative Tradition from a Prophetic Circle at the Ramah Sanctuary," *JBL* 90 (1971): 288-308; "Cultic Elements in the Story of Samuel's Birth and Dedication," *ST* 26 (1972): 33-61; "The Function of Comprehensive Anticipatory Redactional Joints in 1 Samuel 16–18," *ZAW* 85 (1973): 294-314; "The Song of Hannah and Psalm 113," *CBQ* 34 (1973): 139-154; "Samuel Versus Eli," *TZ* 35 (1979): 201-212.

against the Philistines (Judg 13–16). According to Judg 13:1, the Philistine oppression lasted forty years. It must have begun about halfway through the judgeship of Eli (1 Sam 4:18) which can be dated ca. 1145-1105 B.C. The twenty years of Samson's judgeship (Judg 15:20) can be placed between the two battles of Ebenezer (1105 B.C.) and the great Mizpah revival (1085 B.C.).

The Capture of the Ark (4:1b-11)

The First Defeat of Israel (4:1b-3)

4:1b The Philistines, the archvillains of this period, are here mentioned for the first of some 116 times in the books of Samuel.[3] The Philistines are known in secular literature as the Sea Peoples because they came from the islands of the Mediterranean Sea ca. 1200 B.C.[4] After an unsuccessful attempt to invade Egypt, they settled in the coastal plains of Palestine. While they are mainly associated with five cities (Ashdod, Ashkelon, Ekron, Gath, Gaza), from time to time the Philistines would make incursions into the mountains where the Israelites lived. They would seize the harvests and take slaves.

Here the Israelites **went out to fight against the Philistines** in the first united effort on the part of Israelites to defend their land against the incursions by these enemies.[5] The location of **Ebenezer** is unknown except that it must have been within earshot of Aphek (v. 6). The name, which means "stone of help" (lit., "the stone, the help"), was not given to this battlefield until Samuel set up a memorial stone there to commemorate a victory over the Philistines some twenty years later (1 Sam 7:12). Therefore the name here is a prolepsis. **Aphek** means "strength" or "firmness" and is an appropriate name for any fortress. There were several Apheks in Palestine. This Aphek

---

[3]The area which the Philistines occupied lies roughly between Jaffa in the north and the desert beyond Gaza, some fifty miles to the south. The eastern boundary was marked by the junction of the coastal plain and the limestone plateau called the Shephelah, which formed a buffer zone to the hill country of Judah.

[4]According to Amos 9:7, the Philistines came from Caphtor or Crete. An especially valuable study on the Philistines is T. Dothan. See also T.C. Mitchell, AOTS, 404-417; K.A. Kitchen, POTT, 53-78; B. Mazar, WHJP, 3:164-179.

[5]The longer text of the LXX, favored by the NEB, states that it was the Philistines who initiated the hostilities. Campbell (59) here supports the MT over the LXX.

was probably located near the source of the Yarkon river on the northern boundary of Philistine territory (MBA, 84). A site about two miles to the east of Aphek has been identified as Ebenezer.

4:2 After the Philistines deployed their army, **the battle spread,** or the troops clashed.[6] Israel **was defeated**. The use of the passive Niphal hints that the Philistines were merely agents of destruction decreed by a higher authority. The Philistines **killed** (lit., "smote") **four thousand** soldiers **on the battlefield** (lit., "in battle-array in the field"). The Hebrew term אֶלֶף (*'eleph*) translated "thousand" in English versions may be the technical name for a military unit regardless of its size. The losses then equaled four of these units. Since the size of these units is not known, and in fact may have varied from battle to battle, it is impossible to determine how many casualties the Israelites suffered in the first clash with the Philistines.[7] They did not, however, abandon the field to the enemy.

4:3 The **soldiers** (lit., "the people") returned to their camp to regroup and prepare for another day of battle. The use of the term "people" for "army" reflects a time when there was no standing army, but a levy of all the men capable of bearing arms in time of war. The **camp** was a defensive entrenchment which had been prepared just in case they had to fall back in the battle. In the Israelite camp the **elders** of Israel tried to restore morale among the troops. Before the creation of the monarchy, the elders or heads of families were the natural leaders, and especially when the judge of the land was as elderly as Eli.

The elders reacted to the defeat in several ways. First, they expressed shock over the events of the day. They obviously expected victory. Second, they recognized that Yahweh had brought defeat

---

[6]The NIV translation can be defended, although when the term means "spread," it is used in the Niphal rather than Qal as here. G.R. Driver has proposed another meaning for the same root: "when the battle clashed," i.e., in the clash of battle. *JTS* 34 (1933): 379. Cf. ASV, NKJV and essentially NRSV, "when they joined battle"; BV, "when the fight became general"; JB, "the battle was hotly engaged."

[7]McCarter (1:107) takes the military unit called "thousand" to consist of between five and fourteen men. Using this system of interpretation, the four thousand who fell the first day would number between twenty and fifty-six men, and the thirty thousand on the second day would equal 150 to 420 casualties. Klein (41) seems to endorse this reduction. A unit numbering three to four hundred men would seem to be more appropriate. See further Gottwald, 270-282.

upon them. The elders felt that Yahweh had failed them; it never occurred to them that perhaps they had failed Yahweh.

Third, they wrongly attributed the defeat to the absence of the ark on the battlefield. The ark was the symbol of God's presence. In Joshua's day the ark was carried to the scene of battle (Josh 6:4). In 3:3 this sacred chest was called "the ark of God"; here it is called "the ark of the LORD's [Yahweh's] covenant."[8] It was so named because it contained within it the tablets of the ten commandments (Exod 25:21; Deut 10:5). The Israelites had a superstitious belief that the mere presence of the ark would make them unconquerable. Instead of seeking the face of the Lord through national repentance, they attempted to force God's hand to intervene on their behalf by exposing the ark to danger, probably influenced by heathen neighbors who carried the statues of their gods or their symbols into battle (Hindson, 140). The words **from Shiloh** are a link to the preceding chapters and a reminder of all the corruption in which the Elides had engaged at that place.

The Second Defeat of Israel (4:4-11)

4:4 This verse points out, first, the effort which the Israelites expended to secure the ark. Men were sent twenty miles back to Shiloh to bring the ark to the battlefield. Second, the verse indicates the significance of the ark. It was **the ark of the covenant**, the symbol of that ancient covenant which God made with Israel at Sinai. This covenant was often interpreted by Israel to mean that God was obligated to help them unconditionally. Third, the verse reveals the reason they wanted the ark on the battlefield. The ark represented the presence of the LORD Almighty (lit., "Yahweh of hosts"), a title with martial implications (see on 1 Sam 1:3). The LORD Almighty was **enthroned between the cherubim**. Cherubim are angelic creatures first mentioned in Gen 3:24. They are always depicted as guarding something. Their physical features are a mystery.[9] At both

---

[8]Gordon (93) notes that while several titles for the ark are found in chs. 4-6, reference to the "covenant" is confined to the account of the preparations for the second engagement (vv. 3,4,5), as if to suggest that this symbol of the covenant was bound to disappoint expectations once battle was joined.

[9]Klein (41) follows Albright and DeVaux in identifying cherubim as winged sphinxes. Many hybrid human-animal forms were prominent in Assyrian, Babylonian, Hittite, Egyptian and Canaanite art. None of these,

ends of the ark's cover were golden cherubim facing down toward the cover. Their wings extended over the ark and touched one another. The area beneath the wings of the cherubim was called the atonement cover. There God agreed to meet with his people. The atonement cover was like an earthly throne for the invisible God (Exod 25:17-22). Fourth, the verse hints at the disaster to come. Eli's two priestly sons, **Hophni and Phinehas**, accompanied the ark from Shiloh to Ebenezer. Nothing indicates that there was any fault in the manner by which the ark was brought to the camp. Eli's two sons, however, are responsible by their proximity to the ark, for its capture. *They* are the issue here, not the ark (Miller & Roberts, 33). As to the whereabouts of Samuel, the text is silent. He may still have been too young to be going to war with the men.

Eslinger (*Kingship*, 168) calls attention to the structure of v. 4 which underscores the jeopardy of the two priests. Their presence **there** (syntactical emphasis in Heb.) on the battlefield is related between a double reference to the presence of the ark of the covenant. They were trapped there, so to speak, by the awesome presence of Yahweh of Hosts.

4:5 The arrival of the ark in the Israelite camp called forth a **great shout** of joy which doubled as a war cry. The people were now confident of victory.[10] They had accepted the opinion of the elders that the ark would guarantee victory over the Philistines. The noise was so loud that the earth seemed to quake. In their nearby camp the Philistines could hear the commotion. The phrase **that the ground shook** perhaps points to an echo which reverberated through that area.[11]

4:6-8 The reactions of the Philistines to the arrival of the ark are vividly portrayed. First, they were inquisitive. Second, they were astonished. Third, they were afraid. Because they worshiped idols, they regarded the ark as a god. Most heathen feared the might of

---

however, accurately depicts the cherubim as described in the Bible. Josephus (*Ant.* 8.3.3) states that no one knew in the first century A.D. what the cherubim looked like. For a discussion of the problem, see ZPEB s.v. "Cherub; Cherubim" by D.E. Acomb.

[10]Another interpretation is that the people shouted in order to goad Yahweh into action on their behalf.

[11]Mauchline (70) points out that the verb *hm* (הום/הים) usually has a personal reference. He proposes that the meaning here is that "the land [of Israel] was agog with excitement."

the gods of other nations to a certain degree. The Philistines were superstitious, but no more so than the Israelites who supposed the Deity was in some way inseparably connected with the lifeless gold and wood of the symbolic ark and cherubim. Fourth, they lament with the expression of a double *woe*, the first of which is rendered by the NIV **We're in trouble!** The second woe recognizes that they were fighting against **mighty gods** from whom there would be no deliverance. These pagans assumed that Israel, like other nations of that day, had more than one god. Their fear is of **the hand** of the Israelite gods. They knew of what the Israelite gods had done to the Egyptians back in the days of Moses. The Israelite "gods," represented by the ark, had **struck the Egyptians with all kinds of plagues**, lit., "with every kind of smiting." The word translated "smiting" in v. 8 is rendered "slaughter" in v. 10. The allusion is to the overthrow of Pharaoh in the Red Sea which was located **in the desert** (Exod 13:20), not to the ten plagues for which a different word is used in Exodus.

The term **Hebrews** is used (1) by foreigners when referring to Israelites, and (2) by Israelites in speaking of themselves to foreigners; and (3) when Israelites are contrasted with foreigners. The term has been derived from a root which means "cross over" and was used originally of Abraham as one who crossed over the Euphrates.[12] The *Habiru* or *Hebrews* were found in many parts of the Fertile Crescent during this period. They did not constitute one ethnic group, but were to be found as mercenary soldiers, predatory raiders, and slaves. Thus the term may have had a derogatory sense as meaning something like "outlaw." (See discussion on 1 Sam 13:3.)

4:9 When the Philistines recovered from the initial panic, they resolutely determined to fight the battle. The Philistines were afraid that now the lowly Hebrews would be able to gain the victory over them. In that case the Philistines would become slaves to those who had served them for some time.[13] With desperate determination the Philistine soldiers urged one another to fight all the harder. The reaction of the Philistines in vv. 6-9 prepares for the conclusion that

---

[12]Kirkpatrick, 1:71. Others regard "Hebrew" as a patronymic from Eber (Gen 10:21,24), signifying "the descendants of Eber."

[13]That the Israelites had been slaves to the Philistines describes primarily the plight of the Judahites, Danites and Simeonites who bore the brunt of Philistine forays into the Judean hills (Bierling, 128).

whatever happens in the battle to come must be the will of Yahweh, for the Philistines as mere men, could never compete with him.

4:10-11 The verbs describing the Israelite defeat in vv. 10-11 are passive. The Philistines did their part. They **fought**. The defeat, however, was brought on Israel by Yahweh. **Every man fled to his tent**, i.e., the soldiers were deserting the army in fear. The **slaughter** (מַכָּה, *makkāh*) was very great. The psalmist Asaph would later sing of this crushing defeat by the Philistines and the spiritual lessons which it afforded (Ps 78:59-61). The number of Israelites who were **lost** (lit., "fell") is over seven times the losses in the battle on the first day. Probably the figure includes deserters and wounded as well as the dead. On the meaning of the word **thousand** (*'eleph*), see on v. 2. The slaughter in the close combat which characterized ancient warfare was immense. Those who fell are identified as **foot soldiers** because in this period the Israelites had neither cavalry nor chariots.

The ark of God was captured is a refrain found five times in the next twelve verses. The capture of the ark of God was the greatest calamity that had befallen Israel to this time. Yet the Narrator reports the fact without emotion. That ark which had been constructed by Moses in accord with God's command at Sinai, which had accompanied Israel through the wilderness, at the waters of Jordan, and in the march around Jericho — *that* ark was taken by pagan hands to pagan temples. One of the marvelous evidences of the inspiration of Scripture is the restraint with which such devastating tragedies are reported.

Just as the anonymous prophet had predicted in 2:34, **Hophni and Phinehas** both died on the same day. Probably the last stand was made round the ark, and the two may have died defending it.

William Shea has deciphered a five-line inscription which appears to allude to this battle with the Philistines. If his reading holds up under further analysis, this inscription contains the earliest known extrabiblical reference to an Old Testament event (the capture of the ark) and person (Hophni).[14]

The Death of Eli (4:12-18)

4:12 A soldier from the tribe of Benjamin ran back to Shiloh with a battle report. The route was predominantly uphill into mountain-

---

[14]See "The 'Iizbet Ṣarṭah Ostracon," *AUSS* 28 (1990): 62; "Ancient Ostracon Records Ark's Wanderings," *Ministry* (1991): 14.

ous country, but this Benjamite covered the twenty miles **the same day**. His message was urgent. People would need to scatter and hide their valuable possessions because there was no longer any army left to resist the Philistine advance. This man had torn his clothes and thrown dust on his head as a sign of deep mourning.

4:13 Eli was sitting on his chair by the side of the road waiting for any word from the battle. He was **watching** (מְצַפֶּה, *mᵉṣappeh*) i.e., "waiting expectantly." The blind man, who can still hear well, is concentrating on the road leading to the temple. The **chair** (lit., "the throne") may have been Eli's official seat as the judge of the land. He **feared for the ark** that had been taken to the battlefield, perhaps against his advice. He was mindful of the judgment which had been pronounced against his house. He must have known that the presence of the ark would not thwart that judgment. The messenger entered the town gate on the main road[15] which appears to be on the side of town farthest from the temple complex.

4:14-17 Eli was now totally blind. He had not seen the man enter the city; but he heard the cry of the people around him. There must have been total confusion and panic as the messenger blurted out the report. Eli then asked for an explanation. Had he been able to see, he would have known from the dress of the messenger the outcome of the battle. The **man who brought the news** (מְבַשֵּׂר, *mᵉbaśśēr*), i.e., messenger,[16] came over to him and introduced himself. He then broke the news to him with great compassion. He wanted to spare the old man as much as possible. The fourfold announcement grew increasingly alarming. The messenger reported that (1) Israel had fled before the Philistines and (2) the army had sustained heavy losses. He then added the worst news of all: (3) Eli's two sons had been killed and (4) the ark had been captured.

4:18 The news that the ark had been captured caused the old man to tumble off his chair or stool (v. 9). Eli was **heavy** either because of his weight, or because of his age. He fell in such a way that he broke his neck and died.[17] Eli was ninety-eight years old. He is mentioned,

---

[15]Goldman (24) conjectures that the messenger ran past Eli to bring the news to the townspeople, then had to backtrack to give the report to the old priest.

[16]1 Sam 4:17 is the only clear exception to the general meaning of this word, viz., a bearer of good news.

[17]Eslinger (*Kingship*, 179) strangely suggests that Eli was being punished for the crime of being old and feeble. Nothing in the text, however, even hints that Eli's death was a punishment (contra Miller & Roberts 38).

not as the high priest of Israel, but as one who **led** (lit., "judged")
Israel forty years,[18] ca. 1145-1105 B.C. He had not become leader
(judge) until he was fifty-eight. Such obituary notices for Israel's
judges are usually prefaced by a description of how the judge delivered Israel from the hand of some enemy (cf. Judg. 3:10,31; 8:28).
Eli's notice, on the other hand, comes immediately after one of
Israel's most humiliating defeats.

The Birth of Ichabod (4:19-22)

4:19-20 The wife of Phinehas was pregnant and ready to deliver.
The news that her husband and father-in-law were dead, and the ark
captured caused her to enter into premature labor (lit., "she
crouched and gave birth"). The NIV takes **but was overcome by her
labor pains** (lit. "because pains turned upon her," i.e., came on her
suddenly) to refer to what happened after the birth. The clause is better taken as an explanation as to why she gave birth at the moment
of the bad news. She gave birth to a son, but the birth was difficult;
her life was in the balance. The women who attended her during the
birth tried to comfort her with the news that she had borne a son (cf.
Gen 35:17). The woman was too weak or too despondent to respond.

4:21-22 With her dying breath the woman named her new son
Ichabod, which means "no glory." In her view **the glory** had **departed**
(lit., "was taken into exile") from Israel because the ark had been **captured** (לָקַח, lāqaḥ). The term "glory" represents the Presence of God
dwelling in the tabernacle.

The repetition of the thought that the glory had departed shows
how deeply the wife of godless Phinehas had taken to heart the
seizure of the ark. For her, and probably most of her fellow citizens,
Israel could not be brought any lower. This woman's death is recorded because (1) it is further confirmation of the fulfillment of the
prophecies on the doom of Eli's house, and (2) she summarizes in one
word how the average citizen interpreted the events of that day.

---

[18]"Forty years" in some contexts may be a figure of speech for a generation. J.B. Segal, "Numerals in the Old Testament," *JSS* 10 (1965): 11;
Cundall & Morris, 32. The LXX, perhaps under the influence of 1 Sam 7:2,
has "twenty years."

1 SAMUEL 5

After the battle of Aphek, the Narrator concerns himself with the future of the ark. He says nothing of the fate of Shiloh after the rout of the Israelites and the death of Eli. The Philistines probably at once marched on Shiloh where they inflicted a terrible massacre and then razed the sacred buildings of the city to the ground (Ps 78:60-64). The awful fate of the priestly city seems to have become a proverb in Israel (Jer 7:12; 26:9).[1] These events can be dated to ca. 1105 B.C.

The Defeat of Dagon (5:1-12)

God's Hand against Dagon (5:1-5)

5:1 The Hebrew sentence structure is such as to emphasize a new scene. Lit., the verse begins, "Now as for the Philistines, they captured the ark. . . ." As compared to the passive verb in 4:22, this verse stresses the initiative of the Philistines. (There is no need for the pluperfect ["had captured"] as in the NIV.) The point of this emphasis is to stress that the Philistines deserved the punishment which the following verses depict. They acted presumptuously as though *they* had won the victory. They treated the ark as a trophy of victory over Yahweh.

Ebenezer had been the Israelite camp before the battle. See comments on 4:1. The ark, the most important object of plunder, was taken from that place to **Ashdod**, a distance of about thirty miles (MBA, 84). Since the Philistine city of Ekron was much closer to

---

[1] A Danish excavation under Hans Kjaer excavated Shiloh (Tell Seilun) from 1926-29 and again in 1932, revealing that it certainly had been destroyed by fire ca. 1050 B.C. which was undoubtedly the work of the Philistines (Hindson, 140). Both biblical (1 Kgs 11:29) and archaeological testimony indicate, however, that Shiloh was occupied until the exile. See ABD, s.v. "Shiloh" by Baruch Halpern.

Ebenezer than Ashdod, it may be inferred that Ashdod was chosen because it was the location of the main sanctuary of their god.

5:2 Apparently for stylistic reasons, the NIV has condensed v. 2 and thereby concealed an important point which the Narrator is making. The verse reads lit., "and the Philistines took the ark of God, and brought it into the house of Dagon and set it beside Dagon." The verse continues the emphasis on Philistine initiative, for they are the subject of all three active verbs.

The Philistines **carried** the ark of God. How they carried it is not stated. Presumably it was by hand. They probably had little respect for the object now that they had so thoroughly defeated the Israelites in battle. In those days a god was considered only as powerful as the army of the people who worshiped him. The ark was placed in the temple of **Dagon** evidently as a dedicatory offering.[2] The placement of the ark symbolized that Dagon, through his worshipers, had defeated Yahweh.

Dagon was a Semitic deity which had been adopted by the Philistines when they entered the land in force ca. 1200 B.C. In Ugaritic texts he is described as the father of Baal who appears throughout the Old Testament as the enemy of Yahweh (Gordon, 98). Some link the name Dagon to words for "grain," others, to a root meaning "clouds" or "rain." In either case, Dagon was a fertility god.[3] Though archaeologists have not yet uncovered the remains of the Dagon temple in Ashdod (Bierling, 131), temples of this god are attested in several other cities of Syria-Palestine (e.g., Ebla, Mari, Ugarit).[4]

5:3 The next day when the Dagon worshipers went to the temple they discovered that the image of their god had fallen over in front of the ark as though worshiping before the God of Israel.[5] The

---

[2]Another view is that the Philistines were honoring Yahweh as if he had abandoned his own people to acknowledge the power and superiority of their god (Klein, 49; Miller & Roberts, 43).

[3]Older commentaries follow Jerome and Kimchi in connecting Dagon with the word "fish." This view, which is still defended by Goldman (27), has been rejected by most scholars.

[4]Two towns in Israel have names which mean "temple of Dagon" (Josh 15:41; 19:27). Saul's head was attached to the wall of a Dagon temple in Beth Shan (1 Chr 10:10). The temple in Ashdod seems to have survived until the time of Jonathan, the Maccabean leader, who destroyed it in 147 B.C. (1 Macc 10:83f.; 11:4). ZPEB, s.v. "Dagon, Temples of" by H.B. Stigers.

[5]Miller & Roberts (44) call attention to the use of the same terminology

Philistines **took Dagon and put him back in his place**,[6] supposing that it had fallen over due to some accident. They must have considered this, however, a very bad sign. A temple from this period uncovered at Tell Qasile had a "holy of holies" where the image of the god was enshrined on a stepped, raised platform. It is easy to picture Dagon falling off such a platform to a prostrate position before the ark of God (Bierling, 134).

5:4 On the second morning the priests went to the temple early. They must have feared for the safety of their god. The image of Dagon again had fallen on the ground before the ark. This time the head and hands **had been broken off** (lit., "cut off"). The verb (כָרַת, *kārat*) suggests that the head and hands had not been broken off by the fall of the image, but had been severed with deliberate care, and placed contemptuously upon the **threshold**. Some take the term to refer to the entrance to the temple proper, others, to the threshold of an inner chamber or recess in which the idol stood. Only **the body** (lit., "only Dagon") of the image remained. Any theory that the idol had fallen accidentally the previous day now had to be abandoned.

The symbolism in the fate of Dagon is striking. (1) Decapitation was the ultimate humiliation inflicted in ancient warfare (cf. 1 Sam 17:51; 31:9). (2) The hands on the threshold suggest that Dagon was seeking refuge in his own temple. (3) Just as the Philistines had defeated Israel twice on the battlefield, so Yahweh had twice defeated Dagon on his own turf. "Dagon was reduced to a stump, without a head for thinking or hands for acting" (Klein, 50). Scholars sometimes refer to what transpired in the Dagon temple as a contest of the gods. There was no contest. The events in Dagon's temple demonstrated Yahweh's absolute superiority, and that without any recorded effort on his part.

---

in 1 Sam 17:49 to describe what happened to Goliath when he was hit by David's missile. Thus the terminology can be used in Hebrew to refer to one who has fallen victim in individual combat. The cutting off of Dagon's hands and head the following morning may support this understanding of "fallen on his face on the ground."

[6]In v. 1 and again in v. 2 the Philistines *took* the ark of God and set it beside Dagon. Now the tables were turned, and they were forced to take Dagon and return him to his place. The same Heb. verb is used to underscore the irony of what the Philistines had to do with their god as a result of what they had done to God's ark.

5:5 Sanctuary thresholds were commonly treated with respect in the ancient world because they marked the boundary dividing sacred from profane (Gordon, 99). Because a portion of Dagon's body had touched it, a custom developed in Ashdod that no person could thereafter step on the threshold of Dagon's temple so as to defile it with their feet. The purpose for this etiological note is to provide empirical proof to the original readers that the events as told in vv. 3-4 did in fact happen (Miller & Roberts, 46).

God's Hand against Dagon's People (5:6-12)

5:6 The realization that Yahweh had defeated Dagon was reinforced by the fact that the citizens of Ashdod experienced a terrible plague. While Dagon's hands (palms) had been cut off (v. 4), **the LORD's hand**, a symbol of his power,[7] was very much active in the land of the Philistines. First, the Lord brought **devastation** upon them. This term is used in the Old Testament to refer to the destruction of crops. Second, the Lord smote the men of the city with **tumors**, or swellings (עֳפָלִים, *'ăphālîm*). According to ancient Jewish authorities, these swellings were in the anus (cf. Deut 28:27).[8] Modern commentators, however, regard these tumors as inflamed swellings (buboes) of the lymph glands, especially in the armpit or groin, characteristic of bubonic plague.[9] This plague is known to kill more than half the people who contract it (Baldwin, 74).

5:7 The men of Ashdod quickly concluded that their physical affliction was due to the presence of the ark. The same hand that

---

[7]Cf. Campbell, 86. The theme of the Lord's "hand" is a major theme in this unit, appearing some nine times (4:8; 5:6,7,9,11; 6:3,5,9; 7:13). The expression is common Near Eastern language for speaking about plague and pestilence, which are seen as coming from the deity (Miller & Roberts, 48).

[8]Other explanations are (1) sores resulting from dysentery (Josephus, *Ant.* 6.1.1) and (2) boils (Kirkpatrick, 1:77). The Masoretes supplied the consonants עפלם with the vowels for the word טְחֹרִים (*tĕḥōrîm*, which appears in 6:11,17) which seems to mean something like "to strain at the stool." Some think the Masoretes were trying to explain the meaning of the term, and others that they were trying to avoid an offensive term. Because of this, the noun is rendered "hemorrhoids" in the BV and NASB and "emerods" in the KJV. The ASV, JB, and NRSV agree with the NIV in rendering "tumors."

[9]See Miller & Roberts, 49; J. Wilkinson, "The Philistine Epidemic of I Samuel 5 and 6," *ET* 88 (1977): 137-141. John Geyer, "Mice and Rites in 1 Samuel V-VI," *VT* 31 (1981): 293-304.

had smitten down the image of Dagon, had smitten Dagon's worshipers with the tumors. They concluded that the ark could remain no longer in their city.

5:8 The men of Ashdod called together the rulers[10] of the Philistines and asked their advice on what to do with the ark. There were five lords of the Philistines associated with their five chief cities (cf. 6:17). As to whether they were elected or hereditary rulers, there is no information. The Philistine rulers operated together when necessary (cf. Judg 16). To pacify the Ashdodites, the rulers directed them to send the ark to **Gath** (MBA, 84).[11] This decision indicates their unrepentant will to retain Israel's ark. The exact location of Gath is still disputed.[12] Perhaps the Gathites arrogantly volunteered to take the ark off their hands. On the other hand, Gath may have been chosen because there was no Dagon temple there, the Philistines attributing the plague to the antagonism between Yahweh and Dagon (Kirkpatrick, 1:78). In any case, the Philistine rulers would be reluctant to part with this trophy of their victory over the Israelites.

5:9 Once the ark was in Gath, the Lord's **hand was against that city.** The tumors this time affected the **young** as well as the **old**, lit. "from small to great." The detailed description of the human object of the divine attack emphasizes the insignificance of Yahweh's opposition (Eslinger, *Kingship,* 196). The whole city was thrown into a **panic**, perhaps caused by a combination of fear and suffering. The words **an outbreak of tumors** literally mean "the tumors broke out to them," i.e., the tumors broke the surface of the skin.[13]

---

[10]The word translated "rulers" (סְרָנִים, *s*rānîm*) is a special word which always appears in the plural. This is a foreign word which probably was their native title for political leaders. The title seems to be cognate with the Greek term *tyrannos* ("tyrant"). Mitchell, AOTS, 413.

[11]McCarter (1:101) suggests that the ark traveled to Ashkelon and Gaza before arriving in Gath. There may be a hint to support this suggestion in 1 Sam 6:4.

[12]The most widely accepted location of Gath is Tell es-Safi, twelve miles north of Ashdod. Albright argued against this identification and suggested Tell el-Manshiyeh about seven miles further south.

[13]The verb שֹׁתֵר (*štr*) appears only here. It has been related to an Arabic word meaning "to have a cracked eyelid or lip." This would suggest that the tumors broke open and suppurated. Others find this verb to be a mere spelling variation of סתר (*str*), "to hide." In this case the tumors "hid themselves in them," i.e., they gnawed and burrowed into the flesh like a cancer

5:10 The citizens of Gath did not wait for direction from the Philistine rulers. They sent the ark inland to **Ekron** (MBA, 84), twelve miles north of Gath, and ten miles northeast of Ashdod. It was the closest Philistine city to Israelite territory. Having heard about the troubles of the first two cities, the Ekronites did not welcome the ark. They thought the men of Gath who moved the ark were trying to kill them. "As the ark moves on to Gath and then to Ekron the story begins to read like a parody of a victory tour, in which the roles of victor and vanquished are reversed" (Gordon, 100).

5:11-12 The Ekronites[14] called for the Philistine rulers.[15] They urged them to send the ark back **to its own place**, i.e., to the Israelites, before it killed the people of the city. Circumstantial evidence was overwhelming that it was the ark which had caused havoc and suffering wherever it was located. There was power in that ark, a power which Dagon could not neutralize. Philistine armies might subdue the power of Israel, but not the power of Israel's God.

For the second time the text speaks of the **panic** of the Philistines, now caused by the fact that people were dying in the city. Yahweh's **hand** which was "heavy" upon the Ashdodites is now **very heavy** upon Ekron. Those who did not die suffered terribly from the tumors. From the description given here, it would appear that the visitation against Ekron was even worse than that at Ashdod and Gath. The longer the Philistines resisted the chastening hand of the Lord, the more the pressure against them intensified. The **outcry** (שַׁוְעָה, *šaw'āh*) of the city went up to heaven. This suggests that the Ekronites were forced by their circumstances to call on the one true God to relieve their suffering (cf. Exod 2:23).

---

or abscess. The KJV understands the expression to refer to the location of the tumors, hence "they had emerods in their secret parts."

[14]Ekron at this time was surrounded by a massive mudbrick wall nearly eleven feet thick. Archaeologists have uncovered a gateway that may have been the location for the scene where the Ekronites tried to prevent the ark from entering their town. One of the buildings unearthed had a huge hall with three large hearths which Bierling (136) suggests may have been the location for the gathering of the Philistine rulers in 1 Sam 5:11.

[15]For a comparison of the political structure of Philistine and Israelite societies at this time, see B.D. Rahtjen, "Philistine and Hebrew Amphictyonies," *JNES* 24 (1965): 100-104.

1 SAMUEL 6

The Disaster at Beth Shemesh (6:1–7:2)

The ark of God was in the land of the Philistines for seven months overlapping the years 1105-1104 B.C. The humiliating defeat of Israel's army at Ebenezer and the capture of the ark caused the Israelites to fear the Philistines. They were so afraid that they made no effort to free their land from these invaders.

Preparations for the Return of the Ark (6:1-9)

6:1-2 For seven months the ark was moved about within the territory (lit., "in the field" or "cultivated plain") of the Philistines. In spite of the calamities which its presence had brought on their land and people, the Philistine rulers were unwilling to relinquish such a prize. Finally, however, it became obvious that the ark would have to be returned to Israelite territory. Since the ark was a sacred object, the move back needed to be handled very carefully lest the God of the ark unleash even greater plagues against them.

The Philistines consulted their **priests and diviners**, i.e., specialists in the interpretations of signs and omens. The Philistine diviners were acclaimed highly in the ancient world (cf. Isa 2:6). What means of divination they may have employed in this particular case is not indicated in the text.[1] The general question **What shall we do with the ark of the LORD?** is not asking whether or not the ark should be sent back to the Israelites. That is made clear by the mandate given the priests and diviners: **Tell us** [lit., "make known to us"] **how we should send it back to its place**. The issue was, "What is the most appropriate way to return the ark?" The priests would decide

---

[1]The Hebrew term קֹסְמִים (*qōsᵊmîm*) means literally "dividers or partitioners," because it was their duty to separate activities into two classes, viz., lucky and unlucky. On the role of diviners in the Ancient Near East, see A. Guillaume, 133-144; J. Lindblom, 47-104.

what ceremony should accompany the movement, while the diviners would decide what day and hour and special method would be most favorable. **To its place** is not a reference to Shiloh, for it is unlikely that place was any longer suitable as a sanctuary. The words are to be interpreted generally to mean, "where it belongs." Recent events had made clear that the ark did not belong in Philistine territory.

6:3 The verb **return** (also in vv. 4,17) implies giving back something that was taken wrongfully. The priests and diviners evidently thought that the Israelite deity, in some way resident in the golden chest, was angry at the insult offered him either (1) by being taken from his land and people and/or (2) being placed in an inferior position in the Dagon temple. They advised the rulers not to send the ark back without a **guilt offering**.[2] This type of offering was offered when an offense had been unintentional (Lev 5:15). The offering would acknowledge that they had committed an inadvertent trespass against Yahweh by treating the ark of God as common war booty.

You will know (lit., "it will be made known to you") is an assurance that healing would take place when the guilt offering was made. Hebrew syntax permits, however, and the context (v. 9) requires, that this sentence be understood conditionally, "If you will be healed, then you will know, etc." (KD, 171f.). The priests and diviners believed that such an offering would make the God of Israel amenable to forgiving the wrong they had done. Should the Philistines be healed, they would then clearly understand that their land had been punished because of the treatment which the ark had received.

6:4 The Philistines further asked the priests and diviners for a suggestion regarding the guilt offering that should accompany the return of the ark. They suggested a double guilt or reparation offering. First, they should send five golden tumors, one golden tumor from each of the five rulers of the Philistines. Being of gold, these items constituted a valuable gift that would render due honor to Yahweh.

---

[2]Klein (56) suggests that in this context the "guilt offering" would more appropriately be understood as a "reparation offering." KD (171) point out that the verb "return" (Hiph. of שׁוּב [šûb]) is the technical term for the payment of compensation for a fault in Num 5:7 and for the compensation for anything belonging to another that had been unjustly appropriated (Lev 5:23 [Eng. 6:4]).

Second, they should send five golden **rats**.[3] Rats, which are here mentioned for the first time,[4] may have been the carriers of the bubonic plague, which raised buboes or tumors on the people. The biblical narrative, however, does not make this connection. The fact that the rats were included in the offering suggests that rats were part of Yahweh's devastation of the land of the Philistines. The golden "rats" are probably to be identified as the short-tailed field-mouse which often swarms in prodigious numbers, and commits great ravages in the cultivated fields of Palestine. The term **plague** (מַגֵּפָה, *maggēphāh*) is also used to describe the plagues against Egypt (Exod 9:14).

The last clause, **because the same plague has struck both you and your rulers,** reads lit., "because one plague was to all of them and to your rulers."

6:5 The golden tumors and rats were to be **models** of that which was causing the problems in the land of the Philistines. These items of gold would be a way of acknowledging that the plagues of boils and rats were inflicted by the God of Israel, not by chance. By such acknowledgment they would give **honor** or tribute to the God of Israel.

The word **perhaps** maintains Yahweh's freedom to act or refuse to act as he sees fit. Relief from their predicament was not automatic. These pagan priests were more committed to the sovereignty of God than were the priests at Shiloh who thought they could compel Yahweh to act on behalf of his people by lugging his ark to the battlefront. The priests and diviners suggested that this gesture of repentance might move God to remove his **hand** from the people, their **gods** and their **land.** The lifting of the hand would lead to forgiveness or expiation and consequently healing from the tumors.

6:6 In v. 5 the diviners recommended that the Philistines "give honor" to Yahweh. In v. 6 the Philistine priests follow their own advice by (1) advising the proper response of submission; and (2) by pointing out the folly of resisting the mighty deeds of Yahweh (Eslinger, *Kingship,* 210).

---

[3]The Hebrew עַכְבְּרִים (*'akb°rîm*) is rendered "rats" (NIV, NKJV, JB) and "mice" (ASV, BV, NRSV). The only other references to rats/mice in the Old Testament are Lev 11:29 and Isa 66:17 where they are numbered among unclean animals.

[4]The LXX text inserts references to the rodents at 5:6 and 6:1.

Evidently some opposition to the proposal of the diviners surfaced. The priests and diviners had a warning for the Philistines. They must not **harden** their hearts as Pharaoh had done many years before. The question then is whether the Philistines would restore the ark on the warning of one plague, or whether they will hold out till they have been smitten with ten as were the Egyptians. Eventually the Egyptians were forced to release the Israelites, and eventually the Philistines would be forced to release the ark. Better to submit now while the damage was relatively light. This is now the second allusion to the events of the Exodus by the Philistines (cf. 4:8). The phrase **he treated them harshly** may be interpreted in two ways: (1) Pharaoh treated the Israelites harshly and the Egyptians were later forced to send them out of their land, or (2) God treated the Egyptians harshly forcing them to send out the Israelites. In light of the fact that the same verb is used in Exod 10:2 of how God treated Egypt, the latter interpretation is best. This verb (עָלַל, *'ālal*) connotes the rough play that a child might give to a toy.[5] The mighty Egypt was but a toy in the hands of God. The memory of Israel's triumphant departure from Egypt was still fresh among these religious leaders. On the hardening of heart by Pharaoh, see Exod 8:15,32; 9:34.

6:7-9 The religious leaders give instructions for the conveyance of the guilt offering. They advised that the ark be handled with the greatest reverence. First, they needed to **get a new cart ready** (lit., "take and make a new cart," i.e., set to work to make). Only a cart which had never been used for common labor would be suitable for transporting the sacred ark (2 Sam 6:3).[6] Second, they needed to secure **two cows** which had just given birth to calves, cows which had **never been yoked** for labor, i.e., they were unbroken. This served the purpose of (1) confirming the absence of human interference in their movements, (2) anticipating their future sacrificial role (v. 14), and (3) displaying reverence for the offended God[7] (cf. Num 19:2;

---

[5]BDB suggests "how I have made a toy of Egypt" as the translation for the Hithpael of the root עלל in Exod 10:2. Elsewhere this verb is used to describe the all-night ravishing of the Levite's concubine (Judg 19:25), and the abusive behavior which both Saul (1 Sam 31:4) and Zedekiah (Jer 38:19) expected from their bitter adversaries.

[6]Mosaic law stipulated that the ark was to be hand carried; but the Philistines cannot be expected to know such matters.

[7]Certain points of similarity between this account and a Hittite plague rit-

Deut 21:3f.). Nothing was to be employed in God's service which had been previously used for worldly purposes.

Beside the ark they were to put a chest[8] containing the ten golden objects. They should then start the cart on the road to Israelite territory. If the cows followed their natural instinct, they would turn back to their calves. If, however, they moved straight forward on the road, this would indicate that natural instinct was being overruled by Israel's God. This test would confirm the Philistine suspicions that it was the ark in their midst that had caused havoc to their land for the past seven months. The Philistines were only providing Yahweh with yet another opportunity to demonstrate his superiority.

The destination of the ark was **Beth Shemesh**, a priestly city (Josh 21:16) in the tribal area of Judah (Josh 15:10), the valley of Sorek, about eight miles southeast of Ekron (MBA, 84).[9] The name means "House of the Sun" and is probably the same as Ir Shemesh ("City of the Sun") in Josh 19:41. The town seems to have been in territory disputed by the Philistines.[10] By returning it only to disputed territory, some have suggested that the Philistines aimed to maintain some jurisdiction over the ark (Klein, 58).[11]

The idea that anything could happen **by chance** is not common in the Old Testament, but it does occur (e.g., 2 Sam 1:6; Ruth 2:3). Here the expression means "for no known reason." Thus if Yahweh had not smitten them, they had no idea why their land had been devastated.

The Return of the Ark (6:10-12)

6:10-11 The Philistines did as the priests and diviners directed. The models of the mice and the tumors may have been crafted there

---

ual, which involved the dispatching of a ram toward the territory of an enemy god, have been noticed by Miller & Roberts (55). See ANET, 347.

[8]Other authorities would render אַרְגַּז (*'argāz*) in vv. 8,11,15 to mean "bag." See discussion in McCarter (1:130).

[9]J.A. Emerton surveys the archaeological discoveries at Beth Shemesh. AOTS, 197-206.

[10]Large quantities of Philistine pottery found in the ruins of Beth Shemesh attest to Philistine cultural influence there during the period of the judges. A Philistine destruction of Beth Shemesh is attested shortly after 1050 B.C. (Youngblood, 604).

[11]EAE, s.v. "Beth Shemesh" by G.E. Wright.

at Ekron.[12] The transportation instructions were precisely followed. They penned up the calves, hitched up the cows, and started them on the road to Beth Shemesh.

6:12 The dumb beasts did what the pagan priests and diviners scarcely considered possible, for God's hand drove them. They headed **straight up** the Sorek valley **toward Beth Shemesh.**[13] They stayed right on **the road.** The **lowing** of the cows attested their ardent longing for their young, and at the same time the supernatural influence that controlled their movements in a contrary direction. Not to turn **to the right or to the left** is frequently used to express total obedience (e.g., Deut 5:32). The awestruck rulers of the Philistines followed the cart right up to **the border of Beth Shemesh.** This they did to (1) leave the cows free to choose their own course, (2) guard their treasure from theft, and (3) verify by firsthand observation that the cows continued to act contrary to natural instincts.

The Reception of the Ark (6:13-16)

6:13 Here is the first picture of Israel since the agonizing lamentation in ch. 4 over the loss of the ark. Things had gotten back to normal in the land. **The people of Beth Shemesh were harvesting their wheat** (lit., "now Beth Shemesh was reaping its wheat harvest") when they saw the ark approaching. This notice fixes the time of year as the end of May or beginning of June. **In the valley** alludes to the unusual geography of Beth Shemesh which was located at the conjunction of two valleys, Sorek to the north, and Illin to the south. The mere sight of the ark, without any knowledge of the circumstances leading to its return, evoked spontaneous joy.

6:14 The cart finally stopped near a large rock in the field of a man named **Joshua.** Nothing further is known about this man. The beasts **stopped beside a large rock** as if restrained by the hand of

---

[12]Kilns and other industrial installations have been uncovered at two locations in Ekron (Bierling, 138f.).

[13]The Hebrew brings out forcibly the directness with which the cows traveled the road to Beth Shemesh: "And the cows went straight in the way upon the way to Beth Shemesh; they went along one highway, lowing as they went," i.e., they went in one direct course, without deviating from it. The point is that the cows were under divine compulsion to go by the most direct route to their destination.

God himself. The actions of the animals made it seem as if that large rock was their destination.[14]

The Israelites interpreted the actions of the beasts to indicate that God wanted a sacrifice from them. He had provided both the firewood and the sacrificial animals. **The people** (not in the Heb. text) chopped up the cart for wood, and slaughtered the cows for the sacrificial offering. They burned the meat as a **burnt offering** (עֹלָה, 'ōlāh) to the Lord. This offering expressed thanksgiving (Lev 22:17-19; Num 15:1-16), total commitment and expiation (Lev 1:4).

Technically, the cows were not proper sacrificial animals (cf. Lev 1:3; 22:19 which stipulates only *males*); and furthermore, the sacrifices were not being offered at the tabernacle as stipulated in the law. The ark, however, was there, and that signaled the presence of God. Under extraordinary circumstances holy men did offer sacrifices at places other than the tabernacle (cf. 2 Sam 24:22; 1 Kgs 19:21). Because of the supernatural way God was guiding them, the cows might have been viewed as consecrated to the Lord. The text may suggest that the large stone was used as the altar for this sacrifice. On the other hand, other stones hastily heaped up in front of the large rock may have served as the altar. The following verses point to this second alternative.

6:15 A change of scene is signaled by the structure of v. 15, the opening words of which could be rendered, "Now as for the Levites, they . . . ." The verse provides more details, not in chronological order, regarding the sacrificial service which was conducted at Beth Shemesh on the day the ark was returned. Levites **took down** (better, "had taken down") **the ark**, i.e., from the wagon. The concern here is to show how the ark was not mishandled. Levites alone were consecrated to transport the ark (Num 4:4-15; Deut 10:8). **They placed them** (better, "had placed them"), i.e., the ark and the chest, on the large rock. Since Beth Shemesh was a priestly town, the term **Levites** here appears to be used in a general sense to mean "members of the tribe of Levi," not in its technical sense of "Levites" as distinguished from "priests."

Apparently other sacrifices were offered **on that day** before the ark which was elevated on the large rock. The initial burnt offering

---

[14]In v. 14 the Heb. seems to emphasize the spot where the cart stopped by a back-to-back use of the adverb שָׁם (šām, "there"): "and it stood there and there a great stone was."

of v. 14 now is plural **burnt offerings.** The **sacrifices** were thank-offerings to the Lord for his goodness in restoring the ark to Israel.

6:16 The same day (lit., "on that day") links this verse with the previous. From a distance the five Philistine rulers **saw** this great celebration, but their reaction was quite different from that of the Israelites when they "saw" the ark approaching in v. 13. They **returned** to the now devastated city of **Ekron.** They were now convinced beyond any doubt that Yahweh had been at work in the recent calamities in their land.

Footnotes to the Return of the Ark (6:17-18)

6:17-18 The purpose of this footnote is (1) to provide evidence of the accuracy of the account to the original readers and (2) to stress that the offering represented all of Philistia, both its lords and all its towns, from fortified cities to unwalled villages and hamlets. The proposal by the priests in v. 4 was that five golden rats be sent. The people went beyond the recommendation because the countryside had been ravaged by the rodents, while the plague of tumors was concentrated in the cities.

The phrase **the large rock** which the NIV takes as the subject of a sentence, in the Hebrew text expresses the extent of the villages which sent golden rats, thus "villages as far as Greater Abel" as indicated in the NIV note. Greater Abel would then be (1) one of the distant villages of the Philistines or (2) the name of the large stone upon which the ark had been placed in the field of Joshua. The latter is probably intended.[15]

The Narrator next presents a geographical verification of his narrative. The place on which the ark had rested, i.e., the large rock in the field of Joshua, became a **witness**[16] or monument to this important event, when the rulers of the Philistines paid tribute to the Lord

---

[15]In the Hebrew text "Abel" must be regarded as a proper name. The NIV translation is based on "a few Hebrew manuscripts" and the LXX. The emendation of Abel (אבל) to אֶבֶן (*'eben,* "stone") is endorsed by Kirkpatrick (1:84) and KD (175). It is reflected in the ASV, NASB, BV, and NRSV. N.H. Tur-Sinai, following Kimchi, takes Abel to mean "mourning" and interprets it as a descriptive name of the stone in the field of Joshua (cf. KJV and NKJV). "The Ark of God," *VT* 1 (1951): 282-283.

[16]The translation "witness" is based on a slight change in vowel points, from עַד to עֵד (*'ad* to *'ed*).

(cf. Gen 31:52). It was easily distinguished by future generations, because it formed no part of the cultivated land. Situated as it was on the border of Philistine territory, that large rock served as a warning of what would befall the enemies who showed disrespect for the Living God or his people. At the time this narrative was written, Joshua's rock was still pointed out as the site of one of the greatest triumphs of Israel's God.

Problems in the Return of the Ark (6:19-21)

6:19 The Israelites treated the ark with less reverence than the Philistines did. For this reason, **God** [lit., "he"] **struck down** [נָכָה, *nākāh*] **some of the men of Beth Shemesh**. This is the same Hebrew verb in the same form which was used to describe the devastation which Yahweh inflicted against the men of Ashdod and Gath (5:6,9). For emphasis the verb and derivatives are used four times in this one verse.[17] If Yahweh held the Philistines accountable for their treatment of his ark, how much more those to whom he had given this revelation of himself.

The Hebrew is ambiguous as to exactly what the men of Beth Shemesh did to trigger the outpouring of God's wrath. Some think the sin may have been looking *on* the ark with profane curiosity (Kirkpatrick, 1:85).[18] The priests of Beth Shemesh must have known that even Levites were prohibited from looking on the ark upon penalty of death (Num 4:19f.). Certainly the people in Beth Shemesh were not punished for the unavoidable sight of the ark as it approached them. At that point, however, the priests immediately should have placed a covering over the ark (Num 4:5). They, however, left the ark exposed to public gaze. The NIV adopts the other alternative, viz., that they pried *into* the sacred chest, possibly with good intentions, to see if the Philistines had removed any of the sacred objects contained in the ark. "To leave the ark without a veil was neglectful; to pry into it was sacrilege" (R.P. Smith, 113).

Putting seventy thousand of them to death is literally "and he smote among the people . . . ." The number who were put to death

---

[17]For stylistic reasons the NIV renders these occurrences as (1) "struck down," (2) "putting to death," (3) "heavy blow," and (4) "dealt."

[18]KD (176) points out that רָאָה בּ (*rā'āh* + preposition *beth*) means to look *upon* or *at* a thing with lust or malicious pleasure. Thus here it would signify a foolish staring which was incompatible with the holiness of the ark of God.

by the Lord at this time is one of the thorny problems of Old Testament exegesis. The majority of Hebrew MSS literally read "seventy men fifty thousand men," which is not the usual way of indicating the number 50,070.[19] The text appears to distinguish between those the Lord struck down "among the men of Beth Shemesh" and those he smote (struck down) "among the people." Perhaps the *seventy* were the local residents and the *fifty thousand* (אֶלֶף, *'eleph*) was the toll of the plague in the wider population, including the Philistines. The NIV has elected to follow three Hebrew MSS in omitting reference to the fifty thousand.[20] The sudden death of even seventy men in a rural district, especially if they were heads of priestly families there, would be viewed as a terrible calamity, worthy of great mourning. They knew that this **heavy blow** was an act of God.

Actually the Hebrew text of v. 19 can be read in a manner which removes the numerical and grammatical difficulties of this verse. Some years ago Tur-Sinai pointed the way by suggesting a different division of the letters of the word translated "seventy," and by recognizing that the word translated "fifty" also means "armed men" or "warriors." Recognizing these two possibilities, the text would read: "And he smote in the people old men with warriors one thousand men."[21]

---

[19]The two numbers with no conjunction between them and with the smaller number first is contrary to Hebrew usage. For this reason, most authorities regard the "fifty thousand" as a gloss which should be omitted from the text (e.g., J. Davis, 89). Some retain "seventy men, fifty thousand men" as the proper reading here. This is explained as meaning (1) "fifty of a thousand" (five per cent of those guilty), which in this case was *seventy* men (Jamieson, 149f.); (2) fifty thousand was the total population of which seventy were slain. Would, however, a village like Beth Shemesh have such a large population? News of the return of the ark had not yet spread so as to bring in others from a distance. (3) The plague from Philistia first smote seventy men in Beth Shemesh, then spread throughout the land of Israel killing fifty thousand. Those who insist that the "fifty thousand" should be dropped from the text have offered no credible explanation as to how this figure got into the text in the first place.

[20]Josephus (*Ant.* 6.1.4) gives the number who died as seventy. If the fifty thousand is a transmission error, that would not affect the general historical trustworthiness of the narrative nor preclude a full belief in the inerrancy of Scripture in the autographs.

[21]For details of the argument, see N.H. Tur-Sinai, "The Ark of God," *VT* 1 (1951): 279-282. For the MT שִׁבְעִים (*šib'îm*, "seventy") read שָׂב עִם (*śāb 'im*, "old men with"). For חֲמֻשִׁים (*ḥămušîm*) in the sense of "armed men" or "warriors," see Josh 1:14; 4:12; Judg 7:11.

6:20 The men of Beth Shemesh were afraid to have the ark in their midst. They began to wonder if anyone could **stand in the presence** of the Lord and his ark. They felt that none of them was any better than those who had fallen, and that sinners could not approach the holy God. The verb "stand" has a double meaning: (1) to serve before God[22] or (2) to exist before God (cf. Exod 9:11). While one can detect in their words a bit of superstition regarding the ark, their sense of sinfulness is also evident. So they began to look around for another village that might be willing to accept responsibility for the ark. Their question, **To whom will the ark go up from here?** is literally "to whom will he/it go up from here?" The question is ambiguous, and could be a reference to Yahweh himself. This would mean that they regarded the ark and Yahweh as inseparable. The ark could not be returned to Shiloh because that city had been devastated by the Philistines at the same time the ark had been seized.

6:21 The men of Beth Shemesh sent messengers to the village of Kiriath Jearim[23] about nine miles away (MBA, 84). A former Gibeonite city (Josh 9:17), Kiriath Jearim, about eight miles west of Jerusalem, was one of the frontier cities of Judah (Josh 15:9). It was neither a priestly nor Levitical city. The ark was probably taken here because this was the nearest place of importance on the road to Shiloh (Kirkpatrick, 1:86). Without revealing the full story, they invited that town to take charge of the ark. Beth Shemesh being located in a low plain, and Kiriath Jearim on a hill, explains the message **Come down and take it up to your place**. The ark remained in Kiriath Jearim until David removed it to Jerusalem.

---

[22]"To stand before" frequently is used of priests who officiate in religious rituals. According to McCarter (1:136f.) the men of Beth Shemesh were admitting their guilt in profaning the ark and were suggesting that they find a suitable attendant for the ark.

[23]The name *Kiriath Jearim* means "city of woods" or "wood-ville." The place was also called *Kirjath Baal* (Josh 15:60; 18:14) and *Baalah* (1 Chr 13:5,6; Josh 15:9; 2 Sam 6:2). These names point to the former existence of Baal-worship in this place.

1 SAMUEL 7

The Ark at Rest (7:1-2)

7:1 At the invitation of the men of Beth Shemesh, the **men of Kiriath Jearim** came and took the ark of God away. They took it to **Abinadab's house** on the hill overlooking their town. This location may have been chosen (1) for the security which the lofty heights might provide for the sacred ark or (2) because high elevations were considered fit places for Yahweh's worship. **Eleazar**, Abinadab's son, was **consecrated** or set apart by the men of the town to guard or keep the ark. His duties are not indicated.

It is not stated that Abinadab was a Levite; but this is very probable, because otherwise they would hardly have consecrated his son to be the keeper of the ark. The Narrator, however, is not concerned to make this connection. He intends to depict the ark as no longer having any significant role in the active religious life of Israel.

7:2 After the return of the ark ca. 1104 B.C., some twenty years are passed over in silence in 1 Samuel. During the time the ark remained in the village of Kiriath Jearim, the Philistines oppressed Israel. The adventures of Samson fit into this period of time (Judg 15:20). Religiously, during these two decades Israel sank into gross idolatry (v. 3). Through his preaching Samuel kept hope alive in this dark period. Gradually a change of heart came over the people. A great spiritual awakening occurred as all the people **mourned** their sins against God.[1] The death of Samson may account for this spiritual awakening. After twenty years, Israel's champion was dead (Judg 15:20). The people knew that unless God raised up another deliverer, the Philistines would soon bring the entire land of Israel under their dominion.

---

[1]Eslinger (*Kingship*, 231) suggests that the mourning was because the ark, and by implication Yahweh, was interred in Kiriath Jearim.

5. General Recognition of Samuel (7:3-17)

Samuel was about fourteen when the ark was returned by the Philistines. For twenty years he pled with the people to get right with the Lord. At age thirty-three Samuel finally felt that the people were ready to renew their commitment to the Lord and deal with the Philistine problem. About the year 1085 B.C. Samuel summoned the people to Mizpah. He led the people in a great revival service after which Israel was able to inflict a smashing defeat upon the Philistines.

Spiritual Renewal (7:3-9)

7:3 The words **If you are returning to the LORD** suggest that the turning to Yahweh already had commenced inwardly; and the use of the participle in this clause suggests that this turning was an ongoing process. The phrase **with all your hearts** is emphatically placed in the Hebrew to emphasize that God required genuine repentance. When he sensed that the time was right, Samuel indicated that the inward turning of the heart should also be manifested outwardly. They must get rid of all their foreign gods and **the Ashtoreths**. Ashtoreth was a female deity of sex and war who was worshiped in that region (cf. 1 Sam 31:10). A great number of figurines of this goddess have been discovered in Palestine in recent years by archaeologists. They would need to commit themselves (lit., "hearts") anew to the Lord and serve him exclusively (Deut 6:13f.). Samuel promised that if they would make this total commitment, the Lord would deliver them out of the hands of the Philistines.

7:4 The Israelites responded to Samuel's preaching in a positive way. They put away their **Baals** and **Ashtoreths**.[2] Baal was the leading male deity worshiped in that region. He was the Canaanite storm god Hadad, and hence the source of fertility. Each community had its own version of Baal. On Ashtoreths, see v. 3. The plural is used to indicate (1) the many images of these deities; or (2) the different forms under which they were worshiped in local shrines. Though Philistine rule was probably not the cause of Israelite unfaithfulness,

---

[2]The Baals and Ashtaroth are joined in denoting Israel's sin in Judg 2:13; 10:6; 1 Sam 12:10. Both deities had been embraced by the Philistines. The Israelites were not only dominated by Philistine culture, they were influenced by Philistine religion.

it certainly must have encouraged it. Once the Israelites excluded these false gods, they served the Lord exclusively.

7:5 When he felt that the people had demonstrated sincere repentance, Samuel dispatched messengers throughout the tribes to invite **all Israel,** i.e., probably tribal representatives, to assemble **at Mizpah** (MBA, 84). This town was in Benjamite territory (Josh 18:26), on the main road across the hills, about eight miles north of Jerusalem.[3] The name means "watchtower" and so is not an uncommon name for spots among the hills commanding an extensive outlook. At Mizpah Samuel promised to **intercede,** i.e., pray, for Israel that God might forgive their sins and give them victory over their enemies. Thus Mizpah was a consecration for a holy war against the Philistines. This spot was selected for two reasons. Historically, the tribes had met at Mizpah to prepare for war against the wickedness of Gibeah (Judg 20:1ff.). Geographically, Mizpah, situated as it was on the western border of the mountains, was a site which was difficult to surprise; it was a most suitable spot from which to commence conflict with the Philistines. The public repudiation of foreign gods together with the gathering of the people at Mizpah was an assertion of national independence and virtually a declaration of war against the Philistines.[4] The child of prayer was also a mighty man of prayer (cf. 8:6; 12:19,23). He stands alongside of Moses as one of the greatest intercessors of the Old Covenant (Jer 15:1; Ps 99:6).

7:6 The people responded enthusiastically to Samuel's invitation. Three acts of worship are mentioned in this verse. First, they performed a ceremony of pouring out water **before the Lord**. Without exact parallel in the Old Testament, it is difficult to ascertain the precise significance of this action. It has been taken to symbolize (1) repentance, (2) contrition, (3) total surrender, (4) humility (cf. Ps 22:14; Lam 2:19), and (5) self-denial. On the other hand, the action may have been a proclamation that Yahweh, not Baal or Ashtart, was

---

[3]Mizpah is probably to be identified with Tell en-NacBeh (D. Diringer, AOTS, 331). The city of Samuel's day boasted an impressive stone wall which enclosed an area of some 35,000 square yds. There was no methodical plan of construction, and there are also differences in the masonry and thickness of the wall. Like Nehemiah's wall in Jerusalem, it may have been built by groups of men with different building traditions and varying skill.

[4]Contra Hertzberg (67) who is of the opinion that what was done by Samuel and Israel is not to be regarded as a preparation for hostile action against the Philistines.

the true source of life and fertility in Israel (Gordon, 107). Second, the people **fasted**. Going without food was a way of showing that they were focusing on spiritual, not material things. Fasting was a sign of their inward distress of mind on account of their sin. Third, the people also publicly **confessed,** i.e., acknowledged and renounced, their national and personal sins before the Lord. No doubt the major sin which was now renounced was that of worshiping other gods.

The words **And Samuel was leader of Israel at Mizpah** are literally "And Samuel judged Israel at Mizpah." Samuel acted in the capacity of chief magistrate, adjudicating cases which were brought before him. He became the acknowledged ruler of Israel in things temporal, both civil and military, as he previously had been in things spiritual by virtue of his office as prophet. When they answered Samuel's call to assemble at Mizpah, the people were recognizing him as their leader. Through his intercession, Samuel secured for Israel the renewal of God's favor.

7:7 Such a large assembly of Israelites could not go unnoticed by the Philistines. They regarded this show of national unity as a threat to their twenty-year domination in the area. The fact that the Philistines had time to muster an army and advance on Mizpah suggests that the assembly there must have lasted several days. Though they were terrified, the Israelites did not flee. In faith they determined to await the attack.

7:8 The Israelites urged Samuel not to **stop crying out to the Lord,** lit., "be not silent from us from crying unto Yahweh our God." The petition was that Yahweh might **rescue** them from the **hand** (power) of the Philistines. The verb "rescue" (יָשַׁע, yāšāʻ) is used frequently in reference to deliverances effected by the judges.[5]

7:9 In response to the request of the people, Samuel took a **suckling** (very young) **lamb** and offered it up as **a whole burnt offering to the Lord**. The lamb would be at least seven days old, for so the Mosaic law required (Lev 22:27). In the whole burnt offering[6] the entire carcass of the animal was burned on the altar. This offering symbolized the complete dedication of the worshiper to the Lord.

---

[5]See Judg 2:16,18; 3:9,15,31; 6:14f.; 10:13f.; 13:5; and 1 Sam 9:16.

[6]The expression is עוֹלָה כָּלִיל (ʻôlāh kālîl). The first term means "that which ascends." This symbolized devotion and consecration to God. The second term intensified this concept and showed that all was God's and no part was to be reserved for the priest or the offerer.

While offering this sacrifice, Samuel continued to pray for the people. God heard that prayer. While most commentators view Samuel functioning in the role of priest, the language does not necessitate such a conclusion. It may simply mean that Samuel selected and presented the lamb to Aaronic priests to be offered up on behalf of the nation. If Samuel personally officiated in a priestly capacity, it was only because (1) there was no one available from the Aaronic line to officiate and/or (2) he was authorized by divine revelation to do so. The fact that the Lord **answered** the prayer which accompanied the sacrifice indicates that the sacrifice was acceptable to him. This is Yahweh's first positive action towards Israel or an Israelite since he answered Hannah's petition in 1:19 (Eslinger, *Kingship,* 240).

Military Victory (7:10-12)

7:10 Even while Samuel was **sacrificing** and praying, the Philistines were drawing near in battle formation. Before they attacked, however, the Lord **thundered with loud thunder**, lit., "with a great voice," in response to Samuel's prayer. Thunder was poetically regarded as God's voice (1 Sam 2:10; Ps 29). By so "speaking" from heaven, the Lord **threw them** [the Philistines] **into a panic**. The Hebrew verb הָמַם (*hāmam*) means "to move about noisily in total confusion." It is frequently used in accounts when enemies were defeated supernaturally (e.g. Josh 10:10). The Philistine army was **routed** (וַיִּנָּגְפוּ, *wayyinnāgᵉphû*) or smitten[7] before Israel in a reversal of Israel's being "defeated by" (וַיִּנָּגֶף, *wayyinnāgeph*; "smitten before") the Philistines in 4:2. The passive verb in both places suggests that Yahweh was responsible for the outcome of both battles.

7:11 Seeing the consternation of the enemy, Samuel gave the signal for the attack. Emboldened by the "voice" of Yahweh, the men of Israel **rushed out of Mizpah**. Instead of fleeing before their enemies as in 4:10, the Israelites **pursued the Philistines.** All along the roads Philistines were cut down by Israelite swords.[8] The chase continued to a point below Beth Car. **Beth Car** ("House of the Lamb") was

---

[7]Not enough evidence exists to assert with Goldman (38) that the Philistines were smitten down by God before any active effort was made by Israel.

[8]Josephus (*Ant.* 6.2.2) asserts that Israel gathered to Mizpah without arms. If this is true, then the Israelites smote the Philistines with their own weapons. A more modern view sees the Mizpah assembly as preparation for a holy war.

probably a Philistine fortress where the scattered remains of the defeated army were able to rally and defend themselves.[9]

7:12 To commemorate that great victory — the first ever over the Philistines — Samuel erected a memorial stone between Mizpah and Shen, in the midst of the area where the battle had taken place. Shen ("tooth") was a steep, pointed rock, but it is not mentioned elsewhere.[10] Samuel named the stone **Ebenezer** which means "stone of help." He explained the significance of the name by proclaiming: **Thus far has the LORD helped us!**[11] In these words there is a plain indication of the need of further assistance. "The deliverances of the past are a pledge of continued help for the future" (Kirkpatrick, 1:90). To name the memorial stone "Ebenezer" was no doubt intended to offset that other Ebenezer where Israel had been defeated and the ark captured some twenty years earlier (cf. 4:1ff.).[12]

Faithful Service (7:13-17)

Verses 13-17 echo "the formulae which mark the end of the story of a judge (cf. Judg 3:30; 8:28)."[13] The verses describe both the foreign policy and domestic successes of the Samuel administration.

7:13-14 As a result of Yahweh's help, and under the leadership of Samuel, Israel enjoyed a fourfold benefit. First, the Philistines were **subdued**. The word implies "brought low," but does not imply total subjugation. The forty years of Philistine oppression now came to an end (Judg 13:1). Second, the Philistines were so thoroughly defeated that they **did not invade Israelite territory again,** literally,

---

[9]Excavations at Tell Qasile, the Philistine port north of Joppa on the Yarkon River, show that it was destroyed in the middle of the eleventh century B.C., probably by the Israelites at the time of Samuel's victory (Hindson, 146).

[10]The NRSV reads *Jeshanah* (cf. 2 Chr 13:19) for *Shen*, a reading supported by the ancient versions (LXX, *Peshitta*).

[11]Eslinger (*Kingship*, 243) thinks the phrase *'ad hēnnāh* refers geographically to Ebenezer. Yahweh had helped his people back to the place where they were undone and their relationship with Yahweh seemed at an end.

[12]Some think the two Ebenezers refer to the same battlefield. Geographical considerations, however, render this unlikely (Gordon, 108). See discussion at 1 Sam 4:1.

[13]D.J. McCarthy, "The Inauguration of Monarchy in Israel: A Form-Critical Study of 1 Samuel 8–12," *Int* 27 (1973): 402. A new paragraph should therefore start at the beginning of v. 13, not in the middle (as in the NIV). See Youngblood, 609.

"they did not add again to come into the border of Israel."[14] From
that day the power of these determined enemies began to decline.
The words **throughout Samuel's lifetime, the hand of the LORD was
against the Philistines** show that the Philistines made attempts to
recover their lost supremacy. As long as Samuel lived, however, they
were unsuccessful in these efforts. Later chapters will reveal the
Israelites groaning under Philistine oppression (9:16), a forced disarmament (13:19), and three invasions (13:5; 17:1; 23:27) all in
Samuel's lifetime. Therefore his "lifetime" must be understood as
the period of his *active* leadership as Israel's judge. During that period the "hand" (power) of the Lord was against the Philistines.
Samuel, the man of prayer, was able to accomplish what Samson, the
man of muscle, could not accomplish.

Third, several Israelite towns between Ekron and Gath were liberated from Philistine control. It is doubtful that the cities of **Ekron**
and **Gath** themselves fell into Israelite hands.[15] Fourth, the strength
of Israel at this time caused the native **Amorites** ("highlanders") who
lived within the borders of Israel to cease their hostilities.[16] The
Hebrew for **peace between** (שָׁלוֹם בֵּין, *šālôm bên*) appears twice elsewhere (Judg 4:17; 1 Kgs 5:12) in contexts which suggest a mutual
nonaggression pact (Youngblood, 609). Thus during the judgeship
of Samuel, Israel had peace with both external and internal enemies.

7:15-16 With the calling of the people to Mizpah, and the victory at Ebenezer, Samuel assumed the government of the entire
nation. Although he had labored as a prophet from the death of Eli,
at this point he began to function as judge. Samuel served as judge
in Israel **all the days of his life**, i.e., the rest of his life. Saul was made
king a considerable time before Samuel's death. Yet even when Saul

---

[14]Kirkpatrick (1:90) points out that the same language is used in 2 Kgs
6:23, where the very next verse speaks of a fresh invasion. It is obvious, then,
that the phrase can be used in a relative and not an absolute sense, to
describe a cessation of the Philistine inroads *for the time being*.

[15]Perhaps what is meant is that the cities *up to* the borders of Ekron and
Gath were restored to Israel. The excavations at Ekron have not detected
any type of destruction or transition of material culture during this time,
but it is possible that the environs around the city were taken by Israel
(Bierling, 140).

[16]Hertzberg (69) thinks the peace with the Amorites is to be attributed to
the powerful personality of Samuel rather than the consequence of the victory over the Philistines.

became king, Samuel retained a certain civil and religious influence over the nation.

For the convenience of the people, Samuel annually made a circuit of three cities where he judged Israel, i.e., he settled disputes and ruled on various local issues. His three-city circuit began at **Bethel** (MBA, 85) in the hills about ten miles north of Jerusalem. **Gilgal** (MBA, 85) was in the Jordan valley near the ruins of Jericho.[17] **Mizpah** (MBA 85) was about seven miles north of Jerusalem. These places were all on the border between Benjamin and Ephraim, south of Shiloh. Each was a holy site, and at different periods of the year, no doubt, were crowded with pilgrims. Samuel's judgeship was limited to a relatively small area within the tribal region of Benjamin in central Canaan. This subtle reminder of the local nature of judgeship in ancient Israel serves as a preface for the request for a king in the following chapter (Youngblood, 609).

7:17 For the third time in vv. 15-17 Samuel is said to have **judged Israel**.[18] After he completed his visit to the three cities each year he would return to Ramah where he made his residence after the devastation at Shiloh. Following the custom of the Patriarchs, he built an altar there where he would regularly offer sacrifices to the Lord. It is probably going too far to say that Samuel served as the priest at the altar. The language may simply mean that Samuel gave prophetic sanction to the establishment of the Ramah altar. Clearly there was a need for such an altar. The established worship center at Shiloh had been destroyed. The ark of God was housed at a private dwelling. As the accredited prophet of God, Samuel had the authority to designate provisional places of worship until such time as God would make clear his will regarding the matter. In any case, Yahweh sanctioned the erection of this Ramah altar by continuing to accept the person and services of the one who authorized it, and who, presumably, was a regular worshiper there. There is no sign, however, that Samuel had taken the place of Eli as chief priest.

---

[17]Some think that Samuel's annual tours took him to a Gilgal in the hill country of Ephraim just north of Bethel. The argument in favor of this site is that the three cities named would then form a true circuit. This Gilgal, however, had no religious significance and would not therefore attract so many people to it as one that was frequented for sacrifice.

[18]In all three verses the verb שָׁפַט (šāphaṭ) is used which is camouflaged for stylistic reasons by the NIV in the two previous verses as "continued as judge in Israel" (v. 15); and "judging Israel" (v. 16).

1 SAMUEL 8

B. THE RISE OF SAUL (8:1–11:15)

1. Samuel's Leadership Rejected (8:1-22)

The Mizpah revival and subsequent victory over the Philistines were the highlights of Samuel's long judgeship of some forty-two years. These events occurred ca. 1085 B.C. The anointing of Saul took place ca. 1043 B.C. Thus about four decades of Samuel's judgeship are passed over in silence between chs. 7 and 8. When he was about seventy-five, the leaders of the nation came to Samuel and requested that he select for them a king. Clearly chs. 8–12 constitute a major unit within the book. The ambiguity within Israel toward the new development is indicated by alternating negative and positive attitudes toward monarchy.[1]

The Demand for a King (8:1-5)

8:1-2 The Hebrew text emphasizes the age of Samuel by reversing the normal noun/adjective order. The text is literally "and it came to pass when old Samuel became." This emphasis is reminiscent of the picture of Eli earlier (2:22,32; 3:1f.; 4:15,18). Like Eli (2:11-13,22-25) Samuel had two sons. He appointed them as judges[2] for Israel. They were not appointed to replace Samuel, but to assist him. His two sons, Joel and Abijah, had been given names which tes-

---

[1] E.g., Youngblood (611) breaks down the material as follows: 8:1-22, negative; 9:1–10:16, positive; 10:17-27, negative; 11:1-11, positive; 11:12–12:25, negative. See also D.J. McCarthy, "The Inauguration of Monarchy in Israel," *Int* 27 (1973): 401-412; J.R. Vannoy, 197-239.

[2] The root שפט (*špṭ*, "judge") appears five times in ch. 8. The Narrator apparently intended to link the old order of judgeship with the new institution of monarchy.

tified to the faith of their father, viz., "Yahweh is God" and "Yah is my Father" respectively.

Samuel stationed his sons in **Beersheba** (MBA, 104), the southernmost major city of Israel. That he was able to place his sons in authority there proves (1) that Samuel's rule was acknowledged throughout the land, or at least south of Ramah, and (2) that the Philistines were not at this time interfering with the internal government of Israel. Why two judges were appointed to one city is not clear.[3] Samuel must have trusted his sons. He must not have seen any evidence of their weakness and wickedness prior to the appointment.

8:3 Samuel serves as the standard of uprightness against which the Narrator measured his sons. Out from under the watchful eye of their father, Samuel's sons did not **walk** in the **ways** (lit., "way") of their father, i.e., they did not pursue the upright administration of justice which characterized the judgeship of Samuel (cf. 12:4). The sons **turned aside** (וַיִּטּוּ, *wayyiṭṭû*) from the upright path after **dishonest gain**. They took **bribes**. **They perverted** (וַיַּטּוּ, *wayyaṭṭû*; lit., caused "to turn aside") **justice**. This sin is roundly denounced in the Mosaic law (Deut 16:19; Exod 23:6,8).

Unlike Eli, Samuel was not punished for the waywardness of his sons (1) because the offense of his sons, though serious, was not blasphemous like that of Eli's sons; and/or (2) because of the distance from Ramah to Beersheba, he was unaware of their delinquency. While the sons of Samuel were unworthy successors, his grandson Heman came to occupy a prominent position in the royal court of David.[4]

8:4-5 The elders of Israel were the general assembly or council of the nation which is earlier called "the people" in ch. 5, i.e., the people as represented by their elders. In the words of the elders there are five grounds for the request for a king. First, they cited the age of Samuel. The prophet would have been in his seventies at this time. His energies were waning. In order to check the increasing power of the Philistines, a leader was needed who was daring, resolute, and skillful in war.

---

[3]Josephus (*Ant.* 6.3.2) states that only one of Samuel's sons was stationed at Beersheba, and the other was in the north at Dan. It could be that, while the young men started out in Beersheba, one of them was later dispatched to the north.

[4]See notices in 1 Chr 6:33; 25:4f. Heman, the grandson of Samuel, was the king's seer and chief of the choir in the house of God.

Second, the elders cited the degeneracy of Samuel's sons. These elders showed great courage in citing this problem, not only because they were speaking to one who must have loved his sons, but because Samuel had appointed them to their high office. Yet these words also suggest that the elders had the utmost confidence in Samuel. They knew that he would not condone nor tolerate the wickedness of his own sons, but would do what was in the best interest of the nation. Yet should Samuel die, those sons might not yield their office so easily.

Third, they couched their request for a king almost in the very terms used in the prophecy of the law (Deut 17:14). They ask that Samuel **appoint** a king. This is the same verb which was used of Samuel's sons in v. 1, perhaps suggesting that Samuel had made the wrong appointment. Implicit in their language is the thought that the law anticipated this day, and they had a legal right to have a king.

Fourth, the elders wanted the king **to lead them**, lit., "judge them." No doubt they used this verb to soften their radical proposal. The kingship which they envisioned would be a natural progression from the office of judge which they as a people had known for the past three centuries.

Fifth, the elders grounded their request in the observation that most of the other nations of that day were led by kings who passed the leadership down to their sons. The term nations (הַגּוֹיִם, *haggôyim*) stresses the non-Israelite heathen element. This suggests that the elders were willing to scrap the political status of a nation chosen and ruled by God in order to become simply one among many ordinary nations (Hertzberg, 72). To these five grounds, a sixth will be added in v. 20.

The Decision Regarding a King (8:6-9)

8:6 The request for the appointment of a king **displeased Samuel**, lit., "the thing was evil in the eyes of Samuel." Why was this so? First, on the personal level, he probably thought their request was a rejection of his own leadership. Second, Samuel probably thought that such a visible ruler, while not entirely subverting their theocratic government, would necessarily tend to throw out of view their unseen King and Leader, viz., Yahweh. Third, Samuel must have been displeased by the fact that the elders had determined to have a king without consulting the will of God. Fourth, the elders had demanded the wrong kind of king. They did not ask for a man after God's own heart, but for a king like all the nations.

Samuel did not fume at the elders or call them ungrateful for making such a request. Rather he took the matter to the Lord. Had the request been inherently evil, Samuel would have simply refused the request as ungodly. He did not let his own personal feelings decide, but endeavored to learn what the will of the Lord was concerning the matter. Though he and his sons stood to lose governing power, he was willing to do what was in the best interest of the nation as determined by the Lord.

8:7-8 Yahweh soon responded to Samuel's prayer for direction, probably in a vision. The Lord gave to his prophet, first, a word of direction. Twice he was told to **listen** to the request of "the people" which the elders had articulated, i.e., grant their request. The rationale for Yahweh's acquiescence is not offered in the text. A parallel may be found in God's granting Balaam permission to go with the princes of Midian even after he told him that was not the divine will (Num 22:12,20).

Second, God gave him a word of consolation. He assured the prophet that this request was not what on the surface it appeared to be, viz., a repudiation of Samuel's long years of service. Rather the people were rejecting the kingship of the Lord.[5] The term translated **rejected** (מָאַס, mā'as) is a technical term for the people's sin (cf. 2 Kgs 17:15). They wanted a king because they imagined that Yahweh was not able to secure their continuing prosperity.

Third, the Lord gave Samuel a word of perspective. Since the day Israel came out of Egypt, these people had forsaken the Lord and served other gods. The present request was but one more evidence of how rebellious they were.

8:9 Finally, the Lord gave Samuel a word of commission. He should go along with the request for a king. These people would have to be educated in the painful school of experience. First, however, he should **warn them solemnly** (lit., "bear witness") by outlining for the people all the disadvantages of having a king. They must not be able later to excuse their request on the grounds that they had acted without knowledge.

Samuel's second task was to **let them know what the king who will reign over them will do,** lit., "declare to them the manner (מִשְׁפַּט, mišpaṭ) of the king." At this point the details of the nature of

---

[5]The Hebrew word order here is emphatic: "not you [their judge] have they rejected, but me [their true king]."

the kingship are not spelled out. Later it will become clear: Yahweh will accede to their demand for a king; but the king will be completely answerable to Yahweh.

Up to this point, Yahweh had been the supreme political head of Israel. The elders had not suggested that the nation abandon the worship of Yahweh. They did not desire a change in their law code. Their demand was limited to a change in the executive form of government. Thus they were expressing dissatisfaction with the way the Lord had been leading them through the directives he gave to his prophet. This answer serves to console Samuel, and point out the true sinfulness of their request. The sin lies in (1) a failure to trust in the Lord to provide for them what he promised he would give them, viz., kings; (2) a desire for the splendor of a visible monarch; and (3) a desire to order their national affairs by sight and not by faith.

The Disadvantages of Having a King (8:10-18)

8:10-12 Samuel reported back to **the people**, i.e., their representatives, all that the Lord had said. He introduced his speech by saying, **This is what the king who will reign over you will do**, lit., "this will be the manner (*mišpaṭ*)[6] of the king who will rule over you." The Hebrew term may indicate (1) the customary behavior of the king (cf. 1 Sam 2:13 where the customary behavior of priests is mentioned) and/or (2) the legal rights of a king. In the verses which follow, the verb **take** (לְקַח, *lāqaḥ*) appears six times in seven verses. In each case, that which the king "will take" is placed before the Hebrew verb for emphasis. Family, land, wealth — nothing will be left untouched by their king. The verb translated "appoint" in vv. 1,5 ironically is used twice: in v. 11 (NIV: "make them serve") and v. 12 (NIV: "assign"). Samuel can *appoint* a king for them, but thereafter that king will do the *appointing*, and not necessarily in a way that will please the people.

First, the king would take some of their sons to serve as personal retainers (v. 11). He would **make them serve** (lit., "set for him") **with his chariots and horses**. Here, however, war is not in view so much

---

[6]Klein (76) calls attention to the subtle wordplay in this chapter between מִשְׁפָּט ("custom, justice") in vv. 9 and 11 and the root from which that word comes (שָׁפַט) which is used six other places in this chapter. While the people had protested the perversion of "justice" by Samuel's sons, Samuel indicates the kind of "justice" (מִשְׁפָּט) which they could expect from future kings, a miscarriage of all that was considered right in Israel.

as the personal grandeur of the king. The king would ride about in his state chariot (2 Kgs 9:21) escorted by horsemen and runners on foot (cf. 2 Sam 15:1; 1 Kgs 1:5). The old simplicity of the days of the judges would be gone.

Second, the king would **appoint** (lit., "set") some of their sons to serve as military officers (v. 12a). **Thousands** and **fifties** were the largest and smallest divisions of the Israelite army. A price would have to be paid for having a well-organized army.

Third, the king also would take some of their sons to perform manual labor for the crown (v. 12b). Some would have to work in the king's fields, and others would be assigned to work in factories producing war equipment. The king's interests came first. Farmers particularly would be irked by having to leave their own fields to plow the king's ground and reap his harvest just when their presence at home was most needed. Such forced labor was one of the chief reasons for the revolution of northern Israel after the death of Solomon (1 Kgs 5:13-16; 12:4).

Fourth, the king would even press their daughters into royal service (v. 13). The Hebrew text places the emphasis on **your daughters**, as if that would especially be a terrible price to pay for kingship. The daughters would become **perfumers**, i.e., makers of the ointments and scents, of which the people of that region were so fond. The daughters would also serve in the royal kitchens as "cooks" (cf. 1 Sam 9:23-24) and **bakers**. It is not clear whether these women would be considered part of the king's harem (cf. 1 Kgs 11:3) or merely palace servants.[7]

8:14-17 In these verses Samuel continued to outline the powers of the despotic king to confiscate whatever he wanted for his own ends. First, the king would **take** the best of their **fields, vineyards** and **olive groves** to give to **his officials**[8] **and attendants** (lit., "servants"). Again the Hebrew emphasizes the tragedy of this seizure, by placing the three types of property before the verb. Since the king

---

[7]Ackroyd (72) takes the word translated "perfumers" as a possible euphemism for concubines.

[8]The Hebrew term סָרִיס (sārîs) means lit., "one at the head." At times the word takes on the meaning of "eunuch." There is no reason, however, to assume that the officials here mentioned had been castrated. Castration in Israel would have very serious religious consequences (cf. Lev 22:24; Deut 23:1).

took "the best" for himself, making a living on less than the best would become increasingly difficult for his subjects. The seizure of Naboth's vineyard by Ahab and Jezebel is one illustration of how this warning became a reality in Israel (1 Kgs 21:1-16).

Second, the king would take in royal taxes ten per cent of their **grain,** lit., "seed,"[9] and **vintage,** lit., "vineyard."[10] Here again the Hebrew syntax emphasizes that which will be subject to the royal tithe. Though the citizens would have less property, and that of inferior quality, yet the king would still demand his taxes from what they did farm.

Third, the king would take for his own use their male and female servants as well as the best of their **cattle** (lit. "young men")[11] and donkeys **for his own use,** lit., "for his works." With the king appropriating for himself the available manpower, the average farmer might face the bleak prospect of seeing his crop die in the field. Whereas vv. 11-12 refer to leadership positions for their **sons**, the present verse speaks of corvée labor for the slaves.

Fourth, the king would demand one tenth of their flocks (v. 17a), as much as the King of kings required to maintain all the ordinances of their religion.

The climax of the disadvantages in monarchy is reached in v. 17b. With the monotonous use of second person possessive pronouns, Samuel gradually had accustomed his audience to the radical adjustments which monarchy will necessitate. Now he blasted them with this

---

[9]The NIV appears to be correct in interpreting "seed" here as grain product as in Lev 27:30; Gen 47:24; Isa 23:3; Hag 2:19; Job 39:12. BDB suggests that in this context the term means "arable lands" since it is parallel to "vineyards."

[10]The NIV has correctly understood "vineyards" here to refer by metonymy to that which the vineyards produce. Since Samuel has already mentioned how the king would take the best of the vineyards (v. 14), it would not be likely that he would here be said to take ten per cent of a vineyard considered as a piece of property. The reference must be to that which the vineyard produces.

[11]The NIV has chosen to follow the LXX which requires the change of one consonant (בַּחוּרֵיכֶם [baḥûrêkem] to בִּקְרֵיכֶם [biqrêkem]) in the Heb. text probably on the ground that Samuel would not have placed "their choice young men" between the female servants and the donkeys. If their "best young men," however, were in fact servants, or at least from the underclass, there would be no need to depart from the MT. Ruth 3:10 uses the term "young men" for both the rich and poor. The ASV, NASB, NKJV, and BV retain the MT. The JB and NRSV support the NIV in altering the MT on the basis of the LXX.

devastating announcement: **and you yourselves will become his slaves.** The appointment of a king would return Israel to the slave status from which Yahweh had set them free (cf. 2:27).

8:18 What is depicted in the preceding verses is an accurate and graphic representation of the despotic governments which were found in the ancient East.[12] Gradually the Israelite monarchy slid into conformity with this kind of government, especially in the northern kingdom, in spite of the restrictions prescribed by law. Samuel here anticipated the day when the people would **cry out** to the Lord **for relief** from the oppression of their chosen king just as they had cried out under the oppression of Pharaoh (Exod 3:7) and under the oppression of foreign kings during the period of the judges. The sting here is in the fact that their misery will have been self-inflicted. God assures his people, however, that he would not answer them in that day.

The Determination to Have a King (8:19-22)

8:19-20 That Israel had lost the theocratic spirit is clear in these verses First, despite this gloomy picture, the people, through their representatives, **refused to listen.** Second, they insisted that they wanted a king, and make no reference to the great King who had been leading them from the time of the Exodus. Third, they rejected any notion that as Yahweh's people, they should be different from surrounding nations (Num 23:9; Deut 33:28). **Then we** [emphatic in Heb.] **will be like all the other nations.** Yet Israel's glory was to be unlike other nations in having the Lord for their King and Lawgiver. Fourth, they wanted a visible and permanent leader. Fifth, they wanted someone who could lead them out to fight **our battles.** The theocratic spirit regarded Yahweh as the leader in battle (Deut 20:1-4; Judg 4:14; 2 Sam 5:24), and the holy wars were considered Yahweh's wars (1 Sam 18:17; 25:28). The emphasis here, however, is on "our," not Yahweh's, battles.

---

[12]See I. Mendelsohn, "On Corvée Labor in Ancient Canaan and Israel," *BASOR* 167 (October 1962): 31-35; and "Samuel's Denunciation of Kingship in the Light of the Akkadian Documents from Ugarit," *BASOR* 143 (October 1956):17-22. There is therefore no reason to follow the critics who contend that this antagonistic depiction of kingship was written long after the time of Samuel by someone who was bitter regarding abuses of the monarchy.

8:21 Samuel heard all that the people said perhaps implies that he grasped the full significance of their request for the first time. Again Samuel went to God and **repeated it** (lit., "spoke it") **before the LORD**, lit., "in the ears of the Lord." For the third time (see vv. 7,9) the indignant and reluctant old prophet was told to **listen** to the people, i.e., give them what they desired. He told the leaders to return to their homes. No doubt he assured them that in due time he would provide them with a king. Their demand was conceded, for the government of a king had been promised to Abraham, foreseen by Moses, and provided for in the law. The selection of that king, however, God had reserved to himself (Deut 17:14-20). Such was their reverence for God and their confidence in his prophet that Samuel was trusted to pick the one to whom he would cede his governing authority.[13]

---

[13]Helpful insights into the acquiescence of Yahweh to the demands for a king are found in J.B. Payne, "Saul and the Changing Will of God," *BS* 129 (1972): 321-325; R.E. Clements, "The Deuteronomistic Interpretation of the Founding of the Monarchy in I Sam VIII," *VT* 24, 4 (1974): 398-410.

1 SAMUEL 9

2. The Anointing of Saul (9:1-10:16)

Though the people indicated the kind of king they desired, they left the appointment of the candidate up to God's prophet. The year was ca. 1043 B.C. Probably only a few months separate the events of this chapter and those of ch. 8.

Introduction of Saul (9:1-27)

A Task Unbecoming a King (9:1-13)

9:1 Three things are said about the father of the first king of Israel. First, he was **a Benjamite**, i.e., he was of the tribe of Benjamin. His tribe is mentioned first because that was critical in the selection. Benjamin was the smallest of the tribes of Israel. It had nearly been wiped out in a civil war some years earlier (Judg 20–21). Leaders of the larger tribes would have less reason to be jealous of one another if the first king came from the smallest tribe.

Second, the father of Israel's first king was a **man of standing** (גִּבּוֹר חָיִל, *gibbôr ḥāyil*). The Hebrew can mean either (1) a mighty man of valor as in 1 Sam 16:18, or (2) a wealthy man as in Ruth 2:1 (cf. 2 Kgs 15:20). The LXX rendering "a powerful man" incorporates both ideas. He was as prosperous in peace as he was valiant in war.

Third, the father of Israel's first king is introduced by name and genealogy. The unusually lengthy genealogy underscores the prominence of Kish in the tribe of Benjamin. This is only a very abridged account of Saul's descent. Other than **Abiel**, the ancestors of Kish mentioned here are not elsewhere mentioned. This indicates that his claim to kingship could not be based on genealogical considerations. Saul was a virtual nobody before Yahweh made him a royal somebody.

9:2 Here the focus shifts from Kish to his son about whom four pieces of information are given. First, Kish's son was **named Saul**, which means "asked (of God)." The Hebrew root of this word occurs in 8:10, where the people were "asking" for a king. Second, he is called a **young man**. Though he had a grown son at this time according to 13:2, in contrast to his father, he was young. The term בָּחוּר (*bāḥûr*) refers to one in the prime of manhood; one who is capable of war, inheritance, and marriage. The emphasis in the word is not on Saul's age, but his physical fitness for kingship. Third, Saul was **impressive** (lit., "good"), i.e., good looking (cf. 16:12). Fourth, he was **without equal** (lit., "none better than he")[1] **among the Israelites**. He stood a head taller than any of his countrymen (cf. 10:23). His regal stature (1) made him so impressive, and (2) had the potential of intimidating those who opposed him (cf. 16:7). The people had requested a king like all the nations. This initial description of Saul supports the conclusion that God was giving the people exactly the kind of person who would fulfill their kingly expectations.[2]

9:3 This verse further underscores the prominence of Kish, for he had a drove of **donkeys** (lit., "she-asses") and several servants. Kish may have been in the business of breeding donkeys. When some donkeys belonging to his father got lost, Saul was the likely person to go looking for them. So his father dispatched him[3] and a servant to start the search.

Saul's immediate obedience to his father's directive is an important prerequisite for his selection as king. Disobedient sons have been rejected in previous chapters by both God (in the case of Eli's sons) and man (in the case of Samuel's sons).

Saul and his servant left from Gibeah, three miles north of Jerusalem (MBA, 86). Boundaries in this period were marked by stones, not by fences. For this reason, animals could easily stray. In the rural regions these animals would roam at large during the grazing season. The Lord used these straying donkeys to bring Saul into contact with the prophet Samuel.

---

[1]The Heb. טוֹב (*ṭôb*) first refers in v. 2 to Saul's physical appearance. The second usage (in the NIV phrase "without equal") is ambiguous. The word *ṭôb* originally meant "good" in general and "good looking" by extension. It is not clear whether the text is saying that Saul was the best looking man in Israel, or the best available man (M. Sternberg, 355).

[2]So G.C. Luck, "The First Glimpse of the First King of Israel," *BS* 123 (1966): 61.

[3]In the Heb. the imperative "take" is softened by the particle נָא (*na'*, a particle of entreaty) which is left untranslated in the NIV.

Traveling searches as the one here commissioned must have been common. Each owner had his own stamp marked on his livestock. Mention of the mark to the shepherds along the way gradually would lead to the discovery of the straying animals. The servant is not identified, but it is clear that he was no slave for (1) he is on familiar terms with Saul throughout the narrative, (2) he is in charge of the money (v. 8), (3) he offers wise advice to Saul at times (v. 8), and (4) he was treated as an honored guest by Samuel later in this chapter. Tradition identifies him as Doeg the Edomite who later will be such a ruthless partisan for King Saul (1 Sam 22:18).

9:4-5 From Saul's home in Gibeah, the two donkey seekers proceeded northwest through **the hill country of Ephraim**, a spur of the mountains of Ephraim which ran south into the territory of Benjamin where Kish lived. Though there is some disagreement about the location of **Shalisha** ("three-land"),[4] it is probably to be identified with the town of Baal Shalishah of 2 Kgs 4:42 located about fifteen miles southwest of Shechem (OBA, 63). Here Saul and the servant turned south toward **the district of Shaalim** ("land of foxes"). The place is otherwise unknown, but probably is to be equated with Shaalbim of Judg 1:35 located twenty miles south-southwest of Baal Shalishah (OBA, 63). **The district of Zuph** appears to have been the region in which Ramah was located (cf. 1 Sam 1:1; 9:5).

The journey occupied parts of three days (v. 20). Saul became concerned that his father might be worrying about his well-being. When he and his servant came to the land of Zuph, Saul suggested that they return home. Saul's tender concern for his father's feelings is a favorable indication of his character and a refreshing contrast to the sons of Eli and Samuel.

9:6 The servant had a better idea.[5] They were near a town where there was a **man of God**, i.e., prophet. See comments on 2:27. Later the text will identify this prophet as Samuel. The **town** is probably Ramah, but the text never explicitly says this. Nor does the text say that the man of God actually lived in the town.[6] What is clear in this

---

[4]The name probably denotes an area in which three valleys converged.

[5]The fact that this servant had more creative imagination than Saul is an early hint of the leadership inadequacy of Israel's first king.

[6]Some of the older commentaries prefer a town further to the south near Bethlehem in order to accommodate the traditional location of Rachel's tomb near Bethlehem (10:2; Cf. Gen 35:19). See discussion on 10:2.

verse is that Samuel was held in high regard by the servant. This man of God had the reputation of never making any prediction about the future which failed to come to pass. The servant thought that Samuel might be able to tell them what road to follow in order to recover the lost donkeys. From this verse commentators assume that Saul knew nothing about Samuel. It would not be likely, however, that Saul had never heard of Samuel. The servant was surprised that Saul did not propose going to Samuel. So this verse constitutes his arguments as to why the trip should be prolonged by a visit to the man of God. The fact that Saul did not think of the prophet is indication that (1) he did not think the matter was of sufficient importance to trouble such an eminent prophet, or (2) that he did not have any appropriate gift to present to the man of God in exchange for his services, or (3) it was getting late in the day and Saul was anxious to get home.

9:7 There was one problem with the servant's suggestion. It was customary to give a gift to the man of God in exchange for his counseling services. The two men, however, did not even have any food left in their sacks which might be used as a present (cf. 1 Kgs 14:3).[7] Neither did they have anything suitable for a **gift** (תְּשׁוּרָה, *t⁾šûrāh*), the technical term for a fee of this kind, half payment and half gift.[8]

9:8 Fortunately the servant had with him a quarter of a shekel of silver (about ¹⁄₁₀ of an ounce). This is not in coin form, because coins did not come into use in Palestine until much later. There is no way to compute the purchasing power of this silver. A more literal rendering of the servant's words brings out another point obscured by the NIV. Rather than the usual wording for "I have," the servant said: "Behold, there is found in my hand . . . ." The language suggests that the servant did not himself know that he had on his person the silver until that very moment. Its presence, though a mystery to the servant, is another indication of Providence at work in this narrative.

9:9 This parenthetical statement is very important in the history of Old Testament religion. It sets forth two points. First, it was customary for a person to go to a prophet **to inquire of God** or seek a word from God about some problem in his life. Second, the term **seer** used in this passage was no longer in common use at the time

---

[7]Another interpretation is that they had no money left even to buy bread.

[8]See Shalom Paul, "1 Samuel 9:7: An Interview Fee," *Biblica* 59, 4 (1978): 542-544.

the materials in Samuel were put in their final form. The person who formerly was called a **seer** (רֹאֶה, *rō'eh*) was called a **prophet** (נָבִיא, *nābî'*) at the time the final redaction of the book of Samuel was made. See on 3:20. Thus "seers" and "prophets" are not two separate offices in ancient Israel, but one. The term "seer" stresses the mode of revelation, i.e., dreams and visions; the term "prophet" stresses the communication of the word of the Lord.

9:10 Saul agreed to set out immediately for a meeting with Samuel. **The town** is probably Ramah, but might be some other town where Samuel was ministering that day.

9:11 The city was on an elevation, with the water supply consequently at the foot of the ascent. As they were going up the hill to the town, the two men met some girls coming out of the city to draw water from the city well on the edge of town. In that region the drawing of water was a daily task for the teenage girls. The men asked the girls if **the seer** was in town.

9:12 The response of the girls to Saul and his servant indicated several important points. First, it so happened that Samuel was in town. He had just arrived that very day, perhaps from an extended tour of his regular circuit (7:16). Second, Samuel had come to that town because **the people had a sacrifice** that day. The term translated sacrifice (זֶבַח, *zebaḥ*) comes from a verb which can refer to either what a butcher does (Deut 12:15,21; Ezek 34:3) or to what is done by someone who slaughters an animal as part of a religious ritual. Third, the sacrifice of the people was to take place at the **high place** (בָּמָה, *bāmāh*) or the elevated area of town. The term is connected with Canaanite worship prior to the entrance of Israel into the land (Num 33:52). In the Samuel books the term is used ten times and in no instance clearly with cultic connotations. In the present text there is no mention of an altar or a temple in connection with the high place.

9:13 The girls indicated that the men should intercept Samuel on his way to the high place because only invited guests would be allowed to attend the sacrifice. The people would not begin eating the sacrificial meal until Samuel first came to **bless the sacrifice**, i.e., offer the thanksgiving prayer before the meal. This is the only religious activity mentioned at this event. The term **invited** (הַקְּרֻאִים, *haqq²ru'îm*) appears to be a technical term in the later coronation ritual of Adonijah (1 Kgs 1:41,49). This meal was set up by Samuel in anticipation of a coronation banquet. Samuel seems to have returned to the city from the high place, after the ritual of sacrifice had been performed (cf. v. 23), expressly to meet Saul, of whose coming he had been informed.

A Greeting Suitable for a King (9:14-21)

9:14 Saul and the servant went **up to the town** for the unnamed town was on a hill. As they entered the town, the two met Samuel, who here is mentioned by name for the first time in this narrative. He last was mentioned in 8:22 where he sent the people home to await the leading of the Lord in anointing Israel's first king. Now God providentially had brought that candidate before him. His name has been withheld until this moment to pique curiosity in the reader about the mysterious man of God's choosing. Samuel was **on his way up to the high place** for the sacrifice.

9:15-16 These verses are retrospective. At last the information is revealed which makes sense out of the story of the lost donkeys. What was implicit in the previous verses is now made explicit, viz., that God's hand had been guiding events of recent days toward this climax.

On the previous day, God **had revealed** (lit., "uncovered the ear")[9] to Samuel that within twenty-four hours he would send a man from the tribe of Benjamin to him. This is the first divine communication to the prophet since he was told to anoint Israel's first king. The verb "send" indicates the overruling providence of God by which Saul would be brought in contact with Samuel.

Samuel was directed to **anoint** that man **leader** (נָגִיד, *nāgîd*), i.e., "one who has been announced" or "designated." This command is a specification of the manner in which Samuel was to make a king for Israel (cf. 8:21). The king will be under the authority of Yahweh and his representative (Samuel). Hertzberg (82) points out that Saul was given the provisional title *nāgîd* until political honor was added to theological recognition by the acclamation of the people in 11:15.[10] Thereafter he is called "king" (מֶלֶךְ, *melek*). Perhaps the term

---

[9]The idea of "uncovering the ear" is used of divine revelation in 2 Sam 7:27; 1 Chr 17:25; Job 33:16; 36:10,15; Isa 22:14. The expression can also be used of ordinary human disclosure as in 1 Sam 20:12f.; 22:8,17. The figure is taken from the action of pushing aside the headdress, in order to whisper more conveniently to the ear.

[10]The term *nāgîd* appears here for the first of forty-four times in the MT. The title is distinguished from the title *melek* ("king"). It is generally God

nāgîd indicates something like "king-designate." Anointing symbolized impartation of divine gifts for the fulfillment of the task to which one was being called (1 Sam 16:13; Isa 61:1-3).

Three reasons are given for the anointing. First, that man would **deliver my people** from the growing Philistine menace. Though the Philistines were not an immediate problem (cf. 7:13), Yahweh foresaw the danger looming on the horizon. See on 7:13. Second, God had **looked upon** his people. This was not a quiet, inactive awareness, but an energetic look which brought help in trouble (cf. Exod 2:25; 3:7,9; 4:31). Third, God was looking upon his people in active involvement because **their cry has reached me.** These words repeat Exod 3:9. The Philistines were now assuming the role of the Egyptian oppressors. It was time for God to send them another Moses to set them free. The king was to fill that role. This verse raises a question: How could God be displeased with the request for a king (8:7ff.) if he in fact recognized a legitimate need for one to fill that office? The only answer can be that his displeasure was in the state of heart from which the desire for a king arose (KD, 194). The triple use of **my people** in v. 16 reminds everyone that God had not abdicated his throne in favor of the king designate. Yahweh was Israel's king.

9:17 The Hebrew uses syntax — a series of perfect verbs — which suggests the simultaneity of the actions in this verse (McCarter, 1:179). As soon as Samuel saw Saul, Yahweh **said to** (lit., "answered") **him**, i.e., revealed, that this was the man of whom he had spoken the day before. Again the NIV ignores the Hebrew הִנֵּה (*hinnēh*, "behold"), which conveys the excitement of viewing the future king. This was the man who was to **govern** (lit., "restrain") Israel. The term, used only here and in 10:1, is appropriate for the role of the monarch, because during the period of the judges "every man did that which was right in his own eyes" (Judg 21:25) with devastating social and

---

who appoints a *nāgîd*. In two cases, however, a king appointed his son to be *nāgîd* (1 Kgs 1:35; 2 Chr 11:22). J.J. Glück has attempted to demonstrate that *nāgîd* and נֹקֵד (*nôqēd*, "shepherd") are etymologically related and that the former terms means "shepherd." He maintains that through "a natural transfiguration, 'shepherd' became first, an attribution of the title of the ruler and later, a synonym for the title itself." "Nagid-Shepherd," *VT* 13 (1963): 144-150.

moral consequences.[11] The term indicates a special form of rule, under the kingship of the Lord (Baldwin, 89).

9:18-20 That neither Saul nor the servant recognized Samuel indicates (1) that they were not personally acquainted with him, (2) that he was undistinguished from any ordinary citizen by his dress or appearance, and (3) that Saul was innocent of any complicity in the plan revealed by Yahweh.

In his reply to Saul, the prophet achieved several purposes. First, Samuel identified himself. He accepted the title "seer" (see on 9:9) for himself. Second, Samuel invited Saul to eat with him at the special meal in the high place. Saul (the verb is singular) was to **go up ahead** of Samuel. Letting a person go in front was a sign of great esteem. The verb **you are to eat** is plural, including Saul's servant.

Third, Samuel promised that **in the morning** he would tell Saul all about what was in his heart. What Saul had been pondering in his heart is not indicated. Perhaps he had been thinking about what might be done to defend Israel from attacks by neighboring enemies. Fourth, as a down payment on that promised revelation of the next day, Samuel assured Saul that he need not worry any longer about the lost donkeys. They had been found. Since nothing had been said previously to Samuel about the lost donkeys, this statement proved to Saul that Samuel was a "seer" with supernatural insight.

Fifth, Samuel laid the groundwork for the announcement of the next day that God had appointed Saul as the leader of Israel. He did this by asking a rhetorical question: **To whom is all the desire of Israel turned, if not to you and all your father's family?**[12] Kingship is the clear implication of this question. The meaning is this: Saul would be the man the whole nation would take pleasure in honoring as their first king. The reference to **your father's family** may hint that a dynastic understanding of kingship was in view.

---

[11]McCarter (1:179) proposes for עָצַר (*'āṣar*, NIV, "govern") the meaning "muster" with reference to Saul's martial responsibilities. Eslinger (*Kingship*, 310) thinks the word is meant sarcastically: Yahweh will use his kind of king to "restrain" Israel from its stated goal of becoming like all the nations.

[12]The word translated "desire" (חֶמְדָּה, *ḥemdāh*) can mean "desirable things" as well as "desire" or "pleasure." Samuel's question has been interpreted to mean: "And for whom are all the good things that Israel can offer?" This rendering is supported by the LXX. The point would be: Why should you be concerned for a few donkeys when you will be the recipient of great material wealth?

9:21 Saul sensed that some great honor was about to be conferred on him. He could not understand, however, why the desire of all Israel would be focused on him. He was from Benjamin, the smallest tribe in Israel. In that tribe his **clan**[13] was the most insignificant. Originally there were ten clans in the tribe of Benjamin (Gen 46:21), but how many of them survived after the civil war recorded in Judges 20 cannot be determined. Saul does not mention his father's house which, in the light of v. 1, must have been one of the more prominent ones in Benjamin. Nothing in Saul's answer suggests that he understood the prophet to be referring to the kingship. The elevation of Saul from the smallest tribe and most insignificant clan is a concrete illustration of the principle articulated by Hannah in 1 Sam 2:8.

A Meal Fit for a King (9:22-24)

9:22-24 That Samuel intended to distinguish and honor Saul above all his other guests that day is evident in what he did and said. First, Saul and his servant were escorted by Samuel into **the hall**, (לִשְׁכָּה, *liškāh*), a word which most frequently refers to the side chamber of a temple or sacred building. There are places, however, where the term is used of chambers which were not part of a cultic structure (Jer 36:12,20,21). The most that can be said with certainty is that the hall where the banquet was taking place was part of a larger structure of some kind.

Second, the prophet seated them at the head of a table with about thirty guests. These were all honored guests, for they had been invited by Samuel. The seating arrangement indicated that Saul was the most honored of all. What, if any, significance there is in the number thirty is not indicated.[14] Third, Samuel had made prior arrangements with the cook to reserve a specific piece of meat for the honored guest. The advanced planning indicates honor.

Fourth, Samuel directed the cook to bring that special piece of meat — a leg[15] — and set it before Saul. This was the largest and best

---

[13]Other English versions choose to render מִשְׁפַּחְתִּי (*mišpaḥtî*) as "my family." The NIV "clan" is better as indicating a subdivision of a tribe. The term "family" in English generally refers to immediate blood kin, which in Hebrew would be called "father's house."

[14]Klein (90) calls attention to the thirty chief men associated with David (2 Sam 23:13,18).

[15]The expression **what was on it** (הֶעָלֶיהָ, *he'ālêhā*) is a grammatical anom-

portion of the meat, and most suitable for the special guest at that meal. Fifth, Samuel explained[16] that this portion of meat had been set aside from the moment that he had ordered this meal to be prepared. This explanation further underscores the fact that Samuel had foreseen Saul's coming. Sixth, the great prophet and the future king dined together that day. By these actions Samuel was (1) signaling those present that they should be treating this man like a king; and (2) preparing Saul for the announcement he would make the next day. The news that Saul was treated royally that day must have spread rapidly through the land.

A Conversation with a King (9:25-27)

9:25 After the meal, the old prophet took Saul to the roof of his house, i.e., his own house or one made available to him when he was in town. The topics discussed by the prophet and the future king are not indicated. Perhaps they spoke of the deep religious and political degradation of Israel, and the rising menace of the Philistines to the west. Saul must have slept on the roof that night.

9:26-27 The next morning Samuel called Saul down from the roof. It was time for Saul to leave, and Samuel wished to give him a special send off. **When Saul got ready** is literally "and Saul arose." The text is emphasizing Saul's immediate obedience to the prophet. **He and Samuel went outside together** is literally "and the two of them went out, he and Samuel, to the outside." The redundancy of the subject in the original stresses the solidarity between the two men.

The two walked to the edge of town together. There Samuel, illustrating the appropriate chain of command, directed Saul to send his servant on ahead. Samuel wished to speak privately with Saul. He had a message from God for him.

---

aly, being a preposition preceded by a definite article functioning as a relative pronoun (BDB, 209).

[16]The NIV, following the LXX and Vulgate, inserts Samuel's name in v. 24. In the Hebrew text it is the cook who speaks these words to Saul. The NIV also ignores the interjection "Behold" (*hinnēh*) with which the explanation to Saul was introduced. The word serves to introduce that which is unexpected, or even shocking. The word translated "from the time I said" is one which means "saying" and nothing else. It is clear that there is an ellipse here. If the cook is speaking, he is referring to the time when the food arrangements had been made, viz., when Samuel had informed him that he had invited the guests.

1 SAMUEL 10

The Anointing of Saul (10:1-16)

Saul was anointed Israel's first king ca. 1043 B.C. Probably only a few weeks elapsed between the demand of the elders in ch. 8 and the anointing in ch. 10. Saul's rise to kingship took place in three distinct stages: He was (1) anointed by Samuel (9:1–10:16), (2) chosen by lot (10:17-27), and (3) confirmed by public acclamation (11:1-15).

The Private Anointing at Ramah (10:1-8)

10:1 Early in the morning Samuel and Saul stood alone at the edge of the unnamed town. Samuel took **a flask**, lit., "the flask," a narrow-necked vessel from which the olive oil[1] mingled with spices flowed in drops over the head of the anointed. The act of anointing signified (1) the consecration to the service of God, (2) the bestowal of the gift of the Spirit which qualified a person for office, and (3) the identification of an individual as sacred and inviolable (cf. 26:9; 2 Sam 1:14). In this ceremony Samuel was merely acting as the agent of the Lord. It is Yahweh himself who did the anointing.[2]

---

[1] Youngblood (624) thinks this oil was the distinctive formula prescribed for use in anointing priests (Exod 30:23-33), the so-called holy oil (Ps 89:20). In a pit near Qumran, a clay flask was found which dates to the first century A.D. It contained a small amount of well-preserved reddish oil which may be the only surviving sample of the kind of oil used to anoint ancient Israelite kings. Joseph Patrick, "Hideouts in the Judean Wilderness," *BAR* 15, 5 (1989): 34-35.

[2] A survey of the verb "anointed" indicates (1) cases where the people or their representatives perform the rite (e.g., 2 Sam 19:11); and (2) cases where God is said to have acted through a human intermediary, as in the present case. In David's case the anointing was both by Samuel (1 Sam 16:1-13) and by the representatives of the people (2 Sam 2:4; 5:3). The anointing of kings was not practiced in Egypt or Mesopotamia. There is, however, evidence of the practice among the Hittites (Mettinger, 209).

Twelve times the text refers to Saul as Yahweh's "anointed."[3] Priests (Exod 40:15; Lev 8:12), prophets in some cases (1 Kgs 19:16), and kings were consecrated by anointing. These anointings foreshadowed the Messiah (the Anointed One par excellence) who united in himself the offices of prophet, priest and king.

After he anointed Saul, Samuel **kissed** him on the cheek. In this case the kiss probably was not so much a gesture of friendship — he had only met Saul the previous day — as a sign of reverential homage (cf. Ps 2:12). Samuel replied to the look and gesture of extreme astonishment with an announcement by means of a question[4] that the Lord had made Saul **leader** (see on 9:16) over his **inheritance**. The nation of Israel had been acquired by Yahweh as his own possession through their deliverance out of Egyptian bondage (Deut 4:20; 9:26). Saul would need to remember that he was ruling God's people and that he was acting as God's agent. He would have to give an account someday for the way he governed God's inheritance (people).

10:2 Samuel knew that the timid Saul would be reluctant to assume such a public leadership role. He knew that Saul needed first to be convinced in his own mind that he was chosen by God. So Samuel announced three signs that would occur on his return trip to Gibeah. Each of the three signs was designed to strengthen Saul's faith and at the same time teach him a solemn lesson.

First, near **Rachel's tomb**[5] Saul would encounter two men. The exact location where this encounter would take place was **Zelzah on the border of Benjamin**. The place is mentioned nowhere else and cannot be identified with certainty.

One purpose of this first sign was to confirm by neutral mouth what Samuel had previously asserted. The two men would inform Saul that the donkeys had been found. They would further tell Saul that his father was very worried about his whereabouts. This "chance" encounter would serve (1) to establish Samuel's prescience

---

[3]The title "Yahweh's anointed" designates the king as the vicegerent of God. It is characteristic of the books of Samuel and Psalms, but never occurs in Kings, when the true idea of the kingdom had been lost.

[4]In Hebrew a strong affirmation often takes the form of a question, especially when, as probably was the case here, surprise is manifested.

[5]See Gen 35:19. The present-day tomb of Rachel, just north of Bethlehem, was erected by the Crusaders. Jeremiah 31:15 suggests that the tomb may have been in or near Ramah, about 10.5 miles north of Bethlehem.

and hence credibility in the announcement made to Saul, and (2) to relieve Saul's mind of lesser cares so he could concentrate on preparing to be the leader of his people.

10:3-4 The second sign would take place at **the great tree at Tabor**, a famous landmark on the road to Bethel. At that tree Saul would encounter three men who would be **going up to God**, a striking way of referring to worship at a sanctuary. At this time there was still a place of sacrifice consecrated to the Lord at **Bethel,** where Abraham and Jacob had erected altars (Gen 12:8; 13:3f.; 28:18f.; 35:7). Samuel describes exactly what each of the three men would be carrying. The first man would be carrying **three young goats**, the second, **three loaves of bread**, and the third **a skin of wine**, i.e., an animal skin prepared as a liquid container. The goats were for sacrifice, the loaves for the offering, and the wine for libations.

The strangers would first **greet** Saul, lit., "ask of you for peace."[6] This refers to the usual friendly greeting of travelers. That in itself would not particularly be unusual. Then, however, the men would give him two loaves of the bread intended for their offering at Bethel. This act is meant to refer back to 9:7 and is to be regarded as (1) a providential act of God in providing what Saul was lacking, and (2) a preview of what was ahead for Saul. Here Saul learned that, as king, people willingly would bring presents to him. Samuel told Saul to accept the present as being his due, for he had been designated to be the future king.

10:5 The third sign would transpire near **Gibeah of God**, the full name of Saul's hometown (cf. 11:4; 13:2).[7] The town was probably given this name because there was a special high place or sacrificial height nearby. At or near Gibeah was **a Philistine outpost** (נְצִיב, n°ṣîb) (cf. 1 Sam 13:3), a detail which helps further to identify "Gibeah of God." The Hebrew term can refer to (1) a monument (Gen 19:26); (2) an officer (1 Kgs 4:19); and (3) a garrison (1 Chr 11:16). The choice here lies between the second or third meaning of

---

[6]The same idiom is used in 17:22; 30:21; 2 Sam 8:10. The verbal root is שָׁאַל (šā'al, "ask"), another example in these chapters of the familiar pun on the name שָׁאוּל (šā'ûl, "Saul").

[7]Mettinger (246) and others have argued that Gibeah ("hill") of God is another name for the high place at Gibeon. Some scholars have advanced the hypothesis that Saul made Gibeon the capital of the young monarchy. This view is worthy of serious consideration but falls short of definitive proof.

the term. Gibeah was either the official residence of a Philistine officer who collected taxes from the local inhabitants, or of an entire
garrison of soldiers. This reference along with others like it (13:3;
14:4) shows that the tribe of Benjamin was subject to the Philistines
at this time. It is somewhat ironic that the empowerment of Israel's
first king would transpire in the shadow of a Philistine outpost.

The first sign involved two men, the second, three. Now in the
third sign, Saul would encounter **a procession of prophets**. In this
period groups of prophets who lived together in dormitories are
mentioned. Samuel was the leader of this group. That these
prophets would be **coming down from the high place** at Gibeah has
been taken by some to mean that they lived there. It may be, however, that this prophetic group traveled about the country visiting
the various centers of worship.

Samuel told Saul three things about the prophets. First, they
would be making their way down from the high place. Hills or high
places were sometimes used as worship areas. These prophets must
have been engaged in some kind of religious activity on that particular high place. Second, all manner of musical instruments would be
played in front of this procession. Third, the prophets would be
prophesying (lit., "they shall be acting the prophet"), an apt expression for men who were under prophetic tutelage. Such group
prophesying, in this case at least, consisted of rhythmic singing. The
group was probably singing songs which were designed to kindle
patriotic fervor and faith in the hearts of God's people.

Four different musical instruments are named. The **lyre** (נֶבֶל,
nēbel) was a sort of harp of ten strings stretched across a triangular
frame, the longest string being at its base, and the shortest at its
apex. The **tambourine** (תֹּף, *tōph*) was a percussion instrument struck
with the hand, not unlike the modern instrument of the same name.
The **flute** (חָלִיל, *ḥālîl*) was a hollow reed in which the air was blown
against one edge of the mouth hole. Others interpret this instrument as a pipe of one or two reeds into which air is blown. The **harp**
(כִּנּוֹר, *kinnôr*) had a body with two arms joined by a crossbar, the
strings going from the body to the crossbar. It was chiefly used to
accompany the voice.[8] "Prophesying" is used of playing instruments
of music (1 Chr 25:1-3) and chanting (1 Kgs 18:29).

---

[8]ZPEB, s.v. "Music; Musical Instruments" by H.M. Best and D. Huttar
4:319f.

10:6 In the presence of that band of prophets, three things would happen to Saul. First, Samuel predicted that the Spirit of Yahweh would **come upon** Saul **in power** (lit., "rush upon him"). The terminology describes the empowerment of Samson in his amazing physical exploits against the Philistines (Judg 14:6,19; 15:14). Saul would be so overwhelmed with God's Spirit that he would be able to do things he normally would not or could not do.

Second, as a result of that Spirit empowerment, Saul would **prophesy** with the prophets. Their spiritual gift would pass over to him, enabling him to prophesy along with them. The nearest analogy to what is predicted here is the reference to the seventy elders who prophesied when God placed some of the Spirit that was upon Moses on them (Num 11:25-29).

Third, in this experience Saul would be **changed into a different person.** The verb used here (הָפַךְ, *hāphak*) is the same that is used for the "overthrow" of Sodom and Gomorrah. The old personality of Saul would be completely overthrown by God's Spirit. New thoughts and emotions would take possession of him. He would be able to make decisive decisions and exercise other leadership skills.

10:7 The **signs**[9] would assure Saul of God's assistance in all that he undertook as king. He could take whatever action he thought was appropriate. He should act according to the strength he would be given through the Spirit. In the context of 1 Samuel this is best exemplified by Saul's attack on the Ammonites (11:6) and by the initiative he took against the Philistine menace (9:16; ch. 13).

10:8 The NIV understands this verse as a command by Samuel for Saul to go down to Gilgal. While this is possible, contextual considerations point to the first clause as independent and conditional. Samuel presupposes that Saul, once he established himself in the monarchy, would in fact go down to Gilgal. Perhaps in the conversation on the roof the preceding evening Samuel and Saul had discussed the campaign to drive the Philistines out of the hill country (cf. 9:16). Gilgal was the most suitable place to launch the campaign because (1) it was an ancient shrine, (2) it was easily accessible to Israelites from both sides of the Jordan, (3) it was sufficiently remote

---

[9]A sign (אֹת, *'ōth*) is an object or occurrence through which a person comes to recognize, learn, remember, or perceive the credibility of something. A sign serves to support an understanding or to motivate behavior (F.J. Helfmeyer, TDOT, 1:170f.).

from advanced Philistine positions to allow for the gathering and organization of an army, and (4) it was the spot from which Joshua had launched Yahweh's holy war against the Canaanites centuries before. Thus the first clause should probably be translated: "And if you go down before me to Gilgal." Saul would go down to Gilgal *before* Samuel in the sense that he would determine the appropriate time for the campaign against the Philistines.

The second clause appears to be circumstantial and is introduced as a parenthesis: "and behold I am going down to you." This clause indicates that Samuel foresaw that Saul at some future time would in fact go down to Gilgal, and the prophet was intending to join him there at that time. The word "behold" (ignored in NIV) indicates that this commitment was unexpected in view of Samuel's (1) advanced age, and (2) retirement from political leadership.

The infinitive clause **to sacrifice burnt offerings**, etc. the NIV takes as dependent on **I will surely come down to you** rather than on the main clause. This infinitive clause, however, is clearly dependent on the main clause, yielding the following translation: "And if you go down to Gilgal before me (and behold I am going down unto you) to offer up burnt offerings and sacrifice peace offerings, seven days you shall wait until my coming unto you; and I will tell you what you are to do." Saul's purpose for going to Gilgal was to offer various sacrifices. In the context of Saul's mission, this must refer to the religious rituals which preceded the launching of a holy war.

The fourth clause stipulates that when the anticipated trip to Gilgal took place, Saul must wait a full week for the arrival of the prophet. This wait would serve to (1) try the faith of Saul, and (2) underscore the idea that the Philistine war was in fact a holy war.

The fifth clause indicates that when Samuel arrived in Gilgal, he would tell Saul what he was to do. Not only would Samuel give him guidance regarding the religious observances, he would also communicate to him Yahweh's battle plan for ridding the land of the Philistines. Clearly Samuel intended to occupy a position of influence as a counselor to the king.

The Signs on the Road to Gibeah (10:9-16)

10:9 Two questions arise in connection with this verse. First, did the "change" (same verb used in v. 6) in Saul occur when he turned to leave Samuel, or later that day when the Spirit rushed on him as predicted in v. 6? The previous verse spoke of an outward manifes-

tation of change which indeed was the result of the overpowering
Spirit. This verse speaks of inward change of disposition. God began
his work in Saul immediately. Second, how did God change Saul's
heart? The text need not be made to say that the Lord directly
altered Saul's thinking by erasing all his doubts and overriding his
freedom of choice. The Lord changed the heart of Saul through the
words and actions of Samuel, God's agent and spokesman. The
heart in Hebrew denotes the center of the whole mental life of will,
desire, thought, precepts and feelings.

The Hebrew wording of this verse is striking: "When he turned
his shoulder to go from Samuel, God also turned for him another
heart," i.e., God turned him round by giving him a changed heart.
His personality changed, at least for the moment. He received from
the Lord the spirit of regal power. Gone were the concerns about
lost donkeys. He now was thinking as a prince and a general.

All the signs predicted by Samuel came to pass **that day.** Though
the town in which Samuel and Saul had this conversation cannot be
identified with certainty, the distance from Zelzah (where the first sign
was fulfilled) to Gibeah was only about ten miles. As Saul left Samuel
early in the morning, he could easily reach Gibeah in one day.

10:10-11 Only the third sign is minutely described, because it created the greatest public interest. At the outskirts of Gibeah Saul met
the procession of prophets. The Spirit of God came upon him in
power, and he joined them in their prophesying. The purpose here
is not so much to narrate the fulfillment of the sign, but to focus on
the reaction of the locals to the sign.

The people of Gibeah who had known Saul since he was a lad
were shocked by his sudden outburst of energetic prophesying
(singing). They asked two rhetorical questions. The first, **What is this
that has happened to the son of Kish?** presupposes that Saul's previous life was altogether different from that of the prophetic band.
The second question, **Is Saul also among the prophets?** implies that
considerable respect for the band of the prophets already had grown
up among the people. The people could not believe that one so timid
would be part of this group of extrovert prophets![10] The coming of

---

[10]Youngblood (627) thinks the coming of the Spirit authenticated Saul as
Israel's ruler. The neighbors questioned the genuineness of that behavior
and therefore questioned Saul's legitimacy in his new office. The "prophesying," however, was not a sign to the public, but to Saul himself.

the Spirit of God upon Saul may be looked on as the sequel of the divine gift of the new heart bestowed on him earlier that morning when he left Samuel. The questions of the crowd should not be considered as either positive or negative evaluation of either Saul or the prophets. The point is that the people were shocked by the sign, but they did not understand its significance.

10:12 Another man responded to the shock of his fellows by asking, **And who is their father?** This question has been interpreted in a variety of ways. Some think it is a disparaging remark, as if to say, Why is a fine young man like Saul associating with such a disreputable band which has no father, i.e., men who have no family standing? (Mauchline, 100). Others take the term "father" to refer to the leader or interpreter of the prophetic group (Ackroyd, 85). Later Samuel is depicted as standing as head over this or a similar prophetic group (1 Sam 19:20). The question suggests that one is not born a prophet. God's Spirit is what compelled men to join the prophetic band and lift up their voice in persuasive speech and holy song. Understood in this way, this question forms an appropriate retort to the expression of surprise that Saul would be singing with the prophetic choir.

Though Saul was a man of great natural ability, he was not the kind of person the people expected would demonstrate such outgoing spiritual qualities. So this question, **Is Saul also among the prophets?** became a **saying** or proverb in Israel applied probably to the unexpected appearance of any person in a novel character alien to his personality and prior manner of life.

10:13 After Saul ceased **prophesying**, he was more or less on his own (cf. v. 7). He went up to **the high place** (the one mentioned in v. 5?), presumably to offer his prayers and praise to the Lord and to meditate in the solitude of the sanctuary. The secret of Saul's anointing has passed the first test. The people of his home area were unable to comprehend the significance of what they had witnessed.

10:14-16 A strong test of the secrecy of Saul's anointing comes in the form of a direct question from **Saul's uncle**. Commentators are divided on whether this uncle is Abner, Ner or someone else.[11] It is

---

[11]Other views of Saul's "uncle" are (1) a priest and/or a city official who had to answer to the Philistines for law and order (Ahlström, 436); and (2) the Philistine commander at Gibeon (D.R. Ap-Thomas, "Saul's Uncle," *VT* 11 [1961]: 241-245).

not clear whether this conversation took place at the high place or after Saul had gone to his own home in Gibeah — probably the latter. The uncle asked Saul and his servant where they had been. Perhaps he was moved to ask about the trip by the change in the personality of Saul which was now very obvious. Saul told him that when they had not been able to find the donkeys, they had gone to Samuel. The uncle wanted to know what Samuel had said to him. Saul told his uncle that Samuel had assured him that the donkeys had been found. Saul withheld the information about **the kingship,** i.e., the secret arrangements surrounding Saul's anointing as *nāgîd,* because (1) he interpreted Samuel's manner to suggest the matter was to be kept secret for the present, (2) he intended to forestall any ill-advised efforts of his kinsmen to press the issue prematurely, (3) he was demonstrating modesty and humility, and (4) he thereby would leave the fulfillment of Samuel's predictions to the Lord.

3. The Initial Leadership of Saul (10:17-27)

A candidate had been psychologically primed (9:1-24), privately instructed (9:25-27) and anointed (10:1). His heart had been transformed (10:9-11) and his loyalty had been tested. Samuel now put into motion a plan to obtain public support and acclamation for Saul (Eslinger, *Kingship,* 337).

10:17 Samuel convoked the national assembly which had made the request for a king through its representative leaders (1 Sam 8:4). This body was composed of all Israelites of twenty years old and upwards (Num 1:8). He summoned them to **Mizpah**, the spot at which he had led the people to a victory over the Philistines some four decades earlier. He summoned the people **to the LORD**. The Lord's presence may have been symbolized by an altar, or the high priest, wearing on his person the Urim and Thummim.

10:18-19 Samuel delivered a word from the Lord to the assembly. The first person pronoun in v. 18 is emphatic and contrasts with the emphasis on the second person pronoun in v. 19. Samuel reminded the people how God had **brought Israel up out of Egypt**. Over the subsequent years he had brought deliverance to his people, the very thing for which they had requested a king. He had delivered them, not only **from the power of Egypt**, but all the other **kingdoms** which over the years had oppressed the people of God as well.

In spite of Yahweh's past record of mighty deliverances, Israel was now pursuing a course of rebellion. **But you** [emphatic] **have now** (lit., "today") **rejected your God** who continued to save (Heb. participle) them from calamities and distresses (cf. 1 Sam 8:6). This is the first time when Samuel publicly charged the people with rejecting their God by requesting a king (cf. 1 Sam 8:7). Yahweh's deliverances were tied to national repentance, the confession of sins and the purging of idolatry. What the nation really wanted was political independence divorced from spiritual responsibility. **You have said** is literally "you have said unto him."[12] The request made to Samuel for a king was virtually addressed to God himself. No one present objected to Samuel's interpretation of the implication of their request for a king.

Since they had insisted on becoming like all the other nations, he ordered them to present themselves **before the LORD**, i.e., in front of the altar at Mizpah (1 Sam 7:9), or perhaps before the high priest who represented the Lord. The people were to present themselves by their **tribes and clans** (אֲלָפִים, *'ǎlāphîm*), the same word translated "thousands" in other contexts. The term here is equivalent to "clans" in v. 21.[13] In this manner he would point out to them the man God had chosen for their first king. The process was similar to that which was employed to find Achan in Josh 7:17f.

10:20-21 In the person of their elders, each tribe drew near to Samuel. The tribe of Benjamin, presumably last in line because it had descended from the youngest of Jacob's twelve sons, **was chosen**, lit., "was snatched out." This technical term points to the use of the sacred lot. The lot was not viewed as a chance decision, but as a legitimate method of ascertaining the divine will (Prov 16:33).[14] Some think the selection process involved each tribal representative

---

[12]The NIV follows the ancient versions and some Hebrew manuscripts in reading לֹא (*lō'*, no/not) for לוֹ (*lô*, "to him"). There is no necessity for this exchange as the Hebrew *kî* which follows *lô* often has the sense of "no but" as in Ruth 1:10.

[13]Baldwin (93) has this helpful comment: "The word that later meant 'a thousand' had at this early date a less precise meaning. For that reason, numbers based on this sub-unit cannot be used to compute the size of the population, nor indeed of the army."

[14]The sacred lot was used for (1) selecting an attacking force (Judg 20:9f.), (2) the allotment of conquered territory or spoil (Josh 18:10), (3) detecting criminals (Josh 7:14; 1 Sam 14:42), (4) the choice of officers (1 Chr 24:5;

drawing a piece of pottery from a pot. Others think that the selection process was effected by use of the Urim and Thummim of the high priest. Verse 22 certainly seems to point to inquiry by the Urim and Thummim, and the word **further** there suggests the method in the selection of Saul was the same. While it is clear that the Urim ("curses") indicated "yes" and the Thummim ("perfections") indicated "no," the mechanics of the use of this priestly oracle are not known.[15] In any case, the designated king could not be found when the process was over. Foreseeing what would happen, Saul had concealed himself. **Matri** is not mentioned elsewhere.

10:22 They **inquired further of the Lord**, i.e., they asked Samuel or the high priest with his Urim and Thummim for further revelation from God. Their question literally is this: "Is any one else as yet come here?" i.e., had anyone else come besides those who were present before the Lord. Since Saul was not found among them, they wanted to know where they might look for him, whether at home or somewhere else. By this means they learned that Saul had hidden himself among the baggage, i.e., all the wagons and provisions which the people had brought with them. His concealment must have been the result either (1) of modesty or (2) a sudden nervous excitement under the circumstances. Whatever his motives, his hiding in the

---

Luke 1:9; Acts 1:26), (5) the selection of the scapegoat (Lev 16:8,10), and (6) the settlement of disputes generally (Prov 18:18). Kirkpatrick, 1:111.

[15]The Urim and Thummim are mentioned together in Exod 28:30; Lev 8:8; Deut 33:8; Ezra 2:63; Neh 7:65; Urim alone in Num 27:21; 1 Sam 28:6. No mention is made of these objects being made. This has led to the conclusion that (1) they were gems passed down from Patriarchal times; or (2) that they are to be equated with the breastplate of judgment or its jewels. The earliest interpretation is that these stones were on the breastplate of the high priest and that they were capable of shining out to give divine guidance (Josephus, *Ant.* 3.8.9). Modern scholars speculate that they may have consisted of two flat objects. One side of each was called Urim, the other was Thummim. When cast forth from the pouch of the breastplate, the objects had to match up for a definite answer; otherwise the oracle was inconclusive. Others think that two almost identical stones were in the pouch of the breastplate. The high priest simply reached in and pulled one out (1 Sam 14:41). See ZPEB, s.v. "Urim and Thummim" by H.L. Ellison. McCarter (1:250) proposes that Urim means "accursed" and Thummim "acquitted." Klein (140) wonders if there is some significance in the fact that Urim begins with the first letter of the Hebrew alphabet and Thummim with the last.

baggage provided another opportunity for Yahweh to demonstrate his control of the entire procedure and his determination to place his man on the throne.

10:23-24 The people **ran and brought him out.** When Saul emerged from hiding, the people marveled over his height. He was a head taller than any of the others. Samuel presented Saul to the people as Yahweh's **chosen.**[16] Among the surrounding nations the kings were also thought of as chosen by their various gods. There was, however, this difference in Israel. An elect king could also be rejected (1 Sam 15:23-28; 2 Sam 6:21). Samuel pointed out to the people the uniqueness of the height of this man. In respect to his size, there was no other like him among all the people. Physically he was the kind of king Israel desired. They ratified the selection by shouting: **Long live the king!**[17]

10:25 Samuel yet had four items of business to transact. Only after the people had made a public commitment to Saul did Samuel explain **the regulations of the kingship.** God designated the king, but Samuel set forth the principles for the new form of government. These "regulations" (מִשְׁפָּט, *mišpāṭ*) would include (1) the duties of the human king in respect to Yahweh, and (2) the mutual obligations which would govern the relationship between the new king and Yahweh's people. Perhaps the prophet intended from the outset to erect a barrier against all excesses on the part of the king. The custom (*mišpāṭ*) of the king already recited in 8:9-18 was threatened as the penalty of the people's decision to ask for a king. Since they had persisted in their choice, that threat would be carried out.

Second, Samuel **wrote down** the regulations of the kingdom on a scroll. This document was not so much a "constitution" (Eslinger, *Kingship,* 355) or even a "covenant"[18] but a charter defining the position

---

[16]Mettinger (112) points out that in some passages the verb רָאָה (*rā'āh,* "see") is used in the sense "choose" or "appoint." There is then the possibility of interpreting the question in v. 24 to mean: "Do you appoint the one whom the Lord has chosen?" i.e., do you ratify his choice? The formal consent of the people was then expressed by means of the acclamation.

[17]This acclamation occurs eight times in the Old Testament, six of those in connection with the investiture of a king (1 Sam 10:24; 2 Sam 16:16; 1 Kgs 1:25,31,34,39; 2 Kgs 11:12 // 2 Chron 23:11). The exact translation is disputed, but the language certainly recognizes the new king's authority (Mettinger, 133-137).

[18]As, for example, Z. Ben-Barak, "The Mizpah Covenant (I Sam 10:25): The Source of the Israelite Monarchic Covenant," *ZAW* 91 (1979): 30-43.

of the king in relation to Yahweh and to the people. The document probably included a historical prologue containing the very information which now appears in the opening chapters of 1 Samuel. It surely included a legal section based upon what Moses already had written on the subject (Deut 17:14-20).

Third, Samuel **deposited** this document before the Lord, either (1) by the side of the ark of the covenant which was still housed at Kiriath Jearim or (2) in the shrine at Mizpah or (3) in the tabernacle which appears to have been rebuilt about this time (cf. 1 Sam 21). The document was so deposited (1) to preserve it for future reference and (2) that it might serve as a witness against the king and/or people should its provisions be violated. Depositing this document in a holy place recognized that the written words of Samuel possessed divine authority like those of Moses (Deut 31:24-26) and Joshua (Josh 24:26) before him.

Fourth, Samuel then **dismissed the people, each to his own home**, i.e., he sent the people to their homes. It is noteworthy that even after the formal popular ratification of Saul's selection as king, it is *Samuel* who dismissed the assembly. Throughout the remainder of his life, whenever Samuel appeared on the scene, he was the principal person, occupying a position superior to both king and priest. Following this incident, however, Samuel made but few public appearances. He seems to have retired from public service for the most part, and only reappeared during national emergencies.

10:26 The first action of the new monarch was to obey the command of God's representative to return to his home **in Gibeah**.[19] He was escorted by **valiant men**, i.e., those eager to affirm God's choice. These men were volunteering to be a kind of bodyguard for the new king. They were men **whose hearts God had touched**, i.e., they feared God, accepted Saul as God's chosen one, and regarded allegiance to their king as a conscientious duty. Probably most of Saul's earliest supporters were fellow Benjamites.

10:27 Not all enthusiastically rallied to the side of Saul. There were some **troublemakers** (lit., "sons of Belial"), i.e., worthless, good-for-nothing persons as in 1:16; 2:12. This came to be the standard designation for those who were accused of undermining the monarchy (cf. 2 Sam 16:7; 20:1; 23:6). These worthless troublemak-

---

[19]Gibeah was excavated by W.F. Albright. He believed he discovered the remains of what might have been Saul's citadel. Y. Aharoni, *Archaeology*, 191.

ers rejected God's choice for their first king in three ways. First, they openly questioned whether the tall farmer from Benjamin could save them from their enemies. There is more than a touch of contempt in their question. Second, **they despised him** and no doubt showed their disrespect by their comments and body language. In no way had this man distinguished himself either in war or in peace. Furthermore, he came from the tribe of Benjamin, a tribe despised by the others ever since the civil war which had all but decimated that tribe. Third, they brought him no gifts as tokens of their allegiance. Refusing to do so was tantamount to a deliberate and contemptuous rejection of his authority.

In response to this criticism, Saul **kept silent**, lit., "was as one that is deaf," refusing to take notice of their insulting remarks. A strong reaction on his part at the beginning of his reign would have intensified opposition. He would let his deeds silence their criticism. Had he not restrained his anger, a civil war may have been the result.

1 SAMUEL 11

4. The Challenge by the Ammonites (11:1-11)

The time lapse between the public anointing of ch. 10 and the events of ch. 11 is not indicated. Josephus (*Ant.* 6.5.1) sets the time as one month.[1] Even before Saul's selection, an Ammonite attack was threatened (12:12). Probably the actual invasion took place not long after. Ironically, the test of Saul's leadership came, not from the Philistines in the west, but from the Ammonites across the Jordan.

The Attack on Jabesh (11:1-3)

11:1 The Ammonites lived to the east and southeast of the Israelites. They, along with the Moabites, were descendants of Lot (Gen 19:38). While the Moabites were more of a settled people,

---

[1]In the Qumran manuscript 4QSam[a] an extra paragraph introduces this incident, and Josephus reveals that it was part of the text he used. As translated by McCarter (1:198) the addition reads:

> Now Nahash, the king of the Ammonites, had been oppressing the Gadites and the Reubenites grievously, gouging out the right eye of each of them and allowing Israel no deliverer. No men of the Israelites who were across the Jordan remained whose right eye Nahash, king of the Ammonites, had not gouged out. But seven thousand men had escaped from the Ammonites and entered into Jabesh-gilead. About a month later . . . .

Among modern English versions the NRSV alone incorporates this addition in its text of 1 Sam 10:27. Many scholars think this addition was omitted by accident from the MT. For arguments for including this expanded text in the Bible, see F.M. Cross, "New Directions in Dead Sea Research," *BibRev* 1:3 (1985): 26-29. The addition, however, does not appear in the LXX. For arguments against the inclusion of this addition, see Youngblood, 635. See also T. Eves, "One Ammonite Invasion or Two? 1 Sam 10:27–11:2 in the Light of 4QSam[a]," *WTJ* 44 (1982): 308-326; A. Rofé, "The Acts of Nahash According to 4QSam[a]," *IEJ* 32 (1982): 129-133.

their cousins the Ammonites were a fierce marauding tribe. Generally the Ammonites and Moabites were allies against Israel. Twice during the period of the judges they "oppressed Israel," even to the point of crossing the Jordan and occupying Jericho (Judg 3:12-14; 10:6–11:40). Recent evidence has shown that there was actually a Philistine-Ammonite alliance at that time and the two nations were pressing against Israel from both directions.[2]

Though he is not so designated, **Nahash** ("snake"[3]) was the current king of the Ammonites. He was a successor of that king who asserted Ammonite claims over the region of Gilead about eighty years earlier (Judg 11:13). This surely is not the Nahash who showed kindness to David during his wanderings (2 Sam 10:2), but probably his father or grandfather.

Nahash **besieged** (lit., "encamped against") the Israelite outpost of **Jabesh** in the region of Gilead, in the tribal area of Manasseh, almost due east of Mt. Gilboa (MBA, 87). Obviously the town had been reconstructed since it was destroyed in the civil war of Judges 21.[4] Jabesh was located on the Wadi Yabis, about two miles east of the Jordan.

Realizing that they had no chance of successfully resisting the siege, the men of Jabesh expressed willingness **to make a treaty** (lit., "cut for us a covenant") with Nahash. The term covenant (בְּרִית, $b^e rith$) is used here of a solemn agreement between two parties in which the stronger party dictated the terms of a settlement. The weaker party than assumed the status of a servant. A covenant was not the equivalent of total surrender, however, because the stronger party also put himself under sacred obligations.

11:2 Nahash was not willing to settle for this type of submission. He had nothing but contempt for an enemy which would surrender without a fight. He wanted to inflict a humiliating defeat upon the Israelite town, probably in retaliation for the humiliating defeat of the Ammonites by Jephthah (Judg 11). Only if the men of Jabesh

---

[2]G.E. Wright, "Fresh Evidence for the Philistine Story," *BA* 29 (1966): 110-134. Wright shows how the Philistines were also pushing south into the upper Jordan Valley in an attempt to divide Israel for conquest.

[3]According to F.M. Cross, *Nahash* is a shortened form of "good luck." *BibRev* 1:3 (1985): 26.

[4]It is difficult to date the civil war in Judges 21, but it probably occurred shortly after the death of Joshua. If this is the case, Jabesh would have had over three centuries to be rebuilt.

would allow Nahash to **gouge out**, lit., "to scoop or hollow out,"[5] **the right eye** of every man would he be willing to enter into a treaty with them. This was not demanded out of any special spite for the citizens of Jabesh, but rather to bring disgrace on all Israel. The disgrace would be that the other Israelites allowed such a monstrous thing to happen to one of their own cities. In ancient times mutilation was the standard treatment for rebels, enemies of long standing and treaty violators.

Did Nahash actually intend to gouge out the right eyes of the citizens of Jabesh? Some say that he did. Certainly parallels to blinding captives are not lacking (cf. Judg 16:21; 2 Kgs 25:7). Josephus (*Ant.*6.5.1) indicates that Nahash had used this tactic on several cities of the area, and had actually gouged out the eyes of the men there in order to keep them in perpetual servitude. Such maiming would have the practical effect, so Josephus says, of incapacitating these men from ever warring against him again, since in battle a shield would conceal the left eye. Certainly other Scripture attests to the cruelty of the Ammonites (Amos 1:13). The issue here, however, is that of entering into a covenant with the Ammonite king. Nahash would agree to that only on the gory terms stated. In other words, under no conditions would he enter into a covenant which might put him under some kind of obligation to this city. He wanted total surrender in which citizens would be enslaved and everything they owned would be seized.

11:3 When they realized that Nahash was in no mood to negotiate, the elders of Jabesh requested a seven-day reprieve so that they might seek deliverance from other tribes. **Throughout Israel** is literally "in all the borders of Israel." Their intention, as indicated in the next verse, was to go immediately to their new king for help. Nahash granted this request because (1) he was not in a condition to take the town immediately by storm; (2) he believed that the Israelites were in a state of political disarray; and (3) he was arrogantly confident that he was strong enough to deal with any potential threat which the Israelites

---

[5]This verb קָר (*nāqar*) is used in the Qal stem in Prov 30:17 of a bird picking out the eye; and in the Piel stem in Num 16:14 and Judg 16:21 of gouging out the eye. Ahlström (446) references Assyrian inscriptions which refer to a punishment in which eyes were gouged out. In one campaign 14,400 men were given this treatment.

might pose. The men of Jabesh agreed to **surrender** (lit., "go out")[6] after seven days if no help was forthcoming from across the river.

The Actions of Saul (11:4-11)

11:4 The elders had proposed that they would send messengers throughout Israel. Josephus (*Ant.* 6.5.2) indicates that the messengers went to every city. This text, however, reports that the messengers went directly to Gibeah of Saul, a distance of about forty miles. Between Jabesh and the tribe of Benjamin there had been the closest of ties for many years (Judg 21:8-12). Upon hearing of the plight of Jabesh, a city so near and dear to their hearts, the people of Gibeah **all wept aloud**, lit., "lifted up their voice and wept." Yet no one seems to have had any plan by which aid might be rendered to the beleaguered city.

11:5 King Saul had returned from Mizpah to his former work until circumstances called him to royal duties. Since certain citizens vocally opposed his appointment, Saul may have decided not to press his rule until he could prove himself. **Just then** is literally "behold." Returning from the fields, Saul heard the weeping of the people. He inquired about its cause. The people repeated to him what the messengers had said.

11:6 When Saul heard what had transpired at Jabesh, **the Spirit of God came upon him in power**, lit., "rushed upon him." When this happened in 10:10 Saul's personality was changed and he joined the prophetic band in vigorous praise. Here the rushing of the Spirit conveys courage, wisdom, and determination. The decisive action and brilliant military planning by Saul in this situation is described as God-given. Being possessed by the Spirit of God is differentiated from human anger. Yet righteous anger is not incompatible with Spirit empowerment. In fact, here, as in Judg 14:19, anger is presumably a sign of Spirit possession. He **burned** with righteous anger. Disregarding the previous snub he had received from many of his countrymen, Saul knew he needed to move decisively to save the town of Jabesh.

When the people observed that the Spirit had fallen on Saul, the terror of Yahweh fell on them. Normally in holy war accounts the

---

[6]The verb יָצָא (*yāṣā'*) is used of surrender in 2 Kgs 24:12; Isa 36:16; and Jer 38:17.

terror of Yahweh falls upon the enemy (e.g., Gen 35:5; 1 Sam 14:15). Here it is the motivating force which leads Israel to a united response against the Ammonite challenge. In Saul's energetic appeal, the people discerned the power of Yahweh, which inspired fear and motivated them to immediate obedience. They **turned out as one man.** The same Spirit which empowered Saul with courage to assert his leadership over the nation, now laid hold of all the people binding them together as one, filling them with boldness and the mighty confidence that God was with them in this venture (cf. Judg 20:1). Verse 6 is a summary of what happened in respect to the mustering of an army; vv. 7-8 give the details of how that was accomplished.

11:7 In his initial manifestation of righteous anger, Saul slew the (two?) oxen standing before his plow. He hewed them into pieces, probably twelve in number. The verb used here for **cut them into pieces** is used for cutting animals into portions for sacrifice (Lev 1:6; 1 Kgs 18:23) "and this association of thought was doubtless present in the action" (Mauchline, 105). At this point, Saul threw off his role as farmer and took on the task of deliverer (Eslinger, *Kingship,* 366).

Saul then issued his first explicit command as king. He ordered messengers to carry the pieces throughout the tribes of Israel. The chunks of meat were a visual aid to reinforce Saul's first royal edict. If any man failed to report for military duty to follow Saul and Samuel, his oxen would be slaughtered. Saul thus signaled that he would no longer tolerate the passive resistance to his leadership. The threat was moderate in that it did not threaten their persons, but severe as regards their property. Normally the army was assembled by the blowing of a trumpet throughout the land. Saul decided that this dramatic action was necessary on this occasion. Saul's action here is similar to that of the Levite of Judg 19:29, an action which, ironically, had brought the tribes together to attack Gibeah.

The mention of **Samuel** suggests that Saul was still not confident enough in his own authority to order the mobilization of the troops. He knew that many would come just out of respect for the old prophet Samuel. Saul's message put **the terror of the LORD** into the people throughout the land. This is not so much the fear of divine judgment, but the perception that Yahweh was demonstrating his power in the appeal of Saul. This impelled them to immediate obedience. They turned out **as one man,** i.e., the whole population responded. The tribes united behind Saul.

11:8 The Israelite troops assembled **at Bezek** in the tribe of Issachar,[7] about eleven miles west of Jabesh on the west side of the Jordan (MBA, 87). The site was ideal for assembling a large host because (1) it was situated in the plain of Jezreel in open country; (2) it was within a day's march of the besieged city; and (3) it was opposite the ford for crossing the Jordan to Jabesh. There Saul **numbered** his forces. This would involve (1) counting the troops, and (2) organizing them for battle. Here Saul appears as commander-in-chief of the army. Judging from previous mustering, Saul formed his men into units of thousands, hundreds and fifties and appointed officers over each unit.

Some **three hundred thousand**[8] from the northern tribes of Israel and some **thirty thousand** from Judah responded to the summons. The figures are large, but in line with those reported in Judg 20:2 (cf. Num 2:32). Those who regard these figures as inflated explain them by one of two methods. Some resort to the theory of scribal corruption of the numbers, but for this there is no evidence in the MSS. Others suggest that the Hebrew word translated "thousands" does not in all cases have a numeric significance, but means something like "military unit." Thus three hundred military units of uncertain size mustered from Israel, and thirty similar units from Judah. Estimates of their size range from ten or twenty to multiple hundreds. Saul's force was obviously large. This was not the standing army, but a general levy of all able-bodied men.

Why was the contingent from Judah numbered separately? Some see here an indication of the date of the composition of this material, viz., after the division of the kingdom. This, however, is not necessarily the proper conclusion. By this notation the author may have been hinting at three things. First, while helping in this engagement, Judah

---

[7]This Bezek should not be confused with the Bezek of Judg 1:4f. There is this interesting coincidence: At Bezek two tribes united for a great victory over the Canaanites at the beginning of the Judges period; at another Bezek the tribes mustered for an attack which would lead to the defeat of the Ammonites at the beginning of the Israelite monarchy.

[8]Hertzberg (93) labels these numbers "fantasy." He suggests that the number 1,000 has simply been added to the three hundred men with which Gideon defeated the Midianites. The figures in other textual traditions are even higher. The 300,000 becomes 600,000 in the LXX and Old Latin and 700,000 in Josephus (*Ant.* 6.5.3). The 30,000 becomes 70,000 in the LXX, the Old Latin, Josephus and 4QSam[a].

did so as an independent unit. Second, the author may have been suggesting that the rich and prosperous Judah did not really contribute
its fair share to the operation in comparison with the other tribes.[9]
Third, the unity of the nation as portrayed in v. 8 was superficial. Just
beneath the surface the old tribal rivalries were ready to erupt into
full-blown division, as they in fact did after the reign of Solomon.

11:9 The men of Israel, now emboldened by their leader's decisive actions and the national response thereto, sent the messengers
from Jabesh back to assure their fellow citizens that before high
noon the following day they would be **delivered**, lit., "have salvation." A deliverance by noon on the morrow means that the army
marched by night so as to escape detection.

11:10 Now that they were assured that Saul was on his way with
the army, the citizens of Jabesh used deception to lull the
Ammonites into a false sense of security. They promised that the
next day they would **surrender** (lit., "come out to you"), and the
Ammonites could do with them as they pleased. These words have
a hidden double meaning which must have made this deception
especially amusing to later raconteurs. No doubt it was understood
by the Ammonites to mean "come out" in surrender; by the citizens
of Jabesh it meant "come out" in battle. The response from Jabesh
led the attackers to let their guard down.

11:11 Saul organized his army into three divisions so as to attack
the Ammonites from different directions, a strategy earlier employed
by Gideon against the Midianites (Judg 7:16) and by Abimelech (Judg
9:43). He attacked during the last watch of the night (between 2:00
and 6:00 a.m.).[10] Night attacks were very rare in ancient warfare. The
attack was not discovered until the Israelites were already within the
precincts of the Ammonite camp. The enemy was taken totally by
surprise. They must have offered some resistance for the fighting
went on for five or six hours. Finally all three divisions of Saul's army

---

[9]Ten tribes besides Judah (assuming all the tribes participated except the
exempt tribe of Levi) would have contributed an average of 30,000 men
each. Judah should have been able to do much better than that. Jamieson
(160) observes: "The small contingent furnished by Judah suggests that the
disaffection to Saul was strongest in that tribe."

[10]The Israelites divided the night into three watches, the earlier two of
which were "the beginning of watches" (Lam 2:19) which lasted from sunset
until 10 p.m.; and the "middle watch" (Judg 7:19), from 10 p.m. till 2 a.m.

were able to enter into the battle. The enemy was crushed, their army dispersed. The Israelites continued to chase down Ammonites until noon. Surviving Ammonites fled for their lives. No two of them remained together in any sort of organized military unit.

5. General Recognition of Saul (11:12-15)

11:12-13 The Israelites were now quite enthusiastic about Saul's leadership. He had acted decisively and brilliantly in defeating the Ammonites. The people were ready to execute all those who had shown disrespect for Saul at the Mizpah anointing. This demand for the execution of the sons of Belial was legitimate in that they had not only shown disrespect for the king, they had also implicitly slandered Yahweh.

Samuel apparently was with the army during the rescue of Jabesh. The great influence of this prophet among the people is strikingly shown here. In the first flush of Saul's initial victory, they looked to Samuel to punish the men who had dared to question the wisdom of electing Saul as king. Perhaps they looked on Saul primarily as a military leader, and the old prophet and judge as supreme judicial leader.

Saul again asserted his leadership. There is no indication in the text that Samuel regarded this as an intrusion into his area of responsibility. Saul issued the edict that no one would be put to death that day. By this edict Saul (1) assumed the prerogatives of the supreme magistrate and (2) signaled that he was not vindictive.

Saul supports his decree of amnesty by professing **this day the LORD has rescued Israel,** lit., "worked salvation in Israel." The fact of deliverance after the offense was enough to indicate that Yahweh had forgiven those who had maligned his anointed, for the Lord easily could have arranged for those dissidents to have been slain in the battle. This was a day of celebration. Saul's gracious spirit probably helped cement support for his reign among those who were skeptical of his leadership. "Saul began his reign with wise discretion, as well as with heroic valor" (Spence, 337). Saul's heart, as yet unspoiled, was full of humble piety. For all that had been accomplished, he gave Yahweh the credit.

11:14 Samuel wanted to take advantage of the enthusiasm of the people to solidify support for Saul. Since Saul, in his humble frame of mind, would not demand any further affirmations of commitment from the people, Samuel took the initiative. He proposed that the people assemble at the prominent shrine at Gilgal to **reaffirm** (lit., "make new, renew") **the kingship** which had been inaugurated at Mizpah. Everyone would be given the opportunity to express allegiance to the new king. Exactly what ceremonies may have been performed in the reaffirmation of kingship cannot be determined. **Gilgal** is about thirty-eight miles southwest of Jabesh Gilead, about eight miles north of the Dead Sea on the west side of the Jordan (MBA, 87). Gilgal was an appropriate site for such a meeting because here Israel had renewed its covenant with Yahweh in the days of Joshua (Josh 4-5).[11] For emphasis Gilgal is mentioned seven times in vv. 14-15 (four times as שָׁם [šām], "there").[12]

11:15 Samuel's suggestion met with universal approval. **All the people**[13] went to Gilgal in the Jordan valley and **confirmed Saul as king**. Because it was held after the general levy for war, this assembly was probably larger and more representative than the previous one at Mizpah (Kirkpatrick, 1:117). Was Saul anointed again as David was anointed a second time (2 Sam 2:4; 5:3)? The reference to Yahweh's "anointed" would seem to take on added significance if an anointing ceremony had just been concluded. The LXX also preserves the tradition that an anointing did take place at Gilgal. On the other hand, one would think that anointing would have been mentioned had it occurred. The matter must be left open.

Saul was confirmed as king **in the presence of the Lord**. This means that the confirmation ceremony was done before the altar, or

---

[11]Scripture records three fateful meetings between Saul and Samuel at Gilgal: (1) after the Ammonite victory when Saul was confirmed as king (11:14-15), (2) before the campaign against the Philistines when Samuel rebuked Saul for disobedience (13:12-14), and (3) after Saul's victory over the Amalekites when Saul was rejected as king (15:12-30).

[12]KD (211) think the Gilgal here mentioned was not the famous Gilgal in the plains of Jordan, but another town of the same name near Ramah. The argument is that Samuel did not say, "Let us go down," but simply, "Let us go" to Gilgal. If, however, that decision was made on the return trip from Jabesh while the troops were still in the Jordan valley, one would not expect Samuel to say, "Let us go down."

[13]The term עַם ('ām), "people" is used both in reference to the militia summoned to arms, and as the legal and worship assembly. Here the עַם which shortly before had operated as the militia in the battle at Jabesh, was now acting as cultic assembly (Mettinger, 109).

the high priest wearing the Urim and Thummim, or the ark of God.[14] The proceedings there had Yahweh's approval. Saul and all his supporters had a great celebration at Gilgal. They offered up to the Lord **fellowship offerings**. In these offerings a token portion of the animal was burned on the altar and the reminder was eaten by the worshipers in a joyous meal of gratitude. Since fellowship offerings were associated with ratifying the covenant at Sinai (Exod 24:5), some have proposed that here confirming Saul as king involved making a covenant with him or with God. At the very least, the fellowship offerings imply reconciliation between Saul's supporters and his former detractors. The Gilgal meeting represents the third phase of Saul's rise to power, viz., confirmation by public acclamation, following (1) his private anointing by Samuel (10:1); and (2) his choice by lot at Mizpah (10:17-25).

---

[14]Less likely, but not completely impossible, is the suggestion of Jamieson (160) that the tabernacle itself was located at Gilgal at this time.

1 SAMUEL 12

III. SAMUEL'S VALEDICTORY:
RETROSPECT AND PROSPECT (12:1-25)

The assembly at Gilgal marked an important milestone in Israelite history. Consequently 1 Samuel 12 is a watershed chapter in biblical history.[1] This assembly (1) ratified the work of the Mizpah assembly, (2) finally closed the period of the judges, and (3) formally inaugurated the monarchy period. Here Samuel, though he was still to retain his influence and authority as prophet, resigned his office as judge. In so doing he delivered a solemn address to the assembled people. This is one of the speeches made by Israelite leaders which has been used by the biblical Narrator to punctuate the narrative at the close of important epochs. The bulk of ch. 12 (vv. 6-15; 20-25) is sermonic in form. It resembles in many respects the written sermon with which the period of the judges commenced (Judg 2:6-3:6). These passages — one at the beginning and one at the end — serve to explain what happened in the period of the judges from a theological perspective.

A. A TESTIMONY FOR SAMUEL (12:1-5)

12:1-2 The time and place of Samuel's address are not given, but all the indications are that he delivered this speech to the Gilgal assembly of the previous chapter. Samuel began his final speech by reminding Israel that he had **set a king** over them even as they had requested (1 Sam 8:7,9,22). The NIV omits *hinnēh* ("behold") which introduces the initial statement of Samuel. The word connotes that which is unexpected.

---

[1]D. McCarthy, "II Samuel 7 and the Structure of the Deuteronomistic History," *JBL* 84 (1965): 131.

Now (lit., "and/but now") indicates a switch to a new concern separate from the details of installing a king. Samuel points out that the path to monarchy had been followed to its conclusion. **You have a king as your leader** is literally "now behold the king is walking before you." The construction of the clause (*hinnēh* + participle) points to what was happening, and would continue to happen. The metaphor is taken from the position of the shepherd who walked before his flock to guide and guard it. From now on, they must accept Saul's authority on all occasions; he must lead, and they must follow.

When he says **I am old and gray,** Samuel was repeating the elders' own words at Ramah (8:5) which triggered the series of events leading to monarchy. He mentions this to emphasize his long years of service and the wisdom which comes with years of experience. He now would have been about seventy-five years old. Over forty years had passed since the great Mizpah revival when Samuel stepped to the forefront as the leader of Israel.

Samuel's reference to his sons has been interpreted as (1) a way of underscoring his age, i.e., he now had grown sons; (2) a father's way of admitting the painful truth that his sons were not in fact worthy of succeeding him in the office of judge; or (3) a challenge to their dissatisfaction with his sons at least as far as any connivance on his part was concerned. Perhaps a literal rendering of the reference provides a clue to its meaning: "And as for my sons, behold they are with you." The structure of the clause is intended to emphasize the sons. The term "behold" introduces an unexpected occurrence. The sons were now *with* the people, a part of the assembly, not *over* them in leadership capacity. The thought would be either (1) that in response to the criticism of them, Samuel had removed his sons from office; or (2) that in view of the anointing of Saul the people would no longer have to put up with those sons.

Samuel had been their **leader** (lit., "have been walking before you") **from my youth until this day.** The contrast in this verse is between the leadership style and integrity of the new king, which was as yet untested, and that of Samuel whose life had been subject to public scrutiny from his youth. Samuel's public life may be said to have commenced when God first spoke to him in Shiloh (3:11).

12:3 Samuel used *hinnēh* ("behold"), ignored by the NIV, to redirect attention to himself and to introduce a shocking action. In effect he put himself on trial. Samuel wanted to close out his political leadership on a high note. He invited the people to **testify**, lit., "answer," **against** him. They were to be the accusers responding as in a court of law to the formal questions of the judge. This they were to do **before the Lord** (see on 11:15), the supreme heavenly Judge, and **his anointed**, i.e., the king, the supreme judge in the land. The people then must be very careful to answer specifically and honestly. This was the first time when the title "anointed" is publicly applied to the king, though it had been employed before in prophecy (cf. 2:10,35). The title connotes both the honor due the king and the intimate relationship between him and the Lord. Heretofore only priests had been so designated.

By means of five rhetorical questions Samuel affirmed the integrity which he had maintained throughout his years of public leadership. Could any person charge him with theft? Ox and donkey were the most valuable property among an agricultural people, and for this reason they are linked in the tenth commandment (Exod 20:17). Would anyone charge Samuel with oppression?[2] with accepting bribes? If anyone could point to an instance of such abuse of office the old man pledged to make it right. The word **bribe** signifies literally "a covering." It refers to money given by a guilty person to induce the judge to close his eyes to the crime that had been committed (cf. Exod 23:8; Deut 16:19). Samuel's language here contrasts with his description of "the manner (*mišpaṭ*) of the king" in 8:11-17. Kings tended to err in those very areas where Samuel's record was unblemished.

12:4 Though the elders had accused Samuel's sons of unjust dealing (8:3), no one could level a similar charge against Samuel himself. The people readily acknowledged that he had never cheated nor oppressed them nor had he taken any bribe from anyone's hand. His administration had been just and righteous.

12:5 Samuel called the Lord and the king to witness what the people had just stated. Never in the future would they be able to make such accusations against Samuel. With the declaration which the people had made concerning Samuel's judicial labors they had condemned themselves, inasmuch as they thereby had acknowledged on oath that there was no ground for their dissatisfaction with

---

[2]The verb "cheated" (עָשַׁק, *'āšaq*) refers to appropriating another's property by whatever means. "Oppressed" (רָצָה, *rāṣāh*) is a stronger word, and means "to pound or crush in pieces." The two verbs are frequently connected (e.g., Deut 28:33; Amos 4:1).

Samuel's administration. Consequently, they had no good reason for their request for a king. **They said** is literally "he said," apparently viewing Israel as a unit. **He is witness** is literally "a witness."

B. A TESTIMONY FOR THE LORD (12:6-12)

12:6 Here Samuel reminds the people that the witness to his integrity as mediator was Yahweh.[3] He went on to describe Yahweh as the God who **appointed**, lit. "made," Moses and Aaron,[4] i.e., he made them the leaders which they became. The term "made" has nothing to do with physical birth, but relates to the introduction of Moses and Aaron on the stage of history. Creating the office of covenant mediator was the first act of Yahweh as Israel's King. The covenant mediators then **brought your forefathers up out of Egypt**. They took them to Mt. Sinai, and led them in making a covenant binding them to be subjects of their heavenly King. The theocracy began with the Exodus. In the following summary of Israel's history, Yahweh's name is highlighted so as to leave no doubt that he was the ultimate King of Israel.

12:7 Samuel demanded that the people **stand here**, lit., "stand forth," as a criminal about to be condemned is told to stand and face the judge. The figure of a trial (v. 3) was maintained; but the relation of the parties has changed. Samuel was now the accuser, Israel the defendant. He explained that he was about to **confront** them **with evidence** (lit., "that I may enter into judgment with you"), i.e., bring to bear upon them all the authority of his office. The recitation of charges is most solemn and necessarily accurate because it is being done **before the LORD**. What is about to be presented is the evidence of **the righteous acts**, i.e., manifestations of righteousness (cf. Judg 5:11), **performed** [lit., "made"] **by the LORD for you and your fathers**. The **righteous acts** (צִדְקוֹת, *ṣidqôth*) are the benefits

---

[3]There is no verb in the saying of Samuel in this verse. The NIV has supplied words to make sense in English. McCarthy (213f.), however, accepts the MT and designates the nonsentence as "cult invocation" or cry announcing the presence of the Lord on this solemn occasion. For a brief analysis of similar passages, see W.G. Robinson, "Historical Summaries of Biblical History," *EQ* 47, 4 (1975): 195-207.

[4]The rendering "appointed" is not entirely adequate, because parallels of the verb עָשָׂה (*'āśāh*) in this sense where no office is indicated are lacking.

which Yahweh had conferred upon Israel as a result of his covenant faithfulness. The purpose of the following words, then, is to vindicate God's dealings with them against the charge implied in their request for a king, viz., that he had failed to protect them. Samuel regarded both punishments for sin and deliverances from crisis as righteous acts of Yahweh in his covenant with Israel.

12:8 Samuel began his recitation with the bondage in Egypt. Jacob entered Egypt with his family ca. 1877 B.C. Eventually the Egyptians enslaved them. Yahweh effected their deliverance through the covenant mediators — Moses and Aaron — he had sent to Israel. Forty years later the people were able to settle **in this place**, i.e., Canaan, and Gilgal specifically. This one verse summarizes 470 years of Bible history. Here the great things accomplished in the past through covenant mediators is implicitly contrasted with Israel's recent demand to replace the current God-appointed covenant mediator (Samuel) with a king.

12:9 Under the Israelite theocracy the basic obligation of the people was to love the Lord their God with all their heart. This necessitated total abhorrence for idolatry and all the immorality associated with it. Once they came into the land, however, Israel forgot the Lord their God. So God **sold** (i.e., delivered) them into the hands of a series of foreign oppressors. God's abandonment of his people to their enemies is described under the figure of "sale" (cf. Judg 2:14; 3:8; Ps 44:12), just as the deliverance of them is called "redemption" or buying back (Kirkpatrick, 1:119). Under the theocracy unfaithfulness to the Lord was punished by the withdrawal of divine protection for the nation. Samuel mentions (1) Siscra the commander of the army of Hazor[5] who oppressed Israel for twenty years (Judg 4:2-3), (2) the Philistines who had oppressed Israel several times (Judg 3:31; 10:7; 13:1), and (3) the king of Moab (Eglon) who oppressed Israel for eighteen years (Judg 3:12-14).

12:10 In the midst of their suffering, the people cried out to the Lord. They confessed their sins. They admitted that they had served the Baals and the Ashtoreths, the male and female deities worshiped under various names in each Canaanite city (see on 1 Sam 7:3f).

---

[8]Hazor is mentioned as the capital city of the Canaanites in Josh 11:1,10,13, and again as a royal residence in Judg 4:2. Y. Yadin surveys the archaeological discoveries at Hazor. AOTS, 245-263.

They asked God to deliver them from these enemies. They promised to serve the Lord if he would deliver them.

12:11 In response to the prayers of the desperate people, the Lord raised up a series of deliverers four of whom are named: (1) **Jerub-Baal** (Gideon)[6] who delivered Israel from Midianite oppression, (2) **Barak** (lit., "Bedan"),[7] (3) **Jephthah** who routed the Ammonites, and (4) **Samuel**. Following each deliverance the people for a time **lived securely**, lit., "in confidence."

Since the figure of a trial is being employed, the third person reference to Samuel is appropriate[8] for the following reasons: First, "Samuel, the accuser, dissociates himself from Samuel, the savior, who is cited as evidence against his people" (Goldman, 65). Second, in the light of ch. 7, Samuel was certainly justified in placing his own actions on Israel's behalf among Yahweh's "righteous acts." Third, it was necessary, in order to rebuke the Israelites for ingratitude, to point out that Yahweh had not forsaken them, but had continued his deliverances down to the present. The people, then, could not argue that the deliverances of the Lord were a thing of the distant past.

12:12 The rise of Nahash the Ammonite in Transjordan caused the Israelites to ask for a king. This information has not been made explicit previously in the text. There must have been threats of war, if not outright incursions into Israelite territory prior to the attack upon Jabesh Gilead (1 Sam 11). The Lord had been their King (cf. Judg 8:23). He had delivered them from every attack, yet the new enemy

---

[6]The name "Jerub Baal" means "Let Baal contend." This name was given to Gideon for his bold act of piety in destroying an altar of Baal (Judg 6:31f.). Gideon may be mentioned first because (1) his very name challenges apostasy in Israel, (2) he was the most important of the judges, and (3) he specifically refused to accept kingship when it was offered to him (Judg 8:22-23).

[7]The NIV justifies departing from "Bedan" of the mt on the basis of some lxx manuscripts and the Syriac. "Bedan" (בדן) and "Barak" (ברק) are very similar in the older Hebrew script (ﬤﬧﬢ vs. ﬤﬧﬢ). "Bedan" has been taken to be (1) a scribal corruption of "Barak," (2) an alternate name for Barak, (3) the name of a judge not mentioned in the Book of Judges, (4) a shortened form of the name Abdon (Judg 12:13,15), (5) a name of Samson meaning "son of Dan" or as a nickname meaning "corpulent," (6) an alternate name for Jephthah the Gileadite (based on the mention of a Bedan who was a Gileadite in 1 Chr 7:17).

[8]Contra R.P. Smith (209) who thinks a marginal gloss has worked its way into the text at this point. Having Samuel refer to himself already was considered a problem by the Syriac version which reads "Samson."

made them feel that they needed to have an earthly king. In this crisis they had departed from the response pattern of their past history. They said **No** in rejection of the theocratic framework for national defense which had worked so well for so long. As soon as the Ammonites invaded Gilead they had asked for a king **even though the LORD your God was your king,** i.e., had proved himself to be their King repeatedly by sending deliverers to them. As Samuel saw it, their request was incomprehensible unless it be viewed as another example of Israel's stubbornness and spiritual blindness.

C. A TESTIMONY AGAINST ISRAEL (12:13-18)

12:13 Now (= "behold" in Heb.) signals a change in focus. The emphasis in midverse begins to shift from the people's will regarding the king, to Yahweh's. Three steps leading to the present circumstances had taken place. First, they had **chosen** this king. The reference is not to the choice by lot in 10:17ff., but to what had just happened at Gilgal. Now after the victory over Nahash it could be said that Israel had chosen Saul of their own free will. Second, they had **asked** for a king. Though chronologically prior to the previous act, it is mentioned in second place to show that the demand for a king was the strongest act that the people could perform. Third, Yahweh **has set a king over** them. The word **see** (*hinnēh*) emphasizes that this development was unexpected in view of the fact that the request of the people had been an act of hostility to God. This verse sets forth beautifully the kingship as viewed from two perspectives. The people had desired a king, chosen by themselves, to represent the nation in temporal matters; Yahweh had given them a king to represent himself, with authority granted by God and limited by God (R.P. Smith, 210).

12:14 The speech turned more positive and hortatory at this point. Samuel piled up one after the other the conditions of prosperity under the monarchy. They must first **fear the LORD,** i.e., reverence him above all others. Second, they must **serve** the Lord, i.e., render to him public worship. Third, they must **obey** (lit., "hearken to the voice of") the Lord. Fourth, they must not **rebel against his commands,** lit. "his mouth," i.e., they must obey the commands of the Lord in the right spirit and not merely go through the motions. Fifth, all of this is summed up in the requirement that both the people and their king must **follow the LORD your God**, i.e., recognize him as the ultimate King and Shepherd of Israel. As sheep in simple trust follow their shepherd, so Israel and their king must humbly follow wherever the Lord might lead. The word **good** with which the NIV concludes the verse is absent in the Hebrew text. The emotion of the moment may have caused Samuel to break off the sentence, leaving the blessed consequences of their obedience unstated.

12:15 Samuel offered his audience a clear-cut choice. Israel and her king could either be for Yahweh, or against him. He warned of the consequences of national disobedience. Yahweh's mighty **hand**, which had rescued them from their many foes in the past, would be **against them.** The "hand" is a symbol for God's power. The last words of the verse read literally "against you and against your fathers."[9] An ancient Jewish interpretation takes the "fathers" to be a metaphorical reference to their future kings.[10]

12:16-17 Now then (גַּם־עַתָּה, *gam 'attāh*) signals a new stage in the proceedings. Samuel in these verses does four things. First, as in v. 7, he again ordered the people to **stand still**. The Hebrew verb (הִתְיַצְּבוּ, *hithyaṣṣ°bû*) has the meaning "to stand quietly at attention so as to witness a great work of the Lord" (Exod 14:13; 2 Chr 20:17).[11] Second, Samuel asks a question so as to call attention to the time of year. Wheat harvest falls between the middle of May and the middle of June, during the dry season when it rarely rained. Third, Samuel announced what he was about to do and what the results would be. He would call upon Yahweh in prayer to send **thunder** (lit., "voices") and rain. Fourth, Samuel spelled out the purpose of this demonstration. He wanted to leave these people with a supernatural manifestation which would impress upon them how serious their request for a king had been.

---

[9]The conjunction *waw* in the sense of "as," i.e., in a comparative sense, is most frequently placed before whole sentences. KD (215) explain its use here as due to the fact that בַּאֲבֹתֵיכֶם (*ba'ăbōthêkem*) contains the force of an entire sentence. Thus the NIV translation is appropriate.

[10]This view was proposed by D. Kimchi. The relationship of a king to his people is comparable with that of a father to his son. The LXX reads "against you and your king."

[11]In contexts like these the verb יָצַב (*yāṣab*) seems to be a formal expression. The emphasis lies not so much on the physical act of standing as on the psychological attitudes and religious meaning of the act of assembling before the Lord (Eslinger, *Kingship*, 407).

12:18 Samuel **called upon the LORD,** i.e., prayed. The results were as he predicted. The Lord sent **thunder** (lit., "voices") and rain. This caused all the people to stand **in awe** (wonder; amazement) of the Lord and of Samuel. This miracle showed that (1) Israel was still subject to the power of Yahweh; (2) Samuel, because of his closeness to God, was a man to be respected; and (3) they would still need the mediatorial power of Samuel.

D. A FINAL TESTIMONY (12:19-25)

12:19 The direct intervention of Yahweh drove the people to fear and repentance. They asked Samuel to **pray** for them. The request acknowledged a need for Samuel's continuing service as national intercessor (cf. 1 Sam 7:5,8). **Your God** conveys the sense of isolation which the people now felt from God in the light of Samuel's indictment. In the face of this proof of God's displeasure, they actually feared that they might **die** for having rejected the kingship of the Lord. In vv. 4-5 the people had acknowledged Samuel's innocence; here they confessed their own sin. They regarded the thunder and rain as Yahweh's witness against them.

12:20-21 Samuel told the people not to be afraid. Using an emphatic construction in the Hebrew, Samuel said: **You have done all this evil.** They had done evil in asking for a king. That, however, was in the past. The key was to go forward from this point. They should not **turn away** from the Lord, but **serve** him with all their heart. They certainly must stay away from **useless idols**, lit., "emptiness" (Isa 41:29; 44:9). Any object of dependence beyond Yahweh is empty, worthless and ultimately disappointing.

12:22 As bad as their request for a king had been, there was still the possibility of deliverance when necessary. Yahweh would not reject his people **for the sake of his great name**. His reputation was wrapped up in the fate of his people. The nations knew that God had chosen Israel as his people. Were he to abandon them, it would lower his honor in the sight of Gentiles.

12:23 Here Samuel makes two solemn commitments to the people. First, he would not fail them in prayer. He regarded it as a sin if he failed to pray for this people. Though he was retiring from political leadership, he was still God's prophet. Second, Samuel promised that he would continue his teaching ministry. He would instruct them in the way that was good and right. Not only did Samuel faithfully fulfill this commitment on the personal level, through the schools that he founded he made provisions for an abundance of preachers and teachers in the future.

12:24 In his final admonition Samuel repeated the words **fear** and **serve** which were the first two conditions listed in v. 14 for the continued blessing of God upon the monarchy. The basis for this final appeal was either (1) the great sign of rain in harvest time or (2) the many righteous acts by the Lord (v. 7) which stand as the backdrop of this entire passage. They should never forget the great things that the Lord already had done for them as a people. Gratitude for God's past favors encourages continuing faithfulness.

12:25 Samuel gave the people a final warning concerning disobedience. If they persisted in doing what was evil, then both the people and their king would be swept away by some other nation in spite of the prayers which might be offered on their behalf.

1 SAMUEL 13

IV. THE FAILURE IN MONARCHY (13:1–15:35)

The purpose of 1 Sam 13–15 is to document the deterioration of the reign of Saul. Assessed positively, these chapters are the preamble to the rest of 1 Samuel which addresses the theological issue of how it came to be that Israel's kings traced their descent from David, not Saul.[1]

A. SAUL'S INITIAL REBUKE (13:1-15a)

The time lapse between the Gilgal reaffirmation of Saul's reign (11:14-15) and the Gilgal rejection of Saul's dynasty (family) recorded in ch. 13 cannot be determined.

1. Beginning of Hostilities (13:1-7)

13:1 The NRSV has rendered this verse: "Saul was . . . years old when he began to reign; and he reigned . . . and two years over Israel." Notes inform the reader that numbers have dropped out of the text. This verse is viewed as problematic textually and chronologically.[2] According to the majority of scholars, the verse follows the custom of the Israelite historians in giving a statement of the age of the king when he began to reign, and the number of years that his reign lasted. According to this view, the first figure has dropped out of the text or never was there to start with, and the second is

---

[1] D. Jobling, SBN, 6.

[2] If there are textual problems here, they must antedate the LXX, as the MT is represented there. Some Septuagint codices, however, omit the verse entirely.

obviously corrupt. If, however, Saul's age at the commencement of his reign is not present, what has happened to it? Was it deliberately omitted because the "compiler" did not know his age? Has it accidentally dropped out of the text?[3] The NIV follows some Greek manuscripts in conjecturing that Saul was **thirty years old** when he began to reign. Actually *thirty* may be a bit low. Saul already had a son, Jonathan, who commanded a division of the army in the very first years of his reign, and therefore must have been at least twenty, if not older. It would be very unlikely that Saul himself was less than forty at the commencement of his reign.

The second clause in this verse is thought to state the total number of years which Saul reigned (cf. 2 Sam 2:10; 5:4). Here the Hebrew text has what appears to be a partial number, viz., "and two years." There seems, then, to be no other conclusion than that part of the number for the years of Saul's reign has dropped out of the text. The NIV conjectures that Saul reigned **forty-two years**. This conjecture is informed by Acts 13:21 where Saul is said to have reigned, in round numbers, forty years.[4]

Obviously the Narrator is attempting to convey chronological information in this verse. One has to conclude that either his intentions were frustrated by some inept copyist along the way, or that he is to be taken at face value. The verse consists of two clauses, and there is no need to add numbers in either one of them. According to the Jewish scholar David Kimchi,[5] the first clause is lit., "a son of a year was Saul in his reign," i.e., Saul had been king for a year when his rule was confirmed at Gilgal. The events recorded in the two previous chapters are to be assigned to Saul's first year. The second

---

[3]KD (218) opine that the numbers in Hebrew were not written in words, but only in letters that were used as numerals. A single letter, which dropped from the text would remove the age of Saul from this verse. E. Robertson (123) thinks the age of Saul is present, disguised in the word "son" (בֵּן, *bēn*), the consonants of which (ב[2] + נ[50]) = 52.

[4]Josephus (*Ant.* 6.14.9) thought that Saul reigned eighteen years while Samuel was alive, and twenty-two years after his death. This would yield the forty years of Acts. Cf. *Ant.* 10.8.4 where the figure is twenty years. Ahlström (452) contends that Saul's reign would have to have lasted for at least twenty-two years, if not ten years more, in order for him to accomplish everything ascribed to him in the text.

[5]Cited by Goldman, 68.

clause sets forth the length of time between confirmation of kingship at Gilgal and the establishment of a standing army as being
"two years." This reading is incontestable on textual grounds. It
should be read as a circumstantial clause introducing v. 2: "When he
had reigned two years[6] over Israel, then Saul chose for himself," etc.
Such a statement is necessary, else one would conclude that the
selection of the standing army was made from the men who had
accompanied him to Jabesh Gilead and thence to Gilgal.[7]

13:2 How long Saul reigned before he entertained plans of dealing
with the Philistines cannot be determined from the text. It must have
been early in his reign that Saul began to organize a standing army with
which he could defend the land from enemies. As a nucleus he **chose
three thousand men.**[8] Of these, **two thousand** stayed with Saul at

---

[6]Normally in Hebrew numerals from two to ten take the object numbered
in the plural. The numerals eleven and above generally have the object numbered in the singular. The plural *years* (שָׁנִים, *šānîm*) used here would argue
that *two* was the original reading. Cf. GK § 134e. Whereas it is true that "two
years" is usually written (שְׁנָתַיִם, *š°nātayim*), there is nothing syntactically
incorrect about the numeral in the construct preceding the substantive as
here (שְׁתֵּי שָׁנִים, *š°tê šānîm*). See GK§134a. Cf. Judg 11:37f. where "two
months" is written two ways with the numeral in the construct and the
numeral in the absolute in two succeeding verses.

[7]Some think the MT reading "two years" is correct. M. Noth (176-178), for
example, compresses the entire reign of Saul into two years. Saul's reign,
however, must have lasted longer than two years for he could not possibly
have carried on all the wars attributed to him in 14:47 in such a short time.
Others think the "two years" refers to Saul's reign before the Spirit departed
from him, when in God's eyes his reign ceased (Mauchline, 111). E.A.
Niederhiser interprets: Saul spent one year exercising his kingship and two
years being officially anointed king. "One More Proposal for 1 Samuel 13:1,"
HS 20 (1979): 44-46. R. Althann has marshaled evidence from Ugaritic studies to suggest that the verse be viewed as a poetic couplet which mentions
neither Saul's age at his accession, nor the length of his reign. The verse is
merely declaring that early in his reign Saul performed certain actions
detailed in the following verse. His rendering of the verse is: "More than a
year had Saul been reigning, even two years had he been reigning over
Israel." "1 Sam 13:1: A Poetic Couplet," *Biblica* 62 (1981): 241-246. These
interpretations would ignore the supposed analogy in structure to the passages in which both the age of the king at coronation and the duration of his
reign are given. Youngblood (654), however, dismisses as "doomed to failure" any attempt to maintain the integrity of the present Hebrew text.

[8]To raise an army of three thousand men must have been done by con-
scription. This cannot be called a private army.

Micmash about two miles north of Geba.[9] The last thousand was under the command of Jonathan at Gibeah. Jonathan, Saul's son, appears here for the first time. The positioning of these forces suggests that Saul's objective was merely to check any further advance of the Philistines into the hill country. In all probability Saul realized that the Israelites were not ready for a general war against the Philistines. He only wished to force the Philistine outposts to withdraw.

After selecting his force of three thousand, Saul sent the rest of the men **back to their homes.** This assumes that a larger assembly had been held out of which Saul selected his standing army. While this may have been the Gilgal assembly of the previous chapter, in all likelihood another assembly was convoked about two years after the confirmation assembly. In any case, one of Saul's earliest acts after confirmation was to organize a standing army.

13:3 How much time elapsed between vv. 2-3 is not indicated. Perhaps a number of months of stalemate was broken when Jonathan attacked the Philistine **outpost** (נְצִיב, n³ṣîb) **at Geba**. Geba was only about four miles from Gibeah, and for this reason some think that this outpost is the same as the outpost mentioned in 10:5. The text does not indicate whether Jonathan was following his father's orders, or whether he was acting on his own initiative. In any case, the Philistines regarded this as rebellion against them.

Saul sent heralds throughout the cities of Israel to blow the trumpet (שׁוֹפָר, šôphār, i.e., ram's horn) (1) as a warning alarm that general war was imminent and (2) as a summons for troops to gather for the conflict (cf. Judg 3:27; 6:34f.; 2 Sam 20:1). A proclamation accompanied the trumpet blast: **Let the Hebrews hear.** The word **hear** often has the idea of observing, laying to heart what is heard. Some understand the term "Hebrews" in 1 Samuel 13–14 to refer to non-Israelite mercenaries. According to this view Saul was appealing to a "third force" of *apiru* warriors who had previously been serving the Philistines, but were now invited to come over to the Israelite side (Gottwald, 423). In this verse, however, and the following one, "the Hebrews" are obviously the same as "all Israel."[10] The term is

---

[9]Ahlström (438f.) references the excavation of a small fortified site near ancient Micmash dating to the time of Saul. The site had a commanding view in three directions. It was strategically important because it protected the entrance to the hills from the Jordan Valley.

[10]NBD s.v. "Hebrews" by M. G. Kline, 511.

generally used only by foreigners, or in conversation with foreigners. The use of the term here on the lips of an Israelite is unusual.[11] Perhaps Saul used the term sarcastically.

13:4 Through the messengers **all Israel** heard the news that Saul's troops had attacked the Philistine outpost. Though the achievement was actually Jonathan's, yet it belonged to Saul as the commander. The Israelites realized that the attack against Geba would cause Israel to be a **stench** to the Philistines, i.e., they would become offensive to these people who were dominating them. Jonathan's bold attack proved that the Israelites would no longer allow themselves to be oppressed. By means of the trumpet blast and the proclamation, the people were summoned **to join Saul at Gilgal**. Saul withdrew to Gilgal when the Philistines advanced with a large army. There he made preparations for the war of liberation. Gilgal was chosen because (1) the place would recall the victory of Saul over Jabesh Gilead and strengthen Israelite morale, (2) it was a place removed from the central hill-country where the army could be mobilized without danger of immediate Philistine attack, (3) Saul might have hoped for help from the Israelites east of the Jordan, especially from the Jabesh Gilead area, and (4) Saul probably had to abandon the Micmash-Bethel area for the time being.

13:5 The Philistines mobilized their forces for a major invasion of Israel. They had **three thousand chariots.** The MT reads "thirty thousand," a number generally regarded as a copyist's error.[12] The NIV is probably correct in regarding the six thousand פָּרָשִׁים (pārāšîm) as **charioteers** rather than "cavalry." Since two warriors often rode in one chariot, the actual number of chariots would be three thousand.[13] A vast number of infantry accompanied the chari-

---

[11]Baldwin (103) proposes that "Let the Hebrews hear" may have been a Philistine cry meaning "The Hebrews have rebelled!"

[12]This number of war chariots is never found elsewhere either in the Bible or in the literature of the time, not even in the case of nations that were much more powerful than the Philistines. Pharaoh had six hundred chariots (Exod 14:7), Sisera nine hundred (Judg 4:13) and Zerah the Ethiopian three hundred (2 Chr 14:9). Kirkpatrick (1:124) and R.P. Smith (227) opine that the original reading here was "a thousand." The final letter in the word "Israel" served also as the numeral "thirty," and was accidentally repeated before the next word "thousand." Hence "a thousand" chariots became "thirty thousand" chariots in the process of manuscript copying.

[13]Two-man chariots are known from Egypt (ANET, 172, 183-184). Y.

ots. The gathering of the chariots must be understood to be on the Philistine plain. As chariots are not particularly useful in hill-fighting, the strategy of the Philistines must have been one of intimidation. They went up through the western passes and occupied the city of **Micmash east of Beth Aven** ("house of iniquity"),[14] Saul's former headquarters, in the heart of the hills of Benjamin. From Micmash the Philistines commanded the chief approach from Gilgal to the heart of the country.

13:6-7 Verse 6 in the Hebrew is a curious mixture of singulars and plurals which creates a grammatical dissonance. This may be intended to emphasize that individuals were acting independently, but acting in the same way. **When the men of Israel saw** is literally "when a man of Israel (they) saw." **That their situation was critical** is literally "that distress was to him." **And that their army was hard pressed** is literally "because the people [sing.] was hard pressed [sing.]." The idea is that the army was hemmed in and unable to turn in any direction. All the details are not given, so it is hard to reconstruct the course of events. Either (1) the Israelite forces were forced back by the Philistine advance, or (2) Jonathan remained in position with his men while Saul went to Gilgal to gather reinforcements. **They hid themselves** is literally "the people [sing.] hid themselves [pl.]." The Israelites realized that their small army was no match for that Philistine invasion force. Instead of assembling at Gilgal as ordered by their king, most of them fled into hiding in every conceivable hiding place, viz., **in caves and thickets, among the rocks, and in pits[15] and cisterns**.

Again in this verse the issue of the identity of the **Hebrews** surfaces. Verses 6-7 are frequently said to distinguish between *Hebrews* and *Israelites*. Rather two groups of Israelites are being described. Verse 6 refers to those who had been excused from military service

---

Yadin (1:250, 336) has shown that the Philistines and Hittites had three-man chariots.

[14]The name "Beth Aven" is given pejoratively to Bethel by Hosea (4:15; 5:8). A Beth Aven in the vicinity of Ai is distinguished from Bethel in Joshua 7:2, and some think this is the place mentioned here.

[15]The word rendered "pits" occurs elsewhere only in Judg 9:46,49 where the NIV renders it "stronghold." It seems to refer to an excavation or underground chamber. In related languages the word refers to niches for bodies in a sepulchral chamber.

in v. 2b and later hid in the hills west of Jordan. Verse 7 refers to certain Israelites, called *Hebrews*, who had been selected by Saul in v. 2a but afterwards deserted and sought refuge east of the Jordan. See on v. 3. The land of the tribe of **Gad and Gilead**, refers to the area immediately adjacent to the east side of the Jordan. Those who did obey Saul's summons to assemble in Gilgal were terrified at the prospects of facing the Philistines in battle.

2. The Presumption of Saul (13:8-15a)

13:8 Saul waited seven days at Gilgal as Samuel had stipulated (10:8).[16] For some reason Samuel delayed his coming. Perhaps he could not reach Gilgal because the Philistines controlled the major roads. Maybe he was putting Saul to a test. Because of the delay, even the members of the standing army began to desert (scatter). Because he was chosen by Yahweh expressly to deliver Israel out of the hand of the Philistines, Saul was not at liberty to begin the war of independence upon his own authority, but was to wait until duly commissioned to do so by Samuel (Kirkpatrick, 1:125).

13:9 Saul began to worry that the people would abandon him altogether if there were any further delay. He then took matters into his own hand and **offered up the burnt offering**. The definite article points to the fact that the offerings were ready, awaiting Samuel's arrival. In the burnt offering the entire animal (minus the skin) was burned on the altar. This offering symbolized complete consecration to God. The text does not necessarily mean that Saul offered the sacrifice with his own hand, i.e., that he performed the priestly function on this occasion. The cooperation of the priests in performing the duties belonging to them on such an occasion is taken for granted (cf. 2 Sam 24:25; 1 Kgs 3:4; 8:63). The imperative "bring" points in the direction of officiating priests. Ahiah the priest was in fact with the army, apparently (1 Sam 14:3). The burnt offering would entreat God's favor before entering the battle.

13:10 Just as Saul finished offering the burnt offering, and before he had a chance to offer the fellowship offerings, Samuel arrived. Saul

---

[16]Baldwin (104) thinks the reference can hardly be to 1 Sam 10:8, but presupposes a similar instruction given for this occasion also. Another possibility is that Samuel always tried to come within seven days in any time of crisis.

went out **to greet** (lit., "bless") him for he thought that he had complied with the prophet's orders. The reverence which the king, in spite of his disobedience, felt for Samuel is displayed in his public greeting.

13:11-12 Samuel rebuked Saul with a question: **What have you done?** Saul defended his actions. He felt compelled to offer the sacrifice when (1) the men were scattering, (2) Samuel — the "you" is emphatic — did not appear at the set time, and (3) the Philistines were assembling at Micmash (MBA, 88) about ten miles distant for an all-out attack. Thus Saul blames the troops and Samuel himself for his actions. All of Israel's defensive battles were considered holy wars. Sacrifice preceded such battles. Saul was determined to try to expel the Philistines from the land. Before that effort he needed to seek **the Lord's favor** (lit., "make the face of the Lord sweet or pleasant"). He wrongly thought that he needed to offer sacrifice in order to seek Yahweh's favor.[17] Circumstances overcame conscience and commitment to wait and **compelled** Saul to offer the sacrifice. What is clear here is that Saul was more interested in the psychological impact that the sacrificial rituals would have on his troops, than on pleasing God so as to win his favor.

13:13-15a It is hard to pinpoint Saul's fault, but the overriding issue was one of obedience to the Lord.[18] Perhaps this is a case where the obedience was in the letter rather than the spirit (Gordon, 132). Samuel did not bother to answer any of Saul's excuses, but rather rebuked the king in four ways. First, he pronounced Saul's presumptuous sacrifice as **foolish.** To act foolishly is a defect of wisdom, rather than faith or virtue. Second, Saul had not obeyed **the command** that the Lord had given him through Samuel. If he had obeyed God's command, the Lord would have **established your kingdom over Israel for all time.** This means that his sons after him would have continued to reign over Israel in perpetuity. Saul was not doomed from the start (Gordon, 134). Third, now, however, Saul's kingdom would not endure.

---

[17]In the Old Testament there is no clear case where the expression חִלָּה אֶת־פְּנֵי (ḥillāh 'eth-pᵉnê "sought the face of") appears in a context where sacrifice was a necessary accompaniment (Youngblood, 656).

[18]Gunn (39) argues that the instruction in 10:8 is ambiguous with regard to time. Samuel never promised to come within seven days or even on the seventh day. The emphasis could be placed on the "wait until I come" portion of the instructions. Yahweh, through Samuel, required this understanding of the instructions. On Saul's understanding, he had obeyed the directive.

Fourth, the Lord already had sought out Saul's replacement.[19] The man **after his own heart** is clearly David. This phrase does not refer to David's personal piety or virtues of private and personal character. Rather it refers solely to his official fidelity in the service of Yahweh in Israel.[20] From this point of view, David was fully entitled to such a designation because of his ardent zeal and unceasing endeavors in the interests of the true faith. Since David was only thirty at the time of Saul's death, at this time he could only have been a child, if indeed he had even been born. Thus there was time for Saul to repent and seek divine forgiveness.

The man after God's own heart would be appointed **leader** (*nāgîd*, "crown prince") of his people Israel. Samuel speaks here prophetically, but he does not yet know who the king will be. This would happen because Saul had not obeyed the commandment of the Lord.

If Saul waited the seven days, however, why was Samuel upset with him? No hint can be found in the text that Saul was being condemned for usurping to himself the prerogatives of priesthood. The king's fault was a lack of full and confident faith. He was acting as if God, having chosen him for this work, would forsake him in the hour of need. Perhaps Saul did not wait until the *end* of the seventh day. Loosely speaking, he waited seven days. Strictly speaking, however, he had not waited seven *complete* days. The important thing is that he needed the prayers and support of the old prophet of God. Furthermore, he needed Samuel's advice (cf. 10:8). By proceeding with the sacrifice, Saul was indicating that he thought he could make war upon the enemies of his kingdom without the counsel and assistance of God through his prophet. He therefore had acted presumptuously.[21]

---

[19]The verbs here may be prophetic perfects and therefore could be translated: "will seek out" and "will appoint."

[20]McCarter (1:229), followed by Gordon (134), has suggested that the emphasis in this designation is not on any exalted likeness of David to Yahweh, but on the sovereign will of Yahweh who chose David as the instrument of his purpose. The expression "a man after God's own heart" is quoted by Paul in his discourse at Antioch (Acts 13:22). Cf. Ps 89:20.

[21]G.E. Wright ("Fresh Evidence for the Philistine Story," *BA* 29 [1966]: 70-86) speaks of "the Samuel compromise" in which the charismatic savior's (judge's) responsibilities were divided. Saul was assigned the responsibility to lead in battle. Samuel retained the right to authorize holy wars in the name of Yahweh. If this is the case, then Saul was violating the principles of holy war, and Samuel's outrage is understandable.

Twice in vv. 13-14 Samuel asserted that Saul had violated the commandment of the Lord. That this assertion was not contradicted by Saul shows that Saul's actions were an act of overt rebellion against the will of God. Early on Samuel needed to establish once and for all the essential difference between Israel's monarchy and that of the nations.

Samuel did not as yet break off friendly relations with Saul. Perhaps this noble old man still hoped that Saul would recognize the error of his way. From Gilgal Samuel ascended to Gibeah of Benjamin, the home of Saul. What his business was there is not stated.

B. SAUL'S HEROIC SON (13:15b–14:23)

1. The Dire Circumstances of Israel (13:15b-23)

13:15b Saul's plight continued to worsen. When he numbered his troops, he found that he had only six hundred men left **of the people.** That was a small number, but twice the number Gideon used to rout the Midianites (Judg 7:22). These would be the volunteers who joined the standing army during this crisis. The standing army of three thousand men *may* still have been intact. Even so, 3,600 soldiers would not be nearly enough to resist the Philistines effectively.

13:16 The account does not directly mention the return of Saul from Gilgal to the hill country. The MT reads "Geba" (rather than **Gibeah**) of Benjamin, and this was the rendering in earlier editions of the NIV. It seems that the Israelites had taken up their position in Geba (MBA, 88), immediately opposite the Philistines at Micmash less than a mile away. Jonathan most likely had occupied Geba when he attacked the outpost there, and Saul now joined him in anticipation of the Philistine counterattack. Though his disobedience cannot be condoned, Saul was a skillful soldier and a brave man.

13:17-18 The Philistines were sending out **raiding parties** (lit., "the destroyer") throughout central Palestine through the three valleys which radiate from the high country around Micmash. The three raiding parties moved (1) toward the north (Ophrah), (2) toward the northwest (Beth Horon), and toward the southeast, **the borderland** (between Judah and Benjamin) **overlooking the Valley of Zeboim** near Micmash. Saul's army blocked the way to the south. Ophrah was 14.5 miles north of Micmash. Beth Horon was ten miles northwest of Jerusalem. Saul's forces were not able to prevent the

Philistine raids. The tense of the verb **turned,** used three times in the MT, expresses repeated action, indicating that these ravages continued for some time. These raiding parties reveal the strategy of the Philistines. They were attempting either (1) to entice Saul's army to leave its secure positions at Gibeah and Geba or (2) to reduce the land to submission without having to fight a pitched battle.[22]

13:19-22 These verses can be interpreted in two ways. They may be taken to explain why the Israelites were not able to mount a more effective resistance to the Philistine raids; or they may indicate the result of the Philistine raids into the Benjamite territory. The former view would see the general disarmament as a lasting subjugation of a large district in the later years of Samuel's judgeship and the beginning of Saul's reign. The second view would see the disarmament as the temporary result of the present invasion. If the second view is taken, then some period of time — perhaps a year or two — must have elapsed between the events of ch. 13 and the outbreak of the Philistine campaign in ch. 14.

Some interpret v. 21 to mean that the Philistines deported all the blacksmiths. This prevented any serious effort at making weapons in Israel. They had disarmed the Israelites, as far as they had penetrated. While this is a possible interpretation, it should be noted that the text does not say the Philistines deported the blacksmiths. The Philistines knew the secret of smelting iron. The text could be interpreted to say that the Philistines guarded that secret from the Israelites. This prevented the Hebrews from making effective swords or spears.[23]

The situation was so bad that the Israelites had to go down to the Philistines to have their farm implements **sharpened,** lit., "forged." The Philistines charged the Israelites dearly for their services — lit., a *pim*, which is now known to equal **two thirds of a shekel**.[24] The identity of some of the six implements mentioned is uncertain:[25] (1) **plowshares** (BV, "plow point"), (2) **mattocks** (BV, "coulter"), (3) **axes**, and (4) **sickles** (NJPS, "colters"; NASB, "goad"). In v. 21b the NIV takes

---

[22]Hindson (151) suggests that the Philistines made an unwise move by spreading out their forces instead of concentrating them at Micmash.

[23]On the use of iron in Palestine, see James D. Muhly, "How Iron Technology Changed the Ancient World — And Gave the Philistines a Military Edge," *BAR*, 8, 6 (1982): 40-54.

[24]IDB, s.v., "Pim" by O.R. Sellers (4:817f.).

[25]For a typical attempt to identify these implements from an archaeological standpoint, cf. G.E. Wright, "I Samuel 13:19-21," *BA* 6, 2 (1943): 33-36.

the words לִשְׁלֹשׁ (*lišlōš*, lit., "for three") to be a unit of value, viz., **a third of a shekel**. They then supply the words **for sharpening** to make sense of the sentence (cf. NRSV).[26] The reference, however, seems to be to (5) **forks** with three teeth rather than to a second price level (cf. NJPS, "three-pronged forks"). **For repointing** (NRSV; NJPS, "setting"; BV, "sharpening"; NASB, "fix the goad points") (6) **goads**.

Obviously what few soldiers Saul had were not equipped adequately. Only Saul and Jonathan had a sword or spear. The rest of Saul's men were armed with clubs, slings, farming implements and perhaps other weapons made of bronze rather than iron.

13:23 The showdown with the Philistine invaders began when the enemy moved a **detachment** (lit., "outpost") south toward the pass of Micmash. The courage of Saul in facing this force with such a small army of inadequately armed soldiers is to be commended. Between Geba, where Jonathan was stationed, and Micmash there was a **pass**, i.e., deep valley that ran down to the plains of the Jordan. The Philistines had pickets posted on one of the cliffs on the very edge of the valley. From that vantage point they could watch the Israelites in Geba opposite, thus preventing a surprise attack on their camp. The stage was now set for the heroic deed of Jonathan which is narrated in the following chapter.

---

[26]Others think שְׁלֹשׁ קִלְּשׁוֹן (*šᵉlōš qillᵉšôn*, "forks") is a unit of value greater than the *pim* for one would think that sharpening an ax and setting a goad would cost more, not less, than the previously mentioned implements, since they had the potential of being used as weapons of war.

1 SAMUEL 14

Chapter 14 focuses on a battle in the mountainous area around Gibeah and Micmash. The date of this event cannot be determined. It must have been early in the reign of Saul. In spite of a difficult text, this chapter makes sense. The account is quite vivid. In this chapter Saul is depicted, not so much as wicked as foolish and frustrated. His intentions were good, even pious, but he pursued them in self-defeating ways. On the other hand, Jonathan here receives "such marks of divine approval, and such acclaim of the people, as befits a king" (Jobling, SBN, 7f.).

2. The Initiative of Jonathan (14:1-15)

14:1 After some time of inactivity by both armies, Jonathan decided to take matters into his own hands. Without telling his father, he and his armor-bearer decided to attack a Philistine outpost. The young armor-bearer, mentioned some nine times in vv. 1-17, was not merely a servant used to transport weapons. He and Jonathan fought as a team (Klein, 135). No one was aware that Jonathan had left camp. He did not tell his father because (1) Saul would have forbidden such a foolhardy action, (2) secrecy was essential to any chance of success, and (3) perhaps because the plan came to him as an impulse inspired by God.

14:2-3 Saul had set up his force on the **outskirts of Gibeah**, i.e., the part nearest Geba. Here Gibeah seems to denote a district, rather than a city. Saul was camping under **a** (lit., "the") **pomegranate tree**,[1] i.e., the well-known tree at **Migron**. Pomegranate trees

---

[1]The pomegranate was a smallish tree with numerous spreading branches, dark green leaves, occasional thorns, large tough calyxes, and bright red flowers. When fully ripe, the apple-shaped fruit is a mixture of yellow, brown, and maroon in color, and contains multitudinous seeds covered

(רִמּוֹן, *rimmōn*) are common in the state of Israel to this day. Migron
("cliff") is a common name for localities in this mountainous region
(cf. Isa 10:28). With Saul were about **six hundred men**. There was
only the breadth of a ravine between the two enemy forces.

Ahijah the priest was a descendant of Eli who had been dead for
about fifty years. The rebuked King Saul was in the presence of the
representative of the rejected house of Eli.[2] Ahijah was dressed in
the priestly **ephod** indicating that he was there in his official capacity (Lev 8:7f.). Though Saul's position was desperate, it was not hope-
less, not as long as God's priest and the ark (v. 18) were in the camp.
Ahijah is not mentioned in the rest of the Samuel books. Some suppose him to be the same as the high priest Ahimelech, who subsequently was murdered in ch. 22;[3] others think he was Ahimelech's
older brother (KD, 228).

14:4-5 The scene of Jonathan's adventure is here described carefully so that the reader will be able to understand that (1) Jonathan's
efforts were truly heroic, and (2) the valley between Geba and
Micmash was rocky and, in consequence, offered cover and gave
opportunity for a surprise attack. **On each side of the pass** is literally
"between the passages," i.e., ravines running down into the main valley, the great east-west valley known as Suweinit. Jonathan intended
to use these ravines to go down from his high position to the main
valley. On each side of that pass was a **cliff**, lit., "a tooth of a rock."
These two cliffs were given names because they were prominent
landmarks in the area. The southern cliff was called *Seneh* (סֶנֶּה,
"thorny") because of the abundance of blackberry (?) bushes which
grew there. The northern cliff was called *Bozez* (בּוֹצֵץ, "shining" or
"slippery"). The impassable landscape with its high rock formations
made the contemplated undertaking either sheer madness or faith.

14:6-7 Jonathan challenged his armor-bearer to go with him up
the hill against the Philistine outpost with three thoughts. First, the

---

with thin skin and surrounded by red pulp. Some think that a pomegranate
tree would be too low of stature for Saul to erect a tent under its shade.
Therefore, they take the word to be the proper name of a town ("Rimmon")
a little northeast of Gibeah and Micmash (Judg 20:45-47; 21:13).

[2]D. Jobling, "Saul's Fall and Jonathan's Rise: Tradition and Redaction in
1 Sam 14:1-46," *JBL* 95, 3 (1976): 368.

[3]Ahijah means something like "brother" or "friend" of Yahweh.
Ahimelech means "brother of the king" which may be another form of the
same name.

Philistines, unlike most of the peoples of the region, did not practice circumcision. Circumcision was one of the marks of those who stood in a covenant relationship with Yahweh. The epithet **uncircumcised** was one of disgust, a kind of ethnic slur.[4] Jonathan's hope of success was based on the reflection that the Philistines stood in no covenant relationship to Yahweh, as Israel did. The language marks Jonathan's attack an act in a holy war (Mauchline, 116). Second, Jonathan indicated that he was trusting in the Lord for victory. The words **perhaps the LORD will act in our behalf** did not imply doubt, but signified that (1) Jonathan did not presume to dictate to the Lord what he would do, and (2) that he depended, not on his own strength or merit, but on the strength which God supplies. "He protected God's freedom with the word 'perhaps'" (Klein, 136). Third, victory with the Lord did not depend on the numbers who were fighting for the right. Jonathan thought that the Lord might choose to reward their bravery with a victory.

Verse 7 seems to preserve the very words of the young man. It is difficult to render this phrase in English because it is a colloquialism. First, he encouraged Jonathan to **do all that you have in mind**. Second, he urged Jonathan to **go ahead**, lit., "turn yourself." Third, the armor-bearer assured his boss that he was with him **heart and soul**, lit., "I am with you according to your heart," i.e., whatever Jonathan wanted to do, the young armor-bearer was prepared to back him.

14:8-10 Jonathan sought assurance that Yahweh was with him and was guiding him. He determined that if the Philistines wanted to come down the hill to challenge them, they would not advance. Those who have visited the site where this incident occurred have noted the difficulty which the proposed attack presented. Jonathan anticipated being challenged by the Philistine sentries at some point. If the Philistines challenged the two to come up the hill, they would climb the hill and fight them at the top. Such a challenge would indicate that they were overconfident, and even careless in their defense of that hill. They would understand the invitation to come up the

---

[4]This ethnic slur is used elsewhere of Samson's in-laws (Judg 14:3); Goliath (1 Sam 17:26,36); and the Philistines in general (Judg 15:18; 1 Sam 31:4). Archaeological evidence, however, suggests that at least some of the Philistines did adopt the local custom of circumcision. See W.G. Dever, "Further Excavation at Gezer, 1967-71," *BA* 34 (1971): 131.

hill as a sign that the Lord would give them the victory. There was nothing wrong with Jonathan seeking a sign to encourage him in this hazardous undertaking for he did so (1) in the exercise of his calling when fighting not for personal reasons, but the kingdom of God (cf. Judg 7:11), and (2) in the most confident faith that the Lord would deliver and preserve his people. The words **the LORD has given them into our hands** are characteristic of holy war rhetoric.[5]

14:11-12 At some point as they mounted the sides of Bozez, Jonathan and his armor-bearer revealed their position to the Philistines. The Philistines at the top of the cliff mocked them in two ways. First, they hurled at them the pejorative term **Hebrews**. The word in the original text has no definite article as in the NIV. They thought that cowardly Hebrews, like frightened creatures, were **crawling out of the holes they were hiding in**. The Philistines mocked the two by challenging them to **come up to us**. Obviously the words are spoken sarcastically. They regarded the rock face as too steep for anyone to climb. The Philistines boasted **we'll teach you a lesson**, i.e., teach them a few things about warfare. Jonathan was now confident that the Lord would give the victory. He started up the hill with his armor-bearer following close behind.

14:13-14 The ascent up Bozez must have been very difficult. The Philistines could have rolled a single bolder down upon the two men and sent them crashing off the face of the cliff. Owing to (1) the youthful appearance of the two climbers, (2) the overconfidence of the Philistines, and (3) the notion that the cliff would prove too steep to be climbed, the Philistines made no effort to knock the two young men off the cliff. Josephus (*Ant.* 6.6.2) indicates that Jonathan's feat was performed very early in the morning, when the Philistine army was mostly asleep, and some had only recently awakened. It may be that Jonathan and his armor-bearer were hidden from the view of the Philistines as they climbed the rocky slope to the outpost (Mauchline, 116; Hertzberg, 113). Others think the Philistines watched as the two advanced with strange rapidity and were virtually paralyzed by what appeared to be a superhuman feat (Spence, 348).

Jonathan was ready, as soon as he reached the summit, to commence the attack. Caught off guard, the Philistines made but little resistance. It is not clear whether Jonathan struck them down in hand-to-hand fighting or shot down the sentries from a distance with

---

[5]See Josh 6:2; 8:1,7; 10:8,12,19; Judg 11:30,32; 12:3.

arrows. Perhaps the Philistines fell to the ground in fear. In either case, the armor-bearer, who carried his sword, dispatched them. Some **twenty** of the enemy fell before Jonathan and his armor-bearer within the area of about **half an acre**, lit., "within about a half furrow of a yoke of land." The Israelites measured land by the quantity which a yoke of oxen could plow in a day which would be about an acre. "A half furrow of a yoke" would then denote half the distance across an acre field, or about 15-20 yards (Klein, 137). The point is that although the outpost was cut to pieces in a very small area and the Philistines were close to one another, they could not withstand Jonathan's assault.

14:15 The enemy was thrown into panic when the garrison came rushing down the pass with tidings of the attack. Imagined fears and ignorance of what actually had happened caused a situation which the Philistine leaders could not control. Four bodies of men are enumerated. The NIV, rearranging the word order of the original, has three divisions of the whole Philistine army. The true order is as follows: (1) **those in the camp and field**, lit., "those in the camp in the field," i.e., the main army of the Philistines camped in the open country; (2) **all the people** (which the NIV takes as a reference to the entire army) which perhaps denotes the camp-followers; (3) the outpost (sing.) attacked by Jonathan, and (4) **the raiding parties** (lit., "the destroyer") of 13:17f. The notice that **the ground shook** has been taken (1) literally of an earthquake which accompanied the attack of Jonathan, and (2) poetically of the widespread terror and confusion which prevailed among the Philistines. The first explanation is probably correct for two reasons: (1) it is unlikely that the overthrow of a small outpost could by itself account for the widespread panic among the Philistines, and (2) the earthquake and fear of the Lord in other holy war contexts favors this view (cf. 1 Sam 4:5; Amos 8:8; Joel 2:10). The earthquake showed that God was involved in the attack. Thus the panic is said to have been **a panic sent by God**, lit., "a panic of God." Some think the word אֱלֹהִים (*'ĕlōhîm*, "God") here is used to express vastness, and this accounts for the rendering of the KJV, "a very great trembling."

This chapter portrays the sterling qualities of Jonathan, the man who would have followed Saul on the throne, had not Saul forfeited by his presumptuous deeds at Gilgal the hope of dynastic succession.

3. The Complete Victory over the Philistines (14:16-23)

14:16-17 Saul's lookouts in nearby **Gibeah** could see the Philistine **army**, (lit., "multitude") **melting away in all directions**. The verb "melt" (מוּג, *mûg*) is often figurative for being helpless and disorganized through terror (cf. Josh 2:9,24; Isa 14:16). Saul suspected that someone in his army had attacked them. He brought his forces together to see who was not present. He quickly ascertained that Jonathan and his armor-bearer were unaccounted for.

14:18-19 Uncertain what the absence of Jonathan and his armor-bearer meant, Saul ordered Ahijah the priest to bring forward **the ark of God.**[6] Since the defense of the land was a holy war, the ark apparently had been brought from Kiriath Jearim to the battle front. Saul was expecting the priest to inquire of the Lord regarding the nature of the strange movements in the Philistine camp. The parenthetical words (**At that time it was with the Israelites**) cleans up rough Hebrew syntax which reads literally, "for the ark of God was in that day and the sons of Israel." Summoning the ark was probably a preparation for attack. Before the attack, Saul, like Jonathan, wanted God's guidance. For this reason he **was talking to the priest**, no doubt asking him to inquire of the Urim and Thummim which were attached to his breastpiece as to the viability of such an attack. Saul faced momentary indecision whether to risk his small force by leaving his strong position and attacking the great host of what appeared to be panic-stricken soldiers. Perhaps he thought the Philistines might be setting a trap for him.

The tumult in the enemy camp grew greater. Saul knew now that the Philistines were fleeing. Ahijah was told to **withdraw** his hand, i.e., cease making preparations to inquire of the Lord. Conditions in the Philistine camp indicated to this commander plainly enough the will of the Lord. It was time to press the attack.

14:20-22 Saul and his men **assembled** (lit., "were called together") probably by means of sounding the trumpet. In the panic and

---

[6]The LXX has Saul calling for the ephod with its breastpiece which was used in the priestly oracle. The text does not indicate that Saul's intention was to consult the priestly oracle when he summoned the ark. That consultation only occurred after he *talked* with Ahijah. Another possibility is that the "ark" here is not the ark of the covenant which was last mentioned in 1 Sam 7:2 and will not be mentioned again until 2 Sam 6:2, but a special chest which contained the ephod when it was not being worn for oracular functions.

confusion the Philistines mistook friend for foe. They began attacking each other with their swords (cf. Judg 7:22; 2 Chr 20:23).

The **Hebrews** here are either (1) renegade Israelites who had joined the Philistine army, (2) forced levies from districts occupied by the Philistines, or (3) mercenary outlaws who could choose to fight for hire for either side. Having determined that the Israelites were gaining the upper hand, these Hebrews now turned upon their masters. The name "Hebrews" by which these Israelites were known to the Philistines is used to distinguish them from the "Israelites" who had not submitted to their oppressors. Other Israelites who had hidden out in the hill country of Ephraim joined Saul in pursuit of the enemy (cf. the Philistine taunt in v. 11). According to Josephus (*Ant.* 6.6.3), relying on the LXX, the numbers of soldiers in Saul's army swelled at this point to about ten thousand.

14:23 The Lord is given the credit for this victory over the Philistines. The verb **rescued** (יָשַׁע, *yāša'*) is the language of the holy war in which Yahweh delivers his people from oppressors (cf. Exod 14:30; 2 Chr 32:22). The battle pressed on beyond Micmash to the west and beyond **Beth Aven** (see on 13:5). The Israelites charged down the pass of Beth Horon to Aijalon, where the valley begins to open out towards the plain of Philistia. Nothing in the text supports the assertion of Josephus (*Ant.* 6.6.4) that "many ten thousands" of the Philistines were slain in this rout.

C. SAUL'S FOOLISH CURSE (14:24-46)

The contrast between Saul and Jonathan is sharpened in this unit. Here the king appears to be sincere and pious, but at the same time impractical, foolish and frustrated. He had good intentions, but events thwarted them at every turn.

1. Jonathan's Violation (14:24-30)

14:24 In that glorious day of victory over the Philistines there was one dark spot, brought on by the foolishness of Saul. He had bound his army with an oath by reciting before them the words of the curse, and forcing them to shout their consent. No doubt he intended to implement a religiously motivated fast that would energize the men and fill them with holy zeal. The prohibition against eating until the victory was won meant that the soldiers had to dedicate themselves entirely to winning the battle against the uncircumcised Philistines. No wonder the men were **in distress**. This is the same word used of the terror and alarm to which the Israelites were reduced by the Philistine invasion in 13:6. Here the term refers to their weariness and faintness for want of food.

Saul wanted the men to press the battle all day without stopping to eat. The well-being of his men was of no concern to him **until I take vengeance on my enemies.** Saul had personalized the battle. He stands in stark contrast to Joshua who called upon the Lord to stop the sun in the valley of Aijalon "until the nation took vengeance on their enemies" (Josh 10:13). In spite of their physical need, the people faithfully kept the oath throughout the day. In addition to hindering the Israelite pursuit of the enemy, Saul's rash vow also led to (1) an involuntary trespass on the part of Jonathan and (2) (indirectly) to the sin of the people in v. 32.

14:25-30 At one point in the battle, **the entire army**, lit., "all the [people of the] land," entered the woods. In that woods there was **honey on the ground**. When Saul's troops went into the woods, they saw the honey **oozing out**, lit., "and the people entered the woods, and behold a stream of honey." None of the soldiers put his hand to his mouth, i.e., scooped up some honey in his hand so as to taste it, because they feared the oath. That oath which had been laid on them was stronger than their physical desire.

Since he was not in the camp when the Israelite army marched forth, Jonathan had not heard that Saul had bound the soldiers with an oath. Good soldier that he was, Jonathan did not stop to eat, but dipped the tip of his staff into the honey (or honeycomb) and raised it to his lips (cf. Judg 7:5). Instantly his eyes **brightened**, i.e., his physical energies were revived. This is emphasized again in v. 29.

One of the soldiers informed Jonathan of the royal curse. He offered his opinion that the weariness of the troops could be blamed on the ill-advised curse. Thus this common soldier expressed a negative view of Saul's pious oath, a view which was shared by Jonathan.

Jonathan was openly critical of his father: **My father has made trouble for the country**, i.e., he has brought unnecessary hardship upon the people. The "trouble" was the incompleteness of the victory. By the ban Saul had so enfeebled the Israelites that they did not have the strength to follow up the victory over the Philistines.

The soldiers were weak from lack of food. Had they been able to eat a little from the plunder taken from the Philistines, they would have had a greater victory over the enemy. The NIV renders the final clause as a question and thus lessens the force of the statement. It appears to be an indicative as in the NASB, i.e., "for now the slaughter of the Philistines is not very great." Owing to the increasing weariness of the soldiers, but few of the Philistines were overtaken.

2. A Ritual Transgression (14:31-37)

14:31-32 The roads back to Philistia were littered with arms and abandoned booty. By the time the Israelite army reached Aijalon, about twenty miles west of where the battle was first joined, they were exhausted and starved. Aijalon was near the edge of the Philistine plains. The primary objective of clearing the Philistines out of the hill country had now been accomplished. At evening the oath forced upon them by Saul was over. The troops pounced on the Philistine plunder. The enemy had brought live cattle with them as provisions, and the Israelites slaughtered them for food. These livestock were butchered **on the ground** (lit., "slew them to the earth") so that when they were slaughtered the animal fell upon the ground, and remained lying in its blood. They then ate the meat without proper concern for the law which required that all the blood be drained from an animal carcass before it was eaten (Lev 19:26; Deut 12:16). The sin here was twofold: (1) eating in the very place where the blood had been poured out; and (2) eating the meat **together with the blood,** i.e., eating meat from which the blood had not been properly drained.[7]

14:33-34 Someone called Saul's attention to the infraction of God's law: **Look, the men are sinning against the LORD,** i.e., they were in the very act of sinning. This report was made (1) because of the personal scruples of the man doing the reporting, (2) because

---

[7]Hertzberg (116) argues that the preposition עַל (*'al*) can only mean "upon." Had the Narrator meant to say that the men were eating the blood, he would have used the preposition בְּ (*bᵉ*). For the Hebrew preposition עַל, which usually means "upon," in the sense of "together with" see Exod 12:8; Num 9:11; Deut 16:3; and BDB, 755 4c. A prohibition against eating meat "along with" (עַל) blood is found in Lev 19:26, and the practice is condemned in Ezek 33:25.

this man knew that Saul shared his scruples, and (3) because he was afraid that guilt would fall upon the entire army because of this ritual violation. The particular sin as reported to Saul was that the men were **eating meat that has blood in it**, lit., "by eating upon [or along with] the blood." See discussion on v. 32.

The king charged the men with having **broken faith**, i.e., having ignored the principles of their faith. Saul's seriousness in all his dealings with the Lord is clear (1) from the way his men knew he would be concerned about what was taking place, (2) by the rebuke which he administered to the men, and (3) by the provision for them of a suitable place of slaughtering the animals. Saul ordered a large stone rolled over to the spot. The purpose of this stone was to raise up the carcasses of the slaughtered animals from the ground, so that the blood might drain away from them. By this action Saul showed his soldiers how determined he was that the law of Moses be honored.

Subordinates were sent among the men to issue two orders. First, the livestock were to be slaughtered on the great stone so as to allow the blood to properly drain. Second, they must not continue to sin **by eating meat with blood still in it.**[8] The men followed these instructions with the same unquestioning devotion as they had shown to Saul's command to abstain from food throughout the day. Those who slaughtered the oxen cut their throats on that stone. By laying the animal's head on the high stone, the blood oozed out on the ground and sufficient evidence was afforded that the ox or sheep was dead before the men attempted to eat it.

14:35 The altar built by Saul either (1) was the great stone of v. 33, or (2) was built up around it, or (3) was built beside it. Nothing in the Hebrew requires the erection of an altar distinct from that stone. This altar was probably not intended to serve as a place of sacrifice, but simply was a memorial of the presence of God. This **was the first time he had done this,** lit., "as to it he began to build an altar unto Yahweh." This is not a negative comment on Saul's lack of piety. The meaning is that Saul began on that occasion the custom followed later by David (2 Sam 24:25) of erecting memorial altars as the patriarchs had done in old times.

---

[8]The MT uses here the preposition אֶל (*'el*, usually "unto") rather than עַל ("upon" or "along with") as in vv. 32-33. Several manuscripts have עַל also here. The prepositions here appear to be used interchangeably. In all three cases the reference is to the meat along with the blood which adhered to it.

14:36-37 Saul seems to have realized that by putting his men under the curse earlier that day he had prevented the victory from being as decisive as it otherwise might have been. After the men had rested and taken food, in the depth of the night, he proposed that they continue to press the Philistines. To entice the men to this extra effort, Saul suggested that they **plunder** the Philistines **till dawn.** Saul urged his men **not leave one of them alive.** In a holy war the enemy was often put to the ban, i.e., totally wiped out. The men, as weary as they were, rendered the same unquestioning obedience as earlier in the day; Ahijah, however, counseled that the king should first **inquire of God.** He appears to have had doubts whether such a wholesale bloodbath as would surely have resulted from pursuing a dispersed and vanquished enemy, was in accordance with the will of God. No command to exterminate these Philistines had ever been given. Saul then **asked** (same verb used in 10:22) two questions to the high priest regarding the advisability of pressing the pursuit. The Lord, however, did not answer either question through the priestly oracle (cf. 1 Sam 28:6). God in his displeasure had withdrawn his presence and his aid. On the mechanics of the priestly oracle, see on 1 Sam 10:21.

3. A Rash Oath (14:38-44)

14:38-39 From the silence of the priestly oracle, Saul concluded that sin had been committed within the army that day. He called together **the leaders of the army,** lit., "cornerstones of the people" (cf. Judg 20:2), either (1) the elders of the people, or (2) military commanders. Again Saul made a rash vow in the name of Yahweh that, regardless of the sin committed, the offending person would be put to death. To dramatize how serious he was, Saul bombastically added that even if the offender was his son Jonathan he would die. None of the men said a word. They had obeyed their king throughout the day. They had respected his earlier rash vow. Now they listened in terror to these hasty words which condemned to death the young hero by whom God had given victory to Israel that day.

14:40-42 To determine the source of the sin, Saul ordered the troops to stand apart from the royal family. The men reluctantly complied, sensing what was about to take place. The king **prayed** to God for the **right answer,** i.e., an indication of the source of the sin. Then he ordered the priest to cast the lot between the royal family on the one hand, and the rest of the army on the other. Exactly how the lot was cast is not known. It may have involved writing the names of the two options on pieces of pottery and drawing one from a box. Saul must have been shocked to discover by lot that the sin was with himself and Jonathan. **The men were cleared**, lit., "the people escaped." The verb is used in its legal connotation of "went free from condemnation." Their precipitous and ritually objectionable conduct in slaying the animals and eating the meat with the blood had been put right with the Lord. A second lot was cast between the father and son, and the lot indicated Jonathan was guilty.

14:43-44 There was a natural reluctance to rely on the lot alone in a matter involving the death penalty. Saul asked his son to confess his sin (cf. Josh 7:19). Jonathan explained that he had only tasted a dab of honey. The NIV interprets the last words of Jonathan as a question, **And now must I die?** Literally the words are "Behold I, I will die." His words are not a lamentation over his hard fare as the NIV suggests. Rather he confessed his guilt, though involuntary, and expressed his readiness to give his life for his country even in the hour of victory.

Saul swore again that his son would have to die. The king had made an oath which reinforced the second oath to execute the guilty party. Whereas in vv. 39,40,42 Saul referred to Jonathan as **my son**, now he is called simply **Jonathan**. Saul here was speaking as the chief magistrate, not as Jonathan's father. Under God's law, Jonathan's trespass, committed unintentionally, required nothing more than a trespass offering. Under Saul's law Jonathan had to die! Jonathan, the victim of the vow, was as convinced as his father that the vow, though perhaps hastily and rashly made, must be kept. Only the common sense of the people and their innate sense of justice prevented a great tragedy from occurring that day.

Several points yet need to be made regarding this incident. First, what Jonathan did was not wrong in itself, but became so simply on account of the oath with which Saul had forbidden it. He had transgressed *royal law*, not *divine law*. Second, through the inadvertent act of Jonathan a curse unintentionally had been brought upon Israel. Third, when the lot, which had the force of a divine verdict, fell on Jonathan, sentence of death was not thereby pronounced upon him by God. The lot simply made clear that through his transgression of his father's oath, guilt had been brought upon the army. Fourth, the breach of a command issued with a solemn oath, even when it took

place unconsciously, excited the wrath of God, as being a profana-
tion of the divine name. Fifth, Saul had issued the prohibition without divine authority, and had made that unauthorized command
obligatory upon the people by a solemn oath. Thus any guilt for profaning the divine name was as much his as Jonathan's.

4. Saul Overruled by His Troops (14:45-46)

14:45 At that point the troops intervened. First, they expressed
shock that the death of Jonathan, of all people, should be contemplated. "Should **Jonathan** — the emphasis is on the name — **die?**
Second, they called attention to the fact, were it not for Jonathan,
there would have been no victory that day. The victory is regarded
as confirmation that God did not want the death of Jonathan. The
very word **deliverance** (יְשׁוּעָה, $y^e \check{s}\hat{u}'\bar{a}h$) used by the people testifies
that the success of that day was one of God's saving acts. Third, the
troops put their foot down. **Never!** They would not permit Jonathan
to die. Fourth, the troops swore an oath to the effect that they would
not let Jonathan die. The oath of the many, apparently, took precedence over the oath of Saul. Therefore, **not a hair of his head will
fall to the ground.** Fifth, they justified their oath by again making
reference to the events of that day. Jonathan had shown throughout
the day that God had been with him in a special way. He had acted
with God's help (lit., "with God"), i.e., he could only have gained the
victory with God's blessing. It would be morally wrong, and an
offense against common sense and the law of God to condemn what
God had approved. The stand of the army was right and godly. An
oath to commit a crime, in this case the execution of one who had
not committed a capital crime, was an oath to be renounced, and
not a duty to be performed. Thus the men **rescued** (lit., "redeemed")[9] Jonathan. The lesson in all of this is that the manifestation of the will of God in the events of that day took precedence
over the will of the king as manifested in his oath.

---

[9]By the word "redeem" (פָּדָה, $p\bar{a}dah$) the writer means only that Jonathan's
life was spared because of the resolute stand of the troops. There is no hint
here that they (1) paid money to redeem him as in Exod 21:30; Num 3:46-
51; (2) provided an animal substitute for Jonathan as in Exod 13:13,15;
34:20; or (3) offered another man as a substitute as proposed by some (e.g.,
Budde, Ewald, Wellhausen).

14:46 Because of the emotion over the near loss of Jonathan, followed by the mutiny of the troops, Saul had no stomach for further fighting that night. He gave up any thought of pursuing the Philistines. Those of the enemy who survived the battle returned to their own territory. The Israelite purpose of driving the Philistines from the hill country had been achieved.

D. SAUL'S FIRM CONTROL IN THE KINGDOM (14:47-52)

It is not uncommon with biblical historians to find a narrative of major events interrupted with a summary of events or facts such as appears here. What appears in the following verses sounds very much like an excerpt from the royal annals.

1. Plunderers Defeated (14:47-48)

14:47-48 The summary commences with an assertion that **Saul had assumed rule over Israel,** lit., "had captured the kingdom over Israel." The idea is that he overcame the early opposition to his rule (1 Sam 10:27) by his brilliant military campaigns. He is described as a man who was constantly engaged in wars with neighboring peoples. He fought valiantly against the enemies of Israel **on every side**. In war Saul was all that the people had longed for in a king. He was able to gain independence for Israel, and establish the foundations for the vast empire ruled by David and Solomon. **Moab** was the territory immediately to the east of the Dead Sea. **Ammon** occupied the region north of Moab on the fringes of the desert. The campaign against the Ammonites was previously described in chapter 11. **Edom,** formerly called Mt. Seir, was the mountainous area south of the Dead Sea.[10] The Edomites were descendants of Esau, surnamed Edom (Gen 25:30). **Zobah** was a powerful kingdom north of Damascus.[11] The kings of Zobah were apparently independent

---

[10]For an archaeological survey of Transjordan, see N. Glueck, AOTS, 428-452.

[11]Ahlström (445) suggests that Saul's strategy in his wars in Transjordan and against the Arameans was a preparation for his final thrust northwards. He wanted to eliminate Beth-Shan and then conquer the Jezreel Valley and

chiefs.[12] The **Philistines** occupied the coastal plains southwest of Israel. On these nations Saul **inflicted punishment**, lit., "condemned them," i.e., his wars were the proper response to provocations against the people of the Lord.

In dealing with Israel's enemies Saul **fought valiantly** (lit., "acted with power or ability"). He is also credited with defeating the Amalekites (cf. ch. 15) and other marauding desert tribes who **plundered** Israel from time to time. The language used here parallels that of Judg 2:16 where the judges raised up by God are said to have "saved them out of the hands of these raiders." Thus the Narrator stresses that Saul was a deliverer after the order of the earlier judges of Israel. Here, then, is a balanced view of Saul. He failed God and his people in many ways; but at the same time, Saul, like the judges before him, rescued his people from those who harassed them.

2. The Family of Saul (14:49-51)

14:49-50 Saul had four sons (1 Chr 8:33), only three of whom are here named. The son named **Ishvi** is later called Esh-Baal (Ish-Bosheth).[13] The two daughters[14] are named because of the role they will play in the subsequent history (cf. 1 Sam 18:17-21). Apparently the children named here were by Saul's wife Ahinoam of whom nothing further is known. Abinadab may not be mentioned (1) because he was the son of a woman other than Ahinoam, or (2) because he had fallen out of favor with his father, or (3) because his name had accidentally fallen out through some mistake in copying the manuscripts. Saul had at least one concubine, Rizpah (2 Sam 3:7; 21:1-14).

Galilee. This would place the trade routes both to Damascus and Sidon under his control.

[12]By the days of David, Zobah was ruled by a single king Hadadezer, and the accounts of David's wars testify to the power and importance of this kingdom (2 Sam 8:3-10).

[13]Josephus (*Ant.* 6.6.6) suggested that Ishvi was a second name for Abinadab rather than Ish-Bosheth, and in this he has been followed by Kimchi and Kirkpatrick. Most modern scholars accept the identification Ishvi = Ish-Bosheth.

[14]Clines & Eskenazi have edited a vol. of multifaceted essays exploring the role of Michal in the Bible.

His commander was **Abner**[15] who was Saul's cousin. **Ner**, Abner's father, was the son of Abiel,[16] the same as Kish, Saul's father.[17] Thus Saul chose a close relative to lead his troops, a policy later followed by David.

3. The Philistine Struggle (14:52)

14:52 Conflict with the Philistines was ongoing. The terminology **bitter war** (lit., "mighty war") suggests that Saul held his own and more with this powerful enemy throughout his reign. Ongoing hostilities forced Saul to draft into his army every mighty or brave man that he met. No longer could Israel rely on volunteers who took up arms only during crises.

---

[15]The name is spelled here "Abiner," but elsewhere "Abner."

[16]The Hebrew in v. 51 reads lit., "and Kish was the father of Saul; and Ner the father of Abner was the son of Abiel."

[17]Others read the Hebrew text to indicate that Abner was Saul's uncle. This, however, cannot be. The father of both Ner (v. 51) and Kish (1 Sam 9:1) was Abiel. Thus Ner and Kish were brothers, and their sons, Saul and Abner, first cousins. The genealogy of 1 Chr 8:33 and 9:39 which lists Ner as the father of Kish is referring to an earlier Ner in the distant ancestry of Kish who may be referred to in 1 Sam 9:1 as a *Benjamite*.

1 SAMUEL 15

C. SAUL'S FINAL REJECTION (15:1-35)

The interest of this chapter lies in the unfolding of Saul's character. Several years had been passed in successful military operations against troublesome neighbors, and during those years Saul had been left to act in great measure at his own discretion as an independent prince. Now a new test was presented which would clearly reveal Saul's unworthiness to fill the office of the theocratic monarch in Israel.

1. A Divine Commission (15:1-3)

15:1 Two factors compelled Saul to listen to the commission to exterminate the Amalekites. First, Samuel's standing demanded his attention. Without question Saul regarded Samuel as a bona fide prophet and held him in the greatest respect. His standing as a prophet is underscored by the words **I** [emphatic] **am the one the LORD sent**. Samuel had the right to give Saul directives from the Lord because he was the one who had anointed Saul to be the first king of Israel (cf. 1 Sam 10:1). Second, the standing of Saul demanded that he listen to the commission. He was now **king**[1] over God's people Israel. The point of this verse is to make clear that the expedition against Amalek was not the result of Saul's plans, nor the response to a specific historical situation; it was the directive of the Lord through his servant Samuel.

15:2 The commission begins with the formal and solemn messenger formula with which prophets often introduced their utterances: **This is what the LORD Almighty says**, lit., "thus says Yahweh of hosts."

---

[1]Saul is here described for the first time as having been anointed "king" (*melek*); previously the term *nāgîd* ("leader") was used (9:16; 10:1).

This divine title is especially appropriate for the context of the holy war. See comments on 1 Sam 1:3. First, God announced a divine visitation: **I will punish** (lit., "visit"). Here obviously a judgment visitation is envisioned. Second, God named the object of the visitation, viz., **the Amalekites**, a nomadic people inhabiting the wilderness of Sinai and the Negev (Num 13:29). Third, God stated the reason for his judgment visitation against Amalek. They were to be punished because of what they had done to Israel when they came out of Egypt some four centuries earlier. These desert peoples pounced on the stragglers who got behind the main body as they marched toward Mt. Sinai (Exod 17:8-16; Deut. 25:17-19). From that day forward the Amalekites had a continuous record of oppressing other peoples.[2]

15:3 Saul was to **totally destroy**, lit., "place under a ban" (חרם, ḥrm), the Amalekites and everything they possessed. The verb is plural and thus obligates the Israelite troops as well as Saul. Amalek was to be looked upon as accursed. The verb is used seven times in this account, as though to stress by repetition the action which should have been taken. The cup of iniquity of the Amalekites was full. When a country was put under the ban, all living things were killed; spoil was to be burnt, and things indestructible by fire were brought into the treasury of the Lord (cf. Lev. 27:28f.; Deut 13:16ff.). Though Saul had fought against many of Israel's adversaries during his reign (1 Sam 14:47f.), this is the only nation he was to put to the ban. Those who are bothered by the cruelty of this command need to remember that Israel stood in a peculiar relation to the unseen King. This nation was not infrequently used as the visible scourge by which the Supreme Judge punished hopelessly hardened sinners, and deprived them of the power of working evil in this world. Amalek had been weighed in the balance of divine justice and had been found wanting.

2. Failing: Saul's Disobedience (15:4-9)

15:4 Telaim — probably the same as Telem in Josh 15:24 — was about thirty miles south of Hebron near Ziph.[3] First, Saul **summoned**

---

[2]See v. 33. Cf. Num 14:45; Judg 3:13; 6:3.

[3]Others take Telaim as a common noun meaning "lambs." The assembly area would then be the place of "lambs," some open spot, where, at the proper season, the lambs were collected from the wilderness pastures.

(lit., "caused to hear") **the men,** i.e., called up the troops. There he **mustered them,** i.e., organized them for war. He had at his disposal **two hundred thousand foot soldiers** from Israel and **ten thousand men from Judah.**[4] This large force would be necessary in chasing the Amalekites across the sprawling desert. The numbers may be noted in order to indicate that Saul had complete military superiority in this war. He was, therefore, without excuse for failing to carry out the terms of his commission. As in 11:8 the men of Judah are counted separately, perhaps at their own insistence. The number from Judah compared with the hosts of Israel is very small, especially in view of the fact that Judah was the most exposed to the Amalekite raids.

15:5 Saul concentrated on the **city of Amalek,** the location of which is unknown. It was probably no more than a fortified village. There he set up an **ambush** in a nearby **ravine.** In this strategy the enemy would be enticed to attack a small force. When they did so, the rest of the army would come out of hiding to attack them (cf. Josh 8:2; Judg 20:29).

15:6 After he smote the city of Amalek, Saul sent word to the **Kenites** who lived in the same region to separate themselves from the Amalekites so that they would not be destroyed along with the condemned nation during the operations in that area. The Kenites, an offshoot of the Midianites, had shown **kindness**[5] to all the Israelites when they came up out of Egypt. Jethro, Moses' father-in-law belonged to this tribe. The Kenites accompanied the Israelites as far as Jericho (Judg 1:16) and then settled among the Amalekites in the desert to the south of Judah. The Kenites heeded the warning and left the area.

15:7-9 The attack against the Amalekites began at **Havilah.** This must have been some spot lying on the edge of the wilderness to the south of Judah in or near the country of Amalek,[6] to **Shur, to the east**

---

[4]Some attribute the high numbers here, as in 1 Sam 11:8, to a misunderstanding of the word "thousand" (*'eleph*). They affirm that the term denotes a military unit, not a number. Hence in this case Israel supplied two hundred of these military units, and Judah supplied ten.

[5]For an interpretation of the word "kindness" (חֶסֶד, *ḥesed*) as meaning a covenant and as having reference to defensive or nonaggressive alliance between the Israelites and the Kenites, see F.C. Fensham, "Did a Treaty between the Israelites and the Kenites Exist?" *BASOR* 175 (Oct. 1964): 51-54.

[6]In Gen 25:18 Havilah denotes a district in the northeast of Arabia. It is possible that this is the Havilah mentioned here. Driver (123), however,

of Egypt. "Shur" means "wall," and the name may have derived from the wall which defended the northeast frontier of Egypt (Kirkpatrick, 1:142).

Saul interpreted in his own way the instruction of Samuel. He put to the sword **all** the subjects of Agag. How is it then that later in biblical history Amalekites are mentioned again (e.g., 1 Sam 27:8; 30:1; 2 Sam 8:12)? Two answers are possible. First, the "all" may here be restricted, as frequently in Scripture, meaning *all* that fell into his hands, or *all* in that section of Amalek. Second, the text does not say that he slew *all* the Amalekites, but *all* of those who were subject to Agag.[7] Some may have escaped. Saul and the army also spared the best of the livestock.[8] They could not bear to destroy the good animals.

The sparing of Agag may have been motivated by (1) superstition, i.e., avoid executing royalty lest something similar happen to him; (2) economic considerations, i.e., the potential of economic development among the remaining Amalekites (cf. Ahab under similar circumstances, 1 Kgs 20:31-42) ; or (3) pride, i.e., simply that he might show the people his royal captive. Whatever the motive, Saul was guilty of the very sin of Achan in keeping for himself that which had been placed under the ban (Josh 7:20f.).

3. Rejection Pronounced (15:10-35)

Saul's Confusion (15:10-21)

15:10-11 The Lord communicated with Samuel back in Ramah. First, Yahweh announced: **I am grieved that I have made Saul king**. The Hebrew נִחַמְתִּי (*niḥamtî*) does not express any changeableness in

---

points out that this would be a rather remote spot from which to start an attack against Amalek. He suggests that this Havilah is a place in or near the region of Amalek.

[7]Agag is the only Amalekite mentioned by name in the Bible. The name seems to have been an hereditary title, like Pharaoh, for the kings of this people. See Num 24:7.

[8]The word translated **fat calves** (מִשְׁנִים, *mišnîm*) means those who are second in rank or second in age. It has been rendered in most English versions as "fatlings," a rendering which assumes a corruption in the MT and the transposition of two letters which yields שְׁמָנִים (*šᵉmānîm*). The NJPS translation "second born" is probably correct. The young of the second birth had the reputation of being superior to firstlings.

the divine nature, but simply the sorrow of the divine love at the rebellion of sinners (KD, 241).[9] God never changes his purpose. Here, however, God's attitude toward Saul changed. He could no longer use Saul for his purposes, because **he has turned away from me**, lit., "he has turned round from after me."

Whereas for a time he had scrupulously attempted to please Yahweh in even the smallest matters since his rebuke at Gilgal, more recently Saul was indifferent to the Lord. This was his real sin. He had lost the heart of a servant. He wanted to be absolute ruler in Israel. In his public life Saul **has not carried out my instructions,** i.e., he had failed to carry out the total destruction of Amalek. Pride arising from the consciousness of his own strength, led him astray to break the command of God.

Samuel **was troubled**, lit., "it burned to Samuel," i.e., he was angry[10] because (1) Saul's actions had brought grief to God, (2) Saul had disobeyed a simple, unambiguous order, and (3) Samuel feared the worst results respecting the glory of Yahweh and his own prophetic labors. Samuel's anger, however, was mixed with grief (cf. 16:1). Samuel **cried out to the LORD all that night** (cf. 7:8-9; 12:18). He must have been praying (1) for Saul to be forgiven and (2) that the Lord might reverse his judgment against Saul. His prayers, however, were in vain as the following verses demonstrate.

15:12 The next morning, after receiving the revelation from God, Samuel rose up early to go and meet Saul as he returned from battle. He quickly learned two things either before setting out or shortly thereafter. First, he learned that Saul had gone to **Carmel** eight miles south of Hebron. There Saul had set up a **monument** (lit., "hand") **in his own honor**. Here is another proof that the modesty and humility which once characterized Saul now had disappeared. The monument served (1) to commemorate the victory over Amalek, (2) to claim that victory as a personal triumph (which was entirely out of place when he was fulfilling a commission from God), and (3) to remind Judah of the favor he did them by smashing the enemies on their southern border. The monument was erected before Saul went to offer thank offerings to the Lord, and this too indicates the pride and twisted priorities of the king.

---

[9]The Hebrew נָחַם (nāḥam) is variously translated: "it repenteth me" (KJV, ASV); "I regret" (NASB, NRSV, JB, NJPS, NKJV); "I am grieved" (BV).

[10]In the common English versions, Samuel was "wroth" (ASV); "angry" (NRSV); "grieved" (NKJV); "deeply moved" (BV, JB); "distressed" (NJPS).

Second, Samuel learned that from Carmel Saul had headed down into the plain of the Jordan to Gilgal, evidently to offer sacrifices of thanksgiving. It was toward this destination, then, that Samuel traveled. Saul's movements produced the irony that in the same place where his kingdom had been confirmed, it was to be taken from him; and where the warning of the consequences of disobedience had been uttered (13:13f.), the sentence on disobedience was to be pronounced (Kirkpatrick, 1:143).

15:13-14 Samuel finally caught up with Saul at some point along the way to Gilgal. Saul attempted to hide his consciousness of guilt by a feigned friendly welcome: **The LORD bless you!** (cf. Ruth 2:20; Gen 14:19). He then assured the prophet that he had **carried out** (lit., "established") Yahweh's instructions. Saul's words are the exact opposite of those which God had used of him in v. 11. These words are either a piece of bluster or bravado, or they reveal a lack of awareness that he had done wrong, which almost would be incredible.[11] Saul indeed had kept God's commandment in the halfway manner in which men generally obey the Lord, doing that part which is agreeable to themselves, and leaving that part undone which gives them neither pleasure nor profit. Samuel then stripped away the hypocrisy of Saul with two burning questions: **What then is this bleating of sheep in my ears? What is this lowing of cattle that I hear?** "Bleating" and "lowing" describe the normal noise made by sheep and cattle.

15:15 In his response to Samuel's accusatory questions, Saul attempted (1) to shift the blame from himself, and (2) palliate the offense by alleging a good motive. He blamed the presence of the animals on **the soldiers** (lit., "people"). They had spared the best animals with the most laudable intention, viz., to sacrifice them to the Lord *your* God. All the other animals had been destroyed. In his mind he would have fulfilled the terms of his commission by slaughtering the animals in sacrifice just as well as if he had destroyed them in the land of Amalek. Sacrifice and the *ban*, however, were not the

---

[11]Gunn (41-56) argues that here, as in ch 13, there is no failure on Saul's part for which he can be held seriously culpable. Yet Samuel chose to interpret the command in such a way as to make Saul guilty of having disobeyed it. In Gunn's view, Saul was convicted on a technicality. Since he was already destined for rejection, any detailed justification for Saul's condemnation was irrelevant.

same thing. The *ban* was complete destruction, whereas sacrifice usually presupposed a portion for the men as well. The destination of the spoil to the altar was an attempt to conceal the selfishness of the original motive under the cloak of religious zeal.

15:16 Samuel was in no mood for excuses. **Stop!** is literally "leave off." He interrupted Saul's explanation with the announcement of what the Lord had revealed to him **last night**, lit., "this night." "It is plain from this that Samuel had not gone to meet Saul at Carmel, but on receiving information of his movements had proceeded straight to Gilgal, distant from Ramah about fifteen miles" (R.P. Smith, 266). **Tell me, Saul replied** is literally "Speak, they said to him." Apparently the people spoke up and encouraged Samuel to set forth what Yahweh had revealed.

15:17-19 Samuel first addressed Saul's plea that he had given way to the wishes of the people. He was once **small** in his own eyes, i.e., humble. Yet God had raised him up to be head over all the tribes of Israel. Saul had been **anointed** king over Israel. That gave him sufficient authority to deal with any demands of the people. Second, Samuel reviews the terms of the commission which Saul had received from the Lord. He had been sent on a mission of judgment. He was to make war on **those wicked people** (lit., "sinners")[12] until he had wiped them out. The special sin which marked them for punishment was their opposition to the will of God as regards the destiny of his people Israel. Such enemies of Yahweh deserved total destruction. Third, by means of two rhetorical questions, Samuel rebuked the king for his greedy plundering. He and his men had **pounced** (lit., "swooped," i.e., like a bird of prey) **on the plunder,** the material things which once had belonged to the Amalekites. These words imply that Samuel did not believe the reservation of the choice animals was wholly for the purposes of sacrifice. By sparing the animals they had done **evil in the eyes of the Lord.** While the king tried to distinguish between what the troops did and what he himself had done, Samuel's accusation put Saul at the center of the responsibility.

15:20-21 Saul continued to affirm his innocence.[13] In his own eyes, he had fulfilled the command of God in its essentials. (1) He had gone

---

[12]The same term (חַטָּאִים, *ḥaṭṭā'îm*) is also used of the citizens of Sodom in Gen 13:13 where the NIV renders "*sinning . . . against the Lord.*"

[13]Saul's response to Samuel begins with אֲשֶׁר (*'ăšer*) which the NIV has rendered "but." The word more appropriately would be rendered "in that" or

on the mission which Yahweh **assigned**. Destruction of Amalek and seizure of their possessions was not some grand scheme conceived in the palace. (2) He had completely destroyed the Amalekites. The presence of King Agag proved in Saul's mind that he had in fact destroyed the Amalekites, for what army would permit its king to fall captive? (3) Furthermore, he argues, the soldiers only had taken **the best of what was devoted to God** as the first-fruits for sacrifice. They were not seeking self-gain from the spoil. (4) His intention had been **to sacrifice them to the LORD your God at Gilgal.** The words imply that Samuel should be pleased with the victorious army rendering public homage to the Deity whose prophet he was.

Saul's Condemnation (15:22-31)

15:22 Samuel refused to debate Saul on the meaning of the ban. He responded with a classic statement of the prophetic position regarding sacrifice. Samuel put a stop to any further excuses, first, by raising a question: **Does the LORD delight in burnt offerings and sacrifices as much as in obeying the voice of the LORD?** In the **burnt offering** (עֹלָה, *'ōlāh*) the whole animal went up in smoke; the worshipers had no share in the sacrifice. In **sacrifices** the worshiper in some cases ate a portion of the offering. Both types of offerings are here contrasted with obedience. Second, Samuel responded to Saul with an assertion: **To obey is better than sacrifice, and to heed is better than the fat of rams.** Samuel here was not rejecting sacrifices as worthless; nor was he saying that God took no delight in sacrificial offerings. He simply made a comparison between sacrifice on the one hand and obedience to a command of God on the other. Samuel affirmed the superiority of the latter. It therefore follows that sacrifice without an obedient heart is regarded by the Lord as worthless, in fact displeasing to God (Ps 50:8ff.; Isa 1:11ff.; 66:3; Jer 6:20). **The fat of rams** refers to the fat portions around the entrails and kidneys, and the fat tail. All such fat belonged to Yahweh (Lev 3:16-17; 7:23-25) because it was viewed as the choicest part of the animal. As such it was burned upon the altar.

"because." Verses 20-21 are not merely a repetition of arguments supporting Saul's innocence, but a protest that Samuel could accuse him of disobedience in view of the overwhelming evidence that he had carried out the Lord's command with the purest of motives. A paraphrase of the thought would be this: "Because I have obeyed you, do you reproach me?"

15:23 Having established that obedience to God's commands is more important to him than religious ceremonies, Samuel describes the essence of disobedience. **Rebellion** against God's word and **arrogance** are here essentially synonymous in meaning. Saul presumptuously had arrogated to himself the right to decide how far he should fulfill the divine instructions. **The sin of divination** is the attempt to find out what will happen in the future by means of some material object. It recognizes supernatural powers distinct from God. Here there seems to be an allusion to Saul's zeal in abolishing the practice of witchcraft (1 Sam 28:3). Samuel charges him with being no less guilty than those whom he had been so eager to condemn (Kirkpatrick, 1:145).

Arrogance like the evil of idolatry is literally "emptiness along with teraphim is arrogance." "Emptiness" or "nothingness" (אָוֶן, '*āwen*) is a word used in the prophets for idolatry (Hos 12:11; Isa 66:3). "Teraphim" were domestic and oracular deities (Gen 31:19; Zech 10:2). All conscious disobedience is actually idolatry, because it makes self-will into a deity with more authority than the Creator. Opposition to the word of God is like idolatry because the god of self has usurped God's place. Because Saul had **rejected the word of the Lord,** the Lord had now **rejected** him as the king of Israel. Henceforth Saul reigns only as a temporal king, not as the royal representative of the King of kings.

15:24-25 Saul apparently still did not realize the seriousness of the situation. His only concern seems to have been to keep the breach between Samuel and himself from becoming a public scandal and weakening his authority. First, he admits that he had **sinned** (lit., "missed the mark"). His sin was not that he thought sacrifice was greater than obedience. He was judicially cut off for his disobedience of a positive command, which as a theocratic king, it was his duty to have executed. Second, Saul admitted that he had **violated** (lit., "transgressed") both the command of the Lord, and of the Lord's messenger. Third, he acknowledged his weakness, perhaps in an effort to make his disobedience seem less significant: **I was afraid of the people.** This shows that the consciousness of his guilt did not go very deep. The only excuse he could put forth indicated his unfitness for the leadership post to which God had called him. Fourth, Saul begged for forgiveness. Fifth, he wanted Samuel to come back to Gilgal with him so that he might worship the Lord with Samuel's approval. Saul wanted to **worship,** lit., "pray to," Yahweh. He was asking for Samuel's assistance in intercession for forgiveness. Yet v. 30 will suggest a more sinister motive for his request.

15:26-29 Samuel declined the king's request. He merely repeated the sentence of rejection. As Samuel turned to leave, **Saul**[14] **caught hold** of the edge of his robe and accidentally tore it.[15] The **robe** here (מְעִיל, *mᵉʿîl*) was a garment fitted rather closely to the body. What Saul took hold of was **the hem of the robe**, the outer border, probably at Samuel's neck or shoulder, as he turned to go away. Judging from extrabiblical parallels, grasping the hem was another final act of supplication on Saul's part.[16] Samuel used the torn robe as an object lesson. The Lord now had torn the kingdom out of Saul's hand and had given it to another. One **of your neighbors** indicates that Samuel at this point did not know who Saul's successor would be. The word "neighbor" in Hebrew is used in a very indefinite manner, and here means "someone, whoever it may be." Samuel was confident that Saul's successor would be a better man in respect to discharging his duties than Saul had been. Here, as in 13:14, there is a reference to the better king who was to come. Furthermore, Samuel declared, the **Glory of Israel,** i.e., God, does not **lie**, i.e., by giving a wrong judgment. This title for God is found only here. The term "glory" (נֵצַח, *nēṣaḥ*) signifies constancy, endurance, and then confidence, because a person can trust what is constant. Yahweh does not **change his mind**, i.e., by modifying, on appeal, a harsh judgment (Num 23:19). The Lord will not rescind his decree concerning the kingship.

Commenting on the relationship between v. 29 and v. 11, Kirkpatrick (1:146) has these helpful words: "It is precisely because God

---

[14]The name "Saul" is not in the MT, but it is supplied by 4QSamª and LXX.

[15]The Hebrew text does not make clear whether it was Saul who tore Samuel's garment, or vice versa. Some rabbis opt for the second interpretation, citing 1 Kgs 11:30 as a parallel. Mauchline (125) offers a threefold argument against this view: (1) That Samuel tore off a bit of the skirt of Saul's robe would have represented symbolically the loss of a fragment of his kingdom (cf. 1 Kgs 11:30-33). (2) Why would Samuel have waited until he had turned to go away before doing this symbolical act? (3) If Samuel is subject in the second clause, the final verb ought to be active ("and he tore it"), but it is passive.

[16]R.A. Brauner "'To Grasp the Hem,' and 1 Samuel 15:27," *JANESCU* 6 (1974): 35-38.

is unchangeable, that in His dealing with men He must seem to change His action as they change their conduct. This is one aspect of the great problem which runs through all religion, how human free-will can coexist with the Divine Sovereignty. Scripture is content to state both sides of the question, and leave conscience rather than reason to reconcile them."

15:30-31 Again Saul confesses his sin, but this time he offers no excuses. He does not ask for forgiveness. He begs Samuel to **honor** him before the elders of Israel by accompanying him to the public worship services at Gilgal. Saul is desperately afraid of losing public support. Having made his point most forcefully, Samuel went back to Gilgal with Saul, not to worship along with him, but for two reasons: (1) to help preserve the outward order until a new king had been selected by the Lord and (2) to execute the ban upon Agag whom Saul had spared. Samuel recognized that Saul would retain his office for some time. For the sake of his country, Samuel took no actions which would undercut Saul in the eyes of the leaders or people.

Execution of Agag (15:32-33)

15:32-33 Following the worship service, Samuel called for Agag to be brought forth. Agag came **confidently**[17] toward Samuel. The Amalekite was **thinking** (lit., "said") **surely the bitterness of death is past.** His words were a kind of protest against his life being taken so long after the battle and at such a distance removed from the battlefield. The prophet pronounced sentence upon him. Agag's sword had **made women childless**. Agag had carried on his raids and wars with great cruelty. He therefore had forfeited his life. His **mother** would be **childless among women**. Here it is clear that Agag was executed for crimes he personally committed against many people over the years.

Samuel then **put Agag to death**[18] **before the LORD**, i.e., before his altar. The verb here is in the Piel, and therefore could mean not so

---

[17]The Hebrew term מַעֲדַנּוֹת (ma'ădannōth) is obscure. In the standard English versions it is rendered "cheerfully" (ASV, NASB, BV); "haltingly" (NRSV); "cautiously" (NKJV); "reluctantly" (JB); "with faltering steps" (NJPS). On the basis of the use of the word in Job 38:31, some have proposed that Agag came "in fetters." For discussion of the translation problem here, see R. Bratcher, "How Did Agag Meet Samuel? (1 Sam 15:32)," *BT* 22, 4 (1971): 167-168.

[18]The root שָׁסַף (šāsaph) appears only here. BDB gives the meaning "hew in pieces" which is based on the ancient versions and the context. The word probably only means something like "he executed" him.

much that Samuel personally put Agag to death, as that he commanded that it be done. In any case, Samuel was acting as God's agent of judgment on this wicked man. The Supreme Judge already had sentenced the king of the Amalekites to death!

Separation from Saul (15:34-35)

15:34-35 Samuel left Gilgal for Ramah in the mountains. Saul returned to his home in Gibeah. Until the day Samuel died he did not ever go to see Saul again in the capacity of a spiritual advisor.[19] Saul was no more Yahweh's representative, and consequently Samuel no more came to him, bringing messages and commands, and giving him counsel and guidance from God. Yet Samuel **mourned** for Saul. He had no personal grudge against the man. Saul had accomplished so much that was good. Since the Lord, however, had rejected Saul unconditionally, Samuel felt that he was precluded from making any further intercession for Saul's reinstatement in God's favor. So also did the Lord grieve over what had become of the reign of the first king of his people (cf. v. 11). This is the saddest line in the whole history of Saul (Klein, 155). For Saul this was probably the beginning of that darkening of his mind which led to depression, jealousy, and violent and irrational behavior in the years to come.

---

[19]Saul did see Samuel again in 1 Sam 19:24. Here, however, (1) Saul went to Samuel's dwelling to seize David, not to consult with Samuel; and (2) Saul had been overwhelmed by the Spirit, and consequently did not have all his mental faculties functioning normally.

1 SAMUEL 16

F. THE "CALL" OF DAVID (16:1-13)

Shortly after the rejection of Saul, Samuel was sent by the Lord to Bethlehem secretly to anoint his successor. The year would be ca. 1029 B.C. David would be about eleven years old at the time. During the next year or so David served as a musician in Saul's court. This unit is marked off by the phrase "horn with/of oil" in vv. 1 and 13.

1. Samuel's Trip to Bethlehem (16:1-5)

16:1 King Saul had been rejected, but Yahweh took action to see to it that the kingdom itself did not go down with its king. First, Yahweh rebuked Samuel. He had prolonged his grief almost to a sinful extent. By means of a rhetorical question, God indicated to his prophet that the time for mourning was over. It was time to anoint a new king. Second, Yahweh gave Samuel a commission. He was to take an animal **horn** full of olive **oil** (lit., "the oil") and go to the house of Jesse in Bethlehem. The genealogy of **Jesse** is traced to Boaz (Ruth 4:18-21). Jesse seems to have been a man of note in the village of Bethlehem, esteemed for his piety and general worth of character. Third, Yahweh gave Samuel an explanation. He declared: **I have chosen** (lit., "I have seen") **one of his sons to be king**.[1] These words intimate a difference between this and the former king. Saul was given to the people because he was the type of man they would have as their king. The new king came from that tribe which had been promised preeminence since the days of Jacob (Gen 49:10).

16:2-3 Always before, even in moments when he asserted his self-will, Saul had paid honor to Samuel. That was no longer the case. Saul's unfortunate mental malady must have made rapid progress.

---

[1]For "see" meaning "select," compare here v. 17 and Gen 41:33; 2 Kgs 10:3.

Samuel feared for his life for these reasons: (1) Saul was actually king, and the anointing of another in his stead would be regarded as an act of open treason. (2) Bethlehem was not in Samuel's normal area of activity, which was in Benjamin and southern Ephraim. (3) The trip from Ramah to Bethlehem would take Samuel through Gibeah, Saul's capital. (4) Undoubtedly Saul's agents were watching his every move because any future king would most assuredly be anointed by this old and famous prophet.

The Lord instructed the prophet to take a **heifer** (cf. Deut 21:3-4) with him to Bethlehem. This was intended to give to Samuel's visit to Bethlehem a religious, and not a political, significance. He should announce a public sacrifice and invite Jesse to it. At that point God would show him what to do. Samuel was not told to lie by the Lord. He did in fact conduct a public sacrifice in Bethlehem. He was to tell the truth, but not the entire truth which he was not bound to tell.

16:4 Bethlehem (earlier called Ephrath, Gen 48:7) was located about five miles south of Jerusalem, about ten miles from Ramah. As Samuel entered the city he was met by the city elders. The local leaders **trembled** when they met Samuel, i.e., they were apprehensive[2] that his arrival was occasioned by some extraordinary reason which might portend evil for their village. One of the elders (the verb is sing.) speaking for the rest asked if Samuel had **come in peace.** Perhaps Samuel's visits were often made with the view of rebuking sin and correcting abuses. Certainly they did not wish to do anything which might be interpreted by the king as aiding his enemy.

16:5 Samuel indicated that he had **come in peace** to conduct a **sacrifice to the Lord.** He invited the elders to join him at the sacrifice. First, however, they must **consecrate** themselves. This probably involved the washing of the body and clothing, the outward symbols of spiritual preparation (Gen 35:2; Exod 19:10ff.). Samuel himself supervised the consecration of Jesse's family. This gave him the opportunity of a private interview with them in Jesse's house. There was nothing unusual in his sanctifying Jesse and his sons. This was evidently the principal family of the village and they would be the most fit persons to assist in preparing for, and then carrying out, the sacrificial rites.

---

[2]Goldman (94) argues that in this context the verb חָרַד (ḥārad) is used to describe eager or excited motion, not the trembling of fear.

2. David's Anointing (16:6-13)

16:6-7 The exact time and place of the anointing of David is not clear. It may have taken place (1) before the sacrifice, or (2) after the sacrifice and before the accompanying meal. The best reconstruction is that following the formal sacrifice, Samuel retired to the house of Jesse to await the preparation of the meal. It was there, at the house of Jesse, that Samuel saw the eldest son Eliab (Elihu in 1 Chr 27:18) and **thought** (lit., "said") that this must be **the Lord's anointed.**[3] Samuel uses the word "anointed" only in his verdict on Eliab, but he must have said this to himself. The Lord, however, told Samuel not to **consider** (lit., "look on") the man's **appearance** *or* **his height**, i.e., the very things which had made Saul stand out. Men look on **the outward appearance** (lit., "the eyes," symbol of the outward form), but God looks on the heart. Here again Yahweh's sovereign freedom is clearly expressed by his choosing the youngest of Jesse's sons.

16:8-10 Then the other sons of Jesse passed before Samuel: Abinadab, Shammah[4] and four others who are unnamed. These **seven**, plus David, were the eight sons of Jesse.[5] Three times in these verses Samuel **said** that the Lord had not chosen these sons of Jesse. The verb can sometimes be equivalent to the English verb "think," and thus Samuel might have been saying to himself that the Lord had not chosen these sons. Verse 10, however, indicates that he **said to him** (lit., "to Jesse"), indicating that Samuel must have been verbally expressing the nonchoice of these sons.

16:11 So the prophet asked if he had seen all the **sons** (lit., "lads"). It so happened that the youngest of Jesse's sons was tending sheep. Samuel instructed Jesse to send for David. They would not **sit down** (lit., "we will not surround," i.e., the table)[6] to the sacrificial

---

[3]The term "anointed" is used of a royal person thirty-four times. In each instance it appears with the name Yahweh or a possessive pronoun referring to him. One was called "anointed" by virtue of being anointed by Yahweh and not because he had been anointed by elders or people.

[4]This son's name is spelled various ways: Shimeah (2 Sam 13:3); Shimea (1 Chr 20:7); and Shimma (1 Chr 2:13). This man had two sons of his own: Jonadab, celebrated for sagacity (2 Sam 13:3); and Jonathan, celebrated for courage (2 Sam 21:21).

[5]In 1 Chr 2:13-15 only seven sons of Jesse are named, one apparently having died young.

[6]Mauchline (129) thinks the meaning is that they would not make their

meal until he arrived. This points to the time between the public sacrifice and the (private?) meal which accompanied it. In this period the Israelites sat at a low table, with their legs crossed. David was **tending the sheep** at the time. Kings were often described as shepherds both in Israel and in the ancient Near East. Hence the irony here is that the one who had not been permitted by his father to attend the festivities with Samuel was engaged in duties which symbolize metaphorically his great future.

16:12 David is described (1) as **ruddy,** i.e., he had a reddish tint to his hair and possibly his skin. The term is also used of Esau (Gen 25:25). (2) He had a **fine appearance** (lit., "with beautiful eyes"). (3) He had **handsome features** (lit., "goodly in appearance"). This may mean that he had fair skin which was regarded as a mark of beauty in that region where complexions are generally dark. Samuel was directed to rise up and anoint David. This anointing was a prophetic indication of the man whom God, in his own way and at his own time, would place upon Saul's throne, without either scheming or action on the part of either Samuel or David (R.P. Smith, 294).

16:13 Samuel took the horn of oil and anointed David **in the presence of his brothers**. Subsequent history gives no indication that they had any idea of their brother's royal destiny. The true significance of the anointing appears to have been concealed from them. It is not even clear that it was revealed to Jesse and to David himself.[7] They may have supposed that Samuel had selected David as a pupil in his prophetic school (cf. 1 Sam 19:18ff.). Samuel certainly had good reason for keeping the matter secret, not only on his own account, but still more for David's sake.

At this climactic moment in the account the name David is mentioned for the first time. Scholars are sharply divided over the meaning of the name "David." Some have related the name to a title *dawidum* found within the Mari texts.[8] This theory has it that "David"

---

procession round the altar until David arrived. This understanding would place the anointing of David before the public sacrifice.

[7]Josephus states that Samuel *whispered* the purpose of the anointing in David's ear. KD (254) opine that Jesse and David were informed about the object of the anointing.

[8]The suggestion that *dawidum* means "commander" or "chieftain" has been challenged, but the philological link to David's name has been maintained by A. Parrot, AOTS, "Mari," 136-144.

was a regnal name.[9] Others interpret this name to mean "beloved" or "darling," a name he might have received as youngest of the family.

The anointing of David filled him with the leadership qualities which would enable him to be an effective king for **the Spirit of the LORD came upon** (lit., "rushed upon") **David in power** as he did on Saul[10] (cf. 1 Sam 10:6,10; 11:6). That which the pouring of oil symbolized actually occurred. The result of this descent of the Spirit of the Lord upon David was that the shepherd boy grew up into a hero, a statesman, a scholar, and a wise, far-sighted king.

Having completed his mission in Bethlehem, **Samuel then went to Ramah**. The entire transaction must have been strictly private. Presumably David returned to his sheep, although one cannot rule out the possibility that David went with Samuel to Ramah to become his disciple for a period of time. As for Samuel, his public career now came to an end. Although he made appearances later on, he no longer played an active role in the narrative. Obviously the anointing of David was the apex of Samuel's prophetic career.

V. DAVID'S RISE TO PROMINENCE IN SAUL'S COURT (16:14–21:9)

In the remaining chapters of 1 Samuel the focus is on the declining fortunes of Saul and the rising prominence of David, first in Saul's court (16:14–21:9), then as Saul's rival (21:10–27:4), and finally outside Israel (27:5–31:13). In this material the stories of David and Saul engage and disengage in what Fokkelman (2:17) refers to as "the crossing fates."[11]

---

[9]A.M. Honeyman, "The Evidence for Regnal Names among the Hebrews," *JBL* 67 (1948): 13-25. Those who regard "David" as a regnal name accept 2 Sam 21:19 at face value and have Elhanan (who killed Goliath) as the earlier or preroyal name of David.

[10]Klein (162) suggests that David's spirit endowment is superior to Saul's in two respects: (1) The Spirit came upon David as an immediate result of his anointing, while Saul's was separated in time from his anointing, and (2) David's anointing was permanent, while Saul's appears to have been spasmodic.

[11]Jobling (SBN, 7) has noted that from 16:14–31:13 sections describing the relation of David to Saul, and lacking Jonathan, alternate with sections where Jonathan appears. The Jonathan sections are: 18:1-5; 19:1-7; 20:1-21:1; and 23:15b-18. Jonathan played a key role in transferring the crown from Saul to David.

A. INITIAL RECOGNITION AND DANGER (16:14–17:58)

1. Recognition: Saul's Armor-bearer (16:14-23)

This unit is marked off by the phrase "spirit . . . departed from" which constitutes the first words of v. 14 and the last words of v. 23 (in the Heb text). "The transition at vv. 13-14 can . . . be arguably defined as the literary, historical, and theological crux of 1 Samuel as a whole" (Youngblood, 682). From this time forward David is the central figure of the history.

16:14 The same equipping Spirit of the Lord which came on David departed from Saul (cf. Judg 16:20). Now an **evil spirit tormented** him. It was **from the Lord** in the sense that God *permitted* this spirit to enter Saul when he took his Holy Spirit away from him.[12] Some think the spirit was an angelic spirit which God sent to trouble Saul and bring him to his ruin. In this interpretation "evil" would not mean "sinful or wicked," but rather "disastrous," a meaning that the Hebrew term sometimes has. Another view is that this spirit is a metaphor for the inward feeling of depression which debilitated Saul from time to time. A third view is that the spirit was truly wicked, a demonic spirit which filled the vacuum which was left when God withdrew his Holy Spirit. This third interpretation is probably the correct one. The evil spirit is said to have **tormented** (lit., "fall upon," "overwhelm," or "terrify") Saul. The effect of the departure of God's Spirit from Saul was that from that hour the once generous king became the victim of a gloomy depression and torturing jealousy.

16:15-16 Saul's **attendants** (lit., "servants") also believed that the spirit troubling their king came **from God**. They believed that when Saul got into one of his dark moods, beautiful music might help him to feel better. They asked his permission to search out a harpist who could provide such music. Music exerts a powerful influence on the mind. The Bible furnishes the example of Elisha and his minstrel

---

[12]The spirit which came upon Saul is also called (1) "an evil spirit of Yahweh" (19:9), "an evil spirit of God" (16:15,16; 18:10), (3) "the spirit of evil" (16:23), and (4) "the spirit of God" (16:23). It is never called "the spirit of Yahweh" which always designates the spirit of holiness. In similar passages, God sent an evil spirit between Abimelech and the men of Shechem (Judg 9:23) and a lying spirit in the mouth of the false prophets at the time of Micaiah (1 Kgs 22:19-22).

(2 Kgs 3:15). The word translated **harp** (כִּנּוֹר, *kinnôr*) is actually the smaller lyre.[13]

16:17-18 Saul ordered that such a musician be brought to him. Already David had a reputation as a skilled harpist, a brave man and a warrior. One of Saul's servants knew of him. The term translated **servants** in v. 18 (הַנְּעָרִים, *hann°ʿārîm*) is not the same word used in vv. 15,16 and 17. This term lays stress on the royal attendant in question being a young man.

Six attributes qualified David, in the eyes of Saul's young attendant, to stand before the king. First, David knew **how to play the harp**.[14] Second, he was **a brave man**, lit., "a hero of valor." His reputation for bravery must have been earned in doing battle with the bear and the lion which had attacked the flock while he was watching it (cf. 1 Sam 17:34f.).[15] Third, David was a **warrior**. It is possible that David from time to time had to fend off Philistine raiding parties which might have tried to steal his sheep.[16] On the other hand, the term warrior may describe David's capacity and promise rather than actual warlike experience. Fourth, David spoke well. He had a way with words. Possibly he already had composed psalms. Fifth, he was a **fine-looking man**, lit., "a man of form."[17] See on v. 12 above. Sixth, people had observed that the Lord was with David. His life gave evidence of the blessing of God.

16:19-20 Saul sent for David, not knowing, of course, that David had been anointed to be his successor. The command of a king was imperative; and Jesse, however reluctant and alarmed, had no alternative but to comply. Jesse sent with David a donkey loaded with foodstuffs and a young goat as presents for the king. In that time and

---

[13]The lyre usually had two arms rising up from the sound box. The strings were all the same length. They were attached to the crossbar at the top of the instrument.

[14]For pictorial representations of harps from the time of David, see *BAR* 8, 1 (1982): 22, 30, 34.

[15]The same terminology (גִּבּוֹר חַיִל, *gibbôr ḥayil*) is used of Kish, the father of Saul, in 1 Sam 9:1. There it refers to one who comes from a family of standing.

[16]At least at one point Bethlehem had served as a strong place or garrison of the Philistines (2 Sam 23:14; 1 Chr 11:16).

[17]The term תֹּאַר (*tō'ar*) is used of the beauty of both women (Gen 29:17; 1 Sam 25:3) and men (Gen 39:6). It is linked with the word "good" in describing Adonijah (1 Kgs 1:6).

region it was the custom to acknowledge obedience and subjection with a present.

16:21-22 David came to Saul and **entered his service**, (lit., "stood before him").[18] Servants always stood in the presence of the king, so standing before the king became a metaphor for royal service. Saul **liked him** (lit., "loved him") **very much.**[19] Eventually he promoted him to become one of his **armor-bearers.** The position was one of honor and responsibility. How long David served the king in this way is not stated. By the next chapter he was back with the sheep of his father. He may have served as much as four or five years. The court position enabled David to prepare for his destiny. He became acquainted with the manners of the court, the business of government, and the general state of the kingdom. His position also gave him opportunity for gaining the esteem and love of the people.

16:23 The spirit which came upon Saul is here called **the spirit from God** because it was God's messenger of judgment (cf. 1 Kgs 22:19-22). When the troubling spirit from God came upon the king, David would take his harp and play. This made Saul feel much better, and the evil spirit would depart temporarily from him.

---

[18]Some authorities (e.g., R.P. Smith) think that the invitation that David might become a regular part of Saul's court came after the encounter with Goliath in ch 17. These closing verses of ch 16 would then be like a summary of the relations of Saul and David, detailing events both before and after the Goliath incident.

[19]A close relationship existed between a warrior and his armor-bearer. See 1 Sam 14:1; 31:4-6. The verb אָהֵב (*'āhēb*) has a certain ambiguity of meaning. It is the proper term to denote genuine affection between human beings, husband and wife, parent and child, friend and friend. The verb may also have political implications and point to a covenant relationship. J.A. Thompson, "The Significance of the Verb *Love* in the David-Jonathan Narratives in 1 Samuel," *VT* 24 (1974): 334-338. In 1 Samuel the verb *'āhēb* describes the attitude toward David of Jonathan (18:2; 20:17); all Israel and Judah (18:16); Saul's servants (18:22); Michal (18:28).

1 SAMUEL 17

2. Danger: A Philistine Giant (17:1-47)

When Saul's condition showed some temporary improvement, David returned home. He was about nineteen, still too young for war. A Philistine invasion forced David's brothers to go off to fight in Saul's army. This national crisis gave David the opportunity to put on public display that heroic spirit which equipped him so well for leadership in Israel. His confrontation with Goliath was David's first step to the throne to which Yahweh had resolved to elevate him. This explains why the story is given in such detail. The LXX text of ch 17 is shorter than MT. For this reason some have asserted that the David-Goliath story weaves together two or more separate accounts without regard to possible discrepancies.[1] Others argue for the unity of the chapter in spite of the alleged differences between LXX and MT.[2]

A Military Emergency (17:1-3)

17:1-3 The scene of David's memorable defeat of Goliath is fixed with great exactness. The Philistines had recovered from the terrible defeat inflicted upon them by Saul early in his reign.[3] They gathered their forces at **Socoh** (modern *Shuweika*) in Judah some twelve miles west of Bethlehem. Socoh was in the region known as the Shephelah,

---

[1]E.g., E. Tov, "The David and Goliath Saga: How a Biblical Editor Combined Two Versions," *BR* 11, 4 (1986): 35-41.

[2]E.g., D. Gooding 55-86, 99-106, 114-120, 145-154; and T.A. Boogaart detects in the narrative three instances of a confrontation/challenge/consternation pattern which divides the story into three parts: (1) the challenge of Goliath (vv. 1-11), (2) David witnesses the challenge of Goliath (vv. 12-39), and (3) David meets the challenge of Goliath (vv. 40-54). "History and Drama in the Story of David and Goliath," *RR* 38 (1985): 205.

[3]Jamieson (176) calculates that twenty-seven years have elapsed since the Philistine defeat at Micmash.

a buffer zone of low lying hills between the territories occupied by the Philistines and the mountains where the Israelites lived. The name has been found on jar handles in this neighborhood (Goldman, 98). **Azekah** (modern *Tell ez-Zakariyeh*) is mentioned next to Socoh in Josh 15:35. It was an important fortified city later in biblical history (2 Chr 11:9; Jer 34:7). **Ephes Dammim**, ("Pas Dammim" in 1 Chr 11:13) has not been identified. The name means something like "the boundary of blood," so called, no doubt, because of the continual fighting which took place in that area (R.P. Smith, 316).

Saul countered the Philistine invasion by assembling his troops in the **Valley of Elah** ("terebinth trees"). The valley, now called *wadi es-sant* ("the acacias"), runs northwesterly through the hills of Judah near Hebron past the probable site of Gath through the Philistine Plain to the sea near Ashdod.[4] Some distance from the camp, Saul put his men in a military formation to meet the expected attack from the invaders. The NIV obliterates the features of the scene. The Philistines occupied the western slope of the Elah Valley and the Israelites were on the east. In the middle of this broad valley (עֵמֶק, *'emeq*) was a **valley** (גַּיְא, *gay'*), the narrow stream bed.

The Challenge (17:4-11)

17:4 The Philistines had a **champion**, lit., "the man of the interspaces," i.e., a man who stood in the space between two armies. The term refers to a soldier who was willing to engage in single combat for his army.[5] The name **Goliath** is related by some to a Hebrew word (גֹּלָה, *gōlāh*) meaning "exile" or "migration." Others relate the name to an Arabic word meaning "strong."[6] Goliath haled from **Gath**, one of the chief cities of the Philistines.[7] He was over nine feet

---

[4]The valley of Elah was strategically important for military purposes because it gave access to Hebron, Bethlehem, and the Judean hills.

[5]Another example of such representative combat, with twelve on each side, is recorded in 2 Sam 2:12. Documentation of such combat about this time in the ancient Near East is found in "The Story of Sinuhe," ANET, 20a). See also G. Mavrodes, "David, Goliath, and Limited War," *RJ* 33, 8(1983): 6-8; and Harry Hoffner, Jr. "A Hittite Analogue to the David and Goliath Contest of Champions?" *CBQ* 30 (1968): 220-225.

[6]McCarter (1:291) argues that the name "Goliath" is not Semitic, but Anatolian.

[7]The location of Gath is not certain, but many point to *Tell ets Tsafi* about five miles west of Azekah (Klein, 175). See ZA, 46.

tall (lit., "six cubits and a span"),[8] a great but by no means unparalleled height.[9] He was the descendant of the Anakim, a giant race of people. The remnant of this race had settled in the Philistine plain after the Israelite invasion under Joshua almost four hundred years earlier (Josh 11:22). In the light of 2 Sam 21:19, it is possible that Goliath was a general designation of the monstrous descendants of the ancient Anakim in Gath.

17:5-7 The physical description of Goliath is the most detailed found in Scripture. **Bronze** is a compound of copper and tin. All Goliath's defensive weapons were of bronze, while his attack weapons were of iron. He wore a **bronze helmet** on his head and **a coat of scale armor of bronze** which weighed five thousand shekels (125 lbs.).[10] This coat would have been made of plates of bronze lying one upon another like fish scales. Goliath's legs were protected by form-fitting bronze armor called greaves. On his **back** (lit., "between his shoulders")[11] was slung a **bronze javelin** (כִּידוֹן, *kîdôn*).[12] The shaft of the spear in his hand was as big as **a weaver's rod**, i.e., the shaft of a loom to which the web is fastened.[13] Its iron point weighed six hundred shekels (15 lbs.). A **shield bearer** went before

---

[8]In Palestine no cubit measures as yet have been found. Therefore, there is uncertainty regarding the exact conversion of cubits into feet and inches. IDB (4:838) gives the approximate equivalent of the cubit as 17.49 inches. A "span" was half a cubit. LXX, 4QSam[a] and Josephus (*Ant.* 6.9.1) have the height of Goliath as "four cubits and a span," about 6.5 feet.

[9]Pliny (*Nat. Hist.* 7.16) mentions a giant Pusio and the giantess Secundilla who lived in the time of Augustus who were over ten feet (Roman) in height. Josephus (*Ant.* 18.4.5) mentions a Jew who was seven cubits, about 9.5 feet (Roman). In the 1998 *Guiness Book of World Records* the tallest man ever recorded was Robert Pershing Wadlow (1918-1940). When last measured he was 8' 11 $\frac{1}{10}$". When he died, he was still growing.

[10]Based on a shekel = .403 ounces. IDB, 4:317.

[11]Mauchline (133) argues that the term translated **shoulders** can be translated "weapons," so the meaning would be "among his weapons."

[12]McCarter (1:284, 291-93) thinks the *kîdôn* was a scimitar, a sword with a single-edged, curved cutting blade on its outer, convex side. The rendering "sicklesword" has been proposed. This weapon is mentioned elsewhere in Josh 8:18,26 and Job 39:23; 41:29. The weapon was a very common one used from Anatolia to Egypt. It continued to be used into the twelfth century B.C., the period of the judges. Yadin, 2:349-350.

[13]Yadin (2:355) thinks that Goliath carried a typical Aegean javelin, which had a loop and a cord wrapped around it to facilitate long-distance throws. The loops resembled those on a heddle rod, which lifts alternate threads on a loom.

him carrying a large shield (צִנָּה, *ṣinnāh*) which protected the entire body. The point is that Goliath considered himself invincible, and the Israelites shared his estimate of the situation.

17:8-9 At a distance Goliath shouted to the troops of Saul. His question in v. 8 means: Why are you taking up battle stations instead of accepting my challenge? **Am I not a** [lit., "the"] **Philistine**, i.e., the representative of the Philistine nation? Why should both armies engage in battle? Let one man from Saul's forces come out and face Goliath. Whoever slew the other could then claim victory for his army. The phrase **servants of Saul** can mean "attendants of Saul" or in a sarcastic sense, "slaves of Saul." This latter sense is better suited to the context. Perhaps the mention of Saul was intended to taunt the Israelite soldiers with the memory of the former glory of their warrior king.

17:10-11 When no one responded, Goliath became more defiant. The challenge turned into a taunt. **I** [emphatic] **defy** (חָרַף, *ḥāraph*), i.e., "reproach," "scorn," or "hurl insults at." The Hebrew uses an intensive form of the verb. The sense is that the ranks of Israel were dishonored for not accepting his challenge. Saul and all the Israelites were dismayed and terrified by this intimidation. While the Israelites were terrified individually to challenge Goliath, they were not so terrified as to abandon the field to the enemy. Both armies appear to have occupied strong positions. Unless the issue was settled by single combat the stalemate would have continued indefinitely. Further evidence of the departure of God's Spirit from Saul is found in the absence of inquiry of the Urim and Thummim, and no mention of prayer to the God of the armies of Israel.

The Mission (17:12-19)

17:12 The Narrator's intent here is to bring out distinctly the remarkable chain of circumstances by which David was led to undertake the conflict with Goliath. This is why he links on to the reference to his father certain further notices respecting David's family and his position at that time. David was one of eight sons of Jesse, an Ephrathite. The Ephrathites were a subdivision of the Calebites from the Bethlehem region (Ruth 1:2; 4:11; 1 Chr 2:19). Ephrath was an older name for the district in or around Bethlehem. Jesse must have been one of the older members of the community. In the time of Saul, Jesse was **well advanced in years**, lit., "he came among the weak." Perhaps Jesse's age is noted to account for his absence from the army. David's name appears in the initial position of this verse (as well as vv. 14-15) which highlights it.

17:13-15 While Jesse was too old and David too young to fight, the three oldest sons (Eliab, Abinadab, Shammah) **had followed Saul to the war**[14] with the Philistines, i.e., they had been drafted into the army. David **went back and forth** (lit., "was going and returning") from Saul to tend his father's sheep. He obviously was not in the permanent service of Saul at this time. Some see a problem here between these verses and 16:22 where David was appointed Saul's armor-bearer. One would expect to find an armor-bearer in Saul's company, especially in a time of war. These suggestions have been made: (1) David's appointment in 16:22 was not intended to be permanent. (2) David was only summoned to the palace when Saul's madness required his services as musician. (3) The notice in 16:22 that David became Saul's armor-bearer refers to what happened after the slaying of Goliath, and is recorded there by way of anticipation. In any case, military heroes had many armor-bearers — Joab had ten (2 Sam 18:15) — and there is no reason to think that all of them would go on each campaign. "Armor-bearer" may have been like a royal training program for a young man or even an honorary order. In any case, v. 15 makes clear that David returned home when his services were not required at court, and that he was with his father in Bethlehem at the time of the Philistine invasion.

17:16 This verse takes up the description of the Philistine champion from v. 11, the intervening verses being parenthetical. Goliath mocked the Israelite soldiers twice each day for forty days in a row. He came and **took his stand** defiantly in full view of the Israelite camp.

17:17-19 Jesse dispatched David to the battlefield with an ephah (half a bushel) of roasted or parched grain and ten loaves of bread for his brothers. Roasted grain consisted of grains of wheat or barley, plucked before they were quite ripe, and then roasted. A special gift of ten cakes of cheese was to be given to **the commander of their unit**, lit., "their thousand." David was to bring back from the Valley of Elah **some assurance** (lit., "their pledge you shall take")[15] that the food had

---

[14]The Hebrew here is ponderous, but necessary to bring out clearly the pluperfect: "the three eldest sons followed, had followed, Saul."

[15]Another interpretation is that David was to redeem the pledge given by his brothers for food and supplies which they had borrowed.

been delivered and that his sons were still alive.[16] **Fighting against** the Philistines would perhaps better be rendered "at war" which suggests inactive confrontation rather than active engagement.

The Discussion (17:20-30)

17:20-21 Early in the morning, David left the family flock under the care of **a shepherd** (lit., "a keeper"), i.e., someone outside the family hired for that purpose. He reached the Israelite **camp** (מַעְגָּלָה, ma'gālāh). This term, as a military term, is used also in 1 Sam 26:5,7 and may refer (1) to an entrenchment, (2) a barricade around the camp, or (3) to the camp itself which may have been circular in formation. David arrived as the army was going out from the base camp to its battle positions, **shouting the war cry** as they went. The Philistines were drawing up their battle lines on the opposite hill.

17:22-24 David left the foodstuffs with the quartermaster or supply officer, so that he might run to the battle lines to find his brothers. He **greeted** them, lit., "he inquired his brothers of peace." Just then Goliath stepped out from the Philistine lines and shouted his daily defiance to the troops of Saul. The mere sight of Goliath caused the Israelites to fall back in great fear from the edge of the ravine.

17:25 David overheard the men making three statements about the threefold reward which Saul would bestow on the one who slew Goliath. First, the successful Israelite champion would receive great riches from the king. Second, the king would give his daughter in marriage to the champion (cf. Josh 15:16). Marrying the king's daughter would help pave the way to the throne for David. Third, Saul promised to reward the champion by **exempting his father's family from taxes**, (lit., "and the house of his father he will make free in Israel"). A "free" family certainly was one which was exempt from tax obligations and personal services to the crown. In the Ugaritic literature a parallel has been found where a man could be made *free* by the king because of his bravery (McCarter, 1:304). Nothing is said later about the fulfillment of these promises. Probably they were not kept by Saul after the defeat of Goliath because they had not been made specifically to David.

17:26-27 Apparently David had not heard clearly the murmuring about what the king would do for the man who killed the giant. He

---

[16]Jamieson (178) suggests that the tokens of the soldier's health and safety might include a lock of their hair, a piece of their nail, or such like.

directly addressed two questions to the soldiers in the battle line in order (1) to clarify what the king had decreed regarding the man who defeated the giant and (2) to express his indignation and readiness to fight, not to receive any potential reward, but simply because he found it scandalous that no one would accept the challenge from this idol worshiper. David in effect repeated the three statements of the men of Israel, but he altered them according to his own perspective of the challenge. His abhorrence for the battlefield status quo is indicated by three phrases here. First, the forty-day challenge of Goliath was a **disgrace** to Israel. Second, Goliath was **uncircumcised**, i.e., he was not part of the covenant people of Yahweh (cf. 1 Sam 14:6). Third, the god of the Philistines was a lifeless idol; but Yahweh was **the living God** who had proved his power throughout history. Why would those who represent the living God be intimidated by an idol worshiper? (cf. 2 Kgs 19:4). David's questions elicited verification of the commitments which Saul had made to the man who could defeat Goliath. The tone of his questions gave rise to the supposition that he himself wanted to go and fight the Philistine.

17:28 Having betrayed his own intention of trying to fight Goliath by his questioning of the troops, David was sharply rebuked by Eliab, his oldest brother. First, he charged David with neglect of duty. Of necessity David would have to have left the flock with someone younger than himself, and presumably less qualified. Eliab indignantly asked why David had **come down** to the battlefield. Bethlehem stood on higher ground than the scene of the war. Second, Eliab belittled the shepherd work of David by referring to **those few sheep in the desert**. The term **desert** (מִדְבָּר, *midbār*) does not necessarily mean barren country, but land used for pasture as distinct from arable land. Third, Eliab accused David of **conceit**, i.e., arrogance and discontent with his humble occupation. The term זָדוֹן (*zādôn*) comes from a root which means "to boil over" as water. Eliab is alleging that David had proud, ambitious aspirations. Fourth, the elder brother charged David with morbid curiosity, an immature excitement at the thrill of warfare, and an unseemly eagerness for the sight of bloodshed. He had come to the battlefield just so he could witness the battle.

17:29-30 David replied to his brother modestly so as to put the scorn of his reprover to shame. First, he expressed surprise that his brother was upset. His question suggests that Eliab's scoldings were not an infrequent experience. Second, he asked if he was no longer allowed to speak. He was just asking some questions. As soon as Eliab was occupied elsewhere, David turned to some other men, and brought up the matter of Goliath again. He refused to be discouraged by the negativism of his brother.

The Preparation (17:31-40)

17:31-33 Saul soon heard about the brash young man who showed no fear of the Philistine. He was summoned to the king's tent. David lost none of his confidence in the presence of the king. He told Saul that there was no need for anyone to **lose heart** , lit., "let not a heart of a man fall." This fearlessness of David is one manifestation of the special strength which came upon him by the Spirit of God on the day of his anointing (16:13). The avoidance of the name Goliath shows disdain for the giant. David humbly refers to himself as Saul's **servant**, a term which emphasizes obedience. He volunteered to go out and fight the giant. Saul could not let David face Goliath. Though he was about nineteen at this time, compared with the giant David was but a youth (נַעַר, *na'ar*), i.e., a warrior of lower rank, a young man acting as a squire or servant of one of the nobles.[17]

17:34-36 Undaunted by Saul's lack of confidence in his ability, David responded in two ways. First, he reviewed his past experiences; then he referred to the power of God. David assured Saul that he could handle the Philistine. He had confronted the lion and the bear who had stolen sheep from his flock. He would strike the beast with his staff to force it to drop the sheep. If the animal **turned on** (lit., "arose against") him, he grabbed the beast by **its hair** (lit., "beard, chin") and struck it, apparently with his staff, so that it died. He was confident that the Philistine would fall like that lion and bear because he had dared to defy the armies of the living God. The use in these verses of the singular pronominal suffix indicates that when David speaks of the lion and the bear, he connects together two different events. Both species were common in ancient times in Palestine when the country was more densely covered with woods. Lions[18] seem to have been less feared than bears[19] (Amos 5:19).

---

[17]J. McDonald, "The Status and Rank of the *Na'ar* in Israelite Society," *JNES* 35 (1976): 147-170. David had already shown sufficient promise to be called "a warrior" by Saul's servant (16:18).

[18]Lions are mentioned in the Bible 130 times. The last lion was killed in Palestine at Ledja near Megiddo in the thirteenth century. The Palestinian

17:37 The fact that he had triumphed before against seemingly impossible odds fueled David's confidence that he would triumph again. He did not boast of his own prowess, but ascribes all his achievements to divine aid. Yahweh had delivered him from **the paw** (lit., "hand" = power) of the wild beasts. The Lord also would deliver him from Goliath's **hand** or power. David's courage was grounded in his confidence that the **living God** would not let his people be defied by the heathen with impunity. Finally, Saul was convinced by David's arguments. Saul gave royal permission for David to go forth as the representative of the Israelite army to face the giant. The fate of the entire army and the kingdom rested on the shoulders of one who had no military experience. The NIV suggests that the words **the LORD be with you** are a prayer. That does not appear to be the case. A more literal translation would be, "As for Yahweh, he shall be with you." These are words of assurance, confidence, and even faith more than petition. As early as 16:18 one of Saul's servants had observed that Yahweh was with David in a special way. Here Saul himself confirms that observation.

17:38-39 Saul's motives for dressing David in royal battle dress are not clear. Perhaps he merely wanted the youth to have the best defense possible in his confrontation with Goliath. On the other hand, he may have been attempting to form a bond between himself and the youth so that in this way he could claim a share in the victory.[20] The king attempted to dress David in his own tunic, coat of armor and helmet. In placing the royal weapons at David's disposal, Saul was giving official sanction to the forthcoming duel. David fastened on his (Saul's?) sword and tried to move about in this new equipment. He could not move about freely with it on. This gear would be more of a handicap than a help. The weight of the unaccustomed armor hindered his movements. He knew he could not face Goliath like this. The very fact that Saul would even consider dressing David in his own armor indicates that David must have

---

lion is thought to have been of the Persian variety which was neither so fierce nor so powerful as its African cousin (IDB, 2:256).

[19]The Syrian bear was fairly common in biblical times all over Palestine. The color of this species ranges from dark red-brown to the rare light specimens. The last bear in Palestine was killed just before World War I in Upper Galilee, but the species still survives in nothern Syria (IDB, 2:250).

[20]Such is the view of Boogaart ("History and Drama," 210) and Jobling (SBN, 9).

been a grown man, and not a small man at that. He was not the small lad of Sunday School story and chorus.

17:40 David chose to arm himself with what he knew best. He took his staff in one hand. He selected five smooth stones from the stream nearby and put them into **the pouch of his shepherd's bag**, i.e., something akin to a knapsack. With his sling in his hand he went out to confront the Philistine. Obviously David was skilled in the use of the sling, having practiced endless hours with it while guarding the sheep.

The Confrontation (17:41-47)

17:41-44 With his armor-bearer before him, Goliath kept coming closer to David. When he saw that his opponent was but a youth who did not even carry a sword or spear, he was shocked. He wanted to fight a real man, a battle-tested warrior. Goliath considered it a personal insult that the Israelites would send such an unworthy opponent to face him. He was being treated like a mere dog such as one might try to frighten away with a stick. Goliath used the plural **sticks**[21] as a contemptuous exaggeration of the equipment David carried. He cursed David in the name of his Philistine gods.[22] This curse had the effect of turning the military encounter into a theological struggle (Klein, 180). He swore that he would give David's flesh to the birds and the beasts, i.e., David would not receive a decent burial.

17:45-47 David was not intimidated by the words of the giant. He hurled his own threat back in Goliath's face. You come at me **with sword**[23] **and spear and javelin,**[24] i.e., weapons of man, but I come at you in the name of the Lord Almighty, God of the armies of Israel which you have defied. While the Philistine would not name his god, David did not hesitate. The mere **name** of Yahweh would be sufficient to topple this giant. The Philistines were not ignorant of the

---

[21]The LXX has an expanded text here: "and with stones. But David replied, No, you are worse than a dog."

[22]KD (264) and Spence (367) think Goliath cursed David in the name of his (David's) God. This is a possible understanding of the Hebrew, since *elohim* can be translated "gods" or "God." The LXX, however, took it to be plural. Both the MT and LXX say "his" rather than giving a name. If this does indeed mean "his God," then Goliath defied not David only, but the God of Israel as well.

[23]The חֶרֶב (*hereb*) is the double-edged sword.

[24]On the translation of *kîdôn* (NIV, NRSV, "javelin"), see note on v. 6.

devastating power which Yahweh had demonstrated against those who opposed him (1 Sam 5:11; 6:6). On the title LORD **Almighty** see on 1 Sam 1:3. If David appeared to be lacking in arms, it was because Yahweh had no need of them.

David faced the giant with total confidence. First, he claimed victory over the giant personally. This day God **will hand you over to me**, lit., "shut you up in my hand." David predicted that he would strike down Goliath and cut off his head. Second, David claimed victory over the Philistine army. The battle that day would also belong to the Lord. He would give all of the Philistines into the hands of Israel. David predicted that he would **give the carcasses** (lit., "carcass") of the Philistines to the birds and beasts, i.e., leave their corpses unburied. Thus would all the world come to know that **there is a God in Israel**, i.e., one who was worthy to be called "God" (cf. 1 Kgs 18:36; 2 Kgs 19:19). Third, David articulated a basic principle of Israelite faith, viz., **it is not by sword or spear that the LORD saves.** While Goliath had boasted of his strength, David founded his only assurance of victory upon the Almighty God of Israel. He was confident that **the battle is the LORD's,** i.e., Yahweh would defend his honor against Goliath's taunts, so victory was assured.

3. Danger Averted: Goliath Defeated (17:48-54)

17:48-50 The Philistine **moved closer** (lit., "arose and went and moved closer") to attack David. The language suggests that Goliath may have been seated as he waited for some response from the Israelite side. As the Philistine awkwardly plodded forward, David fearlessly began to run toward the Philistine **battle line** to meet him. This unexpected charge must have unnerved the Philistine warrior. David loaded a stone into his sling and hurled it toward the Philistine.[25] It struck Goliath in the forehead where he had no armor.

---

[25]S. Reimer records his observations about modern slingers in Syria. The sling was not twirled, i.e., it did not go "round and round and round" as the Sunday School song says. Objects were slung with a single whip of the sling, starting with the sling in front and then bringing it back and under before releasing. The action was somewhat like pitching a baseball underhand and the entire body was used. Reimer expresses his surprise at the accuracy of the weapon at 150 feet and the velocity of the projectile which often shattered on impact. *ABW* 1 (1991): 21.

The blow **struck down** the Philistine. Stunned and helpless, he fell forward **facedown to the ground.** Then David killed the giant in the manner which the next verse describes. Presumably Goliath's armor-bearer retreated hastily when his master fell. The Narrator emphasizes the daring of David by underscoring that he felled the giant **without a sword in his hand.**

17:51 This verse contains the second of two notices of Goliath's death. Apparently the historian wished to underscore that Goliath did not die as a result of the blow from the stone, but was only stunned. David ran forward, took Goliath's own sword, and severed his head. This he did for two reasons. First, to be decapitated by one's own sword was the ultimate humiliation (cf. 2 Sam 23:21). Second, the heads of slain enemies were regarded in the East as the most welcome tokens of victory (cf. 2 Sam 4:8). The sword probably was not so monstrous in size as Goliath's other weapons since later the priest Ahimelech considered it fit for David's own use (1 Sam 21:9). When the Philistines saw that their champion was dead, they turned and fled.

17:52-53 Saul's army surged forward in pursuit of the Philistines. They chased the enemy all the way to the entrances of **Gath** (lit., "Gai" = valley)[26] and Ekron, about seven miles from the battlefield. **Shaaraim** is mentioned in Josh 15:36 next to Socoh and Azekah as a town in the Shephelah. It was presumably located down the valley, in the line which the Philistines' flight had taken. The slain Philistines scattered along the road presumably were left exposed to the birds and beasts as predicted by David in v. 46.

17:54 Shortly after the battle, David took the head of the giant to **Jerusalem.** This city, or at least the citadel, was at this time under the control of the Jebusites.[27] The reference has been interpreted to mean (1) that David took the head to the tabernacle at Nob which was near Jerusalem (Kirkpatrick, 1:162), (2) that he took the head to

---

[26]The NIV has here preferred the rendering of the LXX. which requires emendation of the Hebrew text. Because no location by the name "Gai" is known, many conservative scholars endorse this emendation. The word is rendered "valley" (NASB, NKJV); "Gai" (NJPS); and "Gath" (BV, JB, NRSV, the latter with marginal reading "Gai").

[27]At some point prior to the days of David, Israelites did occupy Jerusalem, or at least a part of the city. See Josh 15:63; Judg 1:8. KD (265) think the Israelites were still there in David's day, but this is not certain.

Jerusalem at a later time after he had conquered the place,[28] or (3) that he brought the head to Jerusalem immediately after the battle, perhaps throwing the head over the wall. It may be that David wished to use the giant's head to strike fear into the Jebusites who occupied this strategic city.[29] David kept Goliath's weapons in **his own tent,** lit., "his tent." The term has been taken as (1) an antiquated term for David's dwelling place in Bethlehem (cf. 1 Sam 4:10; 13:2), (2) the tent occupied by David afterward when he was on duty with Saul,[30] (3) the tabernacle of Yahweh which was considered David's because he set it up in his own city (2 Sam 6:17), and (4) Goliath's tent.[31] At some point, the sword of Goliath was deposited in the tabernacle (1 Sam 21:9).

4. The Ramifications (17:55-58)

17:55-56 As Saul watched David going out to face the Philistine, he inquired of Abner, his general, whose son this was. Abner swore an oath on the life of the king that he did not know. Saul twice referred to David as a **young man,** but he used two different Hebrew words (*na'ar* and *'elem* [עֶלֶם]). The second word, which appears elsewhere only in 1 Sam 20:22, is more specific. It refers to a young man who had arrived at the age to marry. Why did Saul not recognize

---

[28]Gordon, 158. The case of the relocation of the bones of Saul from Jabesh-gilead to the tomb of Kish (2 Sam 21:12-14) has been offered as a parallel to what may have happened to Goliath's head.

[29]J.K. Hoffmeir collects evidence to suggest that displaying mutilated bodies of enemies was a standard tactic used to instill fear in other enemies. In particular, the Assyrians regularly displayed heads in various ways. On some occasions the head of a victim was placed on the back or shoulders of the decedent's family member who was marched about. In other instances the head of the dead king was displayed at the city gate in Nineveh. "The Aftermath of David's Triumph over Goliath," *ABW* 1 (1991): 22. On the other hand, Mauchline (135) suggests that the Jebusites may have been allies of Saul in this defensive war against the Philistines.

[30]Hertzberg (154) supported by Mauchline (135) thinks the reference is to the tent of Yahweh, but this involves a slight emendation of the text.

[31]J.K. Hoffmeier ("Aftermath," 18-19) has collected Assyrian and Egyptian evidence to demonstrate that seizing the tent of one's opponent in battle was practiced throughout the Near East at this time. David may have taken Goliath's tent back to Bethlehem, along with his weapons, as a trophy.

David? Had not David served for some time in his court? Various proposals have been made: (1) David may have matured considerably during his absence from the court. He was about fifteen when he served in the court; he was about nineteen at this point. (2) When David served in the court, Saul was in a disturbed state of mind. He may have heard David play only once or twice, and that in a darkened tent. Perhaps he paid little attention to the features of his musician. Abner may not have been involved in the appointment of David as court minstrel either because he had not yet been appointed to his office of commander of the host (1 Sam 14:50), or because he was not involved in nonmilitary decisions. (3) The story of David in Saul's court *may* be chronologically subsequent to the present chapter.

Actually the text does not say that Saul did not recognize David. What he wanted to know was the name of David's *father*.[32] Saul needed this information (1) so that he might fulfill his pledge to make the father's house free of tax obligations or (2) so that he might know the parentage of his potential son-in-law.

17:57-58 David was still holding the head of the giant when Abner brought him before the king. Saul asked him about his father, and David identified his father as Jesse of Bethlehem.

---

[32]Goldman (109) contends that **whose son is he?** means no more than "who is he?" However, in the Hebrew Bible when one asks about another's identity, he simply asks the question "who are you?" (cf. Gen 27:18,32; 1 Sam 26:14; 2 Sam 1:8; Ruth 3:9,16. Only when the identity of the father is crucial is the question asked, "Who is your father?" (Gen 24:23,47; cf. 1 Sam 10:12).

1 SAMUEL 18

B. POST-GOLIATH RECOGNITION AND DANGER (18:1-12)

1. Recognition: A Member of Saul's Court (18:1-7)

Chronologically this chapter follows immediately the previous one. The events here can be assigned to ca. 1021-20 B.C. David was about nineteen or twenty years of age. "David's victory over Goliath was a turning-point in his life, which opened the way to the throne" (KD, 265).

18:1 Jonathan had taken little interest in David as a minstrel; but his heroism, modesty and manly bearing, his piety and enthusiasm kindled in Jonathan, not merely admiration, but affection for the son of Jesse. Jonathan **became one in spirit with David,** lit., "the soul of Jonathan was bound up, knotted firmly together (נִקְשְׁרָה, niqš°rāh) with the soul of David."[1] The thought is that Jonathan recognized in David a kindred spirit. These two men were one in their God, in their faith, and in their devotion to the people of the Lord. David **loved him** (i.e., Jonathan) **as himself.** Yet David's love was not subject to the strains and conflicts which tested Jonathan's love, viz., "the clash of loyalties to father and friend, the willing surrender of royal station, the unenvying recognition of the greater brilliance and popularity of the friend who was to stand in his place" (Goldman, 108).

Considerable attention has been devoted to the verb אָהֵב ('āhēb) ("loved"). It certainly has no connotation of homosexual involvement.[2] Actually the term seems to have political overtones in diplomatic and

---

[1] The relationship between Jonathan's soul and David's is described in the common English versions as "closely bound" (JB), "in unison" (BV), "bound" (NRSV), "bound up" (NJPS), and "knit" (NASB). KD (267) propose a reflexive rendering of the verb: "chained itself" to the soul of David. The closest parallel is Gen 44:30 which describes Jacob's profound love for Benjamin.

[2] Tom Horner (26-28,31-39) asserts that the relationship between David

commercial contexts (cf. 1 Sam 16:21; 1 Kgs 5:1). The word is probably used here because it denoted more than natural affection.[3]

18:2 From that day refers to the day David defeated Goliath. Because of David's military skill and Jonathan's close relationship with him, Saul **kept David with him** (lit., "took him"). He did not allow him to **return to his father's house**, i.e, to engage in his former occupation as shepherd. David became a permanent resident at court. It may be that David's appointment as Saul's armor-bearer, which was reported in 1 Sam 16:21, took place at this time.

18:3 At some point Jonathan went beyond the personal feelings of a friendly disposition and made a solemn covenant with David.[4] Here as in v. 1 the expression כְּנַפְשׁוֹ (kᵉnaphšô, lit., "as his own soul") appears which the NIV correctly renders **as himself**. The covenant was kept by both Jonathan and David until the former died, and by David even afterwards (2 Sam 9:1,7). They were truly brothers (2 Sam 1:26).

18:4 As a symbol of the brotherhood between them, Jonathan gave to David certain articles of clothing and weapons. To receive any part of the dress which had been worn by a sovereign, or his eldest son and heir, was deemed in the East the highest honor which could be conferred on a subject. Cf. Esther 6:8. Specifically, Jonathan gave David (1) **his robe** (מְעִיל, mᵉ'îl), i.e., his long outer robe which was the ordinary dress of the wealthier classes (cf. 1 Sam 2:19), perhaps in this case, the royal robe; (2) his military **tunic** (מַד, mad), lit., "his military garments"[5] which were worn over the robe; (3) his **sword**, (4) his famous **bow** (cf. 2 Sam 1:22), and (5) his **belt** or girdle, probably also part of his military dress. Unlike Jonathan,

---

and Jonathan was homosexual. The Hebrew Bible, however, uses the verb יָדַע (yāda', "know") in the sense "have sex with" for homosexual desire or activity, not אָהֵב. See Gen 19:5; Judg 19:22.

[3] J.A. Thompson, "The Significance of the Verb *Love* in the David-Jonathan Narratives in I Samuel," *VT* 24 (1974): 34-38. R. Ackroyd, "The Verb Love — *'āhēb* in the David-Jonathan Narratives — A Footnote," *VT* 25, 2 (1975): 213.

[4] This is the first of a series of such agreements made over a long period of time until David's kingship was firmly established: 1 Sam 20:16-17; 23:18; 2 Sam 3:13,21; 5:3.

[5] That the term is used of fighting attire is proved by its use in 1 Sam 17:38; 2 Sam 20:8. The term is translated "armor" (NASB, NKJV, JB, BV, NRSV) and "tunic" (NIV, NJPS).

David had no personal possessions to give; he could only give himself in true friendship.

18:5 The NIV fails to translate two Hebrew words at the beginning of this verse, viz., "David went out," i.e., he went out on military expeditions. These initial expeditions were probably not on a very large scale, for it is not until v. 13 that David was made **captain over a thousand**.[6] Every task assigned to David was done **successfully**, lit., "he acted prudently." The Hebrew term embraces the ideas of prudence and consequent success. Eventually Saul **gave him a high rank in the army,** literally "set him over the men of war." It is a testimony to the spirit of David that his sudden promotion pleased both the people and the officers of the army.

18:6 The meaning of this verse is clear even though the original Hebrew does not flow smoothly. When the men were returning after David had killed the giant, the women came out to **meet Saul**, i.e., to honor the achievement of the army which he commanded. The women went out **with singing and dancing**, (lit., "to sing and the dances"). Dancing was the usual expression of rejoicing upon occasions of national triumph (cf. Exod 15:20f.; Judg 11:34) and at religious festivals (Ps 149:3). Dancing was as a rule confined to women, but see 2 Sam 6:14. The women sang **joyful songs** which celebrated the recent victory. The songs were accompanied by musical instruments. **Tambourines** were hoops, sometimes with pieces of brass fixed to them to make a jingling, over which parchment was stretched. It was beaten with the fingers. The tambourine is always associated with joy and gladness in the Hebrew Bible (cf. 1 Sam 10:5; 2 Sam 6:5). **Lutes**[7] were triangular shaped instruments of three strings. Not being a temple instrument, the lute was, like the tambourine, usually played by women.

18:7 The NIV translation **as they danced** (מְשַׂחֲקוֹת, *meśaḥăqôth*) is probably too restrictive. The participle connotes enjoying themselves, playing, having fun, or making merry. The NIV has ignored the

---

[6]Goldman (110) suggests that v. 5 anticipates summarily events which are recorded in their proper place in vv. 13-16.

[7]"Lutes" (שְׁלִשִׁים, *šālišîm*) is derived from the Hebrew word for "three." The term is used here uniquely in a context of celebration. Another possibility is that the term refers to a song pattern of three beats on each line of the Hebrew original which the poetic jingle chanted by the women displays. English versions have rendered the term (1) "cymbals" (BV), (2) "lyre" (JB), (3) "musical instruments" (NKJV, NRSV), and (4) "sistrums" (NJPS).

opening verb of the verse. The verse opens with these words: "The women who were enjoying themselves answered and said." Apparently the women sang alternately, i.e., they formed themselves into two choirs, which sang alternate or responsive lines (cf. Exod 15:21). One group praised Saul for slaying his **thousands,** while the other responded by attributing to David the slaying of **tens of thousands.**[8] The refrain evidently became widely current, as it was known even among the Philistines (1 Sam 21:11; 29:5).

2. Danger: Saul's Spear (18:8-11a)

18:8-9 The question **What more can he get but the kingdom?** is lit., "and there is beside for him only the kingdom." Clearly Saul's jealousy went beyond David's military achievements; he feared for the throne! From that time Saul **kept a jealous eye on** (lit., "he kept eyeing") **David,** i.e., he looked at him invidiously, with secret and malignant hatred.

18:10-11a The jealousy of Saul again opened the door of his mind to invasion by an evil spirit from God (see comments on 16:14). The king was now consumed with a murderous jealousy that filled his own soul and drove him to overt acts of violence and covert schemes of deception. First, Saul began **prophesying** in his house. This language is the same as in 1 Sam 10:6,10 where "the Spirit" came mightily upon Saul and he "prophesied" in the midst of the prophets. The term denotes one under the influence either of a good or a bad spirit, i.e., a higher power. In the present context the action would be something like "raving" (cf. NASB, NRSV, BV, NJPS) like a mad man, acting like a man possessed. David was **playing the harp** (lit., "was playing a stringed instrument with his hand")[9] as he usually did, but without the desired effect. Second, before the mollifying influence of

---

[8]"Thousand . . . ten thousand" is a stock parallel pair in the Old Testament (Ps 91:7; Mic 6:7) as well as Ugaritic literature (Youngblood, 708; Klein, 188). Each element in the pair is hyperbolic for a large number. Only a sick mind would assume that the women were lavishing greater praise on David. Mauchline (138) suggested that the women were attributing to David the slaughter of the Philistines in retreat (cf. 17:52), since that retreat was occasioned by the slaughter of Goliath.

[9]The Hebrew text draws the stark contrast between David playing the harp "with his hand" and Saul having a spear "in his hand."

the music could be felt, Saul suddenly **hurled**[10] his spear at David. He probably swung the spear in David's direction without letting it go out of his hand. This supposition is supported by the fact that it is not stated here that the spear entered the wall, as in 1 Sam 19:10.

Saul's spear was the symbol of his office. Saul held it in his hand when he sat in council (1 Sam 22:6) or in his house (1 Sam 19:9f.); it was kept by his side when he sat at table (1 Sam 20:33) and stuck in the ground by his pillow as he slept in camp (1 Sam 26:7). The NIV takes the words **I'll pin David to the wall** as indicating something Saul was thinking (cf. vv. 17,21). The Hebrew is ambiguous. These may have been words Saul said out loud as he made threatening gestures with his spear.

3. Danger Averted (18:11b-12)

8:11b-12 Twice Saul threatened David with his spear. Both times David **eluded him** (lit., "turned aside from his face"), i.e., hastily withdrew from the room. Even after these incidents, David remained at the court of Saul. He looked on such manifestations of bitter hatred as simple outbursts of a temporary insanity. Even when Saul recovered from his paroxysm, however, he **was afraid of David.** Saul's jealousy degenerated into a sense of powerlessness, as knowing that a higher power was with David, while he himself had lost the divine presence. This is now the third time that the narrative has indicated that Yahweh was (or would be) with David (cf. 16:18; 17:37).

C. MILITARY RECOGNITION AND DANGER (18:13-27)

This unit depicts Saul ever trying to do David undeserved harm, but succeeding only in helping him to move toward his destiny of the crown. The rejected king is constantly frustrated; the future king is always successful.

---

[10]As vocalized in the MT the verb יָטֵל (*yaṭel*) comes from the root טוּל (*ṭûl*) which in the Hiphil means "to hurl." The consonants could also be vocalized יִטֹּל (*yiṭṭōl*) from the root נָטַל (*nāṭal*), meaning "to take up." In this context the verb might mean something like "brandish" or "aim." Even with the present vowels the verb may mean "made as though he would cast," or "aimed the spear" (cf. KD, 269). It then would have been the threatening gesture, not the attack, from which David twice withdrew. This interpretation can be traced back to the Targum.

1. Recognition: Saul's Captain (18:13-16)

8:13 Saul **sent David away from him**. This action was motivated by more than one consideration. (1) Saul no longer trusted David in personal attendance on himself, (2) he wished to appoint him to a post of special danger (cf. vv. 17,21,25), and (3) he wished to get David out of the public eye. Yet David's success in everything that he undertook compelled Saul to promote him. He gave David command over a thousand men.[11] **David led the troops in their campaigns,** lit., "he went out and came in before the people."[12]

18:14-16 From Saul's point of view, David's appointment to the officer corps was a tragedy. David only increased his standing with the people. The military command allowed him to demonstrate before the public the extraordinary leadership qualities which he possessed. In everything he did David had great success because **the Lord was with him.** This made Saul fear David all the more. The word **afraid** (וַיָּגָר, *wayyāgor*) in v. 15 is stronger than the word used in v. 12, denoting primarily the avoidance of the person feared (Kirkpatrick, 1:167). Saul was conscious that his old vigor and ability were deserting him, and in David he recognized the presence of a power he knew once had been his. David was the real leader of the army in those days. Although David was of Judah, the future king was equally popular with the northern tribes. They **loved** David. In this context the verb expresses more than natural affection. It denotes the kind of attachment people had to a leader whom they trusted to fight their battles for them.[13]

2. Danger: Saul's Daughters (18:17-25)

The First Promise of Marriage (18:17-19)

18:17 Saul had found it convenient to forget that he had promised to give his daughter in marriage to the champion who conquered Goliath (1 Sam 17:25). He now made this offer with the purpose of

---

[11]Mauchline (139) regards David's appointment to captain of a thousand men as a demotion in terms of his former military appointment as defined in v. 5.

[12]"Going out" and "coming in" are common expressions denoting "to fight battles," and to do so before a group means to be the leader in fighting those battles. Cf. Num 27:17; 1 Sam 8:20; 2 Sam 5:24.

[13]J.A. Thompson, "The Verb *Love*," 337.

tempting David to give additional proofs of his valor. Though not prepared as yet to put David to death himself, Saul would have felt relief
if he had died by the fortune of war. His plan was to offer David the
hand of his older daughter **Merab** ("increase") in marriage if David
continued bravely to **fight the battles of the Lord,** i.e., engage in battle against the Philistines. Israel's wars were the wars of Yahweh
because they were undertaken for the defense and establishment of
Yahweh's kingdom, and therefore divine aid might be expected in
waging them (cf. 1 Sam 25:28; Num 21:14).

18:18-19 David did not reject the offer, but modestly depreciates
his own worth. By means of two questions he indicates his unworthiness to become the son-in-law to the king. First, he is unworthy on
personal grounds: **Who am I?** Second, he felt unworthy on account
of his social standing as determined by his lineage. The words **what
is my family** are lit., "who is my life?" The interrogative pronoun
"who" (מִי, *mî*) is used in the original to signal that David is speaking
about a class of persons to which he belonged.

When the time arrived for the marriage, Saul humiliated David
by giving his daughter to **Adriel,**[14] a man of whom nothing further
is known. **Meholah** is a shortened form of **Abel Meholah**. The town,
which was the birthplace of Elisha (1 Kgs 19:16), was located on the
west bank of the Jordan, but the precise location is still debated.[15]
Saul's change of promise may be accounted for (1) as a further indication of his capricious nature during this period of his reign, (2) as
an attempt to wound the feelings and provoke resentment and possible indiscretion on the part of David, (3) because Adriel had
offered the king a dowry of such proportions that he could not
refuse, (4) because Merab did not love David and therefore protested the arrangement, a circumstance which might be inferred from
v. 20, or (5) because he saw a better opportunity to destroy David by
marrying him to his younger daughter Michal.

---

[14]Merab had five sons by Adriel, all of whom fell victim to the blood
revenge demanded by the Gibeonites from the family of Saul (2 Sam 21:9).

[15]Proposals for the location of Abel Meholah ("meadow of dancing") have
included two sites on the east side of the Jordan and four sites west of the
river. In the light of all the biblical evidence, the site Tell Abu Sus on the
west bank of the Jordan, about twenty-three miles south of the Sea of
Galilee, seems to be the best candidate. See discussion ABD, s.v. "Abel
Meholah" by D. Edelman.

The Second Promise of Marriage (18:20-25)

18:20-21 David was finding ever-increasing support in the Saulide family (cf. 16:21; 18:1,3). In time Saul's younger daughter **Michal** fell **in love with David**. Saul was **pleased** when he heard this. The Hebrew verb used here means "to be right or just." Of course moral right was no consideration. The meaning is that Michal's love for David was right for Saul's purpose; it played into his hands. No doubt Saul had ascertained privately that David was loyal to him and totally unsuspecting of any intrigue in the marriage offer. Michal would be a **snare** or bait to lure David into some venturesome raid upon the Philistines in which he might lose his life. Therefore, Saul offered David **a second opportunity**[16] to become his son-in-law.

18:22-23 David may have mistrusted Saul and so he made no move to ask for the hand of the princess. Saul dispatched his courtiers to persuade him **privately**, as though they were doing it behind the king's back. They urged David to accept the king's offer for two reasons. First, they assured David that **the king is pleased with you.** In view of all that has been reported, this must have been a hard sell. Second, Saul's **attendants** (lit., "servants") **all like you** (lit., "love you").

As in v. 18 David again expressed his sense of unworthiness to be the son-in-law of the king. He offered two reasons why he would not be a worthy candidate: First, David specifically emphasized that he was a poor man. He would not have the money to offer the customary gift or dowry to the father of the bride. Second, David described himself as **little known** (נִקְלֶה, *niqleh*), lit., "lightly esteemed, dishonored."

18:24-25 The servants reported David's words back to Saul. Word was returned to David that Saul wanted no gift for the bride other than an heroic act on his part. The **price for the bride** (מֹהַר,

---

[16]The meaning of the Hebrew is uncertain. A literal rendering would be something like "with two you shall be my son-in-law today." Most English translations assume that the cardinal number is used here in place of the ordinal. Thus "thou shalt this day be my son-in-law a second time" (ASV); "you can become my son-in-law even now through the second one" (NJPS); "with the second one" (BV); "twice Saul said to David, 'Now you shall be my son-in-law;'" (JB); "Saul said to David a second time . . ."(NKJV, NRSV); "for a second time you may be my son-in-law today" (NASB). On the basis of Job 33:14, KD (271) propose "in a second way." A. Phillips regards the statement of Saul as a formal proclamation over David which declared him legally betrothed to Michal. "Another Example of Family Law," *VT* 30, 2 (1980): 241.

mōhar) is explicitly mentioned elsewhere only in Gen 34:12 and Exod 22:16-17. Strictly speaking, the promise made by Saul in 17:25 bound him to give her without dowry; but perhaps he sensed that David would never marry his daughter without performing the customary obligations of engagement. Saul determined that he would give David the opportunity of winning his bride in a manner which befitted a warrior (cf. Judg 1:12). The king named as the bride price for his daughter a hundred **foreskins** as proof of having slain a hundred Philistines. Why foreskins, and not heads?[17] Several answers to this questions have been proposed, viz., (1) this was "ethnic humor, stirred by long antagonism" (Klein, 190); (2) to ensure that David would slay *Philistines*, not Israelites or other less ferocious neighbors (Philistines at this time did not circumcise, while most of the other peoples in the area did); and (3) Saul was under the influence of the evil spirit, and this may account for this barbaric condition being imposed on David. The stated purpose of this requirement was **to take revenge on his** [Saul's] **enemies**.

Saul's willingness to forgo the customary bridal present signaled a change of heart toward David and an eagerness to have him as a member of the royal family. Under this proposal, however, Saul was cloaking his unprincipled malice against David. Because this slaughter would have to be effected not in regular warfare, but in a sort of private raid, there would be every likelihood of David being slain in a rapid counterattack by the Philistines. He hoped that at some point David would **fall by the hands of the Philistines.**

3. Danger Averted: Philistines Defeated (18:26-27)

18:26-27 When David learned that Saul would not expect a gift of money, he was pleased to accept the offer to become the son-in-law of the king. **So before the allotted time elapsed,** is lit., "and the days were not full." In the time established by Saul, David and **his men,** here mentioned for the first time, slew **two hundred**[18] Philistines.

---

[17]Josephus strangely exaggerates the stipulation for the hand of Michal as being "six hundred heads" (*Antiquities* 6.10.2).

[18]The LXX reads "one hundred" which is sometimes assumed to be correct on the basis of 2 Sam 3:14. The latter verse, however, simply quotes Saul's original figure (v. 25) as the price for Michal's hand.

The number was doubled, partly to show his respect and attachment to the princess, and partly to obligate Saul to fulfill his pledge. He brought **the full number to the king,** (lit., "they made them full to the king," i.e., they placed them in their full number) before him. Saul had no choice at this point but to give Michal to David as wife.

David's marriage to Saul's daughter had political implications. If Saul and Jonathan should die, David would have a strong claim to the throne.

D. GROWING RECOGNITION AND DANGER (18:28–19:6)

1. Recognition: Highly Esteemed (18:28-30)

18:28-29 In these verses Saul's fear of David reaches a new plateau which forms a transition to the plan to assassinate David in the following chapter. This state of affairs was brought about by two things Saul now **realized** (lit., "he saw and he knew"): (1) **that the Lord was with David** (cf. 17:37; 18:14f.), i.e., that he was miraculously protected by Yahweh; and (2) **his daughter Michal loved David.** Saul's plot to rid himself of David by offering him Michal backfired. Michal, as well as her brother Jonathan, showed more love and loyalty to their father's rival than to their father. The marriage only enhanced David's status. This made Saul even more afraid of David. He hated David all the more bitterly, because he could not now openly put to death one so closely connected to him. As for David, he knew that some day in God's own good time he would be the king of Israel. Being married to Michal could only help him in his bid for acceptance by the people as their king.

18:30 A new war broke out with the Philistines, no doubt as a result of David's raid. David proved to be the best officer in Saul's army. He had more success against the Philistines than any other commander. His name became **well known** (lit., "precious"), both among the Israelites and the Philistines.

1 SAMUEL 19

The time lapse between this and the previous chapter is not indicated. One estimate is that David served in Saul's army for about four years before he was forced to flee from the king. The events in ch 19 date to ca. 1016 B.C. The key words in this chapter are מוּת (*mûth*, "die"; in the Hiphil = "to slay") which appears eight times, and מָלַט (*mālaṭ*; in the Piel = "escape") which is used five times. Saul means *to slay* David, and David *escapes* from the danger.

2. Danger: Saul's Intentions Regarding David (19:1-5)

19:1-3 Prior to this chapter, Saul had threatened David's life (18:11) and had assigned him to military tasks virtually certain to bring about his demise (18:13,17,25). Now the king went a step farther. He attempted to enlist the help of Jonathan in getting rid of David. The NIV gives the erroneous impression that Saul issued orders for his associates to kill David. The Hebrew suggests only that he spoke to his court officials of his intention to kill David. Jonathan was present. He is said to have been **very fond** of David (lit., "took much delight"), the same word used by the king's servants to describe Saul's attitude toward David in 18:22. Apparently at this time Saul was unaware how close Jonathan and David were.

Jonathan prudently said nothing in public to oppose his father's plans. He realized, however, that there were always men eager to commit the most heinous crimes at the bidding of the king. Jonathan took swift action. He (1) revealed to David that his father was looking for the opportunity to kill him, (2) warned David to be on his guard the following day, (3) urged him to go into hiding and stay there until it was safe to reappear at court, and (4) promised to spend time alone with his father the next day in order to find out more precisely what his plans might be regarding David. The use of the phrase **my father** twice in vv. 2-3 (three times in the Hebrew text) gives Jonathan's negotiations special poignancy (Klein, 195). Jonathan intended to steer his father into the field where David was hiding. His purpose in so doing was not so that David might overhear the conversation in his hiding place; but that Jonathan might more easily report to him the result of his conversation without having to track him down. The first person pronoun in v. 3 is emphatic, as if Jonathan was saying, "Leave this to me; I will assume the responsibility of being your advocate."

19:4-5 Had Jonathan simply advised David to flee, without endeavoring to reconcile the two men, he would have been acting to the detriment of his father's interests by depriving him of the best support of his kingdom (Kirkpatrick, 1:170). Jonathan kept his word. He **spoke well** to his father about David. The heir to the throne — the one above all men likely to be injured by the growing popularity of David — spoke with great power and intense earnestness on behalf of his friend. (1) He appealed to Saul not **to wrong** (lit., "sin against") David. This in effect was a warning that to take the life of David would be a sin. (2) He argued for the innocence of David. He had not **wronged** (lit., "sinned against") the king, who certainly had the right to execute wrongdoers, but not those who were innocent. (3) Jonathan pointed out that all that David had accomplished had been a benefit to the concerns of the crown (lit., "his deeds are very good for you").[1] (4) David's loyalty to Saul could not be questioned since **he took his life in his hands,** i.e., he voluntarily exposed himself to peril of death,[2] **when he killed the Philistine.** (5) Jonathan also pointed out that God had worked through David to give a great victory to all Israel. (6) He reminded Saul of his previous disposition toward David when he rejoiced over David's defeat of Goliath. (7) By means of a rhetorical question, Jonathan admonished his father not to **do wrong to an innocent man** (lit., "sin against innocent blood") by slaying David.

3. Danger Averted: Saul's Oath (19:6)

19:6 The respectful demeanor, cogent logic and impassioned appeal of Jonathan changed the mind of Saul. To signal his determination not

---

[1]On the basis of extrabiblical texts, McCarter (1:322) sees political overtones in this assurance that David's deeds were "good." The idea is that his deeds were consistent with the loyalty he owed the king.

[2]Kirkpatrick (1:170) suggests that the figure is that of taking a treasure out of a safe place, and carrying it about with the risk of losing it. The figure appears elsewhere in 1 Sam 28:21; Judg 12:3; Ps 119:109.

to give vent to his jealous rage, he took an oath that David would not be put to death. His oath was no doubt sincere at the time, but with no real repentance for his murderous plans.

E. CONTINUING RECOGNITION AND DANGER (19:7-24)

1. Recognition: Restored to Court (19:7)

19:7 Jonathan immediately told David of the conversation. He completed his ministry of reconciliation by escorting David back into the presence of his father. David **was with Saul**, lit., "in his presence," i.e., continued to serve Saul as he had done before the death order was issued. Unfortunately this reconciliation did not last long.

2. Danger: Saul's Arrest Order (19:8-17)

The theme of Saul's frustration and David's success is taken up again in this unit. Here Michal, Saul's daughter, becomes David's ally against her father.

19:8 Verse 8 forms a transition from the account of the reconciliation of Saul and David to Saul's first overt effort to slay David. War broke out again with the Philistines. Saul had been appointed king for the express purpose of freeing Israel from Philistine domination, but now David had become more successful than he in the very task for which he had been chosen. This success again triggered Saul's jealousy and feelings of inferiority.

19:9-10 These verses are particularly damaging to the reputation of Saul. He had sworn a solemn oath that he would not kill David. Since the reconciliation, the only event which has been related is that David had been successful in fighting the national enemies. So the narrative is stressing just how mean-spirited and unjustified and even irreligious were Saul's attacks on David. The king continued to be troubled by the evil spirit from the Lord, i.e., Yahweh.[3] (See comments on 1 Sam 16:14).

---

[3]The spirit is said to be "from Yahweh" here and in 16:14. In 16:15 and 18:10 the spirit is described as being "from God" (*elohim*). Some (e.g., R.P. Smith, 360) think that the latter expression points to a natural influence, while the former points to a direct act of divine punishment upon the impenitent Saul. There does not appear to be, however, any progression

One day while David was playing the harp for the troubled king, Saul **tried to pin him to the wall** (lit., "strike David and the wall") **with his spear**. This is not the same verb used in 18:11 (see discussion) where Saul probably only made threatening gestures with his spear. Though the spear missed David, it went crashing into the wall. The words **that night David made good his escape** anticipate the verses which follow in which the details of his escape are reported. In Hebrew historical narrative the result is stated up front, then the details which led to that result are related.

19:11-13 Saul anticipated that David would attempt to leave the city. The king ordered his men to keep watch all night at David's house to prevent his escape. They were under orders to wait for morning light because (1) to slay a man in his own home was considered the worst breach of cultural mores, (2) waiting till morning light would avoid danger to Saul's daughter, (3) a man just aroused from sleep was presumed to be weaker (cf. Judg 16:1-3), and (4) a night attack might have alarmed the town and brought a mob of angry citizens to rescue their hero.

For the second time in this chapter a member of Saul's own family assisted David in escaping the wrath of the king. How Michal learned of the plot, is not indicated. She warned David to make good his escape that night. Placing her own life in jeopardy, Michal helped her husband climb down from a back window (cf. Josh 2:15; 2 Cor 11:33). It has been proposed that David's house, like that of Rahab (Josh 2:15) was built on the city wall. By lowering her husband to the ground, Michal helped him escape the city and those who were waiting in the street in front of the house.

Meanwhile, Michal attempted to buy some time for her husband by a clever deception. She took **an idol** (lit., "the teraphim," a plural word used here as a singular)[4] that was in the house — perhaps one David

---

from a natural affliction to a divine intervention in the use of these expressions in the text.

[4]"Teraphim" are mentioned fifteen times in the Bible. Those which Rachel stole from Laban were small enough to be hidden in a saddle bag upon which Rachel sat (Gen 31:19,34-35). Teraphim are also mentioned in connection with the unorthodox house shrine of a man named Micah (Judg 17:5; 18:14,17-18,20). The worship of teraphim is described as iniquity (1 Sam 15:23). See also 2 Kgs 23:24; Hos 3:4; Ezek 21:21; Zech 10:2. Because no life-size images have been found in Palestinian archaeology, W.F. Albright (ARI, 114; 207, n. 63) states categorically that the term "teraphim"

had taken as a trophy of war — and laid it in David's bed.[5] This particular idol must have been almost life-size and at least partially of human form. Michal covered it **with a garment** (lit., "the garment"), i.e., the upper garment, which was generally only a square piece of woolen cloth. The text suggests that a particular garment, viz., David's, is intended. She then put a quilt or net of woven **goats' hair at the head,**[6] i.e., either round or over the head of the image in order to hide it, or to imitate human hair.

19:14-15 When David did not come out of his house at the usual hour in the morning, Saul's assassins informed the king. Saul then ordered David's arrest. When the arresting officers came to the door and demanded to see David, Michal lied by telling the soldiers that David was ill. The soldiers, intimidated by Michal's forceful obstruction, reported back to Saul. The king, however, was determined. He sent the men back to **see David**, i.e., to see for themselves just how sick David was. They were not to take Michal's word for it. Sick or not, David should be brought "up" to the palace. The terminology suggests that Saul's residence was on the hill of Gibeah, David's in

---

in this passage cannot have its usual sense. He suggests the translation "old rags" based on the meaning of the root *trp* ("to wear out") in Ugaritic. P.R. Ackroyd opines that the images here referred to were designed to aid healing. *ET* 62 (1950-51): 378-379. Youngblood (716) holds that Michal did not place the household idols *on* or *in* the bed but *at* or *beside it*. The Hebrew *'el* often has this meaning. This would enhance the impression of David's illness.

[5]Apparently the common people superstitiously believed that the *teraphim* brought good luck to the house over which they presided. It is difficult to believe, however, that David personally held to any such notion. KD (273) speculate that Michal kept *teraphim* in secret, like Rachel, because of her barrenness (cf. Gen 31:19).

[6]The NIV does not attempt to translate the Hebrew כְּבִיר (*kābîr*). The word is used only in this chapter and the meaning is uncertain. According to BDB (460) the term refers to something *netted*, i.e., either a quilt or a fly-net spread over the face while a person was asleep. Standard English versions render "quilt" (NASB); "net" (NJPS, NRSV); "pillow" (ASV, BV); "tress" (JB); and "cover" (NKJV). The LXX confused כְּבִיר with כָּבֵד (*kabēd*) = "liver." Based on this version, Josephus has Michal placing a still moving goat's liver in the bed, to make the messengers believe that there was a breathing invalid beneath. Albright (ARI) believes that the expression כְּבִיר הָעִזִּים (*kᵉbîr hā'izzîm*) means "old he-goat." He comments: ". . . it would be easy to see how effective the . . . half-concealed head, with black beard and burning eyes, would be as a substitute for a sick man."

the lower city. David should be brought up, even **in his bed.** If the soldiers did not want to attack a sick man, Saul himself would slay his rival. The "bed" in that time was usually nothing more than a mattress so it would have been easy to transport.

19:16-17 The soldiers went back and burst into David's bedroom only to discover that Michal had made fools of them with her deception.[7] Michal was summoned to her father. He rebuked her for deceiving him and aiding David, his enemy, to escape. Afraid of bringing her father's anger upon herself, Michal told her father that David had threatened her life if she would not aid in his escape. While this may have kept Michal in the good graces of her father, her lie only made Saul all the more determined to kill David.

3. Danger Averted: God's Spirit (19:18-24)

19:18 After this escape and deception, David never again appeared in Saul's court. He fled to Ramah (see on 1 Sam 15:34) where the old prophet Samuel still lived. This is the first recorded meeting with Samuel since the Bethlehem anointing (1 Sam 16:13). Samuel would be in his nineties at this time. The prophet hardly could have been surprised by what he heard. David's reports confirmed Samuel's earlier judgment regarding the king. Samuel's immediate departure with David for Naioth, i.e., "the dwellings," probably indicates that the prophet regarded that place as safer refuge than his own house. These "dwellings" were like apartments where the sons of the prophets lived. The Targum renders **Naioth** as "house of instruction," i.e., a theological school.

19:19-20 When Saul got word that David was in Naioth at Ramah, he dispatched three successive groups of soldiers to arrest him. When they got to Naioth, the first company saw **a group**[8] **of prophets prophesying.** Samuel was **standing there as their leader** (lit., "head"). This is probably the same group of student prophets

---

[7]Ralbag (cited by Goldman, 119) suggests that the bed was brought to Saul and the deception only then discovered.

[8]The Hebrew word לַהֲקָה (lahăqāh) appears only here. According to the rabbis, this form arose from an inversion of the letters of the more common word for congregation/assembly (קְהִלָּה, qᵉhillāh). Possibly the term used here was the prophet's own technical term for some peculiar arrangement of their number for choral purposes (R.P. Smith, 362).

that Saul had encountered on the day he was anointed by Samuel (see 1 Sam 10). Samuel appears to have been the founder of this prophetic movement. Their **prophesying** would be vigorous singing of praises to the Lord.[9] The soldiers **saw** this sight. The Holy Spirit came upon them and **they also prophesied.** This is not a case of these soldiers being carried away by the religious excitement of the chanting prophets. These men where overwhelmed by the Spirit of the Lord in such a way as to rebuke their evil designs.

19:21-22 Two more times Saul sent soldiers to arrest David. Each time the soldiers were overcome by the Spirit of God, and they prophesied. Finally, Saul himself decided to go to Ramah. At the great cistern at Secu — apparently a well-known landmark between Gibeah and Ramah about which nothing further is known — he learned the exact location of the apartments known as Naioth.

19:23-24 As he was walking along the road toward Naioth, even before he got there, **the Spirit of God came even upon him.** This refers, not to the evil spirit from the Lord, but to the Holy Spirit. This king who was rebelling against the divine Spirit felt its influence even more forcibly than his servants. As he walked the remaining distance to Ramah, Saul **was prophesying,** i.e., vigorously praising God as he had done on the day he was first anointed (1 Sam 10:6ff.). The spirit of prophecy which had originally confirmed his calling (1 Sam 10:9-13) now blocked his way and thwarted his will.

At Naioth he became so energetic in his praise for the Lord that he "also" (i.e., like the previous soldiers)[10] **stripped off his robes,**

---

[9]In describing what the prophets were doing, the Hebrew uses the Niphal (passive-reflexive) stem of the verb. In describing what Saul and his soldiers did, the Hebrew uses the Hithpael (reflexive) stem of the same verb. Frequently scholars interpret the Niphal form to indicate delivering intelligent oracles and the Hithpael form to indicate unintelligent raving. E.g., T.H. Robinson, "The Ecstatic Element in Old Testament Prophecy," *The Expositor,* 8th series, 21 (1921): 224; H. Knight, 23. The forms, however, are used interchangeably in 1 Samuel 10. If any distinction was originally intended in the two forms of the verb it cannot now be ascertained. See J.E. Smith, "The Life and Thought of the Pre-literary Prophets," *The Seminary Review* 13:4 (1967): 100.

[10]The NIV ignores the expression גַּם־הוּא (*gam-hû'* = "also he") which follows the verb "stripped off" and stresses that Saul was as vigorous and uninhibited in his verbal praise for the Lord as the three groups of soldiers who preceded him.

probably because of the heat. **Also** like the companies of soldiers, Saul **prophesied in Samuel's presence.** What happened to Saul here was like what happened on the day of his anointing when he joined the prophets in vigorous musical praise to the Lord (1 Sam 10:9-12).

Finally Saul became exhausted. He lay **that way** (lit., "naked"),[11] i.e., without his outer garments, **all that day and night.** The absence of the Hebrew *gam* ("also") in this last clause is noteworthy. Only Saul was laying there the whole day and night with his clothes off, apparently unconscious and perhaps paralyzed.

The overpowering of Saul and his soldiers by the Spirit of God turned the wrath of man into the praise of God. Hereby God preserved the lives of all the prophets, preserved the life of his servant David, and frustrated all the evil purposes of Saul. Since the Lord could have dealt with the king in a much more violent manner, inflicting injury or death, this incident should be regarded as a manifestation of God's grace. This was the last recorded effort of the Spirit of the Lord to break through the hardened heart of Saul and bring him to repentance.

People were stunned by this display of religious devotion on the part of the self-willed and disobedient Saul. They asked again the question which they asked years before: **Is Saul also among the prophets?** (cf. 1 Sam 10:12). The present incident is far more spectacular than the earlier one. No wonder, then, that the old proverb, which apparently originated among friends and family of Saul in the area of Gibeah, was now revived and circulated in all Israel.

How is this episode with Saul prophesying before Samuel to be reconciled with 1 Sam 15:35 which states that Samuel never saw Saul until his death? The LXX solved the problem by having Saul prophesy before *them*, i.e., the prophets. Samuel is not mentioned. This, however, seems to be an obvious effort to harmonize the two passages. The correct understanding of 15:35 is that Samuel did not see Saul in the sense of seeking him out to give him prophetic guidance. In the present passage the overpowering by the Spirit prevented any conversation between the prophet and the king.

---

[11]The term עָרֹם (*'ārōm*) does not always signify complete nudity, but is also applied to a person with his upper garment off, wearing only the long linen garment which was worn next to the skin. Cf. Isa 20:2; Micah 1:8; John 21:7. Kimchi and Ralbag (cited by Goldman, 120) hold that Saul was completely naked.

1 SAMUEL 20

F. JONATHAN'S RECOGNITION AND DANGER (20:1–21:9)

While Saul and his men were overwhelmed by the Spirit, David made his getaway. He went to see Jonathan one last time. David was now convinced that he would have to leave the court of Saul permanently. His departure from the royal court was of as much interest to the Narrator as his arrival there in chs 16–17. He has demonstrated that David's path to the throne was legitimate. His fugitive status, however, and especially his relationship with the Philistines during those fugitive years, might cause some to question David's right to rule Israel. For this reason, the Narrator goes into great detail in order to explain how Israel's rising star temporarily experienced eclipse.

1. Recognition: A Covenant with Jonathan (20:1-17)

David's Fear and Jonathan's Naïveté (20:1-4)

20:1 While Saul lay helpless in his trance-like state, David, perhaps at Samuel's urging, **fled from Naioth**. He had no idea how long Saul might be overwhelmed by the Spirit. Prudence would dictate that he remove himself as fast as possible from that area. Yet his bond of friendship drew him back to the capital. He sought out Jonathan to update him on the most recent events, and to seek his blessing on the course he now felt compelled to adopt.

In three rhetorical questions he blurted out his discouragement and confusion to his friend. The three questions are a virtual assertion of innocence. David could not understand why Saul was trying to kill him. He had committed no **crime**, nor had he **wronged**[1] Saul in any way. David appears unwilling formally to break with Saul until

---

[1]The verb (חָטָא, *ḥāṭāʾ*) means "to miss," "to miss the mark," and so "to fail." In a theological context, it has the meaning of "to sin."

251

absolutely forced to do so. **That he is trying to take my life** is perhaps a fourth and independent question introduced by "Why."[2]

20:2 Jonathan made no attempt to reply to David's questions. He responded to David with an exclamation of horror: **Never!** (lit., "far be it"). He refused to believe that his father was still trying to kill David. The prince forcefully affirmed that David was not in danger of losing his life. He declared that Saul **doesn't do**[3] **anything great or small**, i.e., absolutely nothing, **without confiding in me** (lit., "and he does not uncover my ear"). Had Saul changed his attitude, he would have indicated such to Jonathan. Bearing in mind Saul's oath (19:6), and attributing his recent violence to temporary madness, Jonathan refused to believe that his father had any deliberate design against David's life.

20:3 Jonathan's words of reassurance cannot make David waver in his assessment of the present danger. He repeated[4] his unshaken convictions regarding Saul's murderous purpose. He offered a plausible explanation as to why Jonathan had not been informed about the assassination plot which David had narrowly escaped with the assistance of his wife, viz., Saul knew of the friendship between David and Jonathan. Therefore, he was deliberately hiding from Jonathan his present intentions regarding David. To impress on Jonathan how serious the situation was, David took an oath. **As surely as the LORD lives and as you live** is an oath formula appearing here for the first time in the Bible. David believed he was but a step[5] from death, i.e., he stands, as it were, upon the very brink of a precipice. Jewish commentators refer to the **step** which David took in avoiding Saul's spear. He did not believe that his life could be saved by Jonathan's good offices.

---

[2]For the interrogative use of the Hebrew כִּי (*kî*) introducing a clause following the more common interrogatives, see Youngblood, 639.

[3]The NIV rightly reads the לֹו (*lô*, normally "to him") as the negative לֹא (*lō'*). The NIV follows the *Qere* reading of the verb which suggests an imperfect. The *Kethibh* reading, a perfect, is to be preferred. The translation would then be: "My father has (hitherto) done nothing at all, which he has not told me."

[4]The NIV follows the LXX and Syriac in omitting עוֹד (*'ôd*, "again"), the presence of which is acknowledged by ASV, NASB, NKJV, NRSV, and NJPS.

[5]The word "step" is a *hapax legomenon* though a verbal form of this root appears in Isa 27:4, and there are Aramaic and Syriac cognates according to Driver (161). McCarter (1:335) emends the text, partly on the basis of the LXX, and reads: "he has sworn a pact between me and Death."

20:4 Jonathan, who had claimed a close relationship to his father in v. 2, identified with David. David's discouragement, demeanor, and solemn oath had won him over. He would do whatever his friend asked of him.

David's Plan to Help Jonathan Know (20:5-7)

20:5 The next day was the New Moon festival which, according to the Mosaic law, was celebrated with special sacrifices and blowing of trumpets (Num 10:10; 28:11-15; Ps 81:3). Scholars are divided as to whether this festival was celebrated every month, or four times a year. The present passage suggests that Saul gave a feast at the New Moon which was celebrated as a civil as well as a religious festival. In this civil observance the festival lasted two days. David, as the king's son-in-law and a ranking officer in the army, would be expected to be present. This occasion was chosen by Jonathan and David for testing the king's state of mind and heart following his very public religious exercises at Naioth.

20:6-7 The plan was this: David would hide in the field for the next two days. If Saul missed him at the banquet, Jonathan should tell him that he (Jonathan) had given David permission to make a quick trip to Bethlehem for the **annual sacrifice** of his family clan, which apparently coincided with that New Moon. It is doubtful whether Jonathan was empowered to act in the king's stead. If, however, Saul had changed his spirit toward David, he would excuse this breach of etiquette, especially since he may not have been in the capital when David made the request of Jonathan. On the other hand, if Saul was still hostile toward David he might suppose that David was rallying support for a bid for the throne. If Saul lost his temper, then Jonathan would know that his father was **determined to harm** David, lit., "that evil is finished (or complete) from him," i.e., finally decided and no further appeal would then succeed in changing the king's purpose to do David harm.

How is an annual sacrifice **at Bethlehem** to be explained in the light of Deut 12:5ff. which requires public worship acts to be performed at the central sanctuary? Some explain the practice as due to the disorganized condition of public worship in those days since the destruction of the tabernacle at Shiloh.[6] Others propose that the

---

[6]The phrase "annual sacrifice" occurs only two other places, viz., 1 Sam 1:21 and 2:19, both of which refer to the annual trips of Elkanah to the central sanctuary at Shiloh.

annual sacrifice of the clan at Bethlehem was not primarily a cultic occasion, but a celebration at which meat was slaughtered and eaten as specifically permitted in Deut 12:15,20f. This would be like a family reunion. See further on v. 29.

A Covenant between David and Jonathan (20:8-17)

20:8 David had certain expectations of Jonathan based on the covenant which the latter had initiated in 18:3. **Show kindness** (חֶסֶד, *ḥesed*) means to demonstrate covenant loyalty.[7] David humbly referred to himself as **your servant** twice in the Hebrew text. This showed his loyalty to Jonathan. David reminded Jonathan that he had **brought him into a covenant with you before the LORD,** lit., "into a covenant of Yahweh you have brought your servant with you." A "covenant of Yahweh" is one which is ratified in his name by solemn oath, hence a sacred and binding covenant, one in which Yahweh was both Witness and Guardian. **Yourself** is emphatic in the Hebrew. If Jonathan felt there was any truth in the charges brought against him by Saul — if he deemed his friend a traitor to the crown — let him slay the betrayer himself there and then.

20:9 Again Jonathan used the exclamation of horror (cf. v. 2). He indignantly rejected the idea that David had committed treason. He was shocked at any suggestion that he might deliver David over to his father's wrath. He indicated that if he had the least inkling that his father was determined to harm David, he certainly would tell his friend. He indignantly refused to take David's life or even to allow his life to be touched by his father. Following the exclamation, the rest of the sentence in the Hebrew is broken, indicating the agitation and deep feeling of the prince. A literal rendering would be: "If I knew certainly that evil were determined by my father to come upon you, and did not tell you . . . ."

20:10 Again the sentence in the original is very abrupt and ungrammatical. David asked how that information would get to him if Jonathan was with his father in the palace.[8] The question is suggested by David's assessment of the situation, viz., that Saul would

---

[7]חֶסֶד refers to "the mutual relationship of rights and duties between allies" (N. Glueck, 46-47).

[8]Standard English versions conflate what appear to be two questions in the original: "Who will tell me? or what your father answers you harshly?" i.e., if you should attempt personally to bring me the word. Cf. NKJV. The

be suspicious that there existed some understanding between David and Jonathan, and that he would take steps to prevent Jonathan from informing David about the conversation with his father.

20:11 David's question had shown Jonathan that there were obstacles in the path of his promise to keep David informed about his father's attitude. Therefore Jonathan invited David to go out to the open country with him so the two could have more privacy to work out the details of a plan.

20:12-13 Jonathan began his conversation with David by invoking the name of Yahweh.[9] Jonathan would **sound out** his father, i.e., ascertain his disposition toward David. This he would do **by this time the day after tomorrow,** lit., "the third morrow," i.e., on the morning after the second day of the festival, and so on the third morning after the conversation. If Saul was favorable toward David, Jonathan would send word to him by a special messenger. In the event that the king displayed enmity, Jonathan would himself come and see David because (1) he could not entrust another with that message, since thereby Saul might come to know where David was hiding; and (2) no doubt that would be the last time the two friends would be able to see one another. Jonathan then swore that he would most surely warn David if his father was still hostile. **May the Lord deal with me, be it ever so severely** is a self-malediction formula should the speaker (here Jonathan) be unfaithful to the stipulations of his oath. Following the oath, Jonathan wished the Lord's blessing on David, as the Lord had been with Saul in his early military campaigns.

20:14-15 In v. 14 the roles are reversed and Jonathan began to ask favors of David. The Hebrew of these verses is again very abrupt and ungrammatical. This can be attributed to the violent emotion of the speaker. Jonathan requested that as long as he lived, David might show unfailing kindness such as the Lord had shown to his

---

NIV has followed BDB (15) in rendering אוֹ (*'ô*, normally meaning "or") as "if" and then ignoring the interrogative מַה (*mah*).

[9]Jonathan appears to be directly addressing Yahweh here in almost prayer-like fashion. Instead of putting the follow-up verb in the second person (which would be consistent with direct address), Jonathan repeated the name of Yahweh. Standard English versions, however, translate as an oath formula: (1) "The LORD God of Israel be witness!" (BV, and essentially ASV, JB, NKJV); (2) "By the LORD, the God of Israel!" (NRSV, NJPS).

people.[10] Jonathan realized that David would one day be king. In those days, when the kingship changed from one family to another, the new king would execute all of the family members of the old king. Second, Jonathan requested that David would never cease (עַד עוֹלָם, *'ad 'ôlām*) to show kindness to his family, even after all of his **enemies** were cut off from the face of the earth. Thus on behalf of his descendants Jonathan extended in perpetuity his previous covenant with David. After he became king, David fulfilled this promise by showing kindness to Mephibosheth, Jonathan's son (2 Sam 9:1ff.).

20:16-17 Jonathan and David entered into a covenant there in the field outside the palace at Gibeah. Verse 16 has been interpreted in two very different ways. Some see this as a commitment on Jonathan's part that he would protect the family of David as long as he was alive. If he should be unfaithful to that covenant, he prayed that the Lord would exact the penalty of its breach from David's enemies, i.e., the house of Saul. Others understand v. 16 to refer to the promise which Jonathan had sought from David in vv. 14f., and now that promise was made binding also on **the house of David,**[11] i.e., his posterity, as well. In either case, Jonathan prayed that the Lord might bring David's enemies **to account** (lit., "may Yahweh seek from the hand of David's enemies") for the way they treated him.[12]

---

[10]The general drift of v. 14 is clear, but the exact translation is difficult. A rendering closer to the reading of the MT would be: "And will you not, if I am still alive, yes will you not show me the kindness of Yahweh, that I die not?" The construction of this verse is very difficult if all the negatives of the MT be retained. Read with other vowels, two of these negatives become interjections of desire — "O that." The verse would then read: "And O that, while I still live, yes, O that you would show me the kindness of Yahweh . . . ."

[11]The *house of David* is mentioned twenty-two times in the NIV. Two references to the house of David have been found in extrabiblical texts. A. Lemaire calls attention to line 31 of the Mesha Stela (*BAR* 20.3 (1994): 30-37). A basalt stela set up by an Aramean king at Tel Dan mentions the house of David in line 9. Primary publication: A. Biran and J. Naveh, *IEJ* 43 (1993): 81-98; *IEJ* 45 (1995): 1-18. For a discussion of these two allusions, see K.A. Kitchen, "A Possible Mention of David in the Late Tenth Century BCE, and Deity *Dod as Dead as the Dodo?" *JSOT* 76 (1997): 29-44.

[12]Some modern commentators follow Rashi in understanding David's "enemies" as a euphemism for David himself. The explanation is as follows: Oriental courtesy forbade Jonathan's saying, May Yahweh punish David if he should break the covenant, nonetheless he prayed that God would requite

Then Jonathan asked David to **reaffirm** (lit., "swear again") his oath out of (or perhaps *by*) his love for him. The thought is that Jonathan exacted another oath beside that implied in vv. 14-15, because the intensity of his love impelled him to bind David by the strongest possible obligation (Kirkpatrick, 1:178). Each man loved the other as much as he loved himself. Jonathan wanted an unbroken bond of love between his family and that of David.

2. Danger: Flight Necessary (20:18-42)

Jonathan's Plan to Share Information with David (20:18-23)

20:18-19 Jonathan knew that David would be missed at the New Moon festival on the next day. **Day after tomorrow** is literally "when you have waited three days," i.e., either with his family in Bethlehem, or wherever he felt safe. Nothing in the Hebrew text corresponds to **toward evening**. David should **go to the place** (lit., "go down greatly,"[13] i.e., a long way into the valley), where he had hidden before when **this trouble** (with Saul) **began,** lit., "on the day of the business," i.e., either the incident recorded in 19:1-7, the day of the attack with the spear, or some unrecorded matter. This spot is further identified as being **by the stone Ezel.** This stone (or "heap of stones" according to the LXX), or possibly ruin, is mentioned nowhere else. Some have supposed it to be a road-stone, or stone guidepost. The name of the stone means "departure," and probably got its name from its being the spot where David separated from his friend.

---

the violation on someone. If divine anger, however, visits even David's enemies for the breach of covenant, how much more the guilty perjurer himself. See R.P. Smith, 378. Gordon (167) cites 1 Sam 25:22 and 2 Sam 12:14 as other likely instances of the euphemistic addition of "enemies." He also points out that this phenomenon is paralleled in second millennium texts from both Egypt and Mesopotamia. KD (285) think that the second clause in v. 16 is not a wish by Jonathan, but a statement of the historian ("And Yahweh required it [what Jonathan predicted] at the hand of David's enemies") to the effect that Jonathan's words were really fulfilled in due time.

[13]Cf. NRSV, "go a long way down"; and NJPS, "go down all the way." The ASV and NKJV have "go down quickly." This rendering, while supported by the Vulgate, makes no sense. It did not matter whether David went fast or slow, as he was to hide there for some time, but it was important that he should be far away, so that no prying eye might spot him.

20:20-22 No suspicion would be aroused by Jonathan's carrying the bow which was his usual weapon (18:4). Jonathan would shoot three arrows at the stone Ezel as his mark. He would then send his attendant after the arrows. If he told the boy, **the arrows are on this side of you,** then David would know that he was safe. **You are safe; there is no danger** is literally "there is peace to you and nothing (else), or it is nothing," i.e., to worry about. He could rejoin the royal court. If, however, Jonathan told his servant, **the arrows are beyond you,** then David would know that he must leave forever. That would be God's will for him. The prince was prepared to recognize the divine will in the banishment of David from the court. Jonathan planned these precautions because he did not know whether or not he would be accompanied by friends of his father from the city.

20:23 The **matter** discussed is (1) the agreed upon sign which had just been worked out, and (2) the reciprocal covenant of friendship between the two, viz., that David would not harm the family of Jonathan, and Jonathan would protect the life of David (vv. 14-17). Yahweh was **witness** between the two which made this a solemn commitment the breach of which by either party would be divinely punished (cf. Gen 31:49ff.).

A Friendship Condemned (20:24-34)

20:24-25 David played out the charade to humor his friend. He hid in the field while Saul and his court celebrated the New Moon festival. The king **sat down to eat,** lit., "he sat down beside the bread to eat." Saul **sat in his customary place by the wall,** the place of honor at the table opposite the entrance, the safest place in the room. The NIV has him sitting **opposite Jonathan** (so the LXX). The Hebrew text states that when Saul sat down in his usual place, Jonathan "arose,"[14] (1) to show respect for the entrance of the king, (2) to surrender his seat next to Saul to Abner, or (3) to take his place alongside his father. Abner, the commander of the host, sat beside the king on one side.

20:26 The place of David, as the king's son-in-law, was empty. King Saul said nothing during the first day of the festival. The king thought that maybe David had touched something which was

---

[14]Following the Hebrew text here are ASV, NASB, NKJV, NJPS, BV, and NRSV.

unclean or in some other way had defiled himself. Under the law of Moses a person could be made **unclean** by contact with a dead body, or nocturnal emission (cf. Lev 15:2-26). Apparently it was contrary to social propriety to take part in a public feast in a state of Levitical uncleanness, even though it is not expressly forbidden in the law (KD, 282). The repetition of the thought of David's unclean state may be a skillful reflection of the state of Saul's mind, as if he were trying to convince himself that uncleanness is the only possible explanation of David's absence by repeating the phrase over and over again to himself (Goldman, 126).

20:27 The New Moon festival as celebrated at Saul's court extended over two days, as opposed to the one-day celebration which is prescribed in the Mosaic law. Under Mosaic law, most ordinary impurities lasted only until sundown (cf. Lev 15:16). Uncleanness could not, therefore, be the explanation for David's absence on the second day of the festival. Saul asked casually, and with as great an air of indifference as he could muster, why David had not come to the meal either day of the festival. Saul's contempt for David is conveyed in the way he speaks of the **son of Jesse**;[15] by way of contrast, Jonathan refers to him by his proper name.

20:28-29 Jonathan answered the king's question in the way previously suggested by David. He quoted David as having requested release from the obligation to attend the banquet in Gibeah because (1) **our family is observing a sacrifice in the town,** lit., "we have a family sacrifice"[16] in the city; and (2) **my brother has ordered me to be there,** i.e., the eldest brother[17] who was making the arrangements in Jesse's old age. The reference to the brother may be an embellishment on Jonathan's part. On the other hand, perhaps this detail was simply not reported in v. 6. Did Jonathan lie? It is possible that David had made a quick trip back to his hometown on the first day of the festival. It was only 8.5 miles from Gibeah to Bethlehem. David's request was based on the possibility that he had found **favor** with Jonathan (cf. v. 3). The words **Let me go,** lit., "let me escape," in the modern vernacular between friends might be something like "Give me a break!"

---

[15]"Son of Jesse" is used frequently in a disparaging way to refer to David (see 1 Sam 20:30,31; 22:7,8,13; 25:10; 2 Sam 20:1).

[16]This is the only occurrence of the phrase "family sacrifice" (זֶבַח מִשְׁפָּחָה, zebaḥ mišpāḥāh) in the Bible.

[17]4QSam[b] and LXX read plural, "brothers."

Jonathan was using a light, almost jocose way of speaking as if the requested exemption from attendance was but a mere trifle.

20:30-31 The excuse which Jonathan offered was plausible, but it did not dispel the king's mistrust. Saul's anger **flared up** at Jonathan. Saul referred to him neither as "my son" nor by his name. His outburst may be accounted for by one or more of these considerations: (1) Unlike David, Jonathan had not given first place to his own family, (2) Jonathan's support of David had now been clearly impressed on Saul's mind, and (3) Saul may have viewed David's devotion to his family as an act of self-assertion against the king (Mauchline, 148).

Saul's anger was manifested in four ways. First, he hurled foul-mouthed verbal abuse at his son. He called Jonathan a **son of a perverse and rebellious woman!** (lit., "you son of one perverse in rebellion"). This epithet is intended to cast a shadow over the virtue of Jonathan's mother, and therefore Jonathan's paternity.[18] Saul was not angry with his wife; it was his son alone upon whom he wished to vent his wrath.[19] Second, Saul accused Jonathan of having **sided with the son of Jesse** (lit., "you are choosing for the son of Jesse") to his own shame and the shame of his mother, lit., "to the shame of the nakedness of your mother." In essence Saul was saying that Jonathan was a mistake from the day of his birth.[20] Third, Saul accused Jonathan of stupidity which endangered not only himself (emphatic "you" v. 31), but his family. Did he not realize that as long as David was alive neither he nor his future kingdom would be established? Fourth, Saul ordered Jonathan to send and bring David to him, **for he must die**, lit., "a son of death is he." This order suggests that the murder had been prearranged to take place at the feast.

20:32-33 Jonathan ignored the personal attack by his father and tried to plead mildly for his friend as he had done in the previous

---

[18]The NIV translates euphemistically. While the language is strong, it does not call for the crude language of some modern paraphrases, e.g., TEV ("you bastard!") and LB ("you son of a bitch!").

[19]The word rendered "perverse" (נַעֲוַת, na'ǎwāh) is taken by some to be an abstract noun rather than a feminine adjective. The translation would then run, "You son of perversity of rebellion," a common Hebraism for "a man of perverse and refractory nature." This avoids the difficulty of having Saul insult his own wife.

[20]Kimchi suggested the meaning is this: "Your conduct is so lacking in filial loyalty that people will suggest that you are the son of an adulterous union." Cited by Goldman (127).

chapter. Why should David be put to death? What had he done? Saul answered with his spear.[21] He threatened to kill his own son.[22] Then Jonathan knew that his father **intended** (lit., "it was finished from with his father") **to kill David,** i.e., it was his unalterable resolution.

20:34 Jonathan got up from the table, not in fear, but in fierce anger. His anger seems righteous, while that of Saul in v. 30 is marked by fear and envy. Jonathan ate nothing that day, even though it was a festival day of great joy, **because he was grieved at his father's shameful treatment of David,** lit., "for he was grieved for David because his father had put him to shame." Saul had insulted and wronged David by publicly charging him with treasonable intentions.[23] Here is another indication of the noble character of Jonathan. He did not resent the injury and insult offered to himself so much as the wrong done to his best friend.

A Friendship Confirmed (20:35-42)

20:35-37 The **morning** would be the third day of the month. The festival was now over, and the officers and attendants of the royal court were getting back into their normal routine.[24] Pretending to be going out to the field for archery practice, Jonathan and his boy attendant **went out to the field for his meeting with David,** i.e., he went to the appointed place. The presence of the lad would make Jonathan's movements less suspicious. The boy is described as **small** and thus less likely to ask embarrassing questions about the orders he was given. Hoping that David was still in hiding, Jonathan used

---

[21]As in 18:11, the verb translated "hurled" could be translated "he lifted his spear," i.e., brandished it in a threatening way, without actually casting it.

[22]Such is the usual interpretation. Jamieson (190), however, does not think the text actually says that Saul threatened his son. He regards v. 33 as parenthetical: "Now Saul had cast a spear at him to smite him [i.e., David]; whereby Jonathan knew that it was determined of his father to slay David." The idea is that Jonathan recalled the earlier incident in which Saul had tried to kill David, and concluded that the present threats of his father were not empty words.

[23]Another interpretation: the humiliation which Jonathan experienced at the table involved David, because his plea for David had failed (Mauchline, 148).

[24]Goldman (128) thinks that this was a day later than that which Jonathan had fixed for his appointment with David. He must have felt it was unsafe to keep his appointment in the evening of the day in which he discovered his father's attitude. See comments on vv. 5 and 12.

the prearranged sign to attract his friend's attention. He shot a few arrows and ordered his servant to run to fetch them. **As the boy ran, he shot an** [another] **arrow behind him.** When the lad came to one of the first arrows which Jonathan had shot, Jonathan shouted, **Isn't the arrow beyond you?** This shout signaled David, if he was still in hiding, that all was over for him at the royal court (cf. v. 22).

20:38-40 The repeated call to the boy not to wait is to prevent him from looking round or from looking in the wrong direction and possibly discovering David (Hertzberg, 176). Goldman (128) suggests that while the words **Hurry! Go quickly! Don't stop!** were spoken to the lad, they were intended for David. The staccato commands left no room for doubt as to what David's course must now be. The boy picked up the arrow and Jonathan gave the lad his weapons and told him to carry them back into the city. Jonathan wanted time alone with David. He was throwing caution to the wind, but he had to speak to David one last time.

20:41 When he heard Jonathan dismiss his servant, obviously himself intending to stay behind, David understood that the prince wished to speak to him and that it was safe to emerge from hiding. The "arrow" sign would have been enough to have warned David; and had he not seen that Jonathan was alone and waiting for him, David, from his place of hiding, would have made his escape unseen. After the boy had gone, David came out from hiding **from the south side of the stone** Ezel. He paid homage to Jonathan,[28] the crown prince. Then the two friends greeted each other with a kiss on the cheek. They both wept because they thought they would never see each other again. David, however, **wept the most** probably because his future at this time was so uncertain.

20:42 David's heart was too full to reply to his friend's words; blinded with tears, he seems to have hurried away speechless. Jonathan sent David away in peace, as in v. 13 he had promised he would. He wished David well as he departed, because the two had sworn an oath of friendship between them and their descendants. Then David left, and Jonathan returned to town.

1 SAMUEL 21

David now knew he had no option. He had to flee from Saul or he would be killed. Even Jonathan now realized that this was true. David's flight from Saul can be dated to ca. 1016 B.C. David would now be about twenty-four years old.

3. Danger Averted: Tabernacle Supplies (21:1-9)

21:1 David needed help in his flight from Saul. Nob at this time was a priestly city[1] (cf. 1 Sam 22:19), in which the tabernacle (inferred from v. 6), not mentioned since the death of Eli, was then standing. The town was located between Anathoth and Jerusalem within sight of the future temple mount (Isa 10:30,32).[2] To this place David came in order to obtain food and weapons, and perhaps to inquire of the priestly oracle as to his fate (cf. 1 Sam 22:10). Some think Ahimelech is the same person as Ahijah in 1 Sam 14:3; others think the two men were brothers. Ahimelech is called **the priest,** i.e., he served as high priest in this period. This priest **trembled** when David approached him. Normally David was accompanied by a group of servants or soldiers, but now he was traveling alone. This raised suspicion that he was no longer in the service of Saul. Ahimelech did not wish to be drawn into any controversy between the king and his leading commander.[3] David had left the few servants who were traveling with him in his flight somewhere in the neighborhood because he wished to converse with the high priest alone.

---

[1]Though called in 1 Sam 22:19 "a city of priests," Nob is not specified among the places assigned to the priests by Joshua.

[2]Nob is thought to be modern el-Isawiyeh, 1.5 miles northeast of Jerusalem and 2.5 miles southeast of Gibeah.

[3]KD (290) suppose that Ahimelech thought that David had come to him with a commission from the king which might involve him in danger.

21:2 David would not admit to the priest that he was fleeing from Saul, because evidently he was afraid that Ahimelech would refuse to give him any assistance. David told the priest that **the king** had dispatched him on a secret mission. Was David lying? If he was, no one can justify his lie. It is possible, however, that some mission had in fact been assigned to David before the New Moon festival, perhaps even before the incident at Naioth in ch. 19. It is perhaps significant that David did not say "Saul" had sent him on a mission. The unnamed king may be Yahweh. In addition, Jonathan expressed the conviction that the Lord had "sent" David away (20:22), the same idea contained in the literal rendering of **your mission,** viz., "the mission that I am sending you on" (Youngblood, 727). David indicated that he would rendezvous with his men at some designated spot. No doubt David had supporters at court who were prepared to share his flight. **I have told them** is literally "I have made known."[4] That David was in fact traveling with some of his servants is confirmed by Jesus (Mark 2:26).

21:3 David stated the reason for his appearance at the tabernacle. **What do you have on hand** is literally "what is that under your hand?" **Give me** is literally "give into my hand." He needed provisions — five loaves of bread or whatever the priest could spare.

21:4 The priest indicated that he had no **ordinary** (lit., "common") **bread,** i.e., bread which was not consecrated, on hand. He did have some **consecrated** (lit., "holy") **bread,** the bread of the Presence or showbread which had been removed from the sacred table. If David and his men met the minimal requirement of not having slept with women the previous night, he and his servants would be given that consecrated bread. Abstaining from normal husband-wife relations on the day preceding some religious duty was a requirement under the law of Moses (cf. Lev 15:18). Warriors engaged in holy war were bound by the same rule (Deut 23:9-14; Josh 3:5; 2 Sam 11:11-12). So if David and his men were engaged in a holy mission, the priest would share the holy bread with them.

21:5 In response to the priest, David made two affirmations. First, he and his men had abstained from sleeping with their wives **as usual,** lit., "since yesterday and the day before." Since the raids

---

[4]The latter part of v. 2 is rendered in the standard English versions: "I have directed [my] young men" (NKJV, NJPS); "I have made an appointment with the young men" (NRSV); "I have arranged to meet them" (JB); and "I have appointed the young men" (ASV).

against the enemies of God's people were considered "holy war" such ritual purity was required. The clause **whenever I set out** (lit., "in my going out") is best taken with what follows. The thought is, "When I set out, **the men's things** [clothing, pouches, etc.][5] were holy," i.e., Levitically clean through washing (Lev 15:18). The remaining portion of the verse is best taken as a hypothetical statement which literally would be something like this: "and if it is an unholy way, it becomes holy through the instrument" (KD).[6] The thought is that the mission of these men to the tabernacle was sanctified because David, God's chosen instrument, had come there in his extreme need.

21:6 Ahimelech was convinced. He gave David the **consecrated bread,** i.e., **the bread of the Presence.** This was unleavened bread which was removed from **before the Lord,** i.e., the table in the holy place, each Sabbath (seventh day). It was replaced by **hot,** i.e., freshly baked, **bread.** The law stipulated that these twelve loaves of pure wheat flour were to be placed in the sanctuary before Yahweh (Exod 25:30; 35:13; Lev 24:5-9; 1 Chr 9:32).

How could Ahimelech give David bread which was only to be eaten by priests? The answer seems to be given in 1 Sam 22:10. An eyewitness stated that Ahimelech first **inquired of the Lord,** probably by Urim and Thummim (see on 1 Sam 10:20-21), before he gave provisions to David. Thus it would appear that God himself authorized giving David these provisions. In any case, Jesus cited this incident as an excusable violation of a cultic regulation (Matt 12:3-4; Mark 2:25-26; Luke 6:3-4).

---

[5]The Hebrew כְּלִי (kᵉlî; lit., "vessels") could denote weapons, bodies (NEB), or even be euphemistic for genitalia (Hertzberg).

[6]In the standard English versions, the second half of v. 5 is rendered in this manner: "The vessels of the young men are holy, and the bread is in effect common, even though it was sanctified in the vessel this day" (NKJV). "When I came out, the vessels of the young men were holy, though it was but a common journey; how much more then today shall their vessels be holy?" (ASV); "Whenever I went on a mission, even if the journey was a common one, the vessels of the young men were consecrated; all the more then may consecrated food be put into their vessels today" (NJPS); "Though this is a profane journey, they are certainly pure today as far as their things are concerned" (JB). "The vessels of the young men are holy even when it is a common journey; how much more today will their vessels be holy?" (NRSV); "the young men's kits have been consecrated. Although this is a secular mission, the kits will render it set apart" (BV).

21:7 One of Saul's servants, Doeg, was at the tabernacle that day. He is called the Edomite either (1) because of his race, or (2) because of his place of residence. He is the first of many examples of a foreigner employed in a high position in Israel. Doeg was Saul's **head shepherd,** lit., "the strong one of the herdsmen of Saul." As herds would form the main part of Saul's wealth, his chief herdsman would be a person of importance (cf. 1 Chr 27:29,31).[7] He was **detained before the Lord** because (1) he was participating in purification rites, (2) he was suspected of leprosy (Lev 13:4), (3) he was a proselyte who was seeking admission into the religious community, or (4) he was performing some vow. For whatever reason he would have to remain at the tabernacle until the priests gave him permission to leave. Doeg took note of David's presence, and witnessed what Ahimelech did for the fugitive. David probably recognized that Doeg's presence boded much ill (cf. 22:22), and that is why he elected to flee for refuge to Gath.

21:8-9 The sight of Doeg made David realize how helpless he was in case of attack. David asked the priest if there was any kind of weapon on the premises. He explained the lack of a weapon on his part as due to the urgency of his mission. He had not **brought** (lit., "taken") his weapon before leaving the capital. The king's **business** is the same word translated "a certain matter" in v. 2. As in v. 2 the identity of the king is deliberately ambiguous.

The only weapon which Ahimelech had available was the sword with which David slew Goliath. That trophy was **wrapped in a cloth** (lit., "garment") so as to preserve it from rust.[8] It was **behind the ephod,** i.e., in the place allotted for keeping the sacred vestments, of which the ephod is mentioned as the chief. The reference is probably to that special ephod which the high priest wore when producing oracles from God (cf. 1 Sam 14:3). Ahimelech offered that sword to David. If you **want it** is literally "will take for yourself."

David was overjoyed to have this unique sword. There was no other sword like that one because it was a memorial of David's greatest military achievement. The symbol of God's deliverance in the

---

[7]Hertzberg (181) thinks that the phrase can hardly refer to the office of an overseer; it is rather meant to indicate that Doeg was robust in every way.

[8]The word "cloth" is used in Isa 9:5 of military attire. For this reason some have purposed that the sword was wrapped in the blood-stained war cloak of Goliath.

past was a pledge of his help for the future. It does not appear from the story that the Philistine's sword was of extraordinary size. While it surely was a tried weapon of approved temper and strength, its chief value was its storied associations.

VI. DAVID'S RISE TO PROMINENCE AS AN OUTLAW (21:10–27:4)

David became an outlaw when he was forced to flee from the court of Saul. Still God was blessing him. Gradually his power and influence increased even though Saul was doing everything within his power to track him down. This unit is clearly marked off by accounts of David's flight to Gath.

A. DAVID IN GATH (21:10-15)

21:10 That day David left the land ruled by Saul and entered the city of Gath, ironically Goliath's hometown (cf. 17:4). Gath, the nearest Philistine city, was about twenty-eight miles from Nob. The cause of the desperate flight was (1) the fearful implications of Jonathan's information concerning Saul's implacable hatred and (2) the fear of Doeg, one of Saul's most trusted servants. In the extremity of his peril, he sought refuge with Achish to whom he offered his military services. About five years had passed since the defeat of Goliath. David may have assumed that he would be welcomed there because he was a high ranking commander in Saul's army. He would have valuable information to share with Achish. In any case, the remaining chapters of the books of Samuel will provide ample evidence that foreigners often filled the ranks of armies, even Israel's army.

21:11 Some expositors think that it was Goliath's sword which betrayed David's identity to the Philistines. It seems, however, that he was well known in their land. Although he was recognized, there was no attempt made upon his life, or even against his liberty. David was able to convince Achish that his breach with Saul was genuine, but the king's officers were not so easily convinced. **The servants** ("advisors") of Achish were skeptical about David's intentions. They seemed to realize that David virtually was **king of the land,**[9] i.e.,

---

[9]McCarter (1:356) points to the expression, "kings of the land," in Josh

treated as king by the people. With these words the advisors sought to warn their prince that David was a dangerous man.

21:12-13 Taking note of the attitude of these servants, David began to fear that Achish might order his arrest and execution. So he **pretended to be insane**, lit., "he changed his taste," while **in their presence**, lit., "in their eyes," so that they might regard him as harmless. David rightly conjectured that Achish would not want to retain an imbecile at court. **While he was in their hands**, i.e., when they tried to hold him, **he acted like a madman.** This Hithpolel verb form is used elsewhere to describe behavior resulting from drunkenness (Jer 25:16; 51:7) or terror (Jer 50:38) or driving a chariot recklessly (Jer 46:9; Nah 2:4). The title to Ps 56 suggests that he had been seized and made prisoner by the Philistine nobles in Gath. He made **marks**[10] on the doors of the city or palace gate in the manner of mischievous children. He let his **saliva run down his beard**, i.e., he was frothing at the mouth. Such an indignity to the beard, whether done by another or by one's self, was considered in the East an intolerable insult. This disgusting defilement was sufficient to convince Achish that David was insane.

21:14-15 By his dissimulation David escaped the danger which threatened him in Gath. In ancient times insane people were viewed as being possessed by the spirit of gods or demons. People just left them alone. Achish rebuked his servants for having brought David to his palace **to carry on like this in front of me**, lit., "against me." The words suggest that Achish feared personal injury from David. The question, **Must this man come into my house?** is the king's way of expressing a strong negative. A madman like that would be of no help to the kingdom. For the moment David was safe.

12:1,7 and suggests that David was recognized by the Philistines as a local chieftain. R.P. Smith (397) supposes that the title was given David because, in accepting the challenge of Goliath, he had undertaken what in that time was regarded as the king's special duty.

[10]The Hebrew verb form, used elsewhere only in Ezek 9:4, comes from the root תוה (tāwāh, "to make signs or scribble"). The LXX, "he drummed," i.e., he smote with his fists upon the doors, suggests that the Hebrew text they were reading had a form of the verb תפף (tāphaph = "sound the timbrel" or "beat"). According to D.J. Wiseman, the verb may connote highly aggressive behavior which made David a danger to society. "'Is it peace?'–Covenant and Diplomacy," *VT* 32 (1982): 320-321.

1 SAMUEL 22

Chapter 22 depicts David as growing in power, while Saul continued to spiral out of control to even lower depths of shame. David befriended a runaway priest; Saul slaughtered a community of priests, an action in which the pathetic king could find only a foreigner to support him.

B. DAVID AT ADULLAM (22:1-23)

About 1016 B.C. David fled Gath and found a safe haven at the cave of Adullam. He began to gather around him others who felt that their lives were in jeopardy at the hands of King Saul.

1. Recognized by Warriors (22:1-5)

22:1-2 Adullam was a Canaanite city in the foothills of Judah, about sixteen miles southwest of Jerusalem[1] (Josh 15:35; 12:15). Nearby was the great valley of Elah which formed a highway from Philistia to Hebron in the mountains. In the tributary ravines of this valley are many natural caves, some of great extent, roomy and dry.

Many of David's **brothers** came to join him at the cave of Adullam, which was only about twelve miles west of Bethlehem. **His father's household** would include his parents, family servants, and relatives such as Joab, Abishai, and Asahel, his capable cousins.

Besides the family of David, three other classes of people sought out David at Adullam: (1) those **in distress,** lit., "every man of straits," i.e., those who were in a tight spot,[2] or were hard-pressed by the

---

[1]Youngblood (731) identifies Adullam as Khirbet esh-Sheikh Madhkur, about ten miles east-southeast of Gath.

[2]The term "distress" (מָצוֹק, *māṣôq*) is used of those experiencing the horrors of siege warfare. Cf. Deut 28:53,55,57).

oppressive exactions of the monarchy or its ministers; (2) those who were **in debt**, and therefore in danger of being sold into slavery by a brutal creditor; and (3) those who were **discontented**, lit., "embittered of soul,"[3] i.e., who had real or imagined grievances against the monarch. Among them would be those who were being harassed because of their past associations with David.

Eventually David's followers numbered **four hundred** at this location. Each man in this band was an outlaw and therefore a desperate man. This would be a force of some considerable strength. David quickly asserted his leadership over the group, no doubt organizing it with subordinate officers appropriate to a military unit.

22:3 The text does not indicate what caused David to leave Adullam. He must have become concerned about the welfare of his parents. They could hardly be expected to live an outlaw's life permanently. From Adullam David traveled south a short distance around the Dead Sea to Mizpah ("watchtower"), an otherwise unknown fortress in Moab. Because of his previous position of high standing in the court of Saul, David went directly to the king of Moab. He requested that the king allow his parents to **come and stay with you. Until I learn what God will do for me** points to David's faith and piety. Even before this pagan king, David spoke as a man of God. His life was in the hands of God. David used the generic name Elohim for God, not Yahweh, in his petition to the Moabite king. In general this was the practice when believers spoke to pagan people.

Why did David choose to go to Moab? It may have been because he had some roots in Moab. His great-grandmother was Ruth the Moabitess (Ruth 4:17,22). On the other hand, he may have felt that he would be safe in the territory of one of Saul's adversaries (cf. 1 Sam 14:17). David had less anxiety in seeking an asylum within the dominions of this prince than those of Achish, because the Moabites had no ground for entertaining vindictive feelings against him.

22:4 David **left** his parents **with the king of Moab** is literally "led" his parents into the presence of the king.[4] His parents remained in

---

[3]The phrase occurs again in Judg 18:25 where it is translated "hot-tempered men" (NIV) or "fierce men" (NASB). A bitter spirit characterized people who were homeless, or bereft, or who had suffered great loss (1 Sam 1:10; 30:6; 2 Sam 17:8; Job 3:20).

[4]The MT וַיַּנְחֵם (wayyanḥēm) comes from the root נחה (nḥh = "to lead") which is followed by the ASV, NJPS and NKJV. The NIV, NASB, JB, and

the land of Moab as long as he was in **the stronghold.** This has been taken to refer to all the time he was in (1) Moab itself, (2) in Adullam, or (3) the entire region where David lived before he was enthroned at Hebron. If the stronghold is Moab itself or a place in Moab, then the parents would have stayed only a short time in that land. Probably the stronghold was Adullam. A Jewish tradition affirms that the king of Moab betrayed his trust and murdered them, for which David later exacted a heavy vengeance (2 Sam 8:2).

22:5 The prophet Gad is mentioned here for the first time. He came to David in the stronghold and urged him to return to the land of Judah. Clearly the **stronghold** was considered outside the land of Judah. It has been argued that since Adullam was itself in Judah (cf. Neh 11:30), David could not have been told in v. 5 to leave the **stronghold** (if Adullam) to return to Judah. It would appear that places in the Shephelah such as Adullam were at least popularly considered outside Judah, perhaps because of their proximity to the Philistine territory (cf. 1 Sam 23:3).

From this time on Gad occupied a position of prominence among the followers of David.[5] Gad's advice was grounded in the following considerations: (1) David's claim to the throne might be jeopardized by remaining out of the public eye, (2) David himself might be contaminated by heathen superstitions should he remain long outside the land, (3) he should appear publicly among the people of his own tribe as one conscious of innocence, and trusting in God, and (4) he needed to fill the leadership vacuum created by the incapacitation of Saul due to increasing mental turmoil. David followed Gad's advice and reentered Judah. He camped in a thicket known as the **forest of Hereth,**[6] in the wilderness of Judah. McCarter (1:357)

NRSV take the verb to be from the root נוח (nwḥ = "to leave") which is revocalized as וַיַּנִּחֵם (wayyanniḥēm).

[5]Gad later was designated David's seer (2 Sam 24:11). He is said to have been, along with Samuel and Nathan, a compiler of David's memoirs (1 Chr 29:29). He along with Nathan designed the temple services (2 Chr 29:25). When David sinned by ordering a census, Gad appeared to present to him three options regarding divine punishment (2 Sam 24:11).

[6]Hertzberg (185) is sympathetic to the view that חֶרֶת (ḥereth) is a dialect form of חוֹרֶשׁ (ḥōreš; cf. 1 Sam 23:15-19). The "forest of Horesh" would lie in the Judean wilderness about two miles south of Ziph and thus five or six miles southeast of Hebron.

proposes a location for the Forest of Hereth at the village Kharas near Khirbet Qilah which preserves the name of ancient Keilah.

2. Danger: An Ominous Massacre (22:6-19)

22:6 The remaining verses of ch 22 serve the dual purpose of (1) documenting the next steps in the fulfillment of the prophecy made concerning Eli's house[7] (2:31-33) and (2) demonstrating the contrast between Saul's contempt for priesthood and David's commitment to same. It was not long before Saul was informed that David had surfaced again within his kingdom. He **and his men had been discovered** (lit., "were known"). Saul assembled all his officials to discuss the matter. He **was seated under the tamarisk tree on the hill at Gibeah.** Eastern kings frequently sat with their court under some shady canopy in the open air (cf. Judg 4:5). This species was rare in the hill country and this may account for the importance of this particular tree. Saul's subordinates were **standing around him**. To "stand" before the king is in the Old Testament virtually a technical term for "serving" (cf. 1 Kgs 17:1). The word here seems to mean that they each took their proper posts around the king. Saul held a spear in his hand, the equivalent to the scepter of later kings. It might have been distinguished from common spears by its size or ornamentation.

22:7 Those on the inner circle of Saul's court came from the tribe of Benjamin. Saul here is appealing to tribal jealousy. First, he raises the question about royal grants of **fields and vineyards**. Samuel had warned the nation that one of the abuses of kingship was the redistribution of land (1 Sam 8:14). Second, Saul raised the question of appointment to positions of power as **commanders of thousands and . . . hundreds**. This echoes another abuse forecast by Samuel (8:12). Would not David promote his own fellow-tribesmen rather than the Benjamites? Saul addressed these officials in such a way as to turn them solidly against David. He did not even mention David by name, choosing rather to refer to him with his pejorative term **the son of Jesse**.

22:8 Saul's third rhetorical question targets all of his servants. He accused them all of having **conspired** against him in spite of all that

---

[7]Four times in this chapter (vv. 9,11,12,20) Ahimelech the priest is referred to as son of Ahitub to highlight his membership in the condemned family of Eli.

he had done for them. The word is a strong one. It constitutes a charge, not of having failed in duty, but of positive opposition. This reckless charge is supported by two pieces of evidence. First, no one **tells me** (lit., "opens my ear") when **my son** (he does not mention his name) made a covenant **with the son of Jesse.** The covenant is the more public bonding of the two men mentioned in 18:3, not the private and more specific covenant concluded in 20:12-17.

Second, Saul charged his servants with lack of commitment to his cause. **None of you is concerned about me** (lit., "is sick [at heart] about me"). The proof of this charge is the conspiracy of silence among them in respect to Jonathan's encouragement of David's rebellion against the crown. In Saul's sick mind, having been told nothing is equivalent to betrayal. He accused Jonathan of having incited (lit., "raised up") **my servant,** i.e. David. Supposedly Jonathan had incited David to **lie in wait for** (attempt to ambush) Saul. Here Saul's sick mind was speaking. He actually imagined that Jonathan had turned David against him, and that David was trying to lure him into a trap so as to kill him.

22:9-10 Ps 52 refers to this occasion. **Doeg the Edomite** surfaced again. Three times his gentilic "the Edomite" is given (vv. 9,18,22) doubtless to emphasize that it was not an Israelite who was responsible for the foul deeds that follow (Gordon, 174). He is described as **standing with** (עַל, *'al*) **Saul's officials**. Some understand the Hebrew preposition to imply that he actually presided *over* the national leaders (McCarter, 1:364).[8] Doeg probably spoke up (1) so that he personally could not be accused of failing to keep his king informed and (2) so that the king's suspicions might be turned from the courtiers to the others.

Doeg reported what he had witnessed at Nob a few weeks earlier, viz., that Ahimelech had **inquired of the LORD** for David, i.e., consulted the Urim and Thummim on his behalf. Though not expressly mentioned in the previous chapter, this was probably the chief object of David's visit to Nob. The last clause of v. 10 is actually two clauses in the Hebrew in both of which the direct object stands in the emphatic position before the verb **gave.** This was Doeg's way of expressing his opinion that Ahimelech had committed treason giving David **provisions** and **the sword of Goliath.**

---

[8]KD (296) understand the text to say that Doeg was "superintendent" of Saul's servants.

22:11-13 Doeg's suggestion that the priests were David's allies at once aroused all Saul's worst passions. He sent for Ahimelech and all of his relatives who served in the priesthood at Nob. The sending for all the priestly house when Ahimelech alone shouldered the responsibility suggests that Saul and Doeg had predetermined the wholesale slaughter which followed. Suspecting nothing, the priests all came to the king at Gibeah.

Saul used the same word of Ahimelech as he had used of his servants. Saul accused the priest of having **conspired** with **the son of Jesse** against him. The king had reached the stage when he believed that every man's hand was against him. In proof of the accusation of conspiracy with David, Saul repeated the three points mentioned by Doeg, viz., that Ahimelech had (1) given David bread, (2) provided him with a sword (no longer designated as the sword of Goliath), and (3) inquired of God on behalf of David. It would appear from the fact that Ahimelech only addressed this third charge that it was the most serious of the three.

22:14-15 Ahimelech's defense of his actions was magnificent. He admitted the principal charge, but argued that he had good reasons to comply with David's request. First, Ahimelech listed the credentials of David which made him worthy of help. (1) **David** (he used the name the king thus far had refused to use) was the most loyal servant of the king. (2) He was the king's son-in-law. (3) David was captain of the royal **bodyguard,** lit., "those bound by obedience to the king."[9] Because of all the above, (4) David was the most highly respected member of the royal household. By extolling David's faithfulness, Ahimelech only rubbed salt in the king's wounds. Second, Ahimelech appealed to precedent. He had inquired of the Lord previously on behalf of David.[10] Third, Ahimelech professed total ignorance of any

---

[9]KD (296) understand מִשְׁמַעַת (mišmaʿāh) to refer to a privy councilor of the king, who hears his personal revelations and converses with him about them; and שָׂר (sār, NIV, "captain") to be a verb, from the root סוּר (sûr) meaning "to turn aside from the way, to go in to any one." Here the verb would have the meaning "to have access." So, in this view, Ahimelech described David as one who had access to the most private councils of the king.

[10]Others understand the Hebrew to say: "That was the first day that I inquired of God for him." Ahimelech would then be arguing he had no basis for knowing that Saul would be displeased with him for performing this service for his son-in-law. Mauchline (157) proposed yet another rendering which involves a slight change in vowels: "Have I acted corruptly on this occasion by inquiring of God for him?"

rebellion on the part of David or any threat to Saul's life from that source. Fourth, Ahimelech pled innocence. Conspiracy requires collusion, prearrangement, consultation, and a mutually agreed upon course of action. Neither he nor any other member of the priestly family had any knowledge of David's plans.

22:16 Saul would hear no more. He regarded Ahimelech's straightforward statement as a confession of treason. He had aided and abetted David, the enemy of Saul; and he had failed to inform the king of David's movements. The king sentenced Ahimelech and all the members of his father's house — the main branch of the priesthood — to death. Saul already had lost the support of the prophets represented by Samuel; because of this incident he would lose the support of the priesthood. Without the support of the nation's religious leaders Saul would not be able long to maintain himself on the throne.

22:17 Saul ordered **the guards at his side,** lit., "runners," i.e., those who ran by the royal chariot as an escort, to turn and kill the priests of the Lord because they had sided with David. These "runners" were employed as executioners (2 Kgs 10:25). The king's officials, however, were not willing to lift up their hands against the anointed of the Lord.

22:18-19 The king turned to Doeg who seemed to be the only person present who was offering any help to Saul. The Hebrew gives emphasis to the pronouns in both the command of the king to Doeg, and in his response to the command. The informer became the executioner. At the time the priests were wearing **the linen ephod** as the symbol of their priestly office (cf. 2:18,28). The distinctive priestly dress should have reminded Saul of the sacredness of their persons. Nonetheless, Doeg **killed eighty-five priests.**[11] Some think the number eighty-five may include attendants as well as the priests themselves (Mauchline, 156). Because of this deed, Doeg has been execrated in the ancient Jewish writings above any other of the famous wicked persons who appear in the Old Testament.

Not content with his revenge on the priests themselves, Saul also ordered the extermination of everyone living in the town of Nob including women and children and even infants. **Put to the sword** is lit., "struck with the mouth of the sword." All of the livestock of those who lived in Nob was also to be destroyed. Saul ordered done to this

---

[11]The number is inflated in the LXX (305) and Josephus (385). *Antiquities* 6.12.6.

innocent community what he had failed to do in his attack against the ruthless Amalekites. This atrocity was designed to warn all the subjects of Saul about the consequences of offering aid or asylum to David. The plan, however, backfired. The massacre at Nob alienated all good men in the kingdom. In this tragedy the predicted doom of the house of Eli (cf. 2:31) moved forward to final fulfillment.

3. Danger Averted: Safe In The Desert (22:20-23)

22:20 Whereas Saul severed all connections with the priesthood, David acquired the services and support of the last surviving member of the house of Eli. Abiathar, one of Ahimelech's sons, escaped the slaughter. How he got away is not stated. Perhaps he had been left behind to tend the tabernacle when the others were summoned to Gibeah. Abiathar escaped, with the holy priestly vestments, to join David. With the death of his father Ahimelech, Abiathar became high priest.[12]

22:21-22 Abiathar told David how Saul had slaughtered the priests of the Lord, i.e., had ordered their execution. David felt personally responsible. When he had seen Doeg that day at Nob, he **knew** that Saul's servant **would be sure to tell** the king that he had been to the tabernacle. **I am responsible**[13] **for the death of your father's whole family.** David's conscience pricked him for having been, even indirectly, the cause of so great a calamity.

22:23 David told Abiathar that he could remain with him. Since their lives were in jeopardy from one common enemy, their interests from this point on would be identical. David assured the priest that he would protect him from Saul. Abiathar was the last descendant of Eli to serve as high priest.

The main point of ch 22 is that David, though a fugitive, now has a prophet (Gad) and a priest (Abiathar) supporting his cause. He must in the end prevail over Saul because God is truly with him.

---

[12]Abiathar's career, however, ended under a shadow. He supported Adonijah's bid to take the throne from Solomon. For his participation in that attempted coup, Abiathar was deposed from the high priesthood and banished to his hometown of Anathoth (1 Kgs 2:26).

[13]The verb root סָבַב (sābab) which usually means "to surround, encompass, go around" here appears to have the sense of being the cause of a thing, which is one of the meanings of the verb in the Arabic and in rabbinic Hebrew (KD, 297).

1 SAMUEL 23

C. DAVID AT KEILAH (23:1-14)

The time lapses between the various incidents during Saul's pursuit of David are difficult to ascertain. All of the events of chs 21–27 must fit into a period of a little over four years (ca. 1016-1012 B.C.). Five times during this period David narrowly escaped from his father-in-law. Chapter 23 describes two of those escapes.

1. Recognized by Locals (23:1-6)

23:1 At his camp in the forest of Hereth, David got news that the Philistines, i.e., a marauding company of these enemies, were fighting against Keilah. The appeal to David rather than Saul suggests that the people were coming to regard him as their natural protector. Keilah was located in the lowlands of Judah near the border with the Philistines. It has been identified with Khirbet Qilah which is perched on a steep hill above the valley of Elah, about eight miles northwest of Hebron and some three miles southeast of Adullam (ZA, 114). The raiders were **looting the threshing floors** where the harvest was lying ready for threshing. The threshing floors would be outside the walls of the town. Threshing floors would be obvious objectives for the enemy to plunder, as the whole harvest was laid down, threshed and winnowed on them, and the process took some time.

23:2 David inquired of the Lord, probably through the prophet Gad[1] regarding whether he should go up to attack the Philistines. The answer came back from the Lord that he should go up to **save**

---

[1]Most commentators assume that David inquired through the priestly oracle as administered by Abiathar. The text, however, seems to suggest that Abiathar did not join David until he was at Keilah. That leaders made inquiry regarding the Lord's will through prophets in virtually the same language used here is indicated in 1 Kgs 22:5,7,8. Cf. 1 Sam 28:6.

Keilah in the same manner that the judges *saved* Israel from those who plundered them (e.g., Judg 2:16). By asking for Yahweh's permission, the mission to Keilah was given divine sanction. **These Philistines** evidences David's disdain for these perennial enemies of God's people (cf. 1 Sam 14:6).

23:3-4 David's men were not too enthusiastic about going to battle against the Philistines. They were fearful of the army of Saul there **in Judah**. Keilah belonged to the tribe of Judah (Josh 15:44); so "Judah" here must be used in a limited sense of the highlands of Judah which were more or less firmly under the control of the Israelites. The neighborhood around Keilah must have been under Philistine domination or at least subject to Philistine raiding parties at this time. The term **forces** (מַעֲרְכוֹת, *ma'arkôth*, lit., "battle ranks") is a word that was used six times in the plural and four times in the singular in 1 Samuel 17 where both the Philistines and Israelites had massed armies. It refers to men disciplined and drawn up in martial array. The word appears to be a bit strong to use of a raiding party. Fear always tends to overstate the strength of the enemy. In order to infuse courage into his men, David again inquired of the Lord, through the prophet Gad. Again he received a positive directive to **go down to Keilah** — the forest of Hareth must have been situated on higher ground than Keilah — along with the assurance that the Lord would deliver the Philistines into his hand. The words **I** [emphatic] **am going to give the Philistines into your hand** are taken from the vocabulary of Holy War.

23:5 David and his men marched north to attack the Philistines. They first drove away the Philistine **livestock,** (מִקְנֶה, *miqneh*) a reference probably to beasts of burden which were brought along to carry off the plunder (Hertzberg, 191).[2] Strategically, to attack first the transportation capabilities of the Philistines was a skillful move. By this signal victory over the foraging party, David delivered the people of Keilah from further molestation.

23:6 Abiathar, the lone survivor of the Elide priesthood, had possession of the ephod, the most important insignia of the high priestly office. Abiathar brought the ephod with him when he fled to David **at Keilah**, lit., "towards Keilah." In 22:20 the place where

---

[2]The "livestock" may also have been plunder from earlier skirmishes. Mauchline (159) suggests that מִקְנֶה should here be translated "property" or "gear," i.e., the immediately available plunder, rather than "livestock."

Abiathar joined David is not identified. The account of the meeting of David and Abiathar was inserted in the previous chapter to complete the history of the fate of the priests of Nob. If Abiathar did not actually join David until after he had arrived at Keilah, then the inquiry of the Lord in v. 6 must have been through Gad the prophet. Some, however, understand the present verse to be saying that Abiathar joined David in time to make the trip to Keilah with him. With the priestly oracle now available to him, David would be able always to seek Yahweh's guidance.

2. Danger: Keilah Targeted (23:7-8)

23:7-8 While David enjoyed divine counsel through the priestly oracle, Saul was dependent on human intelligence throughout this chapter. David's location in the walled town of Keilah soon became known throughout the land. He was now **imprisoned,** as it were, within that city. Keilah is said to be **a town with gates and bars,** i.e., a fortified city.[3] Saul anticipated that he would be able to trap David in Keilah. It would be easier to capture his rival by besieging him in a city than by attempting to track him down in the Judean wilderness. **God has handed him over to me,** lit., "has rejected him into my hand."[4] Though his plan was brilliant, and his forces superior, Saul was wrong in assuming that God had handed David over to him. The king still failed to grasp the fact that he was the one who had been rejected. So Saul **called up all his forces** (lit., "the people") for battle.

3. Danger Averted: Priestly Oracle (23:9-14)

23:9 David learned about Saul's plans, i.e., his plans became public knowledge. He must have had those who were sympathetic to his

---

[3]Youngblood (740) opines that Keilah had only one gateway in its wall. Its two reinforced wooden doors were hinged to posts at the sides of the entrance. The doors, which met in the center, were secured with a heavy metal bar spanning the entrance horizontally.

[4]The text reads נִכַּר (*nikkar*) which appears to be the Piel of נכר (*nkr*), a Hebrew root which means "has alienated or rejected." Thus "God has alienated him into my hand," i.e., God treats him as a stranger and so lets him fall into my hand. Mauchline (159), however, points to a Ugaritic root *nkr* which means "has sold or surrendered." The LXX renders "God has sold" and this has influenced the NIV.

cause within the ranks of Saul's advisors. David was alarmed to learn **that Saul was plotting against him**, lit., "forging evil against him." There is no idea of secrecy in the Hebrew verb, which is often used of forging metals. The Hebrew word order in v. 9 suggests that David was upset that Saul was plotting against *him*, rather than *the Philistines*. The text stresses the contrast between the vindictive and vengeful intentions of Saul, and David's unselfish, patriotic, and divinely sanctioned military efforts. David called for Abiathar to **bring the ephod** because the high priest did not always wear this garment (cf. 1 Sam 30:7 and notes on 14:18).

23:10-12 David prayed to Yahweh in the right manner. Twice he referred to himself as **your servant**, a designation which stresses his piety and dependence on the Lord. By contrast, Saul's impiety becomes clear when he **plans**[5] to destroy the city of Keilah in order to kill David (Klein, 230). In his anxiety David asked two questions to be answered through the Urim and Thummim, but he received an answer only to the second, which is the logically prior of the two. Would Saul come down against Keilah? Would **the men** (lit., "the lords")[6] of Keilah deliver him over to Saul? In both cases the answer was **yes**. Since David posed two questions in v. 11, but only received the answer to the second, he had to ask the first question again in v. 12 this time expressing concern for the safety of his men also.

23:13 Any hopes David may have had of making Keilah his head-quarters were abandoned. His men — now numbering six hundred — departed Keilah for the wilderness where they would have a better opportunity of eluding Saul. They **kept moving from place to place**, lit, "they wandered about where they wandered about," i.e., without any fixed plan, as chance or their necessities dictated. Saul called off the attack against Keilah. This was David's first escape from Saul.

23:14 David stayed (1) in the **desert strongholds**, i.e., natural fortresses and places difficult of access in the Judean wilderness; and (2) **in the hills** of the area known as the Desert of Ziph. The Hebrew word מִדְבָּר (*midbār*) is not a "desert" in the narrow sense; it primarily refers to pasture land as opposed to cultivated land. The desert or wilderness of Judah is the barren and for the most part uninhabited

---

[5]The same verb (בקשׁ, *bqš*) is used when Saul was "looking for a chance" to kill David (19:2) and when he "tried" to pin him to a wall (19:10).

[6]The same word (בְּעָלִים, *bᵃālîm*) is used of the leaders of Jericho (Josh 24:11), Shechem (Judg 9:2), Gibeah (Judg 20:5), and Jabesh (2 Sam 21:12).

tract between the mountains of Judah and the Dead Sea. The **Desert of Ziph** was that portion of the desert of Judah which was near to the town of Ziph, usually identified with Tell Ziph, a site about thirteen miles southeast of Keilah and nearly five miles southeast of Hebron (ZA, 43). **Day after day,** lit., "all the days," i.e., of his reign, Saul had men out searching for David.

The various geographical notices in this and this following section indicate how hunted and hemmed in was the life of David and his men once they had given up the idea of trying to reside in a fortified city. This underscores the importance of the remark that **God did not give David into his hands.** Though Saul had all the resources of the kingdom at his disposal, he was powerless against David because the invisible King of Israel declined to permit Saul to touch him.

D. DAVID AT HORESH (23:15-29)

1. Recognized by Jonathan (23:15-18)

23:15-16 The account of the major efforts of Saul to arrest David begins with a brief report of a visit of Jonathan to David's camp. At this time David was encamped at **Horesh** ("thicket"), a district in the **Desert of Ziph** which was overgrown with wood or bushes. The Narrator hints that David was discouraged by the intensified effort of Saul to seek him out and **take his life.** Jonathan, now regarded as a conspirator against the crown and estranged from his father, knew that his friend would need special encouragement at this time. While Saul could not track down David, Jonathan did. The irony of this is underscored by the note that Jonathan was **Saul's son.** Jonathan **helped him find strength in God,** lit., "strengthened his hand in God." The encouragement came, not because Jonathan brought much-needed supplies, but because he reminded David of his innocence, and the promises of God regarding his future.

23:17 Jonathan gave David several words of assurance. First, he began by encouraging David not to **be afraid.** These words respond to the explicit reference to David's fear in v. 15.[7] Second, he assured David that Saul would never be able to find him in order to lay a hand on him. Third, he assured David **you** [emphatic] **will be king**

---

[7]"Don't be afraid" mirror David's words to Abiathar in the face of the same threat (22:23).

over Israel. So far as the record goes, Jonathan knew nothing of the anointing of David by Samuel some years earlier. He reached his conclusions regarding the kingship by observing the conduct of both his father and David in recent years. Jonathan anticipated that I [emphatic] **will be second**[8] **to you** in that day. He would not lessen the glory for David by disputing or opposing his rule. What a marvelous spirit this prince possessed. He was willing to forgo his own destiny to allow one more capable to rule God's people. This is the climax of Jonathan's unselfish generosity. Finally, Jonathan assured David that even Saul knew that one day David would be king (cf. 1 Sam 18:9; 24:21). Saul must have reached this conclusion on the basis of these facts: (1) he had been rejected by Samuel, (2) David had achieved marvelous successes, and (3) the Bethlehemite was growing in popular acclaim. Jonathan never lived long enough to see the day which he forecast in this verse.

23:18 Jonathan and David made a covenant before the Lord, their third. Whereas Jonathan seems to have taken the lead in the earlier covenants between the two, this one seems to be bilateral (cf. 18:3; 20:16). This covenant probably stipulated that Jonathan would be second in authority to David when the latter became king. After the friends parted for the final time, Jonathan returned home.

2. Danger: Betrayed by Ziphites (23:19-25)

23:19-20 At this point Saul got a break. **The Ziphites** (lit., "some Ziphites," i.e., inhabitants of the town of Ziph) went up to Saul at Gibeah and told him where David was hiding at **Horesh**. David was gradually retreating further into the precipitous, deserted hills to the southeast of Hebron. From the site of Ziph a panorama of the whole surrounding district can be viewed. No wonder, then, that the Ziphites saw David and his men passing to and fro in the mountains of the wilderness. The Ziphites gave Saul the precise location of his rival. David was on **the hill called Hakilah**, which some identify with

---

[8]In contexts like this the word generally means to be "second in command" or "next in rank" (e.g., 1 Chr 16:5; 2 Chr 28:7). P.D. Miscall (142) notes that the word can also mean "double" or "copy" (Gen 43:12; Deut 17:18). Jonathan would then be asserting that he would be David's "equal" or "copy." The two then make a covenant as equals.

the ridge called El-Kolah, about six miles east of Ziph. This hill over-
looked the barren and trackless country between the hills of Judah
and the Dead Sea. The hill called Hakilah was **south of Jeshimon,**[9] a
wasteland which paralleled both sides of the Dead Sea. The Ziphites
promised to track David's movements. When Saul came down, they
would hand David over to him.

23:21-23 For their treachery against David, Saul blessed the
Judean Ziphites in the name of Yahweh, for in his twisted view these
men were true patriots. They had shown their **concern** (lit., "spared
him," or "shown compassion") for him. While he appreciated the
loyalty and cooperation of the informants, Saul had no intention of
being taken on a wild goose chase. He directed them to return and
make further preparation,[10] i.e., gather more intelligence on David.

Specifically Saul wanted the Ziphites to (1) **find out** (lit., "see and
know") where David **usually goes,** lit., "where his foot is," i.e., where
one could observe his tracks; (2) identify **anyone who has seen him
there,** i.e., to find any person who could testify to having observed
the movements of David; and (3) to discover **all the hiding places he
uses,** when he would disappear from the public eye. Saul warned the
Ziphites that David was **very crafty.** When they could come back
with definite information, i.e., trustworthy and accurate information, concerning his hiding places and camping spots, then Saul
would come down with his army and track him down.

23:24-25 The Ziphites started out as an advance party ahead of
Saul. Meanwhile, David and his men were on the move again. They
were now in **the Desert of Maon in the Arabah south of Jeshimon.**
When Saul heard this (through the Ziphites), he went into the
Desert of Maon in pursuit of his rival. David retreated to **the rock,**
probably the conical mountain in that area, the top of which is today
covered with ruins, which may be the remains of a watchtower. The
Arabah is the name for the central rift valley of which the Jordan
River and Dead Sea are a part. The Desert of Maon must have
extended sufficiently east to reach a point which could be reckoned
as in the Arabah. Modern Khirbet Main, five miles south of Ziph

---

[9]"Jeshimon" is not a proper name, but means any desert (Ps 107:4; Isa
43:19), though it is used especially of the desert of Sinai in Deut 32:10, and
of that of Judah here and in Num 21:20; 23:28.

[10]The NJPS is similar. A better rendering is "make more sure" (NASB; cf.
ASV, NRSV, NKJV, BV).

marks the location of the ancient site of the town of Maon (ZA, 43). The Desert of Maon would thus most likely have been south of the Desert of Ziph. Maon was the home of Nabal (1 Sam 15:2).

3. Danger Averted: A Philistine Invasion (23:26-29)

23:26-27 With the aid of information supplied by the Ziphites, Saul headed for that rock or mountain. He was right on David's heels. While Saul was moving along one side of a mountain, David and his men were on the other side, **hurrying** — the word expresses anxiety and fear — to get away from the pursuers. Saul's forces were closing in on David and his men to capture them. Just at that moment a messenger arrived from Gibeah to call Saul home. The Philistines had invaded the land. The coincidence of the timing of this invasion was God's plan for saving David from certain death at the hands of Saul.

23:28 Saul was forced to break off his pursuit of David to deal with the Philistine threat. Someone named that spot **Sela Hammah-lekoth** which means either "rock of divisions" (referring to Saul's abandonment of the pursuit, or the fact that the mountain itself had momentarily separated David and Saul), or "rock of smoothnesses," i.e., of slipping away or escaping.[11] The rock became a memorial of David's preservation in the wilderness. This was David's second escape from Saul.

23:29 Apparently David no longer felt secure on the west side of the wilderness of Judah where the Ziphites were watching his every move. So he crossed the arid waste and sought shelter in the beautiful oasis of **En Gedi,** about ten miles east of Hachilah, on the shore of the Dead Sea (ZA, 43).[12] In this area caves offered places of escape in which detection was not easy. Presumably the six hundred supporters followed David in his flight. The name "En Gedi" means "the spring of the wild goats or gazelles," a name derived from the large number of ibexes which inhabit these cliffs.

---

[11]The root of the word used here (חָלַק, ḥālaq) can mean "to be slippery" as well as "to divide (by lot)."

[12]For an archaeological survey of the En Gedi area, see B. Mazar, AOTS, 222-230.

1 SAMUEL 24

E. DAVID NEAR EN GEDI (24:1–25:1a)

Again the exact time lapse between this and the preceding chapter is not indicated. Some months probably went by. This much can be said about chronology: all the events of chs 21–27 fit into a period of about four years (1016-1012 B.C.). David had now escaped from Saul twice. In this chapter he had the most narrow escape yet.

R.P. Gordon has pointed out that chs 24–26 contain a three-part plot in which there is incremental repetition of the motif of blood-guilt and its avoidance.[1] Chapters 24 and 26 mirror each other in many details. Both highlight David's refusal to assault the Lord's anointed. These two chapters form a frame around ch 25 in which Nabal played the role of the antagonist who tempted David to commit assassination.

1. Recognized by His Men (24:1-7)

24:1-2 When the threat from the Philistines was over, Saul again turned his attention to tracking down David. He was told by his informants — perhaps the Ziphites again (cf. 23:14,15,19; 26:1) — that David was **in the Desert of En Gedi**. The seriousness of David's predicament in this passage is indicated by the facts (1) that Saul took with him his standing army of **three thousand men** (cf. Baldwin's "three crack battalions"), five times the number who were with David (cf. 23:13); (2) that these were all **chosen men,** i.e., warriors who were especially skilled and courageous; and (3) that his forces represented the army of **all Israel**. That he would take such a force into such inhospitable territory indicates that Saul did not plan to fail again in his efforts to kill David.

---

[1]R.P. Gordon, "David's Rise and Saul's Demise," *TB* 31 (1960): 53.

Saul was nearer than he realized to David when he came into an area known as the **Crags of the Wild Goats**. The reference must have designated some location in the area of En Gedi in which the wild goats were gathered, rather than the cliffs which were scarcely accessible except to the wild goat, for v. 4 indicates that there were sheep pens and a path in the area. Wild goats (i.e., the ibex) are still found in that area even to this day. The large force which he took with him gave Saul every prospect of success. The overruling providence of God, however, again frustrated his plans.

24:3 Several **sheep pens** made of stone were located in this area, even today built at the mouths of the numerous caves. Saul entered one of those caves **to relieve himself** (defecate), lit., "to cover his feet."[2] Nothing in the text suggests that McCarter (1:386) is right in regarding this account as a mockery of Saul (cf. Judg 3:24). The Narrator is merely trying to explain why it was that Saul was in a cave without the presence of his bodyguards. It so happened that David and his men were hiding far back in that cave. It is not necessary to assume that all six hundred of David's men were in the back of the same cave or in one of the galleries branching off from the entrance.

24:4 The men whispered to David, urging him to slay Saul while he was alone in the cave. They quoted prophetic words to the effect that God would deliver David's enemy into his hands. No record exists of any promise made to David that one day God would deliver Saul into his hands. Perhaps this is something which the prophet Gad had said.[3] It is more likely, however, that prophetic assurances of ultimate deliverance from Saul's hand were here interpreted by David's followers in their own way. **Then David crept up unnoticed** is literally "David arose," i.e., he got up from his place of hiding. Nothing here suggests that David approached the person of Saul.[4] Perhaps the king had removed his outer garment and left it near the entrance of the cave while he went further into the darkness to defecate. David

---

[2]The euphemism "cover the feet" is also used of King Eglon (Judg 3:24). The Syriac version took this expression to refer to a midday nap, and this understanding has been followed by a few modern commentators.

[3]KD (303) think the meaning of David's men was this: "Behold, today is the day when God is saying to you . . .", i.e., the speakers regarded the visit of Saul to that cave as an indication of God's purpose to deliver the king into David's hand.

[4]A number of scholars think that the language "David arose" after his men had spoken suggests that he initially was going to follow their advice.

was able to **cut off a corner** (lit. *wing*) **of Saul's robe** which may have been lying on the floor very near to where David was hiding. The bustle and noise of Saul's men relaxing outside the cave entrance probably covered any sounds made by David as he approached Saul's robe. Scholars have suggested various subtle motives for this action, e.g., symbolism that the kingdom was going to be torn away from Saul and given to David (Gordon, 179).[5] Here, however, the taking of the piece of the robe is a sign of restraint and innocence (Klein, 239). The only motive supported by the text is that David wanted proof to convince the king that his life had been in David's hands.

24:5-7 Afterward, lit., "and it came to pass after thus," i.e., after he cut off the piece of Saul's robe, **David was conscience-stricken**, lit., "the heart of David smote him." David believed that he had sinned by merely cutting off a piece of the king's robe.[6] He regarded this as an injury done to the king himself. Here David had a golden opportunity to rid himself of his adversary, and his closest followers assured him that such was the will of Yahweh. David, however, steadfastly refused to advance his cause with violence. He rejected such a notion with the strongest exclamation: **The LORD forbid**, lit., "far be it (חָלִילָה, *ḥālîlāh*) to me from Yahweh." This effectively countered the argument that it was Yahweh who had spoken either through prophet or providence that he would have his enemy in his hand to deal with as he saw fit. David based his allegiance to the king on religious grounds. Saul was **the LORD's anointed** (see on 10:1), i.e., his person was sacred. With these words David **rebuked** (lit., "tore in pieces; split") **his men**. Perhaps this Hebrew verb is the equivalent of the modern "tongue lashing." The precise connotation of this verb is unclear, but it suggests that it was no easy task to restrain the men. Obviously they were reluctant to give up this opportunity to smite Saul. David **did not allow** (lit., "give") **them to attack** (lit., "rise up against") Saul.[7]

---

[5]Baldwin (146) references 1 Sam 15:28 where robe tearing had been interpreted by Samuel as a symbol of the cutting off of Saul's dynasty. The "piece" or "corner" of Saul's robe is mentioned four times in this chapter (vv. 4,5,11 × 2).

[6]David's heart also "smote him" in 2 Sam 24:10 after he had numbered the people, at which time he confessed, "I have sinned."

[7]Polzin (210) thinks David acted in his own self-interest. He too was the anointed of the Lord. He did not wish to do anything that could provide a precedent for his own assassination later.

2. Danger/Defense: An Appeal to Reason (24:8-15)[8]

24:8 When Saul got a safe distance from the cave, David went out and **called out** to him. He addressed the king respectfully. When Saul turned in his direction David's bearing was that of a loyal and respectful servant. He addressed Saul as **My lord the king**, i.e., his acknowledged superior. He **bowed down and prostrated himself with his face to the ground** in homage. By his lowly bearing David showed that, so far from being a rebel, he still acknowledged Saul's lawful authority, and was true to his allegiance. He then began to reason with Saul.

24:9-11 First, David asked the king why he continued to listen to those advisors who told him that **David is bent on harming you**. This question deflects to a certain extent the irrational conduct of Saul. David refers to men like Cush the Benjamite against whom Psalm 7 is directed. Such men strove to inflame Saul's mind against David. Second, David made reference to what **this day you have seen with your own eyes.** Conceding the point raised by his men within the cave, David pointed out that **the LORD delivered you into my hands in the cave.** He could in fact have dealt with Saul as he pleased within the cave. Third, he informed the king that **some urged me to kill you,** lit., "one said to kill you," or "it was said to kill you."[9] David was under the same external pressure as Saul to kill his rival. **I spared** is literally "she looked on with compassion." The reference is to David's eye (fem. gender) which had looked on Saul with pity.[10] David had withstood that pressure and had spared Saul. The implication is that Saul also should withstand the pressure of his advisors to kill David. Fourth, David indicated the reasons he had not, and would not **lift up** his **hand against** Saul. David called Saul **my master,** i.e., he was a loyal subject of the king. Furthermore, his master was **the LORD's anointed,** i.e., his person was inviolable.

---

[8]The Hebrew word אַחֲרֵי (*'aḥărê*, "after, behind") occurs seven times in vv. 8-15. The term is usually left untranslated by the NIV. It serves, however, to give cohesion to the literary unit.

[9]Another understanding is that "Yahweh delivered you today into my hand and he [Yahweh] said to kill you," i.e., God had created an opportunity for David to kill Saul. By the circumstance of being in the cave, it was as though the Lord was bidding him to kill the king.

[10]Thus the verse depicts a contrast. Saul's *eyes* had seen that the Lord had delivered him into David's hands, but David's *eye* had looked on Saul with pity.

24:11 David then addressed Saul as **my father,** a form of address expressing deference and affection (cf. 2 Kgs 5:13; 6:21). Saul was also David's father-in-law, but that was probably not a factor in the address here. Michal, Saul's daughter, probably already had been given in marriage to Phalti thus technically depriving David of being son-in-law to the king. As he continued to reason with Saul, David confessed what he had done in the cave. He held up the piece of Saul's robe. **Understand and recognize** is literally "know and see." This was proof that David could have killed Saul. Saul must surely now realize that David was **not guilty of wrongdoing or rebellion**. David pointed out the injustice being perpetrated against him. **Wronged you** is literally "sinned [against] you." Though he had not "wronged" the king in any way, Saul persisted in **hunting . . . down** David **to take his life**.

24:12 Convinced of his own innocence and of the guilt of the king, David was willing to let Yahweh **judge between you and me,** i.e., decide the merits of the case and exercise his rule in deciding between the pair (cf. Gen 16:5; 31:53). He asked the Lord to **avenge the wrongs** which Saul had done to him. Under no condition, however, would David take revenge on Saul. He promised **my hand will not touch you.**

24:13 The old saying is literally "the saying of the ancients." David quotes a proverb — just three words in Hebrew — to the effect that only a wicked man could perform wicked deeds, i.e., a man's character is known by his actions.[11] To avenge oneself is wicked, and David's deeds clearly prove that he was not evil.[12]

24:14 Even if David should wish to attack the king, he did not possess the power to do so. Saul was really wasting his time pursuing him. As **the king of Israel,** Saul surely had better things to do. David was as harmless as **a dead dog**. Saul had no reason to be afraid of David. A dead dog cannot bite or hurt.[13] David pictured himself

---

[11]Another interpretation of David's proverb is that the misdeeds of the wicked would recoil upon their own heads. Saul's wickedness therefore would be his own destruction.

[12]A.S. Herbert thinks this proverb is double-edged. It vindicates David's refusal to harm Saul while at the same time condemning the wicked Saul for his malicious pursuit of David. "The 'Parable' [*Māšāl*] in the Old Testament," *SJT* 7, 2 (1954): 183-184.

[13]Probably the punctuation following **a dead dog** and **a flea** should either be periods (ASV) or exclamation marks (JB, RSV). The use of question

as insignificant as **a flea** — which is not easily caught, and if it is caught, is poor game for a royal hunter.

24:15 David concluded with a series of prayers. He prayed that the Lord would judge and decide between the two of them as to who was really right. He asked that God might consider his cause and uphold it; that God might vindicate him **by delivering me** (lit., "judge me") out of Saul's hand. The thought is that by judging him justly, the Lord would effect David's deliverance from his adversary.

3. Danger Averted: Saul Relents (24:16–25:1a)

24:16-17 David's behavior toward him had conquered for the moment the evil demon of Saul's heart. First, he expressed in a question his shock at hearing from David: **Is that your voice, David . . . ?** Second, he hinted at a new relationship between the two by referring to David as **my son**. Four chapters earlier Saul had considered David a son of death, i.e., one deserving to die (20:31). Third, Saul was moved by David's speech. He openly **wept aloud** at David's magnanimous conduct which was almost without parallel in that rude age. Fourth, Saul admitted that **you** [emphatic] **are more righteous than I**, i.e., that David had treated him well, while he had treated David badly. There is nothing strange in this sudden change of feeling in one so nervous and excitable as was Saul. It is clear that for the moment Saul meant to alter his conduct toward David. The sad sequel, however, shows that this resolve was of short duration.

24:18-19 Saul realized that the Lord had delivered him into David's hands; yet David had not taken advantage of the situation. Saul cited a proverb to match the proverb of David in v. 14. If a man comes upon his enemy he will not let him get away unharmed. Since David had done him no harm, David must not consider Saul his enemy. He prayed that the Lord might **reward** David well **for the way you treated me today**, lit., "in return for this day in which you have done for me."

---

marks (NIV, NASB, NKJV, BV, NJPS, NRSV), for which there is no warrant in the Hebrew text, hints at threat as if David were saying, "You have taken on more than you bargained for!" (So Baldwin, 145, following D.M. Gunn (1980; 154).

24:20-21 Saul now admitted that he realized that David would one day be king, that the kingdom of Israel — Saul's kingdom — would **be established** in his hands.[14] This conviction was forced on Saul by (1) his own rejection by Samuel, (2) by the failure of all that he attempted against David, and (3) by the realization that a man who possessed such superior character must eventually wear the crown (Spence). Saul asked David to take an oath that when he became king he would not follow the custom of the time and **cut off** (kill) Saul's descendants thereby wiping out Saul's name from his father's family (see on 1 Sam 20:15).

24:22 This request for an oath must have been a face-saving action by Saul. If David would not kill the king, he would have no reason to kill the descendants of the king. Nevertheless, David was glad to take the oath. This oath led to a temporary truce, and they went their separate ways. Still cautious about Saul, David made no effort to return to his old home and position. He maintained his outlaw status when he **went up to the stronghold.** David probably found it difficult to provide food for his six hundred men in the En Gedi area. He left the En Gedi area (below sea level) and returned to the hill country of Judea around Hebron (about three thousand feet above sea level) and perhaps beyond there to Adullam in the Shephelah west of Hebron. Here he would be in a grain producing area where feeding his followers would be easier. The third escape from Saul enabled David and his followers to return to a more hospitable area of the country.

25:1a During the time when David was living in the desert, Samuel, last mentioned in 19:22, died. That the death of Samuel should be reported at this point is appropriate because (1) Saul had been forced to accept the implications of Samuel's judgment on him when he stated publicly that David would be his successor, (2) Samuel's death represented a setback for any possible reconciliation between Saul and David, and (3) David was now deprived of a very important supporter.

All Israel (cf. Deut 34:8) assembled (probably at Ramah) and mourned for Samuel. The nation, which was in danger of breaking up in tribal factionalism because of the hostilities between Saul and

---

[14]The same Hebrew word translated "established" here is used by Samuel when he announced to Saul, "But now your kingdom shall not endure," lit., "be established" (1 Sam 13:14).

David, was united in lamentation over the grand old prophet. This public mourning honored one who had spent his entire life in the service of his country and who had guided them through one of the most critical transitions in their entire history. Since the days of Moses and Joshua, no man had arisen to whom the covenant nation owed so much as to Samuel, who justly has been called the reformer and restorer of the theocracy (KD, 305). During virtually his entire life he had gone in and out among them as prophet, judge and counselor of the king.

The death of Samuel at a hundred plus years marked the end of an era. He was buried (at his own request?) **at his home** in Ramah. Obviously the text does not mean within the house itself,[15] for that would lead to perpetual ceremonial defilement (Num 19:16). The text probably means (1) in his home town or (2) in a garden or courtyard attached to his house.[16] On the location of Ramah, see on 1 Sam 1:1.

---

[15]Baldwin (146) thinks Samuel was buried under the floor of his house so that veneration of his tomb would be discouraged.

[16]King Manasseh is said to have been buried in his own house/home (2 Chr 33:20). This is further explained to mean "in the garden of his own house" (2 Kgs 21:18). Joab was also buried in his own house (1 Kgs 2:34).

1 SAMUEL 25

F. DAVID IN THE WILDERNESS OF PARAN (25:1b-35)

Probably a few months elapsed between the events of the previous chapter and this one. This chapter addresses the same issue: revenge by David's hand, or by God in his own time? David learned that, if he withheld the avenging sword, God would act on his behalf (vv. 38f.).

1. Recognition of David Refused (25:1b-11)

25:1b David's movement probably had nothing to do with Samuel's death as the NIV rendering implies. He went down into the **Desert of Maon.**[1] The NIV here has chosen to follow the LXX rather than the Hebrew text which reads **wilderness of Paran**. This departure from the Hebrew is based on the assumption that (1) this notice of David's movement is connected to the episode which follows and (2) the wilderness of Paran was too far south to make intelligible the interaction between David and a man who lived in Maon. First, the travel notice may have no connection with what follows. David may have made a trip farther south, perhaps in search of provisions for his people, only later to return to the area of Maon where he had stayed earlier (23:14ff.). Second, it may be that the designation "wilderness of Paran" was used with greater latitude than is generally recognized and included the regions of the wilderness of Judah south of Hebron. In either case the MT should be retained.

25:2-3 The attention now shifts to **a certain man in Maon** and his wife. This man **had property there at Carmel** near his home at

---

[1]Goldman (149) suggests that the incident with Nabal took place prior to David's flight to En Gedi when he was dwelling in the wilderness of Maon (1 Sam 23:24).

Maon. Carmel is not the famous mountain spur of northern Canaan, but the spot where Saul erected a monument (1 Sam 15:12). This man was **very wealthy** (lit., "very great"; cf. 2 Sam 19:32). The size of Nabal's wealth is emphasized by being mentioned even before his name is given. His wealth was measured in flocks and herds — a thousand goats and three thousand sheep. The man was **shearing** his sheep for their wool at this time of the year. Sheep-shearing time was a joyous time of celebration, an occasion of festivity and generous hospitality.

At last the name of the wealthy citizen of Maon is stated. **Nabal** means "fool."[2] Since it is unlikely that parents would give a child such a disparaging name, some have suggested that Nabal was a nickname, or a pun made on his original name which had a more positive meaning. The contrast between the characters of Nabal and his wife **Abigail**,[3] so relevant to the present episode, is briefly but vividly drawn. Abigail is described **as an intelligent** (lit., "good in understanding") **and beautiful** (lit., "lovely in form") **woman** (cf. Gen 29:17; Esth 2:7).

Nabal is described as **a Calebite**. Standard English versions have followed the *Qere* reading of the text, rather than what is actually written. Since the conquest the family of Caleb had occupied the region around Hebron (cf. Judg 1:20). The *Kethib* reading (that which is actually written in the Hebrew text) suggests that Nabal was "like his heart" (cf. Ps 14:1; 53:1), perhaps a sarcastic note which alludes to the well-known statment regarding the fool in Ps 14:1 = 53:1.[4] He was

---

[2]The term נָבָל (*nābāl*, fool) designates not a harmless simpleton, but rather a vicious, materialistic, and egocentric misfit. Other passages present the נָבָל as an embarrassment to his father (Prov 17:21), a glutton (Prov 30:22), a hoarder (Jer 17:11), and even a practical atheist (Ps 14:1). Most significantly, a נָבָל was one who refused to feed the hungry and give drink to the thirsty (Isa 32:6). J.D. Levenson, "1 Samuel 25 as Literature and as History," *CBQ* 40 (1978): 13.

[3]Some think that this Abigail was the half sister of David, the daughter of Nahash (2 Sam 17:25) who is the only other Abigail mentioned in the Bible (1 Chr 2:15-16). She was married to "Jithra" or "Jether" (2 Sam 17:25). "Jithra" was Abigail's first husband, or perhaps the given name of Nabal. See J. Levenson and B. Halpern, "The Political Import of David's Marriages," *JBL* 99, 4 (1980): 511-512.

[4]If the *Kethib* is the correct understanding, then the word alludes to the prideful and ultimately stupid character of this man, who seems to have recognized no authority other than his own. Still another understanding of the

surly, lit. "hard" or "harsh" **and mean** (lit., "evil")[5] **in his dealings,** i.e., rough, stubborn and thoughtless.

25:4-8 David sent **ten** of his young men to Carmel to request a donation of provisions. No doubt most of the sheep-masters were glad to give provisions to one who guarded their flocks and defended them from incursions of the desert tribes. The number of servants perhaps sent a signal as to how big the expected gift should be. First, the young men were told to greet Nabal warmly and respectfully. **Long life to you** translates a Hebrew term of uncertain meaning,[6] although obviously it is some kind of greeting. **Good health** (שָׁלוֹם, *šālôm*) is still a standard greeting today among the Jews.

Second, David's servants called attention to the special season of the year. Third, the young men reminded Nabal of how David's men had behaved in reference to the shepherds who worked for Nabal. They did not **mistreat them**, lit. "we caused them no shame." David's men did not appropriate any of the flocks and herds which they watched. Though David had the might to do so, he never took any of Nabal's flocks for his own use. Fourth, David requested that Nabal **be favorable** toward his young men, **since we come at a festive time** (lit., "a good day"), i.e., a good day for eating and drinking, or a holiday (Esth 8:17; 9:19,22). David anticipated that Nabal might be favorably disposed to be generous at this season.

Fifth, David referred to himself and his men by terms which reinforced the obligation of generosity during the festival. David's young men were **your servants,** and David was **your son.** This self-designation as "son" displayed reverence and respect. Sixth, David left the nature of the donation up to Nabal. He could give **whatever you can find for them,** lit., "what your hand shall find," i.e., what was readily available (1 Sam 10:7). David sought neither to harm Nabal and his family nor to diminish him in any way of his lavish holdings.

---

text derives the disputed word from כֶּלֶב (*keleb*, "dog"). Nabal was then a man of dog-like character, or snappish like a dog.

[5]Gunn (1980; 154, n. 7) has pointed out that each of the Hebrew terms "good" or "do good" and "evil" or "do evil" appear seven times in ch 25. The contrast between good and evil underscores one of the major themes of the chapter, viz., good brings its own reward, while evil always backfires on the perpetrator.

[6]Standard English versions render לְחָי (*leḥāy*) as "to life!" (NJPS); "to him who lives in prosperity" (NKJV, ASV); "Greeting!" (BV). The NRSV and JB ignore the difficult word.

25:9-11 David's men delivered the message, and **waited** (lit., "they rested," or perhaps, "they sat down") for a response. Nabal finally replied. Clearly his intentions were to insult David. First, he acted as if he had never heard of David (cf. Judg 9:28). The expression **son of Jesse**, however, is generally used of David in negative comments.[7] Second, he acted as if David were a nobody, just one of many rebels breaking away from their masters. The fact that Nabal's language may have described some of David's men added sting to his rebuff (cf. 1 Sam 22:2). Third, he emphasized that his festival provisions were his own. He spoke of **my bread and water.** In an area in which water was scarce that would be a valuable commodity.[8] Fourth, he pointed out that all the festival provisions he had made were for the enjoyment of **my shearers.**[9] He saw no reason why he should take his prepared meat and give it away.

2. Danger: David's Anger (25:12-13)

25:12-13 When the young men reported Nabal's words, David was enraged. He felt that Nabal had returned to him evil for good. He ordered his men to put on their swords. David and four hundred of his men began heading toward Carmel. Two hundred men stayed **with the supplies,** i.e., remained to guard the camp.

3. Danger Averted: Abigail's Intervention (25:14-35)

25:14-17 Abigail, no doubt, often had acted as peacemaker between her intemperate husband and his neighbors. This explains why **one of the servants** (lit., "a lad, one of the lads") told her what

---

[7]On the use of "son of Jesse" in a disparaging way to refer to David, see 1 Sam 20:27,30,31; 22:7,8,13; 25:10; 2 Sam 20:1.

[8]The LXX read "wine" instead of "water." This is one of the countless alterations which the Greek translators arbitrarily imposed on the text.

[9]Levenson ("I Samuel 25," 16) points out that Nabal here must either be dangerously out of touch with his own workers or a deliberate liar "who seeks only to cover his callousness and greed with a mantle of humanitarian motivation." The way in which he refers to his workers as "slaves" (עֲבָדִים, 'ăbādîm twice in v. 10), and the way they refer to Nabal in v. 17, suggest that a very bad relationship existed between the master and his servants. Cf. the terminology used of David's men in vv. 5,9,12, and 13.

had happened. His reference to David without further definition indicates that he was well-known in that area. The servant reported that David had **sent messengers from the desert to give our master his greetings,** lit., "to bless our master." This man, however, had rebuffed the gesture and had **hurled insults** at David's servants. The verb (עִיט, *'îṭ*) describes the pouncing of a bird of prey upon its victim. It is used in 1 Sam 14:32 to describe how Saul's troops pounced upon the battle spoils. Thus Nabal "flew upon them like a bird of prey." This servant went on to attest that (1) David's men **were very good to us**; (2) David's servants **did not mistreat us.** (3) **The whole time we were . . . near them** is lit., "all the days we went to and fro with them"; **out in the fields** (lit. "the field," i.e., the common pasture land) **near them, nothing was missing,** i.e., David's men had never stolen any of Nabal's livestock. In fact (4) **night and day,** i.e., constantly, David's men had been **a wall around us,** i.e., they protected Nabal's servants and sheep from marauding desert tribes, thieves and predatory animals.

The servant sensed that David would probably retaliate for the mistreatment by Nabal. He encouraged Abigail to **think it over and see** (lit., "know and see") what she might be able to do to avert the disaster. The servant believed that disaster was **hanging over our master and his whole household.** No one could talk to Nabal because he was **such a wicked man** (lit., "a son of Belial"; see on 1 Sam 1:16), i.e., he was so obstinate that his servants dared not try to reason with him. Nabal had scorned David, just like certain "sons of Belial" had refused to pay homage to Saul when he had been selected by lot at Mizpah (1 Sam 10:26-27).

25:18-19 Fortunately a store of provisions already had been prepared for the shearing feast (v. 11). Abigail gathered a sizable amount of provisions, obviously not enough for six hundred men, but perhaps what David had expected his ten servants to bring back. The inventory of items included **two hundred cakes** (like pancakes) **of bread,** and **two skins of wine.** The "skins" may have been those of goat or ox which would hold a considerable quantity. Abigail took with her **five dressed,** i.e., prepared for cooking, **sheep.** She took **five seahs** (about a bushel)[10] **of roasted grain,** considered a delicacy

---

[10]The LXX altered the measure into five ephahs, probably because they considered the quantity in the text ridiculously small for a group the size of David's.

at that time. She also included **a hundred cakes of raisins** (lit., "a hundred bunches of raisins"). The bunches of grapes when dried were pressed into cakes. She also took **two hundred cakes of pressed figs.** All of these provisions were loaded on donkeys. She and her servants started off in the direction of David's camp. She did not, however, tell her husband what she was doing.

25:20-22 Abigail rode her donkey **into a mountain ravine**, lit., "going down by a secret place." The road by which she descended into the valley was concealed from the view of those descending on the opposite slope. David and his men were **descending toward her**, lit., "and behold David and his men were going down to meet her." The word "behold" suggests that the meeting was coincidental.[11] David was still spewing out his anger against the ingratitude of Nabal, attempting to justify to himself the terrible slaughter which was about to take place. In spite of how David's men had protected his property, Nabal had paid him back evil for good. David muttered an oath. **May God deal with David,** lit., "thus may God do to the enemies of David." Again the NIV has followed the LXX in placing the imprecation upon "David" rather than "David's enemies." The thought is that if God would avenge David's enemies for David's failure to observe this oath, how much more would he avenge David himself should he make and then break this oath. See comments on 1 Sam 20:16 and note. The oath was to the effect that by morning no **male** (lit., "one who urinates against the wall")[12] of the household of Nabal would remain alive. In making this vow utterly to destroy Nabal's household, David committed sin. The fulfillment of this vow by the execution of his vindictive threat was clearly opposed to the will of God. Some see here the first revelation of David's dark side, the fruition of which will be adultery and murder (2 Sam 11-12).[13]

25:23-25 When Abigail saw David, **she quickly got off her donkey.** Dismounting in the presence of a superior was a token of respect. Abigail then **bowed down before David with her face to the ground.**

---

[11]Mauchline (169) proposes that Abigail chose her path so as to come upon David unexpectedly so that he might have no time for taking evasive action. It seems better, however, to think that the Narrator is stressing the providential meeting of the two.

[12]The expression "he that urinates against the wall" appears elsewhere in 1 Kgs 14:10; 16:11; 21:21; 2 Kgs 9:8. In the culture of that time such an expression would not be considered vulgar.

[13]J.D. Levenson, "I Samuel 25," 23.

Her almost exaggerated courtesy stands in stark contrast to her ill-mannered husband. Abigail's address is a masterpiece. Feminine charm and exceptional sagacity stand out vividly. She fell at David's feet and pled that the blame for what Nabal had done be put on her.[14] She then begged that David would let her speak to him. He should pay no attention to what Nabal had said because he was a **wicked man,** lit., "a son of Belial," an assessment which echoes that of the servants in v. 17. He lived up to his name Nabal, which means in Hebrew **fool.** Abigail apologized that she had not seen David's men enter Nabal's encampment. Abigail presented herself to David as loyal and subservient. Twice in v. 24 and again in v. 28 she refers to herself as **your servant.** Seven times she refers to David as **my lord** (vv. 24,25,28,29,30, and twice in 31).

25:26-27 Abigail used sweet but persuasive logic to urge David to accept the gift which she had brought on the donkeys. In these verses she makes three arguments, each introduced with the Hebrew וְעַתָּה (wᵉ'attāh, lit., "and now"). First, she pointed to the leading of the Lord, by which David had been kept from committing murder through her coming to meet him. The NIV has rearranged the clauses of v. 26. The verse begins with the oath formula "and now" **as surely as the LORD lives and as you live.** This formula underscores the certainty of what is about to be uttered. Abigail declared **the LORD has kept you, my master, from bloodshed** (lit., "coming into bloodshed") **and from avenging yourself with your own hands.** Her point is that surely the Lord had used her visit to prevent David from two terrible actions, viz., (1) bloodshed; and (2) avenging himself by his own hand, lit., "your hand has delivered you."

In the second "and now," Abigail points to the fact that Yahweh is the avenger of the wicked, by expressing her desire that **your enemies and all who intend to harm my master be like Nabal.** The meaning of these words are not immediately clear. Nabal at this time was in good health and enjoying himself. Does she anticipate what would happen to Nabal? Or is Abigail saying, May your enemies become harmless and stubborn fools like Nabal, despised by both God and man?

---

[14]Another interpretation is that Abigail was accepting the blame for attempting to persuade David to violate a solemn oath. McCarter (1:398) claims that this clause is merely a conventional way of initiating a conversation with a superior. The guilt in question then refers to responsibility for anything that might be considered blameworthy in the ensuing conversation.

In the third "and now," Abigail tactfully asked David to accept her **gift** (lit. "blessing"; cf. 1 Sam 30:26). In using the term "blessing" the deep religious feelings of the Hebrew mind are revealed. The gift came not from the donor, but from God. She does not presume to offer the gift for David's own use. The gift was designated to **be given to the men who follow you.** She would not have it said that she had offered David a bribe for the sake of her husband.

25:28 Abigail here asks for David to forgive her (the word "servant" is feminine). Some think that she is referring to the irritation of speaking further (McCarter, 1:398). A better interpretation is that the **offense** is that of her husband which this good wife had taken upon herself (v. 24). So she is asking for forgiveness for the rudeness and rebuff which David's messengers had received at her house. She supports her petition with promises of the rich blessings which were in store for David. She announced that Yahweh would give him a **lasting dynasty** (lit., "a sure house"),[15] i.e., would establish him and his posterity on the throne.[16] In her view David deserved to be king because he had been fighting **the LORD's battles** (1 Sam 18:17).

The NIV alone among the standard English versions regards the second half of v. 28 as a wish: **Let no wrongdoing be found in you.**[17] The phrase **as long as you live** is lit., "from your days," i.e., from the beginning of your life. The line is probably better regarded as an observation rather than a wish, along the lines of the NKJV, JB, and NJPS. It constitutes a second reason why Yahweh will make a lasting dynasty for David. He had never been guilty of **wrongdoing** (רָעָה, rā'āh). She was not suggesting that David was sinless, but that he had

---

[15]The phrase בַּיִת נֶאֱמָן (bayith ne'ĕmān) appears three times. An anonymous prophet predicted that the future faithful priest would have an "enduring house" (1 Sam 2:35 NASB; NIV "I will firmly establish his house"). In reference to the house of David, the phrase is used, besides here, in 1 Kgs 11:38. Cf. 2 Sam 7:11,17,26,27; 1 Kgs 2:24; Ps 89:4.

[16]Abigail anticipates the prophecy of Nathan which utilizes identical language (2 Sam 7:16). This led the rabbis to count Abigail among the seven women who were recipients of the Holy Spirit of prophecy.

[17]The second half of v. 28 has been rendered in the standard English versions in these ways: "and no evil is found in you all your life" (BV); "and evil shall not be found in you so long as you live" (NRSV; essentially ASV); "and evil is not found in you throughout your days" (NKJV); "and in all your life there is no wickedness to be found in you" (JB); "no wrong is ever to be found in you" (NJPS).

never precipitated any calamity or misfortune, such as Saul had done at Nob.

The point of the whole verse is this: since David was one who would be greatly blessed, he could afford to be gracious. Abigail implies that killing a man out of personal revenge, unlike the killing of enemy soldiers in fighting the Lord's battles, would be a blot on David's clean record. Abigail is now the fourth person (along with Samuel, Jonathan and Saul) to forecast kingship for David.

25:29 Abigail was aware that someone, viz., Saul, **is pursuing you to take your life**. With exquisite courtesy and true loyalty Abigail refrained from mention in connection with evil the name of her king, the anointed of Yahweh. She believed that David's life **will be bound securely in the bundle of the living by the LORD your God.** This is an allusion to the bundle[18] in which a person might tie together silver or other precious objects so as to carry them on his person. Abigail foresaw a very different fate for those who opposed David. These enemies the Lord would **hurl away as from the pocket of a sling.**

25:30-31 Abigail made skillful appeal to David's peace of mind. She had no doubt that one day Yahweh (1) will have done **for my master**, i.e., David, **every good thing he promised concerning him;** and (2) will have **appointed him leader over Israel** (cf. 1 Sam 13:14). These words suggest that Abigail knew of the anointing of David, and his designation to be the future king. Once David had received every good thing which the Lord had promised him (i.e., the throne), he would not **have on his conscience the staggering burden**[19] [or perhaps stumbling-block] **of needless bloodshed or of having avenged himself.** Abigail asked David to **remember** with gratitude the counsel she had given when he achieved this success of becoming king. These words are almost a hint to David to give her the status of a wife in the royal household if disaster were to befall her husband.

25:32-34 In David's reply to Abigail (her name is spelled "Abigal" in the Hebrew of v. 32), he first praised God for having sent her to meet him. Her providential arrival was understood as the plan of

---

[18]McCarter (1:399) takes צְרוֹר (ṣrôr, "bundle") to mean "a tied up document" (cf. Job 14:17). This "document of the living," as it may be translated, may be equivalent to "the book of the living" of Ps 69:28 (cf. Rev 3:5).

[19]The term פּוּקָה (pûqāh), which appears only here, is rendered "grief" (ASV, NRSV, NKJV); "stumbling" (NJPS); "self-accusation" (BV). The term is obviously a figure for qualm of conscience.

God to keep David fit for the office he would one day hold. **May you be blessed for your good judgment** is literally "may your good judgment be blessed and may you be blessed." Second, David pronounced a blessing on the noble woman for keeping him (1) **from bloodshed this day** and (2) **from avenging myself with my own hands.** He clearly portrayed to her what would have happened had she not undertaken her mission. First, she would have been injured, certainly by the loss of her loved ones, but perhaps even in her own person. Second, **not one male** (see on v. 22) **belonging to Nabal would have been left alive by daybreak.** It is obvious that David now had repented of his vengeful resolve regarding Nabal. The solemn oath to murder the entire house of Nabal was now broken. The only oath a godly person may break with impunity is that which binds him to do some evil deed.[20] There were faults aplenty in David's life, his outburst against Nabal being one of them; but with all his faults he had the spirit of genuine repentance, and this is what made him a man after God's own heart.

25:35 David accepted from Abigail what she had brought to him. With the assurance that he had heard her request for the life of her husband, David sent her home in peace. **Granted your request** is literally "lifted up your face."

G. LAST SCENES OF FUGITIVE LIFE (25:36–26:25)

1. Recognition through Marriage (25:36-44)

The Death of Nabal (25:36-38)

25:36-37 When Abigail got back home, she found her husband **in the house holding a banquet like that of a king.** Apparently he never missed his wife. Nabal was in **high spirits** (lit., "his heart was good"), i.e., a jovial frame of mind, because of the abundance of the wool that year. He was **very drunk,** the result of his high spirits. The banquet after the shearing was traditional in Israel (2 Sam 13:23-28), but not to feast like a king while knowing that hungry and thirsty men were encamped nearby, men who had a legitimate claim to a

---

[20]David broke his oath when he was shown the wickedness of it. Some years before, Saul, had he not been forcibly hindered by his army, would have murdered his own son Jonathan because of a foolish oath. See on 1 Sam 14:24,45. Cf. Judg 11:34,40.

small share of the bounty. Abigail told Nabal **nothing** (lit., "nothing small or great") until daybreak. He was in no condition to understand what she had to tell him. When he was **sober** (lit., "the wine had gone out of Nabal") in the morning, Abigail told him **all these things**,[21] i.e., the entire story of her meeting with David. Nabal's **heart failed him** (lit., "died within him") **and he became like a stone.** This is a way of describing a paralyzing stroke.[22]

25:38 Nabal lingered for ten days. Then the Lord **struck** him, i.e., he had another stroke, and he died. The loss of various perishables and exactly five sheep (v. 18) out of his three thousand (v. 2) brought on the fatal stroke!

David's Marriage to Abigail (25:39-42)

25:39-40 David **praised** God at the news of Nabal's death for three reasons. First, God had **upheld my cause**, i.e., punished the wrongdoing of Nabal thus vindicating David's sense of outrage against the man. Second, God had **kept his servant from doing wrong.** This chapter describes David's fourth escape, not an escape from Saul, but from the consequences of his own temper. Third, God had demonstrated his justice in this world by having **brought Nabal's wrongdoing** [lit., "the evil of Nabal"] **down on his own head**. God had smitten Nabal because of what he had done to David. **Then David sent word to Abigail** (lit., "then David sent and spoke concerning Abigail") **asking her to become his wife** (lit., "to take her to him for a wife"). A woman without a husband or adult sons was in a very difficult position in biblical days. David did not want this gracious woman to suffer any want. Presumably he waited to marry her until after the normal seven days of mourning had passed.

25:41-42 The proposal was received by Abigail with the same courteous humility which marked her behavior earlier in the chapter. She had no hesitation about becoming David's wife. Her words signal that she was willing to perform the most menial of tasks. The entire account makes it clear that Abigail was as well matched with David as she was mismatched with Nabal. She quickly got on her donkey, along with her five maidservants, and followed David's messengers. Shortly

---

[21]In the Hebrew the same expression is rendered "this message" (v. 9) and "every word" (v. 12).

[22]Youngblood (763) thinks it best not to diagnose "like a stone" with a specific illness but understand it figuratively as in Exod 15:16.

thereafter she married David. This marriage was important to David both materially (she was a wealthy widow), and politically. He came to have a marriage bond with an area that Saul had never effectively incorporated in his kingdom.

David's Other Wives (25:43-44)

25:43 Abigail was not David's only wife. Previously during his wilderness wandering he had married a woman from **Jezreel** named **Ahinoam**.[23] The reference is not to the famous Jezreel in the north, but to a town in the hill country of Judah (Josh 15:56), in the neighborhood of Maon and Ziph. The marriage to these two women proves that (1) David's situation was better than it had been for some time, (2) he regarded the truce with Saul as virtually conceding to him southern Judah, and (3) he considered himself safe from the designs of the king. David's marriages to Ahinoam and Abigail helped pave the way for his later anointing in Hebron after Saul's death.

25:44 This verse answers the question which the previous notices of David's marriages raises, viz., What happened to Michal, Saul's daughter and David's first wife? Saul had given her to another man when David fled from Gibeah. **Paltiel** was from **Gallim** which was located a short distance north of Jerusalem (cf. Isa 10:30). This probably had happened when David fled from Gibeah. By this gesture Saul was intending to sever any connection between himself and David.

The giving of Michal to Paltiel raises certain moral questions. Was Michal living in adultery with Paltiel? Under Mosaic law a divorced woman was free to marry another man and that marriage was recognized as legitimate (Deut 24:1-4). David had not divorced Michal, but Saul as chief magistrate probably had the authority to dissolve the marriage on the grounds of abandonment. Thus technically, Michal did not commit adultery when she married Paltiel. More problematic is the return of Michal to David (2 Sam 3:14f.), an action the law labeled "abomination" (Deut 24:4). David clearly thought he was entitled to take back his wife because he had never given her a divorce. Taking Michal back is not condemned in the record.

---

[23]The only other Ahinoam mentioned in the Bible is the wife of Saul (1 Sam 14:50). Some think that David already had asserted his right to the throne by marrying the queen. See J.D. Levenson, "I Samuel 25," 27. The supporting evidence, Nathan's word in 2 Sam 12:8, is too slight "for so monstrous a deed" (Baldwin, 153).

1 SAMUEL 26

2. Danger/Defense: Hill of Hachilah (26:1-20)

Saul made one last effort to capture David ca. 1012 B.C. David was about twenty-eight years old. The differences between the incident recorded in this chapter and the one narrated in ch 24, despite their similarities, are sufficiently significant to mark this as a new attempt in the continuing campaign to capture David and not a variant account of the same event. The story of Abigail in ch 25 depicted David's position as relatively secure. Chapter 27 depicts David's move into Philistine territory. The present chapter forms a bridge between his security and his desperate flight from the land. Here is recorded the last straw which proved to David that he would never be safe as long as he was in the land of Israel. Reinforced by the lesson of the Nabal episode (25:39), David was more resolved than ever that he would not lay violent hands upon Saul (v. 10).

A Pursuit by Saul's Army (26:1-5)

26:1 Again the **Ziphites** went to offer their services to Saul in Gibeah. They reported that David was hiding out on the **hill of Hakilah** (cf. 1 Sam 23:19) which faced the barren **Jeshimon** (cf. 1 Sam 23:19).

26:2-4 The king had relapsed into his old enmity. Leaving the higher elevation of Gibeah, Saul took his standing army of **three thousand men** (cf. 1 Sam 13:2; 24:2) **down to the Desert of Ziph,** i.e., the area around Ziph, to search for David. Saul's soldiers are called **chosen men of Israel** because they were battle-tested veterans. He **made his camp beside the road on the hill of Hakilah facing Jeshimon,** i.e., the high road which led down to Arad. This was the area in which David had last been spotted by the Ziphites. David, however, had moved off the hill and out to **the desert. David saw,** i.e., learned, **that Saul had followed him there**.

26:5 Always before David had run from Saul. The meeting between the two men in ch 24 had taken place by chance. On this occasion David aggressively sought out Saul, first by sending out spies and later by going personally into the king's camp. Having obtained information respecting the locality of Saul's camp, David, accompanied by his nephew, **set out and went to the place where Saul had camped.** From a distance he could see **where Saul and Abner son of Ner, the commander of the army, had lain down.** He noted that Saul's army was camped in a circle. The king was sleeping within **the camp,** (מַעְגָּל, *ma'gāl*), lit., "entrenchment." See on 1 Sam 17:20. The expedition carried no tents. Both the troops and their king slept on the ground. "Abner" has not been mentioned since 14:50,51.

An Intruder in Saul's Camp (26:6-12)

26:6-7 David determined that he would enter the camp of Saul in the darkness. He asked two of his men to **go down into the camp** with him. Ahimelech the Hittite, mentioned only here in the Bible, did not volunteer. As he is mentioned before Abishai, he must have held an honorable place with David, as did subsequently another Hittite (2 Sam 11:3). Abishai is the first of the sons of Zeruiah, David's sister (1 Chr 2:16) to be mentioned in 1 Samuel. The record indicates that he was a daredevil type.[1] Two others, Joab and Asahel, figure prominently in subsequent narratives of this book. Why these brothers are always named after their mother is not clear. Perhaps their father had died young, or perhaps Zeruiah is named because of her relationship to David. Abishai followed David through the rows of the sleeping **army,** lit. "the people." In spite of impossible odds, David was able to breach the security of Saul's camp. The king was **lying asleep inside the camp with his spear stuck in the ground near his head.** Ironically this spear would be the same weapon which Saul had hurled at David in an attempt to kill him (1 Sam 19:10).

26:8 Like David's men in the cave (1 Sam 24:4), Abishai saw in Saul's defenseless condition a proof that it was God's will that he

---

[1]Abishai was a member of the most elite troops of David (2 Sam 23:18f.). It was he who wanted to cut off Shimei's head (2 Sam 16:5-11). He killed a Philistine champion (2 Sam 21:16-17), and he participated in the assassination of Abner (2 Sam 3:30). Other exploits carried out jointly with Joab are reported in 2 Sam 2:18-24; 10:9-14; 18:2-14; 20:6-10.

should die. He whispered to David: **Today God has delivered** [lit., "shut up"] **your enemy into your hands.** In distinction to what transpired in ch 24 where the men urged David to smite Saul, Abishai asked permission to pin Saul to the ground with one thrust of his spear. **My spear** is literally "the spear." The NIV rendering masks the irony of having the king slain with his own spear.

26:9-11 David ordered Abishai not to destroy Saul. He was, after all, the LORD's anointed. Whoever killed the Lord's anointed would be guilty before God. David undergirded his prohibition with an oath grounded in the life of Yahweh. He was confident that one day **the LORD himself will strike him.** The only one with a right to deal the king a fatal blow was Yahweh himself. God is said to smite men with disease (2 Kgs 15:5) as well as some sudden, untimely stroke, as happened to Nabal. The Lord himself must decide when and how Saul's hour would come. By means of a second oath (**the LORD forbid**) David swore not to stretch out his own hand against Yahweh's anointed. Whereas, however, David exercised restraint respecting Saul's person, at the same time he directed Abishai to carry off some things which would show where they had been, and what they had done. He was to take the king's **spear and water jug**. Their size, form and ornamentation would distinguish these objects from those used by the common soldiers.

26:12 Despite his instructions to Abishai in the previous verse, this verse makes clear that David himself was the one responsible for taking the trophies. There is no indication of remorse on his part for gathering this material evidence such as David felt in ch 24 when he cut off part of the king's robe. No one knew about David's entrance into or exit from the camp of Saul. Once again as in ch 19 Saul and his supporters had been immobilized by a supernatural power. All of Saul's men were sleeping because the Lord had put them into a **deep sleep** (תַּרְדֵּמָה, *tardēmāh*). This was a slumber so profound and unusual that it was regarded as sent directly from God. The Hebrew word is used especially of supernaturally caused sleep, as in Gen 2:21; 15:12.

A Voice from Saul's Past (26:13-20)

26:13-14 In ch 24 David fearlessly cried out to Saul when the king was still quite close to the cave. Here David put some distance between himself and the king before calling out to him. David **crossed over to the other side**, i.e., to the side of the valley. **He**

stood on top of the hill some distance away, i.e., on a hill opposite where Saul was sleeping, a safe distance from his enemy. David began to shout to Abner, Saul's general. The noise woke up Abner, but he could not recognize the voice. **Who are you who calls to the king?** suggests that David had offended the king by awakening him.

26:15-16 David did not answer Abner's question as to his identity. The fact that David had been able to penetrate to the center of the encampment through the circular rows of the sleeping soldiers triggered the three-question taunt of Abner. (1) **You're a man, aren't you?** Anyone worthy of the title "man" ought to have guarded his master better than Abner has done. (2) **And who is like you in Israel?**, lit., "who is as you?" Among all Saul's subjects there was no one so powerful and highly placed as the commander-in-chief, and he ought to have shown himself worthy of his position that night. (3) The third taunt question rebuked Abner for dereliction of duty. Someone had come to destroy the king, and Abner had slept through the whole incident. He was a better man than that! David declared that the general and his entire army **deserve to die** (lit., "are sons of death") because they did not perform their duty to guard the king. He told Abner to look for Saul's spear and water jug which were near the head of the king.

26:17 By this time Saul was wide awake. It was still too dark to recognize his face and figure, but **Saul recognized David's voice**. He called out in the same question used in the incident at En Gedi: **Is that your voice, David my son?** (24:16). The term "son" is one of affection, and perhaps reflects the former status of David as the son-in-law of the king. David then identified himself and affirmed his respect, and loyalty to Saul by addressing him as **my lord the king.**

26:18 David then tried to reason with Saul again. Why was the king pursuing him? What had David done, or of what wrong was he guilty?

26:19-20 On this occasion David made no concession to the fact that Saul had addressed him affectionately. David was formal in his address: **my lord the king** (cf. 24:11). He was becoming both more certain of his future role and more desperate to escape his pursuer (Baldwin, 155). David begged the king to **listen to his servant's words.** The king's antagonism against David could only come from one of two sources. First, it may be that **the LORD has incited you against me,** i.e., if God has made you an agent to punish me for my sins, **then may he accept** [lit., "smell"] **an offering**, i.e., accept my offering and forgive me. Smelling a sacrifice is an anthropomorphic term, used to denote the divine satisfaction with an offering (cf. Gen 8:21). The word for offering (מִנְחָה, *minḥāh*) was the meal offering which signified sanctification of life and devotion to the Lord. In this offering a mixture of flour and frankincense was burnt for a sweet odor before God. Second, **men may have done it**, i.e., stirred Saul up against David. If that be the case, **may they be cursed before the Lord.**

David's curse on those who were stirring up Saul is justified on three grounds. First, **they have now driven me from my share in the Lord's inheritance,** i.e., they were intent on driving David out of his share of the Lord's inheritance, i.e., the land of Israel. Second, they did not care if David rendered devotion to the gods of one of the surrounding nations. By driving him from the land and ordinances of true worship, into foreign and heathen countries, they were exposing him to all the seductions of idolatry. They were in effect telling him to **go serve other gods.** David did not want to leave his country. He did not want his blood to fall to the ground **far from the presence of the Lord,** i.e., the place where he revealed himself and was worshiped. Third, King Saul was wasting his time pursuing David who is as harmless as **a flea**, lit. "a single flea."[2] He was chasing David as one **hunts a partridge**[3] in the mountains. No one would think it worth his while to hunt a single partridge in the mountains when these birds could be found in coveys in the fields. The species of partridge common in the Holy Land tries to save itself primarily by running, rather than by flight. It is continuously chased until it becomes totally fatigued. Then the hunters rush upon the birds and knock them to the ground. This was what Saul was trying to do to David.

3. Danger Averted (26:21-25)

26:21 In ch 24 Saul conceded David's superior righteousness and his own evil doing. Here he first frankly confessed his sin (as over against David's "I have not sinned" in 24:12). Second, Saul invited David to **come back** to his position in the royal court which he left

[2]For "a flea" the LXX substituted "my soul," probably with a view of avoiding the repetition of the simile from ch 24.

[3]For "partridge" the LXX substituted "screech-owl," and changed the sense: "as the screech-owl hunts on the mountains."

in 19:11-12. Third, because David had spared his life that day, Saul pledged that he would **not try to harm** David **again.** Fourth, Saul admitted that he had **acted like a fool** and had **erred greatly,** i.e., made a wrong judgment. This admission of foolishness recalls the charge which Samuel had leveled against Saul in 1 Sam 13:13. Saul's words were not untrue subjectively; but his temporary emotion did not last. Perhaps in these words there was, besides sorrow for past failings regarding David, frustration (1) because of the unmilitary arrangements of his camp which resulted (2) in his falling again into David' power.

26:22-24 David ignored Saul's request to return. He told Saul to send one of his servants over to retrieve his spear. His silence about the water jug is a mystery. These explanations have been offered: (1) David wished to keep the jug as a trophy of his bravery that night, (2) the jug was of such little value it was not worth returning, (3) the king would never drink from a jug which had been in the possession of an enemy, (4) the spear (symbol of death) was returned while the jug (symbol of life) was not, and (5) retaining the jug signaled that David saw himself as in control of the situation. David was confident that the Lord would reward him for **his righteousness and faithfulness.** The Lord had delivered Saul into David's hands that day, but David would not lay a hand on the Lord's anointed. Just as he had **valued** the life of Saul (lit., "behold, as your soul was great this day in my eyes"), so he hoped the Lord would value his life and deliver him **from all trouble.** The events of the night once again assured David that he would be safe under the protection of the Lord.

26:25 Saul now pronounced a blessing on David as he previously had blessed the Ziphites who disclosed David's whereabouts (23:21). He knew that David would (1) accomplish **great things**; and (2) **surely triumph** in whatever he set out to do. Saul's predictions about David's future are not as explicit as in 24:20, but clearly he recognized that David would win in the struggle between the two of them. In these words there is a ring of falseness. David understood this, and so he **went on his way.** He placed no confidence in Saul's professions or promises, but wisely kept at a distance, and awaited the course of Providence. Saul then **returned home** to Gibeah. This was David's fifth escape. Saul and David never saw each other again.

1 SAMUEL 27

H. DAVID SEEKS SANCTUARY IN GATH (27:1-4)

About 1012 B.C., after four years of evading Saul, David was tired and discouraged. At the age of twenty-eight he decided to offer his services to the Philistines. Apparently he had been contemplating this move for some time (cf. 26:19).

27:1 David thought to himself, lit., "said to his heart," **"One of these days I will be destroyed** (lit., "be swept away")[1] **by** (lit., "into") **the hand of Saul."** The second betrayal by the Ziphites made David feel that he was surrounded by spies and that he could not continue to dodge military confrontation with Saul. He began to feel that Saul would eventually trap and kill him. **The best thing I can do** is literally "there is nothing better for me than." Saul would then give up searching for him because he would be out of the king's reach. David had fled under very different circumstances to Gath at the outset of his troubles with Saul. As a solitary fugitive who was hated because he was the slayer of Goliath, he narrowly escaped losing his life; now he was the commander of an outlaw band of stalwart warriors, and he was welcomed as an ally.

The resolution of David to leave the land of Israel and go over to the Philistines was wrong for several reasons. First, he was removing himself from the place where the divine oracle intimated to him that he should remain (1 Sam 22:5). Second, he was doing exactly what his enemies at the court of Saul had wished he might do (1 Sam 26:19). Third, he was withdrawing from his people the counsel and aid which he might have given them had he remained in Israel. Fourth, David was furnishing to his enemies ammunition for their propaganda against him, for his actions had the appearance of treason. Fifth, he did not seek the Lord's guidance before he made this

---

[1]The same verb (סָפָה, sāphāh) is also used in 1 Sam 12:25 and 26:10.

move. Finally, it was a faltering trust in God and a craven fear for his own life (cf. 26:20,24) which drove him to leave the land of Israel and seek refuge among his Philistine foes.

Why did David not flee to Moab as he had done in the early phase of his difficulties with Saul? Possibly (1) he doubted the power of Moab to protect him, (2) the Moabites had killed his parents, and (3) he already had conceived the plan which is subsequently reported in this chapter by which he would be able to help his own people and further his own royal claims, viz., destroying the enemies of Israel while at the same time being a loyal servant of the Philistine king.

27:2 David and his six hundred men **went over to Achish** king of Gath. This Achish son of Maoch is probably the same person mentioned in 21:11.[2] Many consider the "Achish son of Maachah" of 1 Kgs 2:39 also to be this same Achish, since Maoch and Maachah are certainly only different forms of the same name (KD, 319). If this is the case, then Achish reigned for fifty years. It is said in 1 Chr 18:1 that David conquered the Philistines, and took from them Gath and other towns. He seems to have permitted Achish to remain there as a tributary king, thus paying back the old debt of kindness to this Philistine.

27:3 David and his men **settled in Gath** with their families. He placed himself under the authority of Achish and offered his men to fight with the Philistine army. David at this time had two wives with him: **Ahinoam of Jezreel** (see on 1 Sam 25:43) and **Abigail of Carmel**, who was the widow of Nabal. Because David had been pursued by Saul for so many years, Achish did not hesitate to give him a place of refuge in his land.

27:4 This verse indicates that up to the moment when Saul heard that David had crossed the frontier, he had not ceased efforts to apprehend him.

VII. DAVID'S RISE TO PROMINENCE
OUTSIDE ISRAEL (27:5–31:13)

David's days outside Israel were a spiritual low for the future king. He became involved in deception and atrocities which cannot be defended. Yet God continued to bless David and groom him for his

---

[2]Jamieson (206), however, argues that the mention of the king's family here creates a presumption that this Achish was a different king from the one who was reigning on David's first visit to Gath.

royal destiny. David's days as a fugitive leader in the highlands of southwest Judah may be recalled in an allusion on an Egyptian monument.[3]

A. DAVID IN ZIKLAG (27:5–28:2)

1. Recognition: Governor of a City (27:5-7)

27:5 David requested that Achish assign him his own city out in the rural area of his kingdom. From David's standpoint, it was important to remove his followers from the corrupting influence of a pagan culture. He also wished to have a more independent position where he might be less exposed to the jealousy of the Philistine lords, and have free opportunity for ruling and organizing his followers. David based his request on two considerations. First, he suggested that by complying with this request Achish would be demonstrating his confidence in David. Second, David suggested that it was not appropriate for him to remain in the royal city with Achish.

27:6 Achish saw the request as an opportunity to place a trusted ally on the outskirts of his territory. David would be a wall of defense against the turbulent inhabitants of the Negev. The king assigned David to the city of **Ziklag** (ZA, 46). The ancient site has been identified with a tell about fifteen miles southeast of Gaza and about twenty-five miles southwest of Gath (Klein, 264).[4] Here David was distant enough from the Philistine pentapolis to have great independence, but at the same time well away from the centers of Saul's jurisdiction. The main disadvantage was that this outpost tended to be the target of marauding bands from the desert. This gift of Ziklag to David suggests (1) that the city was under Philistine jurisdiction at this time and (2) that the site was virtually uninhabited.

---

[3]K.A. Kitchen has called attention to row VIII of the Karnak inscription of Shoshenq I (biblical Shishak) where, in a list of locations in southern Judah and the Negev, he reads "highland/heights of David." The inscription dates to 924 B.C. "A Possible Mention of David in the Late Tenth Century BCE, and Deity *Dod as Dead as the Dodo," *JSOT* 76 (1997): 39-41. For discussions of other possible references to David in the documents of the period, see *BAR* March/April 1994 and each of the following issues of *BAR* for that year.

[4]Mauchline (177) assigns fifteen miles as the distance from Gath to Ziklag. The location of both sites is not certain. On the various suggestions which have been made respecting the location of Ziklag, see Ahlström, 459, and Bierling, 155-159.

The note that Ziklag **has belonged to the kings of Judah ever since** indicates that Ziklag became one of the crown estates of the royal family in Judah. This note offers a clue as to when the history of David was compiled. It must have been after the division of the kingdom in 931 B.C. and before the Babylonian exile. Only in that time frame would it be appropriate to speak of "the kings of Judah."

27:7 David lived in the land of the Philistines sixteen months.[5] Why was he accepted now, when earlier the officers of Achish forced him to flee from there because of their hostility? Achish readily received David for two reasons: (1) he brought with him a sizable force which he offered to place at the disposal of the Philistine king, and (2) David had now become the archenemy of Saul, who was in turn the archenemy of the Philistines. While he resided there, David was joined by additional forces. A band of archers and slingers from Saul's own tribe came to Ziklag, as well as men from southern Judah, and from Manasseh (1 Chr 12:1-7,20-22).

2. Anticipation: Raids on Ancient Enemies (27:8-12)

27:8 David used Ziklag as a base of operations against the ancient inhabitants of that area. The verb **went up** is used (1) in a military sense (the advance of an army against a people or town) and (2) in a geographical sense. The tribes mentioned here probably had their main centers in the mountain plateau of the desert of Paran. The verb translated **raided** (פָּשַׁט, *pāšaṭ*) is a colorful one, meaning to strip off encumbrances so as to make a dash; or to dash from a place of shelter.

The **Geshurites** were a tribe dwelling south of Philistia near the Amalekites (cf. Josh 13:2).[6] The **Girzites** are not mentioned else-

---

[5]Literally the Hebrew reads "days and four months." Apparently the word "days" is here used idiomatically for a year, strictly speaking, a term of days which amounted to a full year. Cf. Lev 25:29; Judg 17:10; 1 Sam 1:3,20; 2:19; 29:3; 2 Sam 14:26. The Hebrew could be rendered "a space of time, even four months." The note in 29:3, however, suggests that he had been there much longer. Josephus says that David's stay in Philistia was four months and twenty days.

[6]The Geshurites here should be distinguished from the Geshurites in Syria (2 Sam 15:8).

where in the Bible.[7] Hertzberg (214) suggests that this is another form of the name **Girgashites**, some of the original inhabitants of Palestine. The Geshurites and Girzites were probably allies of the Philistines (Hindson, 166). Saul virtually had wiped out **the Amalekites** (1 Sam 15:8-9), but a new wave of these desert marauders was attempting to press into Canaan out of the desert.

The mention that the three named peoples had **from ancient times . . . lived in the land extending to Shur and Egypt** locates them geographically. At the same time this statement serves to justify David's violence toward them in that they were counted among the peoples which had been under the ban (extermination order) since the days of Moses. **Shur** is on the border of Egypt, somewhere east of Lake Timsah (cf. Gen 25:18; 1 Sam 15:7). David's raids on the peoples of the Negev were carried out beyond the reach of Philistine observation in an area in which the Philistines had limited political interest. These raids were safe exploits which would not disturb David's relations with Achish. The occasion of David's attacks is not indicated. He may have been attempting (1) to punish these tribes for past or present incursions into the land of Israel, (2) to keep his army active and militarily sharp, and (3) to provide the means of subsistence for his men.

27:9 The verbs in this verse are frequentative, describing David's customary action. David apparently would launch a retaliatory attack against the desert people whenever they attempted to invade southern Judah. He would exterminate these enemies of Israel and take all their plunder. Then he would return to **Achish** at Gath to present to him an agreed upon share of the plunder. From this it can be inferred that Achish expected David to pay a kind of tribute, as well as to render personal service in war.

27:10 David's misleading reports were worded in such a way that Achish assumed the raids were against Israelite territory. The term **Negev** means "dry land," and the area was so called because of the absence of streams.[8] The **Negev of Judah** was probably in the vicinity of Beersheba (2 Sam 24:7). The **Negev of Jerahmeel** extended south of Beersheba. The Jerahmeelites were the descendants of Jerahmeel, the first-born of Hezron (1 Chr 2:9,25,26). The **Negev of**

---

[7]The Girzites were most likely not the Canaanites occupying Gezer, a town to the northeast of Philistia, contra Goldman, 165. Gezer was not in the area which David could have raided from Ziklag.

[8]For an archaeological survey of the Negev, see Y. Aharoni, AOTS, 384-403.

the Kenites was near Hebron (Josh 14:6-14; 15:52-54) and Debir (Josh 15:15-19). Through Jethro the Kenites became allies with the Israelites in the wilderness period (cf. Exod 18; Judg 1:16; 1 Sam 15:6). Probably they lived under the protection of Judah. Thus the Geshurites, Girzites, and Amalekites dwelt close to the southern boundary of Judah, so that David was able to represent the march against these tribes to Achish as a march against Judah.

27:11 On the practical level, David's decision to leave no survivors was wise. He could not risk any survivor coming to Gath to tell Achish what he was really doing. On the moral level, David's actions are more difficult to assess. When Israel entered Canaan under Joshua, wars of extermination were both commanded and commended. Then Israel was simply the stern instrument of divine wrath. There is, however, no indication that David had been given such a mandate by the Lord. If he tried to justify his actions to himself, he may have argued that the extermination order against the original inhabitants had never been rescinded by God. Probably, however, no such ethical questions were raised. Such barbarity was not unusual in those days, and unfortunately David did not rise above the practice of his contemporaries. **And such was his practice** (lit., "the right which he exercised") **as long as he lived in Philistine territory.**[9]

27:12 Achish assumed, from what David had told him, that he was attacking his own people. He thought no more convincing proof of his loyalty could be offered. Achish concluded that **he has become so odious to his people,** i.e., he had made himself to stink (cf. Gen 34:30; Exod 5:21; 1 Sam 13:4; 2 Sam 10:6; 16:21). He thought that David **will be my servant forever.**

No doubt when this story was later told around the cooking fires of Israel the stupidity of Achish would bring howls of laughter. Those who supported David's claim to the throne would point out that while their man spent time in the service of the Philistines, he had spent his time there "whipping old enemies like the Amalekites and duping the hated Philistines" (Klein, 265). David was already beginning the task which he was later to complete: that of conquering the whole of Israel's neighboring peoples.

---

[9]Ahlström (460) references the archaeological discovery of the abandonment and/or destruction of several settlements in the Negev around 1000 B.C. David may have been responsible for some of this abandonment.

1 SAMUEL 28

3. Danger: Drafted for War (28:1-2)

In 1010 B.C. the leaders of the Philistines, led by Achish, planned a major invasion of the land of Israel. In the past they had come up into the mountains of Judah. This time they headed north to the valley of Jezreel, the bread basket of Israel. In this flat terrain their chariots would give them military superiority.

28:1 In those days, while David was still at Ziklag, the Philistines were strong enough to strike a blow at the center of the kingdom of Israel. The death of Samuel, the general dissatisfaction with Saul, and the absence of David all emboldened these enemies for a major effort to split the kingdom of Israel in half. Not since their defeat in the valley of Elah (1 Samuel 17) had there been such a massive invasion by the Philistines. Achish trusted David, and expected him to accompany the Philistine army into battle against Saul.

28:2 David was in no position to refuse Achish, yet to fight against his own people would have violated David's conscience. He gave an ambiguous response to the Philistine, hoping that God would show him a way out of the dilemma. **Then you will see for yourself** is literally "therefore you shall surely know." Achish interpreted this to mean that David would fight heroically for the Philistines. It may be that Achish intended to establish David, his friend and subordinate, on the throne of Saul as a Philistine vassal king.

B. A WORD OF JUDGMENT FOR SAUL (28:3-25)

1. Saul's Desperate Plight (28:3-14)

28:3 The Narrator repeats the fact that **Samuel was dead** and had been buried in Ramah to make the point that Saul had no legitimate source of guidance in the face of the massive Philistine invasion. In his earlier days, when he had been more committed to the Lord, Saul had expelled the **mediums and spiritists from the land** (cf. 1 Sam 15:23). Mediums[1] were those who claimed to have contact with people on the other side of death. They inquired of a demonic spirit or were possessed by one or more of them (Deut 18:11; Lev 20:27). Spiritists[2] were, literally "knowing ones." Their knowledge of the realms beyond was derived from demons. A demon within spiritists often impersonated people who had died. Though outlawed, witches still secretly practiced their Satanic religion. Saul's actions in prohibiting the occult practices accords well with the unanimous biblical tradition and makes the visitation of this chapter conflict with his better knowledge and judgment.

28:4 The Philistines assembled their forces. They marched north along the coast to the plain of Esdraelon, the great battlefield of Palestine, where their chariots and horsemen could easily deploy. They **set up camp at Shunem**, about forty-four miles north of Aphek (northernmost Philistine city) at the east end of the plain of Esdraelon. The enemy had thus penetrated into the heart of northern Israel. Saul countered their move by positioning his troops on the slopes of Mount Gilboa anywhere from five to twelve miles southeast of Shunem.[3] He chose this position in order to (1) have a good view of the enemy troop movements across the valley and (2) minimize the advantage the Philistines would have in the valley with their chariots and horsemen.

28:5-6 Saul was terrified when he saw the size of the invading force. He had experienced some success in defeating the Philistines in battle, but never in their terrain, and never such a vast host. The consciousness that God had forsaken him also, no doubt, con-

---

[1]Hebrew הָאֹבוֹת (hā'ōbôth). The singular אֹב ('ōb) signifies (1) the demon or spirit supposed to speak through the necromancer; and (2) the possessor of such a spirit. The term is generally rendered by the LXX "ventriloquist," because (1) the spirit was supposed to speak from the necromancer's belly, or (2) because the LXX viewed such mediums as charlatans who used their abilities to dupe the credulous.

[2]The term הַיִּדְּעֹנִים (hayyiddᵉ'ōnîm) is rendered "spiritists" (NKJV, NIV); "fortunetellers" (BV); "wizards" (ASV, JB, NRSV); "familiar spirits" (NJPS).

[3]The Philistines may have been moving to counter Saul's intended strategy of conquering the Jezreel Valley and Galilee which would give him control of major trade routes. C.E. Hauer, "The Shape of the Saulide Strategy," CBQ 31 (1969): 153-167.

tributed to his fear. **He inquired of the LORD,** i.e., he sought guidance and consolation from Yahweh.

The Lord did not answer Saul **by dreams or Urim or prophets.** These were the three normal ways that the Lord would give guidance to those kings who pleased him. Saul's wickedness rendered him utterly unworthy to find favor with God. The tragedy here is that Saul did not cry out for divine forgiveness, but only for divine guidance.

28:7 Saul ordered his attendants to find for him a **medium,** lit., "a mistress of a conjuring spirit," i.e., of a spirit with which the dead were conjured up for the purpose of making inquiry concerning the future. He specified a woman, not a man. The wizards, or male practitioners, probably all had been searched out and executed. Anxious inquiries led to the discovery of a woman living in seclusion in the general neighborhood. **Endor** was on the other side of where the Philistines were camped about six miles north of Saul's position, and even north of the Philistine position. According to tradition, the woman was the mother of Abner, Saul's general. This, if true, might explain why she had not been driven out of the land.

28:8 Saul disguised himself (1) to help him elude the Philistines, (2) to conceal his identity from (3) his own soldiers and (4) from the witch who might have refused to cooperate with one who had tried to drive all witches from the land. By night he and two of his men made their way around the Philistine camp to Endor. Saul got right to the point when he came to the medium's house. He wanted her (1) to **consult a spirit** (lit., "divine")[4] for him; and (2) to **bring up,** i.e., from the realm of the dead, the person that he would name. Prophesying by means of the אוֹב (*'ōb*, "spirit") apparently was performed by attempting to call up a departed spirit from Sheol.

In 1 Chr 10:13-14, Saul is condemned for consulting the medium for guidance and for failing to inquire of the Lord. This statement can be harmonized with the present text in the following manner: Saul went through the motions of inquiring of the Lord, but his heart was not changed. Thus, he really did not inquire of the Lord.

28:9 The woman neither admitted nor denied that she possessed the power to do what Saul had asked of her; she wanted first to make

---

[4]The English versions translated the Hebrew verb קָסוֹמִי (*qāsómî*) as "inquire for me as a medium" (BV); "consult a spirit" (NIV, NRSV); "disclose the future to me . . . by means of a ghost" (JB); "divine unto me" (ASV); "conduct a seance for me" (NKJV).

sure that her visitor was not one of the king's officers trying to trap her. The medium reminded the disguised Saul that such activity was illegal. Other mediums and spiritists had been **cut off** from the land, i.e., either killed or driven away. She suggested that the stranger might be setting a trap for her that would result in her execution.

28:10-11 Saul had to take an oath before the woman would acknowledge that she engaged in illicit witchcraft. **Saul swore to her by the LORD** that she would not be punished for doing what he asked. So far as is known, this is the last time Saul invoked the name of Yahweh. What an irony! While engaged in a superstitious practice which was a denial of God, the king swore in God's name! It is evident that the oath, **as surely as the LORD lives** had become a common and established form of swearing in Israel. By means of a question (**Whom shall I bring up?**) the woman acknowledged that she professed the power to call up spirits from beyond the grave. Saul told her to **bring up Samuel**, i.e., from the region of the dead, or *Sheol.* In the popular mind *Sheol* was thought to be under the ground, probably because (1) the dead were buried in the earth; and (2) because heaven was considered to be above the earth.

28:12 This verse is the key to the entire episode. **The woman saw Samuel**, i.e., he immediately appeared, apparently without the hocus pocus which such mediums normally went through in attempting to contact the dead. She **cried out at the top of her voice**. The outcry signaled that the woman saw an apparition which she did not anticipate. The appearance of Samuel differed essentially from everything she had experienced and effected before. The woman was shocked and fearful in the presence of the real spirit of Samuel. This verse asserts that Samuel appeared; it does not assert that he appeared through the power of the woman.

If she had not suspected before, she now knew it was King Saul who was standing before her. These explanations have been offered: (1) such perception would have come to her in the heightened perception of the state of clairvoyance; (2) she had some intuitive perception of a special relationship between the apparition and her unknown guest which prompted her to make an intelligent guess as to his identity; (3) by word or by his posture of bowing, Samuel revealed to her the presence of the king; (4) she made a logical deduction from the fact that there could be only one person who would want to see Samuel in those troubled times; and (5) a light filled the room when Samuel appeared which illuminated the features of Saul.

28:13 Even though his own fear had brought him to that place, Saul urged the woman not to be afraid, just to tell him what she saw. The woman said she saw **a spirit coming up out of the ground**. The word "spirit" is literally "Elohim,"[5] and it is followed by a plural verb.[6] "Elohim" in the Hebrew Bible usually refers to God, but sometimes means "judges." Because the word is plural, Jewish tradition held that Moses appeared along with Samuel. It is unlikely, however, that the woman saw more than one figure, since in the following verse she describes only one. Here the word "Elohim" denotes a supernatural, nonearthly being.

28:14 Saul asked what the spirit looked like. From this it is clear that at the outset only the woman saw the apparition. The spirit looked like **an old man,** probably indicated by his white Nazirite locks (cf. 1:2; 12:2). He was **wearing a robe** (מְעִיל, $m^{e}\hat{\imath}l$). This was an exterior tunic, longer than the common one, without sleeves, worn by persons of rank (cf. 1 Sam 18:4; 24:5,11), and especially by those engaged in the divine service (Exod 28:31; 39:22; Lev 8:7). This is the same robe which, when torn, became the symbol of Saul's downfall as king (15:27-28). The robe was sufficiently characteristic of the prophet to serve as a means of identification (cf. 1 Sam 2:19; 15:27). Saul *knew* **it was Samuel**. His certainty regarding the identity of the apparition is based (1) upon the description by the woman or (2) his personal observation, for at this point Samuel most likely became visible to Saul. In respect for this grand old leader of the nation, Saul **bowed down and prostrated himself with his face to the ground.**

The text gives every indication that the spirit of Samuel appeared in the house of the witch on the eve of Saul's final battle with the Philistines. Nevertheless, the fathers of the church, the reformers, and earlier Christian theologians, with few exceptions, assumed that there was not a real appearance of Samuel, but only (1) an imaginary one, or (2) the demonic impersonation of Samuel.[7] Modern scholars

---

[5]If the woman had meant to equate what she saw with a ghost, she would have used the word *'ôb*. Beuken ("I Samuel 28," 10): "the woman expected a ghost but saw a divine being, divine in terms of her pagan religion."

[6]The standard English versions render (1) "a ghost" (JB); "a god-like form" (BV); "a god" (ASV); "a spirit" (NKJV); "a divine being" (NRSV, JPS).

[7]For a survey of the Rabbinic and Patristic interpretation of 1 Samuel 28, see K.A.D. Smelik, "The Witch of Endor; I Samuel 28 in Rabbinic and Christian Exegesis Till 800 A.D.," *Vigiliae Christianae* 33 (1977): 160-179.

for the most part are agreed that the text is reporting an actual post-mortem appearance of Samuel not, however, as a result of the incantations of the witch, but through a miracle of God. The appearance of Samuel from the kingdom of the dead has an analogue in the appearance of Moses and Elijah on the mount of transfiguration (Matt 17:3; Luke 9:30-31), although the latter appeared *in glory*.

The Lord permitted Samuel to reappear on this occasion for one or more of the following reasons: (1) to make Saul's crime in consulting the witch the means of announcing his impending doom, (2) to show the heathen world the infinite superiority of an oracle from the Lord over the feeble prognostications of those who resort to the powers of darkness, and (3) to confirm the belief in life beyond the grave.[8]

2. Samuel's Ominous Prophecy (28:15-25)

28:15 A conversation took place between Samuel and Saul, apparently without the mediation of the medium. Samuel spoke in the name of the Lord, reiterating that name seven times in vv. 16-19. He seems to rebuke Saul for having **disturbed** him in the peaceful existence of the afterlife. *Sheol* was a quiet, though imperfect and temporary state of bliss, at least for the saints of God (cf. Isa 14:9).

Saul explained that he was **in great distress.** This is a despairing assessment of the king's situation, but it is no confession of sin, no cry for mercy — nothing but the overwhelming desire of self-preservation. The Philistines had launched an attack, and God had **turned away** from him. Saul now recognized what the Narrator reported in 1 Sam 16:14; 18:12. The Lord no longer answered Saul's prayers either in dreams or by prophets. Here there is a contradiction in Saul's reply. If God had forsaken him, how could he expect any answer from him; and if God did not reply to his inquiry through the ordinary mechanisms, how could he hope to obtain any divine revelation through the help of a witch?

28:16-17 Saul's assessment of his spiritual situation was confirmed and heightened by Samuel. Again Samuel rebuked Saul. Why did he consult this man of God now that the Lord had in fact turned away from him and had become Saul's enemy?[9] Yahweh had done what he

---

[8]Dr. Hales quoted by Jamieson (211).

[9]The word "enemy" (עָר, *'ār*) is taken by some to be an Aramaism, found

had predicted through Samuel when he was alive. Because Saul had not obeyed the Lord and carried out his fierce wrath against the Amalekites, the Lord had (1) **torn the kingdom** out of his hands and (2) **given it to one of** his **neighbors — to David.** By the end of that day Saul would no longer be king. An evil spirit impersonating Samuel would never have spoken these words. The devil would not have wished to help David "the man after God's own heart" to ascend the throne of Israel; nor would an evil spirit have announced the punishment which was about to fall on one who was disobedient to God. The name of Saul's neighbor to whom the kingdom would be given was withheld in 13:14. It could now be stated.

28:18-19 The same verb is used in the original in both the condemnation and in the announcement of judgment. Saul did not **obey the LORD.** He did not **carry out** [lit., "do, execute"] **his fierce wrath against the Amalekites** (cf. 1 Samuel 15). For these reasons, **the LORD has done this to you today,** i.e., done what he announced in v. 17. The guilt of the king involves the nation also in punishment.

The Lord would **hand over** to the Philistines both Israel and Saul. In the battle the next day both Saul **and his sons** would be killed and join Samuel in *Sheol,* the abode of the dead. The prophet did not say that *all* of Saul's sons would die the next day, and indeed they did not. Only three fell that day. The expression **with me** does not imply that the condition of Saul and his sons would be the same as that of Samuel, but only that they too would be among the dead. Yahweh would also **hand over the army** [lit., "camp"] **of Israel to the Philistines.** The language here is that of the Holy War. At this point Yahweh's holy war was being waged against Israel, not Israel's adversaries.

28:20 The shocking words from Samuel caused Saul to fall **full length** [lit., "the fullness of his stature"] **on the ground** for he had been kneeling since Samuel had appeared. His strength was gone because he had eaten nothing all that day and night, and he was under enormous mental stress.

---

elsewhere in Hebrew only in one or two doubtful places. Others regard the word as a corruption of the text. The ancient versions had problems with the word, and may have been translating a different Hebrew text. The LXX rendered: "has turned to be with your neighbor"; the Vulgate: "has passed over to your rival." For a discussion, see Driver (216f.). Standard English versions render: "and is with your neighbor" (JB); "has become your adversary" (BV, ASV, NJPS); "has become your enemy" (NIV, NRSV, NKJV).

28:21-22 Here is another irony in this passage. Saul had been forsaken by God, and left without comfort by Samuel. The witch, though a grievous sinner, had compassion on Saul.[10] She **came to Saul** from where she was standing across the room. She **saw that he was greatly shaken.**[11] From across the dimly lit room she had not perceived how terrified Saul was. She reasoned with him. She had obeyed his words, even jeopardizing her own life by agreeing to call up one that he named. Now he must listen to her. He must allow her to prepare some food so that he would have strength to make his way back to the camp of Israel. The witch's actions grew out of (1) natural womanly sympathy for the pitiful king; or (2) cautious regard to her own safety, lest, if the king be found dead in her house, she would be held accountable.

28:23 At first Saul refused. He may have imagined that to eat in that place would seal his rejection by God and his prophet. On the other hand, with a death sentence hanging over him, he could not even think of food. Saul's two companions and the woman keep on urging him to eat. So Saul eventually got up from the ground and sat on the couch to await what the woman might prepare for him.

28:24-25 The woman quickly butchered a fattened calf (cf. Gen 18:6ff.) which she had available **at the house**, i.e., nearby. Because of the need for haste, she baked some bread **without yeast**. The woman set this meal of meat and bread before her king and his men. This was Saul's last supper. Here is the final irony of the passage. The woman gave the king a meal fit for a king even though he had just been informed that all hope of retaining his kingship was now lost.

---

[10]For a more sinister appraisal of the motives of the witch, see P.T. Reis, "Eating the Blood: Saul and the Witch of Endor," *JSOT* 73 (1997): 3-13. According to Beuken ("I Samuel 28," 13), the meal invitation reveals a lack of comprehension of the power of the prophetic word. "In fact, she tries to turn away the death sentence which irrevocably has crossed the path of Saul."

[11]The verb בָּהַל (*bāhal*) can refer to the fright with which people react when an unexpected event enters their life, but often, more seriously, it marks their reaction to a sudden confrontation with death. In a word it refers to the fright in which the grip of death on a person becomes visible. Other renderings of the verb are: "terrified" (RSV), "disturbed" (NEB), "quite terror-stricken" (NAB).

1 SAMUEL 29

C. DAVID ON THE MARCH (29:1–30:6)

1. Recognition: The Bodyguard of Achish (29:1-2)

As they marched toward Shunem in the Jezreel valley, the Philistines stopped at Aphek to organize their forces. Thus this chapter chronologically precedes the note in 28:4. It serves to keep before the reader that whereas Saul had been abandoned totally by the Lord in his moment of crisis, David still enjoyed providential watch care.

29:1 Forces is literally "camps." **Aphek** means "fortress." Several places with this name are mentioned in the Bible. Scholars differ as to whether the Aphek here is the place in the plain of Sharon mentioned in 1 Samuel 4 (ZA, 114) where once the Philistines had achieved a great victory over Israel, or another Aphek in the Jezreel valley. If the former interpretation is correct, then Aphek was the staging area for Philistine troop deployment in the first and last battles against Israel. The army of Israel was **camped by the spring in Jezreel**, probably Ain Jalud, a copious spring at the foot of Mount Gilboa. Jezreel occupied a strong and central position, commanding the route from the plain of Esdraelon east through the valley of Jezreel to the Jordan.

29:2 The Philistine **rulers** were the leaders of their five main cities (cf. 1 Sam 5:8,11; 6:4,12,16,18; 7:7). The Philistine army was organized into units of **hundreds and thousands**. The language here suggests a review of the troops, perhaps at the place of rendezvous of the separate forces from each of the Philistine cities. The Philistine rulers personally participated in the march past the commanders. David and his men were positioned at the rear of the line of march with Achish. They were his personal bodyguards.

2. Anticipation: Loyalty to Israel Assumed (29:3-11)

The Objections of the Commanders (29:3-5)

29:3 The Philistine **commanders** apparently are to be distinguished from the rulers of the previous verse. They observed David's men marching at the rear of Achish's contingent of troops. They would stand out because of their distinctive (1) weapons, (2) dress, and (3) racial characteristics. The commanders immediately challenged Achish about the presence of **these Hebrews**, a disparaging name for Israelites used by foreigners (cf. 1 Sam 4:6,9; 13:3,19; 14:11,21). The commanders were not comfortable with a sizable Hebrew unit as the rear guard.

Achish's defense of David was in keeping with the attitude expressed in 27:12 and 28:1-2 where he was utterly blind to David's duplicity (cf. 27:8-11). Achish defended his trust in David by two arguments. First, he pointed out that David was a former officer of Saul, rightly suggesting that there had been a falling out between the two. Second, David had faithfully served Achish **for over a year,** lit., "these days or these years," i.e., a year or two. This indefinite expression of time is probably equivalent to saying "a year, in fact two years."[1] David had actually been in his service for only sixteen months (1 Sam 27:7). Since the day David **left Saul** (lit., "from the day of his falling away," i.e., desertion) there had been no occasion for Achish to question his loyalty.

29:4-5 The Philistine **commanders,** lit., "princes," became angry. They insisted that David be sent back to **the place you assigned him,** viz., his city at Ziklag. David **must not go** [lit., "go down"][2] **with us into battle**. In support of their demand, the commanders made three points. (1) David could not be trusted in the heat of battle. They had no doubt that David would **turn against** (lit., "become an adversary against") **us during the fighting**. (2) They suggested that David might be looking for just such an opportunity to get back in the good graces of Saul. (3) To justify their suspicions, the commanders reminded Achish that they used to sing in Israel about how

---

[1]See discussion at 1 Sam 27:7 where "days" is equivalent to a complete year.

[2]"Go down" into battle is a technical military expression derived from the fact that armies usually encamped on opposite ranges of hills before descending into the valley to engage in battle.

many Philistines he had slain in battle, i.e., David was a popular Israelite war hero.

This is the second time that the jingle of 18:7 was quoted by Philistines (cf. 21:12). From this one would conclude that (1) the fame of David was widespread and (2) the Philistines were generous in acknowledging military heroism even in an enemy.

Dismissal of David (29:6-11)

29:6-7 Anticipating that his order would hurt and anger David, Achish clothed the news in words of praise and personal trust. First, he assured David on oath that he had been a **reliable** (lit., "upright") ally during the time he had lived in Philistine territory. The use of Yahweh's name in an oath by a pagan king has been explained in various ways, e.g., (1) that this is the Hebrew equivalent of an oath taken in the name of one of his gods, (2) that he used the name Yahweh to impress David with his sincerity, (3) that he had embraced Yahweh as one of his gods, and (4) that he was being courteous to David in not swearing by Philistine gods. Second, Achish said he **would be pleased** (lit., "it would be pleasing in my eyes") to have David serve with him in the army. **Serve** is literally "go forth and come back" (cf. 18:16). Third, Achish never had found in David **any fault**, i.e., evidence of disloyalty. Thus Achish dismissed David with the utmost courtesy, assuring him that his own wish had been that he should remain with him.

Having given David the good news, Achish broke the bad news. The **rulers** did not approve of David. The military commanders must have swayed the other four city rulers with their logic. Even though Achish was *king,* he apparently could not overrule the collective judgment of the other Philistine rulers. Therefore, Achish ordered David to leave in peace. He should do nothing which would **displease the Philistine rulers**. By this advice Achish was warning David not to press his right to go into battle nor take any retaliatory action in response to his dismissal (cf. 2 Chr 25:10-13).

29:8 In this verse the disingenuous Israelite is depicted in sharp contrast to the generous and transparent Philistine king. Partly to vindicate himself against suspicion of disloyalty, and partly to test the sincerity of Achish, David adopted outwardly the attitude of surprised indignation that his loyalty would be questioned. Inwardly he must have rejoiced that he had been delivered from this dilemma of either going to war against his own people, or being disloyal to

Achish. David protested his dismissal with three questions. (1) What had he done? (2) What fault had Achish found in him? In this question David referred to himself as the **servant** of Achish. (3) Why could he not be allowed to go and **fight against the enemies of my lord the king**? Achish interpreted the reference to be to himself. This, however, may be another deliberately ambiguous statement of David which Achish misinterpreted. David may have been referring to Saul with the words "my lord the king"[3] (KD, 331). The Philistine commanders were probably right about David's intentions. He was truly reluctant to quit the march and lose a chance to be an adversary within the Philistine camp (McCarter, 1:427).

29:9-10 For the third time Achish expressed his personal satisfaction with David. He had been as pleasing to Achish as **an angel of God,** i.e., a messenger of God, one sent by God. Nevertheless, the Philistine **commanders** had put their foot down: David could not go into battle with them. Therefore, at first light David must be on his way south to Ziklag along with **your master's** [Saul's] **servants.** This may be a reference to that band of deserters belonging to the tribe of Manasseh who, instead of obeying Saul's summons to the war with the Philistines, joined David about this time (1 Chr 12:19-21).[4]

29:11 In the morning David departed to the south, and the Philistines **went up,** i.e., headed north from Aphek to the valley of Jezreel. If it was on the second day's march that the Philistine lords insisted on David's departure, he would be back at Gath in two days, and on the third day reach Ziklag (cf. 1 Sam 30:1).

The biblical Narrator is concerned in these verses to underscore three points: (1) that David retained the favor of a Philistine king under the most difficult circumstances, (2) that the duplicity of David while living in the land of the Philistines almost landed him in the awful predicament of having to go to war against his own people, and (3) that behind the scenes God so orchestrated events as to rescue David from this untenable situation.

---

[3]The word "lord/master" (*'ādôn*) is used three times in ch 29 (vv. 4,8,10) to designate David's relationship to a superior, and in each case the person indicated is probably Saul.

[4]In the LXX v. 10 is longer than in the MT, adding after **have come with you** these words which appear in the NRSV: "and go to the place that I appointed for you. As for the evil report, do not take it to heart, for you have done well before me." This, however, looks more like a characteristic LXX expansion than a mistaken omission from the MT.

1 SAMUEL 30

Chapter 30 describes the last of David's perils during the time of his flight. This chapter deals with another confrontation with the Amalekites and thus forms an interesting contrast with the expedition of Saul in 1 Samuel 15. Saul's failure in respect to that expedition led to the rejection of the king, whereas David's success in this chapter paved the way for him to ascend the throne.

3. Danger: Rebellion by His Troops (30:1-6)

30:1 After three days of traveling from Aphek (about twenty-five miles per day), David and his men reached the home base of Ziklag tired, hungry and expecting all the comforts of a welcome home. They found the town in ruins. The Amalekites had come in from the desert to attack the place while the men of Ziklag were absent. The **Negev** is the technical name for the district between the hills of Judah and the actual desert to the south. It is a series of rolling hills, with virtually no trees or shrubs to relieve its bareness. The word **raided** is the same word used in 1 Sam 27:8. It implies that the Amalekites spread themselves over the country to drive off cattle and booty, but with no intention of fighting battles. Whereas other parts of the area were simply plundered, Ziklag was sacked and burned, probably in retaliation for David's cruel treatment of the Amalekites over the past several months.

30:2 No resistance could be made to the Amalekite attack because most, if not all, of the men of war were with the Philistine army. Because they were valuable as slaves, the Amalekites spared the women and children. The intention was probably to sell them at the Egyptian slave auctions. **Carried them off** is literally "drove them," i.e., like cattle.

30:3-5 The NIV omits the word "behold" from v. 3, a word which indicates the shock of what David's men saw when they returned home. Even from a distance David's men could see the smoking ruins of their town. Naturally the troops feared for the safety of their wives and children who had been taken captive. David and his men **wept aloud** when they saw what had taken place **until they had no strength left to weep**. Among the captives were David's two wives, viz., **Ahinoam of Jezreel** (see on 1 Sam 25:43) and **Abigail. Widow** is literally "wife," i.e., former wife.

30:6 David suffered a double blow when he returned to Ziklag. Not only did he come home to a city in ruins and to panic over the fate of the women and children, he had to face the hostility of his own troops. David was **greatly distressed**, lit., "in a predicament."[1] The Hebrew term refers, not so much to his grief, but his personal danger. The men held David accountable for what had happened. Because of his allegiance to Achish, David had left the town of Ziklag defenseless. For this reason there was talk of **stoning** David. Every man was **bitter in spirit**, i.e., the grief of each man turned to anger, because of what had happened to his family members. In this crisis, David **found strength in the Lord his God**, i.e., his faith in God enabled him to deal with this crisis effectively (cf. 1 Sam 23:16; Eph 6:10). The contrast with Saul is obvious. Saul sought out a medium in his crisis (ch 28), but David leaned upon the Lord.

D. A WORD OF ENCOURAGEMENT FOR DAVID (30:7-8)

30:7-8 The priest Abiathar, the sole survivor of the Nob sanctuary, had defected to David when David was at Keilah (1 Sam 22:20-23; 23:6,9). Now confident and assured, David asked Abiathar to bring the ephod with its two stones, the Urim and Thummim. Not since his rescue of Keilah (1 Sam 23:9) had David consulted the priestly oracle.

To Abiathar's credit, he had not abandoned the future king of Israel even during those sixteen months when David seems to have all but abandoned the Lord. David inquired of the Lord as to whether or not he should pursue the Amalekites. Whereas in 1 Sam 28:6 Saul could find no divine guidance from Urim, David here

---

[1]The NKJV, NASB and ASV also render "David was greatly distressed." Other versions indicate that David "was in a serious predicament" (BV); "in great danger" (NRSV, NJPS); "in great trouble" (JB).

received an encouraging answer: **"Pursue them, . . . You will certainly overtake them and succeed in the rescue,"** lit., "Pursue; for overtaking you will overtake, and delivering, you will deliver."

E. DAVID IN BATTLE (30:9-31)

1. Recognition: A Mighty Warrior (30:9-20)

30:9-10 David and his old band of **six hundred men** started out in hot pursuit.[2] Because Ziklag was burnt down, of course they found no provisions there, and were consequently obliged to set out in pursuit of the foe without being able to provide themselves with the necessary supplies. So rapid was his march that one third of his men dropped from the ranks. When they got to the **Besor Ravine** about fifteen miles south of Ziklag, **some stayed behind**, lit., "those who were to be left behind stood." This language suggests that David had decided not to take his whole force on the search for the Amalekites in the difficult country of the Negev.

The reason David did not take his full force with him was because a third of his men were **exhausted**. The verb (פָּגַר, *pāgar*) used here and in v. 21 is related to a noun meaning "a corpse." Perhaps the idea is that they were "dead tired." That the men were exhausted is not surprising. They had just covered the eighty miles or so from Aphek to Ziklag in three days and two hundred were too exhausted **to cross the ravine**. Verse 24 indicates that David left with these two hundred as much of the baggage as possible.

30:11-12 David's task was now made much easier by the discovery of an Egyptian lying in the sand. The man was very weak, for he had consumed no food and water for three days. This Amalekite slave (v. 13) had been left behind with no supplies of food. David's men gave him water and some cakes of pressed figs and raisins. The fact that they gave him not only the basic needs of bread and water, but figs and raisins also, shows that they deliberately tried to get his full cooperation by more than usual kindness (Mauchline, 190). The man revived, and became genial and communicative.

---

[2]Those who had come from Manasseh (see on 29:10) to join David did not participate in the chase because (1) they had not lost wives and children in the raid, and (2) they would not have been able to keep up with the original band which was accustomed to forced marches and rapid deployment.

30:13-14 David questioned the prisoner. Because he was unarmed, and wore the garb of a slave, David asked concerning his owner and his country. It turned out that he was an Egyptian who had been the slave of one of the Amalekite raiders. When he had become ill three days before, his master had abandoned him in the desert. His life was of too little value for his master to mount him on a camel, or even to leave with him supplies of food. The descendants of **Caleb** occupied the area of the hill country south of Hebron which included the towns of Ziph, Carmel and Maon. The **Kerethites** were closely associated with the Philistines (cf. Ezek 25:16; Zeph 2:5). The name suggests that they came originally from the island of Crete (Caphtor; cf. Amos 9:7). They may have been mercenaries who fought for the Philistines. The **Negev of the Kerethites** presumably was the region around Ziklag south of Philistine territory. A defeat of the raiders would endear David to other communities living in the area.

30:15 David asked the Egyptian if he could lead him **down to this raiding party**, lit. "troop." The word indicates a band of roving plunderers. He asked David to swear **before God**. The solemn sanction of an oath was recognized throughout the ancient Near East. The slave wanted David to swear that he would neither kill him nor hand him back over to the Amalekites. The Egyptian probably knew where the camp was because he had heard them discussing where they would camp. The Amalekites would be moving slowly because of the large booty of cattle which they had taken during their raid.

30:16 The Egyptian led David to the edge of the Amalekite camp. They were **scattered over the countryside** (lit., "over the face of all the land") in small groups **eating, drinking and reveling**, lit., "behaving as at a festival gathering," because of the great amount of plunder which they had taken. They felt secure because of the distance they had traveled from their last raid. Apparently they had no lookouts on duty.

30:17 The NIV would make it appear that David ordered a night attack on the camp. The word translated **dusk** (הַנֶּשֶׁף, *hanneSeph*), however, most often refers to predawn twilight, i.e., dawn (JB, GNB) Such is the interpretation of the Talmud (*Ber.* 3b; cf. Hertzberg, 228). If this interpretation is correct, David reached the location of the Amalekites in the evening and attacked at dawn.[3] Apparently

---

[3]R.P. Smith (549) thinks that David arrived in late afternoon, attacked immediately, maintained the attack until night fall, and renewed it in the morning.

after their initial surprise, the Amalekites offered stubborn resistance. The battle continued **until the evening of the next day,** lit.,
"until the evening of their morrow." This probably refers to the
evening with which the next day commenced, since the new day
began at sundown. The battle then lasted from early dawn till past
sunset (Kirkpatrick, 1:227). Most of the raiding party got wiped out
except for four hundred young men who fled **on camels.** Yet this
tiny surviving remnant was equal in size to the whole of David's battle group. The completeness of David's victory here contrasts
sharply with Saul's total defeat in the following chapter.

30:18-20 David recovered **all the plunder** the Amalekites had
taken, including his two wives. None of the captives was missing. In
addition to recovering his lost possessions, David captured a rich booty
of flocks and herds which his men drove off in triumph ahead of their
own cattle. The men presented this plunder to David by acclamation.

2. Anticipation: A "Royal" Edict (30:21-25)

30:21 As David approached the Besor Ravine, the two hundred
men who had been too exhausted to follow him came out to meet
the victors. David and his men **greeted them,**[4] lit., "he asked them of
their welfare." **People** (עַם, 'am) is a technical term in this chapter for
"David's men" (vv. 4,6, and the last clause of v. 21).

30:22 David had to settle a dispute at the Besor Ravine. Among
the four hundred who had fought the Amalekites were some **evil
men and troublemakers**. These selfish and mean-spirited men
thought that the spoils of war should go only to those who actually
went into battle. The two hundred did not go out **with us,** lit., "with
me." Apparently each man spoke for himself, in the true spirit of
selfishness. All which had been recovered from the Amalekites was
called by them **the plunder we recovered.** They had risked their
lives in taking this plunder, and previous ownership counted for
nothing. Those who had guarded the baggage should receive only
their family members and **go.**

---

[4]The translation "greeted" (or variations thereof) is found in the ASV,
NKJV, NRSV, and NJPS. The BV, JB and ASV margin rendered "he
inquired after their welfare" (or equivalent). Given the circumstances, the
latter translation is preferable.

30:23-25 David ruled on this dispute. He generously called the troublemakers **my brothers**. Credit for the victory belonged to the Lord, not the four hundred. He had protected them and handed over to them the forces that had attacked Ziklag. That being the case, nobody should listen to these troublemakers. The share of the man who stayed with the supplies should be the same as that of the man who went down to the battle. David made this a **statute and ordinance for Israel** from that day forward. Even as David showed kinglike leadership in battle, now he performed a royal judicial function. He was beginning to act like a king.

3. Anticipation: Distribution of Plunder (30:26-31)

30:26 When David got back to Ziklag, he sent some of the plunder taken from the Amalekites to the elders of Judah who were his friends. This was done (1) to recompense these people for previous losses to marauding desert tribes, (2) to thank them for the encouragement they had been to him during his wilderness wanderings, (3) to remove any doubts about his loyalty to Israel in spite of his sixteen-month alliance with the Philistines, and (4) to position himself to be elevated to kingship by his native tribe immediately after the death of Saul. **Present** is literally "blessing." David's language "carries with it the assertion that, no matter what Saul may be doing, it is David who is successfully fighting Yahweh's battles" (Gordon, 210).

30:27-31 The size of the list of towns which David endowed indicates the quantity of the spoils which he had taken from the Amalekites. A good atlas is essential for the study of these verses.

Once again in ch 30 David appears as an admirable leader. He certainly is depicted as back on track with the Lord. He is energetic and decisive, compassionate and fair. Here he is generous with those who have been kind to him in his wanderings, and as a result he forms friendships which he retained and cherished long afterwards when he became the king of Israel.

1 SAMUEL 31

F. FINAL OBSTACLE TO KINGSHIP REMOVED (31:1-13)

While David was defeating the Amalekites in the desert, Saul was facing the judgment of God on Mt. Gilboa. In the Hebrew the linkage between chs 30-31 is even more clear. Miscall (181-182) points out that in 30:17 David "fought" (הִכָּה, *hikkāh*) the Amalekites and they fled (נוּס, *nûs*). At the same time in the north (ch 31) the Philistines "killed" (*hikkāh*) Saul (v. 2) and Israel (vv. 1, 7) "fled" (*nûs*).

1. The Death of Saul (31:1-6)

31:1 On the day after Saul's visit to the witch of Endor (1 Sam 28), the Philistines launched their attack. The text is literally, "Now the Philistines were fighting against Israel and the Israelites fled." Details of the battle have not been reported, but it most likely was fought somewhere in the Jezreel valley. Obviously the Narrator regarded military details as incidental to his main purpose, the description of Saul's death in fulfillment of the prophecy of Samuel. **The Israelites** is literally "the men of Israel." They were driven back upon their camp, and finally fled in confusion up the heights of Gilboa, pursued by the Philistines. Many **fell slain,** i.e., died, on the slopes of Mt. Gilboa.

31:2 When the Israelites broke ranks and fled, **the Philistines pressed hard after Saul and his sons**. They knew that if they could kill the members of the royal family, the battle would be over. Three of Saul's sons died in the battle, and presumably Saul witnessed their deaths. Saul's fourth son, Ishvi or Eshbaal (also called Ishbosheth), apparently was not present at the battle.

31:3 The **fighting grew fierce around Saul** in that the Philistines focused their attack on him and shot clusters of arrows in his direction. **The archers,** is literally "shooters, men with bows." As the first word would equally apply to men who threw javelins, the explanation is added to make the meaning clear. **They overtook,** lit., "found," Saul, which means either (1) that they got him in range of their arrows or (2) they picked him out in the confusion of battle. **They wounded him critically**, based on the rendering of the LXX, is followed by most English versions. The Hebrew reads: "he writhed (in fear) exceedingly because of the archers."[1] Despair and the fear of insult paralyzed his courage (Kirkpatrick, 1:231).

31:4 Saul was determined to die on his own terms. He requested his armor-bearer to thrust him through (cf. Judg 9:54). Saul's last reference to the Philistines showed his total disdain for them as **uncircumcised** (cf. 1 Sam 14:6; 17:26,36). Saul did not wish to be alive when the Philistines caught up with him. He knew they would **abuse** or torture him before killing him.[2] The word means to inflict upon another all that passion, lust, anger or malice dictated.

The **armor-bearer was terrified** and would not kill his king. He would no more touch the Lord's anointed than David would. So Saul took his own sword and fell on it. Suicide was practically unknown among the Israelites.[3] Saul's divine commission had been to save Israel from the Philistines (1 Sam 9:16), but ironically he took his own life to avoid being humiliated by them.

31:5-6 The armor-bearer then fell on his own sword either because (1) in foolish fidelity he refused to survive his master or (2) he felt remorse because he had failed to preserve the life of his master. So Samuel's prophecy was fulfilled. Saul and three sons all died on the same day. Thus ended the troubled reign of Saul. All Saul's **men died together that same day**. The reference here is to the king's personal guards. To their credit these men fell to a man fighting bravely to defend their king.

---

[1]The JB, NRSV, NASB, NJPS and BV have Saul wounded by the archers. The ASV has correctly translated the clause: "he was greatly distressed by reason of the archers."

[2]The story of Samson (Judg 16:25) illustrates how the Philistines delighted in torturing their former adversaries. Later King Zedekiah had a similar fear if he should surrender to the Babylonians (Jer 38:19). The word is also used of what the men of Gibeah did to a Levite's concubine throughout the night (Judg 19:25).

[3]Prior to Saul the only recorded example is that of Samson who sacrificed his life in order to effect the destruction of a large group of Philistines. Ahithophel, David's counselor, committed suicide, (2 Sam 17:23) as did King Zimri (1 Kgs 16:18) and the betrayer of Jesus.

2. Valor of the Gileadites (31:7-13)

31:7 The Israelites is literally "the men of Israel." This phrase in v. 1 referred to the army; here it refers to noncombatants. While the Philistines concentrated on Saul and his sons, the rest of the Israelite army managed to escape. The news that the king and his sons were dead spread to the Israelites **along the valley** (lit., "on the other side of the valley"), i.e., the north side of the Jezreel valley encompassing the regions of Issachar, Zebulun, and Naphtali. These people abandoned their towns and fled. Those who lived just **across the Jordan** also deserted their towns.[4] Nothing here indicates that the Philistines actually took possession of any territory east of the river, although the threat of occupation by them must have seemed very real to the inhabitants of that area. For a time the Philistines occupied the greater part of north Canaan. Thus at the end of Saul's reign the military superiority of the Philistines was perhaps even greater than it had been at the beginning. The country to the south of the plain of Jezreel does not appear to have been overrun by the victorious army. Perhaps the presence of David, considered a friend and ally by the Philistines, insured immunity from Philistine invasion south of the Jezreel Valley.

31:8-9 The battle must have raged until dusk, as Saul's body was not discovered until the next morning. When the Philistines came to strip the valuables from the dead bodies on the battlefield, they came across the bodies of Saul and his three sons. They cut off Saul's head, and stripped off his armor, thus repaying Israel in a measure for the embarrassing decapitation of their champion (1 Sam 17:51). The translation **they sent messengers** is based on a slight alteration of the MT which suggests that they sent the head and weapons of Saul throughout their land. The Narrator uses the pejorative term **idols** to refer to the Philistine gods thus hinting that whatever triumph the Philistines now celebrated would be of short duration.

31:10 The custom of depositing trophies of war in sanctuaries seems to have been common (cf. 1 Sam 5:2; 21:9). The Philistines put Saul's armor in **the temple** (lit., "house") **of the Ashtoreths.**[5] The

---

[4]The phrase "on the side of the Jordan," which usually refers to the region east of the Jordan, may in this context refer to the area between the battlefield and the river on the west bank. So KD (337) and Kirkpatrick (1:232).

[5]Excavators found the ruins of two temples in Beth Shan, which some

plural may indicate that the pieces of armor belonging to Saul and his sons were divided between the different shrines of the goddess. On "Ashtoreths," see comments on 1 Sam 7:4-5. First Chronicles 10:10 adds this information: "They put his armor in the temple of their gods and hung up his head in the temple of Dagon." First Samuel began with a reference to Yahweh's "house" at Shiloh (1:24) and concludes at the "house" of a pagan deity.

The Philistines fastened Saul's headless body to the wall of Beth Shan (ZA, 114).[6] This strategic city was the easternmost of the line of old Canaanite fortress cities stretching across the Jezreel valley from the Mediterranean to the Jordan. It was located on a hill overlooking the Jordan valley some four miles west of the Jordan and twelve miles south of the sea of Galilee. The royal heads were fixed in the temple of Dagon (1 Chr 10:10). According to 2 Sam 21:12 the men of Jabesh recovered the bodies "from the public square at Beth Shan, where the Philistines had hung them." The spot was probably above the principal gate which opened onto the wide marketplace outside the city walls.

31:11-12 The people of Jabesh Gilead heard what had happened to the body of their king. The valiant men of that town journeyed through the night some thirteen miles to Beth Shan. They took down the bodies of Saul and his sons, and carried them back to Jabesh. There they burned the bodies. Burning corpses was not the custom in Israel and was normally restricted to the worst of criminals (Lev 20:14). Here, however, the partial cremation was done out of respect (1) to prevent the Philistines from finding those bodies and desecrating them further and/or (2) to avoid the risk of infection from the quickly decomposing bodies (Baldwin, 171).

31:13 The men of Jabesh took the bones which did not burn in the fire, and they buried them under a **tamarisk tree** in their city. Sometime later King David had those remains reverently interred in the family sepulchre of Kish, the father of Saul (2 Sam 21:12,14). The men of Jabesh showed their respect for the bodies of their royal family when they **fasted seven days**.

---

have suggested are the temples of Dagon and Ashteroth in which Saul's head and armor were displayed. See NBD, s.v., "Bethshean, Bethshan," by T.C. Mitchell. See also the archaeological survey of Beth Shan by G.M. Fitzgerald, AOTS, 185-196.

[6]Archaeological excavations at Beth Shan are summarized by G.M. FitzGerald, AOTS, 193-196.

2 SAMUEL 1

VIII. THE COVENANT WITH DAVID ESTABLISHED
(1:1–7:29)

The beginning of 2 Samuel is reminiscent of 1 Samuel in that there is a combination of prose and poetry, both of which are used to produce a moving summary of the detailed history to follow. In this unit the Narrator relates how the covenant with David was established.

A. ENTHRONEMENT OF DAVID OVER JUDAH (1:1–3:5)

1. Impediment Removed (1:1-27)

A Battle Report (1:1-10)

1:1-2 David's success and Saul's death are mentioned side by side in such a way as to deflect attention from the gloom of Gilboa. The words **after the death of Saul** link this chapter to 1 Samuel 31, and the following words refer to 1 Samuel 30. Clearly the two books of Samuel were originally one continuous work. David **returned from defeating the Amalekites.**[1] For **two days** he and his men engaged in restoring the ruins of Ziklag (see on 1 Sam 27:6) in order to provide shelter for their families. **On the third day a man arrived from Saul's camp**. The Amalekite had traveled over eighty miles from the Gilboa battlefield in something less than three full days. If one assumes that the man came immediately from the battlefield, one

---

[1]The MT reads literally, "the Amalek." Several Heb. MSS and English versions read as a gentilic: "the Amalekites." The ancestor of the Amalekites was one of the grandsons of Esau (Gen 36:12; 1 Chr 1:36), and thus they were linked with the Edomites. They were a nomadic tribe usually found in southern Palestine and the Sinai peninsula.

must conclude that the Gilboa battle was fought on the same day David returned from his pursuit of the Amalekites. The words **from Saul's camp** suggest that the Amalekite was attached to the Israelite army either as a combatant, or more likely, as a camp follower. The man's clothes were torn and he had dust on his head to symbolize mourning (cf. 1 Sam 4:12), though one should not conclude that he personally felt any remorse. He **fell to the ground** to pay homage to David, thus indicating that he expected David to be Saul's successor on the throne.

1:3-4 David asked for identification. The man said that he had **escaped from the Israelite camp**, i.e., the victorious Philistines who were attacking the Israelite camp; or the Israelites who may have forced him into their service. David's question **What happened?** is literally "what was the matter?" In an ascending climax, the man reported (1) the Israelite rout, (2) the slaughter of the troops, and (3) the death of the king and crown prince. **Many of them** is literally "many of the people," i.e., the army, **fell,** i.e., were wounded, **and died**. To this point the report was accurate. The remainder of the report, however, was fabricated by the Amalekite for self-serving purposes.

1:5-9 David tried to ascertain whether the Amalekite was telling rumors or the truth. He wanted proof that Saul and Jonathan were dead. The man represented himself as accidentally finding Saul while wandering over Mt. Gilboa (1 Sam 28:4) in the confusion of the rout. **There was Saul** (lit., "and behold[2] Saul") **leaning on his spear**, weary, wounded, and deserted by his bodyguards. Some scholars have tried to reconcile the Amalekite's story with the account in 1 Sam 31:3ff. by assuming that Saul had not died immediately after falling upon his sword, but had struggled to his feet again by supporting himself on his spear. More likely, however, the Amalekite was fabricating much of his story. Philistine chariots were bearing down on Saul on the lower slopes to which they had access. Saul supposedly called this Amalekite over and asked him to kill him. **What can I do?** is literally, "behold me," i.e., here I am. **Stand over me**[3] suggests that the king had collapsed to the ground. Two

---

[2]"Behold," used twice in v. 6, is typical of dream reports, and may hint that the Amalekite was fictionalizing (A. Berlin, 81).

[3]ASV renders "stand beside me." Most English versions agree with the NIV.

reasons are given for the macabre request. First, Saul was in **the throes of death,** i.e., he felt death coming on. The Hebrew word שָׁבָץ (*šābāṣ*) occurs only here, and the versions, ancient and modern, have rendered it in a variety of ways.[4] Probably it means "giddiness" or "dizziness" — conditions which could have been caused either by exhaustion or loss of blood — which rendered him incapable of defending himself. Second, **I'm still alive,** lit., "my life is yet whole in me," i.e., I am fully conscious (and in great agony). He feared that he might fall alive into the hands of the Philistines (cf. 1 Sam 31:4).

1:10 The Amalekite reported that he **stood over** Saul and killed him, because he knew that the king would not survive the wound he already had received in the battle. Two pieces of physical evidence were presented to confirm the story. First, the Amalekite had Saul's **crown.** This was probably not the state crown, but a light fillet worn around the battle helmet as the mark of royalty. Second, he had **the band on his arm,** i.e., an armlet such as was worn above the elbow by kings and distinguished warriors throughout the ancient East. He presented them now to David as proof that Saul was dead, and perhaps in recognition that David was now king of the land. Apparently the Amalekite thought that he could curry favor with David by claiming that he had been the one to kill the king. The truth is that he must have been lurking nearby when Saul committed suicide as reported in the previous chapter.[5]

A Just Execution (1:11-16)

1:11-12 David and his men tore their clothes (cf. Gen 37:34; 2 Sam 13:31). They **mourned,** lit., "beat the breast," **and wept and fasted** till evening for Saul, Jonathan, the **army** (lit., "people") **of the Lord and the house of Israel** (the entire nation), now broken and scattered by the Gilboa defeat. The responses here were the expected and customary reactions to death in the community.

---

[4]*šābāṣ* is rendered (1) "agony" (Targum, NJPS, NASB); (2) "terrible darkness" (LXX); (3) "distress" (Vulgate); (4) "convulsions" (NRSV); (5) "weakness" (BV); (6) "anguish" (NKJV, ASV); (7) "giddiness" (JB).

[5]So B. Arnold, "The Amalekite's Report of Saul's Death: Political Intrigue or Incompatible Sources?" *JETS* 32, 3 (1989): 296-297. A different view is taken by Mauchline (197), who thinks that the Amalekite's narrative rings true. He regards David as blameworthy for disregarding the man's "honorable motives and humanitarian considerations."

1:13-14 Apparently after the period of mourning, David began to question the messenger more closely.[6] He asked him where he was from? The king was trying to determine whether the Amalekite was a resident in Israel or in the territory of the Amalekites. Perhaps his crime would have been considered less heinous if he were not a resident in Israel and owed no duty to Saul. The messenger explained that he was **an alien** (גֵּר, gēr) — an Amalekite who had migrated to the land of Israel. Such individuals had legal status (Lev 25:6; Num 35:15; Deut 14:29), but did not enjoy full rights of citizenship. David then asked why he had not been afraid **to destroy the Lord's anointed.** In David's eyes regicide was not merely a political crime, but a religious offense of the greatest magnitude.

1:15-16 The Amalekite had just recognized David as king, and therefore acknowledged his authority. David immediately assumed the ultimate authority of chief magistrate by ordering the execution of the man. **Strike him down** (פְּגַע בּ, pāga‘ bᵉ, lit., "fall on him"). **Your blood be on your own head** is a formula used to underscore that the individual deserved to die and the executioner was guiltless. The idea is that the blood that has been shed was the cause of the blood about to be shed. By his own mouth this man had professed his guilt.

A Bitter Lamentation[7] (1:17-27)

David's poetic lament over Saul and Jonathan, like the Song of Hannah in 1 Samuel 2, stands in a strategic position. It serves to (1) "close the book" on the previous regime, (2) reveal David's intensely emotional makeup and magnanimous character, and (3) set the standard for proper respect for those who might in the future occupy the throne of Israel.[8]

---

[6]Others regard v. 12 as parenthetical. They understand this interrogation of the Amalekite to have occurred immediately after the man had made his report.

[7]For studies of the structure of this lament, see W.L. Holladay, "Form and Word-Play in David's Lament over Saul and Jonathan," VT 20, 2 (1970): 153-189; S. Gevirtz, "David's Lament over Saul and Jonathan," PEPI, 72-96; W.H. Shea, "Chiasmus and the Structure of David's Lament," JBL 105, 1 (1986): 13-25; D.L. Zapf, "How Are the Mighty Fallen! A Study of 2 Samuel 1:17-27," GTJ 5 (1984): 95-126; D.N. Freedman, "The Refrain in David's Lament over Saul and Jonathan," EOR, 115-126.

[8]Cf. Polzin (David, 13f.), who argues that the lament is "politically motivated."

1:17-18 In this dark hour of Israel's history David's only thought was of the misfortune suffered by his people. David took up a **lament** (קִינָה, *qînāh*) over the death of Saul and Jonathan.[9] The word used is the technical term for a death-dirge or mournful elegy. He ordered that **the men of Judah be taught this lament of the bow**, lit., "to teach the men of Judah the bow." The NIV correctly has followed modern interpreters in taking this to be the title of the lament.[10] The song was taught to the men of Judah rather than to all Israel because for the immediate following years, while the memory of Saul was fresh, David reigned only over the tribe of Judah. The lament was also recorded in **the Book of Jashar** ("the upright"). This book, mentioned previously in Josh 10:13, apparently was a collection of poems commemorating remarkable events or great heroes of the national history to which additions would be made from time to time as occasion warranted. The book no longer survives.[11]

1:19-20 Saul and Jonathan who fell in battle with the Philistines are poetically described as the **glory**,[12] i. e., the chief ornament and honor, of Israel. The **heights** refers to Gilboa. The refrain **How the mighty have fallen!** tolls like a funeral bell three times in this lament and sets forth its theme, viz., the death of Saul and Jonathan (cf. vv. 25,27).[13]

---

[9]Saul and Jonathan are both mentioned four times by name in the lament. It may be that the fourfold repetition of "mighty" in vv. 19,21,25,27 also alludes to the king and his son, not to the fallen Israelite warriors in general. While Saul and Jonathan are named an equal number of times, Jonathan is given pride of place when the two are first mentioned together in v. 22.

[10]Some eminent Jewish scholars understand the phrase to underscore the importance of teaching archery to the armies of Judah.

[11]Several medieval rabbinical works have received the title *Book of Jashar*. A forgery from Christian circles is associated with Alcuin, Bishop of Canterbury (d. A.D. 804), who is said to have discovered it in the city of Gazna on a "pilgrimage into the Holy Land, and Persia." The manuscript was supposedly rediscovered in England in 1721. It was first published in 1829, and was reprinted in a fifth edition by the Rosecrucian Order in 1953. ABD, s.v. "Jashar, Book of" by D. Christensen.

[12]The word translated **glory** (שְׁבִי, *ṣᵉbî*) can also mean "roe" or "gazelle" which some commentators take as a reference to the handsome and fleet-footed Jonathan. No evidence has been adduced, however, to show that Jonathan ever received such a title. Furthermore, the poem celebrates both Saul and Jonathan, and the term cannot be limited just to the latter.

[13]JB renders this refrain as a rhetorical question: "How did the heroes fall?"

Though he had been living among the Philistines, all David's
sympathies were with Israel. He could not bear the thought that the
story of Israel's defeat would be broadcast throughout the land of
the Philistines — in Gath and Ashkelon, for example. **Gath** is selected because (1) of its political importance, (2) its nearness to Israelite
territory, and (3) recent residence of David. **Ashkelon** was a great
religious center and possible location of the temple where Saul's
armor was displayed (1 Sam 31:10). **The daughters of the Philistines** refers to the custom of the times where military victories were
celebrated by the women of the country with public songs and
dances (cf. 1 Sam 18:6; Exod 15:20f.). The **uncircumcised**, the common epithet for the Philistines,[14] underscores the bitterness of the
defeat by the heathen over the circumcised, i.e., Yahweh's inheritance. The phrase **tell it not in Gath** became proverbial as is indicated by its use in Micah 1:10 long after Gath had ceased to exist as
a city. In actual fact the Philistines sent the news of their victory
throughout the whole land (1 Sam 31:9).

1:21-22 David here poetically called on nature itself to share in
mourning Israel's defeat by the Philistines. He wished the scene of
the disaster to remain barren to mark the tragedy. Gilboa should no
longer possess fruitful fields which would produce tithes and offerings for Yahweh. For David the greatest curse which could befall the
earth was the incapacity to render service to the Lord.

Gilboa was cursed because there **the shield of the mighty** (plural) was defiled with blood and dirt. Shields left on a battlefield were
a national disgrace. Saul was metaphorically the shield of the army.
No longer rubbed with oil, lit., "without anointing with oil," refers
to Saul who no longer was the Lord's anointed.[15] This defilement

---

[14]With the exception of Gen 34:14, the phrase is used in the historical
books only of the Philistines. See Judg 14:3; 15:18; 1 Sam 14:6; 17:26,36;
31:4; 1 Chr 10:4.

[15]Most English versions understand the reference to be to Saul's literal
shield. Metal shields were cleansed and polished with oil; those made of
wood and leather were rubbed with oil so as to make missiles deflect from
them. A shield unrubbed with oil would be one which had been abandoned
on the battlefield. In the Samuel books and Kings the term **anointed** (מָשִׁיחַ,
māšîaḥ) is used of persons, not objects. The BV translates "the shield of
Saul, the anointed no more"; the ASV margin renders "as of one not anointed." The thought would be that even the shield of Saul, the anointed of the
Lord, shared the fate of those of the common soldiers at Gilboa.

took place in spite of the fact that both Saul and Jonathan had been valiant in battle. In poetry arrows are represented as drinking **blood**, and the sword as eating **flesh** (lit., "fat"). The **bow** was Jonathan's favorite weapon (cf. 1 Sam 18:4; 20:20), and **the sword** and spear, Saul's. The king and crown prince courageously faced the enemy. **Turn back** (נָשׂוֹג אָחוֹר, *nāsôg 'āḥôr*) denotes a reprehensible action associated with disobedience, rebellion, dishonor, shame, disloyalty, or defeat.[16] Their weapons **did not return unsatisfied** (lit., "empty"), i.e., they took their toll of Philistine soldiers.

1:23 David continued by describing the loving relationship between Saul and Jonathan in life. Jonathan remained faithful to his filial duty even when his father was persecuting his closest friend. In spite of temporary outbursts of anger, Saul loved his son to the last. They were not separated in their death. David described their physical abilities as **swifter than eagles** (cf. Jer 4:13; Hab 1:8) and **stronger than lions** (2 Sam 17:10; Judg 14:18). The term נֶשֶׁר (*nešer*, "eagle") is a general term embracing most large birds of prey, including vultures.

1:24 David called for the daughters of Israel, who once cheered and danced to celebrate Saul's victories, to weep over the king's death. The verse hints of a time of increasing prosperity under Saul's rule. From the spoils of his many battles, briefly mentioned in 1 Sam 14:47, the women of Israel had been clothed with the finest garments and accessories. **Scarlet** was the clothing of kings and of the wealthy. **Finery** is literally "delights."[17]

1:25-26 The poem reaches its climax in an outburst of grief over the death of Jonathan. His name is inserted in the repetition of the first line of the lament. **Brother** is used here in the technical sense of "treaty/covenant-brother" (Youngblood, 815). **On your heights** underscores the tragedy that this valiant warrior died in those very mountain strongholds which he had once won and so often successfully defended.

For the first time in the poem the first person is used to underscore David's personal loss in the death of Jonathan. David addressed the deceased as though he were still living, a common

---

[16]Cf. Isa 42:17; 50:5; 59:14; Jer 38:22; 46:5; Ps 35:4; 40:14; et al.

[17]The term עֲדָנִים (*'ădānîm*) is rendered "with delights" (BV); "luxury" (NRSV, NKJV); "fine linen" (JB); "finery" (NIV, NJPS). The ASV and NASB render the term adverbally as "delicately" and "luxuriously."

illusion in bereavement (Baldwin, 181). The last sentence of v. 26 has been alleged to indicate that Jonathan and David had a homosexual relationship. This interpretation is clearly incorrect. Both men were God-fearing; both were married and had children. David would later be tempted to adultery with Bathsheba. Using poetic hyperbole, David simply means that his relationship with Jonathan brought him more satisfaction and joy than his relationship with any woman in his life thus far, including his mother. The term "love" in such contexts has the meaning of covenantal loyalty (Youngblood, 816). See comments on 1 Sam 18:1-4.

1:27 Here, David faced the reality of death. For all he knew, these two great men were still lying untended on the slopes of Gilboa. **The weapons of war** is perhaps a final metaphorical reference to Saul and Jonathan, those two warriors who were Israel's greatest weapons against national enemies. Less likely is the view which takes the phrase literally and understands it to mean that the weapons had failed to save the lives of Israel's two great heroes.

2 SAMUEL 2

2. Recognition by the Elders (2:1-7)

A Royal Anointing (2:1-4a)

2:1 In the course of time (lit., "and it came to pass after this") is a transition-marker.[1] Apparently some time elapsed after Saul's death without an invitation from the leaders in the tribe of Judah for David, formerly greatly beloved in that tribe, to assume the vacant throne. David was forced to take the initiative. Eager to know the divine will, David **inquired** of Yahweh regarding his next step. His inquiry was probably made through the high priest Abiathar as in 1 Sam 23:9f. By this means he ascertained that he should move immediately from Ziklag to the hill country of Judah. The expression **go up**[2] may have a military sense as well as a geographical sense. Further inquiry indicated that he should settle in **Hebron**,[3] the political and geographical center of the region and perhaps the most important city still remaining in Israelite hands after the invasion of 1010 B.C.[4]

---

[1]When the phrase occurs at the beginning of a sentence, it appears mostly to structure the major events within the book according to a general temporal sequence as in 2 Sam 2:1; 8:1; 10:1; 13:1; 15:1; 21:8; otherwise, when it occurs later in a sentence, it simply orders matters within a particular narrative event, as in 2 Sam 3:28; 21:14; 24:10.

[2]Youngblood (819) points out that the Heb. verb translated "go up" is thematic of vv. 1-3 occurring five times in various translation disguises.

[3]Since the location of Ziklag is disputed, the distance from Ziklag to Hebron is indicated in various atlases as eighteen (OBA; Rogerson) or twenty-eight miles (ZA; MBA).

[4]Other factors supporting the selection of Hebron as David's capital: (1) its Patriarchal associations (Gen 13:18); its importance as a priestly settlement (Josh 21:10f.); and (3) its mountainous and defensible situation. It is the highest town in Palestine.

2:2-3 David had two wives (cf. 1 Sam 25:42f.) with him when he made the move to Hebron: **Ahinoam** and **Abigail.**[5] The Hebrew text identifies Abigail as, lit., "the wife" (i.e., former wife) of Nabal. The wives are mentioned to (1) recall David's marriage connections with Judah and (2) show that he was leaving the land of the Philistines for a new chapter in his life. David's force had grown considerably by defections of entire units of Saul's army just before the battle of Mt. Gilboa (1 Chr 12:19-22). This host, with their families, accompanied David to Hebron. They made their permanent settlement in the towns of the district to which Hebron gave its name. On **Jezreel** see on 1 Sam 25:43.

2:4a The men of Judah, either en masse or in the person of the tribal elders (Mettinger, 118), assembled at Hebron to anoint David as king over **the house** (tribe) **of Judah**. The first private anointing of David (1 Sam 16) had been in token of his divine commission; this anointing gave evidence of his recognition as king by the tribe of Judah. Nothing is said about the mechanics of the anointing, whether by the elders of the tribe,[6] or by a priest like Abiathar.

A Proper Recognition (2:4b-7)

2:4b-7 When David was told is literally "and they told David." David may have inquired about the fate of Saul's body; or the report may have been given to him in an attempt to identify the center of opposition to his reign; or those who gave the report may have been hinting that David needed to make some diplomatic gesture towards the important city of Jabesh in appreciation for their heroic action (cf. 1 Sam 31:11ff.). In any case, as his first royal act David sent a message to that city. His message began with a formula of blessing. He wished God's **kindness** (i.e., mercy) **and faithfulness** on them

---

[5]The only other Ahinoam in the Bible was the wife of Saul (1 Sam 14:50), and the only other Abigail was the sister (or half sister) of David (2 Sam 17:25). Some think David married the widow of Saul and his half-sister. See Levenson and Halpern, "The Political Import of David's Marriages," *JBL* 99 (1980): 507-518. Chronological considerations make the marriage to Saul's widow virtually impossible. A marriage to a half-sister was forbidden (Lev 18:9,11; 20:17; Deut 27:22).

[6]Recent study has suggested that anointing had a contractual connotation with the anointer expressing obligations to the anointee. See T.N.D. Mettinger, 111-130, 208-232.

for having buried Saul. He promised: **I** [emphatic] **too will show you the same favor**[7] i.e., that Saul had shown them. The compact between Saul and Jabesh was not terminated by Saul's death. It was this pact which David was seeking to renew.

David encouraged the men of Jabesh to **be strong** (lit., "let your hands be strong") **and brave**, lit., "become sons of power." They needed courage to face the future without their king; they needed courage to hold the land of Gilead against the Philistines.[8] Though the death of Saul had been a tragedy, all was not lost for David had been anointed king of Judah. David was really inviting this prominent town to be the first city of the north to recognize his kingship.

3. Opposition by Abner (2:8-11)

2:8-9 David's oblique appeal for support from the Gileadites moved Abner, Saul's cousin and general, to rally support for Ish-Bosheth,[9] Saul's fourth son and the sole survivor of the royal house. He was a mere tool in the hands of Abner who by kindred, office and personality was the natural champion of the house of Saul. Abner took Ish-Bosheth across the Jordan river to **Mahanaim** about

---

[7] Lit., "do with you this good [thing]." הַטּוֹבָה (*haṭṭôbāh*) has been rendered "goodness" (KJV, NASB); "good" (NRSV); "kindness" (ASV, NKJV). Taken adverbially, it is thought to describe how David would deal with them, i.e., "generously" (NJPS) or "well" (JB). Ahlström (461) thinks these words have covenant implications. David was inviting them to accept him as their new master even as they formerly had accepted Saul.

[8] Ahlström (461) takes these words as a declaration of war if the men of Jabesh would not accept David as their new king.

[9] His original name was "Esh-Baal" (1 Chr 8:33; 9:39) which has been taken to mean (1) "fire (destroyer?) of Baal," (2) "man of Baal," or (3) "Baal exists." "Bosheth" ("shame") became a contemptuous surrogate for the name Baal in books commonly read, while the original spelling was retained in the genealogy. The significance of names with a Baal component is debated. Some conclude that such names indicate the syncretistic nature of religion in those days. Others point out that *baʿal* ("lord") may at one time have been used as a title for Yahweh until discredited by idolatry (cf. Hos 2:16). Thus "Esh-Baal" may have meant "man of the Lord" or "Lordly man." Saul had an ancestor named Baal (1 Chr 8:30), and this son may have been named after him. M. Tsevat also argues that "Ish-Bosheth" may mean "man of strength." "Ishbosheth and Congeners: The Names and Their Study," *HUCA* 46 (1975): 71-87.

fifteen miles south of Jabesh Gilead.[10] Probably the presence of the Philistines made it impossible to maintain a capital on the west side of the Jordan (1 Sam 31:7). **He** (Abner) **made him king,** perhaps with the concurrence of the tribal elders (cf. 2 Sam 3:17). The kingship of Ish-Bosheth had no religious sanctions attached to it, and its only foundation was the hereditary principle.

No statement is made about the time which elapsed between the death of Saul and the elevation of Ish-Bosheth. Presumably this verse refers to what transpired immediately after the battle of Mt. Gilboa. Ish-Bosheth ruled **over Gilead**, the whole territory occupied by the Israelites east of the Jordan (cf. Josh 22:9). As the Philistine grip west of Jordan gradually loosened,[11] the authority of Ish-Bosheth expanded to **Ashuri**[12] (probably the tribal area of Asher north of the plain of Esdraelon),[13] Jezreel, Ephraim, and Benjamin, and finally all the rest of Israel, excluding Judah. **Jezreel** is not merely the city by that name, but the vast plain that was named after it as in 1 Sam 29:1. The areas west of the Jordan are mentioned in their geographical order from north to south.

2:10-11 By the time his reign extended over all Israel (ca. 1005 B.C.), Ish-Bosheth was forty years old. As Saul's reign was only about thirty-two years, Ish-Bosheth must have been born shortly before the beginning of Saul's reign. Apparently Abner was occupied for some four or five years in bringing the northern tribes under the authority of Ish-Bosheth.[14] He reigned two years over the northern tribes

---

[10]Mahanaim is tied to the Jacob traditions (Gen 32:2). It was a Levitical city (Josh 21:38). Later David would take refuge from his son Absalom in this place (2 Sam 17:24). The exact location of the site has not been determined.

[11]Hertzberg (250) suggests that the Philistines may have ceded the districts mentioned in this verse to Ish-Bosheth.

[12]For the MT's "Ashurites," some read "Geshurites," following the Peshitta and the Vulgate. According to Ahlström (399; n. 3) this emendation is unwarranted.

[13]*Asher* here probably includes the adjacent tribal areas of Naphtali, Zebulun and Issachar as well. Youngblood (823) questions this interpretation "since the tribal names are restricted to the last triad in the verse."

[14]In this reconstruction the two years of Ish-Bosheth's reign over all Israel are parallel to the last two years of David's rule in Hebron over Judah. Others interpret the data to mean (1) there was a gap of over five years between Ish-Bosheth's death and David's recognition in the north; or (2) David was recognized as king of Judah for the last 5.5 years of Saul's reign. See Gordon, 214, for references.

(Israel). The house of Judah, however, **followed** (lit., "went after") David who ruled 7.5 years in Hebron. The Philistines would have welcomed the fact that two weak and rival states had arisen in the place of Saul's former kingdom.

4. Growing Power (2:12-32)

The Clash at Gibeon (2:12-16)

2:12-13 Only one battle of the long war between the house of Saul and the house of David (3:1) is described in detail, no doubt because of the impact it had upon subsequent events. Abner and the supporters of Ish-Bosheth **went** (lit., "went out") **to Gibeon.**[15] The text uses the technical expression for going to war. This suggests (but does not prove) that Abner was planning a push into David's territory to the south. The forces of David, led by **Joab son of Zeruiah** (David's sister; 1 Chr 2:16) were shadowing Abner's movements. The two forces met at **the pool in Gibeon**. Gibeon was in the tribal area of Benjamin (Josh 18:21,25) six miles northwest of Jerusalem. The ruins of this pool still remain (cf. Jer 41:12).[16] The opposing forces **sat down,** i.e., encamped, on opposite sides of the pool. Both armies seem to have been reluctant to strike the first blow. This does not appear to be a chance meeting, for the destination of both forces was clear from the outset.[17]

2:14 Abner suggested to Joab that each side put forward some young soldiers to **fight hand to hand** (שָׂחַק, *śāḥaq*), lit., "play" or "make sport," **in front of us**. In a military context **young men** (נְעָרִים, *nᵊʿārîm*) refers to professional soldiers (cf. 1 Sam 21:2-5; 25:5; 26:22).

---

[15]For an archaeological survey of Gibeon, see W.L. Reed, AOTS, 231-243. The ancient site occupied about sixteen acres.

[16]The pool is a cylindrical shaft thirty-seven feet in diameter and thirty-five feet deep. A five-foot-wide spiral stairway winds downward around the inside wall of the pool in a clockwise direction (J.B. Pritchard, 64-74).

[17]Though in Saulide territory, the inhabitants of this place may not have supported the house of Saul because of the atrocities which had been committed against them (2 Sam 21). So Abner may have been trying to reassert control over the place. F.C. Fensham, "The Battle between the Men of Joab and Abner as a Possible Ordeal by Battle?" *VT* 20, 3 (1970): 356-357; Y. Sukenik, "Let the Young Men, I Pray Thee, Arise and Play before Us," *JPOS* 21 (1948): 110-116.

The word "play" is used euphemistically in reference to deadly serious representative combat.[18] Such contests of military skill often preceded the general engagement of the forces and were designed to
(1) entertain the troops; (2) intimidate the enemy; (3) break down
inhibitions to bloodshed by creating a revenge factor on both sides;
or (4) in theory, settle the issue between the two forces. Nothing in
the text, however, suggests that Abner meant this single combat to
decide the battle. That Abner and Joab envisioned a contest to the
death is not likely, since the verb *śāḥaq* and cognates are only used
in reference to less deadly instances of entertainment[19] (Polzin,
David, 32f.).

2:15 Both sides sent forth twelve men to neutral ground between
the two armies. Some have suggested that the number **twelve** symbolized the twelve tribes of Israel and that the ultimate aim of the
contest was the unity of all the tribes. The combatants paired off.
Each **grabbed his opponent by the head**, i.e., the beard. This indicates that none of the twenty-four men carried shields for self-
defense, for with shields on their arms they could not have seized
one another. In the course of the fight, each man on both sides was
stabbed and killed and the contest ended in a draw. That spot came
to be known as **Helkath Hazzurim**. The NIV in the margin interprets this name to mean "field of daggers" (lit., "flints"), or "field of
hostility." Others have interpreted "field of the strong men" (lit.,
"rocks"). The etymology is uncertain.

The Death of Asahel (2:17-23)

2:17 Excited by the spectacle of merciless slaughter, the two
armies rushed headlong into fierce battle. Eventually Abner's army
was defeated.

2:18-21 The three sons of Zeruiah, David's sister, were fighting
in David's army. **Joab** and **Abishai** must have been seasoned warriors. The youngest of the three, Asahel, was as **fleet-footed** (lit.,
"light in his feet") as a **wild gazelle** ("deer"), an animal celebrated for
swiftness, grace and beauty; but he was less experienced in the skills

---

[18]Hertzberg (252) characterizes these activities as "a mock duel" and a
"battle game" in which tempers flared and fatal wounds were inflicted.

[19]The verb is used of the Philistines having Samson play before them
(Judg 16:25); the women playing instrumental music, singing and dancing
(1 Sam 18:7); David's playing before the Lord (2 Sam 6:21).

of war. He chased Abner during the battle and refused to turn aside. To capture a general's armor was considered the greatest trophy. Abner spotted the young man, and verified that he was in fact Asahel. Abner urged him to turn aside to challenge one of the younger soldiers. Then he might be able to win a victory trophy by stripping the dead man of **his weapons** (חֲלִיצָה, ḥălîṣāh). The word may refer to the belt worn by soldiers as a symbol of their military prowess (Gordon, 215). Asahel, however, would not turn aside.

2:22-23 Apparently Abner had known Joab and his family for a long while. He knew that the killing of Asahel would have personal (because of blood-vengeance) as well as political consequences. Abner warned the young warrior a second time to turn aside lest he be struck **down,** lit., "to the ground." Abner would never be able again to look Joab in the face should he be forced to kill his brother. Still Asahel refused to give up the chase. Abner's reluctance to kill Asahel may have been partly on account of his extreme youth, but was chiefly through dread of the vengeance of Joab.

As he closed in on him, Abner abruptly stopped and thrust backward with the butt of his spear. The butt of spears were sharpened and perhaps tipped with iron for the purpose of sticking them into the ground (1 Sam 26:7). The charging Asahel was struck with such force that the butt of the spear ripped through his **stomach,**[20] and exited his back. Asahel fell there and died **on the spot,** lit., "died [on the place that was] under him." Either because of fear, revulsion and/or respect, some of David's troops stopped when they came to the spot where Asahel had fallen. The loss of their dashing leader took all further fight out of these troops (cf. 2 Sam 20:12).

The Conclusion of the Battle (2:24-32)

2:24-25 Joab, Abishai, and such troops as had not come across the body of Asahel, continued chasing Abner. Near sunset they came to a hill called **Ammah, near Giah**. Neither location yet has been identified. Probably this hill was near Gibeon, which would mean that the pursuit was not long. **The wasteland of Gibeon** is the pasturelands to the east of the city. At that hill reinforcements from

---

[20]The KJV following Jewish commentators renders the Hebrew (הַחֹמֶשׁ, haḥōmeš) "under the fifth rib" here and in the three other passages where the word is found (2 Sam 3:27; 4:6; 20:10). The LXX rendered the word "groin."

the **men of Benjamin**, Abner's kinsmen, rallied around the general in a strong defensive position.

2:26 Across the valley which separated the two forces, Abner called out to Joab. By means of three rhetorical questions he proposed a truce. Should the fighting continue, many good men on both sides would be killed. The further prosecution of the battle would result in bitter hostility between the tribes thus making any final settlement all the more difficult. It was time for Joab to call off the pursuit. **How long** usually serves to introduce questions implying a rebuke (cf. 1 Sam 1:14; 16:1).

2:27-28 Joab acknowledged that Abner had made a point. All the men in that battle were in fact brothers. Furthermore, an all-out assault on the position of Abner would be extremely costly in terms of dead soldiers. Had Abner not spoken, Joab's men would have pursued Abner's forces throughout the night.[21] Joab pretends that his men still have plenty of strength in reserve. They were not quitting because all the fight had gone out of them. Since, however, Abner had already sued for mercy, Joab was content to stop at this point. Therefore, Joab blew the signal trumpet halting the attack. **Nor did they fight anymore** points to the end of this particular battle, not the end of the war (cf. 2 Sam 3:1).

2:29 Fearing that Joab might change his mind when he learned of the death of his youngest brother, Abner ordered an immediate withdrawal. All that night Abner and his men marched through the **Arabah** (Jordan valley). They **crossed the Jordan** and eventually made their way back to **Mahanaim**. **Bithron** ("cleft, ravine") is probably the name of the narrow valley leading from the Jordan to Mahanaim.[22] Perhaps the Jabbok valley is intended (Gordon, 216).

2:30-31 Joab returned to Gibeon and there assembled his men. He discovered that he had lost in the battle twenty men, including his brother Asahel. His forces had killed 360 of the **Benjamites who were with Abner**, lit., "of the Benjamites and among Abner's men,"

---

[21]Another rendering of 2:27, reflected in the ASV, has Joab blaming Abner for the initial commencement of hostilities (so KD, Kirkpatrick, Hertzberg). This rendering assumes there had been no hostile intent in Joab's meeting Abner's troops at the pool in Gibeon. The BV has still another rendering: "Had you but spoken sooner, the people would have withdrawn, every man from his brother, this morning."

[22]"Bithron" also has been taken to be a time reference: "marching throughout the morning" (JB); "marching the whole forenoon" (NRSV).

perhaps pointing to the mixed tribal character of Abner's troops.[23] It is not clear whether these numbers include the twenty-four champions who were killed in the military contest which preceded the battle.

2:32 The bodies of ordinary soldiers were probably buried on the spot, but Asahel's relationship to David demanded different treatment. On the day following the battle, Asahel was taken to Bethlehem, about eleven miles from Gibeon. He was given an honorable burial in his father's tomb. Here is the only allusion to Zeruiah's husband, who appears from this notice to have been a citizen of Bethlehem. Joab and his men then marched all that night to arrive back at Hebron by daybreak.

---

[23]The NRSV and JB agree with the NIV in ignoring the Hebrew conjunction. The ASV, NASB, NKJV, NJPS and BV recognize the distinction between Benjamites and Abner's men.

2 SAMUEL 3

5. David's House: Growth (3:1-5)

3:1 The war does not mean continual fighting, but the state of hostility which existed between the supporters of the two royal families. Ish-Bosheth was too weak to assert his authority over Judah, and David was waiting for the Lord to fulfill his promises in his own time. David, however, was gradually getting stronger, while Ish-Bosheth and his supporters were getting weaker.

3:2-5 The Narrator inserts family information about a king at critical points in the history of his reign. Here the list of David's wives and sons serves the purpose of indicating the strengthening of the house of David. The focus of the list is on those sons who were born after David became king. In such lists, only the firstborn son of each wife is mentioned. The language should not be taken to mean that he had only one son by each wife, or that he had no sons before he was crowned king of Judah. No daughters are here mentioned, though they are mentioned later. Beginning with this list of David's sons, much of 2 Samuel is paralleled in 1 Chronicles.

David went to Hebron with two wives (1 Sam 25:42f.), and while there he took to himself four more. Each of the six bore him one son. **Ahinoam** ("my brother is delight") gave David **Amnon** ("faithful"), his firstborn son. Of Abigail David's second son **Kileab** was born. This appears to be a nickname meaning something like "the father prevails" or "entirely the father." Kileab's real name was Daniel (1 Chr 3:1). He must have died young because he had no part in the later succession struggle among the sons.

Maacah, was the daughter of **the king of Geshur**, a small kingdom in Syria north of Israel. This may have been a political marriage designed to gain an ally virtually in the backyard of Ish-Bosheth (Bright, 176). Such a marriage to a pagan princess was contrary to the spirit of the Mosaic law (Exod 34:16; Deut 7:3; Josh 23:12).

Maacah's son **Absalom** ("father is peace") plays an important role in later events (2 Sam 13–19). David's fourth wife, **Haggith** ("festal"), bore **Adonijah** ("Yahweh is lord"),[1] a son destined to lead the final rebellion against his father. David's fifth wife, **Abital** (**"**my father is dew"), bore to him **Shephatiah** ("Yahweh has judged"). David's sixth son **Ithream** ("remainder of the people") was born of **Eglah** ("heifer") who is described as **David's wife**. The addition of this descriptor gave birth to a Jewish tradition that Eglah was another name for Michal, the first and proper wife. She had no children after she ridiculed David in 2 Sam 6:23, but she may have had a child before. The note that Eglah was David's "wife" may (1) serve as a literary device to close out the whole list;[2] or (2) indicate that Eglah enjoyed some special status within the harem, e.g., head wife. David's plural marriages served (1) to ensure, even at this early stage, that he would have a son to succeed him as king; and (2) to enhance his prestige with surrounding nations.

B. ENTHRONEMENT OF DAVID PROSPECTS (3:6-39)

1. Impediment Removed (3:6-11)

3:6 During the civil war among the supporters of the two royal families, Abner had been **strengthening his own position**[3] within the house of Saul, i.e., he exceeded the authority of his position.

3:7 Apparently Saul had only one concubine, **Rizpah** ("glowing stone") who was the daughter of **Aiah** ("falcon"; cf. 2 Sam 21:8). Ish-Bosheth accused Abner of **sleeping with** (lit., "going in to") Rizpah. It was the exclusive right of the successor to the throne to cohabit

---

[1]Only two of the seventeen sons of David named in 2 Sam 3:2-5 and 5:13-16 have names which contain the element *yah*, abbreviation for *Yahweh*. Neither David's brothers nor his father had Yahwistic names.

[2]Cf. Youngblood (830): she is last in the list and her relationship to David therefore "summarizes that of the other women."

[3]The Hebrew uses a participle מִתְחַזֵּק (*mithazzēq*) which normally has a positive sense, "kept faithful to" (Andersen) or "supported" (NJPS) the house of Saul. Influenced by the context, most English versions agree with the NIV that the term here refers to inappropriate seizure of authority. E.g., the JB renders "Abner took complete control in the House of Saul." McKane (190) does not think the term is used here pejoratively. The thought then would be that up to this point Abner was firmly committed to Ish-Bosheth.

with the concubines of the deceased king.[4] The text does not indicate whether or not Abner actually had been guilty as charged.

3:8 Abner was angry because of the charge against him. The accusation was equivalent to treating Abner as a **dog's head**, i.e., a worthless dog.[5] The sexual promiscuity of dogs is proverbial. To be a "dog's head" and be siding with Judah in the civil war would be about as low as someone could sink. At the very time Abner was being charged, he was showing his loyalty to **the house of . . . Saul**, his **family** (lit., "brothers/relatives") and **friends**. He had not **handed over** Ish-Bosheth to (lit., "caused [him] to be found in the hand of") David, though he very well could have done so. Yet his loyalty was now being rewarded by this (false?) accusation.

3:9-10 Smarting from the (unjustified?) rebuke by Ish-Bosheth, Abner swore an oath that he would transfer the kingdom from the house of Saul to David. The formula **May God deal with Abner, be it ever so severely** is a common self-malediction in which one pronounced unspecified disasters upon himself if he failed to perform whatever he had committed himself to do. Delivering over the kingdom to David would fulfill what the Lord **promised him on oath**. No explicit divine oath to David is mentioned in the preceding chapters unless the allusion is to the promise in 1 Sam 15:28f. The oath could be implicit in the anointing of David by Samuel (1 Sam 16:13). That God had designated David to be Saul's successor (cf. 1 Sam 25:28-31; 2 Sam 5:2) seems generally to have been known. The transfer of the kingdom would make David ruler of both **Israel and Judah** from **Dan** in the north to **Beersheba** in the south.

3:11 Abner's outburst was like a slap on the face to Ish-Bosheth. The son of Saul was powerless to deal with his commander. He realized that he had no subordinate powerful enough to execute an arrest order.

2. Recognized by Abner (3:12-21)

3:12 Without waiting for his temper to cool, Abner sent messengers on his behalf to David. The rhetorical question **Whose land is**

[4]M. Tsevat, "Marriage and Monarchical Legitimacy in Ugarit and Israel," *JSS* 3 (1958): 237-243.
[5]The Jewish commentators Rashi and Kimchi take the term "dog's head" to mean "head/commander over dogs." Cited by Youngblood, 836.

it? recognized the sad state of affairs that the land of Israel had two rulers. David claimed rule over all the land by divine fiat; Abner controlled a large percent of the territory.[6] Through his messengers Abner suggested that if David would make an agreement with him, he would help him bring all Israel under his rule. Abner did not stipulate what advantages he expected to derive from this deal.

3:13-14 David was willing to **make an agreement** (lit., "cut a covenant") with Abner on one condition. Abner must bring **Michal the daughter of Saul**, David's first wife,[7] back to him. He had fought for her (1 Sam 18:27), and she had been given to him in marriage. Though she had been given to another man, he had the right to demand her return. This demand served to demonstrate that David would not become ruler over all Israel through treachery. He would not meet secretly with Abner to plot and scheme. Abner must come to Hebron in a very public manner, bringing with him Saul's daughter who would be far more crucial to David's royal plans than Abner. **Come into my presence** and **come to see me** both are literally "see my face," the Hebrew phrase being repeated for emphasis. This response was a slap in the face to Abner who fancied himself able single-handedly to induce the northern tribes to support David. The reasons for demanding the restoration of Michal were probably (1) affection for the wife of his youth who had once saved his life by her cleverness (1 Sam 19:11ff.), (2) a desire to force the sole survivor of Saul's house to reverse the humiliation which had been inflicted on him by his father-in-law, (3) a desire to solidify his claims to the throne by reestablishing his ties with the house of Saul, and (4) the recognition that a son by Michal would unite the two royal houses.

The formal demand for the return of Michal was directed to **Ish-Bosheth** the *de jure* king so that (1) the restoration of Michal might take

---

[6]The language of Abner is ambiguous. He could mean, "The land is yours by promise; therefore I will help bring all Israel under your authority;" or "The land of Israel is mine to give; therefore make an agreement with me." J. Vanderkam opts for the second interpretation. "Davidic Complicity in the Deaths of Abner and Eshbaal: A Historical and Redactional Study," *JBL* 99, 4 (1980): 531-532.

[7]In speaking to Abner, David referred to Michal as "Saul's daughter." If he agreed to bring her to David, he in effect had turned his back on the claims of the house of Saul forever. In speaking to Ish-Bosheth David referred to Michal as **my wife**, thus implying that she never should have been given to another man.

place openly as a public act of justice, (2) the strength of David and weakness of Ish-Bosheth might be placed in juxtaposition, (3) Abner might have an opportunity to go to Hebron as Michal's escort and conclude the plans for the transfer of power, and (4) the head of the house of Saul would be given the opportunity of reversing the injustice done to David by his father. Compliance with David's demand would signal that Ish-Bosheth was ready to relinquish his claim to the throne.

Had David divorced Michal and she then had married another, he could not have reclaimed her (Deut 24:1-4). In this case, however, she had been taken from him and given to another man. Under the common law of the ancient Near East he had a right to reclaim his wife.[8] Saul had required of David **a hundred Philistine foreskins** as the "mohar" (bride price) for Michal. David here understated his accomplishment, for he doubled the price demanded by the king (1 Sam 18:25,27).

3:15-16 Although Ish-Bosheth realized the possible political implications of a David/Michal reunion, he knew that he was unable to take on both David and Abner. He therefore gave orders for Michal to be taken away from her husband **Paltiel** ("God is my deliverance"). She may have been married to him for as long as a decade. Paltiel seems to have moved from his home in Gallim near Jerusalem (1 Sam 25:44) across the Jordan with the supporters of Ish-Bosheth.

Paltiel followed behind the royal procession weeping, helpless to reclaim his wife. Painful as was his fate, this man had done wrong in marrying another man's wife. The feelings of Michal are not indicated. She would not be the first woman of royal blood to be forced to subordinate her personal feelings to the greater interests of the kingdom. When the procession got to **Bahurim** on the Jerusalem/Jericho road to the east of the Mt. of Olives on the border of the tribe of Judah, Abner ordered Paltiel to return home. He would not allow the weeping husband to enter David's realm. Presumably Abner took Michal on to Hebron.

3:17-18 Abner, through his representatives, **conferred** with the **elders** in northern Israel either in individual localities or at some

---

[8]Remarriage after the first husband's return from captivity or exile was the usual practice, even when the wife had married another man in the meantime and had had children by him. See B. Barak, "The Legal Background to the Restoration of Michal to David," *VTSup* 30 (1979): 15-29. So also Gordon (219).

regularly scheduled assembly. This probably took place before he brought Michal to Hebron, and therefore the verb should be rendered in English as pluperfect. Abner's opening words suggest that, at least after the death of Saul, David had many supporters in the north (cf. 1 Chr 12). Now was the time to make him their king. It was only because of the influence and perhaps intimidation of Abner that these tribes had not made David their king immediately after the death of Saul. Abner presented his plan, not as the wisest political course of action, but as the will of Yahweh. God had promised that by the hand of David **my servant**[9] he would rescue his people from the hand of the Philistines and their other enemies. Abner either had in mind some expression used by one of the prophets (Samuel or Gad), or else he regarded the anointing of David by Samuel as tantamount to this promise. Abner virtually acknowledged failure in being able to provide security from the Philistine threat west of the Jordan. The commission which had been given to Saul (1 Sam 9:16) was now David's.

3:19 Abner personally tried to persuade the Benjamites, kinsmen of Saul and Ish-Bosheth, to go over to David's side. They were the main obstacle to a united nation. Then Abner made his way to Hebron to report to David what the northern tribes, and especially Benjamin, wanted to do. Probably the official purpose of this trip was to convey Michal back to her husband.

3:20 The **twenty men** who accompanied Abner to Hebron may not have understood the real purpose of the trip. These twenty have been identified as (1) elders of the northern tribes, (2) the official escort of Michal, and (3) Abner's personal bodyguard. David gave Abner a royal welcome. The feast celebrated the end of the successful negotiations with the northern tribes and the private agreement between David and Abner.

3:21 Having found David amenable to the terms stipulated by the northern elders, Abner was now fully persuaded. He was prepared to go at once and assemble **all Israel**, i.e., the national assembly of leaders, for David so that they might enter into a **compact** or

---

[9]This is the first time that Yahweh (or anyone else) is reported to have called David God's "servant." God subsequently called David "my servant" twice (2 Sam 7:5,8). David echoed God's language nine times in the same chapter. While prophets frequently were honored with this title, David was the only king to receive it.

covenant with him. David dismissed him **in peace** to go on his mission, i.e., he promised Abner safe conduct.

3. Opposed by Joab (3:22-30)

3:22-23 Joab's absence from Hebron during Abner's visit may have been planned by David. In any case, he and his men returned **from a raid** (lit., "from the troop") on some enemy of Judah just after Abner left Hebron. Such raids would have been the main source of support for David's troops during this period. In the Hebrew the verb **returned** is singular because the narrative turns on the actions of Joab, not the men who were under his command. **Sent him away** reflects the etiquette of that region in which the host gives his guest permission to depart. Three times (four in LXX) it is repeated that Abner departed from David **in peace** (vv. 21,22,23), i.e., relations between David and Abner were cordial.

3:24-25 Joab seems to have been totally ignorant regarding the real purpose of Abner's meeting with David. His somewhat rough remonstrance with David may have been supported by an honest suspicion of Abner's intentions. Joab rebuked David for allowing Abner to leave the city. He accused Abner of coming to Hebron to spy on David's activities. **Movements** is literally "going out and coming in." Joab was trying to poison David's mind against Abner, that he might better carry out his revenge. That David made no effort to reply to Joab's complaint is strange. Perhaps he was having second thoughts which caused him to be influenced by Joab's strong assertions.

3:26 Unknown to David, Joab sent messengers, doubtless in David's name, after Abner, and they brought him back on some false pretense. **The well of Sirah**, mentioned only here, tentatively has been identified about two miles north of Hebron. Joab was exceeding his office in taking it upon himself to counter the decisions of the king and frustrate his intentions.

3:27 When Abner returned to Hebron, Joab **took him aside** (נָטָה, *nāṭāh*), the same verb used by Abner to urge Asahel "to turn aside" before he was slain (2 Sam 2:21). Joab lured Abner **into the gateway** (lit., "into the midst of the gate"), i.e., the space between the inner and outer gateways, as if he were going to talk with him privately. The city gate complex was a customary place of conference. Abner suspected nothing. There Joab stabbed Abner **in the stomach** (חֹמֶשׁ,

ḥōmeš), the same place Abner had smitten Asahel (2 Sam 2:23). So the death of Abner mirrors the death of Asahel. This duplicity and violence was **to avenge the blood**, i.e., death, of Joab's younger brother Asahel. Blood revenge certainly was not justified in this instance (if it ever was) because Abner had killed Asahel in self-defense and in battle. The murder of Abner was all the more heinous because it was perpetrated within the gate of a city of refuge where those who had committed manslaughter were supposed to be safe from the avenger of blood.

3:28-29 Later is literally "from after this." Realizing that enemies and skeptics would blame him for Abner's death, David made an exaggerated public display of his innocence. The wording suggests that a public statement was issued. Feeling he was too weak to execute the murderer (cf. v. 39), David administered the most severe punishment which he could. He put a curse on the perpetrator by wishing that Abner's **blood**, i.e., the responsibility for his death, would **fall** (lit., "swirl/storm") upon the head of Joab and all his father's house, i.e., his brother Abishai. He expressed the wish that the assassination might be avenged on the members of Joab's house with disease, infirmity, death or poverty. **May never be without** is literally "may there never be cut off from Joab's house." **A running sore** is literally "a discharge" (NASB, NRSV, NKJV, NJPS), most likely a reference to some venereal disease which would make a person unclean and therefore debar him from public worship (Lev 15:2). **Leprosy** may refer to a whole range of skin diseases, including the dreaded leprosy. In the rendering **who leans on a crutch** the NIV is supported by the ASV, BV, and NKJV. Others prefer rendering "one who takes hold of a spindle or distaff" (NASB, JB, NRSV, NJPS, TEV), i.e., a man fit only for women's work. Context supports the NIV here. The death of Abner put the unification of the kingdom under David's rule on hold.[10]

3:30 Abishai is linked with **Joab** as co-conspirator in the plot against Abner. Personal revenge and family honor were the motives for the crime. Joab also foresaw that if he allowed Abner to have the

---

[10]J.C. Vanderkam argues that David desired and planned Abner's death. See "Davidic Complicity in the Deaths of Abner and Eshbaal" *JBL* 99 (1980): 521-539. Cf. F. Cryer, "David's Rise to Power and the Death of Abner," *VT* 35 (1985): 385-394; P.K. McCarter, "The Apology of David," *JBL* 99 (1980): 489-504; K.W. Whitelam, "The Defense of David," *JSOT* 29 (1984): 61-87.

credit of placing the crown of Israel on David's head, he would lose his own position and influence. The verbs **murdered** and **killed** suggest the difference in what happened to Abner and what had happened to Asahel. The first verb (הָרַג, *hārag*) connotes a violent and unjustified act.

4. Growing Popular Support (3:31-37)

3:31-32 The contrast between David's treatment of Joab and his execution of the murderers of Ish-Bosheth (4:9-12) is striking, reflecting these facts: (1) Joab was a relative of David, and (2) he was too powerful to be treated as he deserved. David ordered a state of mourning throughout Hebron. Everyone — including Joab the murderer — was ordered to tear their clothes and put on **sackcloth,** a dark garment made of coarse camel or goat hair which was used in making sacks. The honor guard, dressed in mourning clothes, walked **in front of Abner**, i.e., in front of his bier, to the tomb. The **bier** is like an open coffin on which the dead were carried to the place of burial. As chief mourner, **King David** walked behind the bier, presumably in royal regalia so as to give all possible dignity to the funeral. David's desire to honor the memory of Abner was also displayed (1) by the fact that he led the expressions of grief, and (2) by the poem he composed for the occasion.

Abner was buried in **Hebron**, rather than his hometown of Gibeon (1 Chr 8:29,33; 9:35). To be buried in a royal city was another honor for Abner. David wept at the tomb, as did all the people.

3:33-34 David sang a lament for Abner. The opening rhetorical question was directed to the mourners, while the rest of the lament was addressed to the dead person. The lament noted that Abner had experienced a death unworthy of him. This great man with so much potential had not died in battle, nor had he been executed as a **lawless** person (lit., "as a fool"), i.e., a most despicable, sociopathic, morally worthless and intellectually deficient person.[11] Abner was an experienced soldier and a seasoned negotiator; he was versed in the procedures of statecraft. Yet he died in circumstances which made

---

[11]A. Phillips, "*Nebalah*: A Term for Serious Disorderly and Unruly Conduct," *VT* 25 (1975): 237-241. Most English translations render "fool" (ASV, NKJV, BV, JB, NASB, NRSV) or "churl" (JPS).

him look like a simpleton, completely duped. Only those who were **wicked men** (lit., "sons of iniquity") — a direct reference to Joab — would slay a man in this treacherous manner.

3:35 David followed the pre-exilic custom of fasting as a funeral rite (1 Sam 31:13; 2 Sam 1:12). They brought food to David, but he refused to eat. David swore that he would not eat until the sun had set. His emphatic refusal further helped to convince the people that the king was not implicated in Abner's death. Apparently he did not enforce this fasting on the rest of the troops.

3:36-37 The people — both David's followers and those who were presently under Ish-Bosheth's rule — were pleased with this demonstration of grief over the murder of Abner. Indeed they were pleased with David's conduct generally. The twenty men who had accompanied Abner would be witnesses throughout all Israel of all that David had done and said. They all realized that David personally had no part in the murder of Abner.

5. David's House: Limitations (3:38-39)

3:38 David's appreciation of the importance and value of Abner indicates that Joab's jealousy was not without ground. One of the great qualities of David was his willingness to recognize the virtues possessed by opponents. He spoke of Abner as a **prince** and **a great man** in Israel. He felt compelled to explain why he did not punish Joab for the murder. Though he was the anointed king, the **sons of Zeruiah** (Joab and Abishai) were **too strong,** i.e., too influential among the troops, for him. Most of the army were intensely loyal to Joab and his brother. All David could do was to wish (or pray) that the Lord might repay the evil deeds of this evildoer. This was a way of leaving the execution of justice in the hands of Yahweh. Until his dying day David carried with him the burden of not having punished Joab for his crime (cf. 1 Kgs 2:5).

2 SAMUEL 4

C. THE ENTHRONEMENT OF DAVID OVER ISRAEL (4:1–5:16)

1. Impediment Removed (4:1-12)

The Assassination of Ish-Bosheth (4:1-8)

4:1 The news of the death of Abner affected both Ish-Bosheth and his people. The former **lost courage**, lit., "his hands became feeble," i.e., he lost heart and became despondent. The strength behind his throne was now gone. Some think that calling Ish-Bosheth simply **son of Saul** suggests a derogatory attitude toward him (cf. 1 Sam 20:30f.). **All Israel**, i.e., the tribes which supported Ish-Bosheth, **became alarmed** because the political situation was now thrown into confusion. They feared that the death of Abner, which they assumed to have been at the instigation of David, might signal an all-out assault against the north which now had only the incompetent Ish-Bosheth as a leader.

4:2-3 Ish-Bosheth had two commanders named Baanah and Recab ("charioteer") who thought they would take advantage of the confusion in the north. As **leaders of raiding bands** — the ancient equivalent of modern commando units — these two were accustomed to hazardous enterprises. They decided to assassinate the king so as to gain some recognition from David. They were both **sons of Rimmon the Beerothite. Beeroth**[1] ("the wells") was one of the four cities of the Gibeonites (Josh 9:17) which had been allotted to the tribe of Benjamin (Josh 18:25). The Benjamites had occupied Beeroth when the original Canaanite inhabitants fled to **Gittaim**

---

[1]Beeroth has been identified with the modern *El-Bireh*, nine miles north of Jerusalem (OBA; Rogerson) and *el-Burj*, 4.5 miles northwest of Jerusalem (ZA; MBA).

("two wine presses"), the location of which is unknown.[2] So Baanah and Recab were Beerothites by residence, but Benjamites by descent. The fact that the murderers of Ish-Bosheth were of his own tribe is made prominent.[3] It would not have been surprising if the non-Israelite inhabitants had murdered Ish-Bosheth, but the Narrator includes a reminder that this was not the case. The expression **to this day** makes it likely that the time of the Narrator was not very far removed from the events which he relates.

4:4 The Beerothites felt confident that the assassination of Ish-Bosheth would lead directly to David's succession. Only one other direct descendant of Saul remained alive, but he was not a viable candidate for the throne.[4] Jonathan had a son named Mephibosheth[5] who was **lame in both feet,** (lit., "smitten of feet"). Before the fateful battle of Gilboa, the Israelite army had been camped at **Jezreel** (1 Sam 29:1). When news came from Jezreel of the death of Saul and Jonathan, the nurse (nanny) fled with the child. Unfortunately she had dropped the child. This caused permanent lameness. The text does not relate where Mephibosheth and his nurse were when they heard the news; they could have been in Gibeah, Saul's hometown. Both his youth (he was twelve at this time) and his disability made Mephibosheth unwilling or unable to press his claim to the throne.

4:5 Recab and Baanah planned to assassinated their king. They arrived at his house in Mahanaim **in the heat of the day** while Ish-Bosheth was taking his daily siesta. At that hour his guard would likewise be asleep, or at least insufficiently alert.

4:6 The commanders went into the inner part of the house **as if to get some wheat** (lit., "takers of wheat") probably as provisions for

---

[2]Beeroth was probably abandoned by its original inhabitants at the time of Saul's bloody assault against the Gibeonites (2 Sam 21:1f.). Hertzberg (264) locates Gittaim in the neighborhood of Lydda in Philistine territory on the basis of the positioning of the name in a list of postexilic reoccupied areas in Neh 11:33.

[3]Others think that the sons of Rimmon were descendants of the Gibeonites. They would have had animosity toward the house of Saul because of the cruel attack upon them referred to in 2 Sam 21:1f.

[4]Saul had sons by a concubine, and grandchildren by his daughter Merab (2 Sam 21:8), but these children were not regarded as the representatives of Saul's house.

[5]Mephibosheth ("exterminator? of shame") is elsewhere (1 Chr 8:34; 9:40) called Merib-Baal ("contender with Baal"). See comments on 2 Sam 2:8.

their troops. Inside the house they quickly found the room where
the king was sleeping. They stabbed Ish-Bosheth **in the stomach** and
slipped away undetected. The LXX (followed by the RSV but not the
NRSV) adds a note to the effect that the female slave who monitored
the door had fallen asleep over her work and thus did not sound the
alarm. The verb rendered **slipped away** is generally used of escaping danger; here, however, the NJPS, RSV and JB understand the
verb to refer to the stealthy entrance into the house of Ish-Bosheth.

4:7 In characteristic style, the Narrator gave in the previous verse
a general account of the incident. He now repeats that information
and adds details to it. The location of the assassination made the
deed that much more dastardly. Ish-Bosheth was **lying on his bed in
his bedroom** unable to make any stand against his attackers. The
bed is the divan or raised bank, which in an ancient home ran along
the wall. It was supplied with pieces of carpet, or cushions, on which
people could sit crossed-legged or recline. The assassins cut off Ish-
Bosheth's head in order to provide proof to David that his rival was
indeed dead. Such bloody trophies of rebels were prized by ancient
rulers, and rewarded handsomely (cf. Matt 14:8-11). The brothers
thought they were doing a service to David by removing the only
existing obstacle to the union of the nation. Recab and Baanah traveled all night **by way of the Arabah**, i.e., the dry rift valley of the
Jordan and Dead Sea, thereby avoiding other travelers. The men tra-
versed some eighty-five miles from Mahanaim to Hebron.

4:8 Your enemy, who tried to take (lit., "sought") **your life** refers
to Saul, not Ish-Bosheth. The two assassins claimed to be instruments of Yahweh's providence to avenge David against the hostilities of **Saul and his offspring**, i.e., Ish-Bosheth. The brothers were
stating what had happened in the way they thought best calculated
to awaken the gratitude of David toward themselves. Ish-Bosheth is
never honored with the title "king" in the text.

The Execution of the Assassins (4:9-12)

4:9-11 Clearly the sons of Rimmon miscalculated David's attitude
to the house of Saul. The king began his response to Recab and
Baanah with a solemn oath formula, **as surely as the LORD lives** to
which is added the clause **who has delivered me** (lit., "my soul") **out
of all trouble** (cf. 1 Kgs 1:29). These words suggest that one who
trusts in God has no need to commit crimes for his own defense, or
sanction such crimes by others. Acting in his capacity as royal judge,

David cited a less serious judicial precedent to justify the action which he was about to order. He told the two assassins what he had done to the Amalekite who thought he was bringing good news about Saul's death (2 Sam 1:2ff.). David had executed this man who claimed to have performed a mercy killing on a battlefield. Of necessity the punishment for Recab and Baanah must be worse for they had admitted to killing **an innocent** (lit., "righteous") **man**[6] in his own house and on his own bed. Ish-Bosheth seems to have been a weak rather than a wicked man. Based on what he had done to the Amalekite, David was of a mind to **demand** Ish-Bosheth's **blood** from the hand of these two men, i.e., they would forfeit their lives. By this execution David would **rid the earth** (or "land") of such wicked men. The verb root בָּעַר (bāʿar) in the Piel form has a technical legal sense. It means to purge evil by means of capital punishment from the land (e.g., Deut 19:13,19). The crime of murder defiled the land until expiated by the execution of the murderer (Num 35:33).

4:12 David gave the order for the execution of Recab and Baanah. His men cut off their hands and feet and hung the bodies by the pool in Hebron. The **hands** were cut off because they had committed the murder; the **feet**, because they had brought the head to Hebron. The mutilated bodies[7] were displayed in a public place as a warning against the commission of such crimes by others. The **pool in Hebron** was probably the most public place in the city. By way of contrast, they took the head of Ish-Bosheth and buried it in the tomb of the greatest champion of the house of Saul, Abner. The sepulcher is still shown at a spot a few yards from a mosque in Hebron. David's actions indicate that (1) such crimes were abhorrent to him, (2) he personally had nothing to do with the death of Ish-Bosheth, and (3) he would not hesitate to fulfill his God-given duties as chief magistrate of the land.

---

[6]It is significant that David did not refer to Ish-Bosheth as "Yahweh's anointed" as in 2 Sam 1:14. This may be an implicit denial of Ish-Bosheth's kingship. The crime charged against the two Beerothites was not regicide.

[7]The Hebrew is unclear as to whether the body parts (Kirkpatrick, Mauchline), or the mutilated bodies themselves (KD, Gordon) were displayed by the pool. The NIV interpretation is probably correct.

2 SAMUEL 5

Chapter 5 has many difficulties, but it is most important. The elevation of David probably occurred only a few weeks after the death of Ish-Bosheth (ca. 1003 b.c.).[1] The chapter contains the highlights of David's establishment as a great king of a united kingdom. These highlights are not necessarily related in chronological order.

2. Recognition by the Elders (5:1-5)

5:1-2 All the tribes[2] of Israel (in the persons of their representatives) came to Hebron in response to the summons of Abner (2 Sam 3:17-19) to recognize David as their king. They stated three reasons for their coming. First, they cited ties of kinship: **We are your own flesh and blood** (lit., "behold we are your bone and your flesh"). The expression has been taken to be an allusion to (1) the common descent of the tribes from Jacob, (2) the kinship established through marriage to Saul's daughter, (3) the compatibility of king and people in terms taken from the marriage experience (cf. Gen 2:23), and (4) a formal treaty formula.[3] Second, they alluded to David's proven military leadership. Even when Saul was king, David had been the

---

[1]Some scholars postulate an interregnum of five years between the death of Ish-Bosheth and the crowning of David based on the fact that Ish-Bosheth ruled but two years, while David ruled seven years in Hebron. See comments on 2 Sam 2:10.

[2]The Hebrew word (or its homonym) can mean "rulers, judges," and this is the translation preferred by Anderson (75). It is unlikely that, literally, all the tribes of Israel came to Hebron. Alternatively, Kirkpatrick (2:80) suggests that the reference is to the assembly of Israel composed of all the warriors of the nation above the age of twenty who chose to come.

[3]W. Brueggemann regards this as a "statement of loyalty in initiating and affirming a treaty relationship. . . . It describes the commitments of partners

371

commander **who led Israel on their military campaigns**, lit., "the one leading out and bringing in Israel." Third, they recognized that David had a divine appointment to be Israel's **ruler** (נָגִיד, *nāgîd*). See on 1 Sam 9:16. The belief that God had promised the kingship to David may have been based on rumors of his anointing by Samuel (cf. 1 Sam 16:13), and/or the signs he had given of being possessed by God's Spirit (cf. 2 Sam 3:18). The course of events seemed to confirm the divine appointment of David since no viable alternative to him existed. The verb **shepherd** is used here for the first time with reference to a king in Israel. The symbol of the shepherd to represent the duties of a ruler was widely used in the ancient Near East. The term was especially appropriate for David who had grown up shepherding his father's flocks near Bethlehem.

5:3 The **elders** were the representatives of the various tribes alluded to in v.1.[4] From 1 Chr 12:23-40 it is evident that a general assembly of the nation took place at this time. The elders negotiated on behalf of the assembly. David **made a compact** (lit., "cut a covenant")[5] with the elders of Israel at Hebron. He either imposed various obligations on these tribes, or, more likely, gave certain assurances and/or promises to them.[6] The northern tribes then **anointed David king over Israel,** thus (1) publicly ratifying the earlier anointing by Samuel; and (2) symbolizing their submission to

---

to each other who have obligations to each other in all kinds of circumstances." "Of the Same Flesh and Bone [Gn 2,23a]," *CBQ* 32, 4 (1970): 536, 538.

[4]Hertzberg (267) and Mauchline (215) think that v. 1 refers to a preliminary exploratory meeting initiated by political activists from the northern tribes, while v. 3 refers to the formal recognition of David by the official body of elders.

[5]On the concept of "cutting a covenant," see on 1 Sam 11:1. The construction normally (excepting Josh 24:25; 2 Kgs 11:4) expresses the obligation of the one who grants the covenant. "If one does not want to count 2 Sam 5:3 among the rare exceptions, one must understand בְּרִית (*berîth*) as denoting David's obligation to the elders of Israel" (Mettinger, 139). See also D.J. McCarthy, "Compact and Kingship: Stimuli for Hebrew Covenant Thinking," *SPDS*, 75-92.

[6]Cf. McCarter (2:132): "David bound himself formally to certain contractual obligations toward the Israelites." The covenant agreement was made on the basis of the shepherd model, which (1) protected the people from the oppression common to ancient monarchies (cf. 1 Sam 8:10-18) and (2) insured the loyal support of the people.

the authority of David.[7] See on 1 Sam 10:1. **Before the LORD** indicates that this anointing was probably performed by a religious figure, perhaps the high priest. The Book of Chronicles goes into
much more detail about the three-day celebration of this anointing
of David (1 Chr 12:23-40). This was the third time David was anointed (cf. 1 Sam 16:13; 2 Sam 2:4).

5:4-5 The reference to the age of David probably refers to the
time he first became king over Judah. This would mean that he was
37 or 38 when he became king of all Israel. In round figures he ruled
forty years (actually 40.5 years). In Hebron he reigned 7.5 years over
Judah (ca. 1010-1003 B.C.), and in Jerusalem thirty-three years over
all Israel (ca. 1003-970 B.C.).

3. Opposition by the Jebusites (5:6-10)

5:6-7 David's first order of business[8] was to establish a new capital closer to the northern tribes which had just endorsed his reign.[9]
He chose the ancient and well-fortified city of **Jerusalem**[10] which was

---

[7]Mettinger (226) argues that the passage exhibits reciprocity: David granted the people his royal promise. By thereafter performing the anointing,
the elders accept an obligation toward David. This anointing had a contractual implication.

[8]Baldwin (195) and Bright (194) suggest that the capture of Jerusalem may
have followed the defeat of the Philistines, described in vv. 17-25. This conquest, however, was so important and far-reaching that it was given pride of
place in the accomplishments of David after his anointing. So also E.H. Merrill,
"'The Accession Year' and Davidic Chronology," *JANES* 19 (1989): 108. Y.
Aharoni (*Land*, 292), on the other hand, retains the order of the biblical text.

[9]The expedition to capture Jerusalem must have taken place immediately
after the coronation in Hebron, since the length of reign over all Israel and
the reign in Jerusalem are said in v. 5 to be the same. B. Mazar places
David's capture of Jerusalem at the very beginning of his reign over all
Israel, but the shift of the capital of Israel only much later, in David's eighth
regnal year. "David's Reign in Hebron and the Conquest of Jerusalem," ITH
235-244. See also N.L. Tidwell, "The Philistine Incursions into the Valley of
Rephaim," (ed., J.A. Emerton; VTSup 30 [1979]: 190-212.

[10]Jerusalem is mentioned frequently in extrabiblical documents, the earliest of which are in the Ebla archives (ca. 2500 B.C.). The base of the Jebusite
fortress was uncovered in 1983 by archaeologist Yigal Shiloh. See Hershel
Shanks, "The City of David after Five Years of Digging," *BAR* 11, 6 (1985):
25-26.

on the border between Judah and Benjamin. The account of the capture of Jerusalem is supplemented by 1 Chr 11:4-9. **The king and his men**[11] marched against the **Jebusites who lived there**, lit., "who lived in the land."[12] Very little is known about the Jebusites, but they appear to have been a Canaanite clan.[13]

The Jebusites engaged in prebattle verbal taunting (cf. 2 Kgs 18:19-27). **You will not get in here** indicates the confidence of the defenders. The Jebusite citadel stood upon a mountain shut in by deep valleys on three sides. In their haughty self-security they imagined that even **blind** and **lame** warriors would surely drive off the attackers.[14] The verb is in the perfect form which expresses an accomplished fact, one not subject to dispute.[15] Nevertheless, David captured the fortress which protected the hill later called **Zion** ("dry or arid mountain").[16] The hilltop of about sixty acres came to be

---

[11]According to 1 Chr 11:4 David took "all [the army of] Israel" with him on this attack. Since David's personal troops effected the capture, the Samuel text focuses on them alone.

[12]Jerusalem at this time consisted of a fortress on the southeastern hill and an open settlement on the southwestern hill. The former did not fall into Israelite hands until David conquered it (Josh 15:63). The latter had at one time at least temporarily been conquered by the tribe of Judah (Judg 1:8). Many Jebusites were living in open areas surrounding the fortress itself. For an archaeological survey of Jerusalem, see D.R. Ap-Thomas, AOTS, 276-295.

[13]Gordon (226) points out that the Jebusites appropriately are last in the list of Canaanite tribes which, according to Gen 15:18-21, were to come under the power of Abraham's descendants.

[14]The KJV and ASV render: "except thou take away the blind and the lame, thou shalt not come in hither." More recent versions agree with the NIV in understanding "blind" and "lame," both plural, as the subject of a singular verb in the perfect form. The grammatical justification of this rendering is discussed in GK §145o.

[15]According to Josephus (*Ant.* 7.3.1), the Jebusites mocked David by placing cripples on the wall. Other explanations: (1) the Jebusites were announcing their intention of fighting to the last man, even to the disabled, (2) blind and lame were paraded before the attackers to remind them of the penalty for not keeping a loyalty oath (alleged to have existed between David and the inhabitants), or (3) to inflict on the attackers some magical restraint (Yadin 267-270).

[16]Originally the site of Zion was identical with that of the Jebusite fortress on the ridge called Ophel. The name was later extended or transferred to that part of the ancient city of Jerusalem north of Ophel on which stood the temple and the royal palace.

called **the City of David** because it was captured with his personal troops.[17]

5:8 David suggested that his men would be able to reach the Jebusites if they used the **water shaft** (צִנּוֹר, *ṣinnôr*) or water supply.[18] In 1867 Sir Charles Warren discovered in the ancient water works of Jerusalem a perpendicular shaft leading up through the solid stone of the hill. A sloping passage connected this shaft with the interior of the Jebusite fortress. During time of siege residents of the fortress could stand on a platform — perhaps made of wooden planks — at the top of the shaft and draw water by means of a bucket at the end of a rope. Warren's shaft may have been Joab's means of access into the Jebusite fortress.[19] Thus David directed his men to capture the city, not by direct assault on the walls, but by a surprise assault from within. The Book of Chronicles adds the thought that the first man to strike down a Jebusite in the city would be made commander of the army. This is how Joab won his position.

David used the expression which the Jebusites had used of themselves, viz., **lame and blind**. Those Jebusites are said to be **David's enemies,** lit., "hated by David," because they had taunted him. A proverb grew out of this episode, viz., **The 'blind and lame' will not**

---

[17]Ahlström (473) references the practice in the Near East of naming cities as property of a king.

[18]T. Kleven classifies the various proposed translations of the Hebrew צִנּוֹר (*ṣinnôr*) in four categories: (1) words that suggest (with the NIV) some kind of water-passage; (2) weapons of attack, e.g., "grappling-iron" (NEB); (3) part of the defenses of the city, e.g., fortress (Scippa, cited by Baldwin); and (4) parts of the body, e.g., throat, joint, socket, private parts. Kleven points to the use of the word in Ugaritic where it refers to some kind of water-shaft. The Hebrew word occurs elsewhere only in Ps 42:8 where it is rendered "waterfalls." "Up the Waterspout," *BAR* 20 (1990): 34-35.

[19]Defended by Kleven ("Waterspout"); Dan Gill, "They Met," *BAR* (July-Aug 1994): 21-33; R. Reich and E. Shukron believe their discoveries have shattered the Warren's Shaft theory. "Light at the End of the Tunnel," *BAR* (Jan-Feb. 1999): 22-33. A literal rendering of the difficult clause is: "let him touch/reach/strike/assault in the *ṣinnôr* the Jebusites." According to J. Simons (172), it was not a case of climbing up the shaft, but simply of obtaining control of the foot of it, since this would effectively cut off the fortress from its water supply and make surrender inevitable. The parallel passage in 1 Chr 11:6, however, uses the verb עָלָה (*'ālāh*, "went up"), which suggests that he did indeed climb one of the shafts connected with the waterworks of Jerusalem.

enter the palace (lit., "the house"). As rendered by the NIV the proverb seems to say that the blind and lame (i.e., those considered David's enemies like the Jebusites) would not be allowed into David's palace. The JB and NJPS take "the house" to be the temple. The ASV renders the proverb: "There are the blind and the lame; he cannot come into the house." The proverb would then describe the impregnability of a dwelling which could easily be defended by the lame and blind. This understanding of the proverb is more appropriate to the context.

5:9-10 Nothing is said about the treatment of the native population once the fortress fell to the Israelites. Josephus (*Ant.* 7.3.2) suggests that the Jebusites were expelled from the city. It is more likely, however, that they were simply incorporated into David's kingdom. See comments on 2 Sam 24:16.

David then took up residence in the fortress of Mt. Zion. The place was thereafter called **the City of David**. Up to this time Jerusalem had been a border town between Judah and Benjamin out of Israelite jurisdiction. Because of its tribal neutrality, central location and superior defenses this city made an ideal capital for David's kingdom.

David built up and strengthened that fortress particularly on its north side which was the least defensible. The exact location and significance of **the supporting terraces** (lit., "the Millo") is not known. Some type of fortification is intended, perhaps a tower at one corner of the wall.[20] Once settled in his new capital, David became **more and more powerful,** i.e., great and influential. **Yahweh God Almighty** (lit., "God of hosts"; see on 1 Sam 1:3) blessed his every move.

The Narrator recognizes two ways in which David consolidated his hold on his new capital: (1) building relations with neighboring nations (vv. 11-12) and (2) building the royal family (vv. 13-16).

4. Gentile Presents (5:11-12)

5:11-12 The chronological placement of the events related in vv. 11-12 is uncertain. **Hiram** did not become **king of Tyre** until late in

---

[20]The possible connection between Millo with מָלֵא (*mālē*, "fill in") is a clue to the meaning: (1) a construction (tower?) built on a filled-in platform of earth or stones, or (2) the artificial terracing on the east slope of the hill on which the ancient city stood. The Millo was also a concern of Solomon (1 Kgs 9:15,24; 11:27).

David's reign.[21] While it is possible that the reference here is to the father of Solomon's ally (2 Chr 2:3), it is more likely that the building of this particular palace occurred as much as twenty-five years after the capture of Jerusalem (Merrill, 244). Hiram was concerned lest Israelite expansion deny Tyre and her trading partners the use of inland trade routes. He was guided by self-interest when he made the overtures mentioned here (Gordon, 228).[22]

Tyre was one of the two great Phoenician cities. It was celebrated for its commerce, its mechanical skill, and its wealth. As a gesture of friendship Hiram sent to Jerusalem **messengers** (i.e., ambassadors), **cedar logs**, and a construction crew which built David **a palace** (lit. "a house"). This may be the same house alluded to in 2 Sam 7:2 and 11:2. On the other hand, this may be an expansion or remodeling of an existing palace. Cedar logs were highly regarded for their durability and they were often used as pillars, as well as roofing and paneling. These logs were imported from the Lebanon mountains, and they were taken in rafts to Joppa on the coast of Palestine, and hauled up through the Judean mountains by mule power to Jerusalem. Hiram's actions encouraged David and made him realize that the Lord had truly established him as king over all Israel. The Lord had exalted David's kingdom **for the sake of his people Israel**, i.e., because he had chosen Israel as his people, and had promised to make it a great and glorious nation.

5. David's House: Growth (5:13-16)

5:13-16 A list of sons born to David in Hebron (3:2-5) concluded

---

[21]David captured Zion ca. 1003 B.C. The famous Hiram did not ascend the throne until 986 B.C. (IDB) or 979 B.C. (Albright) or 969 B.C. (ABD). Katzenstein (96) proposes that the mission was sent by Abibaal, Hiram's father, but that the mission was headed by the young Hiram, just as Toi, king of Hamath, sent his son Joram to congratulate David on his victories over Hadad-ezer (2 Sam 8:10). Thus Hiram is mentioned as the sender of the messengers even though he had not yet become king.

[22]Three factors account for these overtures by Hiram: (1) the proximity of the two countries, the two capitals being but a hundred miles apart; (2) the similarity of the languages spoken by the two peoples; and (3) the economic interdependence of Phoenicia and Israel. Phoenicia depended on Israel for agricultural products; Israel depended on Phoenicia for commercial products, building materials and skilled craftsmen.

Table 5 DAVID'S SONS			
2 Samuel 3:2; 5:14-16	1 Chronicles 3:6-7; 14:6-7	Mother	Location
1. Amnon	Amnon	Ahinoam	Hebron
2. Kileab	Daniel	Abigail	Hebron
3. Absalom	Absalom	Maacah	Hebron
4. Adonijah	Adonijah	Haggith	Hebron
5. Shephatiah	Shephatiah	Abital	Hebron
6. Ithream	Ithream	Eglah	Hebron
7. Shammua ("Heard")	Shammua (Shimea)	Bathsheba	Jerusalem
8. Shobab ("Substitute")	Shobab	Bathsheba	Jerusalem
9. Nathan ("He has given")	Nathan	Bathsheba	Jerusalem
10. Solomon ("Peace")	Solomon	Bathsheba	Jerusalem
11. Ibhar ("May God choose")	Ibhar		Jerusalem
12. Elishua ("God is salvation")	Elishua (Elishama)		Jerusalem
13.	Eliphelet (Elpelet)		Jerusalem
14.	Nogah		Jerusalem
15. Nepheg	Nepheg		Jerusalem
16. Japhia ("May God shine")	Japhia		Jerusalem
17. Elishama ("God has heard")	Elishama		Jerusalem
18. Eliada ("God knows")	Eliada (Beeliada)		Jerusalem
19. Eliphelet ("God is deliverance")	Eliphelet		Jerusalem

the account of his enthronement over Judah. So here a similar list of children born to David in Jerusalem concludes the summary of highlights of his establishment as ruler over all Israel. Disregarding the commandment of Deut 17:17, David took more **concubines and wives**[23] when he was established **in** (lit., "from"[24]) Jerusalem. These

---

[23]This is the first place where concubines are mentioned in connection with David, and the only time when concubines are mentioned before wives when they are mentioned together. Perhaps the Narrator is expressing his antagonism for David's proclivity for the trappings of Oriental monarchy (Youngblood, 859).

were probably marriages of convenience by which David hoped to consolidate the united kingdom. The concubines (wives of secondary rank) are probably mentioned before the wives because David took several of them with him to Jerusalem before he started adding new wives to his harem. Eleven sons were born to him there. The list here is a continuation of the list found in 2 Sam 3:2-5. Table 5 displays the four lists of David's sons by his wives (as opposed to his concubines). Two of the sons must have died young and so are absent from the list in the present text. Suggested meanings of the names are based on Anderson (87f.)

D. ENTHRONEMENT OF DAVID IN JERUSALEM (5:17-6:23)

1. Impediment Removed (5:17-25)

First Philistine Invasion (5:17-21)

The chronological positioning of the two battles with the Philistines is impossible to determine. Some defend the order of the text, viz., that the Philistines attacked David *after* he had captured Jerusalem.[25] Others find evidence in the narrative that at least one, possibly both, of the Philistine invasions took place prior to the capture of Jerusalem.[26] During the seven years in which David ruled in Hebron, the Philistines left the Israelites alone. Perhaps they even regarded David as a friend. Now that the tribes were united, the Philistines determined to crush David.

5:17 Early in David's reign over all Israel, the Philistines went up into the mountains **in full force** (lit., "all the Philistines"). The emphasis is on their total mobilization. They went **to search** for David. The language implies that David had left Hebron to prepare for the attack against the Jebusites, but was not yet occupying Zion.

---

[24]The parallel reads "in Jerusalem" (1 Chr 14:7). At times in the Hebrew Bible there is an interchange in the prepositions *Beth* and *Min*. Nahum Sarna, "The Interchange of the Prepositions *Beth* and *Min* in Biblical Hebrew," *JBL* 78 (1959): 310-316.

[25]In Chronicles the two battles with the Philistines are placed between the unsuccessful and the successful attempts to bring up the ark to Jerusalem.

[26]C.E. Hauer, Jr. defends the chronological order of events in 2 Samuel 5. "Jerusalem, the Stronghold, and Rephaim," *CBQ* 32, 4 (1970): 571-575.

The Philistines were not sure of David's whereabouts or his intentions. Their actions caught David momentarily off guard, and forced him temporarily to interrupt his plans to capture Zion.[27] He hastily **went down to the stronghold,** probably the old cave of Adullam.[28] His initial plan was to resort to the kind of guerrilla warfare to which he had become accustomed during the days of his flight from Saul. Had David been occupying the Zion fortress at this time, he would hardly have left his fortifications when the Philistines encamped just west of Jerusalem.[29]

5:18 The Philistines attacked where David's kingdom was arguably at its weakest. They spread out in the **Valley of Rephaim** ("giants")[30] among the precipitous hills in the southwest approaches to Jerusalem. The Israelites had not been able to hold this area, and David's defenses here were either weak or nonexistent.[31] The Philistines' goal may have been to move south through Bethlehem to attack Hebron. David **inquired of the LORD,** probably through the priestly oracle. Shall I **go and attack** (lit., "go up unto") **the Philistines? Will you hand them over to me** (lit., "give them into my hand")? Yahweh authorized David to **go** (lit. "go up"). **I will surely hand the Philistines over to you** is literally "give the Philistine into your hand."

---

[27]Both sides were relying on military intelligence as is indicated by the fact that the Philistines "heard" and "went up" and David "heard" and "went down" (v. 17).

[28]1 Sam 23:14 alludes to many "strongholds" in the wilderness, so it is not certain which of these David occupied here. When the Narrator refers to Zion as a "stronghold" in vv. 7 and 9 he writes the word defectively (מְצָדָה, *mᵉṣūdāh*). In v. 17 he writes the word *plene* (מְצוּדָה, *mᵉṣûdāh*) suggesting that he intends to make a distinction between Zion and the stronghold to which David fled (Youngblood, 862).

[29]Kirkpatrick (2:86) argues that David left Zion and went down to his stronghold at Adullam in order to cut off Philistine advances up the valley of Elah, the main route leading from Philistia to Hebron. The enemy, however, came up by a different route.

[30]The name of this valley preserves a remembrance of the gigantic races of Rephaim, to which Og the king of Bashan belonged (Deut 3:11; cf. Josh 17:15).

[31]Baldwin (203) also points out that the valley of Rephaim was on the northern border of Judah adjacent to Benjamin, which was a stronghold of Saulide supporters. Perhaps the Philistines were trying to exploit any uncooperative elements in David's newly extended kingdom.

5:20-21 David must have come upon the Philistines from the south. His forces swept down from the higher ground to break through the Philistine ranks in the plain below. After the battle David observed that the Lord had **broken out** against his enemies like a raging torrent breaks through and carries away whatever opposes it. From these words of David the battlefield was named **Baal Perazim** ("Lord of break-throughs"). Here clearly the name has no reference to the heathen deity *Baal*. The Philistines abandoned their idols there. They probably had brought them to the war, as the Israelites once did their ark, to guarantee the victory. David and his men carried off these idols (1 Chr, "gods") and burned them (1 Chr 14:12) according to the stipulation of Deut 7:5,25. The impact of this victory was substantial emotionally if not militarily for it received passing reference by the prophet Isaiah more than two centuries later (Isa 28:21).

Second Philistine Invasion (5:22-25)

5:22-24 The Philistines regrouped and came up to the same Valley of Rephaim with a force which, according to Josephus (*Ant.* 7.4.1), was three times the size of the one which previously had been defeated. They were determined to drive a wedge between David and the northern tribes. It is not clear whether David yet had captured the Zion fortress. No doubt the Philistines prepared for an attack from the same direction as before. Again David inquired of the Lord. He was directed this time not to meet the enemy head-on. Taking advantage of the valleys and the cover of a thicket of trees, David was told to outflank the invaders. He should listen for **the sound of marching,** i.e., the wind blowing in the tops of the **balsam trees.**[32] Then he should **move quickly,** lit., "be sharp," i.e., act decisively. That movement in the trees would (1) signal that the Lord was going out before the army of David **to strike the Philistine army,** (2) drown out the sound of the attack, and (3) identify the timing of the attack as noontime when the sea breezes reach Jerusalem (Herzog & Gichon, 80).

5:25 As always, David was obedient to the directive of the Lord. He won a decisive victory. The details of the battle are not given.

---

[32]There is uncertainty as to the type of tree/shrub. It is also identified as "balsam" in the BV, JB, NASB, and NRSV; but "mulberry" in the ASV and NKJV; and "mastic" in the NAB. NJPS transliterates the Hebrew.

Finding their line of retreat to the west blocked by David's army, the Philistines made a detour north before they could turn downhill toward Philistine territory. The NIV's **Gibeon** in the MT is "Geba."[33] Gibeon was about eight miles northwest of the Valley of Rephaim, and Geba about the same distance north. The two towns were about five miles apart. The Hebrew text here should be retained. The Philistines had a garrison at Geba where this retreating army may have intended to make a stand. From there, however, the Philistines plunged into headlong flight past Gibeon (1 Chr 14:16) down through the valley some fifteen miles to **Gezer** in the lowlands. Gezer was an ancient Canaanite city which only came into the possession of Israel in the days of Solomon (1 Kgs 9:16). It is generally identified as Tell el-Jazar some nineteen miles northwest of Jerusalem (ZA, 117). The text does not indicate that the Philistines became David's vassals, but that very well may have been their status.[34]

---

[33]The ASV, NASB, NKJV, NRSV, NJPS, and BV follow the Hebrew text here which reads "Geba." The JB and NIV regard "Geba" as a scribal slip for "Gibeon" which is the reading of the LXX and the parallel passage in 1 Chr 14:16. Cf. Isa 28:21. Geba ("height") was a common name and might refer to a location nearer the Valley of Rephaim. Cf. A. Demsky, "Geba, Gibeah, and Gibeon — An Historical-Geographical Riddle," *BASOR* 212 (1973): 26-31.

[34]H. Donner, "The Interdependence of Internal Affairs and Foreign Policy During the Davidic-Solomonic Period," *SPDS*, 209 n. 6. Cf. A. Malamat, "A Political Look at the Kingdom of David and Solomon and its Relations with Egypt," *SPDS*, 195.

2 SAMUEL 6

Establishing Jerusalem as a center of worship for the unified nation was the priority of the early years of David's reign. The first step in bringing this about was to transport the ark to Jerusalem. The date would be ca. 1002 B.C. The rout of the Philistines as far as Gezer (2 Sam 5:25) caused David to entertain the possibility of moving the sacred ark of God from the fringe of enemy territory to his new capital in Jerusalem.

2. David's Plan for the Ark (6:1-5)

6:1-2 David **again** brought together the troops of Israel. The previous gathering to which the text refers may have been (1) the gathering for David's coronation in Hebron, (2) the muster for the Philistine wars, or (3) the mobilization for the assault on Jerusalem. **Thirty thousand,** i.e., thirty military units, **of chosen,** i.e., carefully selected, men were designated to form an honor guard for the ark of God. Perhaps David feared that the move might be opposed by the Philistines.[1] These men started out to bring the **ark of God**[2] up to Jerusalem from the city of **Baalah of Judah**[3] where it had lodged for some seventy years. This town, while not in Philistine territory, appears to have been under Philistine domination during most of that time. That may explain why so little is said about the ark in the

---

[1]Mauchline (223) suggests that the thirty thousand may have been a liberation army prior to forming a triumphal procession.

[2]The designations "ark of the Lord" and "ark of God" are each used seven times in 2 Samuel 6, the number of completion/perfection (Youngblood, 869).

[3]The place was also known as Kiriath Baal and Kiriath Jearim (Josh 18:14). It was about seven miles west of Jerusalem, about halfway between Jerusalem and Gezer.

life of Israel. A great throng of people accompanied the procession (1 Chr 13:1-8). The ark was **called by the Name** of the Lord Almighty (lit., "Yahweh of hosts"; see on 1 Sam 1:3), i.e., it belonged to him. **Name** connotes that which the Lord has revealed about himself, especially his personal presence. The ark was his throne. He sat, as it were, on the mercy seat which was **between the cherubim**, the wings of which were stretched out over the ark. Thus the ark was the visible symbol of Yahweh's presence and of his covenant with his people. See comments on 1 Sam 3:3; 4:4.

6:3-4 The Israelites, perhaps following the example of the Philistines in 1 Samuel 6, **set the ark** (lit., "made the ark to ride") on an ox-drawn cart. To honor the ark and to insure against defilement, a **new cart** was used. In their zeal to hasten the ark to Jerusalem, they neglected to follow the precise stipulations of the law of God which required the ark to be hand-carried by priests (Num 7:9). The cart was guided by two brothers, **Uzzah and Ahio, sons of Abinadab** who probably was dead by this time.[4] While the ark reposed at the house of Abinadab, Uzzah and Ahio had been its custodians. Ahio was walking in front of the wagon, leading the oxen, and Uzzah beside it.

6:5 David was leading the representatives of the whole house of Israel in celebration. They were singing songs accompanied by various musical instruments **with all their might**, i.e., enthusiastically. **Before the Lord** here means "before the ark." On **harps, lyres** and **tambourines**, see on 1 Sam 10:5. **Sistrums** (ASV, JB, NRSV, BV: "castanets"; KJV "cornets") are mentioned only here in the Bible. The Hebrew term comes from a root which means to shake or quiver. This instrument was used throughout the ancient Near East to express both great sorrow and extreme distress.[5] It consisted of rings hanging loosely on iron rods and making a tinkling sound when shaken. The term rendered **cymbals** (צֶלְצְלִים, ṣelṣ^elîm) is an ancient term for percussion instruments which produced a clashing sound when struck together. The musicians and singers were organized into seven companies (1 Chr 15).

---

[4]In 1 Sam 7:1 Eleazar, the son of Abinadab, was the keeper of the ark. There is no indication what may have happened to Eleazar. Perhaps he was dead.

[5]Drawings of various ancient sistrums can be found in IDB, vol. K-Q, 471.

3. Opposition: Yahweh's Anger (6:6-11)

6:6-7 When the procession moved past **the threshing floor of Nacon**[6] (location unknown), the oxen may suddenly have turned aside to snatch the scattered grain of the threshing floor. Uzzah reached out and took hold of the ark of God **because the oxen stumbled**[7] and he feared that the ark would come crashing to the ground.[8] The text, however, gives no indication that the ark was in any danger. Uzzah's motives were good. He acted on reflex and without sacrilegious intent. Yet **the Lord's anger burned against Uzzah** because of his irreverent act.[9] His sin was that, as an unconsecrated person, he laid hold of the ark (1 Sam 6:19). **God struck him down and he died there beside the ark of God**. Some speculate that the ark fell on him and crushed him, but it is best to attribute his death to a supernatural stroke.[10] In so far as David had decreed how the ark was to be transported, he was responsible for Uzzah's death. As a Levite, however, and one who had watched over the ark during its stay at Kiriath Jearim, Uzzah should have known the proper manner in which the ark was to be transported. Uzzah's action was the culmination of a cavalier attitude which gave little consider-

---

[6]KD trace "Nachon" to the root נָכָה (*nākāh*), "to smite." Thus the name given to the spot was "threshing floor of the stroke." In Chronicles it is called "threshing floor of Kidon" (1 Chr 13:9), i.e., destruction or disaster.

[7]The verb שָׁמַט (*šāmaṭ*) is usually transitive, hence these renderings have been proposed: "they let the oxen fall" or "the oxen let it fall" which might mean that the oxen ran away or slipped the yoke. Other renderings: "the oxen had slipped" (BV); "the oxen were making it tilt" (JB); "the oxen shook it" (NRSV).

[8]Anderson (104) suggests that the falling of the ark was Yahweh's sign that the procession should stop. By touching the ark, Uzzah was attempting to frustrate or disregard the will of Yahweh.

[9]The rendering of other English versions is instructive: (1) NJPS, "indiscretion"; JB, "crime"; ASV, NKJV, "error"; NASB, "irreverence"; BV, "sacrilege." The NRSV does not attempt to translate the Hebrew term.

[10]Some have attempted to explain the death of Uzzah naturalistically. One suggestion is that the gold-covered chest produced enough static electricity while bumping along the rocky road to electrocute Uzzah when he touched it. Another view is that a member of the ark's military escort used his spear (כִּידוֹן, *kîdôn*) to dispatch Uzzah on the threshing floor of Kidon (1 Chr 13:9). In either case, Hebrew historiography would regard the Lord as the ultimate cause of Uzzah's death (Youngblood, 871).

ation to the sacredness of the ark. Judgments of this kind were temporal and do not give any indication of the treatment of the offender beyond the grave. The Hebrew emphasizes the place of Uzzah's death by twice inserting the word **there** in the last two clauses (one of which is not translated in the NIV). The irony of his death is underscored by the words **beside** (lit., "with") **the ark,** i.e., near that which he had been attempting to rescue from harm.

6:8 David became **angry because the Lord's wrath had broken out** (פָּרַץ, *pāraṣ*; lit., "had broken a breach") **against Uzzah**. He had prepared a great religious festival, and Yahweh had broken in upon them like an enemy. At the time this book was written that location was called **Perez Uzzah** ("outbreak against Uzzah"). David blamed God for what happened to Uzzah, and used the event to opt out of his plan to move the ark to Jerusalem. The term "Perez" conveys in Hebrew the idea of a great calamity (Judg 21:15) or of a sudden attack upon a foe. In 2 Sam 5:20 David experienced how Yahweh could break forth (*pāraṣ*) against his enemies. Here he learns that Yahweh was also capable of sudden outbursts against David's own servants.

6:9-10 David's initial agitation over the incident turned to fear. He became **afraid of the Lord that day**. He may have thought that the punishment of Uzzah might be extended to himself and his people. He began to wonder how[11] he would ever bring such a dangerous object to Jerusalem without making some similar disastrous error. He was not willing to take the ark any further toward the City of David (Jerusalem) until he received further light from the Lord. He took the ark aside out of the road to the house of the Levite **Obed-Edom.**[12] He is called **the Gittite** probably because he was a native of Gath-rimmon (Josh 19:45), one of the Levitical cities (Josh 21:24f.), or Gittaim (2 Sam 4:3).[13]

---

[11]"How" (אֵיךְ, *'ēk*) is used in the Old Testament history only rarely in exclamation (as in 2 Sam 1:19,25,27) and usually indicates a questioning that is often, as here, tinged with fear (cf. 2 Sam 1:14).

[12]Among David's servants were two Levites by this name — one belonged to the family of Merari, a singer and doorkeeper for the ark (1 Chr 15:18,21,24); the other was of the family of Korah (1 Chr 26:4f.). Of this second Obed-Edom Chronicles says, "for God had blessed him" which corresponds to the language of v. 11.

[13]In the gazetteers of MAB and ZA, four Israelite towns have names compounded with Gath. Obed-Edom could have come from any one of them.

6:11 The ark remained at the Gittite's house **for three months**. The Lord blessed the entire household of Obed-Edom in ways that must have been obvious to others.

4. A Solemn Procession (6:12-19)

6:12 David decided to try again to move the ark to Jerusalem because (1) the Lord was blessing Obed-Edom, and (2) David had learned the reason for the initial failure (1 Chr. 15:13). He went down from the heights of Jerusalem and completed the transfer of the ark to the City of David **with rejoicing,** i.e., in a joyful procession accompanied by music and dancing (cf. 1 Chr 15).

6:13 This time the ark was transported on the shoulders of the priests. When they had gone but six steps, the procession stopped. David offered sacrifices, like all Israel in 1 Kgs 8:62, through the ministration of the priests. The purpose was to ask a blessing upon the removal of the ark, and to avert further disaster.[14]

6:14-15 During the march to Jerusalem, David was wearing **a linen ephod,** a short, sleeveless, tightly fitted garment worn by those engaged in the service of God, especially by Levites and priests.[15] This garment left the king free to express his devotion to God vigorously. The removal of his kingly attire, and the assumption of this light garment was done as an act of religious homage indicating his penitence, joy, thankfulness, and devotion. He **danced** (lit., "whirled") **before the Lord**. Such dancing was usually performed by women, but David in his religious enthusiasm could not resist joining them. **With all his might** points to a wild movement of the feet, with violent efforts of leaping. He and the house of Israel brought up the ark of the Lord **with shouts and the sound of trumpets**. Like other ancient people, the Hebrews had their sacred dances which

---

Gordon (233), however, argues that Obed-Edom was from Philistine Gath. He may have been one of those who had been attracted to David's cause during the latter's stay in the region of Gath (1 Sam 27–30).

[14]Chronicles says nothing about this sacrifice at the beginning of the movement, but mentions seven bulls and seven rams offered by the Levites, presumably as a thank offering, at the conclusion of the movement. See 1 Chr 15:26.

[15]Baldwin (209) observes: as king of a kingdom of priests, David was entitled to wear this priestly dress.

were performed on solemn occasions. David wrote a psalm to commemorate this occasion (1 Chr 16:7-36).

6:16 **Michal**, David's wife, was watching from a window as the procession was entering the city. When she saw King David **leaping and dancing before the Lord, she despised him in her heart**. The narrative places in stark contrast the spirit of Saul's house in which Michal had been brought up, and that of David. During Saul's reign the ark had been neglected, and the instruments of true religion had been ignored. Why Michal found David's actions so disgusting is not stated. Perhaps for the first time she was observing the depth of David's devotion to the Lord. Then again, perhaps her idea was that the king should avoid mixing with the people, and be aloof and inaccessible. In any case, the basic problem was that Michal did not share her husband's enthusiasm for the ark. The threefold mention of Michal as the **daughter of Saul** suggests (1) that she was acting more like Saul's daughter than David's wife, and (2) that the pride of her aristocratic rank was offended by her husband's public exhibition of himself in a manner so undignified.

6:17-19 The ark of God was placed **inside the tent that David had pitched for it**. The old tabernacle remained in Gibeon (1 Chr 16:39; 21:29; 2 Chr 1:3). David probably chose to leave it there because it was too large for the Jerusalem location; or because he contemplated the erection of a magnificent temple very soon. In celebration David sacrificed **burnt offerings,** symbolizing total commitment, and **fellowship offerings,**[16] expressing joy, before the Lord. In the fellowship offering only a token portion of the animal was offered on the altar; the rest was eaten by the people in a religious feast of communion with God. Obviously an altar had been prepared for the occasion. These words do not necessarily mean that David functioned as a priest; he may be said to have sacrificed if he provided the sacrificial animals for the occasion. When he was finished, he **blessed the people in the name of the Lord Almighty** (lit., "Yahweh of hosts"). As theocratic ruler of the people, he was entitled to bless the people of God and claim for them the blessing which the Lord had promised. Then he gave a gift of food **to each**

---

[16]Other English versions render "communion sacrifice" (JB); "peace offering" (ASV, RSV, BV, NKJV); "shared-offerings" (NEB); "offerings of well-being" (NRSV, NJPS).

person in the whole crowd.[17] The loaf of bread was an unleavened cake of the sort that was offered in sacrifices (Lev 8:26; 24:5). Compressed cakes of **dates** and **raisins** were considered delicacies. The giving of gifts made the occasion even more joyous. This great celebration of the arrival of the ark in Jerusalem was most impressive as the proclamation of Yahweh as King in Jerusalem, with David as his appointed prince (Baldwin, 212).

5. David's House: Strife (6:20-23)

6:20 After the public celebrations, David returned **to bless** (i.e., invoke God's blessings on) **his own household**. Michal, daughter of Saul, came out to meet him. With sarcasm she accused him of having **distinguished** (lit., "honored") himself by **disrobing**[18] in the sight of the lowly slave girls. **As any vulgar** (lit., "empty, worthless") **fellow would** is literally "as any vulgar fellow, disrobing, would disrobe," thus giving a triple emphasis to what Michal viewed as the disgusting actions of her husband. David had removed his outer royal robe, and his wife viewed that as disrobing himself. The word **today**, used twice in the MT, emphasizes the time of the event. While the actions of the king may have been undignified, they were not immodest. Michal had fallen in love with a brave warrior image (1 Sam 18:20); she was repulsed by the humble worshiper stripped of his royal regalia.

6:21-22 David defended himself by saying that he had been celebrating **before the Lord**, i.e., his dancing had been religious devotion. Michal's approval or disapproval of his behavior was wholly irrelevant. He lashed back at his wife for her comment. The Lord had chosen David over her father Saul, or anyone from Saul's family, to be ruler over Israel. Before the Lord, therefore, he would celebrate.

David in no way regretted what he had done. He pledged that he would become even more undignified than this. David was prepared

---

[17]The MT contains a phrase omitted in the NIV which stresses even more forcefully the universal generosity of the king, viz., he gave a loaf of bread "to all the people."

[18]Other translations render "uncovering himself" (ASV, NASB, NRSV, NKJV, BV); "exposing himself" (NJPS); "displaying himself" (JB). Gunn (*David*, 73) thinks David was not literally disrobing, but "showing off" in Michal's view.

to be **humiliated** (lit., "low") even in his own eyes, if that action would give glory to the Lord. David was more concerned to honor the Lord than to boost his own ego. The **slave girls**[19] would hold him in honor for his vocal and vigorous praise for the Lord. David trusted the good sense of the common people to appreciate his religious zeal. He valued the opinion of the slave girls more than the opinion of his haughty wife.

6:23 The placement of this verse at this point suggests that Michal's condition was connected to her attitude toward the religious zeal of her husband. Her barrenness points to (1) the punishment of Michal herself, (2) the permanent estrangement between David and Michal, and (3) the cessation of the rejected Saulide house. David refused to legitimize his succession to Saul's throne through Michal.

---

[19]Women who are called **slave girls** (sing. אָמָה, *'āmāh*) throughout the books of Samuel and Kings are women who by word or work further the cause of kingship in general and the glory of David's house in particular. Polzin, *David*, 67.

2 SAMUEL 7

E. ENTHRONEMENT OF DAVID'S DYNASTY (7:1-29)

Chronologically, ch. 7 is not in order. Most likely the chapter relates an event which occurred fairly late in David's reign. The Narrator has placed this incident here for topical reasons. He has just spoken of the moving of the ark to Jerusalem. Now he relates how David wished to build a house for that ark. Here is a pivotal text in Old Testament theology.[1] The Nathan oracle constitutes the title-deed of the Davidic house to rule Israel and Judah (Gordon, 235). Yahweh's covenant[2] with David receives more attention in the Hebrew Bible than any covenant except the Sinaitic.[3]

1. David's Plan for the Temple (7:1-3)

7:1-2 The text stresses the fact that David was established as **king** of Israel.[4] He settled in the **palace** which he had built in Jerusalem (2 Sam 5:9,11; 1 Chr 14:1). **Given him rest from all the enemies round about,** taken word for word from Deut 12:10, suggests a time after some if not all of the wars which are narrated in the following chapter. **Nathan the prophet** was the most influential religious figure to arise in Israel since the death of Samuel.

---

[1]Gordon (235) calls this chapter the "ideological summit" of the entire Old Testament.

[2]Although ch. 7 nowhere contains the word "covenant," numerous passages do use that term in reference to what transpires here: 2 Sam 23:5; 1 Kgs 8:23; 2 Chr 13:5; Ps 89:3,28,34,39; 132:12; Isa 55:3; Jer 33:21.

[3]J.D. Levenson, "The Davidic Covenant and Its Modern Interpreters," *CBQ* 41, 2 (1979): 205-206.

[4]In the Hebrew text David is called "king" in three successive verses (vv. 1-3) although the NIV uses a pronoun for him in v. 2. He is not called by his personal name until v. 5.

David's desire to build a suitable house for Yahweh was both a cultural and a spiritual concern. The first person pronoun in v. 2 is emphatic. **Living** (יָשַׁב, *yāšab*) is the same verb translated "settled" in v. 1. David was bothered by the fact that he dwelled in **a palace of cedar** (lit., "cedars"), while the ark of God was **in a tent,** lit., "within the curtain." Most tents were constructed of goatskin curtains. The cedars were those which had been sent by Hiram from the mountains of Lebanon. Cedar was a rare, valuable and durable timber. David was proposing in a round about way that he should build a temple for the Lord to house the ark.

7:3 David's honorable resolve to build a worthy house for the ark gained the immediate approval of the prophet. He assured David that the Lord was with him in any project which he might undertake. Unfortunately, Nathan was expressing a personal opinion, not the word of the Lord.

2. Opposition: Yahweh's Will (7:4-7)

7:4 That night, i.e., before David could take any measures toward temple construction, Nathan got a message from the Lord. The formula **the word of LORD came** occurs some two hundred times in the Old Testament, especially in the books of Jeremiah and Ezekiel. He was to take the message to **David my servant**. While all God's people are his servants, only a few had this special title bestowed upon them.[5] The use of this honorable title was meant to give David gracious assurance that his pious intentions were appreciated (cf. 1 Kgs 8:18). **This is what the LORD says** is the familiar messenger formula which serves to authorize and legitimize the message which follows.

Though David's proposal had divine approval, the timing was not right. The prohibition is administered, not in the form of a blunt negative, but obliquely in a rhetorical question (cf. 1 Chr 17:4). David's plan was rejected, his person was not (Gordon, 237). Through later revelation David learned the reason for this prohibition. Throughout his life he had been a man of war; he had shed much blood (1 Chr 22:8; 28:3). Those wars had been necessary, under the circumstances in which David was placed, and had never been disapproved by God; still the mere fact that he had been a man

---

[5]Besides Israel and David, "servant" is a title for (1) Moses, (2) Nebuchadnezzar, and (3) Messiah.

of blood made it incongruous for him to be the builder of the house of prayer for all people.

7:6-7 Nathan began with two reminders. First, the Lord had not dwelt in a house **from the day that I brought the Israelites up out of Egypt to this day**. This formula appears to point to a turn of events which implies a rejection of the divinely authorized status quo and the embarkation down a path with humanly unforeseen and potentially disastrous results.[6] Up to this point God had designated the tabernacle as his abode. So long as God's dwelling was a tent, he appeared as if traveling or going **from place to place with a tent as my dwelling,** lit., "I was walking about in a tent and in a tabernacle." The reference is to the movements from place to place in the wilderness, and subsequently at Gilgal, Shiloh, Nob and Gibeon in Canaan. Never once had he rebuked **any of their rulers** (lit., "tribes")[7] for not building him **a house of cedar,** i.e., a permanent sanctuary with beams of the most costly timber. Various tribes arose to leadership during the prior history of Israel through the various judges God had raised up. Those God raised up were **to shepherd** the flock of God. A shepherd walked in front of his flock to bear the brunt of danger, to clear the road, and to guide the sheep into safe pastures. The emphasis here is on Yahweh's right to initiate the matter of temple building (Gordon, 237).[8]

3. A Solemn Promise (7:8-17)

Promises to Be Realized in David's Lifetime (7:8-11a)

7:8-9a The repetition of the messenger formula (cf. v. 5) marks v. 8 as the start of a new section of Nathan's oracle. Here Nathan

---

[6]The exact formula appears in 1 Sam 8:8 in reference to the request for a king, which is regarded as an example of continuing apostasy on the part of Israel. Cf. Judg 19:30 where a similar formula occurs.

[7]Here "tribes" is used for the rulers who sprang from those tribes. Cf. Ps 78:67f.; 1 Chr 28:4. The parallel passage (1 Chr 17:6) reads "judges" for "tribes." So Kirkpatrick, 2:98. P.V. Reid suggests revocalizing *šibṭê* as *šōbṭê* (Qal participle) meaning "the one who wields a staff." These "staff bearers" were commissioned to shepherd God's people. "*šbṭy* in 2 Samuel 7:7," *CBQ* 37, 1 (1975): 18.

[8]It is clear that, despite its description as a הֵיכָל (*hêkāl*, "temple") in 1 Sam 1:9, the Shiloh sanctuary was not regarded as a permanent house.

gave David two reminders. First, the term **Almighty** (lit., "of hosts") is added to the name Yahweh to create a regal title. The title reminded David that whereas he may be king of Israel and surrounded by servants, he is a vassal (servant) of the heavenly king. Second, Nathan reminded David that God had selected him to be **ruler** (see on 1 Sam 9:16) over his people. God had blessed his reign thus far. Wherever David went, God **cut off** his enemies before him. The history of David distinguishes between two series of wars: (1) those which established David firmly on his throne; and (2) those which gave him widespread dominion.

7:9b-11a On the basis of what had been, David was called to look forward to what would be. The Nathan oracle made several specific promises to David:. (1) God intended to make the name of David great. His name would rank alongside those of the greatest men of the earth (cf. 2 Sam 8:13). The blessing of a good reputation was most highly esteemed by the Hebrews (cf. Gen 12:2). (2) God would grant to David and his people Israel **a place** of their own, a home where they would no longer be disturbed by enemies (cf. Deut 11:24). God would **plant them**, like a tree with deep roots, in their own land. **Wicked people** (lit., "sons of iniquity"; cf. 2 Sam 3:34) would not oppress them anymore, as they did **at the beginning** of Israel's sojourn in the land of Canaan. Those enemies had oppressed Israel throughout the period of the judges, and into the reign of Saul. Yahweh, however, spoke as if the entry into Canaan was yet future, as indeed it always is for true believers. (3) God promised to give Israel **rest.** These promises — if indeed they are promises — may look forward to the glorious kingdom of David's greater Son, even Christ.[9]

Promises to Be Realized after David's Death (7:11b-17)

7:11b-12 Instead of David building a house of worship for the Lord, God would build **a house,** i.e., dynasty, for David. The switch from the first person divine speech to the third person reference to Yahweh in v. 11b serves the purpose of emphasizing the source of

---

[9]According to normal rules, the verbs would be perfects with consecutive *waw*, making the statements future. Some commentators, however, interpret the Hebrew to be a statement of what God already had done for David and for Israel through David. His conquests had given Israel security in their land. E.g., see R.P. Smith (184), Hertzberg (285).

the choice of David's house. Here the contrast between the kingship of Saul and that of David is most vivid. The emphasis here on dynastic perpetuity is obvious in the use of "house" (fifteen times) and "forever" (eight times).

Rest (lit., "lie down") **with your fathers** is a metaphor for death (cf. Deut 31:16; Gen 47:30). God promised to **raise up your offspring,** i.e., posterity, to succeed David, i.e., elevate him/them to royal dignity. **Will come from your body** (lit., "loins;" cf. Gen 15:4) indicates that David's successor would not be any of the sons whose births have previously been narrated. God would **establish** the kingdom of the offspring of David.

7:13 He (emphatic), i.e., the offspring of David, would **build a house** for God's **Name,** i.e., as the dwelling place of God's Name (cf. Deut 16:2). Implied in these words is the promise that God would be present in that temple in special manifestation. One cannot build a temple for God himself, only for God's Name, i.e., what he has revealed about himself. The Name of God is all of the attributes of God, his character, his personality, all that he has revealed to man through the Word and through events. This verse again emphasizes the foreverness of the Davidic dynasty (cf. Ps 89:29).

7:14 I (emphatic) **will be his father** points to a special relationship between God and the offspring of David, one which did not exist between God and Saul. The result is that the offspring of David would be God's **son.** This sonship was not based on physical descent (as in Egyptian theology) but on a legal relationship.[10] The nation Israel was honored by being called God's son (Exod 4:22; Deut 14:1); now the Davidic ruler, as the representative of that people, was honored with the same title. The father/son relationship implies on the part of God, watchful care and love like that of a parent; on the part of the ruler, loving obedience and unquestioning trust. A father eventually delegated to a son all that he had. For a royal son, sonship includes government. David later quoted these words in reference to Solomon (1 Chr 22:9f.; 28:6). The language, however, can be applied properly to any ruler from the line of David, and ultimately to Christ who is the Son of God in a far more profound sense (Heb 1:5).

---

[10]Anderson (122) calls attention to the fact that father-son terminology was used in respect to partners in the legal transactions of (1) adoption, (2) covenant, and (3) royal grant, all three of which appropriately might be used of the relationship between God and David.

God's favor to David's line would not be unconditional. The high dignity bestowed on David's offspring did not exempt any of these rulers from sin or its consequences. **When he does wrong**, God would discipline him as any father would discipline a son that he loves. The **rod of men** is explained as meaning **floggings inflicted by men**. God would use other men and nations to administer discipline to the offspring of David who followed him on the throne.[11] The sinless Son of David, Christ, was also chastised, but not for his own sins. He bore the punishment for the sins of all men (Isa 53:4-6).

7:15-16 Though from time to time he might discipline David's offspring, God would never take away his love permanently from him as he took it away from Saul. The former king and his house were utterly and permanently set aside. God, however, would never remove the kingship from the family of David. His house and kingdom would endure **forever before me**, lit., "before you." The NIV here follows the LXX, but there is no good reason to abandon the MT. David is envisioned seeing all his descendants pass before him in a vision. His throne would be an everlasting throne. The word **forever** throughout this passage does not refer merely to an incalculable period (cf. Ps 89:29). Such promises could only be fulfilled by running out in a person who lives forever, i.e., by culminating in the Messiah, who lives forever, and of whose kingdom there is no end.

The importance of the Nathan oracle is indicated by the frequent references to it in the subsequent history of Israel. David applied it to Solomon (1 Chr 22:9ff.), Solomon claimed it for himself (1 Kgs 5:5; 8:17ff.), it is confirmed to Solomon (1 Kgs 9:4f.), and it is repeatedly affirmed that, in spite of the sins of individual kings, the kingdom would not be withdrawn from David's house (1 Kgs 11:12; 15:4f.; 2 Kgs 8:19). Numerous prophecies, based upon the promises made here, announced the coming of a glorious ruler from the house of David.[12] The "foreverness" of these promises points beyond David's son Solomon. Jesus the Messiah is a son of David. He is God's son *par excellence*. He is currently building a spiritual temple. On the cross he experienced the disciplinary rod of

---

[11]Other interpretations: (1) chastisement as a human father might administer, i.e., not with the purpose of destroying him, but of correcting him and turning him from the wrong path; (2) punishments such as all men incur when they sin.

[12]See Isa 9:7; 55:3; Jer 29:16; 33:15,17; Ezek 34:23; 37:24; Hos 3:5; Amos 9:11.

God, not for his own sins, but for the sins of others. He sits even now upon the throne of God in the heavenly places.

7:17 Nathan faithfully reported **this entire revelation** (lit., "vision") to David. A vision in the night, as distinct from a dream, came to the recipient in a wakened condition. The word does not imply that Nathan saw anything with the natural eye but signifies the type of revelation which was commonly given to prophets.

4. David's House: Celebration (7:18-29)

David sets the tone of his prayer by centering both his thanksgiving and his petitions around the theme of greatness (גָּדוֹל, *gādôl*). God is great (v. 22) because of what he had done for David (v. 21) and Israel (v. 23). God's name would continue to be great so long as David's house remained (v. 26). In this prayer, David made no mention of the matter that occasioned Nathan's oracle in the first place; the temple was forgotten as David claimed and celebrated God's unexpected promise concerning his familial house.

Thanksgiving for Undeserved Favor (7:18-21)

7:18-19 David went into the tent where the ark of God was located in Jerusalem and **sat**[13] **before the Lord**, i.e., before the ark. The sitting posture in prayer is not mentioned elsewhere in the Bible. David either (1) sat upon the ground in order to demonstrate his humility or (2) sat upon his heels in the kind of kneeling position which is common in the Near East even to this day. **Who am I . . .** is a formula of polite self-depreciation before a person of higher rank. David expressed his unworthiness to have been treated so wonderfully thus far by the Lord. This wonderful past, however, was exceeded by news of the wonderful **future**[14] which God had announced through Nathan for David and his family. David would have an enduring house or family. He and his family had been chosen,

---

[13]Some think that the word in the context means to "remain" or "tarry" (cf. Gen 24:55; 29:19).

[14]Lit., "and you have spoken also unto the house of your servant for a great while to come." The Hebrew לְמֵרָחוֹק (*lᵉmērāḥôq*) is that which points to a remote period, i.e., that of the eternal establishment of David's house and throne.

unworthy as they were, to play a significant role in the long-range plans of the **Sovereign Lord**, lit., "Lord Yahweh."[15] David recognized his own status before God by referring to himself as **your servant**.[16] The last sentence in v. 19 is difficult. Nothing in the Hebrew indicates that this is a question. The literal rendering is "and this is the law of men," i.e., this decree concerning David's kingdom is the will (תּוֹרָה, *tôrāh*) of God, and has implication for all of mankind.[17] These words indicate David's amazement over what the Lord had promised him.

7:20-21 David was virtually speechless before the Lord. He could neither ask nor desire anything greater than what had been now conferred upon him. As words failed him, David fell back on the omniscience of God. **For the sake of your word** refers to the earlier promises of Samuel regarding David, and perhaps also to the foundational messianic prophecies found in the Pentateuch.[18] The choice of David was according to God's sovereign **will**, not because of David's worthiness. The revelation is in keeping with God's character, and therefore typical of his dealings with mankind. Now God had made known to David **this great thing**, i.e., the choice of David's family for perpetual reign in Israel. God not only makes great plans for his servants, but he also graciously makes his plans known (Baldwin, 217).

Praise for God's Dealings with Israel (7:22-24)

7:22 For David, God's goodness was a proof of his greatness. All he could do was to praise the Lord. No other so-called god compared to the Sovereign Yahweh. He alone spoke to his people. With their own ears they (Israel) had heard him speak at Mt. Sinai. David

---

[15]This divine title is used seven times in David's prayer but nowhere else in Samuel. Abraham addressed God with this title in Gen 15:2,8. The title is common in Ezekiel.

[16]David refers to himself as Yahweh's "servant" ten times in this prayer.

[17]Another interpretation is that God was acting towards David in a human manner, as an earthly friend and benefactor would. The parallel passage in 1 Chr 17:17 is quite different: "You have looked on me as though I were the most exalted of men."

[18]E.g., Jacob's prophecy concerning Judah (Gen 49:10). The connection between this Patriarchal prophecy and Nathan's promise is established by 1 Chr 28:4 where David refers to his election as king as being the consequence of the election of Judah as ruler (KD).

knew the greatness of God from his own experience. Here he begins to reflect on the evidence of God's greatness in the history of Israel. **As we have heard with our own ears** should not be restricted to oral tradition because similar language is used of written records.[19]

7:23-24 While the general thrust of v. 23 is clear, the exact translation is difficult.[20] Like their God, Israel was unique upon the earth. God **went out**,[21] i.e., became active in the interest of his people, in order (1) to **redeem**[22] them from the bondage in Egypt (cf. Deut 7:8; 9:26; et al), thereby making Israel his special people; (2) to **make a name for himself**, which he did through the great events of the Exodus; and (3) to perform **great and awesome wonders**,[23] terminology taken from Deut 10:21. The words **by driving out**[24] have been supplied by the NIV to make sense of a difficult Hebrew sentence. The reference is to the expulsion of Canaanite nations at the time of the conquest under Joshua. These acts were performed **before your people**, i.e., before the nation whom the Lord redeemed out of

---

[19]Cf. Deut 4:6; 2 Kgs 17:14; 18:12; Neh 9:29.

[20]A more literal translation of v. 23 would be this: "And who is like your people, like Israel, a unique nation in the earth whose God went to redeem for himself [for] a people, and to make for himself a name, and to do for you (plural) great and marvelous things, for your (sing.) land from before your people which you redeemed for yourself from Egypt, nations and their gods." The whole verse is so full of grammatical difficulties as to make it extremely probable that the text is corrupt.

[21]The word "God" (אֱלֹהִים, *'ĕlōhîm*) usually takes singular agreement when used of Israel's God. Here, however, is one of the few exceptions to this rule. The verb here is plural. The parallel in 1 Chr 17:21 uses a singular verb.

[22]The verb in the Hebrew is plural. The thought is, "What nation is there whom its gods went to redeem?" Another view is that the plural of majesty is being employed in reference to God.

[23]The NIV omits translation of לָכֶם (*lākem*, "for you" [plural]). This word is omitted by the LXX and changed into "for them" by the Vulgate. If the word is retained, it must be understood (1) as a momentary reference to the people or (2) as a plural of majesty referring to the Lord. In other English versions the term is rendered (1) "for them" (BV, NJPS, NRSV); "for You" or "Thee," i.e., singular in reference to God (NASB, NKJV); and (3) "for you," i.e., Israel (ASV).

[24]The NIV substitutes "by driving out" for the Hebrew לְאַרְצֶךָ (*lᵉʾarṣekā*, "for your land"). The NIV is based on the parallel passage in 1 Chr 17:21 and the LXX.

Egypt. Such gracious and mighty deeds had established Israel as his special people **forever**. Israel would have an everlasting existence. The shape of Israel, however, would change over the centuries. The church of Christ is the present and final manifestation of Israel.

Petition for Fulfillment of the Promise (7:25-29)

In this section of the prayer, David uses **now** (וְעַתָּה, *wᵊʻattāh*) three times (vv. 25,28 [omitted by NIV],29) to signal the transition "from antecedent to consequent in speech" (Polzin, *David*, 84). In this prayer David is on a quest for certainty regarding the promises made through Nathan.

7:25-26 The first **now** requested fulfillment of God's word. David prayed that God would keep forever the promise which he had just made concerning his family. By keeping that promise, God's name would be great forever. Men would come to recognize that the Lord Almighty was God over Israel. By keeping his promises to David, **the house . . . of David** would be established before the Lord.

7:27 David had courage to offer this prayer to God because the Lord had **revealed**, lit., "uncovered the ear of your servant," this great promise to David. The figure of speech is probably derived from the practice of removing the hair or a corner of the turban from another's ear in order to whisper a secret into it. The essence of the Nathan oracle is that God would build a house for David. This promise justified a prayer which otherwise would have seemed presumptuous.

7:28-29 In the Hebrew v. 28 begins with "and now." This verse assumes the fulfillment of the previous petition for God to keep his word to David. That which God had spoken was **trustworthy**. **Good things** (lit., "a good thing") is probably a synonym for "covenant" (Kalluveettil, 44). David **found courage**, lit, "found his heart," to utter this prayer. This was a good and trustworthy, i.e., dependable, promise. Therefore, David requested that the Lord **bless** his house (family) that it might continue forever in God's sight.

The third "and now" opens v. 29 in the Hebrew. Here there is a double petition for God's aid and blessing, so that David and his house might be kept faithful to the covenant and faithful to the trust committed to them.

2 SAMUEL 8

IX. THE COVENANT WITH DAVID BLESSED (8:1–12:31)

A. NATIONAL EXPANSION (8:1-18)

David was forced to extend his dominion beyond the boundaries of Israel proper in order to protect his frontiers against possible invaders. To enjoy peace, Israel needed to be surrounded by a ring of friendly states. This chapter may be intended by the author to mark the close of the history of David's public deeds.

Scholars disagree about whether the battles mentioned here chronologically followed (Carlson 115f.) or preceded (Merrill 247) the promises made in the previous chapter. Historians would attribute David's success to the fact that (1) there was no major power in the area to check his expansion and (2) David was a leader of exceptional skill both in politics and in war. The biblical Narrator, however, and his contemporaries recognized the achievements of David to be the result of divine intervention. Twice he states in this chapter **The LORD gave David victory wherever he went** (vv. 6,14).

1. Geographical Growth (8:1-14)

Expansion against Old Enemies (8:1-2)

8:1 On the temporal marker, **In the course of time** (lit., "and it happened after thus"), see on 2 Sam 2:1.[1] David was able to take **Metheg Ammah** (lit., "bridle of the mother-city") away from Philistine control. The name points to the city which held the bridle

---

[1]Anderson (131) suggests that this opening phrase may imply that David's victories were seen as the fulfillment of Yahweh's promise that wicked men would no longer oppress Israel (2 Sam 7:11). This was accomplished by eliminating the sources of potential danger.

or control over the territories of the Philistines.[2] This is probably metaphorical for Gath, the chief city of the Philistines at this time[3] (cf. 1 Chr 18:1). Although the Philistines were subdued, there does not appear to have been any attempt to reduce them to vassalage as in some of the other cases in this chapter.

8:2 David was especially harsh with Moabite captives. He measured off the bodies of his prostrate enemies with a line divided into three equal parts. Such as were found under the two first parts of the measuring line were put to death, those under the third part were spared.[4] It is reasonable to assume that only males were executed, and probably only fighting men. These men had committed such notorious atrocities that David considered the death penalty appropriate. The sparing of one third of the captives[5] would have been viewed in the ancient world as an act of kindness. The surviving Moabites became subject to David and paid tribute (taxes) to him. Why David inflicted such terrible vengeance on the Moabites can only be conjectured. A Jewish tradition relates that the king of Moab betrayed his trust and murdered David's parents. Another possibility is that the Moabites were guilty of some act of treachery against David during one of his campaigns against the neighboring states of Edom and Ammon.

Expansion against the Arameans (8:3-12)

8:3-4 The Arameans[6] were ruled by **Hadadezer,** king of **Zobah,** a small mountainous kingdom north of Damascus. David may have

---

[2]Ahlström (469) takes "Metheg Ammah" to be a metaphor for David's replacement of the Philistines as the lord of Palestine.

[3]See 1 Chr 18:1 where the capture of Gath is specifically mentioned, and the suburbs of Gath are literally called "her daughters." On the location of Gath, see on 1 Sam 5:8.

[4]Lit., "he measured two lines to execute and the fullness of the line to keep alive." The word "fullness" may suggest that mercy was given more generously than punishment.

[5]The LXX and Vulgate change the ratio: half were put to death and half were spared.

[6]On the Arameans, see A. Malamat, "The Kingdom of David and Solomon in its Contact with Egypt and Aram Naharaim" *BA* 21, 4 (1958), 96-102; B. Mazar, "The Aramean Empire and Its Relations with Israel," *BA* 25, 4 (1962): 97-120. Both articles are included in *Biblical Archaeologist Reader 2* (New York: Doubleday, 1964). See also M.F. Unger.

fought in Saul's army in earlier campaigns against this kingdom (cf.
1 Sam 14:47). **To restore his control** is literally "to turn his hand
against," i.e., establish his dominion.[7] Apparently while Hadadezer was
campaigning along the Euphrates (lit., "the river") in the north, David
invaded his kingdom from the south. The Arameans were not equal to
war on two fronts, so David defeated Hadadezer. He was able to capture a thousand of Hadadezer's chariots, seven thousand of his charioteers, and 20,000 foot soldiers. See comments on 2 Sam 10:15ff.

A problem arises in the numbers in 2 Sam 8:4 when compared
to the account of prisoners taken in the same battle in 1 Chr 18:4.[8]
See Table 7. KD proposed that the word for "chariots" dropped out
of the text of 2 Sam 8:4 in an early stage of copying. When that happened, a later scribe changed seven thousand to seven hundred
because Hebrew would never write seven thousand after one thousand in recording one and the same figure. The defective copy of
the Samuel text was then copied through the centuries, even though
the scribes surely realized that the present Hebrew reading is at
odds with that of 1 Chronicles. In all probability 1 Chr 18:4 is the
correct reading. The NIV has translated 2 Sam 8:4 in the light of
1 Chr 18:4. Whether this is a legitimate function of an English translation is questionable.[9]

Table 6 Booty in the Aramean Campaign		
	2 Samuel 8:3-8 (MT)	1 Chronicles 18:4
Charioteers (*pārāšîm*)	1,700	7,000
Chariots (*rekebh*)	1,000	1,000
Chariot Horses	100	100
Foot Men (*'îš raglî*)	20,000	20,000

[7]Ahlström (482, n. 1) references an Assyrian inscription in which Ashur-
rabi II (1012–972 B.C.) recaptured territory that "the king of the land of
Amuru had seized by force." This king of Amuru would most probably be
Hadadezer, who had expanded his kingdom around 1000 B.C. and whose
power, through vassals, reached the Euphrates.

[8]For a harmonization of 2 Sam 8:4 and 1 Chr 18:4 see Archer (184). Haley
(382) points out that in all probability in ancient times letters were used for
numerals. The difference between 7,000 and 700 when Hebrew letters represent numbers is only two dots over the letter marking the numeral.

[9]ASV, NASB, JB, NRSV, NJPS follow MT here. The term *pārāšîm* is
usually rendered "horsemen," with JB and NIV rendering "charioteers."

David's victory, using Israelite infantry against a powerful force of cavalry and chariots, shows again his great military genius. Following the prior example of Joshua (Josh 11:6), David **hamstrung** the chariot horses. This refers to a cutting of a tendon in the hoof or knee of the horse which makes it impossible for the animal to be used again in war. At this time the Israelites did not use war horses.[10] **All but a hundred of the chariot horses** is literally "he left a hundred chariots" or "chariot horses."[11]

8:5-6 The Arameans of Damascus, who may have been vassals[12] or at least allies of Hadadezer, intervened against the Israelites. David struck down "twenty-two thousand" of them on the battlefield. He established **garrisons**[13] of soldiers throughout the kingdom of Damascus by which he could keep the populace under subjection. These Arameans became subject to David and brought tribute to him. The words **The LORD gave David victory** (lit., "Yahweh delivered David") **wherever he went** are theologically important. This is the same language used throughout the Book of Judges (at least fifteen times) to refer to the actions of Yahweh in delivering his people, through the instrumentality of judges, from the hand of their enemies. These words (1) explain David's success against military forces with superior weaponry and (2) justify these military operations beyond the borders of Israel. These nations against whom

---

Other versions understand the "one thousand" to refer to chariots, and the "seven hundred" to "horsemen" (NKJV) or "cavalry" (BV).

[10]The same Hebrew word *rekebh* can be translated "chariot," "chariots" or "chariot horses." The verb translated **hamstrung** (עָקַר, *'āqar*) could refer to the wrecking of the chariots. This would avoid giving to *rekebh* different meanings in the same verse. Josh 11:6,9, however, makes clear that the hamstringing of horses was a regular military tactic in ancient Israel.

[11]The KJV renders "he reserved of them a hundred chariots." More recent versions understand the text to say that he left untouched the horses used with a hundred chariots, i.e., from one hundred to four hundred horses depending on how many horses the Arameans assigned to each chariot. This is the understanding of the ASV, NASB, NRSV, NKJV, BV and JB.

[12]A. Malamat has argued that Damascus must have been "a conquered territory" ruled by Hadadezer since there is no mention of the "king" of Damascus. See "Aspects of Foreign Policies of David and Solomon," *JNES* 22 (1963): 5.

[13]The term נְצִיב (*nᵉṣîb*) is translated "outpost" in 1 Sam 10:5. See discussion of the term there. Other than JB ("governors"), the standard English versions here render the word "garrisons."

David warred are viewed as oppressors of Israel from whom God needed to deliver his people.

8:7-8 The gold (plated? embossed? fitted?) **shields**[14] which belonged to the **officers** — probably only the personal bodyguard — of Hadadezer were brought to Jerusalem. They were eventually placed in Solomon's temple (2 Kgs 11:10). **From Tebah** (or Betah) **and Berothai,**[15] towns formerly controlled by Hadadezer, David captured a large quantity of **bronze,** an alloy of copper and tin. These towns lay close together, about fifty miles north of Damascus in the valley between the Lebanons and the Anti-Lebanons, an area rich in copper.[16]

8:9-10 Tou (or Toi) ruled **Hamath,** an Aramean kingdom north of Zobah with a capital of the same name situated on the Orontes river. When he heard that David had defeated Hadadezer, Tou sent his son Joram **to greet** (lit., "ask him of his welfare") David and to **congratulate** (lit., "bless") him. Tou **had been at war** with Hadadezer for some time (lit., "a man of wars of Tou was Hadadezer"). He was grateful to David for smiting his rival. **Joram** ("Yahweh is exalted")[17] may have been the name this prince adopted when Hamath became a satellite of David (Malamat, 7). He brought with him articles of silver, gold and bronze as presents for David.

8:11-12 All that David captured or was given he **dedicated** to the Lord, i.e., set apart to be used in the temple which his son would later build (cf. 1 Kgs 7:51). Here is a hint of the lavish preparations by David for temple building which is itemized in 1 Chr 22:2-5. This

---

[14]The word translated "shields" (שֶׁלֶט, *šeleṭ*) is of uncertain meaning. It comes from a root which means "to have power or authority." Hence these "shields" imply they were a symbol of rank. The Syriac rendered it "quivers"; the LXX, "bracelets." In the parallel passage (1 Chr 18:7), the Syriac and Vulgate render the term "quivers"; the LXX, "collars."

[15]In 1 Chr 18:8 the cities of Hadadezer are called "Tibhath" and "Cun." These are either (1) alternate names for the cities of 2 Sam 8:8 or (2) additional cities from which David took tribute.

[16]4QSam[a] and LXX have a long addition to vv. 7-8 which relates that these gold and bronze items were taken away by Pharaoh Shishak when he came against Jerusalem in the days of King Rehoboam (1 Kgs 14:26).

[17]This son's name in 1 Chr 18:10 is "Hadoram" ("Hadad [the storm god] is exalted"). Gordon (245) suggests another possible explanation for the name Joram: the divine name "Hadad" was simply paraphrased with an Israelite one.

included items taken from wars with Edom, Moab, Ammon, the Philistines, Amalek[18] and Hadadezer of Zobah.

Expansion against the Edomites (8:13-14)

8:13-14 During Israel's campaign in the north, Judah must have come under attack by the Edomites. David dispatched Abishai with a detachment of troops to repel them. He **became famous** (lit., "made a name") when he returned to Jerusalem after his forces struck down eighteen thousand **Edomites**[19] in the **Valley of Salt,** the exact location of which is unknown.[20] He left behind **garrisons** (cf. v. 6) **throughout Edom,**[21] so establishing a trade monopoly there and opening the way to communications with Arabia and Africa. Again the text emphasizes that all these victories were gifts of the Lord to David.

2. Bureaucratic Growth (8:15-18)

Having described the external security of David's kingdom, the Narrator now presents a list of the chief officers of state who administered the internal affairs of the kingdom. Another list of these officers is given in 2 Sam 20:23-26 (cf. 1 Kgs 4:1-6).

---

[18]Saul "utterly destroyed" Amelek (1 Sam 15), but they were a nation of many tribes, and Saul's victory must have been over only one branch. This is the only mention of David's war with Amalek. Perhaps the spoil taken in the encounter recorded in 1 Sam 30:10ff. is meant.

[19]The NIV has departed from the majority of Hebrew MSS which here name the enemy defeated in the Valley of Salt as "Aram," i.e., the Arameans. "Aram" and "Edom" can be almost indistinguishable in an unvocalized Hebrew manuscript. A scribe might easily have confused the two names. Reference in v. 14 to garrisons throughout the land of Edom suggests that "Edom" was the original reading in v. 13, a reading supported by a few Hebrew MSS and the LXX. The reading of the MT, however, is not impossible (cf. Y. Aharoni, *Land*, 318 n. 17). That David's troops did slay 18,000 of the Edomites in the Valley of Salt is attested in 1 Chr 18:12. Joab followed up with a larger force. He slew 12,000 in a second battle (Ps 60, title) and remained six months in the land ruthlessly putting every male to death (1 Kgs 11:15f.).

[20]In attempting to locate the Valley of Salt commentators use such language as "east of Beersheba;" "south of the Dead Sea;" and "in the neighborhood of Sela," i.e., Petra. Clearly the place was near or in Edom (2 Kgs 14:7).

[21]The Hebrew is emphatic through redundancy: "put in Edom garrisons, in all Edom he put garrisons."

8:15-18 David is depicted in v. 15 as the ideal king. He did what was **just and right** for all his people. This may suggest that David was chief justice of the land. He was accessible to his people and was prepared to act personally in the capacity of judge in order to hear their claims and, if necessary, redress their wrongs. **Joab** was commander of David's army, i.e., the Israelite tribal levies which were separate from the mercenaries commanded by Benaiah. **Jehoshaphat** was the state **recorder** (*mazkîr*), lit., "remembrancer," the officer who brought state business to the king's notice and advised him on it.

Zadok and Ahimelech were **priests**. Questions arise over both names. Zadok has not been mentioned previously in the text. According to 1 Chr 6:3-8 he was a son of Ahitub, and his genealogy is traced back to Eleazar and Aaron. Yet the Narrator earlier mentioned only Abiathar the son of Ahimelech as having escaped the massacre of the priests of Nob (1 Sam 22:20). Two explanations of Zadok's identity have been offered: (1) he was the chief priest in Jerusalem before its seizure by the Israelites. His retention in office represents the integration of the old Jerusalem cultus (cf. Gen 14:18-20) into the Israelite religion (Gordon, 246); and (2) he was an Aaronide priest from Hebron or southern Judah,[22] i.e., he escaped the Nob slaughter because he did not live there.

Elsewhere Zadok and *Abiathar* (not Ahimelech) are mentioned as the principal priests of David's reign. Some see here a problem in that Abiathar is not named in v. 17 as a priest, and he is listed as the father, rather than the son, of Ahimelech (1 Sam 22:20). Commentators have made these suggestions: (1) the names of the father and son here have been accidentally reversed by scribes and (2) Zadok and Ahimelech were assistants to Abiathar the high priest whose position here is assumed. Certainly Abiathar held office throughout the reign of David (1 Kgs 2:26); but according to 1 Chr 24:3,6,31 Ahimelech is mentioned along with Zadok as head of the priests of the line of Ithamar. Perhaps Abiathar is not here named because his office of high priest was not a royal appointment. According to 1 Chr 16:39, Zadok officiated in the high place at Gibeon where at this time the tabernacle was located. Ahimelech probably assisted his father Abiathar in the Jerusalem sanctuary.

---

[22]F. Cross, CMHE, 207-215. S. Olyan, "Zadok's Origin and the Tribal Politics of David," *JBL* 101 (1982): 177-193.

Seraiah[23] was the state **secretary** (סוֹפֵר, *sôphēr*). He would have been charged with the task of drafting and custodial care of official documents, and perhaps also the task of recording the principal events of the reign. Benaiah was over **the Kerethites and Pelethites**, the foreign troops which were hired to serve as a royal bodyguard. These troops are known by this name only during the reign of David. On the Kerethites see on 1 Sam 30:14. The Pelethites[24] cannot be identified certainly. Some assume that they were Philistines.[25] David's sons served as **royal advisors** (כֹּהֲנִים, *kōhănîm*), the term which normally means "priests." 1 Chr 18:17 calls these two sons "chief officials at the king's side." This suggests that in a few instances the term *kōhănîm* denotes a civil and not a sacerdotal minister.[26]

---

[23]He is called "Shavsha" in 1 Chr 18:16, and may be the same as Sheva (2 Sam 20:25) and Shisha (1 Kgs 4:3). The many variants of this scribe's name may indicate its foreign (Egyptian?) origin and the Hebrew scribes were not entirely sure how to transliterate it.

[24]The name "Pelethites" (פְּלֵתִי, *pᵉlēthî*) is a possible dialectical variant of פְּלִשְׁתִּי (*pᵉlištî*, "Philistines").

[25]By employing foreign guards to ensure the safety of the king, David would minimize the possibility of becoming the victim of intertribal rivalries; these men could give wholehearted allegiance to him (Baldwin, 224).

[26]Youngblood (913) calls attention to 1 Kgs 4:5 where Zabud is called, literally, "a priest, a personal adviser to the king."

2 SAMUEL 9

Chapters 9-20 of 2 Samuel present a continuous narrative that displays remarkable literary qualities. Because the emphasis is upon the establishment of the hereditary succession principle in Israel, these chapters (together with 1 Kgs 1-2) are commonly called "the Succession Narrative."[1]

B. ROYAL BENEVOLENCE (9:1-13)

Nothing indicates when the event narrated in ch 9 took place. Mephibosheth was only five years old at the time of his father's death (2 Sam 4:4), and now he had a young son (v. 12). This necessitates that the incident took place several years after David began to reign. See, however, the comments on v. 12. For the chronological relationship between this account and David's execution of the descendants of Saul, see comments on 2 Sam 21:1-14.[2]

1. The Search for Jonathan's Son (9:1-5)

9:1 Perhaps the deaths of Abner and Ish-Bosheth (chs 3-4) provide the explanation for David's question. He was asking about figures of public or political standing (Gunn, *David*, 68). The form of

---

[1]For a discussion of literary excellence of this material, see R.N. Whybray, 56-95; G. von Rad "The Beginning of History Writing in Ancient Israel," in PHOE, 166-204. Youngblood (914) suggests that "court history" could be a more appropriate title. See also J.W. Flanagan, "Court History or Succession Document? A Study of 2 Samuel 9-20; 1 Kings 1-2," *JBL* 91, 2 (1972): 172-181.

[2]R.P. Smith estimates that this incident took place seventeen or eighteen years after the battle of Gilboa.

his question here and in v. 3 suggests that he did not expect to hear of many if any survivors. The term **kindness** (חֶסֶד, *ḥesed*) comes from the vocabulary of covenant obligation. The rendering "keep faith" (NJPS) captures the meaning of the original. The term conveys the idea of loyalty to a solemn commitment. This diplomatic move would bring to David the support of any remaining supporters of Saul.

9:2-3 Apparently when Saul died, his estate became crown property. These lands were being managed by Ziba, who previously had served Saul but was now a loyal servant of David. The king summoned Ziba and asked if there yet remained members of Saul's house to whom David could extend kindness. **God's kindness** (cf. 1 Sam 20:14) is love and mercy such as God shows to men, unfailing and unlimited. Ziba told the king of a crippled son of Jonathan[3] who was still living. Ziba mentions the physical condition of this son in order (1) to explain to David why he had never heard of him and (2) to signal that neither this son nor his friends were any threat to David's throne.[4]

9:4-5 Ziba informed David that the surviving son of Jonathan was living at the house of a man named **Makir** in the village of **Lo Debar** on the other side of Jordan in the same general region which Saul's son Ish-Bosheth had ruled for a time. Makir was a rich man (cf. 2 Sam 17:27f.) who had received into his home the lame son of Jonathan after the death of his father in the battle of 1010 B.C. Mephibosheth resided with Makir because (1) he no longer had access to the lands of his father or grandfather and (2) because he feared the king. In that time the rise of a new dynasty usually led to the massacre of all the members of the old dynasty. David immediately had the son of Jonathan brought to Jerusalem.

2. The Provisions for Jonathan's Son (9:6-13)

9:6-7 Mephibosheth[5] came to David and **bowed down** (הִשְׁתַּחֲוָה,

---

[3]Other survivors of Saul's house are mentioned in 2 Sam 21:8. Perhaps these men were already dead at the time David befriended Mephibosheth.

[4]Mephibosheth was five years old at his father's death. David probably had never seen this child, because those were the years of his flight into the wilderness to escape Saul. The lameness of the child had prevented him from playing any significant part in public affairs during the days when his uncle Ish-Bosheth was ruling over the remnants of Saul's kingdom.

[5]Mephibosheth's proper name was *Merib-Baal* (1 Chr 8:34; 9:40).

hištaḥwāh) to pay him the homage due a king. As in v. 2, he referred to himself as **your servant**, and in the Hebrew prefaces those words with "behold" which the NIV leaves untranslated. David sensed that the man was afraid. Mephibosheth would not have remembered the affection between David and his father. David assured the man that he had nothing to fear. He intended to show kindness to him for the sake of his father Jonathan with whom David had a close friendship.

David's kindness expressed itself in two concrete actions. First, he ordered that **all the land** (lit., "field") formerly owned by Saul should be restored to Mephibosheth. Second, from that day on Mephibosheth would **eat at my table** (lit., "eat food at my table"), i.e., he would have free access to David's court.[6] The privilege of being the king's friend, and eating at his table, was an honor that would be more highly prized than even the possession of the estates. More suspicious commentators think that David intended to keep this grandson of Saul under careful scrutiny to prevent any conspiracy to recapture the throne for the house of Saul.

9:8 Mephibosheth expressed his gratitude for this manifestation of royal favor with the deepest obeisance. He could not believe his good fortune. Because of his handicap, he considered himself to be **a dead dog**, i.e., a person of no account (cf. 1 Sam 24:14; 2 Sam 3:8; 16:9).[7]

9:9-11 Mephibosheth was in no physical condition to oversee large land holdings. David again summoned **Saul's servant** (lit., "personal attendant"). He told Ziba that he had returned to Mephibosheth everything that belonged **to Saul and his family** (lit., "house"). Ziba was appointed Mephibosheth's estate manager. He, his sons and servants were ordered to **farm** (lit., "serve, work") **the land,** lit., "the ground," for Mephibosheth, and harvest the crops off those lands. **May be provided for** is literally "have food and eat it." This arrangement suggests that Ziba already occupied the land, the only change being that Mephibosheth would now receive the fruits instead of David. Thus the crippled son of Jonathan would have the income to support his family in the style of a prince. The parenthetical note regarding Ziba's sons and servants serves (1) to underscore

---

[6]This need not necessarily mean that he shared in the king's personal table, as did David at the court of Saul (1 Sam 20).

[7]In the ancient Near East, dogs did not have the beloved status that they have today. The use of the term "dog" as an expression of contempt or self-abasement is well attested in that time. See Anderson (142) for references.

the extent of the estate and the capacity of Ziba to manage it and (2) to indicate the prominence to which this former servant of Saul had risen. He now had several wives and many slaves of his own. Herein lies the seed for the rift between Mephibosheth and Ziba that will play out in subsequent chapters. From that day on, he **ate** (lit., "was eating") **at David's table** (see on v. 7).

9:12-13 Whether **Mica** was born before or after Mephibosheth came to reside at David's court cannot be ascertained. He is mentioned here to underscore the unending loyalty of David to the house of Jonathan. This son fathered numerous offspring who were leaders in the tribe of Benjamin until the captivity (1 Chr 8:35-40; 9:40-44). All the members of Ziba's household became servants of Mephibosheth. The Narrator mentions for the second time (cf. v. 3) that Mephibosheth **was crippled in both feet** because (1) ordinarily people with physical infirmities would not be permitted in the presence of a king and (2) Mephibosheth's condition would figure prominently in the narratives to follow (cf. 16:1-4; 19:24-30).

The account of David's kindness to Mephibosheth serves several purposes: (1) It demonstrates that David kept his word to Jonathan. (2) It introduces two characters (Ziba and Mephibosheth) who figure prominently in David's later struggles. (3) The account also underscores that David sensed no threat from the former royal family. (4) The kindness toward this son of Jonathan also indicates the soft side of David's personality.

2 SAMUEL 10

C. GLORIOUS VICTORIES (10:1-19)

A war against Ammon was briefly noticed in 2 Sam 8:12, but scholars debate whether that notice refers to the campaign of chs 10–12 or to a later third campaign.[1] The Narrator devotes considerable attention to the war with the Ammonites and their allies because (1) this was the fiercest struggle which Israel faced under David's reign and (2) it is in the background of David's great sin. The parallel to this unit is 1 Chr 19:1-19.

1. The Background of the Campaign (10:1-5)

10:1-2 Chapter 10 begins with the temporal marker **in the course of time** (see 2 Sam 2:1). Nahash, king of the Transjordanian kingdom of Ammon, died and was replaced by his son Hanun. The Nahash who attacked the city of Jabesh Gilead, early in Saul's reign was probably the father of this Nahash, and the grandfather of Hanun. Apparently Nahash had been a friend to David, probably because he hated Saul so much. **Show kindness** (*ḥesed*), as in 2 Sam 9:1,3, is faithfulness to a covenant. The **kindness** which Nahash had shown David may have been some unreported aid during David's flight from Saul, or during the war with Ish-Bosheth. In order to cement the alliance already existing between Israel and Ammon, David sent a delegation of high-ranking diplomats to **express his sympathy to Hanun** (lit., "comfort him") on the death of his father and to congratulate him on his ascent of the throne.

---

[1]Gordon (250) concludes that the respective sets of data are more satisfactorily explained by interpreting 8:3-8 as a reference to a third and final Israelite campaign against the Arameans.

10:3 Hanun's advisors raised two questions designed to create doubt about the sincerity of David's diplomats. The first question anticipates a negative answer, the second a positive one. **The city** is Rabbah, the strongly fortified capital of Ammon. Knowledge of its interior would be important to an enemy. Perhaps the nobles were suspicious (1) because of David's growing power; and (2) because of David's recent severe treatment of their neighbors and kinsmen, the Moabites (2 Sam 8:2). Convinced that they had come to gain military intelligence, Hanun seized the diplomats. He inflicted the greatest insult on these men and the king they represented by shaving off **half of each man's beard**. The reference is not to half of the length of the beard, but to one entire side. Adult Israelites wore a full beard. It was the mark of their manhood. One shaved his beard only as a sign of deepest mourning (Isa 15:2; Jer 41:5). Otherwise only children, women and eunuchs were beardless. Hanun increased the insult by cutting off a portion of the robes of the diplomats. Exactly how the robes were cut is not clear.[2] Severing the robe at the hips would accord with the treatment given war captives (Isa 20:4). It may be, however, that the robes were cut vertically, like the beards, so as to expose one side of the body, while the other side remained covered. The object then would be to make the envoys look ridiculous. In this condition Hanun sent the diplomats back to David. Hanun must have intended his actions to be a declaration of independence from Israel and therefore also a declaration of war.

10:5 When David heard what had happened to his diplomats, he sent messengers to meet them. He directed them to remain at Jericho until their beards had grown back. Then they could return to Jerusalem. He did not wish to expose these men to the humiliation of entering the capital looking as they did. **Jericho** had been destroyed by Joshua. He placed a curse on anyone who would rebuild, i.e., fortify, that city. An unfortified settlement at that location seems to have existed under the name "city of palm trees" (Judg 1:16; 3:13).[3]

---

[2]"In the middle as far as their hips" (NASB); "in the middle, even to their buttocks" (ASV); "in the middle at their hips" (NRSV); "in the middle at their buttocks" (NKJV); "cut off their robes halfway, just below the belt" (BV); "cut away half of their garments at the buttocks" (NJPS); "cut their clothes halfway up to the buttocks" (JB).

[3]For an archaeological survey of Jericho, see K.M. Kenyon, AOTS, 264-275.

2. The First Campaign against Ammon (10:6-14)

10:6 Bravado turned to panic when the Ammonites saw how seriously David treated the humiliation of his ambassadors. They **realized** (lit., "saw") that they **had become a stench in David's nostrils**, (lit., "they had made themselves stink"), i.e., had become offensive.[4] The Ammonites prepared for retaliation from David. **They hired** (lit., "sent and hired") twenty thousand foot soldiers from the Aramean cities of Beth Rehob and Zobah.[5] The region of **Beth Rehob** lay just north of Dan in Lebanon's Beqa valley (ZA, 117).[6] On **Zobah** see 2 Sam 8:3. The **king of Maacah** contributed a thousand men, and the city of **Tob** twelve thousand. The term foot soldiers (*raglî*) probably is the ancient equivalent of "troops," without specification as to what branch of service those troops belonged. The parallel text in Chronicles indicates that cavalry and chariotry came to the assistance of the Ammonites.[7] **Maacah** was a small Aramean kingdom south of Mt. Hermon, encompassing the areas east of the Jordan and probably also northern Galilee in the pre-Davidic period (cf. Deut 3:14; ZA, 29). **Tob** was the district northeast of Gilead between Aram (Syria) and Ammon (cf. Judg 11:5; ZA, 117).[8]

---

[4]The expression has been rendered "antagonized David against themselves" (BV); "made themselves repulsive" (NKJV); "had become odious to David" (ASV, NASB, NRSV); "incurred the wrath" (NJPS) or "enmity" (JB) of David. See comments on 1 Sam 13:4; 27:12.

[5]According to 1 Chr 19:6, Hanun paid a thousand talents of silver for the service of these soldiers. Anderson (147) points out that a thousand talents of silver could purchase some hundred thousand slaves in that day.

[6]This assumes that Beth Rehob is the same place mentioned in Num 13:21 and Judg 18:28. Others identify this place with Rehoboth by the river (Gen 36:37), a site in Mesopotamia. This would account for the reference to the Mesopotamians mentioned in 1 Chr 19:6. For discussion see G.W. Ahlström (397ff.).

[7]1 Chr 19:7 seems to suggest that the Aramean forces consisted of 32,000 "chariots." No mention is made of infantry. Since the number corresponds to the total number of "foot men" and "men" hired in the Samuel account, one should probably read: "And they hired 32,000 along with chariots." Another possibility is that the term "chariots" includes not just the vehicles themselves, but all the troops, both infantry and cavalry, which supported the chariots in battle. In either case, it would appear that the total mercenary force was 32,000 plus the additional thousand from the king of Maacah.

[8]On the location of Tob, see discussion of Ahlström, 400. The corre-

10:7 David was forced by the alliance of the Arameans and the Ammonites to act sooner than he had intended. David was obligated to liberate territories already lost, and to crush any potential of an invasion across the Jordan into the Israelite heartland. He dispatched Joab and **the entire army of fighting men** (lit., "all the host, the mighty men"). Elsewhere the "mighty men" are the elite corps that is distinguished from the host or conscripted militia. If the conjunction has dropped out here between "host" and "mighty men," then this passage also would distinguish between the two contingents of the army. Otherwise the meaning would be either (1) that the entire army of David was by this time considered an elite body or (2) that Joab took with him only the elite professional soldiers.

10:8 Joab found the enemy forces drawn up in battle formation at the entrance to the city gate. Chronicles names the city as Medeba (1 Chr 19:7) located twenty miles southwest of Rabbah (ZA, 117). Medeba was a city assigned to the tribe of Reuben at the time of the Israelite conquest (Josh 13:9). After humiliating David's ambassadors, Hanun had invaded Israelite territory and occupied this city. The Ammonites **came out** from the city[9] and massed directly in front of the gate. The Arameans positioned themselves in **the open country** (lit., "the field") around the city where their chariots and cavalry could more easily maneuver. They probably were in hiding until the right moment when they sprang up to surprise Joab.

10:9-12 Joab apparently marched into a trap. He found **battle lines** (lit., "the face of the battle") **in front of him** (lit., "from faces") and behind him. If he attacked either force separately, his rear would be exposed to the other. David's general showed great tactical skill in dealing with this military emergency. Certain select troops were deployed to the rear to fight the more formidable Aramean force. Joab personally led these troops. He deployed **the rest of the men** (lit., "people") against the Ammonites. They were under the command of his brother Abishai. The words **be strong and let us fight bravely** are lit., "be strong and let us show ourselves strong." The two generals must do their best for the people and **cities of our God,** i.e., the cities God had given to Israel. The cities in the tribal areas of

---

sponding text of Chronicles (1 Chr 19:6-7) omits the lesser known cities of Beth Rehob and Tob and adds Aram Naharaim (Mesopotamia).

[9]In spite of the distance between Rabbah and Medeba, Mauchline (246) still thinks the city here is Rabbah.

Reuben and Gad were in immediate danger. Should the Israelites taste defeat, the entire land of Israel would be open to occupation by the Arameans. The words **the LORD will do what is good in his sight** express both Joab's trust in the Lord and his resignation to God's will.

10:13-14 While Abishai held the Ammonites in check, Joab and his troops advanced to the rear against the Aramean troops, who fled before Joab. Hirelings generally place personal safety above whatever cause for which they fight. The rout of the Arameans freed Joab to help Abishai. The Ammonites also broke ranks and took refuge within the city walls. At this point Joab was not prepared to undertake a protracted siege of the city. So he withdrew the army and returned to Jerusalem.

3. The Defeat of the Arameans (10:15-19)

10:15-16 The war with the Arameans is probably the same as that recorded in 2 Sam 8:3-6. King Hadadezer personally reorganized the Aramean forces. He summoned additional troops from **beyond the River,** i.e., the Euphrates River.[10] The term **brought** (lit., "caused to go out") is a technical term for going out to war. These Mesopotamian auxiliary troops were under the direct command of **Shobach,** the commander of King Hadadezer's army. The Aramean forces assembled at **Helam** (exact location unknown[11]), a region or city on the northeast border of Israel.

10:17-18 David regarded this massing of troops at Helam as a threat to his kingdom. He **gathered all Israel,** i.e., the entire army. David personally led his forces across the Jordan and moved toward Helam on the edge of the desert. David surprised the enemy with the rapid mobilization and deployment of his troops. In the battle of Helam, the Arameans again fled from the Israelites, experiencing mammoth losses. Shobach, the commander of the Aramean forces, was also killed in the battle. Certain discrepancies between this passage and parallels in Chronicles are displayed in Table 7 (next page).

---

[10]Assyrian records from the time of David document that the Arameans had conquered various Assyrian districts. This accords well with the biblical tradition concerning Hadadezer's rule on both sides of the Euphrates. See A. Malamat, "The Kingdom of David and Solomon in Its Contact with Egypt and Aram Naharaim," *BA* 21 (Dec 1958), 97f.

[11]Baldwin (230) identifies Helam as modern 'Alma, some thirty-five miles east of the Sea of Galilee.

Table 7 AMMONITE WAR CASUALTIES		
	2 Sam 10:18 killed	1 Chr 19:18 killed
rekeb charioteers	700	7,000
pārāšîm horsemen (NIV note)	40,000	
raglî foot soldiers		40,000

The discrepancy between the seven hundred and the seven thousand charioteers may be a scribal miscopying in one or the other of the two texts (Haley, 382). Another possibility is that in Samuel the term *rekeb* means something like "(men of) chariots," while the same term in Chronicles means "charioteers."[12] The terms for "foot soldiers "and "horsemen" may be used interchangeably in these passages, referring to a combination of forces (Youngblood, 925f.). Samuel emphasizes the cavalry component, and Chronicles emphasizes the infantry component. The forty thousand would then be part foot soldiers and part horsemen.

10:19 After the battle of Helam, the kings who were vassals (servants) of Hadadezer transferred their allegiance to David, paying him the tribute which they previously had paid to the Aramean. The Israelites now effectively controlled a large portion of Aram (Syria). According to 2 Sam 8:6 (assuming that it refers to the same war), the kingdom of Damascus was subjugated and secured by military outposts. Hadadezer, though in a much weakened position, apparently still maintained his independence in Zobah.[13] With the Arameans firmly under control, a second campaign against the Ammonites could be undertaken without fear of involvement from their allies in the north (cf. 11:1).

---

[12]Z.C. Hodges, "Conflicts in the Biblical Account of the Ammonite-Syrian War," *BS* 119, 475 (1962): 241-242.

[13]A. Malamat believes that David took over Hadadezer's kingdom structurally as well as geographically. "Aspects of the Foreign Policies of David and Solomon," *JNES* (1963) 2. Other historians (e.g., Miller and Hays) are skeptical of such a total incorporation.

2 SAMUEL 11

D. PERSONAL FAILING (11:1-27)

The Bible in no way glosses over the heinousness of David's sin. The ugly episode recorded in this chapter is the key to the history of the rest of David's reign. Herein lies the explanation of the sudden gloom which settles over his kingdom. David's sin with Bathsheba occurred ca. 995 B.C. David was forty-five at the time.

1. The Setting of the Sin (11:1)

11:1 Normally military operations were suspended in the rainy season. When the rainy season ended in the **spring** (lit., "the turn of the year came"),[1] the troops would make their moves. Grass for pack animals was abundant. Roads again were passable. Armies could raid fields for provisions. The phrase **when kings** (lit., "messengers")[2] **go off to war** may point to David's self-indulgence which is the proximate cause of the crimes which follow. Rather than leading forth the army, David sent Joab and **the king's men** (lit., "servants"), i.e., either (1) troops normally assigned to guarding David or

---

[1]The text does not suggest that the attack against Ammon took place in the Spring immediately following the defeat of the Ammonites at Medeba (2 Sam 10:9-14). David may have been occupied in Aramean territories during the following year (2 Sam 8:8; 10:15-19). During this time Judah seems to have come under attack from the Edomites. See comments on 8:13-14. These facts would point to a respite of about a year and a half in operations against the Ammonites. Kirkpatrick, however, places the assault after the new year (March-April) following the first campaign.

[2]Most commentators follow the *Qere* reading of the text which necessitates the dropping of a letter from the word. Fokkelman (1:50-51) defends the *Kethibh* reading. He understands the text to be saying that David sent forth the troops a year after the messengers had made their disastrous visit to Rabbah.

(2) high ranking officers.[3] **The whole Israelite army** is literally "all Israel," i.e., troops gathered from all the tribes. Before beginning the siege of Rabbah, Joab **destroyed the Ammonites**, i.e., devastated the country, putting all whom they found to the sword. The Ammonites retreated behind the walls of Rabbah, their capital, where they hoped they could outlast the siege efforts of Joab.[4] During this time David remained in Jerusalem.

2. The Magnitude of the Personal Failings (11:2-27)

The Sin of Adultery (11:2-4)

11:2-4 One evening is literally "at the time of evening." **From** in both instances in v. 2 is literally "from upon." In Palestine it was the custom to take a siesta in the heat of the day (cf. 2 Sam 4:5). Upon awakening from his siesta, David went to the roof of the palace to enjoy the cool evening breezes. Dwellings had flat roofs accessible by either interior or exterior stairs (cf. 1 Sam 9:25). **Walked around** in the Heb. is a verb form which connotes (1) activity undertaken for one's own personal benefit and (2) unstructured activity. The palace was no doubt built on the highest point of the city and commanded a view of the courts of the surrounding houses.[5] On the roof or in the courtyard of a house below, the wife of one of David's high officers was **bathing**. Surely the woman at this point is without blame.[6] Rooftops were

---

[3]The term "servant" in Oriental courts was used to designate those high in rank near the king's person. Cf. R.P. Smith, 265.

[4]One of the most significant witnesses to the organized political authority and vitality of the Ammonite state at this time is the strong line of circular tower fortresses forming a well integrated defensive system protecting the western approaches to Rabbah. These fortresses contain massive stones ($10 \times 3 \times 3$ ft.) the positioning of which would have required a most advanced technology. These towers "in arrangement, design, composition, strength and number remain unparalleled by any similar phenomenon in Western Palestine." G.M. Landes, "The Material Civilization of the Ammonites," *BA* 24 (1961): 68-72.

[5]From his roof David could have seen much of what was going on in town. Jebusite Jerusalem was a small and narrow city (459×164 yds.). Archaeologists estimate the population at this time to have been about 2500. See Ahlström, 486, n. 1.

[6]Hertzberg (309) and others suggest that Bathsheba is not without blame and may even have planned to use her bathing to entice the king. Cf. G.

secluded, private areas. Probably neither she nor her husband ever suspected that what went on there could be (or would be) observed from the palace. **The woman was very beautiful**. Her physical charms excited sensual desire as David played the role of a voyeur.

David sent someone to find out about the woman. It is unusual that Bathsheba was identified to him by the name of her father as well as that of her husband. This suggests that her father **Eliam** is the same Eliam who was the son of Ahithophel (2 Sam 23:34), one of David's closest advisors who later betrayed him.[7] Bathsheba was also the wife of one of David's finest officers (cf. 2 Sam 28:39), **Uriah the Hittite**.[8] His name (meaning "Yahweh is light") suggests that he had renounced the religion of his ancestors to embrace the Living God.

The knowledge that Bathsheba was a married woman, and that her husband was a trusted servant of the king did not deter David. He **sent messengers to get** (lit., "take") **her.** Bathsheba appears not to have offered any resistance either because of (1) personal vanity or (2) fear of refusing the demands of such a powerful man. The writer explains that Bathsheba **had purified[9] herself from her uncleanness**. This detail is noted (1) to explain the bath of the preceding verse, (2) to underscore the hypocrisy of the incident, and/or (3) to underscore that Uriah could not have been the father of the child. Under the law of Moses, a woman was required to bathe after her monthly period before her husband was permitted to sleep with her. How ironic. David broke no ritual rule in sleeping with this woman; but he did break the seventh commandment. After she slept with the king, Bathsheba went back to her home. Kings of other

---

Nicol, "The Alleged Rape of Bathsheba: Some Observations on Ambiguity in Biblical Narrative," *JSOT* 73 (1997): 43-54.

[7]Bathsheba is spelled *Bathshua* as in 1 Chr 3:5, and she is said to be the daughter of "Ammiel" ("people of God"), which is a transposition of "Eliam" ("God of the people"), both names being compounded of עַם (*'ām*, "people") and אֵל (*'ēl*, "God"),

[8]4QSam[a] adds that Uriah was Joab's armor-bearer (cf. Josephus *Ant.* 7.7.1).

[9]The Hebrew employs a participle which has more accurately been rendered by the NRSV "she was purifying herself after her period." This suggests that the messengers interrupted Bathsheba's ritual bath to bring her to the king. Another possibility is that Bathsheba performed the ritual bathing after the sexual intercourse as required by Lev 15:18. Cf. Spense (471) and KD (416).

lands could take any woman they pleased, married or not. Israel's kings were bound by the law which considered adultery as a capital crime. David could not take this married woman into his harem.

The Attempted Cover-up (11:5-13)

11:5-9 Bathsheba is not named in v. 5. To David she had been merely **the woman**, rather than a person (Baldwin, 232). She sent word to David that he might devise some plan to shield her from the consequences of her sin (Lev 20:10). Both she and the king were in great alarm over the pregnancy. **I am pregnant** are the only words Bathsheba speaks in this narrative.

The king quickly set in motion a plan by which he hoped to cover up his transgression. He sent a messenger to Joab across the Jordan river at Rabbah. He ordered Uriah the Hittite[10] to return to Jerusalem. The pretext was that David wanted a detailed report on the status of the siege. The real purpose was to give Uriah an opportunity of spending a few days with his wife, so that it might be supposed that the child she was carrying was his. The officer reported to the king without first stopping to greet his wife.

David used his initial meeting with Uriah as an opportunity to size up his potential adversary. He asked Uriah a series of questions about the war effort. The answer Uriah gave is not included in the narrative which signals that David was not paying any particular attention to his account. David probably hoped that Uriah would be like himself; instead he proved to be a man of integrity, whose first loyalty was to the king's interests rather than to his own pleasure (Baldwin, 233).

Following his report, David encouraged Uriah to go down to his house to **wash his feet**. Obviously Uriah still had battlefield grime on him. Washing the feet after a long, dusty journey was a way of relaxing and preparing for meals and for retiring for the night. Here, however, the expression meant more than merely bathing the feet, as can be seen by Uriah's comment in v. 11.[11] David sent **a gift** of food which was a special mark of favor from a superior (cf. Gen

---

[10]Several times Uriah is referred to as "the Hittite" (vv. 3,6,17,24) as if to emphasize that this foreigner had stronger principles than did Israel's king.

[11]M. Pope (515), commenting on the same expression in S of S 5:3, understands the phrase "wash your feet" as a euphemism for marital intercourse. Gordon (254) thinks the expression refers to a ritual ablution releasing a soldier from the vow of sexual abstinence during a military campaign.

43:34). By giving this gift David was (1) trying to relieve his guilty conscience and (2) encouraging Uriah to have an enjoyable evening with his wife.

Three times the text emphasizes that Uriah did not go down to his house that night. He spent the night with the soldiers and others who were the king's attendants. All of them would be eager to learn of the news of friends and relatives who were on the front lines in Ammon. The servants' quarters must have been off to one side of the main entrance to the palace.

11:10-11 David expressed surprise and displeasure that Uriah had not done as men usually do on their return from a **distance** (lit., "way"[12]). When questioned about his reluctance to avail himself of the comforts of home, Uriah cites his loyalty to his comrades. Men from **Israel and Judah** were staying in tents on the campaign at Rabbah.[13] Even **the ark of God** was in the field (cf. 1 Sam 4:3-4) signaling that the war with Ammon was considered a holy war. Perhaps David sent it along with its priestly attendants so that Joab might make inquiry of the priestly oracle concerning strategic moves during the course of the siege (cf. 1 Sam 14:18). Uriah did not feel right going to his house to eat and drink and to sleep with his wife when his fellow soldiers could not enjoy these same privileges.[14] **Tents** may be a proper noun, "Succoth," identifying the geographical location of the Israelite base camp (Youngblood, 934).[15] **My lord's men,** lit.,

---

[12]The Heb. term is used elsewhere of military campaigns (Judg 4:9; 1 Sam 21:5 (6); 1 Kgs 8:44), although English versions do not always give this sense to it.

[13]The separate mention of *Israel* and *Judah* gives no indication of a late date for this book. These two parts of the nation had already been separated, and even hostile to each other. Had Uriah been in David's service since he was king only at Hebron, it would be most natural for him to refer to the entire nation as "Israel and Judah."

[14]Others think that Uriah may have learned of the night visit of Bathsheba to the palace from one of his friends in the palace guard. If doubts about his wife's fidelity were the true reason for his refusal to sleep at home, the answer which he gave to David must be considered a chivalrous and discreet avoidance of a delicate subject.

[15]Cf. the NIV margin at 1 Kgs 20:12,16. Yadin (274-275) presents the case for "Succoth" here. One would not expect to find the ark in a סֻכָּה (*sukkāh*, "hut") but in an אֹהֶל (*'ōhel*, "tent"). Succoth is located about twenty miles north-northwest of Rabbah. See ZA, 53. It might be possible to understand Uriah's words to mean that the national militia (Israel and Judah) was being

"the servants of my lord," i.e., David, are probably the same as "the king's men" in v. 1. **Lie with my wife** would be a jarring, albeit unintentional, rebuke of David's adultery. Uriah's refusal to sleep at home may reflect the old rule that those who engaged in holy war should avoid contact with women (cf. Deut 23:10-15; 1 Sam 21:5).[16] Uriah swore an oath[17] that he would not go down to his house. The soldier's conduct suggests that his suspicions had been aroused.

11:12-13 His first attempt at cover-up having failed, David tried again. He ordered Uriah to remain one more day before returning to the army in the field. That night, however, David entertained Uriah at the palace. Although Uriah would not seek the comforts of his own house, he had no scruples in the king's house. David got Uriah drunk on wine in the hopes that he would forget his oath and go down to his wife. David adds sin to sin in order to accomplish his ugly goal. However, "Uriah drunk is more pious than David sober" (Ackroyd, 102).

The Sin of Murder (11:14-24)

David's Orders to Joab (11:14-17)

11:14-17 When David realized now that he would never succeed in getting Uriah to visit his wife, he resorted to an even more wicked scheme. David composed a letter to Joab and sent it by Uriah. The letter ordered Joab to put Uriah where the fighting was the fiercest. Then Joab was to withdraw from him so he would be left to face the enemy alone. Uriah would then be killed by the Ammonites. David did not explain his orders to Joab. All the general could conclude is that in some manner Uriah had incurred the wrath of the king on his recent visit to Jerusalem. Presumably the dispatch to Joab was sealed or if not, Uriah could not read.

---

held in reserve, encamped in booths, while Joab and the professional troops were in the open field in an advance position (Cf. Gordon, 254).

[16]Anderson (154) thinks that David was attempting to lure Uriah into an infringement of "war regulations" which might enable the king to get rid of him by legal means. The penalty for a soldier violating the regulation about sexual abstinence during war is not stated in the Bible.

[17]The form of the oath has been abbreviated in the NIV. Literally, the oath formula was "as you live and as your soul lives." This form of the oath formula does not occur elsewhere.

While Joab had the city under siege is literally "and it was in Joab's keeping watch unto the city." This probably refers to the assignment of his men to their posts in the siege operations. Joab put Uriah at the place where he knew the strongest defenders of the city were fighting. He situated his men in such a way as to invite the Ammonites to attack them. When the men of the city sallied forth to try to drive off the attackers, some of **David's army** (lit., "servants") were killed. Among them was Uriah. Joab did not carry out David's orders to the letter. He did not order his men to retreat thus leaving Uriah exposed to enemy fire. That plan would have been difficult to carry out without being charged by his men with treachery. He devised a plan which would accomplish David's purpose, but which would be blamed on bad generalship. Joab's plan, however, involved a greater loss of life than did David's. For this reason Joab feared the reaction of the king when he heard the battle report.

Joab's Report to David (11:18-24)

11:18-21 Joab sent David a full account of the battle. He knew that David would explode in anger when he heard about the many casualties. Joab told the messenger what to say when David asked why the troops had gone so near to the walls. Joab surmised that the king would compare this folly to the stupidity that had gotten Abimelech killed by a millstone thrown from the wall of Thebez by a woman[18] (Judg 9:50-53). The Abimelech incident must have been cited frequently in Israelite camps as an example of military recklessness. **Jerub-Besheth** is "Jerubbaal" in Judg 6:32.[19] The messenger was to save the worst news (from his point of view) till last. After the initial rage had settled he would inform David of the death of one of his bravest soldiers, viz., Uriah the Hittite.

11:22-24 The messenger did as Joab instructed him. He reported to David how the Ammonites came out against the Israelites, but **we drove them back** (lit., "we were against them"), i.e., to the city gate. The Ammonite **archers** (lit., "shooters")[20] then rained down arrows

---

[18]The fact that a woman was involved in the death of Abimelech hints that Joab had guessed the reason for the death warrant which had been issued against Uriah.

[19]On the substitution of "Besheth" or "Bosheth" for "Baal," see notes on 2 Sam 2:8; 9:6.

[20]Goldman (248) thinks in this case the weapons were more likely to have been catapults and stones than bows and arrows.

on Joab's men **from** (lit., "from upon") the wall. Some of the king's men died. Following Joab's instructions, the messenger quickly added, **Uriah the Hittite is dead!**

The Aftermath of the Incident (11:25-27)

11:25-27 Don't let this upset you is lit., "do not let this matter be evil in your eyes." In his reply to the messenger David did not register the explosive anger which Joab had anticipated. He professed to be satisfied with Joab's report. He should not let the losses at the wall upset him. **The sword devours one as well as another**, i.e., anyone can get killed in a battle. Such are the fortunes of war. Joab should continue to press the attack against Rabbah and destroy the place. This message from David was intended to placate his own conscience as well as give encouragement to Joab. The conclusion of this war against Rabbah is recorded in 12:24-31.

The NIV condenses v. 26 which, in the Hebrew, twice mentions the name of the murdered man and three times underscores his relationship to Bathsheba: "When the wife of Uriah heard that Uriah her husband was dead she mourned for her husband." In this way the Narrator distances himself from the illicit liaison and pays his respect to Uriah. Bathsheba went through the ritual of public mourning over the death of her husband. How long this lasted is not indicated.[21] After that time of mourning, David **had her brought** (lit., "sent and gathered her") to his house. His scheme to make the child look legitimate required swift action on his part. As was the case with Abigail (1 Sam 25), the immediate marriage to Bathsheba would not necessarily have raised a question in that culture. David may have been praised for taking into his harem the widow of his servant. She became David's wife and bore him a son. David thought he had gotten by with his sins of adultery and murder. **The thing David had done displeased** (lit., "was evil in the eyes of") **the LORD** (cf. v. 25). This statement not only expresses a moral judgment on what transpired, but it furnishes the key to all that is recorded through ch 20.

---

[21] Public mourning for Aaron and Moses were for thirty days (Num 20:29; Deut 34:8) while that for Jacob and for Saul was seven days (Gen 50:10; 1 Sam 31:13).

2 SAMUEL 12

E. PROPHETIC REBUKE (12:1-14)

The Lord left David almost a whole year in his sin before sending his prophet to confront him about his misdeeds. In Ps 32 David describes the miserable state of his heart during this period. Before there could be forgiveness, the sin had to be exposed and rebuked.

1. Nathan's Parable (12:1-4)

12:1-4 To charge the king with his transgression, Nathan resorted to a parable by which he led the king to pronounce a death sentence upon himself. The genius of Nathan's parable was that it so aptly depicted the baseness of David's behavior without the latter's realizing it. Nothing in his words suggested that the prophet was speaking a parable. He approached David as if to ask his decision in a case of oppression of a poor man by a rich neighbor. The parable, carefully constructed with only sixty-one words, concerned two men, one rich and one poor. The rich man had flocks of sheep and cattle. The poor man had one little ewe lamb which he treated as a pet.[1] The custom of keeping a pet sheep in the house apparently was quite common. The lamb shared **his food**, lit., "piece of bread," i.e., his meager fare. He treated the lamb as **a daughter**. A traveler[2] came

---

[1] The verb **bought** suggests that the lamb was not a gift or an inherited possession, but something which the poor man had to buy out of his meager savings. The verb rendered **he raised it** means lit., "he made it live, he revived it." This may mean that he saved its life, and this may provide the reason for the adoption of the lamb as a family pet.

[2] Three expressions are used in the Hebrew to describe the visitor: (1) "traveler" (lit., "walker"), (2) "wayfarer" (NASB), and (3) "the man who had come to him." Nathan probably uses these terms chiefly to diversify his

427

to visit the rich man. Instead of preparing a meal using meat from one of his own sheep or cattle, he stole the ewe lamb from his poor neighbor and prepared it to serve to his guest.

2. David's Anger (12:5-6)

12:5-6 Understanding the story as an actual case of oppression, David's anger **burned** against that rich man. In an outburst of anger he swore an oath to the effect that this particular man was worthy of death, lit., "is a son of death." The man, however, had not committed a capital crime. Hence the judicial decision was that he must pay his neighbor **four times over**[3] for that stolen lamb (cf. Exod 22:1).

3 Nathan's Application (12:7-9)

12:7-9 How shocked David must have been when Nathan courageously announced the condemnation in two simple Hebrew words: **You are the man!** This may well be the most dramatic sentence in the Old Testament.

So as to convict the king, not only of a heinous crime against his subjects, but of base ingratitude toward the Lord, God's many favors to David are enumerated. The list begins with two assertions, both of which contain an emphatic first person pronoun. God had **anointed** David king over Israel. He had **delivered** him from the hand of Saul. Like the rich man in the parable, David had been blessed beyond measure. God had given David (1) deliverance from the hand of Saul; (2) your master, i.e., Saul's house; (3) Saul's wives;[4] and (4) the house of Israel and Judah, i.e., the entire nation. The custom was that when a king died his successor inherited his harem. Though David could

---

language, but it has served as a handle for much allegorizing in the past both in Jewish and Christian circles. See R.P. Smith (287).

[3]The LXX has "sevenfold." This reading is defended by Carlson (163-169) on the basis of the structure of chs. 13–21 and P.W. Coxon on the basis of a play on the name Bathsheba. "A Note on Bathsheba in 2 Sam 12:1-6," *Biblica* 62 (1981): 247-250.

[4]Saul's wives would have included Ahinoam (1 Sam 14:50) and probably his concubine Rizpah (2 Sam 3:7) and possibly others who are not named in the text.

have married Saul's wives, there is no evidence that he actually did so. God would have **given** (lit., "added") him even more.

Great as was David's sin against Uriah and Bathsheba, his sin against God was greater. His actions **despise the word of the LORD** in violating three of the commandments of the Decalogue: the tenth, seventh and sixth. He had struck down Uriah the Hittite and taken his wife as his own. David had **killed** (lit., "murdered") the man **with the sword of the Ammonites**. He was as guilty of murder as if he had slain the man with his own hand. Still worse, he employed the enemies of God's people as the instruments for the commission of this heinous act. **Sword** is not to be taken literally since Uriah was actually shot with an arrow (2 Sam 11:24).

4. Nathan's Announcement (12:10-12)

12:10-12 To despise the word of God (v. 9) is to **despise** Yahweh personally. The threefold penalty answers to David's sin. First, for the murder of Uriah the sword would never depart from David's **house**, i.e., not his descendants, but his immediate family. **Never** (עַד עוֹלָם, *'ad 'ôlām*; lit., "forever")[5] is to be understood relatively, as equivalent to "all the days of your life" (cf. 1 Sam 1:22). Second, because he had brought calamity upon the army and the nation, out of his own household the Lord would bring calamity upon David. The fulfillment was the rebellion which Absalom launched against his father. Third, because he had committed adultery, God would take his wives (i.e., permit his wives to be taken) and give them to one who was close to him. David had committed his sin with Bathsheba in secret, but this terrible punishment would happen to his wives **in broad daylight** (lit., "before the sun") in the sight of the entire nation.

5. David's Forgiveness (12:13-14)

12:13-14 David now realized the magnitude of his sin. He sincerely confessed that sin (cf. Ps 51). His words are few, but they are evidence of a thoroughly broken spirit. He made no excuses. He

---

[5]Polzin (*David*, 81) points out the irony that the very next "forever" to follow the eight forevers of 2 Sam 7 in God's promises to David is the promise of perpetual punishment for David's house.

asked for no sympathy or mitigation of the sentence against him. As an adulterer and murderer David deserved the death sentence. As absolute monarch he had no reason to fear any such punishment from judicial officers. The Lord alone could execute that sentence against him, and the Lord had now forgiven the sin. The sentence he had pronounced upon himself was remitted because of (1) David's heartfelt repentance, (2) God's fatherly grace, and (3) the promises previously bestowed upon David by this same prophet (2 Sam 7:11-12). Nathan then assured David that the Lord had taken away his sin. **You are not going to die**, i.e., he would not be smitten dead because of his sin with Bathsheba. The fact that God does not hesitate to strike people down for what might be regarded lesser infractions (cf. 2 Sam 6:7) makes his forbearance here all the more noteworthy (Youngblood, 946).

David's actions had caused the Lord's enemies then, and even to this day, to **show utter contempt** for true religion.[6] Yahweh's enemies include unbelieving Israelites as well as those who worshiped other gods. David's crime had been against a Hittite (v. 9) and he had used the Ammonites, without their knowledge, to promote his own ends. The point is that David must act honorably even with regard to the Lord's enemies. God would punish him by taking away from him the child who recently had been born. Thus the visible occasion for any further blasphemy against the Lord and his people would be removed from the scene. This is not the case of an innocent child being punished for the sins of the father, for that concept was abhorrent to Mosaic faith (Ezek 18). The death of the adulterous offspring would demonstrate to all skeptics that the righteous rule of Yahweh could reach and punish the king himself.

F. DIVINE DISCIPLINE (12:15-23)

1. David's Prayers for the Sick Child (12:15-17)

12:15-17 The last mentioned punishment was inflicted immediately. After Nathan departed, **the Lord struck the child.** The words **that**

---

[6]Anderson (163) takes "the enemies of Yahweh" to be a euphemism for Yahweh himself. For a parallel, see notes on 1 Sam 25:22. By his actions David had shown contempt for Yahweh. The verb, however, is in a form (Pi'el) which sometimes has a causative connotation. See discussion in Hertzberg (315).

Uriah's wife had borne to David point to the fact that the sin of David was about to claim another innocent life. The child became very ill. This is one case in which Scripture associates illness with the sin of a parent, but as in the case of the man born blind (cf. John 9:2), the purpose was the glory of God. The biblical writer does not hesitate to attribute directly to the Lord the sickness of this child.

David pleaded with God for the life of the child. He **fasted** and slept **on the ground**.[7] The words **into his house** are not represented in the Hebrew text.[8] An inner courtyard of the palace is probably meant. This was David's acknowledgment before all his subjects of his iniquity and of his sorrow for it. He assumed the position of a condemned criminal. His grief was for his own sin as well as for the condition of the child. **The elders of his household** — the oldest and most influential servants — tried to get him up from the ground, but he refused. He would not eat any food with them.

2. David's Reaction to the Child's Death (12:18-23)

12:18-20 On the seventh day of illness, the child died. David's servants were afraid to tell him. He had been so upset by the sickness of the child that the servants feared that he might do something **desperate** (lit., "evil"), like harm himself. David noticed the advisors whispering among themselves. He guessed that the child had died. Reluctantly his advisors confirmed David's suspicions.

Then David got up from the ground. He **washed, put on lotions** (perfumes) **and changed his clothes**, i.e., he laid aside all the signs of penitential grief. Next he went to the house of the Lord (the tent in which the ark was housed) and worshiped. He then returned home and requested food to be brought to him. These actions indicated that his fasting and prayer during the sickness of the child were primarily an indication of personal repentance.

12:21-23 The servants could not understand David's behavior. There should have been a seven-day mourning period for the child. David, however, had engaged in actions which were normally curtailed during mourning. Why would he fast and weep while the child

---

[7]4QSam[a] and some Greek texts add that David lay "in sackcloth." Cf. vv. 18,20.

[8]The last half of v. 16 might be rendered literally: "and he went and he spent the night and he laid on the ground."

COLLEGE PRESS NIV COMMENTARY

was still living, and then resume normal activities immediately after hearing that the child was dead?

In reply David gave the palace officials "a short sermon on the futility of prayers for the dead" (Gordon, 259). David explained that while the child was alive there was always a chance that the Lord would hear his prayers and be gracious and allow the child to live. Now the child was dead. Nothing David could do would bring that child back from the dead He was confident that one day he would go to be reunited with the child in the afterlife (heaven). David's statement suggests a belief in infant salvation and immortality.

G. TOKENS OF GRACE (12:24-31)

1. The Birth of Solomon (12:24-25)

12:24-25 David went to comfort his wife Bathsheba. The text leaves open the way in which David expressed his sympathy to Bathsheba. In time[9] he went to her and slept with her.[10] She gave birth to a son. They named the child **Solomon** ("the peaceful"). David regarded the birth of this child as a pledge that he should now become a partaker again of peace with God. Although Solomon most likely was not born until after the Ammonite war was concluded, his birth is mentioned here because of what immediately precedes. The Lord loved that child and indicated such by giving him a special name: **Jedidiah** ("beloved of Yah"). This name was intended only to express the divine acceptance of Solomon; it never came into use as a personal title. **He sent word through Nathan** is literally "he sent by the hand of Nathan." The giving of such a name was a declaration on the part of Yahweh that he loved Solomon. From this David discerned that he had been restored to fellowship with the Lord.

---

[9]Kirkpatrick (2:132) estimates that Solomon's birth did not take place until some four or five years after the death of the first child.

[10]In 2 Sam 5:14 and 1 Chr 3:5 Solomon is the last of four sons of Bathsheba. Some take this to mean that Bathsheba had given David three sons before the birth of Solomon. Some place the birth of these three sons before the death of the child; others, after his death.

2. The Conquest of Rabbah (12:26-31)

This unit chronologically follows ch. 11. The author wished to wrap up the story of the sin with Bathsheba and its consequences before he concluded the story of this war against the capital of Ammon.

Joab's Invitation to David (12:26-28)

12:26-28 Joab had captured **the royal citadel,** lit., "the king's city," i.e., the entire capital of the Ammonite kingdom with the exception of the acropolis. He also captured the city's **water supply,** lit., "the city of waters," i.e., the fortress which guarded the water supply for the rest of Rabbah. This capture made the fall of the capital imminent. Joab then sent messengers to David to inform him of the result of the siege and to encourage him to bring the rest of the army. He wanted David to have the credit for capturing this major city (cf. 2 Sam 5:9).

David's Subjugation of Ammon (12:29-31)

12:29-31 So David mustered **the entire army,** i.e., all the soldiers who had remained behind in the land, and went to Rabbah. He attacked and captured the acropolis.[11] He took the crown of **their king,** lit., "Malcam" (cf. BV, JB, NRSV), a variant of Milcom (1 Kgs 11:5) the Ammonite god.[12] The crown weighed one **talent** (about 75 lbs.[13]). **It was set with precious stones** is literally "and a precious

---

[11]So far as is known, this is the only time in the six centuries of Ammonite history when their ring of defensive fortresses was breached and their capital taken. G.M. Landes, "The Material Civilization of the Ammonites," *BA* 24 (1961): 74. See note on 2 Sam 11:1.

[12]If the crown here mentioned was in fact that of the king, most likely its great weight required that it be fixed on a canopy above his throne. The idea that the crown was that of the Ammonite deity has been rejected by most commentators because it is thought unlikely that David would have worn the crown of an idol. Nevertheless, it is not so unlikely if the wearing of the crown showed the superiority of Yahweh over Milcom (Baldwin, 246). A more formidable argument against the view that the crown was that of the deity is that a god-statue with its crown was usually made in one piece (Ahlström, 485, n.3). Another way of interpreting the phrase is that the crown of Milcom was the crown worn by Milcom's viceroy, viz., the king of Ammon. For the Egyptian style of the Ammonite crown, see S. Horn, "The Crown of the King of the Ammonites," AUSS 11 (1973): 174.

[13]*IDB* 4:830-833 s.v., "Weights and Measures."

stone" (cf. NRSV, JB, BV). Perhaps the meaning is that the crown had a notable stone. **It was placed on David's head** may refer to a symbolic ceremony in which the heavy crown was placed over the head of David. This line may also be interpreted to mean that the notable jewel from that Ammonite crown was placed in David's crown as a symbol of his victory. From this conquest David carried away a great quantity of plunder.

The NIV has given an interpretive paraphrase of the second half of v. 31 which is probably correct.[14] David consigned to forced labor those captured in Ammon. Josephus (*Ant.* 7.7.5) speaks of David torturing the Ammonites before putting them to death. The Ammonites may have been set to raze their own city with iron picks and mattocks. The word translated **brickmaking**, variously rendered in English versions,[15] is now known to refer to the brick mold, the wooden frame in which the clay was pressed into shape.

---

[14]Lit. the Hebrew reads, "he put them in the saw," etc. KD (425) emend the text and read: "he sawed them in pieces with the saw . . . ." "He made them work at brickmaking" is literally "he made [them] pass through the brickkiln." KD understand this to mean that David burnt them in the brick-klin. Those who understand the text to indicate that David tortured the Ammonite captives cite 1 Chr 20:3, "he brought out the people who were in it, and cut them with saws . . . ." Here, however, the verb rendered "cut them" is of uncertain meaning. The NRSV, BV, JB, NKJV and NJPS support the NIV understanding of v. 31. The ASV and NASB maintain the ambiguity of the Hebrew. See G.C. O'Ceallaigh, "And so David did to all the cities of Ammon," *VT* 12 (1962): 179-189.

[15]"Made them cross over to the brick works" (NKJV); "made them pass through the brickklin" (ASV, NASB); "sent them to the brickworks" (NRSV). "forcing them to keep working at the brick molds" (BV); "employed them in" [or "assigned them to"] "brick making" (JB, NJPS).

2 SAMUEL 13

X. THE COVENANT WITH DAVID IN JEOPARDY
(13:1–20:26)

A. TESTED BY FAMILY TURMOIL (13:1–14:33)

There is no indication as to the passage of time between this and the previous chapter. That David now had ruled over all Israel for about fifteen years seems a reasonable estimate (R.P. Smith 324). It is probable that the events narrated here occurred soon after the war with the Ammonites and David's marriage with Bathsheba. Clearly attention shifts here from affairs of state to family problems which tested in both the short term and the long term the covenant made with the house of David.

1. Amnon's Plot (13:1-10)

Amnon's Lust (13:1-4)

13:1-2 The Hebrew word order in v. 1 is the reverse of the NIV. Literally the verse opens: "And it came to pass after this, that Absalom the son of David had a fair sister." Absalom and Tamar were the children of Maacah, the daughter of Talmai, king of Geshur. Amnon, David's firstborn, was the son of Ahinoam the Jezreelitess (2 Sam 3:2). He fell in love with his half-sister Tamar. He **became frustrated to the point of illness** is literally "and it was narrow to Amnon, even to becoming sick." In Scripture narrowness points to distress, while in joy there is a sense of largeness and expansion.

13:3-4 Jonadab, Amnon's friend and cousin,[1] was a **very shrewd** (חָכָם, *ḥākām*) but unprincipled man. The word indicates sagacity

---

[1]Jonadab was the son of Jesse's third son Shimeah, who is called Shammah in 1 Sam 16:9.

whether rightly or wrongly used. Every morning Jonadab observed how sickly and tired Amnon looked.[2] When he inquired about the condition, Amnon told Jonadab about his attraction for Tamar. The reference to Tamar as **Absalom's sister** underscores the special care and protection of the uterine brother in a polygamous society. He had greater responsibility than the father for guarding the interests and honor of his sister.

Jonadab's Suggestion (13:5)

13:5 Jonadab had a plan which would bring Amnon and Tamar together. Amnon should **go to bed** (lit., "lie down") and pretend to be ill. David apparently was in the habit of visiting any of his children when they were sick. When this occurred, Amnon should ask his father to have Tamar come and give him something to eat. He should act as if he wanted her to prepare the food in his sight, and then feed him. A sick man's request was likely to be granted with a less strict regard for proprieties. Referring to Tamar as **my sister** was designed to hoodwink David. Perhaps the idea is that a sick person craves certain food, and will eat only what he craves. On the other hand, Ackroyd (121) suggests that there may have been a belief that food prepared by a virgin in the presence of a sick man might have a special curative quality.

Amnon's Duplicity (13:6-7)

13:6-7 Since he was not returning immediately to the palace, David naively **sent word to Tamar**. He suspected nothing. The phrase **make some special bread** contains a verb and noun derived from the Hebrew word for "heart." The terms are used only here. Some envision heart-shaped cakes (a specialty of Tamar?); others think of a meal such as the heart might desire, i.e., whatever the sick person might request. McCarter (2:322) argues that dumplings are intended.[3]

Tamar's Gullibility (13:8-10)

13:8-10 Tamar was probably flattered to respond to this special request for her culinary talents. When she entered Amnon's house,

---

[2]The Hebrew is literally "Why are you thus sick, O son of the king in the morning [and] in the [following] morning?"

[3]McCarter bases his conclusion on the use of the term בָּשֵׁל (bāšal) (v. 8) which normally means "boil."

he was lying down. She set about preparing to bake her specialty. Six verbs set forth the girl's bustling activity. Sandwiched in the midst of these verbs is the phrase **in his sight** implying that Amnon was watching her every movement. She took some dough and **kneaded** (worked it back and forth), and **baked** (lit., "boiled/cooked") it. Then she set the cakes on a table in full view of Amnon. Probably a servant took the food into the bed chamber and offered it to the prince. That he refused to eat seemed natural enough in a whimsical invalid, and for the same reason his next order apparently aroused no suspicion in Tamar. As sick as he was he could not bear all these people around! With a plural imperative,[4] Amnon ordered everyone out of the house. He then summoned Tamar into the bedroom so that he might eat the food directly from her hand.

2. Tamar's Rape (13:11-19)

Tamar's Protests (13:11-14)

13:11-14 When she complied with his request, Amnon **grabbed** (יַחֲזֶק, *yaḥăzeq*) **her,** i.e., "overpowered" her. At first he spoke lovingly to her, calling Tamar **my sister,** a term which is used figuratively for the beloved in Song 5:1. He asked her to **come to bed,** lit., "come, lie down," with him.

She protested vigorously. **Do not force me** is literally "do not humble me." Hebrew women regarded chastity as their crown of honor, and Tamar was about to have that honor taken from her by force. She opposed his request on three grounds. First, she cited public opinion. **Such a thing should not be done in Israel!** Rape and incest might be accepted among the Canaanites, but it was abhorrent to Hebrew morality. Second, Tamar called this a **wicked thing** (נְבָלָה, *nᵉbālāh*), i.e., "a senseless and disgraceful thing."[5]

---

[4]Youngblood (960) thinks this is the indefinite/impersonal plural imperative.

[5]The term is used of the rape of Dinah in Gen 34:7. It connects the concepts of crime and stupidity. By using נְבָלָה (*nᵉbālāh*) and "in Israel" from Genesis, Tamar was attempting to impress on Amnon how heinous his deed would be. A. Phillips, "NEBALAH — A Term for Serious Disorderly and Unruly Conduct," *VT* 25, 2 (1975): 237.

Third, Tamar begged Amnon to consider how both of them would be ruined by this act. **What about me?** is literally "as for me, where shall I go?" She would be disgraced for the rest of her life! He would be regarded as one of **the wicked fools** (נְבָלִים, $n^e b \bar{a} l \hat{i} m$), i.e., "wanton, profligate men," in the nation.[6] Would this be the kind of person Israel would want for their king?

Finally, Tamar argued that forced sexual intercourse was unnecessary. She suggested that he ask the king's permission to marry her. Marriage between close relatives was illegal (Lev 18:9,11; 20:17). Therefore Tamar must have been (1) stalling for time; (2) ignorant of the law; or (3) convinced that such a marriage, though illegal, would not be as bad as this rape.

Amnon **refused to listen** to Tamar (cf. v.16). **He raped her** is literally "forced her and laid her."

Amnon's Contempt for Tamar (13:15-17)

13:15-17 Once he had forced Tamar, Amnon wanted nothing more to do with her. In fact, he **hated her** now more than he **loved her** before the act.[7] This sudden revulsion of feeling indicates that Amnon's "love" was nothing more than lust. He ordered her out of his house. She pled with him not to send her away. Tamar assumed that, for better or for worse, she now belonged to Amnon. She counted his abandonment of her a greater wrong than his act of brutality because that abandonment made it appear that Tamar had initiated the seduction. Amnon ordered his servant to throw her out. **This woman** in the Hebrew is simply "this," a most contemptuous way of referring to Tamar. Perhaps in English it would best be rendered "this thing." **Out of here** is literally "from upon me," a word used of dismissing one whose presence was obnoxious. By such an order the servant and all Amnon's people would be led to believe that Tamar was the guilty person, and Amnon the victim of her enticements.

---

[6] A fool was one who was guilty of every conceivable wickedness, one who had cast off the fear of God and the restraints of decency. Ungodly acts were not only criminal, they demonstrated that the guilty person was incapable of rightly estimating his privileges.

[7] A rapist's emotional response following his crime is unpredictable. Amnon *hated* Tamar; but Shechem *loved* Dinah after he raped her (Gen 34:2-3). Hatred following sexual intercourse can also occur after marital sex (Deut 22:13,16; 24:3).

Tamar's Humiliation (13:18-19)

13:18-19 The servant pushed Tamar out and bolted the door after her. Tamar normally wore **a richly ornamented robe.** All of the virgin daughters of the king were similarly dressed. The fact that Tamar wore such a distinctive dress is mentioned to show that she immediately would have been recognized as a royal princess by all who saw her. She was so distressed after the incident with Amnon that she tore her garment. She threw ashes on her head from the very fire which she had just used in cooking. She **put her hand on her head** probably to replace the veil which had been ripped off in Amnon's chamber. She wept as she ran toward her brother Absalom's house. **Weeping aloud as she went** is literally "she went going and cried." Tamar behaved like a mourner, as if she were a widow (cf. 2 Sam 20:3).

3. Absalom's Revenge (13:20-29)

Immediate Reactions to the Rape (13:20-22)

13:20-22 When Absalom saw his sister, and the direction from which she was coming, he suspected what had happened. **Been with you** is a euphemistic reference to the rape. For **Amnon** the Hebrew has "Aminon," possibly a contemptuous diminutive. Absalom urged Tamar to gain control over her emotions because Amnon was her **brother.** All must be kept in the family. A public scandal must be avoided. While it was Absalom's duty to avenge the honor of his sister (cf. Gen 34:31), for the time being they must both wait to see what action David would take. After all, David was her father, and the chief law enforcement officer, and one who personally had been manipulated in this matter. Only if David failed in his duty would Absalom undertake revenge. Absalom urged Tamar not to **take this thing to heart** (lit., "do not set your heart for this matter"), i.e., pay undue attention to it or worry about it (cf. 1 Sam 4:20; 9:20).

Absalom was the full brother of Tamar. He loved her as a brother should love his sister. He tried to comfort her about what had happened. Tamar could no longer live in the quarters of the virgin daughters, so she took up residence in Absalom's house. She lived as a **desolate woman,** i.e., as a widow — childless, despondent and humiliated.

When David heard about what had happened **he was furious**. Unfortunately, he took no action against Amnon.[8] The Narrator refers to David by his title **King** which points to the irony of his impotence in respect to punishing his son for the crime.

From that day forward Absalom never spoke a word to Amnon **either good or bad** (cf. Gen 24:50; 31:24), i.e., he did not speak a single word. This outward demeanor of indifference masked Absalom's hatred and determination to avenge his sister's honor. Amnon must have interpreted this silence as ominous.

Absalom's Plot (13:23-27)

13:23 After **two years** (lit., "two years days-wise," i.e., two full years) both David and Amnon had been lulled into a false sense of security. Absalom hired some men to shear the wool from his sheep. This would take place at **Baal Hazor** near the border of Ephraim about fifteen miles north of the capital (ZA, 119). **Near the border of Ephraim** is literally "with Ephraim." The preposition here suggests that "Ephraim" is not the name of a territory, but of a town otherwise unknown.[9]

Absalom's plan was to ensure, without arousing suspicions by inappropriate insistence, that Amnon would attend the sheep-shearing celebration. He pretended that it was **the king and his officials** (lit., "servants") whose presence he most desired, certain that they would not accept. David declined the invitation because providing for such a group would be **a burden** (lit., "heavy on") to his son. If the entire court went, Absalom would have to provide a meal for a considerable number of people.

Absalom's next step was to suggest that in lieu of the king he would be honored by the presence of the king's eldest son. He asked that Amnon, the eldest of the king's sons, be permitted to come to the festivities in Baal Hazor as a stand-in for his father. David's **Why?** suggests that he was suspicious about the request. He knew how much Absalom had hated Amnon immediately after the incident

---

[8]An early explanation of David's perplexing lack of decisiveness is found in this addition to the LXX: "but he did not curb the spirit of Amnon his son, because he loved him, because he was his firstborn."

[9]Ephraim here may be identified with the Ephron of 2 Chr 13:19. It may be the same town to which Jesus once withdrew (John 11:54). Others think the reference is the place better known as Ophrah northeast of Bethel.

with Tamar. **My brother** is designed to assuage any lingering fears David may have had about allowing Amnon to attend this festival. Absalom kept insisting that Amnon be allowed to attend. David finally gave in and **sent** Amnon along with the rest of the king's sons with Absalom, probably thinking that there was safety in numbers.

The Murder of Amnon (13:28-29)

13:28-29 Absalom ordered his men to strike down Amnon when he gave the signal. He would wait until Amnon was in **high spirits,** i.e., intoxicated, from drinking wine. Absalom urged his men not to be afraid. **Have not I** [emphatic] **given you this order?**, i.e., he would take responsibility for the murder. **Be strong and brave** is literally "become sons of power." The plot was carried out as planned. When Amnon was slain, then the rest of the king's sons fled the scene fearing that they too might become victims. Even though David possessed horses (2 Sam 8:4), **mules** at this time were the mount of royalty (cf. 2 Sam 18:9; 1 Kgs 1:33).[10]

4. David's Agony (13:30-36)

Initial Reports of Amnon's Death (13:30-33)

13:30-33 Some of the royal servants traveled faster than the fugitives. Rumor exaggerated the calamity. Initial reports back at the palace had all the king's sons slain by Absalom. David tore his clothes and **lay down on the ground** in agony over this news (cf. 2 Sam 12:16). His palace servants joined their king in mourning by tearing their clothes.

Jonadab, David's nephew and Amnon's friend, again (cf. v. 3) showed his wisdom by advising David to discount rumor. He surmised correctly that only Amnon was dead. **This has been Absalom's expressed intention** is literally "upon Absalom's mouth had it been set." Absalom had revealed his intentions to confidants.

---

[10]This is the first mention of mules in the Bible. Since the breeding of hybrids was forbidden (Lev 19:19), these animals were probably imported. Up to this time the donkey had been used for riding. Horses seem to have been used chiefly for chariots at this time.

Arrival of the King's Sons (13:34-36)

13:34-36 While the members of the royal family fled toward the capital, Absalom fled in the opposite direction. David's watchman spotted the group coming down **the road west of him**, lit., "from/on a way behind him."[11] **Horonaim** ("the two Horons") refers to Upper and Lower Beth Horon, towns located some ten miles northwest of Jerusalem (ZA, 117). Apparently in their fear and confusion, the princes had fled by an unusual route and were returning from a direction opposite to that in which the watchman was looking for them. He reported this to the king. Jonadab saw this report as a confirmation of what he had just told the king that not all the king's sons were dead.

As Jonadab finished speaking, the king's sons came in. They were all **wailing** (crying) **loudly. The king** and **all his servants** continued to weep with them.

5. Absalom's Flight (13:37-39)

13:37-39 Absalom fled to **Geshur** in Syria northeast of the Sea of Galilee. This city was ruled by **Talmai**, his mother's father. He knew he would be safe with these relatives. At the same time he was forfeiting any likelihood of inheriting the throne of Israel. Meanwhile, David continued to mourn for his son Amnon every day. As his first-born son, Amnon had a special place in David's affections. For a time the situation reached a deadlock. David was powerless to punish his son, and Absalom could not return home.

Absalom stayed three years in Geshur. The passing of time took the edge off bitter feelings. By that time David had ceased grieving over his son Amnon. He longed to be reunited with Absalom. **Spirit** is not in the Hebrew text, but is demanded by the feminine verb **longed**.[12]

---

[11]Peoples of that region orient themselves to the directions of the compass by facing east. Hence, "behind" the watchman would be west. For a defense of translating Heb. *min* as "on," see comments on 2 Sam 5:13.

[12]So also ASV, NASB, BV, NKJV. Another translation of the phrase is that the soul of David "desisted from going forth against Absalom," i.e., he gave up plans of pursuit and retribution. Such is the rendering of the Vulgate. This understanding is reflected in JB: "the king's heart was now no longer set against Absalom." The Hebrew verb is Piel conjugation, while the sense "failed with longing" is generally expressed by the Qal.

2 SAMUEL 14

Absalom spent three years in exile in Geshur. David missed his son and longed to be reunited with him. David, however, thought that if he invited his son to return home it would appear that he was condoning Absalom's murder of his half-brother. Joab decided to engineer the return of Absalom.

6. The Plan to Bring Absalom Home (14:1-20)

Joab's Action (14:1-3)

14:1-3 Joab has not been mentioned since 2 Sam 12:27. His full name here signals a new beginning in the narrative (Youngblood, 975). Literally, v. 1 reads, Joab "knew that the king's heart was upon [or against] Absalom." This has been taken by most to mean that David missed Absalom a great deal. The words could just as easily be taken to mean that David was still hostile to his son.[1] In either case Joab had to employ an elaborate deception to effect a policy change that would recall Absalom from Geshur. Joab's concern was not so much for David in his grief as for the future of the royal house. When Amnon died, Absalom possibly became heir apparent, and Joab considered it necessary for him to be present in Jerusalem.

Joab devised a plan to help David deal with the Absalom problem more objectively. To assist him, Joab sought out a wise woman. **Tekoa**, a town about six miles south of Bethlehem, is famous as the home of the prophet Amos. In order to present her fictitious story

---

[1] Other translations of v. 1: the king's heart was "concerned about" Absalom (NKJV); "was toward" (ASV) "went out toward" (BV); "was inclined toward" (NASB); "again turning to" (JB); "was on" (NJPS, NRSV). On the other hand, KD (433-34) argue that the view that David was now favorably disposed toward Absalom is "neither philologically sustained, nor in accordance with the context." Kirkpatrick (2:142) and Baldwin (253) concur.

successfully, the woman had to come from some outlying district, otherwise she might have been recognized.

The woman was to pretend to be in **mourning** for the dead. She was to dress like a woman who had spent many days grieving over a dead loved one. She was to abstain from any cosmetic lotions (perfumes). The woman was then to go to David and recite a certain script. Joab gave her the outline of what to say.

The Woman's Parable (14:4-11)

14:4-5 The king was accessible to citizens whose complaint had not been settled to their satisfaction by local judges. The woman from Tekoa sought out the king, paid him homage, and then pled for his assistance. She pretended to be a widow who had two sons. **What is troubling you?** is literally "what to you?" an idiom which sounds more harsh in English than in Hebrew.[2] The redundant **my husband is dead** (v. 5) serves to evoke sympathy from the king. The boys got into a fight in the field, and one struck and killed the other.

14:6-7 The woman referred to herself as **your servant,** lit., "your handmaid." She implied that since there were no witnesses, the crime could just as well have been manslaughter as murder (cf. v. 6). Now the rest of the clan (extended family) demanded that the second son be handed over to them to be executed for killing his brother. **The only burning coal** is a graphic and moving figure. The last coal still left among the embers would provide the means by which the fire, almost extinct, could be rekindled.[3]

14:8-10 The king responded to the woman's problem in three stages as she continued to press for a more binding commitment. First, David tried to brush aside the woman by saying that he would issue orders granting protection to the woman and her son.[4] The woman indicated that if any guilt was incurred in allowing the blood of her son to go unavenged, she was willing to bear it. The implication

---

[2]Cf. the use of the idiom in Josh 15:18 (Caleb to his daughter); 1 Kgs 1:16 (David to Bathsheba) and 2 Kgs 6:28 (the king to a desperate woman).

[3]Verse 7 may provide a clue as to why David hesitated to heal the breach with Absalom. Other members of the royal family may have been agitating for executing the murderer as soon as he crossed the border.

[4]Another interpretation is that David in effect granted a pardon to the son. This he could reasonably do, as it was a case of manslaughter and not premeditated murder.

of v. 9 is that David simply had put her off with a vague promise. David responded by giving a more specific assurance of his sympathy and help. He promised that if she would bring her tormentors to him he would order them not to harass (lit., "touch")[5] her about the matter any longer.

14:11 The woman pressed for something more. She wanted the king to **invoke the LORD his God**, i.e., take an oath, that **the avenger of blood** would not be permitted to destroy her last son. The avenger of blood was a person who was given the responsibility of executing a murderer. Some understand the avenger to be a relative of the murder victim; others suggest that the avenger was a government official. In response, David swore in the name of the Lord that not a hair of her son's head would fall to the ground.

The Woman's Plea for Absalom (14:12-15)

14:12-13 Humbly the woman requested to speak further to the king. She applied the parable to the case of Absalom. While the king was willing to guarantee the safety of the widow's son, he would not guarantee the safe return of Absalom, favorite prince of the people. In ruling as he did for the woman, David in effect was condemning himself. The woman did not ask for a pardon for Absalom's fratricide. Rather she asked that his crime be evaluated in a broader context, viz., the suffering and disaster which would befall others if the murderer was executed. David was doing to the people of God what the avenger of blood sought to do to the woman, viz., depriving them of the heir to the throne.

14:14-15 In that region nothing was as precious as water, and water wasted was a monumental tragedy. Life is **like water spilled on the ground**. It cannot be gathered up again. Therefore David should waste no time restoring his son.[6] In so doing he would be acting in a Godlike way, for the Lord is constantly looking for ways to restore the wayward. **Does not take away life** is a poor rendering of the Hebrew נשא נפש (nśʾ npš, lit., "lift up his soul"). In this context the expression seems to mean "dedicate himself." Here it is best to translate this

---

[5]The verb נָגַע (nāgaʿ) often has a legal overtone of interfering with the legal rights of a person. See Gen 26:11,29; Josh 9:19; Ruth 2:9; Jer 12:14; Job 1:11; Prov 6:29.

[6]Another interpretation is that Amnon was dead and could not be brought back by any harshness to Absalom.

expression as part of a rhetorical question, "But will not God dedicate himself, and will he not devise ways to make sure that a banished person does not remain banished from him?" (Youngblood, 980).

Verse 15 is ambiguous, perhaps deliberately so. The woman sought to excuse her boldness in addressing the king by the pressure brought to bear on her from **the people**. Is she referring to her bold words regarding Absalom, or of her family problems? If the former, then "the people" would mean the nation generally. If the latter, then she is referring to family members. Certainly in the next verse she returned to her own affairs to keep up the pretense of reality. Verse 15, however, is best viewed as the conclusion of her Absalom appeal.

The Ruse Continued (14:16-17)

14:16-17 To continue to throw off David, the woman returned to her fictitious story. She wanted the king to think that was her only reason for coming to him. The allusion to Absalom merely had occurred to her during the course of the conversation.[7] She only came to the king with her request because the people made her afraid with their demand for the life of her son. She thought that the king might be persuaded to deliver her and her son from the hand of the man who was trying to **cut off** (lit., "destroy") both herself and her son from their inheritance. If her second son were to be killed, the estate of this family would be lost at the death of the woman. It would pass on to other people. The avenger of blood had no wish to kill her, but by the death of her son her family would become extinct and she too would lose her share in **the inheritance God gave us**, i.e., the family's property in Yahweh's land. The woman prayed that the king's word might **bring me rest**, lit., "be for a resting-place," from those who were making these demands upon her.

The woman rounded off her speech with enough flattery to silence any possible rebuke from the king (Gordon, 268). She praised David for being **like an angel of God** in **discerning** (lit., "hearing"), i.e., distinguishing, between **good and evil**, i.e., good and bad decisions.[8] She was ascribing to David a more than human

---

[7]Hertzberg (333) suggests that there is a double entendre in vv. 16-17. The woman appears to describe her own case when, in fact, she is referring to the king's case.

[8]Others think "good and evil" form a merism, a way of expressing totali-

ability to discern the right. The king had absolute competence to deal with all legal cases since he was Yahweh's earthly representative. The woman concluded by wishing God's blessing upon the king as he made his decision.

The Ruse Exposed (14:18-20)

14:18-19a By this time David was beginning to suspect that there was more to the woman's story than met the eye. He ordered that she not **keep** (lit., "hide") anything from him. He demanded to know from her if Joab had anything to do with sending her to him.

14:19b-20 To underscore the truthfulness of her reply, the woman took a solemn oath. **As surely as you live** is literally "by the life of your soul" (cf. 1 Sam 17:55; 25:26). The woman indicated that she would not attempt to **turn to the right or to the left** from what the king said, i.e., she would not attempt to evade his question. She acknowledged that Joab had coached her regarding what to say to the king. Joab had so acted in order **to change the present situation,** i.e., bring about a change in the relationship between Absalom and his father. The woman then praised again the wisdom of David.

7. Absalom's Return (14:21-27)

Authorization of the Return (14:21-22)

14:21-22 David knew that he had been tricked into a course of action he could not avoid, because it was backed by his oath. He now turned to Joab who must have been standing nearby. David dispatched Joab to bring Absalom back. The words **the young man** may be intended to justify the recall order by alluding to his son's youth and the hasty acts which fathers must learn to tolerate at that stage of life. Joab fell **with his face to the ground** to pay homage to David. He **blessed** the king for his decision, i.e., directed a prayer to God that David would receive a divine blessing. Continuing in an attitude of humility mingled with courtesy, Joab thanked him for the favor in granting the request. KD (437) detect in these words and actions that Joab frequently had appealed to David for Absalom's return.

---

ty, in this case: *all, everything* or at least all moral knowledge. The idea is that God is morally inerrant.

This may be why David suspected that he had instructed the woman of Tekoa.

Actual Return of Absalom (14:23-27)

14:23-24 Joab went to Geshur personally to bring back the people's prince. Though David permitted Absalom to return to Jerusalem, he did not restore his son to the palace. Apparently Absalom was confined to his own house. Thus he was still being punished for what he did to his brother.

14:25-27 Absalom was a favorite of the people. No one in all Israel was as handsome as Absalom. He had no blemish on his body from head to foot. Apparently for reasons of vanity he let his hair grow. **From time to time**[9] when the hair became burdensome he would crop it. The weight of the shorn locks was **two hundred shekels,** about two lbs. The normal weight of the hair, however, may have been increased by the lavish use of oils.[10] Various systems of weights and measures were used in ancient Israel.[11] The text indicates that for the weighing of his hair the **royal standard**[12] (lit., "the stone of the king") was used.

Absalom was the father of three sons and a daughter. The sons are not named, perhaps because they died in infancy. He named his daughter Tamar because she was beautiful like his sister Tamar who had been disgraced and humiliated.

8. Absalom's Restoration (14:28-33)

14:28-30 Absalom lived two years in Jerusalem without seeing the king's face. He seems to have been under house arrest (cf. 1 Kgs

---

[9]Literally the Hebrew reads that Absalom cut his hair "at the end of days to the days." Josephus (*Ant.* 7.8.5) interprets the text to say that Absalom cut his hair once each week. The phrase can mean "from year to year" or "at the end of every year" and that is the way most English versions render the phrase.

[10]Others have suggested that the text is actually declaring the value of the hair, not its weight.

[11]Jewish tradition asserts that the royal shekel was half the weight of the sanctuary shekel. Gen 23:16 speaks of "weights current among the merchants"; Exod 30:13,24 mentions "the shekel of the sanctuary."

[12]The king was custodian of the standard by which all other weights were judged.

2:36). Absalom tried to make an appointment with Joab to see if something could be done to effect his restoration to the court. Joab refused to come to him perhaps because he did not wish to incur David's displeasure by visiting Absalom while he was still in disgrace. A second request to Joab was also ignored. Then Absalom thought of a sure way to get Joab's attention. He ordered his servants to burn Joab's barley field which was next to his own. **Next to mine** is literally "near to my hand."

14:31-32 Joab hurried immediately to Absalom's house when he heard that the servants had burned his field. Absalom pointed out that he had twice sent for Joab and he had chosen not to respond. He wanted Joab to carry a message to the king. Why had David brought him back from Geshur? He would have been better off to have remained there with his in-laws. Absalom declared that he wanted to **see the king's face**, i.e., be restored to court. He argued that either he should pay the full penalty for the death of Amnon or be completely forgiven. **If I am guilty of anything** is not a profession of innocence. Rather Absalom means, "if my offense is still unpardoned, I would rather be dead."

14:33 Joab conveyed Absalom's message to the king. He made the king realize that by allowing Absalom to return he had recognized that the murder of Amnon was justifiable homicide. There was, therefore, no legal grounds to deny the prince his rightful place in the royal court. David then summoned the prince. Absalom came **before the king** (lit., "to the king's face") and did homage with his face to the ground. The **kiss** on the cheek seems to have been more court protocol than a token of fatherly affection. Though a small step toward reconciliation had been taken, both men apparently remained cold and unforgiving.

2 SAMUEL 15

B. TESTED BY DYNASTIC UPHEAVAL (15:1–19:43)

1. Absalom's Revolt (15:1-18)

Preparations for the Coup (15:1-6)

Verses 1-6 describe the four years preceding Absalom's revolt. The paragraph uses several verb forms which indicate habitual or repeated action. The Narrator is describing how Absalom continued to act over the course of those years.

15:1 In the course of time in the Hebrew is a more precise phrase than that which is used in 10:1 and 13:1. It suggests that Absalom began his scheme soon after obtaining his liberty. He rode about the city in **a chariot** pulled by two horses. **Fifty men** ran ahead of his chariot to announce Absalom's approach. Absalom imitated the magnificence of foreign monarchs in order to make an impression on the people.

15:2-4 Absalom rose early every morning to stand by the road leading to the **city gate**, lit., "gate." Probably the gate of the royal palace is intended. In this complex of buildings the king would give audience and administer justice. Absalom flattered the common people by feigning personal interest in them. He would strike up a conversation with those who were coming to place their complaints before the king for a decision. A **representative** would listen to the complaints and summarize the facts in the case to the king, who would then make the pronouncement. The king was the supreme court for the settlement of legal disputes. The complaints which were brought to the palace gate were probably those that concerned royal issues, e.g., taxation, forced labor, or military duty.

Absalom did not accuse the king himself of wrong, rather he insinuated that the system of government was defective. He would listen to the complaints. Then he would assure each person that his claims were valid and proper. Unfortunately, he would point out, there was no representative of the king to hear these complaints. Thus Absalom insinuated that David was not really concerned about his people. Certainly Absalom's tactics suggested that David's increasing remoteness from the people was a major source of dissatisfaction. Absalom planted the thought that if he were a **judge**[1] then everyone with a complaint would get justice. Absalom's words were purposely ambiguous. The people could interpret his words as aspiring to be king. If challenged, however, he could plead that his only concern was with justice for the common man. The words **to me** stand first in its clause in v. 4 for emphasis.

15:5-6 Absalom played the role of the people's prince. He refused to accept homage from those he greeted at the city gate. He would take their hand, hug and even kiss them upon the cheek. Using the favorite trick of the demagogue, he treated every person as his friend and equal. Simple people must have been greatly impressed by the way this prince treated them. **Stole the hearts** refers not so much to their affections (he already had that), but stole their understanding, i.e., he deceived or duped them.[2]

The Launching of the Coup (15:7-12)

15:7-12 The NIV has followed Josephus, some of the ancient versions and a few MSS in reading **four years**,[3] i.e., four years after the

---

[1]The Hebrew שֹׁפֵט (šōphēṭ, "judge") is a participle of the verb šāphaṭ, which means "to rule, to govern," which includes the functions of decision making and the dispensing of judgments. A ruler was the supreme court. In the west-Semitic world the root šāphaṭ was often used for rulers and administrators. Cf. 1 Sam 8:5.

[2]Another understanding is that the expression means he "won over their loyalties."

[3]The Hebrew text reads "forty years." Those who accept the traditional text understand the forty years to be counted from (1) the time when the Israelites demanded a king, (2) the anointing of David by Samuel, or (3) the anointing of David at Hebron. The latter is most likely. This would date Absalom's rebellion to the last year of David's reign. The reading "four years" of the NIV is thought to be less problematic than forty years. Yet it is not without its own difficulties. The four years would be counted from the final reconciliation between David and Absalom. This would mean that six years had elapsed since Absalom returned from Geshur. The excuse which he offered David for wishing to go to Hebron would hardly have deceived the king after six years.

reconciliation between David and Absalom. Absalom approached his father with a request for permission to travel to Hebron to **fulfill a vow**. He claimed — it was probably a lie — that while he lived in the land of Geshur he promised the Lord that if he was ever permitted to return to his native land he would worship the Lord in Hebron. David was completely hoodwinked by this profession of religious devotion. He gave permission for Absalom to leave Jerusalem. Ironically, **Go in peace** were the last words David ever spoke to his son.

Why did Absalom choose Hebron as the spot from which to launch his rebellion? It was (1) in the heart of Judah, Absalom's base of support; (2) it was a royal city long before Jerusalem became the capital; (3) it was the town where Absalom was born (2 Sam 3:3); and (4) it was a safe distance from Jerusalem where David's soldiers might crush the revolt before it gained momentum. By choosing Hebron, Absalom made the rebellion from the start the revolt of Judah. Before the war broke out, Absalom deprived David of those forces which he would normally count on in an emergency. He deprived his father of the territory where David would be most comfortable fighting. If he could succeed in fomenting rebellion among the northern tribes, he would have David caught between two hostile forces (Herrmann, 164ff.).

Absalom sent **secret messengers** throughout the tribes of Israel to notify his supporters that the rebellion was about to be launched. The prince had established in every major city a cadre of sympathizers with whom the messengers could make contact. **The sound of the trumpets** (lit., "trumpet") is that which accompanied coronation. News of the royal proclamation would rapidly spread.[4] Absalom's agents would be able to explain what had taken place. At the same time they would urge the people to confirm what had transpired in Hebron. Absalom invited **two hundred** of the leading men of Jerusalem to accompany him to Hebron.[5] These men knew nothing of the plot which was unfolding. However, their absence from Jerusalem at the time Absalom was proclaimed king would make it

---

[4]Jamieson (252) speculates that trumpeters had been stationed at convenient stations throughout the land whose job it was to relay the signal that Absalom had been proclaimed king.

[5]Conroy (105n), on the other hand, thinks that the two hundred were from the poorer element in Jerusalem.

appear to the citizens in Hebron and in Jerusalem that they were supporting the rebellion. Some of them probably did join Absalom out of fear if not conviction. If they refused to embrace his cause, they could be held as hostages. **Offering sacrifices** refers, not to the fulfillment of the fictitious vow, but to the ceremonies which accompanied Absalom's coronation. Others throughout the land who were key leaders were notified to come to Hebron. Among these was David's most trusted advisor, Ahithophel **the Gilonite,** i.e., from the town of Giloh six miles northwest of Hebron. The fact that Absalom sent to call Ahithophel to come **from Giloh** suggests that he was no longer functioning as the counselor to the king.[6] During the several days of the sacrificing in Hebron the conspirators continued to assemble. David was totally unaware of what was happening. **The conspiracy gained strength** (lit., "was strong").

Initial Response to the Coup (15:13-18)

15:13-18 A messenger — obviously someone loyal to David — arrived from Hebron with the news that the hearts of the men of Israel were now with Absalom. The news took the king by complete surprise. Probably he had dismissed reports of Absalom's intentions.

David ordered an immediate evacuation of the government **officials** (lit., "servants") from Jerusalem. Verse 14 suggests two reasons for the order: (1) David feared that, if he waited there any longer, his escape route might be cut off; and (2) he desired to spare the city the destruction which would result from a clash with Absalom's forces. Other motives may have been at work as well. It has been suggested that (1) his courage failed him for the moment, (2) he suspected the loyalty of the Jerusalem population, (3) he felt he would be trapped there between the northern tribes and Absalom marching from the south, and/or (4) he would be able to maneuver his troops better in the open field.

David evacuated the palace with **his entire household**; but he left **ten concubines** to take care of the palace. He did not imagine that they would be in any particular danger. David probably thought that

---

[6]Ahithophel may have been the grandfather of Bathsheba (cf. 2 Sam 11:3 with 23:34). The affair with Bathsheba may have triggered his hostility toward David. Others think that Ahithophel's defection resulted from a growing dissatisfaction over the diminishing influence of Judah within the expanding Davidic empire.

his absence would be of short duration. The king led the procession to **a place some distance away,** lit., "Beth-merhak [the last house]."[7] The reference is probably to the last house of Jerusalem in the direction of the Mount of Olives. There he stopped to review the troops. All of his men marched past him, along with the **Kerethites and Pelethites,** the palace guard which was made up of Philistine mercenaries. See notes on 2 Sam 8:18. Among those troops were **six hundred Gittites** (men of Gath)[8] who had been serving David since the days he had been in Gath many years before. It is clear that David had the support of the professional soldiers, while Absalom was backed by the militia (Mettinger, 118).

2. David's Flight (15:19–16:14)

The Committed (15:19-37)

David and Ittai (15:19-22)

15:19-22 The commander of the Gittites was **Ittai.** His loyalty to David stands in stark contrast to the treachery of Absalom. He appears to have been a political exile or soldier of fortune who only recently had come to reside in Israel.[9] In his first question to Ittai, the **you** is emphatic, i.e., why would you of all people choose to abandon the city? **Stay with King Absalom** is literally "stay with the king." David considers Absalom's coup a *fait accompli.* As a foreigner he need not feel any obligation to continue with David. His best course of action would be to transfer loyalty to the new king.

Ittai swore an oath in the name of Yahweh[10] that he would stay with David no matter where he went. He was willing to face death to

---

[7]The NIV is based on the Targum, the Aramaic version of the Old Testament. The Hebrew is unusual, hence the uncertainty.

[8]Others think the reference is to David's original band of followers (1 Sam 23:13) who are called "Gittites" because they had followed David since the days of his residence in Gath. This corps seems to have been afterwards maintained as a guard with the title "the Gibborim," i.e., "the mighty men" (2 Sam 10:7; 16:6; 20:7; 1 Kgs 1:8). In place of Gittites in v. 18 the LXX reads "Gibborim."

[9]The term "exile" (גֹּלֶה, *gōleh*) does not necessarily imply compulsory change of residence, but may be used of one who moves voluntarily from place to place.

[10]Swearing by the name of Yahweh suggests, but does not prove, that Ittai

honor this oath. Here is unselfish devotion to what at the time must
have appeared to be a losing cause. So David told Ittai **to march on**,
lit., "pass over," i.e., over the Kidron valley. So the Gittites marched
on, taking their **families** (lit., "all the children") with them.

David and Zadok (15:23-29)

15:23-24 As the procession marched away from Jerusalem, the people of the countryside wept aloud as **all the people**, i.e., the army and
retinue of followers accompanying David, passed over the Kidron. The
Kidron Valley is the deep ravine to the east of Jerusalem which sepa-
rates the city from the Mount of Olives. On the procession moved
toward the desert (lit., "over the face of the road with[11] the desert"),
i.e., the wilderness of Judea and beyond that to the Jordan river.

Zadok the priest accompanied David in his exodus from Jerusalem. With him were **all the Levites** who were carrying the ark of
the covenant.[12] They set the ark down near the road. Of the standard
English versions, the NIV alone states that Abiathar **offered sacrifice** (lit., "went up") before the ark until all the followers of David
finished leaving the city.[13] The text is actually suggesting that
(1) Abiathar the priest came up to where the ark had been placed,
implying that he was late arriving or that (2) Abiathar led the multitude forward up the Mount of Olives until they had all come out of
the city. The situation certainly did not permit time for sacrifices.

15:25-26 David encouraged Zadok to take the ark of God back
into Jerusalem. He had no superstitious feelings about the need to

---

had embraced the religion of Israel. The Philistine king Achish also swore
in Yahweh's name (1 Sam 29:6).

[11]The NIV has read *'el* ("to/unto") for *'eth* ("with"/sign of direct object)
which is absent in several MSS.

[12]Apart from 1 Sam 6:15, this is the only direct reference to Levites in the
books of Samuel. In both places the Levites are the custodians of the ark of
God.

[13]"Abiathar came up" (NASB, NRSV, NJPS); "Abiathar went up" (ASV,
NKJV); "Abiathar had come up" (BV). The NIV rendering is not supported
by the ancient versions. Passages can be cited where the verb can be rendered "offered sacrifices" without the addition of the word sacrifice; but in
these places the context makes the sense plain. Baldwin (261), however,
thinks that a makeshift altar, a small fire, and grain offerings would be possible in the emergency, as an accompaniment to prayer for the king's protection and victory.

have the ark with him as apparently Saul did (1 Sam 14:18). David placed himself in the hands of the Lord. If he found favor in God's eyes, he would bring David back to see that ark. **His dwelling place** refers to Jerusalem in general and the tent where the ark was kept in particular. If the Lord was not pleased with him, then David was prepared to endure whatever might lie ahead. Sending the ark back to Jerusalem was for him an act of faith and an act of surrender to the will of the Lord.

15:27-29 Aren't you a seer? is more accurately rendered "Do you see?" i.e., understand (NJPS, BV).[14] Zadok, Abiathar and their two sons (Ahimaaz and Jonathan)[15] could do much good for him in the city. Verse 28 begins in the Heb. with "see" which is left untranslated in the NIV. They could find out what Absalom's intentions were and send word to David at the **fords in the desert,**[16] i.e. the fords of the Jordan in the wilderness of Judea. So Zadok and Abiathar took the ark back into the city. David believed that he would be safe in Transjordan. It is possible that Joab and the army were deployed in that region.

David and Hushai (15:30-37)

15:30-37 David **continued up the Mount of Olives** (lit., "the ascent of the olive trees"). He was weeping. His head was covered and he was barefoot. These were signs of deep mourning (cf. Jer 14:3; Ezek 24:17). Those with him joined in this mourning. News that his close friend and advisor **Ahithophel** had joined the conspirators made the sorrow all the worse. His political wisdom had become proverbial (2 Sam 16:23). With Ahithophel guiding him,

---

[14]The ASV, NASB and NKJV agree with the NIV. The JB and NRSV follow the LXX and render: "Look." KD revocalize the *hē* interrogative as an article and translate it as a vocative, "Thou seer!" If "seer" is correct, then perhaps David hoped that he would receive a vision from the Lord that would provide guidance. Every indication here, however, is that David expected the priests and their sons to provide ordinary intelligence, not supernatural revelation.

[15]"You and Abiathar take your two sons with you," lit., "your two sons with you." The plural pronouns have caused the NIV to speculate that David was addressing both Zadok and Abiathar. The MT makes sense if David is addressing Zadok as Abiathar's superior.

[16]The ASV, BV, NASB and NRSV so render. The NKJV and JB follow a different reading: "plains of the wilderness"; NJPS, "steppes of the wilderness."

Absalom was not likely to make any stupid moves. David prayed that the Lord would turn the counsel of Ahithophel into foolishness. The Lord was not long in providing the answer to that prayer.

The summit of the Mount of Olives is **where people used to worship God**. This could refer to some Canaanite sanctuary or high place which once was located there or to the actions of people coming from the east when they first caught sight of Jerusalem. There **Hushai the Arkite**[17] was waiting for David. His robe was torn and he had dust on his head. Hushai's coming was the beginning of the answer to David's prayer in v. 31. Hushai was probably old and unable to undergo the rigors of fugitive life. He would be a **burden** to David, perhaps because of his age or infirmity. David wanted Hushai to return to Jerusalem. Hushai was another noted counselor. His job would be to do what he could to frustrate or contradict any advice that Ahithophel might give that would be detrimental to David. If he learned what Absalom's plans were, he should pass that information on to Zadok or Abiathar. That information would then be relayed to David through the sons of those two priests. Hushai never hesitated to accept this dangerous assignment. Here again (cf. vv. 27-28) David showed that he did not think that his trust in Yahweh absolved him from the responsibility of taking all possible measures on his own account for the success of his cause.

David's friend is probably a court title for the king's confidential adviser (cf. 1 Kgs 4:5). Hushai arrived back at Jerusalem just about the time that Absalom was entering the city. Presumably he had time to clean himself up before this meeting with the rebel.

---

[17]The Arkites lived between Bethel and Ataroth (Josh 16:2).

2 SAMUEL 16

As he was fleeing from Jerusalem, David was met by two individuals with links to the house of Saul. The first professed loyalty to the king; the second abused him.

The Opportunist (16:1-4)

16:1-4 Just beyond the **summit** of the Mount of Olives, Ziba, the steward of Mephibosheth (cf. 2 Sam 9), was waiting to meet David. His intention apparently was to demonstrate his loyalty to David. He had with him **a string of donkeys,** lit., "two donkeys," loaded with food and beverage for the king and his supporters. **A hundred cakes of figs** is literally "a hundred of summer fruits," i.e., fruits belonging to late summer. Here is a clue as to the season in which the rebellion was staged. The donkeys were offered to David for the convenience of **the king's household,** probably his wives. They would be able to take turns riding on the donkeys. The royal fugitives were traveling on foot because that was suitable to their present state of humiliation and penitence. Ziba was an opportunist. He was one of the few people who correctly calculated that Absalom's rebellion ultimately would fail. He was trying to position himself for a greater influence and power when David was restored to his throne.

David asked Ziba about the whereabouts of his master's (Saul's) **grandson** (lit., "son"),[1] i.e., Mephibosheth. Ziba stated that he was staying in Jerusalem hoping that in the confusion caused by Absalom's rebellion the people of Israel would give back to him his grandfather's kingdom. The accusation was clearly improbable.[2] Yet

---

[1]The term "son" is used very indefinitely in Hebrew. The NIV has correctly interpreted the term here to refer to a grandson.

[2]Mephibosheth, who had never made any claim to the throne before, could not possibly have thought now that the people of Israel, who had just chosen Absalom as king, would give the throne of Saul to a cripple like

it was not inconceivable that the Saulides might take advantage of
the confusion of the moment to rally behind Mephibosheth in a bid
to recapture the throne. Ziba, however, probably was lying. Nonetheless, David believed Ziba without asking any further questions.
He was rash and hasty in decreeing that all which belonged to
Mephibosheth would now belong to Ziba. This illustrates the royal
prerogative to confiscate land from an enemy and redistribute it.
Ziba bowed and thanked David. The land grant would be valid only
if the cause of David prevailed. If Ziba deserves any credit in this situation it is that he attached himself to a ruined man; but his motive
was selfish calculation, not love for David.

The Antagonist (16:5-14)

Shimei's Abusive Conduct (16:5-8)

16:5-8 Near **Bahurim** (cf. 2 Sam 3:16) east of the Mount of
Olives, Shimei, a relative of Saul, came out to meet David. He cursed
David and threw stones at him and his officials. He was not intimidated by the fact that special guards were walking on David's right
and left. The **troops** (lit., "the people") has been understood to refer
to (1) the general body of his followers or (2) the mercenary soldiers
(the Cherethites, Pelethites, and possibly the Gittites), while the **special guard** (גִּבֹּרִים, *gibbōrîm*) probably formed David's personal bodyguard. Shimei was on the side of a hill (v. 13) which apparently over-
looked the road followed by David's company, but was separated
from it by a narrow valley (v. 9). At the risk of his own life he could
not resist taunting David in his hour of humiliation.

Shimei called for David to **get out** (lit., "go forth"), i.e., into banishment and exile. He called David a man of blood and a **scoundrel**
(cf. 1 Sam 1:16). His flight from Jerusalem was just payment from
the Lord for all the blood David had shed in the house of Saul. The
reference is (1) to the war between the house of Saul and the house
of David (2 Sam 3), (2) David's suspected complicity in the deaths of
Abner and Ish-Bosheth, or (3) the humiliating execution of seven
descendants of Saul who were delivered over to the Gibeonites by
David (2 Sam 21:7-9).

---

himself. He had a son, however, who would have been about twenty (cf.
2 Sam 4:4; 9:12). Therefore the house of Saul had at least one potential candidate for the throne.

David's Humble Response (16:9-14)

16:9-10 Abishai, Joab's brother, asked David for permission to slay Shimei and cut off his head. This man's zeal for David was consistent (cf. 1 Sam 26:8; 2 Sam 19:21). Abishai referred to Shimei with an insult formula, **a dead dog**, i.e., one who was as good as dead (cf. 2 Sam 3:8). Joab probably joined Abishai in this request. According to Exod 22:28 it was a crime to curse the ruler of God's people. For this reason, Abishai was prepared to execute the man.

On other occasions David gave in too readily to the sons of Zeruiah, but not now. **What do I have in common with you,** lit., "what have I to do with you?" This formula signifies that a person did not wish to have anything in common with the feelings and views of another (cf. 1 Kgs 17:18; Josh 22:24). The **sons of Zeruiah**, David's (step)sister, were Abishai and Joab (see on 1 Sam 26:6). The underlying assumption in v. 10 is that Shimei's curses were the result of the irresistible power of Yahweh.

16:11-14 Widening his audience, David addressed **his officials** as well as Abishai. He accepted this treatment by Shimei as part of God's judgment against him, and no one should question God's actions. If David's own flesh and blood was trying to take his life, why should not this Benjamite feel as he did toward the king? David ordered his men to leave Shimei alone, for he viewed Shimei as an instrument of God's chastening hand. **See my distress** is literally "look on my iniquity," i.e., the iniquity done to me (so ASV).[3] David was confident that the Lord would look upon his humble demeanor and would change the unjust curses being hurled at him into blessings.

As David and his men continued along the road, Shimei was keeping a safe distance on the ridge of the hill overlooking the road. He continued to curse the king and throw stones and dirt at him, not so much to inflict injury as to express hatred.

The steep climb up the hill and down through the wilderness exhausted David and his men. They paused on the west side of the Jordan river to await word from agents in Jerusalem regarding Absalom's plans. **At their destination** has been supplied by the NIV.[4]

---

[3]The MT has "look on my eye," i.e., on my tears. The word is translated "my affliction" (NASB); "my misery" (JB, BV); "my punishment" (NJPS); "my distress" (NRSV). KD (449) understand David to mean "on the guilt which really belongs to me, in contrast with that with which Shemei charges me."

[4]The ASV margin regards the word translated "exhausted" as a proper

3. Absalom's Counselors (16:15–17:23)

Hushai Joins Absalom (16:15-19)

16:15-19 Absalom and his forces entered Jerusalem without opposition. **Men of Israel** refers to Absalom's supporters, not the northern tribes as distinct from Judah. The language suggests that Absalom had the support of the tribal leaders. By contrast, David's followers throughout this narrative are called simply "the people." Ahithophel, David's former friend and adviser, was with Absalom.

Hushai, David's friend, went out to meet Absalom. He acted completely in the spirit of the commission which David gave him in 15:34. He hailed Absalom as the new king. Hushai greeted the rebel with a repetition of **Long live the king!** (lit., "let the king live"). Perhaps it is significant that Hushai avoided saying, "Long live King *Absalom!*"

Absalom was suspicious about Hushai's loyalties. He asked him why he had not left the city with the other supporters of David. **Your friend**[5] is an ironic play on Hushai's title (cf. 2 Sam 15:37). Hushai indicated that he would give himself to whatever person the Lord chose to be king. The implication is that events had convinced Hushai that Yahweh had chosen Absalom. **His I will be**, i.e., I will support his cause. He pledged himself to serve Absalom just as he had served his father David.

Ahithophel's Initial Advice (16:20-23)

16:20-23 Absalom first asked Ahithophel for his advice about what move he should next make. The verb **give** and pronoun are plural, suggesting that others as well as Ahithophel were addressed. Ahithophel advised Absalom to sleep with the **concubines** (see on 2 Sam 3:7) of his father whom he had left behind to care for the palace. This action would accomplish two objectives. First, Absalom would become **a stench** (בָּאַשׁ, *bā'aš*) in his father's nostrils. The term refers to disloyalty so egregious as to shatter forever an existing relationship (1 Sam 13:4; 27:12). The cohabitation may have served as

---

name, "to Ayephim." No such place is known, but it would be an appropriate name for a resting-place for travelers. KD (449) insist that only by understanding "Ayephim" as a proper name does the verse make any sense.

[5]Absalom twice uses the ordinary word for friend (רֵעַ, *rē'a*) rather than the technical name (רֵעֶה, *rē'eh*) for Hushai's office.

an indication that as far as Absalom was concerned, David was dead.[6] Ahithophel was afraid that if Absalom's cause began to decline, he might come to terms with his father, who would readily forgive a son if he submitted, but would certainly punish Ahithophel. For his own selfish purposes, then, he led Absalom on to a crime which rendered a reconciliation with David impossible. Second, this single act, Ahithophel said, would strengthen the hands of his supporters, some of whom may have been having second thoughts about what they were doing, or fears that David might be able to force his way back into the capital.

Absalom's going in to sleep with the ten concubines was done publicly. **A tent** (lit., "the tent," i.e., the bridal tent or (חֻפָּה, *ḥuppāh*) was pitched on the flat roof of the palace (cf. Ps 19:4-5).[7] This may have been he same roof from which David lusted after Bathsheba several years earlier. Everyone could see Absalom entering that tent each evening. Thus was fulfilled the prophecy of Nathan (cf. 2 Sam 12:11f.). Absalom's actions were a flagrant breach of divine law (Lev 20:11), a greater crime than that of Reuben who forfeited his birthright (1 Chr 5:1).

The Narrator explains why Absalom followed Ahithophel's advice, as filthy as it was. This man's advice was regarded both by David and Absalom like that of one who inquired of God, i.e., his wisdom was considered as God-given. In this case, however, the counsel of Ahithophel was setting Absalom on the road to disaster, as will become apparent later.

---

[6]Scholars dispute whether the cohabitation with concubines would have conferred special legal claim to the kingship. Anderson (214) takes note of the arguments pro and con and concludes that it would not.

[7]Others think the tent was that used by David and his family for the enjoyment of the cool evening breeze, the tent which citizens of Jerusalem had often seen erected on the flat roof of the palace.

2 SAMUEL 17

Ahithophel's Battle Strategy (17:1-4)

17:1-4 Ahithophel was confident that he had bolstered Absalom's claims to kingship in the eyes of the citizens of Jerusalem. He now proposed a bold military strike against David with **twelve thousand men**. **I would choose** is literally "let me choose . . . let me attack him . . . let me strike him."[1] Ahithophel apparently was requesting to be made commander-in-chief of the army. He requested permission to move **tonight**, i.e., the night following the day in which David had fled from Jerusalem. The rationale for this attack was threefold. First, a swift attack would catch David **weary and weak** (lit., "limp/ feeble of hands"), i.e., discouraged and dispirited. Second, such an attack would **strike him [David] with terror,** i.e., throw him and his supporters into a panic since they would be unprepared to make a stand. Third, the attack would focus on the king himself. Once he was slain, **all the people**, viz., his supporters, would return to Jerusalem and give their allegiance to Absalom. **Bring . . . back** and **return of all** are words of subtle flattery suggesting that by following David the people were deserting their lawful sovereign, Absalom.

Ahithophel's plan seemed good to Absalom and to **all the elders of Israel**. Their presence seems to indicate that Absalom professed to act in an orderly and constitutional manner, and upon the advice

---

[1] The NIV alone among standard English versions renders the verbs as optative. This translation is defensible only by deleting the enclitic particle *na'* which follows the verb *choose*. The Hebrew cohortative standing alone, or co-ordinated with another cohortative, and strengthened by the addition of the particle *na'* is used to express (1) self-encouragement, (2) a wish or (3) a request for permission (GK §108).

[2] Thus David was betrayed by precisely the same official body from the northern tribes that had earlier entered into a contractual agreement with

of those in authority.[2] David's unpopularity in the north may have been due to his failure to seek the advice and consent of the old tribal leaders.

Hushai's Conflicting Advice (17:5-13)

Hushai's Criticism of the Previous Advice (17:5-10)

17:5-6 Uncertain of the degree of his popular support, Absalom thought he should consult at least one more advisor. He sent for Hushai, who had not been allowed to attend Absalom's council. **What he has to say** is literally "what is in his mouth." He told him what Ahithophel had advised and asked if Hushai shared that opinion. **Give us your opinion** is literally "you [emphatic] speak."

17:7-10 Hushai (who supported David) labeled Ahithophel's advice as **not good**. The words **this time** are a subtle flattery of Ahithophel's wisdom as a counselor, i.e., his present advice was an exception to his generally impeccable counsel. Hushai was seeking to dispel any suspicion that his disagreement with his rival was due to jealousy. The truth is that Hushai knew that Ahithophel's plan was flawless and would prove fatal to David. He set about to gain time for David so he could (1) collect more troops and (2) prepare to fight in more favorable circumstances.

First, Hushai argued that David may not have many men with him, but those who supported him were **fierce,** lit., "bitter of soul," i.e., embittered. They would fight like a mother **bear** whose **cubs** were being taken away. The Syrian bear is said to be particularly ferocious under such circumstances. Second, a night attack would not surprise David, for most likely he was not even with the troops. As a shrewd and experienced man of war, he would make plans to avoid being captured in a surprise attack. He probably had taken refuge in some cave or other inaccessible place. Third, David might be preparing an ambush for Absalom's troops. A panic was more likely to arise among the volunteers fighting for Absalom than among David's veterans. **If he should attack your troops first** is literally "in the falling on them," i.e., at the first onslaught of David's mighty men.

---

him at his investiture over those tribes (cf. 2 Sam 5:3). There are hints in ch 19 that the elders of Judah had also betrayed David (Mettinger (122f.).

Hushai's Counterproposal (17:11-13)

17:11-13 Hushai's counterproposal had two points. First, before pursuing David, Absalom should raise a huge army. He should recruit men from **Dan** in the north to Beersheba in the south. **As sand on the seashore** is a common figure for an innumerable multitude (cf. 1 Sam 13:5). Second, Absalom himself (as opposed to Ahithophel) should lead that grand force into battle. The literal Hebrew is quite dramatic: "your face going out in the battle." The picture of the young prince leading a great army into battle would have appealed to the vanity of Absalom.

Hushai described in vivid terms the decimation of David's army. **Wherever he may be found** suggested that before the attack Absalom should make certain of his father's whereabouts. **As dew settles on the ground** suggests inescapablity and certainty. David's entire force should be slaughtered, not one man left alive. Should David take refuge in a fortified city, Absalom's huge force could attach ropes to its walls and pull them down[3] to **the valley,** a ravine or gorge worn away by erosion. Such ravines are common in Palestine, where the streams rush along furiously after the rains, but in summer are dry. A city thrown into such a place would be totally swept away during the next rainy season. By using first person plural pronouns three times in these verses, Hushai gave the appearance of being wholeheartedly committed to the cause of Absalom.

Hushai's Message for David (17:14-22)

The Alert Relayed to the Priests (17:14-16)

17:14-16 Both Absalom and his counselors liked the advice of Hushai better than that of Ahithophel, probably because it was more dramatic, democratic and safe. Ahithophel had given the right advice. Yahweh, however, used Hushai's persuasive abilities to frustrate that good advice in order to bring disaster on Absalom.

Hushai secretly reported the two sets of advice to Zadok and Abiathar, the priests who were also (secretly) supporting David. Hushai was not really sure which direction the king might in the end

---

[3]Jamieson (257) thinks in siege operations the construction of defensive walls and towers was tested by actually attaching ropes to them and applying the brute strength of the attackers and their beasts.

choose to go. So he urged the priests to tell David to get across the Jordan as soon as possible. Otherwise the supporters of David might be swallowed up in the swiftness of Absalom's attack. On **fords in the desert** see on 2 Sam 15:28.

The Narrow Escape of the Runners (17:17-20)

17:17-20 On **Jonathan and Ahimaaz** see 2 Sam 15:36. **En Rogel** was at the junction of the valleys of Kidron and Hinnom south of Jerusalem. Here two fleet-footed messengers were waiting for news of what was happening up in Jerusalem on the hill. **A servant girl** was to go and inform them about the possible plans of Absalom, so they in turn could carry the word quickly to David. Those two ardent supporters of David could not be seen in the city, for it was well known that the chief priests and their sons were on David's side. Their movements would be watched carefully.

Unfortunately, somebody spotted Ahimaaz and Jonathan in En Rogel and reported that sighting to Absalom. Realizing that they had been spotted, the two messengers went racing up the Mount of Olives opposite Jerusalem. Apparently the servant girl already had given them the message just before Absalom's men entered En Rogel in hot pursuit. Absalom's men could probably see the two men running just ahead of them up the mountain. Ahimaaz and Jonathan went toward **Bahurim** east of the Mount of Olives to the house of a man who must also have been a supporter of David. They quickly climbed into **a well**, probably a rock-cut cistern for storing rain water. If such a cistern were dry, it would serve as an excellent hiding place. **A covering** (lit., "the cover," i.e., the usual cover of the cistern)[4] was placed over the well and **grain**[5] was put upon it by the lady of the house.

---

[4]The term מָסָךְ (*māsāk*) is generally used of a curtain used at the entrance of a place (e.g., Exod 26:36). Thus it may be that she hastily stripped off a near-by door hanging to throw over the mouth of the cistern or well. Alternatively, the usual covering of the cistern was made of the kind of cloth used at entrances. In any case, the spreading of a covering over the opening of a cistern or well must have been common practice, else it would have raised the suspicions of Absalom's agents.

[5]The meaning of the Hebrew *riphôth* is uncertain. The reference must be to some produce which was usually dried in the sun. Dates and bruised grain, i.e., wheat or barley beaten so as to remove the hull, have been proposed.

Absalom's men came into the house demanding to know the whereabouts of Ahimaaz and Jonathan. The woman of the house misdirected the pursuers when she told them that the two already had crossed over **the brook**.[6] The soldiers searched the premises but never thought of looking into the well. It was a narrow escape for David's messengers.

The Delivery of the Warning (17:21-22)

17:21-22 As soon as the pursuers had gone off on the false trail, Ahimaaz and Jonathan climbed out of the well and went to inform David. When David learned of Ahithophel's advice, he ordered a nighttime crossing of the Jordan river. By daybreak none of his supporters were left on the west bank of the river. Crossing the river at night would have been a very dangerous undertaking, but it was necessary in view of the possibility of being trapped there by Absalom. **No one was left** is literally "even to one there was not any one missed."

Ahithophel's Suicide (17:23)

17:23 When Ahithophel saw that his advice was not followed, he rode back to his hometown on his donkey. He put his house in order, i.e., made final arrangements of his affairs, and committed suicide by hanging himself. Ahithophel's motives may have been (1) wounded pride, (2) disappointed ambition, or (3) the anticipation that Absalom's cause was doomed. Ahithophel was in a no win situation. If David should be victorious, he would be executed as a traitor. If Absalom should win, he would be replaced as chief advisor by Hushai. Since he was buried in his father's tomb, there must not have been any stigma attached to an act of suicide at this time (cf. 1 Sam 31:4-5).

4. The Confrontation In Transjordan (17:24-18:16)

Absalom's Pursuit of His Father (17:24-26)

17:24-26 In Transjordan David chose **Mahanaim** on the River Jabbok, about fifty miles from the fords of the Jordan, for his head-

---

[6]The term *mîkal* ("brook") occurs only here. It probably was a local name for some stream near Bahurim, and should be rendered in English as a proper name. The NIV margin suggests "they passed by the sheep pen towards the water."

quarters (ZA, 119). This was the city Ish-Bosheth had used as his capital (2 Sam 2:8). The defenses of the city must have been substantial. Meanwhile, Absalom was wasting time gathering **all the men of Israel** for his attack. Eventually Absalom went across the river in pursuit of his father. He appointed Amasa, his cousin and David's nephew, as the commander of his army. Thus the two army commanders in this civil war (Amasa and Joab) were nephews of David by different sisters (Abigail and Zeruiah). Absalom's forces made their camp in **Gilead,** that region on the east between the Dead Sea and the Wadi Yarmuk.

The details of Amasa's ancestry are obscure. His father **Jether**[7] is called **an Israelite** (lit., "the Israelite") here, but "the Ishmaelite" in 1 Chr 2:17. The man must have lived among the Ishmaelites where he was known as "the Israelite."[8] Jether is said to have **married Abigail** (lit. "that went in to Abigal"). The language is unusual to describe a marriage. It may refer to an illicit sexual encounter.[9] Amasa would then be an illegitimate son. **Nahash** may have been (1) another name for Jesse, (2) the first husband of Jesse's wife, (3) David's mother, or (4) a second wife of Jesse. Amasa was probably the Amasai who brought a powerful reinforcement to David while he was living at Ziklag (1 Chr 12:18).[10] The ambition of supplanting Joab made him now forget David's long friendship. The details of the family history are given to enable the reader to understand the animosity between Amasa and Joab as they commanded the opposing forces. By placing his name after the mention of his troops in the

---

[7]The NIV has followed the spelling of 1 Chr 2:17. A more accurate rendering here is "Ithra" or "Jithra." The spelling difference in the Hebrew is slight, Ithra being the emphatic form of Jether (R.P. Smith, 419).

[8]The reverse could also be true. He could have been an Ishmaelite who assimilated into Israel after his encounter with Abigal (Abigail). Others see a textual corruption here with Chronicles preserving the original reading. Ahlström (493, n.3) defends the reading "Israelite." One MS of the LXX has "Jezreelite," another has "Ishmaelite. "

[9]Gordon (283), however, thinks that the language implies an Arab ṣadiqa type marriage in which the wife and children lived with the mother's people.

[10]Kirkpatrick (2:168) argues persuasively for the view that Nahash was the first husband of Jesse's wife, so that Abigail and Zeruiah were only step-sisters to David. He points out the guarded statement of 1 Chr 2:16, which does not say that Abigail and Zeruiah were Jesse's daughters, but "sisters of his sons." Some have even conjectured that Nahash here may be the king of the Ammonites defeated by Saul.

last sentence of v. 26, the Narrator aims to dishonor Absalom and foreshadow his dishonorable end (Conroy, 141).

David in Mahanaim (17:27-29)

17:27-29 How long David was in **Mahanaim**[11] before the battle with Absalom is not indicated. While he was there, the most powerful chieftains in Gilead showed their support for him. **Shobi** was an Ammonite.[12] He appears to have been the son of the Nahash who attacked Jabesh Gilead in the days of Saul, and the brother of Hanun (2 Sam 10:1). After the capture of Rabbah (2 Sam 12:36-41) David seems to have made him the governor of the Ammonites. **Rabbah** was some twenty miles south of Mahanaim. The second benefactor was **Makir** of Lo Debar thirty-three miles to the northwest. He had been a supporter of the house of Saul (cf. 2 Sam 9:4). Perhaps David's treatment of Mephibosheth won him over. David's most generous supplier, however, was **Barzillai** from Rogelim some thirty miles to the north.[16] These friends supplied David and his people with utensils, bedding, grain, meat, and other food products. They were moved to compassion because David's people had become hungry, tired, and thirsty as they made their way through the desert (uninhabited area) to reach Mahanaim.

---

[11]It is possible that Shobi was an Israelite living in the old Ammonite capital of Rabbah.

[12]Barzillai has a non-Hebrew name. Ahlström (404, n.1) contends he was the Gileadite ruler and vassal to David.

2 SAMUEL 18

David's Preparations for Battle (18:1-5)

18:1-2 During the days or weeks in which Absalom was raising his army, David **mustered**, i.e., organized his men into a fighting force. Commanders were appointed over **thousands** and **hundreds**, the usual military divisions[1] (1 Sam 22:7; Num 31:14). Obviously the force which had accompanied David on his departure from Jerusalem had been augmented by loyal followers, especially those living in Transjordan. Following military custom of the day,[2] the force was organized into three main divisions **under the command** (lit., "hand") of (1) Joab, (2) Abishai, and (3) Ittai the Gittite. The latter probably commanded all the foreign mercenaries. David intended to **march out with,** i.e., accompany but not lead, his troops. Five times in vv. 2-5 the Narrator calls David **the king** which stresses that (1) he was the legitimate ruler of Israel and (2) he was still in charge of his troops.

18:3-4 The troops refused to permit David to lead the army into battle (cf. 2 Sam 21:17). If the battle were lost, and the soldiers fled, the enemy would chase down David. **You** [emphatic] **are worth ten thousand of us** is literally "now there are ten thousand like us."[3] David would support the effort by heading the reserves which would

---

[1]Anderson (224) points out that the terms "thousands" and "hundreds" are technical terms for military units and are not necessarily indicative of the numerical strength of these units. Traditionally this organization goes back to Mosaic times (Exod 18:21; Deut 1:15).

[2]The tripartite military organization is indicated in Judg 7:16; 9:43; 1 Sam 11:11; 13:17.

[3]The NIV has followed the LXX and Vulgate in reading "you" for "now." Putting together the phrases "if half of us die" and that David "is worth ten thousand," some have drawn the reasonable conclusion that David's force numbered about twenty thousand. Others read the remark to mean that the force numbered ten thousand. Josephus (*Ant.* 7.10.1) gives the figure as four thousand.

(1) secure a retreat if one should be necessary; or (2) reinforce the frontline troops **from the city**, i.e., Mahanaim. The king agreed to remain behind. He stood beside the gate while the men marched out in units of hundreds and of thousands.

18:5 The three supreme commanders were ordered to be gentle with Absalom **for my sake.** On the eve of the battle which could have cost David his throne and even his life, his sole concern was for the welfare of the son who had cast off every vestige of filial affection. His charge to his generals grew out of (1) his unbounded affection for his son, (2) his recognition that his son was an instrument of chastisement in the hand of divine providence, and (3) his desire that his son not die in a state of rebellion and sin. All the troops heard these specific orders given to each of the three commanders.

The Battle in the Forest (18:6-8)

18:6-8 David's army (lit., "the people") marched out to confront **Israel,** i.e., Absalom's forces (cf. 2 Sam 16:15). The battle was joined in **the forest of Ephraim.** Commentators are all but unanimous that this was some part of the great forests of Gilead, probably not far from Mahanaim.[4] David had selected this terrain, where the experience and courage of each individual soldier counted more than sheer numbers. The association of the name Ephraim with this forest may go back to the slaughter of the Ephraimites by the Gileadites in a civil war during the period of the judges (Judg 12:6).[5]

Absalom's citizen **army of Israel** was **defeated by David's men,** i.e., his trained mercenaries. The casualties were **twenty thousand men.** The figure seems large; but nothing has been said about the size of the forces engaged on either side.[6] Obviously the defeated

---

[4]KD (457) argue that the forest must have been west of Jordan in the tribal territory of Ephraim. The theory is that initial skirmishes in Gilead forced Absalom to withdraw back across the Jordan. The general tenor of the account, however, and especially the return of the army to Mahanaim on the same day (19:2-5) make it likely that the battle was fought east of Jordan in Gilead. Because there is no other instance of the name in connection with Transjordan, it should not be emended on that account as in the NEB (to "Ephron").

[5]Less likely is the explanation of Mauchline (284) that Ephraim had gained ground east of the Jordan.

[6]McCarter (2:405) estimates the losses as between a hundred and 280 men. He thus reduces the size of the "thousands" unit to between ten and fourteen soldiers. Of necessity the "hundreds" unit would be even smaller.

rebels were vigorously pursued. The phrase **that day** may be used to include the whole campaign of which this battle was the culmination. **The battle spread out** is literally "the battle became a scattering,"[7] i.e., it was a series of disconnected encounters. The wooded landscape removed all sense of direction so that soldiers wandered aimlessly and got lost. It may have been that David's forces attacked Absalom's men while they were still on the march, without giving them an opportunity to form themselves into battle order. The treacherous forest area **claimed more lives** (lit., "the forest was greater to devour among the people") than died by the sword (lit., "that which the sword devoured"). They must have perished in pits and crevices which were concealed in the dense growth of the forest.[8]

The Death of Absalom (18:9-16)

The Reluctance of a Soldier (18:9-13)

18:9 In the course of the battle Absalom became separated from his troops. Perhaps he was attempting to flee the scene. He suddenly came face to face with **David's men** (lit., "servants," probably his elite bodyguard). When he spotted David's men, he spurred his mule[9] forward into the denser part of the forest. The mule went under the thick branches of **a** (lit., "the") **large oak.**[10] **Absalom's head got caught in the tree,** i.e., his head got wedged into the fork of a branch from which he could not extricate himself. There he hung stunned and helpless in **midair,** lit., "between the heaven and the earth," as the mule rode on without him. His predicament may have been further complicated by the entanglement of his long thick

---

[7]Standard English translations have followed the Masoretic *Qere* which turns what appears to be a noun into a participle.

[8]Kirkpatrick (2:171) opines that owing to the nature of the ground more were slain in the pursuit through the forest, than in the actual battle.

[9]Normally mules were only for use on the march, and were sent into the rear when the fighting began. This mule was perhaps David's mule, a mark of royalty (1 Kgs 1:33,38).

[10]The article seems to show that the tree was well known in later times. The Heb. אֵלָה (*'ēlāh*) is generally said to denote the terebinth or turpentine tree, which is similar to the oak in general appearance. In the forests east of Jordan, however, oaks are far more common, and the NIV may be correct in here rendering the term "oak tree."

hair.[11] Since Absalom had become utterly defenseless, to kill him now would not only violate a royal directive, it would be the equivalent of killing a man in cold blood. Absalom's plight was reported to Joab.

18:10-11 Joab rebuked the soldier for leaving Absalom alive. **What!** is literally "behold" which the NIV regularly ignores in translation. Had he killed the young prince, Joab would have given him a reward of ten silver shekels (four ounces) and a special **warrior's belt**. Presumably Joab was tempting the soldier with a bribe to go back and kill Absalom rather than referring to a previously promised reward.

18:12-13 The soldier replied that he would not disobey David's orders regarding Absalom even if he were to feel the weight of a thousand shekels (25 lbs.) in his hands.[12] **Protect** is literally "have a care, whoever you are, of the young man Absalom." **If I had put my life in jeopardy** is literally "if I had dealt treacherously against his life." He knew that Joab would not have come to his aid had the king ordered him executed for killing Absalom.

The Execution by Joab (18:14-16)

18:14-16 Joab decided to take matters into his own hands. He took **three javelins** (lit., "rods" or "staves"). Perhaps these were merely sharp sticks readily available in the forest. Joab thrust them into **Absalom's heart,** not anatomically his heart, for the blows did not kill him outright; but i.e., "into the midst of his body." Joab knew his blows would not kill Absalom, nor were they intended to do so. Joab's action was meant to (1) inflict pain without killing, (2) shed blood, (3) perhaps symbolize the impalement of a traitor, and (4) signal his troops that they could kill the king's son with impunity. Ten of Joab's armor-bearers then surrounded Absalom and struck him until he was dead. By letting his ten attendants dispatch Absalom, Joab ensured that his death was not the act of one man alone. Absalom was slain not so much out of Joab's personal revenge for

---

[11]The popular notion articulated by Josephus (*Ant.* 7.10.2) that Absalom's hair got caught in the tree finds no support in the text. He probably was wearing a helmet. Youngblood (1019), however, argues for the traditional interpretation by pointing out that here, as in 2 Sam 14:26 (where "hair of his head" is lit. "his head"), "head" is used as synecdoche for "hair."

[12]More literally v. 12 reads, "though I were feeling the weight of a thousand shekels of silver in my hand."

property damage inflicted by Absalom (2 Sam 14:30), but out of a sense of public duty. Events had convinced Joab that he had been wrong in thinking that Absalom was the son who should succeed David. He did not believe that the king would be safe nor the kingdom at peace so long as that turbulent prince was alive.

In language reminiscent of the conclusion of an earlier battle (2 Sam 2:28), Joab **sounded the trumpet** to call off the pursuit of Israel. He knew that with the death of Absalom the rebellion had collapsed. Further bloodshed was unnecessary.

5. The Aftermath of the Battle (18:17–19:8)

The Burial of Absalom (18:17-18)

18:17-18 The soldiers threw Absalom's body into **a** (lit., " the") **big pit** in the forest. The definite article suggests either (1) that the spot was well-known or (2) that he was buried in a mass grave. David's men piled up a **large heap of rocks over him** as a monument to shame over the rebel's grave (cf. Josh 7:26; 8:29).[13] Meanwhile the Israelites who had fought for Absalom fled to their **homes,** lit., "tents," on the other side of the Jordan.

Absalom had erected a monument in the King's Valley (the Kidron Valley?) near Jerusalem. He thought this monument would perpetuate the memory of his name since he had no son to do so. Apparently the three sons mentioned in 2 Sam 14:27 died young.[14] That pillar was called **Absalom's Monument** (lit., "hand"). This fact is mentioned to underscore the contrast between this splendid cenotaph, and the heap of stones which marked the rebel's grave in the forest of Ephraim.[15] Thus two memorials sum up the life story of Absalom (Gordon, 285).

---

[13]Some think the cairn was symbolic of the stoning which was the penalty of a rebel son (Deut 21:20,21).

[14]Whether the monument was erected before or after Absalom had sons is not clear. Josephus (*Ant.* 7.10.3) suggests that he erected the monument with a view of keeping alive his memory, even if he should have no children.

[15]A structure known as Absalom's tomb exists in the Kidron Valley today. It is about forty feet high and pointed like a pyramid. This monument may occupy the spot, but cannot itself be the work of Absalom since it comes from Hellenistic times.

The Notification of David (18:19-33)

The Runners Dispatched (18:19-23)

18:19-23 Ahimaaz, is one of the two runners who carried intelligence from Jerusalem to David when he was camped beside the Jordan (2 Sam 17:17). This close friend of David requested permission to carry the news of the victory to the king. **Has delivered him from the hand** is literally "has judged him out of the hand of his enemies," i.e., pronounced a favorable verdict in his cause and delivered him. Twice Joab told Ahimaaz that he was not to take the news **today** (lit., "this day").[16] He could carry the news **another time** (lit., "another day"). Joab refused to allow him to do so **because the king's son is dead.**[17] Why did Joab not let him run? The text does not say. Scholars have proposed three reasons: (1) because he did *not* wish to have the news of Absalom's death softened by this friend; (2) or just the opposite, because he wished to soften the blow by sending a more detached messenger; (3) or because Joab, out of friendship, wished to spare Ahimaaz the unpleasantness or even animosity of David when he heard the bad news.

Joab then dispatched **a** (lit., "the") **Cushite** (Ethiopian)[18] to go and tell the king what he had seen. Passing over all Joab's personal friends to send a slave was proof that the message was not expected to bring the bearer honor or reward. Joab was quite right in supposing that David would be more displeased at his son's death than pleased with the victory of his troops.

Again Ahimaaz sought permission to run behind the Cushite. The NIV omits an emphatic phrase "also me" which is used in Ahimaaz's second request. Perhaps he felt that the Cushite would not present the news of Absalom's death in a sympathetic manner. Joab was perplexed as to why he was so insistent. **My son** probably denotes the youth of the runner and is not used in any condescending sense.

---

[16]The second time Joab underscores his point by placing "today" in emphatic position.

[17]The NIV takes the last clause of v. 20 to be the words of Joab. The Hebrew is more ambiguous, and this clause may be the comment of the Narrator rather than part of Joab's explanation to Ahimaaz. The clause in Hebrew is verbless and could just as easily be rendered: "the king's son was dead." This leaves open the possibility that at the time Ahimaaz asked to carry the news of the battle he did not yet know that Absalom was dead.

[18]It is also possible that "Cushi" is here a proper name of an Israelite.

There would be no special **reward** (lit., "you have no news finding," i.e., no message that will find for you, the king's favor and reward.[19] Still Ahimaaz wanted to run. Joab finally gave in. The lack of precision regarding the location of the battlefield makes tracing the routes taken by the rival runners impossible. In all probability the Cushite had taken the direct but more difficult route over the hills and through the thick forest, while Ahimaaz ran by a longer but faster route **by way of the plain**, i.e., the Jordan valley.[20]

The Runners Spotted (18:24-27)

18:24-27 Waiting for news of the battle, David was sitting **between the inner and outer gates** (lit., "between the two gates," i.e., in the space between the outer and inner gates of the city gatehouse. The gatehouse had an upper chamber, the roof of which provided a view over the walls. A watchman reported seeing a single runner. David speculated that the news must be good because had his troops been defeated many men would be streaming back to Mahanaim.

Then the watchman reported seeing another man running. Again David speculated that he must be bringing good news. By this time the watchman was able to identify the first runner. He was running in the unique style of Ahimaaz. David knew Ahimaaz to be **a good man**, i.e., loyal supporter, a trustworthy and honest messenger. He was too brave a man to have fled from the battle, and must therefore be carrying a dispatch from the field. David assumed that a distinguished messenger like Ahimaaz would not have been chosen as the bearer of bad news. In the case of victory the fastest runner would be sent, and in the case of defeat there would be no eagerness to bring news of it.

The Runners Reporting (18:28-32)

18:28-32 As he drew near, the breathless Ahimaaz called out to the king: **All is well**, (lit., "peace"). The word is a shortened form of the usual Hebrew salutation, not a message of victory. He then bowed down before his king and praised the Lord. **Delivered up** is literally "shut up," i.e., restrained and confined within bounds,

---

[19]KD (460) understand the phrase to mean that there is no striking message for Ahimaaz to deliver, i.e., no message that strikes the mark or affects anything.

[20]For the suggested routes of the two runners see MBA, map 110.

instead of leaving them at large to work their evil schemes. The news of victory in battle is received without comment by David. He immediately asked: **Is the young man Absalom safe?** (lit., "is there peace to the young man"). It appears that David would excuse the rebellion as some youthful indiscretion by his son. Ahimaaz did not directly answer the king's question. He knew how hurt David would be. He skillfully, though untruthfully, evaded the question. At the time both he and **the king's servant** (the Cushite) were dispatched, he saw only great confusion among the men just as Joab had dispatched the runners. He said he did not know what the confusion was all about. Apparently now that he was face to face with the king, Ahimaaz could not bring himself to tell the king that Absalom had been slain. He pled ignorance regarding Absalom's welfare. David told Ahimaaz to stand aside while he waited for the second runner to arrive. Compassion not greed for reward (Anderson, 226) motivated the withholding of the whole truth. Ahimaaz now understood Joab's unwillingness to let him carry such painful news, and he was glad that this part of the news had been entrusted to the Cushite.

Then the Cushite arrived. **Hear the good news** is literally "let my lord the king receive tidings." He delivered his message professionally, and yet kindly. Yahweh had delivered David from those who had rebelled against him. On **delivered you**, see on v. 19. Again David asked about Absalom. The Cushite was candid but kind. He referred to Absalom along with all the enemies of the king, omitting his name and avoiding the word "dead."

The Reaction of David (18:33)

18:33 Shaken comes from a Hebrew word referring to agitation of body. A violent trembling must have seized the king. The king immediately sought a place of solitude where he could mourn for his son. David's grief was not merely that of a father for his son, but for that son slain in the very act of outrageous sin. Perhaps the grief was multiplied by his anger that his men had paid no heed to his expressed orders regarding Absalom, and that he had listened to them when they insisted that he not go into battle. **If only I** [emphatic] **had died**, i.e., David would have gladly sacrificed himself, had it been possible, to save the life of his son. The psychological dimension of this tragedy for David is summed up in the fivefold repetition of "my son."

2 SAMUEL 19

The Morale Problem among the Troops (19:1-8)

David's Inconsolable Mourning (19:1-4)

19:1-4 David grieved over the death of Absalom. The army, which should have been celebrating victory (lit., "deliverance"), was depressed because their king was so sad. Out of respect for the king's sorrow, the troops slipped back into Mahanaim as if they had deserted the battlefield. There were no parades and celebrations after this victory. The men were acting like they were sorry they had won the battle. **That day** indicates that the battle had been fought in the vicinity of Mahanaim. See notes on 18:6. All this while David covered his face (see on 2 Sam 15:30) and continued crying out over his dead son.

Joab's Sharp Rebuke (19:5-8)

19:5-8 Joab went into the house where the king was lodging. The hard and unsympathetic character of the old veteran here comes to the fore. He told David that his actions had **humiliated** or disappointed **all your men** (lit., "all your servants"), i.e., loyal, obedient and dependable troops. Their hopes of rejoicing that night over the victory were dashed by his extravagant display of grief. Joab reminded David that those men had just risked their lives to save him and the royal family. The significance of what the troops had accomplished is stressed in the Hebrew by the use in v. 5 of the word נֶפֶשׁ (*nepheš*, "life") four times [one omitted by the NIV]. David's other sons and daughters, wives and concubines would have been in jeopardy had Absalom won the battle.

Joab accused David of not knowing who his real friends were. His actions made it appear that he loved his enemies and hated his friends. His troops had gotten the impression that David would have preferred that they had been slain in battle, and that Absalom had survived. The urgency of the situation is indicated by the use five times of the word **today,** twice in v. 5 [once rendered **just** by the NIV) and three times in v. 6 [one omitted in the NIV].

Joab urged David to go out to **encourage** the men, lit., "speak to the heart of your servants." If he did not, not a man would remain in the ranks of his army by nightfall. The loss of his loyal followers, Joab said, would be the worst calamity which David ever had experienced. **I swear** is not a threat that he will persuade the army to desert David (contra Gordon, 288); but the strongest possible assertion that these men would not continue to serve a king who allowed private grief to outweigh his gratitude for their services.

Joab's hard and unsympathetic speech aroused David from his exaggerated grief to a sense of his duty. He took his seat in the gateway where kings were accustomed to give audience to their people (cf. 2 Sam 15:2). The troops **came before him**, i.e., passed in review, and received his thanks for their support in this crisis.[1] By following Joab's advice David had probably saved the nation from years of anarchy, and perhaps a fresh civil war. **Meanwhile, the Israelites** (as contrasted with "the people," i.e., David's army) **had fled to their homes** (lit., "tents"). This common expression refers not only to a defeat in battle, but to a complete collapse of the military structure. This sentence resumes the narrative from 18:17 and prepares the way for the account which follows.

6. David's Restoration (19:9-43)

The Bickering (19:9-10)

19:9-10 It is surprising that the first conciliatory moves with respect to the restoration of David came from the northern tribes. The return of the king became an issue of protocol, and a highly contentious one at that (Gordon, 288). **The people were all arguing with each other,** i.e., hurling recriminations at one another. They were angry with their leaders for the delay in restoring David. Perhaps the leaders were hesitating in this matter because they feared reprisals for having acquiesced in Absalom's rebellion. The movement to recall David arose out of a sense of having done an injustice to **the king**. (This title on the lips of the northerners is

---

[1]Others take the words to mean that David again appeared in public and was accessible to his people.

significant.) The people were recalling how David had delivered
them from all their enemies, especially the Philistines. Without a
strong king they might again fall into the hands of those enemies.
They felt guilty that they had **anointed**[2] Absalom as their ruler, and
that their rightful king had been forced to flee beyond the Jordan.
Now that Absalom was dead,[3] why was no one organizing a special
effort to bring the king back to Jerusalem?

The Reluctant (19:11-15)

19:11-15 David could have marched on Jerusalem and reclaimed
his throne by force, but he preferred to return peacefully at the invitation of his subjects. The elders of Judah had been instrumental in
launching the coup. They were consequently among the last to get
behind the movement to recall David from Transjordan. By inviting
them to take the lead David was signaling that there would be no
reprisals against them. He sent a message to the priests **Zadok and
Abiathar**. These two priests had remained behind at Jerusalem to
watch over David's interests. By means of a messenger (perhaps
Ahimaaz or Jonathan) he directed the priests to approach **the elders
of Judah**, those who would naturally be the leaders in the restoration of the king. David had either heard rumors of a movement for
his restoration among the northern tribes, or he had actually
received overtures from those tribes. In the question **Why should
you be the last to bring the king back to his palace?** there is an element of reprimand.[4] Certainly his own tribe should take the lead in
this matter. **You are my brothers, my own flesh and blood** is literally "my brothers are you, my bone and my flesh are you."

---

[2]The anointing of Absalom is not elsewhere mentioned. The language
suggests some solemn anointing and appointment of Absalom by the tribal
elders. This accounts for the manner in which Absalom's partisans are
always described as "Israel," while David's men are simply "his servants."
Anderson (236) suggests that David had to be anointed anew at Gilgal
before he could again be accepted as legitimate king. David, however, is
repeatedly called king prior to crossing over to Gilgal. Cf. Mettinger, 119.

[3]The words "died in battle" suggest that the people did not hold Joab
guilty for slaying Absalom.

[4]Mettinger (123) points out that the question is not introduced by מַדּוּעַ
(*maddûa'*) which has cognitive value and is used in real questions, but by
לָמָּה (*lāmmāh*), which has emotional connotations and conveys a note of a
reprimand.

Zadok and Abiathar were also told to communicate to **Amasa** (emphatic in v. 13) that David had taken an oath to make him the commander of the militia in place of Joab.[5] **Are you** [emphatic] **not my own flesh and blood** (lit., "bone")? Amasa was David's nephew,[6] and the commander of Absalom's army. A commander-in-chief cannot tolerate battlefield insubordination even on the part of a popular and capable general. Clearly David was so angry with Joab (also his nephew) for disobeying his orders that he wished to remove him. Furthermore, by appointing Amasa, David would signal those who had supported Absalom that there would be no recriminations against them. He would also turn Amasa's powerful influence on the men of Judah in his favor. On the formula **May God deal with me, be it ever so severely** see on 2 Sam 3:9. **From now on** is literally "all the days." This may be the only time in history when a defeated general was made the commander of the army which defeated him.

He (David? or Amasa?) **won over the hearts of all the men of Judah.**[7] Even those who had fought to oust David as king were now behind him. They sent word to the king to return. They promised to meet him at the Jordan to escort him back into the land. **Gilgal** near the Jordan river is the place where kingship was born, broken, renewed, and now restored. It was the entrance to the territory of Judah. On this occasion only the tribe of Judah was officially invited to assemble there to meet the king and bring him across the river.

The Desperate (19:16-23)

19:16-23 Shimei had cursed David and had thrown stones at him as he left Jerusalem in humiliation (cf. 2 Sam 16:5ff.). Though he was a Benjamite, he hurried down to the Jordan with the men of Judah to meet David, his zeal no doubt sparked by fear of royal revenge. With him were a **thousand Benjamites**. This indicates that Shimei was a person of influence who could either raise a force against or in support of the king. Shimei was also accompanied by Ziba, **the steward of Saul's household**. Hence this Ziba had been a

---

[5]It is unlikely that this command extended also over the mercenaries and the elite troops (Anderson 236).

[6]Amasa was the son of David's sister or stepsister Abigail. See 2 Sam 17:25.

[7]Baldwin (275) argues that David erred by taunting Judah with the readiness of the other eleven tribes to receive him.

trusted member of Saul's court. He must have been a man of wealth for he brought with him fifteen sons and twenty servants. Like Shimei, Ziba was anxious about his future. He wished to curry favor with the king. The support of these two influential Benjamite leaders would signal that no significant opposition would be put forward by partisans of Saul's house.

While the delegation from Judah remained on the west bank, the Benjamites impetuously dashed into the ford of the river and crossed to the east side to show their zeal to serve the needs of the royal family. **Where the king was** is literally "before the king," i.e., in the sight of the king. **They crossed** is literally "she/it crossed."[8] Probably some conveyance (perhaps a raft)[9] was used to ferry the women and children across the river. **Whatever he wished** is literally "to do the good thing in his eyes." They obviously are showing respect for David in hopes that he would not use the Absalom rebellion as an excuse for eliminating those whose loyalty was suspect.

Prostrating himself, Shimei admitted **I** [emphatic] **have sinned**. He begged for forgiveness for the way he had acted at the time David fled Jerusalem. **Hold me guilty** could also be rendered, "devise punishment for me." He asked that David put the whole incident out of his mind. He acknowledged that his conduct was sinful. In support of his petition for amnesty, Shimei pointed out that he was the first of the **house of Joseph** (northern tribes)[10] to come to meet David.

True to his fierce, impetuous character (cf. 2 Sam 16:9), Abishai thought that Shimei should be executed because he had cursed God's anointed king. Technically he was right. What Shimei had done was equivalent to blasphemy (cf. Exod 22:28). David, however, rebuked the vengeful Abishai by asking for the second time: **What**

---

[8]The ASV and NKJV understand the reference to be to a ferry-boat; the BV, NASB, and NIV emend the text to make the verb plural. The NRSV and NJPS translate the verb (in the Qal stem) as a passive: "while the crossing was taking place."

[9]Josephus thinks a bridge of boats stretched across the Jordan (*Ant.* 7.11.2). On the other hand, the LXX refers this to the "men," the attendants of Ziba and Shimei, who helped carry the members of the royal household across the river.

[10]For the name "Joseph" applied to the northern tribes, cf. Amos 5:6; Ezek 37:16; Ps 78:67. They are thus named because Ephraim (Joseph's son) was the most powerful tribe among them.

do you and I have in common, you sons of Zeruiah? See on 2 Sam 16:10. His spirit was totally different from that of the sons of his sister Zeruiah (viz., Abishai and Joab). By suggesting such an execution, **you** [plural, i.e., Abishai and Joab) **have become my adversaries,**[11] i.e., they were prompting him to act against his better judgment. Trouble and discontent would certainly have followed an attempt on David's part to punish any of his enemies, and there might even have been armed resistance to his crossing. This was a day of celebration that David was still king in Israel. So the king asserted his royal authority. There would be no executions to mar the joy of that day (cf. 1 Sam 11:13).[12] David took the risk of granting Shimei on oath a free pardon in spite of his earlier reprehensible conduct.[13]

The Aggrieved (19:24-30)

19:24-25 Mephibosheth, Saul's grandson, **went down,** apparently **from Jerusalem,**[14] **to meet** David at the Jordan. **He had not taken care of his feet,** i.e., washed them, **trimmed his mustache** (lit., "the upper lip") or washed his clothes from the day David left Jerusalem. This neglect of his person indicated that he was in mourning for what had happened to his king. David asked him why he had not joined the rest of his loyal supporters during the exile across the Jordan. Because Ziba had accused Mephibosheth of disloyalty, David was suspicious of him.

---

[11]The Hebrew term is שָׂטָן (śāṭān, sing.) from which is derived the name of the arch-adversary of all mankind. The word may have the connotation "accuser" as in Zech 3:1. Abishai acted as if he were a prosecuting attorney (Anderson, 237).

[12]The text does not support those who see David's leniency with Shimei as an indication that he was forced to negotiate his restoration to the throne. Mettinger (119) is more correct in comparing what transpired at Gilgal as equivalent to a second coronation. Amnesty for criminals was frequently associated with the inauguration of a new national leader (cf. Num 35:25-28; Josh 20:6).

[13]Despite this magnanimous act of forgiveness, David did not forget Shimei's abuse. His final advice to Solomon was not to let Shimei go unpunished (1 Kgs 2:8f.).

[14]No preposition appears with "Jerusalem" in the Hebrew text. Context suggests, and Hebrew grammar permits, the insertion of the preposition "from." Several Greek minuscules have this reading which is followed by the NASB, JB, and NRSV. Others think this incident is not reported in chronological order. Mephibosheth went down *to* Jerusalem from his home in

19:26-28 Mephibosheth explained how he ordered his donkey to be saddled when he heard of David's flight from the city. Ziba took the saddled donkey, along with another animal loaded with provisions, and went off himself to David with his fictitious story, leaving Mephibosheth behind (2 Sam 16:1ff.). Furthermore, Mephibosheth alleged that Ziba had slandered him before David. Yet David was as **an angel of God** (i.e., one who sees all just as it really is) in wisdom (cf. 2 Sam 14:17,20). He therefore would do what was right in respect to the conflicting charges of these two men. Mephibosheth already had benefited from David's mercy by being given a place at the royal table. He did not feel it was right for him to make any further appeals to the king. **Deserved nothing but death** is literally "all the house of my father were only men of death." Normally all the descendants of the preceding royal house would have been killed by the new king. David, however, had shown kindness to them.

19:29-30 That Mephibosheth was telling the truth should have been clear to David by both the appearance of the man, his demeanor, his explanation, and the corresponding silence of Ziba. He must have instantly seen that his decree in 16:4 giving Ziba the properties which he formerly had given to Mephibosheth was completely unjust. Since he could bear to hear no more, David cut short Mephibosheth's speech with an impatient question and issued a new decree. The two men would **divide the fields** which were formerly owned by Saul. Some see this as a confirmation of the original arrangement in which Ziba would be Mephibosheth's tenant, cultivating the land for him and probably sharing half of the harvest (2 Sam 9:7,9f.). More likely, however, this is a revocation both of the original arrangement and the grant made to Ziba in 2 Sam 16:4. That this is a compromise between the rival parties is seen in that Ziba now owned more than he did originally, but less than David had granted him during the flight from Jerusalem. David resorted to

---

Gibeah where he may have stayed during the revolution to avoid all suspicion of supporting Absalom. Cf. the ASV and NKJV. The BV and NJPS also render in such a way as to suggest that the meeting between Mephibosheth and David took place in Jerusalem. R.P. Smith (467) combines both ideas by suggesting that Mephibosheth first met David at the Jordan, then later conferred with him in Jerusalem. Still another possibility is that Jerusalem is the subject of the sentence, i.e., Jerusalem (i.e., its inhabitants) along with Mephibosheth had gone down to meet the king.

the course of compromise either (1) because he had some doubt about who was telling the truth, (2) more likely that he was unwilling for political reasons to offend Ziba, or (3) he was testing the sincerity of Mephibosheth. Though Ziba perhaps had committed treachery against his master, his treachery had been most useful to David in his hour of need. Ziba had put his life on the line to befriend David. He also had been active in bringing over the tribe of Benjamin to David's side. Though his motives had been selfish, yet David had reaped the benefit of his actions. The king here aimed to reward Ziba for his assistance regardless of the way he had treated his master.[15]

The new disposition of the land holdings of the former king could not have pleased the opportunist Ziba. Outwardly Mephibosheth professed to regard the loss of his property with indifference. He said he would rather have David returned to power than to own any of the property. Was he sincere? Who can say?

The Benefactor (19:31-39)

19:31-39 The kindly old Barzillai — he was eighty — came down to the Jordan to see David off. Social etiquette required that a parting guest should be accompanied on the first stage of his journey (cf. Gen 18:16). **He** [emphatic] **had provided** for the king during his stay in Mahanaim (cf. 2 Sam 17:27). David wished to return the hospitality Barzillai had shown him. **Cross** [Heb. adds "you" for emphasis] **over with me,** i.e., over the Jordan, to go to Jerusalem. There the king would provide for Barzillai until his dying day.

Barzillai thanked the king for his generous offer. Just as Hushai was too old to leave Jerusalem during David's forced exodus (2 Sam 15:33), so Barzillai was too old to leave his hometown of Rogelim to march to the capital with David. A series of questions indicates that his sense of sight, taste and hearing were failing. **Tell the difference between what is good and what is not** refers to what is pleasant and unpleasant rather than to ethical values. **The voices of men and women singers** were the professional singing groups which were a prominent appendage to the courts of Eastern rulers. He would not, therefore, gain much benefit from living in the royal palace. He

---

[15]David has been praised for the wisdom of his decision (Hertzberg, 367), and excoriated for the impetuosity and irresponsibility of it (Jamieson, 265).

would only be a potential **burden** to David (cf. 15:33). **How many more years will I live** is literally "how many are the days of the years of my life." Barzillai wished to remain near the tomb of his father and mother so that he might be buried there when he died. However, he was glad to present Kimham to David. He is generally understood to be Barzillai's son, although there is no explicit mention of the fact. If David wished to show kindness to Barzillai, let him take Kimham with him to Jerusalem. David's response is particularly charming in the way in which he assents to Barzillai's proposal with a slight alteration. Barzillai's **Do for him whatever pleases you** becomes I [emphatic] **will do for him whatever pleases** *you.* Furthermore, he would do for Barzillai personally whatever the old man might request. David kissed, blessed and dismissed Barzillai thus relieving the old man of making the crossing over the river.

The Childish (19:40-43)

19:40 David **crossed over** the Jordan, probably at Adam where the Jabbok flows into the Jordan (ZA, 54). He was escorted across the river — perhaps carried across — by **all the troops of Judah** and by **half** (a portion) **the troops of Israel**., i.e., the thousand men from the tribe of Benjamin and perhaps other Israelites who lived in the vicinity. Perhaps the note that only half of the people of Israel came to escort David back is meant to underscore the divided attitude towards David (cf. v. 9) among the northern tribes. **Kimham**[16] crossed over the river with David. The royal entourage paused for some time at **Gilgal**, a shrine close to the fords of the Jordan.

The rest of the troops from Israel began to arrive at Gilgal. Because they had not been invited to the Gilgal gathering to welcome the king, they complained that the men of Judah had stolen (i.e., kidnapped) the king away from them. Before they could arrive, the men of Judah had brought the king and his household across the river.

The men of Judah were quick to defend their actions. David was from their tribe. They had come down to show their support for one of their own people. The men of Judah had not derived any advantage from their tribal relationship to David.[17] Why should the men of Israel be angry about what had taken place at the Jordan? David's

---

[16]The name is here spelled "Kimhan" in the Hebrew.

[17]Some see in the response of the elders of Judah a side-thrust at the tribe of Benjamin which had enjoyed special privileges during the previous reign.

discrimination in favor of his own tribe (vv. 11-15) had driven a wedge between Judah and the other tribes.

The **men of Israel** (northern tribes) responded to the argument of the men of Judah by noting that David was king of the entire nation. (1) The ten tribes[18] of the north had **ten shares** (lit., "hands") of David.[19] The king belonged equally to all, and not to his own tribe only. (2) Since they had a greater claim on David, it was not right for the men of Judah to treat the northern tribes **with contempt,** lit., "humble (them)." (3) Furthermore, the plans to bring the king back to Jerusalem had originated among the northern tribes.[20] While the Israelites stated their case calmly, the men of Judah met their complaint with harsh and bitter rejoinders. This silly argument indicates how deep the tribal animosity ran. One can only guess what must have been going on in David's mind when he heard this bickering.

---

[18]Some think Simeon is here considered part of Judah. Others reckon Israel as ten tribes by counting Ephraim and Manasseh as one (cf. 1 Kgs 11:31). Still others think that one tribe (Simeon) is regarded as having disappeared.

[19]The clause "we have a greater claim on David than you have" in the LXX is "we are older than you" (reading בְּכוֹר [bᵉkôr] = "firstborn" for בְדָוִד [bᵉdāwid] = "in David"). Cf. the NEB "and also we are senior to you."

[20]Throughout v. 43 the pronouns are singular. Apparently one individual was speaking on behalf of all the northern tribes.

2 SAMUEL 20

C. TESTED BY TRIBAL REVOLT (20:1-22)

1. Rebellion in Gilgal (20:1-2a)

20:1-2a The animosity between Judah and the northern tribes offered an opening to a bold and ambitious leader who apparently hoped to restore the sovereignty to the tribe of Benjamin. Sheba is identified as a **troublemaker**,[1] **a Benjamite**, the **son of Bicri,** i.e., of the clan of Bicrites,[2] a clan tracing its descent from Becher the second son of Benjamin (Gen 46:21). This man happened to be present at Gilgal to watch the ridiculous quarreling among the tribes over who had the greater share (or claim) in David. Sheba **sounded the trumpet** to gain the attention of the crowds there. He called for rebellion — more of a secession than an armed uprising — in the rhythmical parallelism of Hebrew verse. He spoke for those who wanted no part of David (cf. 1 Kgs 12:16). There is a touch of contempt in the words **Jesse's son.**[3] **Every man to his tent**, nominally a call to disperse and return to their homes, was the usual watchword of national insurrection (cf. 1 Kgs 12:16). All the men of **Israel** (i.e.,

---

[1]Heb. בְּלִיַּעַל (bᵉliyya'al). The NIV renders this term "wicked" (1 Sam 1:16; 2:12; 25:17,25); "troublemaker(s)" (1 Sam 10:27; 30:22); "scoundrel" (2 Sam 16:7); "evil men" (2 Sam 23:6). See comments on 1 Sam 1:16.

[2]Some link "Bicri" with "Becorath" (1 Sam 9:1) and propose that Sheba was a kinsman of Saul. It is unusual that Sheba is given his full name every time he is mentioned in this narrative, discounting two occurrences where the NIV has inserted his name for clarity. This suggests that the Narrator is making a point about his name. "Bicri" is close in sound with the word rendered "a swift she-camel" running helter skelter (Jer 2:23). Perhaps the thought is that Sheba is a true son of a camel — stubborn, rebellious, and self-willed. (Clines quoted by Youngblood, 1043).

[3]The implication is that David did not come from royal stock. See 1 Sam 20:27,30,31; 22:7,8,9,13; 25:10.

the northern tribes) who were present at the Gilgal meeting followed Sheba. They felt slighted by what had transpired at the
Jordan. **Deserted David** is literally "went up (i.e., to the mountains
from Gilgal) from after David." **To follow Sheba** is literally "after
Sheba." Sheba's hostility was directed particularly against the house
of David; but unlike Absalom's rebellion, it had nothing directly to
do with the succession to the throne.

2. Reinstatement in Jerusalem (20:2b-7)

20:2b David's negotiations with Judah resulted in a total reversal
of the positions of the tribes toward him. **Stayed by** (lit., "clung to")
their king is a strong expression indicating that they followed David.
The Absalom rebellion had started in the tribe of Judah, and that
tribe had been tardy in returning to their allegiance to David. Now
they were fiercely loyal. Israel, which joined the Absalom rebellion
belatedly, and which first proposed the return of David, now was in
the forefront of rebellion. The men of Judah, who had brought David
back across the Jordan, escorted their king all the way to Jerusalem.
The trip was about fifteen miles, mostly uphill all the way.

20:3 Absalom had slept with David's concubines (secondary
wives) as his first public act after entering Jerusalem (2 Sam 16:22).
So David's first act after returning to Jerusalem was to deal with the
problem of these concubines. To continue to claim these women as
his concubines would be a terrible violation of God's law. David
decided that they should be treated as though they were **widows**[4]
since Absalom, who had claimed them as his wives, was now dead.
Because they had once been married to a king, however, they could
not be permitted to marry other men. David removed the women
from the palace and set them up in a house by themselves. He provided protection for them and food. The women were shut off from
society until the day of their deaths. In addition to the moral recti-
tude of David's treatment of the concubines, his actions may have
had political significance. He may have been sending a signal to the
tribes of the north that he was distancing himself from his own former practice in respect to concubinage, and from that of Absalom
as well (Brueggemann, 330).

---

[4]"Living as widows" in the LXX is, in the Targum, "widows whose husband was alive."

20:4-5 The next order of business for the restored king was to deal with the incipient revolution being fomented by Sheba. David ordered Amasa, who now was the commander of the army, to summon the men of Judah (cf. 19:14). The necessity for a levy of Judahite forces shows that they already had disbanded. Within three days Amasa and the men of Judah were to meet David in Jerusalem in order to undertake a campaign against Sheba. For some unexplained reason, Amasa did not reappear within the three days. The text hints that Amasa went out of the bounds of Judah into Benjamin in his efforts to raise an army. This had consumed more time than had been allotted by the king. Perhaps he was having a difficult time recruiting soldiers so soon after the Absalom rebellion. Amasa's failure on his first assignment showed how difficult it was to find a substitute for the vigorous and popular Joab.

20:6-7 David next dispatched other troops to track down Sheba. He feared that (1) Amasa had gone over to the rebellion of Sheba and (2) he might do more harm than Absalom had done. **Escape from us** is literally "tear out our eye." Standard English versions are united in understanding this expression to mean "elude our sight." Another sense of these words is "to harm us irretrievably" (KD, 469). So David dispatched Abishai **with your master's men**, i.e., Joab's men, to pursue Sheba. Speed was important lest Sheba escape to some fortified city. David was still determined not to call upon Joab who for the moment accompanied the expedition in a subordinate position.

Abishai took Joab's men (i.e., troops formerly under Joab's command) and the **Kerethites and Pelethites** (see on 2 Sam 8:18) and all the other **mighty warriors** (see on 2 Sam 10:7) he could muster, and set out after Amasa. David left himself largely unprotected in Jerusalem. This indicates how urgent he felt it was to deal with the current rebellion.

3. The Murder at Gibeon (20:8-13)

20:8-13 Gibeon was six miles north of Jerusalem in the tribal territory of Benjamin. The **great rock** must have been a prominent landmark in the area. How it came about that David's men encountered Amasa at this spot is not stated.[5] Perhaps Amasa was en route back to

---

[5]Amasa had been assembling his army in Judah, and Gibeon was in Benjamin. It is reading too much into the text to suggest that Amasa was

Jerusalem to report to the king as ordered (v. 4) that he had raised the force. Suspecting nothing amiss, Amasa approached David's men, assuming perhaps that David had sent reinforcements. Amasa seems to have been separated from his troops at the time that he came to meet Abishai's force.[6] Perhaps Amasa had designated Gibeon as the point of muster, and most of his troops had not yet arrived.

Joab, who was among the troops of his brother Abishai, decided to assassinate Amasa. The description of Joab's dress is intended to explain how he contrived to stab Amasa without his purpose being suspected. In the girdle which he wore over his military dress he carried a dagger. As he met Amasa he contrived[7] to let this dagger fall out of its sheath on the ground.[8] This would cause Amasa to let his guard down. Supposedly both he and Joab, former enemies in the Absalom rebellion, were now on the same side. Amasa did not realize that his loyalty to David was suspect. Apparently Joab picked up the dagger with his left hand. Amasa still suspected nothing because that was not Joab's "fighting" hand.[9] It is clear that Joab had planned from the beginning of the expedition to kill Amasa at his first meeting with him.

Joab gave a verbal greeting to Amasa, calling him **my brother**. The two were blood relatives and also comrades in arms. Following the custom of the time, Joab **took** (lit., "seized") **Amasa by the beard** with his right hand to kiss him. Kissing of the beard was a token of warm greeting and a mark of respect (Jamieson, 267) and therefore would not likely have excited Amasa's suspicion. He paid no heed to the dagger in Joab's left hand. Joab plunged the dagger into **the**

---

organizing a force in Israel to continue the opposition to David (Mauchline, 295). Some think that Amasa followed Abishai to Gibeon (e.g., Goldman, 315). It is more likely, however, that he already had started north in pursuit of Sheba, and Abishai caught up with him on the outskirts of Gibeon.

[6]Others, however, think he was accompanied by the levy of men he had raised in Judah.

[7]R.P. Smith (493) argues that the fall of the dagger was an accident of which Joab took instant advantage.

[8]Another view is that Joab's tunic was girded up to facilitate marching. The dagger did not fall to the ground, but rather into the folds of the soldier's garment.

[9]Gordon (294) suggests this alternative: Joab brought two swords, one of which he contrived to let fall to the ground in order to give Amasa the impression that he was unarmed.

belly (see 2 Sam 2:23) of Amasa with such force that **his intestines spilled out on the ground**. Joab delivered but one blow, but clearly it would have been more merciful to have delivered more. The intention was that Amasa[10] should suffer a horrible, painful and humiliating death. The brothers then continued their march north as though the death of Amasa was of little importance.

One of Joab's men was stationed beside the body to invite Amasa's soldiers who came upon the scene, if they truly were for David, to **follow Joab**. That Joab's name is mentioned before that of the king suggests that he may have commanded more personal loyalty among these particular soldiers than did David.[11] Joab's agent saw that **the troops** (lit., "all the people," i.e., Amasa's force) shocked by what they had witnessed, would not walk over or around Amasa who was wallowing in his blood as he died. He therefore dragged the dying soldier off the road into a field, and covered it with a garment. After Amasa had been removed from the road, all the men went on with Joab to pursue Sheba. It is clear that Joab was extremely popular with the troops. Abishai probably was glad to see his older brother back in command.

4. The Siege at Abel (20:14-22)

20:14-22 Staying one step ahead of his pursuers, Sheba[12] made his way through the tribes of Israel in an unsuccessful attempt to win popular support for his rebellion. Eventually he came to Abel Beth Maacah (lit., "Abel and Beth Maacah").[13] Elsewhere this town is

---

[10]Gunn (*David*, 140, n. 21) calls attention to the cruelly comic portrait of Amasa: He gained his command by losing a war. He was late for an appointment for which he was relieved of command. He failed to observe the dagger in the hands of his rival. His writhing body temporarily halted the advance of a military expedition.

[11]Gordon (295) suggests the mention of Joab's name first hints of "the mixed motivation of Joab and his supporters."

[12]The NIV has supplied "Sheba" as the subject of the verb. Kirkpatrick (2:188) takes the reference to be to Joab who was gathering forces as he made his way north in pursuit of Sheba.

[13]Beth Maacah is not elsewhere mentioned as a distinct place. Perhaps Abel was near Beth Maacah. "Abel and Beth Maacah" is a variant of Abel of Beth Maacah (v. 15), or, in the more usual form, Abel Beth Maacah (1 Kgs 15:20).

called simply Abel. It was four miles west of Dan. Apparently the only support he was able to rally was among **the Berites**, a people otherwise unknown.[14]

Joab and his troops besieged the city of Abel. They built **a siege ramp** which would give them a platform level with the top of the city's walls from which to fight those who defended the city. The siege ramp **stood against** [or "in"] **the outer fortifications** (חֵל, *ḥēl*). The term includes the low outer wall and the space — often a trench — between it and the main wall. **Battering the wall to bring it down** is literally "destroying the wall to make it fall." It is possible that these words refer to undermining the wall rather than battering it. These operations must have gone on for several weeks.

In Abel a wise woman lived. When she saw that the city was about to fall, she called for a conference with Joab. The woman pointed out to Joab some things about her city that he may not have known. First, this city was famous as a place of wise counsel. For many years people had come there to find the answers to their personal problems. **And that settled it,** i.e., the counsel which they received completely satisfied them. The implication is that Joab would do well to heed her advice. Second, the city of Abel was peaceful and faithful to the crown.[15] Third, this city was **a mother in Israel**,[16] i.e., a mother city, a metropolis, the chief town in that district, a place which had given birth to many people for the nation. Fourth, this city was part of the inheritance of the Lord. This was not some foreign city. The siege would **destroy** (lit., "slay") part of God's heritage.[17]

---

[14]Traditional Jewish interpretation identifies the Berites as the Beerothites (cf. 2 Sam 4:3). Modern scholars have proposed reading "Bicrites." Sheba was a Bicrite. If this reading is accepted, then Sheba's following came largely from his own kinsfolk.

[15]"We are the peaceful and faithful in Israel" is lit., "I am peaceable faithful ones of Israel." The woman was speaking in the name of the community.

[16]Lit., "a city and a mother in Israel." A "mother-city" was an important city with dependent villages. For the concept of "mother" as applied to a city, see comments on 2 Sam 8:1.

[17]On the concept of the land as Yahweh's "inheritance," see 1 Sam 26:19; 2 Sam 10:12; 14:16. There may be in these words the claim that the people of Abel held an inalienable title to their land in accordance with the tradition of Yahweh's allocations to the tribes at the time of the settlement (Gordon, 296).

In his private disputes Joab was ruthless; in his public business he was usually conciliatory (cf. 2 Sam 2:27f.; 18:16). It would appear from v. 21 that the citizens of Abel did not quite understand why Joab was besieging them. Joab assured the woman that it was not his desire to destroy or swallow up the Lord's inheritance. He was only there to arrest Sheba the son of Bicri. The mention that Sheba was from **the hill country of Ephraim**[18] stresses that the culprit was from a distant part of the land. This man had lifted up his hand in defiance against King David. If this one man were handed over, Joab promised to withdraw from the city. The woman promised to do even more than that. She promised to throw Sheba's head over the wall! This woman had the authority to speak for the whole community.

The wise woman advised the citizens of Abel to decapitate Sheba. They cut off Sheba's head and threw it **from the wall,** probably from one of the apertures made for the archers.[19] The implication is that Sheba had only a few supporters with him, or he had lost all support. Thus the war came to a satisfactory end with a minimum of casualties, thanks to the intervention of a wise woman.

Joab immediately sounded the trumpet to signal the men to withdraw from the city and return home. When he returned to the king, Joab was restored to his office as commander of the entire army. The king's views on Amasa's death are not indicated. Joab, however, was never forgiven for this murder (1 Kgs 2:5,31f.). For the moment he escaped unscathed because he had crushed Sheba's rebellion.

D. DAVID'S COURT (20:23-26)

20:23-26 The second half of the history of David's reign closes, like the first (2 Sam 8:16-18) with a list of the leading officers of state. The earlier list began with the statement that David "reigned over all Israel" (cf. 1 Kgs 4:1). The absence of a similar statement here perhaps signals David's weakened position at this time (Youngblood, 1049). For the most part the two lists are the same, but over time there were changes in some positions. (1) **Joab** was

---

[18]The "hill country of Ephraim" extended far enough south to include part of the territory of Benjamin (see on 1 Sam 1:1).

[19]Most English versions render "over the wall." The NIV here has correctly translated the preposition which is rendered "from a window" in Gen 26:8.

reinstated as army commander. Whatever his private wishes, David found that he did not possess the power of removing Joab from office. (2) **Benaiah** was over the Kerethites and Pelethites. See on 2 Sam 8:18. (3) **Adoniram** (Adoram) was in charge of **forced labor** (מַס, *mas*), those who were required to work for the government without pay.[20] This office is not mentioned in the earlier list. Adoniram continued to hold this office during the reign of Solomon (1 Kgs 4:6; 5:14). (4) **Jehoshaphat** was the **recorder**. (5) **Sheva** has now replaced Seriah as secretary. (6) **Zadok and Abiathar** served as priests; and (7) **Ira the Jairite**[21] is not mentioned in the other list of the king's officers. He replaced the king's sons in the office of **David's priest**, probably a personal adviser to the king. See on 2 Sam 8:18. The term "priest" in this context probably refers to a civil and not an ecclesiastical minister.

---

[20]The mention of this office is an indication that David had followed the practice of oriental kings in respect to the imposition of *corvée* — forced labor. This practice became a burning social issue in Solomon's reign, and a major cause of the division of the kingdom after his death. See I. Mendelsohn, "On Corvée Labor in Ancient Canaan and Israel," *BASOR* 167 (1962): 31-35; J.A. Soggin, "Compulsory Labor under David and Solomon," SPDS, 260-267.

[21]"Jair" was the name of a group of villages of Manasseh in Gilead. Ira may have become attached to David's court during the latter's stay in Gilead (2 Sam 17:24ff.).

2 SAMUEL 21

XI. THE COVENANT WITH DAVID IN RETROSPECT
(21:1–24:25)

The last four chapters of 2 Sam contain a sixfold appendix to the book. This material comes from different periods of David's life. The contents of the appendices are of varied character. Two are narratives, two are poems, and two are lists. These chapters offer "a highly reflective, theological interpretation of David's whole career" (Childs, 275).

A. DAVID'S DISCIPLINE: A FAMINE (21:1-14)

Shimei had charged David with wrongly shedding the blood of the house of Saul (2 Sam 16:7). No doubt there were others in Israel who shared that sentiment. The account which follows may have been intended to be a rebuttal to that charge. David is presented here as just in his dealings with the Gibeonites, loyal to his covenant with Jonathan and completely devoid of any personal animosity toward the Saulides (Anderson, 251).

1. The Offended Appeased (21:1-6)

21:1-6 In Palestine a famine was the almost certain consequence of a failure of the winter rains. Famines are mentioned quite frequently in the biblical record. The text gives no indication as to when the famine occurred apart from the fact that it probably was before David befriended Mephibosheth (2 Sam 9:1ff.).[1] When the

---

[1]Commentators agree that the present incident occurred in the early years of David (1) because it would have been unjust to punish a nation for the sins of a king who had long passed away; and (2) because the burial of the bones

famine persisted **three successive years** (lit., "three years, year after year"), i.e., into the third year, David knew that this was not a natural disaster. He concluded that the Lord must be punishing the nation for something. So David **sought the face of the LORD,** i.e., he prayed or requested enlightenment, probably in the Gibeon sanctuary. The Lord answered David, probably though a prophet, that the famine was the punishment for what Saul had done to the Gibeonites. **Blood-stained house** signifies the house upon which blood that had been shed still rested as guilt. Murder that was not punished by the shedding of blood polluted the land and involved the nation in guilt (Num 35:33f.).

The text stresses that the **Gibeonites were not a part of Israel**. They were survivors of the **Amorites** who inhabited Palestine before the Israelites arrived on the scene. Specifically they were of the Hivite people (Josh 9:7). **Had sworn to spare them** is literally "had sworn an oath to them" (Josh 9:3,15-27). In his **zeal for Israel and Judah,** Saul had engaged in some ethnic cleansing of the land. His motives are a matter of speculation.[2] Probably practical and political motives masqueraded behind religious zeal to cleanse the land from the remnant of the heathen.[3] In view of Saul's massacre of the priests of Nob (1 Sam 19), his attempt to wipe out the Gibeonites is certainly in character.

Two questions about this famine must be addressed. (1) Why was the punishment of Saul's sin delayed? and (2) why did it fall upon David and his people who had no part in the sin? Saul's actions were those of Israel's king. A national crime had been committed since a *national treaty,* rather than a personal oath, had been violated. The

---

of Saul and Jonathan as an act of respect makes such probable. Mephibosheth had a young son at the time David sent for him (2 Sam 9:12). He was five years old when his father died (2 Sam 4:4), twelve and a half when David completed his reign in Hebron. The famine lasted three years. If the famine occurred four or five years into the reign of David over all Israel, then Mephibosheth would have been about twenty when he was summoned before David. The famine likely occurred before Absalom's rebellion because there is probably an allusion to the execution of Saul's sons in 2 Sam 16:7.

[2]J. Blenkinsopp amasses circumstantial evidence to suggest that at some point Saul had adopted Gibeon as his capital. "Did Saul Make Gibeon His Capital?" *VT* 24 (1974): 1-7.

[3]There is no justification for linking the slaughter of the Gibeonites with the massacre of the priests at Nob as suggested by Hertzberg (382).

people were guilty in that (1) they permitted their king to act in this lawless manner, (2) they assisted Saul in the execution of the ethnic cleansing policy, and (3) they took advantage of the result of Saul's attacks and thus gave their approval to them. The penalty may have been delayed (1) to allow Israel's leaders to take the initiative in repentance and reparations, (2) to teach the continuity of national commitments from one regime to the next, (3) to warn David about the possible national implications of actions which he might take as Israel's king, and (4) to highlight the divine displeasure with this particular act of Saul. There were so many other grievous sins for which Saul was to be punished, that it was hardly possible to bring out during his lifetime just how bad these lawless acts against the Gibeonites really were. If the slaughter of the Gibeonites had occurred in the last year or so of Saul's reign there would not have been time to bring upon his kingdom such a prolonged expression of divine displeasure.

The text does not indicate whether David's consultation with the Gibeonites was a spontaneous act or a command of God. There are two indications that the latter was the case. First, the suggestion of the Gibeonites involved at least one violation of Israelite law which David would not have presumed to authorize apart from divine authorization. Second, only God would know what it would take to appease his anger over the violation of the national covenant by King Saul. David asked them what it would take to **make amends**, lit., "cover up the incident." The idea is that of a veil drawn over the offense to conceal it by means of a gift or offering. David was probably thinking of monetary compensation for the illegal shedding of blood by Israel's king. He wanted them to **bless**[4] rather than curse the Lord's inheritance (Israel). Only then, he believed, would the famine be removed.

The Gibeonites mention two alternatives for compensation, one of which was not adequate, and the other not legally permissible for them. **We have no right to demand silver or gold from Saul or his family** is literally "it is not to me a matter of silver and gold with Saul and his house." Monetary payments might be required in some cases for wrongful death (Exod 21:30), but not for murder (Num 35:31f.).

---

[4]The Heb. uses an imperative in a voluntative sense which gives greater force to the intention of the previous verb. David is looking for the kind of reconciliation with the Gibeonites which would compel them, as it were, to reverse the curse which they had pronounced on Israel.

Money could not compensate them for the atrocities committed by Saul. They made it plain that only a blood-penalty would appease their anger. It was not their place, however, to execute any Israelite either in blood revenge or in judicially executed capital punishment. To do so would only bring on them the wrath of the more powerful Israelites around them. David then committed himself to do for these Gibeonites whatever they stipulated as being just. **What do you want me to do for you?** is literally "what are you saying I should do for you?"

The Gibeonites first spoke of their current plight. They had been **decimated** (virtually wiped out) by Saul. Their territories had been seized so that at present they had no place to live anywhere in Israel, at least no place was *safe* for them to live. This suggests that Saul had triggered a race war against the Gibeonites which was still being carried out in local communities.

Since the Gibeonites were in no position to initiate judicial executions, the responsibility rested with David. They demanded that **seven sons** (descendants) of Saul be handed over to them to be killed. Why seven? It is not likely that only seven Gibeonites had been slain by Saul. Seven may be (1) symbolic of the total number of slain Gibeonites; or (2) it may point to the number of guilty Saulides who remained; or (3) it was a sacred number, denoting the performance of a work of God; or (4) the number may have been specified in the treaty Joshua had made with the Gibeonites. Even the manner of executing treaty violators may have been specified in that treaty. **Killed and exposed** is a single verb in Hebrew the meaning of which is disputed. It obviously refers to some form of execution, probably impalement[5] presumably after execution as in Num 25:4. The bodies would not be buried, but would be left out in public view of both God and man. **Before the LORD** underscores the judicial and public nature of the executions.[6] Since the offense had been outrageous, the punishment must be conspicuous. **Gibeah** was Saul's home. It was selected by the Gibeonites as the spot where the bodies should be

---

[5]The obscure verb occurs elsewhere only in Num 25:4. The NJPS, JB, and NRSV render "impale them"; ASV, NASB, and NKJV, "hang them up"; BV, "expose their broken corpses"; NEB, "hurl them down"; NAB, "dismember them."

[6]The words "before the LORD" may suggest that the Gibeonites regarded the seven executions to be demanded by divine justice.

exposed to add to the humiliation and shame of the fallen dynasty. That Saul was **the LORD's chosen one** aggravated his guilt and made his crime a national offense. That these heathen people made use of the name of Yahweh is not unexpected since the original covenant with the Gibeonites had been made in Yahweh's name.

2. The Guilty Punished (21:7-9)

21:7-9 David spared Mephibosheth the son of Jonathan from this execution. Thus he honored the oath he had made with his friend Jonathan some years earlier (1 Sam 20:12ff.). David handed over to the Gibeonites, however, five grandsons of Saul and two sons. The two sons were sons of Rizpah, Saul's concubine (cf. 2 Sam 3:7). One of the sons of Saul who was executed had the same name as Jonathan's son who was spared: Mephibosheth. The grandsons were children of **Merab**[7] by **Adriel son of Barzillai the Meholathite.**[8] David granted the request of the Gibeonites (1) possibly because God had directed him to consult with the Gibeonites; (2) because, according to the law, blood-guiltiness when resting upon the land could only be expiated by the blood of the criminal (Num 35:33); and (3) because those handed over participated in the acts of genocide committed against the Gibeonites.

The seven descendants of Saul all **fell together**, i.e., they were all executed at the same time. Then the executioners exposed (impaled on a post) those bodies on a hill **before the Lord**, i.e., under the open sky. This execution took place during the first days of the

---

[7]The NIV follows two Hebrew MSS and the ancient versions which read "Merab." Most MSS and the printed editions of the Hebrew Bible read "Michal" and this is the reading followed here by the ASV and NKJV. Merab was married to Adriel (1 Sam 18:19). Michal was childless (2 Sam 6:23). Traditional Jewish interpretation of the reading "Michal" is that she reared the five boys orphaned by the death of their parents (*Sanh.* 19b). The KJV and NKJV were influenced by this tradition in rendering v. 8 "whom she brought up for Adriel." Josephus (*Ant.* 7.4.3) says that Michal bore these five lads to Adriel after a second divorce from David.

[8]It is not likely that this is Barzillai the Gileadite who supported David during Absalom's rebellion. This Barzillai was a "Meholathite," i.e., he came from the town of Meholah or Abel-meholah. This town was a site along the route of Gideon's pursuit of the Midianites (Judg 7:22). It was in the same district as Beth Shan (1 Kgs 4:12) and was the home of Elisha (1 Kgs 19:16).

barley harvest in April about the time of the Passover (Deut 16:9). If these seven were innocent of any involvement in the crimes of Saul, then David violated God's law. No innocent family member was to be executed for the crimes of another member of the family (Deut. 24:16). Since David was not condemned for any violation of the law, one must assume that these seven personally had been involved in the ethnic cleansing attributed to Saul.

Is it chronologically possible for these seven to have participated in the campaign against the Gibeonites? Certainly the two sons of Saul could have done so. What about the grandsons? That depends on when this episode is dated. A careful study of all the clues in the text suggests that Saul's grandsons would have been at least in their teens by the time David assumed rule over all Israel. That is certainly old enough for them to have participated in the atrocities initiated by their grandfather.

Cynics have suggested that the execution of Saul's seven descendants was a political crime committed to render David's throne secure. This can hardly be the case. If these seven had any claim on the throne, it was minimal. Mephibosheth was the heir of Saul, and David protected him and Mica his son.

3. The Devoted Rewarded (21:10-14)

21:10-14 The law required those who were impaled to be taken down and buried that same evening (Deut 21:23).[9] Yet the seven Saulides remained exposed for weeks as a grim trophy of Gibeonite vengeance. Rizpah, the mother of two of the executed men, could not give the corpses of her sons proper burial without violating the royal edict. She did the next best thing. The grieving mother spread sackcloth (a coarse cloth like burlap) **on a rock.** The preposition *'el* is better rendered "at," "unto" or "against." The sackcloth formed either a rough tent to shelter her from the sun during her vigil, or a bed upon which to rest. Rizpah remained there to guard the decaying bodies of her sons from scavengers. Her intention must have

---

[9]KD (477) argue that the law of Deut 21:22-23 had no application in this case where expiation of guilt that rested upon the whole land was concerned. In this instance the expiatory sacrifices were to remain exposed before Yahweh till the cessation of the famine showed that his wrath had been appeased.

been to protect the dead bodies so that eventually they could be given proper burial. She was at her post from the beginning of the harvest until **the rain poured down from the heavens**. Unless there was a special and unseasonable downpour, the reference would be to the October rains. This means that Rizpah kept her devoted vigil some six months. By the time the rains came, only skeletons remained. Rizpah did not let the vultures feed on those carcasses by day, nor the wild beasts by night. After the rains came, the corpses could be openly taken down from the stakes and buried.

When David heard of what this loyal mother had done, he was deeply moved. Therefore he issued two commands. First, he ordered that the bones of Saul and Jonathan be secured from the **citizens** (lit., "lords" or "owners") of Jabesh Gilead and then reburied in the tomb of Kish. The people from this town had **taken them secretly** (lit., "stolen them") when the Philistines had hung them on the wall of the **public square** (lit., "broad place")[10] at Beth Shan (1 Sam 31:11-13). Second, David ordered that the bones of the recently executed seven descendants of Saul also be buried in the tomb of Kish, Saul's father. By this act David publicly indicated that he had no personal grudge or enmity toward the Saulides. This tomb was located at **Zela,** a city in Benjamin (Josh 18:28) not yet identified. **After that,** i.e., after the execution of the men, **God answered prayer in behalf of the land,** lit., "God was entreated for the land." The famine was over (cf. 2 Sam 24:25).

B. DAVID'S HEROES: A LIST (21:15-22)

This unit is closely related to 2 Sam 23:8ff. from which it is separated by the two poems which follow. It has no connection with the preceding narrative. At one time this list may have been part of a more extended history which recorded the individual accomplishments of David's men. Verses 18-22 are also preserved in 1 Chr 20:4ff., where they are placed immediately after the account of the capture of Rabbah Ammon. Four episodes are related. All are

---

[10]This statement is in no way inconsistent with 1 Sam 31:10 where the Philistines fastened the body of Saul "to the wall of Beth Shan." The exact place where the Philistines fastened the body was the broad space or square just inside the gate where the people would gather for commerce.

connected with Philistine campaigns which resulted in the defeat of an opponent of unusual size.

1. The Rescue by Abishai (21:15-17)

21:15-17 Once again indicates this account was taken from a larger document available to the Narrator. The wars against the Philistines which are mentioned in this list were probably connected with the campaigns recorded in 2 Sam 5:17ff. early in David's reign. Here the Israelites took the offensive. David and his men **went down** to confront the Philistines. During one battle David became exhausted.

Ishbi-Benob was a descendant of **Rapha**. The Rephaim were a tall race which once inhabited Canaan. A few were still living among the Philistines in the days of David. The Philistines used these giants to intimidate the Israelites before battles. Ishbi-Benob's spear had a head weighing three hundred shekels (7.5 lbs.), half the weight of the spearhead of Goliath (1 Sam 17:7). He also was **armed** (lit., "girded") with a **new sword**.[11] When he saw that David could no longer defend himself, he **said** (probably to himself) that he would kill David.

Abishai (see on 1 Sam 26:6) **came to David's rescue** (lit., "help"). **David's men swore to him**[12] (David) that never again would their king lead them into battle. David was **the lamp of Israel** — the guiding light of the nation — and they did not wish to risk the loss of his life. The record indicates that David led his armies in many campaigns following the final defeat of the Philistines, so he must not have felt bound by the oath which his men took.

2. The Exploits of Three More Heroes (21:18-22)

21:18-22 Two battles were fought with the Philistines at **Gob** near Gezer (cf. 1 Chr 20:4) about twenty miles southeast of modern Tel

---

[11]The word "sword" is not in the Hebrew which reads חֲדָשָׁה (ḥădāšāh), i.e., "new." Perhaps the giant had girded about him some strange weapon for which the Israelites had yet to devise a name.

[12]KD (478) understand the Hebrew to mean that the men administered an oath to David, i.e., made him promise by oath not to lead into battle. This, however, is the same construction used of the Israelite oath to the Gibeonites in v. 2.

Aviv. The second hero here honored was **Sibbecai the Hushathite**, i.e., a descendant of Hushah of the family of Judah (1 Chr 4:4). He slew **Saph,** (spelled Sippai in 1 Chr 20:4) another (giant) descendant of Rapha.

The third hero was **Elhanan the son of Jaare-Oregim**[13] who came from Bethlehem. He was able to slay **Goliath the Gittite.**[14] 1 Chr 20:5 makes it clear that this was actually Lahmi, the brother of the famous Goliath who had been killed by David.[15] After the death of Goliath, this giant may have been known, at least to Israelites, as "Goliath."[16] Like his famous brother, he also carried a spear **with a shaft as big as a weaver's rod,** lit., "the wood of his spear was like a rod of weavers" (cf. 1 Sam 17:7). Modern scholars have suggested that the point of comparison was not the size of the weapon, but its construction. It may have had loops attached to it to improve its effectiveness (Yadin as cited by Anderson, 255).

The fourth hero was David's nephew **Jonathan.**[17] **Shimeah** is a variant reading of "Shammah" (1 Sam 16:9). In a battle at Gath he slew a **huge man**[18] who had twenty-four fingers and toes. This giant was another descendant of Rapha. He **taunted** or mocked Israel. Jonathan accepted the challenge, and slew him in hand to hand combat.

---

[13]"Jaare-Oregim" is generally regarded as a corruption (cf. KD, 479). The parallel passage in 1 Chr 20:5, where the name is simply "Jair," is regarded as the original text. "Jair" there is taken to be the same as "Jaare" here with a slight transposition of the letters. "Oregim" means "weavers." The term may have crept in from later in the verse by oversight on the part of a copyist. It may be, however, that the writer saw irony in the fact that a man who was from the weavers defeated a man whose spear was like the rod of weavers.

[14]Jewish tradition regarded Elhanan as the prethrone name of David. This position is defended by Baldwin (286). Under this view, "Jair" (see previous note) is equivalent to "Jesse."

[15]Some take the term "Bethlehemite" which appears here but is absent in Chronicles as a corruption of "Lahmi the brother of" which does appear in Chronicles.

[16]Hertzberg (387) suggests that the name "Goliath" had come to designate a type of warrior in which case there may have been more than one "Goliath."

[17]Jonathan was brother to the worldly-wise Jonadab who helped Amnon devise a rape strategy.

[18]English versions agree that the word מָדוֹן (*mādōn*) is related to מִדָּה (*middāh*). The parallel passage reads אִישׁ מִדָּה (*'îš middāh*), "a man of size or stature" (1 Chr 20:6).

The descendants of Rapha were a giant race which intimidated the Israelites back in the days of Moses and caused them to lose heart (Num 13:33). For this reason the sacred writer makes special mention of the fact that David and his men were able to defeat them.

2 SAMUEL 22

C. DAVID'S TESTIMONY: A SONG (22:1-51)

David's Song of Deliverance also appears as Ps 18. Because of its length, these two chapters are important for the theory of textual transmission. Several variations appear.[1] Scholars debate which text is the more original. Probably both drafts of this poem go back to David himself. The Ps 18 recension was crafted (or edited) to fulfill the liturgical purpose of the Book of Psalms. The poem is a powerful celebration of the deliverance of David from the power of all his enemies.

The poem was composed after the Nathan oracle of 2 Samuel 7 (cf. v. 51). It comes from David's happiest time when he had won for Israel security and empire. Were it to be given a chronological placement in the book, the poem would appear after ch 8. The placement here at the conclusion of the book suggests that the compilers intended for the history of David to be read theologically, i.e., in the light of this psalm. It is not David, the great and powerful king, upon whom readers should focus, but David's great and powerful God.

1. Background (22:1)

22:1 David composed this song to celebrate his deliverance from **the hand of all of his enemies**. Deliverance **from the hand of Saul** is specially mentioned, not because it was chronologically last, but because it was the greatest and most glorious — a deliverance out of the deepest misery into regal might and glory (KD).

---

[1]Critics have noted some seventy-four variations (Jamieson, 272). Of these, the NIV documents four readings in which the wording of Ps 18 has been preferred over the wording of this chapter.

2. David's Testimony (22:2-25)

Opening Praise (22:2-4)

22:2-4 Nine figures, organized into three groups of three, express David's dependence on God. The Lord is (1) his **rock** (סֶלַע, *sela'*) in which he might take refuge as he had taken refuge frequently in the caves of the wilderness, (2) his **fortress**, and (3) his **deliverer.** He is David's (1) **rock** (צוּר, *ṣûr*),[2] (2) his **shield** from all hostile attacks (cf. Gen 15:1; Deut 33:29), and (3) his **horn of salvation**. As with the horn of a wild beast, God routed all who attacked him (cf. Deut 33:17; 1 Sam 2:1). God was (1) his **stronghold** (מִשְׂגָּב, *miśgāb*), a high place where a person is secure against hostile attacks (cf. Ps 9:9); (2) his **refuge,** lit., "my place of retreat" and (3) his **savior** who delivered him from the violent men who sought his life. The **violent men** were Saul and his supporters. **I call to the LORD, who is worthy of praise** is literally "the praised One, I call to Yahweh," i.e., I proclaim Yahweh to be the one worthy to be praised. David found that when he praised God (as he does in the preceding verses) he was saved from his enemies. The Hebrew root יָשַׁע (*yāša'*, "save, help") occurs four times in this introduction to the psalm and five more times in the remaining verses.

Divine Deliverance (22:5-25)

David's Peril (22:5-7)

22:5-7 David poetically describes the desperate situation from which the Lord rescued him. He was like a drowning man sinking beneath the waves. **The torrents of destruction** is literally "the floods of Belial," i.e., calamities that proceed from worthless or base fellows.[3] Death had ensnared him as a hunter might catch his prey in a net. David cried out to God. The Lord heard his prayer from his heavenly temple (cf. Ps 11:4).

---

[2]*Sela'* (v. 2) is used in the sense of concealment; *ṣûr* (v. 3) connotes immovable firmness. The concept of Yahweh as "Rock" harks back to Moses (Deut 32:4). God is called "my rock" seventeen times in the Old Testament.

[3]The term "Belial" is commonly used in the phrase "sons of Belial," i.e., worthless, base fellows. The term has the derived meaning of "ruin" or "destruction."

Divine Intervention (22:8-15)

22:8-15 Theologians label what is depicted in these verses as a theophany, a visible manifestation of God's presence. This theophany had its analogue in the miraculous phenomena which accompanied the descent of God on Mt. Sinai. In highly figurative language the poet paints a picture of the awesome power which God displayed on behalf of his people. These words should not be taken as an account of the actual form in which the divine help was given to David.

God became angry at what the enemies were doing to David. The heavens and earth seemed to quake at his anger. **The foundations of the heavens** may be the mountains on which the heavens seem to rest; alternatively, the expression may simply indicate that the whole universe is moved when God comes in judgment. They **trembled** is literally "they swayed back and forth," i.e., continuously swayed. **He was angry** is literally "it burned to him," i.e., his wrath flared up like a fire. **Smoke rose from his nostrils** is literally "smoke went up in his nostrils." The figure is that of snorting or violent breathing, which indicates the rising of wrath. Smoke was followed by **consuming fire** which burst forth **from his mouth** devouring all that opposes him. This figure is reinforced by the parallel **burning coals blazed out of it**, i.e., out of his mouth as out of a glowing furnace. The coals are fiery messengers of God's vengeance (Kirkpatrick). This description is based upon Exod 19:18 where the Lord descended on Mt. Sinai in smoke and fire.[4]

God **parted the heavens** (cf. Isa 64:1) and **came down** to earth, i.e., he manifested his power in the world. **Dark clouds were under his feet** (cf. Exod 19:6; Deut 5:22). Darkness symbolizes the mystery and terror of his coming (Kirkpatrick). Those stormy clouds are likened to **cherubim** (lit., "a cherub") — a type of angel — upon which the invisible God rides to the aid of the needy (see comments on 1 Sam 4:4). This figure is borrowed from the fact that God was enthroned between the two cherubim upon the lid of the ark of the covenant (Num 7:89). **He soared on the wings of the wind** is language common to ancient poets. Here it is exegetical of the preceding clause. The poet thus underscores how quickly in answer to the prayers of his servant, God came to the deliverance of David.

---

[4]Others think the figures are derived from the phenomena of (1) a volcanic eruption or (2) a thunderstorm with its black clouds and flashing lightning.

God in his wrath withdraws his face from man. The darkness of the storm was a **canopy** (lit., "pavilions") which shrouds God's majesty (cf. Exod 20:18). **Dark rain clouds** is literally "the gathering of waters." Thus God is described as surrounded by impenetrable darkness which shields the blinding light of his glory. Out of the darkness the **bolts of lightning** (lit., "coals of fire") streaked across the sky. David imagines that those lightning bolts were but a small manifestation of the brightness of God's presence.

Thunder here, as frequently in the Old Testament, is called the **voice** of God (cf. Ps 29:3). **Most High** is a name for God found forty-nine times in the Old Testament, mostly in poetic texts. This name celebrates Yahweh as supreme ruler of the universe. The bolts of lightning were like **arrows**[5] (cf. Ps 77:17f.) being hurled at the enemies. The heavenly display **scattered** and **routed** (lit., "confused") the enemies (cf. 1 Sam 7:10). It is not clear whether David actually had witnessed a time when Saul's forces were dispersed with a thunderstorm, or whether he is simply poetically describing how God might help him on any occasion.

Divine Rescue (22:16-20)

22:16-20 Stormy wind and earthquake are added to thunder as symbols of the wrath of God. The earth is pictured as convulsed to its lowest depths. The presence of God divided the water and exposed **the valleys** (lit., "channels") **of the sea,**[6] i.e., the bottom of the sea. At the word of the Almighty, **the foundations of the earth** were exposed. David imagines great geologic upheavals accompanying God's **rebuke**[7] of the wicked. **The blast of his nostrils** is a violent wind which is the evidence and result of his anger (cf. Job 4:9; Isa 30:33). God's anger parted the waters of death which were about to engulf David. Into the deep abysses which had been uncovered through the threat of God's wrath, he **reached down**, as it were, and drew out the sinking man, i.e., David. The **deep waters** are the floods of calamity (v. 5) which had engulfed him.

[5]Arrows, when applied metaphorically to God, sometimes signify calamities inflicted upon men, such as famine and pestilence.
[6]This poetic description may have been inspired by what transpired at the Red Sea.
[7]The term is used of the rebuke of God upon his enemies, which occasioned their destruction (e.g., at the Red Sea) or in any circumstance (Ps 76:6; 80:16; 104:7; Isa 50:2).

The exaggerated poetry of vv. 16-17 is explained in v. 18: God delivered David from his **powerful enemy.**[8] That enemy was **too strong** for human strength alone to overcome. Without God's help that enemy surely would have prevailed over him. The enemy had confronted David **in the day of my disaster,** i.e., the period of his persecution, when he more than once ran imminent risk of being captured or killed by surprise. Yahweh was David's **support** or staff on which he could support himself. The Lord brought David out **into a spacious place.** When one is in trouble, he is in a narrow place. To be brought into a spacious place is to be set free from difficulty.[9] David ascribed his wondrous deliverance to the fact that **he delighted in me,** i.e., God extended his grace to David.

Ground of Deliverance (22:21-25)

22:21-25 The deliverance from his enemies was a reward for David's righteousness (right living). These words are not intended as boasting, but as testimony to the faithfulness of Yahweh to guard and reward those who are faithful. David found in the divine mercies towards himself clear evidences of his standing with God. His **hands** had not been stained with sin. He had **kept the ways** of God. He had never committed the evil of **turning away from** (lit., "acted wickedly from") **my God.** He had made a sincere attempt to keep all of God's laws or decrees. They were always **before me,** i.e., constantly on his mind.

David claims that he was **blameless** before the Lord. He does not mean that he was without sin. The context here is that of his persecution by Saul. He had done nothing deserving of such vicious treatment by Saul. **His laws are before me,** i.e., constantly on his mind. Verse 25 essentially repeats v. 21. David's righteousness and cleanness consist of endeavoring earnestly and sincerely to walk in the ways of God.

---

[8]The singular may be used as a collective; or perhaps Saul is meant.

[9]Jamieson (276) suggests these words may be interpreted literally. David had been brought out of the caves and deserts, where he had been compelled to seek refuge, to the comfort and freedom of royal rank.

3. David's Prayer and Testimony (22:26-51)

David's Perception (22:26-28)

22:26-28 David recognized that God treats every person in accordance with that person's conduct toward him. The Lord responds positively to (1) the **faithful** or pious,[10] (2) the **blameless**,[11] (3) the **pure** (lit., "the one who purifies himself") and (4) the **humble**. On the other hand, with the crooked God shows himself **shrewd**, i.e., he can outsmart them every time. Morally distorted people are given over by God to pursue perversity to their own destruction.

Verse 28 divides people into two classes, viz., the humble and the haughty. God intervenes to save the **humble** (lit., "afflicted people"), the pious and depressed in the nation, i.e., those who through the discipline of suffering have learned humility. His eyes focus on the **haughty** (lit., "the high") to bring them down. The haughty are those with no fear of God and no respect for a neighbor's rights, the godless rich and mighty in the nation.

David's Confidence (22:29-37)

22:29-37 As the Lord had delivered him out of the danger of death, so he also had given David power over all his enemies. He confessed that Yahweh was his **lamp**.[12] The light of a lamp was a common figure for prosperity while its extinction signaled calamity (Esth 8:16; Job 18:5-6; Ps 97:11; 132:17). God had lifted David out of a condition of depression and contempt into one of glory and honor. He provided strength and courage for David to **advance against a troop**, i.e., charge through the enemy,[13] or **scale a wall**, i.e., leap over the defenses of his enemy.[14] With God on his side, David felt invincible.

---

[10]The word includes love to God as well as to man. See note on 1 Sam 2:9.

[11]"Blameless" (גִּבּוֹר תָּמִים, *gibbôr tāmîm*), lit., "an upright hero." The phrase refers to the man strong in innocence, i.e., who manfully maintains his integrity.

[12]Verse 29 begins with the Hebrew *kî* which refers to the thought implied in v. 28, that David belonged to the "afflicted people."

[13]Some think this might be an allusion to David's successful pursuit of the Amalekites (1 Sam 30:8).

[14]If the reference is to a specific event in David's life, it probably refers to the capture of the stronghold of Zion (2 Sam 5:6ff.). The capture was effected so easily that it seemed that David had leaped over the walls.

David derived his confidence from both the acts of God and from his word. **As for God** is literally "the God" (הָאֵל, *hā'ēl*),[15] i.e., "the Mighty One."[16] David's God, Yahweh, is *the* God. His way (activity) is **perfect**, without blemish. Yahweh's word is **flawless,** lit., "tested," i.e., refined like pure gold. The Lord is **a shield** to all who take refuge in him, i.e., put their faith in him.

Who is God besides the LORD? is a monotheistic formula (McCarter, 2:469) which underscores that there is no help except by Yahweh. The Lord alone is a **Rock** or ground of hope as in v. 2. God **makes my way perfect,** lit., "he leads the innocent his way."[17] He provided David with swift and agile feet, like a **deer**. This would be an indispensable qualification for success in ancient warfare. Thus David could escape his enemies and climb to the inaccessible heights. These **heights** may be the mountain strongholds which David occupied during his flight from Saul.[18]

The Lord **trains his** [David's] **hands for battle,** i.e., gave him battle skills. He provided David with strength to use **a bow of bronze**. This is a symbol for the most powerful weapon available in those days.[19] The Lord also gave David **the shield of victory**, i.e., deliverance or protection. This shield consisted of salvation — the helping grace of Yahweh.

In vv. 36-37 David switched to second person, i.e., praise prayer. **You stoop down** (lit., "your answering," i.e., to David's prayers[20]) to

---

[15]Hertzberg (398) thinks the article in *ha'el* (vv. 31,33,48) has demonstrative significance, i.e., *this* God. David's whole career points like a finger to this God of salvation.

[16]The name *ha'el* occurs twenty times in the Old Testament, six of which are in poetic texts in Samuel (1 Sam 2:3; 2 Sam 22:31,32,33,48; 23:5.

[17]Various translations of 22:33b: "makes my way without blame" (JB); "guideth the perfect in his way" (ASV); "he makes my way perfect" (NKJV); "who kept my path secure" (NJPS); "He levels for me his good way" (BV); "has opened wide my path" (NRSV); "he sets the blameless in his way" (NASB).

[18]KD (490) think the "heights" are the high places of his own land, which he maintained triumphantly, so that he ruled the land from them.

[19]Mauchline (310) argues that the bow itself could not have been of bronze since such a bow would lack pliancy and resiliency; the reference must be to bronze-tipped arrows.

[20]The NIV is influenced by the reading of Ps 18:35. Various renderings of v. 36b: "your help" (NASB, NRSV); "thy/your gentleness" (ASV, BV, NKJV); "your providence" (NJPS); "your armor covers me over" (JB).

make him great in time of war. God made the path of his feet **broad** (cf. v. 20) so that his **ankles** did not turn aside or turn back. This means that with God's help David had been able to walk with bold steps of confidence. God removed all obstructions and stumbling blocks out of the way.

David's Success (22:38-46)

22:38-46 God had enabled David to pursue and **crush** (destroy) his enemies, to walk right over their fallen bodies. Switching again to second person address, David praised God for girding him with this battle strength. The enemies had to **bow at my feet** (lit., "beneath me"), i.e., submit to David's authority. **My foes** is literally "those who hated me." God made his enemies **turn their backs in flight**. David caught and destroyed them. They **cried** (lit., "looked") **for help**[21] from any source, even Yahweh.[22] God, however, did not give those enemies deliverance. David was able to pulverize them as fine dust. He trampled them under his feet like mud.

God delivered David from the attacks of his own people (Israelites) as well as foreign enemies. The reference is to the efforts of Saul to kill David and/or the long war between the house of Saul and the house of David (2 Sam 3:1). The Lord had preserved his position as **the head of nations**, i.e., his power and influence were acknowledged by neighboring nations. Being preserved from Saul enabled David to conquer several other nations. Foreigners who merely heard rumors of his approach were surrendering their fortresses and **cringing**[23] (in fearful homage) before David (cf. 2 Sam 8:9f.). **As soon as they hear me** is literally "at the hearing of an ear." **They all lose heart** (lit., "languish, fade, wilt") before David, i.e., despair of ever being able to resist his victorious power. **They come**

---

[21]The NIV is influenced by the reading of Ps 18:41. The difference between "cried" and "looked" in the Hebrew text is one consonant. The JB renders "cried"; the BV, NKJV, NRSV, JPS, ASV and NASB render "looked."

[22]Anderson (265) suggests the enemies here may have been fellow Israelites.

[23]The NJPS, BV, and NRSV agree with the NIV. The verb comes from a Hebrew root which means "to deceive," so that the meaning here is that foreigners feign obedience. Hence the NASB: "Foreigners pretended obedience to me." The ASV and NKJV adopt the neutral "submit to me." The JB renders "foreigners come wooing my favor."

trembling is literally "they gird themselves,"[24] i.e., they muster enough courage to come out of their strongholds to surrender to David.

Concluding Praise (22:47-51)

22:47-51 David concluded his song with praise for the God he loved so much. In contrast to the lifeless idols, Yahweh **lives**, i.e., he really exists. The experience of David's life was to him convincing evidence that God was the living, acting Ruler of the world. Again he referred to the Lord as **my Rock**, i.e., his steadfast Savior. **The Rock, my Savior** is literally "the rock of my salvation." God executes vengeance against the enemies of David. Vengeance — righteous retribution for evil otherwise unpunished — is a divine prerogative and responsibility (Ps 94:1). The faithful looked forward to the execution of that vengeance as the vindication of God's righteousness and the innocence of his people. God again and again rescued David by lifting him out of the reach (so to speak) of his enemies. **My foes** is literally "those who rose against me." **Violent men** is literally "a man of violences," i.e., of multiple acts of violence. Some commentators see here a reference to Saul. The NIV, however, is probably correct in understanding the words to mean men of violence in general.

David owed the Lord a debt of gratitude. He unashamedly would give his thanks to the Lord among the nations (pagan peoples) which he had conquered.[25] He would testify to the world that Yahweh **gives his king great victories** is literally "great deliverances are to his king," i.e., belong to him. In the light of the great promise of 2 Samuel 7 David was confident that Yahweh would show **unfailing kindness** (חֶסֶד, *ḥesed*), i.e., covenant faithfulness, **to his anointed**, i.e., to David personally and to his descendants **forever**. "The king whose salvation the Lord had magnified, was not David as an individual, but David and his seed for ever — that is to say, the royal family of David which culminated in Christ" (KD, 493).

---

[24]The NIV and most English versions are influenced by the reading of Ps 18:45.

[25]Paul quotes v. 50 along with Deut 32:43 and Ps 117:1 as proof that the salvation of God was intended for Gentiles also (Rom 16:9).

2 SAMUEL 23

D. DAVID'S HOPE: A SONG[1] (23:1-7)

1. Introduction (23:1-3a)

23:1 These are not the last words David ever spoke, but rather the last inspired song which he ever composed.[2] It must have been composed very near the end of his life in 970 B.C. An **oracle** (*nᵊ'um*) is a direct utterance from God. The introduction to the poem is a fourfold portrait of the writer. In this case, God was delivering his oracle through the pen of **David son of Jesse**. David introduced himself by the announcement of his name and parentage in order to demonstrate his own insignificance, and to magnify the supernatural prophetic power which had been imparted to him. Second, he was **the man** (*haggeber*), an almost exclusively poetical word which implies strength. **Exalted** is literally "raised on high."[3] Third, David identified himself as **the man anointed**. He was anointed with sacred oil by Samuel the prophet when he was but a boy. Finally, David referred to himself as **Israel's singer of songs**, lit., "he who is pleasant in the psalms of Israel."[4] He was God's instrument for stim-

---

[1]See N.H. Richardson, "The Last Words of David: Some Notes on II Samuel 23:1-7," *JBL* 90 (1971): 257-266; G. Del Olmo Lete, "David's Oracle [2 Samuel XXIII 1-7]: A Literary Analysis," *VT* 34 (1984): 414-437.

[2]Jamieson (281) further restricts the meaning to the last divine communication which David received of the kingly character and glory of the Messiah.

[3]The adverbial accusative עַל (*'al*) leaves it to the imagination to picture the greatness and extent of sovereign power and glory to which the shepherd son of Jesse was raised. The NIV alone among standard English versions treats *'al* as an abbreviated divine epithet, "Most High." That rendition, however, is endorsed by Youngblood, 1081f.

[4]Recent commentators have taken זְמִרוֹת יִשְׂרָאֵל (*zᵊmîrôth yiśrā'ēl*) to be a divine epithet, meaning something like "the protector of Israel" (McCarter 2:476). The plural is taken as a plural of majesty. Thus David would be described as favorite of the Strong One of Israel" (NRSV). The traditional

ulating the spiritual life of his people through his psalms. Songs
(זְמִרוֹת, z³mirôth) are not songs generally, but songs of praise in honor
of God. Some seventy-three of the psalms in the Book of Psalms
were written by David.

23:2-3a David made a fourfold claim to divine inspiration. First,
he claimed that **the Spirit of the LORD spoke through** [lit., "in"] **me,**
i.e., he realized that the Holy Spirit of the Lord was guiding him in
the composition of this song. Second, David claimed that God's
word[5] **was on my tongue.** That which God revealed to his mind (revelation) was communicated accurately in word (inspiration). To this
claim of inspiration, Jesus himself gave witness (Matt 22:43). Third,
David affirmed that **the God of Israel spoke,** which underscored that
what he was about to say was the word of God. *The* God (as opposed
to *my* God) indicates that the content of this prophecy relates to the
people of Israel. Fourth, he identified the one who spoke as the **Rock
of Israel.** This emphasizes that the prophecy is guaranteed by God's
unchangeable nature (see on 1 Sam 2:2). **Said to me** in this context
is equivalent to "promised me" (cf. Deut 6:3; 19:8).

2. God and the Righteous Ruler (23:3b-4)

23:3b-4 The brevity of the Hebrew makes for difficult translation
and interpretation of these verses. The NIV sees here a general principle, viz., that a righteous king is a blessing to his people. That tru-
ism would hardly be worthy of the elaborate introduction in vv. 1-3a.
It is better to regard these words as prophetic, an announcement of
the coming of a wonderful ruler. **When one rules over men in righteousness, when he rules in the fear of God** is literally "a ruler[6] over
men [i.e., mankind], a righteous one who rules in the fear of God."
David envisioned one who would rule over men in righteousness.[7]

---

rendering is not impossible and has been followed, in slight variation, by
most standard English versions: "the favorite of the songs of Israel" (NJPS);
"the singer of the songs of Israel" (JB); "the sweet psalmist of Israel" (ASV,
NASB, NKJV, and essentially BV).

[5]"His word" (מִלָּתוֹ, millāthô) is an exclusively poetic term.

[6]The Hebrew uses the participle מוֹשֵׁל (môšēl, "ruler, prince") from the
root māšal, "to make decisions, have power, to rule." Gideon was offered a
chance to rule (מְשֹׁל, māšal) the people (Judg 8:22-23). This term is applied
to Messiah in Micah 5:1.

[7]Following the lines of interpretation suggested by Kirkpatrick (2:214).

His government would be upright, i.e., encouraging all that is morally beautiful, and restraining that which is morally reprehensible and
destructive. The justice of this ruler would be founded in his **fear of
God**. He would be godly in his personal life and keenly aware that he
was God's agent in maintaining orderly society. The ruler over men
whom David saw in the Spirit is not anyone who rules righteously,
nor is he the seed of David collectively, but Messiah, as was recognized long ago by the Aramaic Targum.

Two figures describe the blessing of the future king's righteous
and godly reign. First, his reign would be like **the light of morning
at sunrise**, i.e., a sunrise which drives away darkness, and gives men
by precept and example the clear knowledge of their duty.[8] The
comparison of a king to the sun is not surprising in the light of Gen
1:16,18 where the sun was appointed to rule the day. The morning
sun symbolizes gladness, illumination, and a new beginning. Thus
"the light of the rising sun on a cloudless morning is an image of the
coming salvation" (KD 496). Second, his reign would be like the
refreshing **rain** which renews life in vegetation. "Rain" is figurative
of blessing generally (cf. Isa 44:3). The green **grass** which springs up
from the earth is an image of the blessings of the messianic salvation
(Isa 44:4; 45:8) and the steady but silent growth of piety and virtue
among the peoples who submit to the reign of David's greater son.

3. God and the Davidic Dynasty (23:5)

23:5 Verse 5 contains three negative rhetorical questions expecting positive answers. David understood that it was through his
house (dynasty) that the new day so beautifully described in the preceding verses would dawn. David's family was in the right relationship with God. This is indicated by the fact that God had made an
everlasting covenant with David. God's covenants contain promises
and commitments to his people. **Arranged and secured in every
part** indicates that this covenant had been formulated with legal cor-
rectness and was valid. It had been secured against every form of
tampering. It covered every contingency. In 2 Sam 7:12ff. Nathan
the prophet had promised David that one from his family would

---

[8]Jamieson (282) calls attention to one ancient MS which reads: "and as the
morning light shall Yahweh, the Sun, arise, even an unclouded morning."

rule forever. No obstacle — not even the apostasy of some of David's successors — would invalidate that divine commitment (2 Sam 7:14-15). This covenant could not be invalidated or called in question. Because of that covenant, David was confident that God would provide for him personal **salvation** or deliverance from physical threat. **My every desire** is literally "all the good pleasure," i.e., the stated purpose of God as revealed in the Nathan oracle. He could anticipate that the righteous ruler, who would bring such abundant blessing, would arise out of his family. God would **bring to fruition** (lit., "cause it to spring forth") the salvation promised to David's house and the sovereign promises concerning the future Davidic ruler.

4. God and Evil Men (23:6-7)

23:6-7 The fate of evil men is contrasted to the blessing on David and his house. The development of salvation under the righteous ruler is accompanied by judgment upon the ungodly. The **evil men** (lit., "belial")[9] are those who rise up to oppose the righteous king. They are compared to **thorns** which injure all who come in contact with them. Men dig up and burn thorns in order to clear the land. Those who do the clearing, however, must protect themselves, especially their hands. Hard instruments and violent means must be taken to destroy or uproot those thorns. For this reason God himself will remove or destroy those thorns who are opposed to this kingdom (cf. Matthew 13:40-41).

E. DAVID'S HEROES: A LIST (23:8-39)[10]

1. Supreme Honor (23:8-12)

Three warriors received the supreme recognition from King David. This group was known simply as **the Three** (v. 8). Nothing is

---

[9]"Belial" signifies "worthlessness" and especially "vicious worthlessness." See note on 1 Sam 1:16. The word here is used collectively and is probably an ellipsis for "sons of Belial." The godless are depicted as "personified worthlessness" (KD, 497).

[10]For a helpful study of David's military organization, see B. Mazar, "The Military Elite of King David," *VT* 133 (1963): 310-320.

said outright about their relationship to the Thirty mentioned later. Presumably they belonged to the Thirty, but were distinguished within that group.

Josheb-Basshebeth (23:8)

23:8 The first hero is Josheb-Basshebeth or Jashobeam (1 Chr 11:11).[11] His family name was **Tahkemonite**[12] (Hachmonite in 1 Chr 11:11). This hero joined David at Ziklag. Josheb was **chief of the Three,** lit., "chief captain."[13] **He raised his spear against eight hundred men is** literally "he swung his spear over eight hundred slain at once." The idea is not that he killed eight hundred in one blow, but that in one battle he slew eight hundred men.[14] Eventually he was appointed the commander of the first division of David's army (1 Chr 27:2).

Eleazar (23:9-10)

23:9-10 Next in rank in the group of the Three was Eleazar son of Dodai the Ahohite.[15] In one battle he was with David when the

---

[11]The standard English versions agree with the NIV in the rendering of the name of the first hero. KD (499) and others think the name as it stands in the Hebrew text of Samuel is corrupt. Most scholars think the Chronicles reading ("Jashobeam") is correct. On the basis of the LXX, Mauchline (315) would read "Ishbaal" and this reading is followed by the JB.

[12]"Tahkemonite" (ASV, NASB, NKJV, NRSV, BV, NJPS) appears to be a faulty spelling, and the parallel in Chronicles is the correct reading. Jashobeam was a son (or descendant) of the family of Hachmon (1 Chr 27:32).

[13]The Hebrew רֹאשׁ הַשָּׁלִשִׁי (rō'š haššāliší) has been rendered "chief among [of] the captains" (NKJV, ASV, NASB); "chief of the military leaders" (BV); "the chief officer" (NJPS); "chief of the Three" (JB, NRSV). Some commentators alter the text on the basis of Chronicles to read רֹאשׁ הַשָּׁלִשִׁים (rō'š haššᵉlōšîm, "chief of the thirty"). KD (500) point out that the singular of the word used here refers to the royal aide-de-camp (e.g., 2 Kgs 7:2,17,19; 9:25) and in the plural to the royal bodyguard (e.g., 2 Kgs 10:25). The plural form in Chronicles can be explained on the simple ground that David's thirty heroes formed his whole body of adjutants. Thus no emendation of the text of either Samuel or Chronicles at this point is necessary. The word for "captain" and the word for "three" are similar and it is not always clear which meaning is intended.

[14]The number of men whom he slew at one time is stated in Chronicles to have been three hundred, but as Abishai accomplished this feat, and yet held only inferior rank, eight hundred is probably correct.

[15]Eleazar was probably descended from Ahoah, a son of Benjamin (1 Chr

Israelites **taunted the Philistines**, i.e., goaded them into a battle. **At Pas Dammim** does not appear in the Hebrew text of Samuel. It needlessly has been supplied from the parallel passage in Chronicles.[16] **The men of Israel retreated** (lit., "went up") is a proper translation (cf. 1 Kgs 15:18; 2 Kgs 12:19) and that idea is reflected in the standard English versions. The verb, however, may simply mean that the men of Israel went up into battle. Eleazar **stood his ground** (lit., "arose" as in the ASV, NKJV, and NASB; "advanced" as in BV). Thus the Hebrew is not clear whether Eleazar stood alone when others fled, or led a charge against the enemy. 1 Chr 11:13-14 clarifies the situation. The Israelite army did flee before the Philistines and "they" (Eleazar and his men) stood their ground defending a field of barley. In this battle Eleazar gripped his sword so tightly that his hand "froze" to the sword, i.e., the muscles of his hand became so stiff that he could not relax them. Through his courage **a great victory** (lit., "salvation, deliverance") was won. The term commonly means a deliverance given by God and not achieved by human agency alone. **The troops returned to** (lit., "after") **Eleazar.** This does not imply that they had fled, but simply that they turned in whichever way he turned, and followed him. **Only to strip the dead** suggests that Eleazar alone was responsible for that victory, but his men benefited by removing valuables from Philistine corpses.

Shammah (23:11-12)

23:11-12 Third in rank among the Three was **Shammah** the son of Agee the Hararite. **The Philistines banded together**, lit., "gathered to Lehi,"[17] i.e., massed for a new invasion of Judah. In a battle

---

8:4). He, however, is not named among the Benjamites who joined David at Ziklag (1 Chr 12:1-7) probably because he had joined David at an earlier date.

[16]Pas Dammim (Ephes Dammim in 1 Sam 17:1) was in the valley of Elah where David slew Goliath. Numerous battles between the rival peoples were fought in this border area, hence the place name meaning "the boundary of blood." A more literal reading would be: "one of the three mighty men with David when they defied the Philistines who were gathered there to battle and the men of Israel had gone up [to battle]."

[17]So the JB and NRSV. This reading requires a slight change of vocalization of the Hebrew consonants. Maintaining the reading as vocalized in the MT are the NASB and ASV; NKJV, "gathered into a troop"; BV, "mustered into a combat group"; JPS, "gathered in force."

with the Philistines, Shammah took his stand in a patch of lentils (beans)[18] and defended it even after the other soldiers had fled. The Philistines seem to have made this incursion in order to carry off or destroy the crops of the Israelites.

2. Superior Honor (23:13-23)

A Daring Requisition of Water (23:13-17)

23:13-17 Within a military order known as the Thirty certain men stood out. Though their exploits were not considered as valiant as those of the Three, yet they enjoyed superior honor within their group. David was in **the stronghold** at the **cave of Adullam**. The Philistines were **encamped in the Valley of Rephaim.** Not yet entrenched in Jerusalem, David had taken refuge in the wilderness.

At the cave of Adullam three men heard David express his longing for some water from a well in Bethlehem.[19] The problem was that Bethlehem was some twenty-five miles distant, and the Philistine encampment blocked access to the village. David's men, however, **broke through the Philistine lines** to fetch the water. When they returned to Adullam, David refused to drink water which had been secured at the risk of the lives of his soldiers. As if that water were a sacrificial libation, **he poured it out before the LORD.**[20] David did this (1) to consecrate that water to God because it had been bought with blood, and only Yahweh was worthy of such a costly offering; (2) to express thanksgiving for the safe return of the three brave men. **Is it not the blood of men** in the Hebrew is a striking interrogative exclamation, i.e., "the blood of men?"[21] Because the water was secured at the risk of life, it is compared to **blood**. Drinking this water, therefore, would be nothing less than drinking their blood. By this action David taught his troops that their well-being was more important to him than his personal comfort. Nonetheless, the bravery of these three soldiers earned them the title **the three mighty men**.

---

[18]"Barley" in 1 Chr 11:13. The difference in reading is probably caused by a transposition of letters.

[19]Rather than a mere sentimental longing, David may have been sick, and burning with fever when he uttered these words (R.P. Smith, 571).

[20]The text uses the technical term for a sacrificial libation.

[21]In 1 Chr 11:19 the text reads: "Shall I drink the blood of these men?"

The Fame of Abishai (23:18-19)

23:18-19 One of the three mighty men who fetched the water from Bethlehem was **Abishai the brother of Joab,** David's commander. **Chief of the Three** is better rendered, "chief captain"[22] as in v. 8. He had once slain three hundred with his spear in one battle. **So he became as famous as the Three** (lit., "and to him was a name among the Three"). This deed made him the most honorable of the second rank of Three. Yet he **was not included among them** (lit., "but unto the Three he did not come"). According to 1 Chr 11:20-21 this verse means that Abishai, though famous among the second trio, did not attain to the highest honor among the first Three.[23]

The Bravery of Benaiah (23:20-23)

23:20-23 The second member of the second Three was Benaiah. He was from **Kabzeel** ("Jekabzeel" in Neh 11:25), a town in the Negev near the border of Edom (Josh 15:21). He was the son of Jehoiada who is identified as a priest. He led a group of 3,700 martial priests who did so much to make David king of all Israel (1 Chr 12:27). Benaiah is called a **valiant fighter.** Three of his great exploits earned his position on this list of worthies. First, he struck down two of **Moab's best men,** lit., "two of ariels of Moab." The exact meaning of "ariel" in this context is not certain. The LXX regarded "Ariel" as the proper name of the king of Moab.[24] Others translate the term "altar-hearth" (Goldman, 339), but this hardly fits with the verb **struck down,** i.e., slew. Still others see Ariel as a compound of two terms *ari* (lion) and *el* (God). The reference would then be figurative for two lion-hearted men or fierce warriors.[25] One would not

---

[22]The MT "Chief of the Three" is followed by the NIV, NJPS, ASV, and NKJV. The idea is that Abishai was the chief (commander) of the second group of Three — those who fetched the water from Bethlehem. The rendering "chief of the thirty" (NASB, BV, NRSV, and JB) is based on the reading of two Hebrew MSS and the Syriac version.

[23]KD (503) think *haššǝlōšāh* in v. 19 should be emended to *haššǝlōšîm,* "the Thirty." Thus the verse would read: "he was honored before the Thirty and became their chief, but he did not come to the Three."

[24]The LXX has "two sons of Ariel." So the ASV, NASB, NJPS, and NRSV. Ariel is the name of a person in Ezra 8:16.

[25]So "lion-like heroes" (NKJV). This is the interpretation given to Ariel in the Syriac version. The BV transliterates but then notes that the term probably refers to military champions. So also Anderson (276).

expect to find, however, the use of poetical language in a prosaic catalog like this. Another possibility is that a "lion of God" would be a way of referring to "a gigantic lion."

Second, Benaiah faced **a lion** in the middle of a pit on a snowy day. The exact circumstances of this deed are left to speculation. Lions inhabited the thickets on either side of the Jordan in biblical times. Perhaps this unfortunate animal had wandered into a populated area and had become a menace to the locals. The pit may have been a cistern. The **snow** is mentioned because (1) it may have betrayed the tracks of the lion, (2) the event was more than usually impressed upon the memory because of the rarity of such snowy days, and (3) the slippery ground made the confrontation with the beast even more dangerous. At the risk of his own life, Benaiah went down into the lair and slew the beast.

Third, using only an ordinary club, Benaiah disarmed **a huge** (lit., "who was a sight") **Egyptian** warrior[26] who may have been a mercenary in the service of the Philistines. He slew the Egyptian with his own spear. This fight was probably a single combat between champions of opposing armies.

Benaiah was as famous as the top three mighty men. He was held in greater honor than any of the group known as the Thirty, but he was not included in the top Three. His deeds were daring, but they were not *saving* deeds. Eventually David **put him in charge of his bodyguard,** lit., "appointed him to his audience," i.e., his privy council (cf. 2 Sam 8:18). He was also commander of the third division of twenty-four thousand men (1 Chr 27:5). Subsequently he took the side of Solomon against Adonijah, and was rewarded by being made commander-in-chief in place of Joab (1 Kgs 2:35).

The third member of the second group of three is not named for some reason. Perhaps he later disgraced himself in some way or proved himself to be disloyal to the king. Some think that Joab was the missing member of the group. Others have nominated Amasa and Ahithophel.

---

[26]1 Chr 11:23 sheds light on the meaning of this text. The Egyptian was "a man of measure," i.e., a tall man, "five cubits tall," i.e., over seven feet.

3. Secondary Honor (23:24-39)

23:24-39 A third group of heroes was called the Thirty. This group may have been like a supreme military council responsible for maintaining discipline, recommending promotions, and prescribing training for David's army. Nothing is known of the exploits of these heroes. The group may have started out with thirty warriors; but as others performed equally valiant deeds, they were added to the rolls. It is also possible that vacancies in the ranks due to death were filled by new soldiers so that there were never more than thirty at one time. The names seem to be listed chronologically, i.e., in the order in which the honor was bestowed (Mauchline, 321), or the order in which these men attached themselves to David (K. Elliger, cited by Gordon, 314). The order was initiated in David's fugitive period (when his friends were mostly in Judah) and was later expanded after the establishment of his kingdom. The list in Chronicles contains sixteen additional names of those who attained this honor after the list in 2 Samuel was composed.

The figure **thirty-seven** here probably refers to all the heroes of the three groups: The First Three (3), the Second Three (2), the Thirty (31) equals 36. As noted above, one of the names of the Second Three (probably Joab) was omitted from the list because of later failings. He probably was the thirty-seventh hero.[27]

Many of the heroes came from Judah, especially from the area of Bethlehem. Several are David's own relatives. Seven towns or families produced sixteen on the list. One father and son, and a couple of pairs of brothers are included. Several foreigners made the list: Hittites, Ammonites, Moabites, an Aramean from Zobah, and Gibeonites. These men had earned their right to this honor by their battlefield feats and by their fidelity to David. Twelve of these heroes (viz., the five belonging to the first two classes and seven of the third) were appointed by David as commanders of the twelve divisions into which he divided the army. Each division served one month each year on active duty.

---

[27]KD's restoration of the text of v. 34 would yield these numbers: three in the first class, two in the second, and thirty-two in the third class.

#	Samuel Text	Chronicles Text	Town S = Samuel C = Chronicles	Location	Notes
			Table 8 **THE ORDER OF THE THIRTY**		
1	Asahel	Asahel		Judah	The brother of Joab. Slain early in David's reign (2 Sam 2). Mention of him here indicates that David established this honorary group while he was ruling in Hebron before he became king over all Israel.
2	Elhanan	Elhanan	Bethlehem	Judah	Not to be confused with another Elhanan from Bethlehem who was also a mighty warrior (2 Sam 21:19).
3	Shammah	Sammoth	Harorite	Judah?	Commanded the fifth division of David's army. Not to be confused with the Shammahs in vv. 11 & 33.
4	Elika		Harodite	Judah?	
5	Helez	Helez	Paltite (S) Pelonite (C)	Judah	Chronicles tells us he was from Ephraim, so he must have migrated south into Judah to commit himself to David's cause early on. He commanded the seventh division of David's army (1 Chr 27:10).
6	Ira	Ira	Tekoa	Judah	He commanded the sixth division of David's army (1 Chr 27:9). He should not be confused with his namesake who was David's priest (2 Sam 20:26).
7	Abiezer	Abiezer	Anathoth	Benjamin	Commanded the ninth division of David's army (1 Chr. 27:12).
8	Mebunnai	Sibbecai	Hushathite	Judah	Commanded the eighth division of David's army (1 Chr 27:11).
9	Zalmon	Ilai	Ahohite	Benjamin	
10	Maharai	Maharai	Netophathite	Judah	Commanded the tenth division (1 Chr 27:13).
11	Heled	Heled	Netophathite	Judah	A descendant of Othniel, the first judge of Israel. He was commander of the twelfth division (1 Chr 27:15).
12	Ithai	Ithai	Gibeah	Benjamin	Not to be confused with Ittai the Gittite of 2 Sam 15:19.

13	Benaiah	Benaiah	Pirathonite	Ephraim	Commander of the eleventh division (1 Chr 27:14). Not to be confused with his namesake in v. 20.
14	Hiddai	Hurai	Gaash	?	
15	Abi-Albon	Abiel	Arbathite	Judah	
16	Azmaveth	Azmaveth	Barhumite (S) Baharumite (C)	Judah	
17	Eliahba	Eliahba	Shaalbonite	Dan	
18	Sons of Jashen	Sons of Hashem	Gizonite (C)		Apparently these sons were so well known that their names did not need to be given. Probably two brothers had been involved in the same brave deed and thus earned a spot in the Thirty jointly.
19	Jonathan	Jonathan	Hararite	Judah	The son of Shammah who was one of the First Three. Both father and son earned military honors.
20	Ahiam	Ahiam	Hararite	Judah	
21	Eliphelet	Eliphal	Maacathite (S)	Naphtali	
22	Eliam		Gilonite		The son of Ahithophel, the adviser who betrayed David during the Absalom rebellion. He may have been the father of Bathsheba.
		Hepher	Mekerathite		
		Ahijah	Pelonite		
23	Hezro	Hezro	Carmelite	Judah	
24	Paarai	Naarai	Arbite (S)	Judah	
25	Igal	Joel	Zobah (S)	Foreigner	
26	Bani		Gadite	Transjordan	
		Mibhar			
27	Zelek	Zelek	Ammonite	Foreigner	
28	Naharai	Naharai	Beerothite (S) Berothite (C)	Foreigner	Descended from the Gibeonites, who inhabited Palestine before Israel. **Armor-bearer** is plural in the Hebrew, referring to both Zelek and Naharai. Both of Joab's chief armor-bearers were foreigners.
29	Ira	Ira	Ithrite	Foreigner	
30	Gareb	Gareb	Ithrite	Foreigner	
31	Uriah	Uriah	Hittite	Foreigner	The man David sentenced to death in his orders to Joab in ch 11. Thus the list ends with the name of one who did not betray the king, but was betrayed by him.

2 SAMUEL 24

F. DAVID'S DISCIPLINE: A CENSUS (24:1-25)

1. The Proposal of David (24:1-4)

24:1 Again the anger of the LORD burned against Israel is literally "the anger of Yahweh added to burning against Israel." Yahweh previously had displayed anger toward Judah during the three years of famine (2 Sam 21). The reason for the divine anger here is not indicated. Perhaps it was because God saw in the king and his subjects a rising spirit of sinful pride and reliance on earthly strength. It may also be because the people of Judah had followed Absalom in rebellion against their rightful king David.

In the Hebrew the verb translated **incited** has no stated subject. According to the parallel account in Chronicles (1 Chr 21:1), Satan moved David to take a census of Israel and Judah.[1] The Evil One may have planted this idea directly in the heart of the king, or he may have used a royal advisor. The Lord permitted David to fall into temptation by withholding his supporting and restraining grace. God himself tempts no person (Jam 1:13). "This is a striking instance of attributing directly to God whatever comes about under His permission" (Spence, 507). Though the taking of the census was a sin, in its final result it led to good, in that the chastisement cured the people of their thirst for war (R.P. Smith, 596). **Take a census** is a different word from that used in the rest of this chapter, and means simply to "count," while the other conveys the idea of a military muster. On the designation of the people as **Israel and Judah,** see on 1 Sam 17:52.

Merely taking a census could not be wrong, for Moses took two censuses of Israel (Num 1, 26). Yet some think that David's sin was

---

[1]For a discussion of who incited David, see J. Sailhamer, "1 Chronicles 21:1—A Study in Inter-Biblical Interpretation," *TJ* 10 (1989): 33-48.

in the action itself. A census may have been viewed as presumptuous because it seemed to contradict the promise in Gen 15:5 that the seed of Abraham would be past numbering (cf. 1 Chr 27:23). Others think the census was not conducted in the proper manner. Perhaps it is condemned because David failed to collect the atonement money as Moses did in the wilderness census (Exod 30:12-16).[2]

Another approach is to see the sin of the census in the motives which inspired it, rather than in the action itself. David's motives are unclear, but these possibilities have been suggested: (1) He was attempting to lay the groundwork for fiscal reorganization of the whole kingdom, or at least of the newly conquered territories. (2) He was contemplating a more ambitious military expedition. Perhaps he wished to extend the boundaries of his country beyond that which God had promised to Abraham, Isaac and Jacob. To the sacred historian the sinfulness of the census was self-evident.

24:2-4 David delegated the responsibility for the census to Joab and the army commanders. When Moses numbered the people, the census was taken by the priests (Num 1:3; 26:1,2), and from the payment of the half-shekel to the sanctuary, it appears that it was to some extent a religious ceremony. All this David neglected. The appointment of Joab proves that David wanted an accounting of the military resources of his kingdom.

The commanders were to go throughout the tribes of Israel from **Dan to Beersheba**, i.e., the entire land. They were to enroll all the **fighting men** (lit., "people"), those who had attained the age of twenty (1 Chr 27:23). **That I may know how many there are** is literally "that I may know the number of the people," i.e., troops.

Joab expressed a wish that the manpower available to the king might be multiplied a hundred times over. He expressed the desire that David might live long enough to see that huge increase in the population. Joab, however, could not understand why David would **want** (lit., "be pleased") to take this military census. He recognized that the census would be of no essential advantage to David's government, and he realized that it might produce dissatisfaction

---

[2]Josephus *Ant.* 7.13.1. KD (506-507) brush aside this interpretation "for the Mosaic instructions concerning the atonement money had reference to the incorporation of the people into the army of Jehovah, and therefore did not come into consideration at all in connection with the census appointed by David as a purely political measure."

among the people. His protest as recorded in Chronicles is even stronger than here. Joab's objections were sustained by his subordinate officers.

The text does not clearly state why Joab objected to the proposal of the king. Perhaps he considered it nothing more than a waste of time. Something more, however, seems to be involved. Previous victories had shown that Yahweh did not depend upon great numbers to achieve his purposes. Joab may have regarded it as sheer presumption that a man should try to measure his power and his glory by the number of his subjects. The king should continue to put his reliance in Yahweh, not in national resources. In any case, the strong objection of Joab shows that there was something obviously wrong in the action of David.

In spite of their protests, Joab and the commanders were **overruled** (lit., "overpowered") by David. **They left the presence of the king** implies that they acted as a royal commission, having received their instruction from the king. So they left on their mission to enroll the fighting men of Israel.

2. The Implementation of the Proposal (24:5-8)

24:5-8 The commanders started their count in Transjordan. The census takers first **camped** near **Aroer**, i.e., **south** [lit., "right"] **of the town in the gorge. And then went through Gad** represents a major departure from the Hebrew text.[3] Literally the words are a further description of the location of Aroer: "the right side of the city which is in the middle of the valley of Gad."[4] Apparently they fixed their headquarters in the open field because great crowds assembled for

---

[3]Kirkpatrick (2:225) supports the view that the text refers to Aroer on the Arnon because (1) it is natural to suppose that the census began from the southern boundary of the Transjordan territory, which was the river Arnon, and (2) the description of the place as "the town in the gorge" is repeatedly mentioned in connection with Aroer on the Arnon (Deut 2:36; Josh 13:9,16).

[4]The NASB so translates and essentially the ASV, NKJV, BV, and NJPS. The NRSV and JB insert the conjunction "and" making the reference to a second city. The MT distinguishes the Aroer where the Joab commission encamped from the more famous city of that name on the Arnon in the tribe of Reuben. Aroer of Gad was "before Rabbah" (Josh 13:25).

the census.[5] From there they made their way north through the tribal territory of **Gad** and on to the Levitical town of **Jazer**[6] (Num 32:1, 3,35; Josh 13:25; 21:39) some seven miles west-southwest of modern Amman.

From Jazer the commanders proceeded through the mountainous region of **Gilead,** the territory between the Jabbok and Yarmuk rivers. There seems to be an attempt here by the Narrator to trace the outer boundaries of the Davidic kingdom. The implication is that all the towns within those boundaries were subject to the census. The region of **Tahtim Hodshi** has not yet been identified. It must have been north of Gilead and east of the Jordan. The name may be corrupt.[7] The team eventually came to **Dan Jaan**[8] (elsewhere simply Dan), the northernmost city of Israel. The group then moved **toward Sidon**. The great Phoenician seaport was probably not part of David's kingdom, but the northwest corner of his kingdom bordered on the territory of Sidon.

The census takers then swung west toward **the fortress of Tyre** which was twenty-seven miles from Dan.[9] They then proceeded south through the old towns which were occupied primarily by the native peoples. The old inhabitants apparently had not been exterminated in the north, but had been made tributary. The **Hivites**[10]

---

[5]While the majority of commentators emend the text so as to make Aroer the more famous city in Reuben, R.P. Smith (596) presents an admirable defense of the view adopted here.

[6]Jazer was a city captured by Israel from the Amorites (Num 21:32), and rebuilt by the tribe of Gad (Num 32:35; Josh 13:25), allotted to the Levites (Josh 21:39).

[7]P. Skehan proposes emending the text to read *tht hrmwn* i.e., [the region] below [Mt.] Hermon. "Joab's Census: How Far North [2 Sam 24,6]?" *CBQ* 31, 1 (1969): 45 and n. 19, 47, 49. A similar suggestion is found in Y. Aharoni, 318, n. 19; and McCarter, 2:504-505.

[8]The meaning of "Jaan" is uncertain. Several commentators have followed the LXX and Vulgate in reading "Dan-jaar," i.e., "Dan in the forest." Youngblood (1098) thinks "Jaan" may be a corruption for "Ijon," a town mentioned together with Dan in 1 Kgs 15:20, located nine miles north-northwest of Dan in the direction of Sidon.

[9]Spence (508) suggests that the census team may have been permitted by the friendly governments of Sidon and Tyre to enumerate the Israelites living there.

[10]The term may be a variant of "Horites" (i.e., Hurrians) which is used eight times in the NIV. The LXX renders "Hurrians."

were the original inhabitants of Shechem (Gen 34:2) and Gibeon (Josh 9:7) in central Canaan. **Canaanites** refers to the other tribes which occupied the area before the Israelites conquered the land under Joshua. Eventually the commanders reached **Beersheba**, the border city of Judah in the south. Beersheba is located **in the Negev** about forty-five miles southwest of Jerusalem. Joab and his officers traveled through the land in a horseshoe path which moved from the southeast border of the kingdom through the territories in the north to the southwest border. The entire census effort took **nine months and twenty days**.

3. The Result of the Census (24:9-10)

24:9-10 Joab reported the results of his census to David back in Jerusalem. Those who were numbered were **able-bodied men**, an idiom suggesting unusual courage. These men could **handle** (lit., "draw") **a sword.** The separate numbers of Israel and Judah attests to the continued rivalry between north and south in the reign of David. Perhaps his kingdom was looked upon as a confederation of the two kingdoms which, for a short time after the death of Saul, had been independent of one another. The reported census results are considerably different in Chronicles (30,000 less in Judah, and 300,000 more in Israel, for a total difference of 270,000). The discrepancy may be due (1) to textual corruption in the one text or the other or (2) differences in the subgroups which were included.

According to 1 Chr 21:6 Joab refused to number Levi and Benjamin, the former because they were exempt from military service (Num 1:47 ff.), the latter possibly in order to avoid exciting disaffection in a tribe especially ready to take offense (Kirkpatrick, 2:226). The larger figure for Israel in Chronicles probably includes an estimate of the fighting men in the omitted tribes, and perhaps of portions of other tribes as well.[11] The larger figure for Judah in

---

[11]Another possibility is that the militia of 288,000 (1 Chr 27:1-15) + another 12,000 bureaucrats associated with the twelve tribal overseers (1 Chr 27:16-22) are included in Israel in one case and excluded in the other. In the case of Judah, the thirty mighty men may have had command of a special force of 30,000, not included in the lower figure, which kept watch on the Philistines. Still another possibility is that the descendants of the old Canaanites were counted in one account, but not in the other (cf. 2 Chr 2:17).

Samuel may (1) be simply a rounding off of the actual number given in Chronicles or (2) include an estimate of the officiating priests and Levites reckoned to Judah. No doubt the original report was broken down into various categories — by age, race, skills, tribes, etc. The two biblical writers have added together the categories which they thought were most significant and this would account for the different totals. In any case, the figures suggest a total population at this time of about five to six million,[12] and a population density of 415 to 500 per square mile. Chronicles claims to have an inclusive figure ("in all Israel") while Samuel makes no such claim ("in Israel").[13] According to 1 Chr 27:24 "Joab began to count the men but did not finish." The final report, therefore, must have contained estimates to a certain extent.

At some point after Joab had submitted his report to the king, David's **conscience** (lit., "heart") was awakened. He realized that the census was (1) an act of arrogance, (2) a manifestation of distrust of Yahweh, and (3) the action of a worldly king, not the anointed of the Lord. He confessed his sin to God. David asked that he might be forgiven of the foolish thing he had ordered. Still it must be observed that ten months had passed (v. 8) before David recognized his sin.

4. The Punishment of Israel (24:11-17)

The Mission of Gad (24:11-14)

24:11-14 In consequence of his repentance, God dispatched the seer Gad to David in the morning. Gad last appeared in 1 Sam 22:5 when he warned David to return from the land of Moab (1 Sam 22:5). **Seer**[14] is a name sometimes given to a prophet because of the visions he saw. Gad was **David's seer**, i.e., a personal counselor.

Because he was in a penitent state, God in his grace allowed David to name the punishment. Gad confronted David with three

---

[12]Those who perceive the numbers to be too large have proposed that the term *thousand* (*eleph*) designated a unit of fighting men composed of a much smaller number of men than one thousand.

[13]Cf. J.B. Payne, "Validity of Numbers in Chronicles," *NEASB* 11 (1978): 23.

[14]The word for "seer" is חֹזֶה (*ḥōzeh*, lit., "gazer") a term first used here in place of the older word for seer (*rō'eh*) used in 1 Sam 9:9.

options: (1) **three years**[15] **of famine** in the land; (2) **three months of fleeing** from before his enemies; or (3) **three days of plague**[16] in the land. **Think it over and decide** is literally "know and see," i.e., David was to make a careful choice.

David was in **deep distress** because it was impossible to regard one punishment as lighter or harsher than the other two. He decided against the second punishment. He knew the hardships of flight from human enemies. So he left it to the Lord to decide between the first or the third. He placed himself in God's hands rather than suffer those other punishments in which the will of man seemed to have a greater share. War would place the nation at the mercy of its enemies; famine would make it totally dependent on foreign grain merchants. Only plague would bring a punishment which came directly from God and depended totally on his will. David's choice also involves that form of punishment from which his own royal position would afford him no immunity. He preferred to fall into the hands of God because **his mercy is great**.

The Plague against Judah (24:15-17)

24:15 The Lord sent the plague against Israel. It started that very morning and lasted to **the end of the** [lit., "a"] **time designated**. The reference is not to the end of the three-day period, for it is clear from v. 16 that the plague ceased before the end of that time. It may refer (1) to a time determined in the counsel of God before the expiration of the period originally named; or (2) to the time of the afternoon sacrifice.[17] If this is the case, then the time of the plague was reduced to a single day. Some **seventy thousand** people from **Dan to Beersheba,** i.e., throughout the length and breadth of the land, died in the plague during the few hours of that day. Was this a general plague (NIV) or a targeted plague (similar to the death of the firstborn in Egypt)? Youngblood (1100) suggests the latter, based on

---

[15]The Hebrew reads **seven years**. The NIV has followed the LXX and the parallel in Chronicles. Following the principle of *lectio difficilior potior* ("the more difficult reading is the more likely one"), the reading "seven years" should probably be retained here.

[16]The reading in 1 Chr 21:12 is: "three days of the sword of the LORD — days of plague in the land, with the angel of the LORD ravaging every part of Israel.

[17]The LXX renders "until the time of the evening meal."

the use of the term translated **people** (*'am*) throughout this chapter. Until v. 15 the term is rendered in the NIV "fighting men" (v. 2,4,9,10) and "troops" (v. 3).[18] This suggests that the term *'am* should also be translated "fighting men" in vv. 15-17,21. Wanting more land and people to rule — the apparent reason for the census — David found himself with seventy thousand fewer soldiers. The plague seems to have broken out at the opposite extremities of the country, and to have advanced rapidly from all points, till it was ready to concentrate its violence upon Jerusalem.

24:16 The administration of the plague had been assigned to an angel (1 Chr 21:15). This angel stretched out his hand against the population center of Jerusalem. Yahweh, however, **was grieved**[19] **because of the calamity**. He therefore ordered the angel to cease afflicting the people of Israel. At that time the angel of the Lord was at the threshing floor of **Araunah,** lit., "the Araunah."[20] Threshing floors were constructed on knolls to catch the wind for winnowing the grain. The owner was a **Jebusite**, i.e., he descended from the pre-Israelite occupants of Jerusalem. By restraining the death angel at that spot Yahweh was signaling that the threshing floor of Araunah was to become a sacred spot.

24:17 Verse 17 explains the reason for Yahweh's compassion. He had been moved by David's prayer for his people. The king **saw**[21] **the angel.** The text clearly implies that the death angel was visible. This destroying angel hovering over Mount Moriah, and brandishing his deadly sword over the inhabitants, must have been an awesome

---

[18]In addition, the term אִישׁ (*'îš*, "man/men"), left untranslated in vv. 9,15 clearly here means "soldiers."

[19]English versions reflect significant diversity in the rendering of the Hebrew root נָחַם (*nāḥam*): "repented" (KJV, ASV); "thought better of this evil" (JB); "relented" (NRSV, NKJV, NASB) "renounced further punishment" (NJPS); "felt grief" (BV). The Hebrew verb is used to describe a change of action on God's part triggered by man's (1) repentance, (2) faithfulness, or (3) in some cases, disobedience. The word does not imply admission of wrong, nor does it indicate regret concerning previous action. See notes on 1 Sam 15:11,29.

[20]Chronicles calls the owner of the threshing floor Ornan, using what is thought to be the Hebrew spelling of the man's name. Others think Araunah is a title rather than a name since the definite article has been attached to it in v. 16.

[21]A pluperfect would better convey the sequence of events.

spectacle.[22] The account in Chronicles adds these details: "David looked up and saw the angel of the LORD standing between heaven and earth, with a drawn sword in his hand extended over Jerusalem. Then David and the elders, clothed in sackcloth, fell facedown" (1 Chr 21:16).[23] The visible appearance of the angel excluded any thought of a natural disaster. The drawn sword was a symbolical representation of the purpose of the angel's coming (cf. Num 22:23; Jos 5:13). Therefore David prayed to the Lord. His prayer emphatically[24] admitted again the responsibility for the wrong. He confessed **I have sinned**, i.e., missed the mark in respect to duty; and (2) **done wrong,** lit., "done crookedly," i.e., acted in a crooked or perverse way by following the leading of self-will rather than the straight path of righteousness. He pointed out that the people were but innocent **sheep** in the matter of the census. David pled that God's hand might be on him personally and on his family. This willingness to accept all the blame and all the punishment is probably what moved the Lord to call off the plague.

The sentiment of David's prayer was right, but his facts were not accurate. Israel had in fact sinned. By supporting the rebellion of Absalom in such large numbers they had repudiated for a time God's anointed king. Thus in the plague God was "killing two birds with one stone." Israel was punished for tolerating the Absalom and Sheba rebellions. David was punished by seeing his potential military force devastated. Because the wrath of the Lord came upon Israel, the census figures were not recorded in the royal chronicles of King David (1 Chr 27:24).

5. The Place of Sacrifice (24:18-25)

Instructions by the Seer (24:18)

24:18 On the day the plague stopped, Gad the prophet came again to David, according to Chronicles, by direction of the angel

---

[22]Some think that "the angel of the Lord" is figurative of the plague, but "the introduction of a bold poetical figure into a narrative of plain, unvarnished prose is most improbable" (Jamieson, 289).

[23]The Chronicles reading may have been an original part of the text of Samuel, for the Chronicles reading is supported by the oldest MS (4QSam[a]).

[24]In the Hebrew a repetition of the first person pronoun communicates the emphasis.

(1 Chr 21:18). He encouraged David to **go up** to the hill where the Jebusite had his threshing floor. There he should build an altar. The threshing floor was on Mount Moriah, the hill immediately to the north of the oldest part of the walled city of Jerusalem. Later Solomon would build his temple there.

Negotiations for Purchase (24:19-24)

24:19-21 David immediately complied with the directive of God's prophet. When he saw the royal entourage, Araunah **went out**. Again Chronicles fills in details lacking in Samuel. Araunah was threshing wheat. He and his sons turned and saw "the angel," lit., "messenger," probably a servant sent ahead to announce the approach of the king. The four sons hid themselves (1 Chr 21:20). Araunah bowed before the king[25] with his face toward the ground. He asked the king the reason for his visit. David indicated that he had come to buy the threshing floor so that he might build an altar. The king assumed that only by building that altar could the plague against Israel be stopped permanently.

24:22-23 Araunah offered David anything he wanted to carry out his noble purpose. He offered his **oxen** for a burnt offering. He even offered David some items about the place as wood to burn for the sacrifice. **Threshing sledges** were large sleds which had sharp stones set in the under side. When they were pulled by oxen over grain, the kernels were separated from the stalk. **Yokes** were bars which fit over the necks of the oxen which enabled them to pull wagons or plows. An ancient tradition connects the opening **O king** (lit., "king") with the name "Araunah," thus making him the last Jebusite king of Jerusalem.[26] **Araunah gives** [i.e., "offers"] **all this to the king**. The opening words of v. 23 were not intended to be taken literally (cf. Gen 23:11); they are a typical opening gambit in Middle Eastern bargaining. Araunah not only offered these items to the king, he also uttered a prayer on his behalf. He prayed that the Lord might **accept David**, i.e., accept the sacrifice and grant David's request for

---

[25]4QSam[a] has David and his servants clothed in sackcloth.

[26]N. Wyatt, "'Araunah the Jebusite' and the Throne of David," *ST* 39 (1985): 40. He concludes that Araunah is derived from Hurrian, and means "the lord." F.M. Cross (210) objects to seeing Araunah as the last Jebusite king.

the end of the plague. **Your God** seems to put some distance between this Gentile and Yahweh.

24:24 David would accept no gifts from Araunah. He would not offer a sacrifice to the Lord which cost him nothing, for that would contradict the essential concept of sacrifice. David pointedly refers to Yahweh as **my God**. This is the principle which underlies all true sacrifice and all real giving to God. So David bought the threshing floor, the oxen and the wood instruments for **fifty shekels** (1.25 lbs.) **of silver**, a rather small price.[27] Later he must have paid a larger sum to Araunah for the whole hill (1 Chr. 21:25).

The Construction of the Altar (24:25)

24:25 David quickly offered **burnt offerings** and **fellowship offerings** on the new altar. Then the Lord heard David's prayer on behalf of the land, and terminated the plague. Chronicles adds this information: The tabernacle and the altar of burnt offering were at that time in the high place at Gibeon. David was afraid to go there "because of the sword of the angel," i.e., the plague. When David offered sacrifices on the new altar in Jerusalem, Yahweh answered him from heaven by fire upon the altar (1 Chr 21:26-30). David then recognized this as the future location for the house of Yahweh (1 Chr 22:1). So the Samuel material began at the "temple" of God in Shiloh (1 Sam 1:9) and concludes at the site of the future temple in Jerusalem.

---

[27]Rashi has argued that the fifty shekels was the price paid on behalf of each of the twelve tribes. See J.M. Myers, 149.